Company Acquisitions

8th edition

Company Acquisitions Handbook

8th edition

Tottel Publishing Ltd, Maxwelton House, 41–43 Boltro Road, Haywards Heath, West Sussex, RH16 1BJ

© Tottel Publishing Ltd 2007

A CIP Catalogue record for this book is available from the British Library.

ISBN: 978 1 84592 457 7

Typeset by Phoenix, Chatham, Kent
Printed and bound in Great Britain by Antony Rowe, Chippenham, Wilts

Contents

Table of statutes   xi
Table of statutory instruments   xvii
Table of cases   xxi

Chapter 1:   Introduction   1
Professor Patrick Dunne, 3i Group plc
   Summary   5

Chapter 2:   Accounting   7
Ian Connon, Senior Technical Manager, PKF (UK) LLP
   Introduction   7
   Accounting framework   8
   UK GAAP   9
   Consolidation exemptions   13
   Small companies and the FRSSE   15
   Acquisition or merger accounting?   16
   Merger accounting   17
   Acquisition accounting   18
   Acquisition costs   26
   Disclosure in accounts   27
   International Financial Reporting Standards   29
   Associates and joint ventures   35
   Shares or assets?   37
   Possible future developments   38
   Conclusion   38

Chapter 3:   Corporate Rescue and Insolvency   39
John Anderson, Senior Associate, Eversheds LLP, Newcastle upon Tyne
   Introduction   39
   Administration – a new priority, on paper   42
   Administration – entry (and exit) routes   47
   Administration – a brief note on Chapter 11, the day before
         yesterday in Parliament and a conflict of roles   49
   Pre-packs – in administrations and otherwise   52
   Phoenix companies – a ruse by any other name   54
   A trap for the unwary   57
   Employees and employment claims – Paramount lost,
         Huddersfield worsted   60

Pensions on insolvency – a very expensive problem, only
    expensively solved   69
The 'hive down' – a moribund concept   71
Work outs   72
Lessons from America   78
Some conclusions   84

Chapter 4:   Defence Tactics   **87**
Darren Bryant, Corporate Finance Partner,
    PricewaterhouseCoopers LLP
Introduction   87
The regulatory environment   88
Defensive measures prior to a bid   90
Defensive measures following announcement of a bid   95
Conclusion   103

Chapter 5:   Employee Share Schemes   **105**
Monica Ma, Partner, Simmons & Simmons
Introduction   106
Identifying the employee share schemes   106
Institutional investors' guidelines   111
Impact of the acquisition   112
Treatment of 'early leavers'   114
Share option schemes in acquisitions   115
Employee benefit trust   118
New employee share schemes after the acquisition   119

Chapter 6:   Employment Responsibilities and Objectives   **121**
William Dawson, Partner, Simmons & Simmons
Introduction   121
Identifying the contract of employment   123
Pre-contractual considerations   123
Directors (executive directors)   123
Managers and all other employees   133
All employees – the purchaser's legal obligations   135
Share acquisition   135
Unfair and wrongful dismissal   136
Internal reorganisation   139
Purchase of assets only   144
Purchase of a business or undertaking   145
Reorganisation   157
Collective matters   163
Key points for the purchaser/transferee   174
Key points for the seller/transferor   174
Precedents – employment warranties and indemnities   175

Chapter 7:   Environmental Responsibilities   **183**
Claire Sheppard, Partner, Addleshaw Goddard with contributions by
    Lucy Fletcher, Associate, Addleshaw Goddard
Introduction and purpose of chapter   183

The structure of environmental liabilities 184
The key differences between share and asset transactions 186
A question of semantics 188
Identifying and assessing environmental issues 189
Due diligence and disclosure 191
Using environmental consultants 194
Instructing local lawyers 197
Legal environmental issues 197
Overview of main authorisations 205
Overview of other general legislation 216
Allocating risks and liabilities between the parties 220
Money laundering 226
Environmental Information Regulations 227
Environmental permits and the transfer process 228

Chapter 8: Legal Aspects of Acquisitions   **235**
Nigel Boardman and Richard de Carle, Partners, Slaughter and May
Introduction 236
Sale or purchase of a private company 236
The basic structure of a private acquisition 239
Pre-contractual considerations 243
The conduct of negotiations 249
The purchase consideration 251
The identity of the seller 256
Immovable property 257
Restrictive covenants 259
Continuation of services and intra-group relations 260
Gap between exchange and completion 261
The sale and purchase agreement and disclosure letter 261
Consents 266
Warranties, indemnities and covenants 268
Protections and limitations for the seller 274
Specific limitations 276
Assignments of warranties and indemnities 280
Other matters for the seller to consider 282
Other regulations 282
Practical steps – checklists 284
Comparison of the Companies Act 1985 and the Companies Act
2006 289

Chapter 9: Pensions Aspects of Acquisitions   **293**
Jason Eshelby and John Harvey, Hewitt Consulting – M&A team
Introduction 293
This chapter 294
Pension benefits 294
An outline acquisition 296
Interested parties 298
Benefits to be provided 301
Transfer provisions of the seller's scheme 302

Contents

Methods 303
The participation period 303
Pension clauses of the sale agreement 304
Adjustment to the purchase price 305
Pensions regulatory framework 305
Debts on employers for defined benefit schemes (section 75 debt) 306
Debts on defined contribution employers 309
Approved withdrawal arrangements 309
Moral Hazard provisions 311
Clearance 312
The Transfer of Undertakings (Protection of Employment)
     Regulations 2006 ('TUPE') 314
Funding occupational defined benefit schemes 315
The Pension Protection Fund (PPF) 315
Accounting for pension costs 316
Conclusion 316

Chapter 10:   Post-Acquisition Management **317**
Professor Patrick Dunne, 3i Group plc
Introduction 317
Why acquisitions fail 318
Why acquisitions succeed 319
Degree of integration 320
People issues 324
Communication 326

Chapter 11:   Regulatory Aspects of Acquisitions in the EU **331**
Robert S. K. Bell, Partner, Nabarro
Introduction 332
EU merger control 332
Principal aims 333
General issues 333
History 334
The Merger Regulation 335
Procedure 345
Substantive assessment 353
Notice on a simplified procedure 355
Penalties 356
Ancillary restrictions 357
EEA Agreement merger control rules 360
United Kingdom 361
The Netherlands 375
France 379
Germany 393
Italy 405
Spain 411
Poland 418
Ireland 423
Sweden 432
Czech Republic 437

Hungary	440
United States	448
Finland	456
Acknowledgements	461

Chapter 12:   Strategy and Tactics   **463**
Professor Patrick Dunne, 3i Group plc
Developing an acquisition strategy	463
Establishing the team	467
Identifying targets	471
Approaching targets	475
Valuing the target	479
Detailed investigation	482
Financing the acquisition	488

Chapter 13:   Tax Planning   **493**
Sara Luder, Partner, Slaughter and May
Introduction	493
Share sales and asset sales	494
Share sales – seller's tax planning	499
Share sales – purchaser's tax planning	509
Consideration	515
Warranties and indemnities	521
Clearances and consents	525
Tax losses	529
Close companies	531
Public mergers and acquisitions	532

Chapter 14:   Corporate Acquisitions involving Real Estate   **539**
Peter Hardy, Partner, Addleshaw Goddard
Introduction	540
Shares or assets?	540
Assessing the importance of property in target	542
Property due diligence	543
Property documents	550
Dealing with landlords	551
Post completion	554
Overseas properties	554

Chapter 15:   Private Equity Finance and Buyouts   **557**
Simon Witney, Partner, SJ Berwin LLP
Introduction	557
Objectives of a private equity house	560
The buyout process	568
The structure of a buyout	569
Key legal documents	579
The main terms of a buyout	586
Impact on the M&A deal	597
Secondary buyouts	598

Contents

Exit routes   599
List of Figures   601

Appendix A   Glossary of terms   **603**

Appendix B   Specimen: Confidentiality Undertaking   **615**

Index   *623*

Table of statutes

PARA

Civil Liability (Contribution) Act
  1978 .... 8.40
  s 1, 2 .... 8.40

Communications Act 2003 ..... 11.49,
                          11.55, 11.58
  s 319, 373, 375 .... 11.58

Companies Act 1985 ..... 2.1, 2.2, 2.3,
                 2.4, 2.10, 2.12, 2.23,
                 2.28, 2.39; 4.2; 9.29;
                          11.68
  s 1(3) 8.1, 8.63
  30 .... 8.1, 8.63
  80 .... 8.19
  81 .... 8.1, 8.63
  88 .... 8.63
  95 .... 8.62, 8.63
  103 .... 2.41; 8.19, 8.63
  104-108 .... 8.19, 8.63
  123 .... 8.63
  130 .... 2.5, 2.41
  131 .... 2.5
  133 .... 2.5, 2.18, 2.36
  150 .... 8.19, 8.63
  151 .... 8.22, 8.58, 8.63; 15.36
  152-153 .... 13.36
  155 .... 8.22; 15.36
    (4), (5) 8.60, 8.63
  156 .... 8.60, 8.63; 15.36
    (4) 8.58
  157, 158 .... 15.36
  163(2) 8.63
    (b) 8.2
  225 .... 8.63
  227 .... 2.6
  228, 228A 2.7
  229 .... 2.9
  248 .... 2.8
  249 .... 3.2
  258 .... 2.6, 2.9
  263 .... 8.22, 8.63
  287, 288 .... 8.63
  303 .... 6.7
  312-314 .... 6.11

PARA

Companies Act 1985 – *contd*
  s 316(3) 6.11
  318B 8.59
  319 .... 6.6
  320 .... 3.11; 6.11; 8.15,
                8.24, 8.31, 8.58, 8.63
  321(2)(b) 3.11
  322(2), (3) 3.11
  346 .... 3.11; 8.24, 8.63
  381B 8.63
  394 .... 8.61, 8.63
  395 .... 8.63
  425 .... 3.2; 13.56
  429 .... 5.14; 8.3, 8.63
  736 .... 2.6
  741 .... 3.11
    (2) 15.51
  Sch 4 .... 2.20
  Sch 4A
    para 9 .... 2.16
      10 .... 2.12

Companies Act 1989 .... 11.63, 11.64,
                          11.68

Companies Act 2006 .... 2.1, 2.8; 3.6,
                    3.11; 4.2; 6.6, 6.7,
                    6.11; 8.1; 15.36
  s 4(1)-(3) 8.63
  60-62, 86, 87 .... 8.63
  162, 167 .... 8.63
  172 .... 7.22
  173(1) 8.31
  190 .... 8.63
  191 .... 3.11; 8.63
    (5) 3.11
  193 .... 3.11
  223, 252-255 .... 8.63
  275, 276 .... 8.63
  392 .... 8.63
  417 .... 7.22
  519-521, 555, 557 .... 8.63
  569-573 .... 8.63
  584, 592-604 .... 8.63
  609, 670 .... 8.63

PARA

Companies Act 2006 – *contd*
s 678 .... 8.22, 8.63
  689, 680 .... 8.63
  693(3) 8.63
  755, 760 .... 8.63
  793, 803 .... 4.4
  829, 830 .... 8.63
  849, 850 .... 8.63
  860(1) 8.63
  861(5) 8.63
  870(1) 8.63
  874(1)-(3) 8.63
  895, 896 .... 13.56
  977-980 .... 8.63
  1150 .... 8.63

Company Directors Disqualification Act 1986 .... 3.2

Competition Act 1998 .... 8.26;
                 11.45, 11.50

Contracts (Rights of Third
  Parties) Act 1999 ..... 7.11; 8.29,
                  8.52
s 1(1) 8.50

Data Protection Act 1998 .... 6.58; 8.16

Employment Act 1989 .... 6.65

Employment Rights Act 1996 .. 6.18,
              6.54, 6.65
s 1 .... 6.2, 6.42
  4 .... 6.2
  43A-43L 6.30
  86 .... 6.6, 6.21
  94 .... 6.18
  95 .... 6.18, 6.19
  98 .... 6.19, 6.28
    (1)(b) 6.19
    (2)(b) 6.19
    (c) 6.19, 6.30
    (4) 6.19, 6.28, 6.30
  104(4) 6.44
  105 .... 6.30
  108(1), (3) 6.18
  118 .... 6.20
  123 .... 6.23
  139(1), (2) 6.30
  141 .... 6.26
  203(1) 6.11
  218(2) 6.37
  231 .... 6.25

PARA

Enterprise Act 2002 ...... 3.1, 3.4, 3.5,
            3.6, 3.7, 3.8, 3.9,
            3.13, 3.37; 8.26;
           11.45, 11.47, 11.50,
           11.51, 11.53, 11.55,
           11.56, 11.58, 11.60,
              11.61, 11.62,
                 11.69
Pt III (ss 22-130) 11.70
s 22 .... 11.56
  31 .... 11.65
  33 .... 11.56
    (1) 11.50
  57A 3.37
  58 .... 11.55, 11.58
    (2A)-(2C) 11.58
  70 .... 11.59
  99 .... 11.65
  110(1), (3) 11.70
  117 .... 11.66
  120 .... 11.50, 11.70

Environment Act 1995 .... 7.17

Environmental Protection Act
  1990
  Pt I (ss 1-28) 7.23, 7.48
  s 6 .... 7.48
  Pt II (ss 29-78) 7.4, 7.23, 7.34
  Pt IIA 7.16, 7.17; 8.4
  s 29 .... 7.48
  33 .... 7.34
  36 .... 7.30
  40, 78 .... 7.48
  Pt III (ss 79-85) 7.37
  s 79 .... 7.37

Fair Trading Act 1973 .... 11.45

Finance Act 1930
  s 42 .... 13.47

Finance Act 1967
  s 27(3) 13.47

Finance Act 1988
  s 132 .... 13.40

Finance Act 1996 .... 13.16, 13.34
  s 87 .... 13.34
  100 .... 13.32

Finance Act 2002 .... 13.5

PARA

Finance Act 2003
Sch 7 . . . .   13.18
para 2, 3 . . . .   13.18
Sch 22 . . . . 13.35; 15.26
Sch 23 . . . . 5.14; 13.55

Financial Services Act 1986 . . . .   4.2

Financial Services and Markets
Act 2000 . . . .   4.2
s 21 . . . .   8.8
Pt IV (ss 40-55) 2.8
s 86 . . . .   8.56
(1) 8.2
102 . . . .   8.20
397 . . . .   8.30

Fraud Act 2006 . . . .   8.30
s 2, 3 . . . .   8.13

Freedom of Information Act
2000 . . . .   7.48

Goods Vehicles (Licensing of
Operations) Act 1995 . . . . .   7.3

Income and Corporation Taxes
Act 1988
s 15 Sch A 13.20
94 . . . .   13.16
213 . . . .   13.54
214 . . . . 13.40, 13.54
215-217 . . . .   13.54
343 . . . . 3.4, 3.19; 13.47
410 . . . .   13.20
703 . . . .   13.42
704 . . . . 13.42, 13.45
705, 706 . . . .   13.42
707 . . . . 8.31; 13.42, 13.43,
13.44, 13.45
708, 709 . . . . 13.42, 13.45
765 . . . . 8.31; 13.43,
13.46
765A 13.46
767A 13.42
768, 768A, 768B 13.47
776 . . . .   13.42
Sch 18 . . . .   13.34
para 1(3) 13.33

Income Tax (Earnings and
Pensions) Act 2003 . . . .   13.35
Pt VII (ss 417-554) 15.26
s 401, 403 . . . .   13.30

PARA

Income Tax (Trading and Other
Income) Act 2005 . . . .   13.25

Industrial Training Act 1982 . . .   6.65

Insolvency Act 1986 . . . . 3.4, 3.5
s 8, 9 . . . .   3.7
19 . . . .   3.13
(5) 3.6
(6) 3.13
29(2) 3.4
37 . . . . 3.12, 3.14
44 . . . . 3.12, 3.13, 3.14
72A-72H 3.5
110 . . . .   3.2
115 . . . .   3.6
123 . . . .   3.7
127 . . . .   3.2
175 . . . .   3.8
(2)(a) 3.6
176A 3.6, 3.9
176ZA 3.6
213, 214 . . . .   3.2
216, 217 . . . .   3.10
238 . . . .   3.2
239 . . . . 3.2, 3.8
245, 423 . . . .   3.2
Sch B1
para 3(1) 3.4
6 . . . .   3.10
10-12 . . . .   3.7
13 . . . .   3.7
(i)(f) 3.8
14 . . . . 3.4, 3.7
15-35, 37, 38 . . . .   3.7
42-44 . . . .   3.7
52 . . . .   3.7
(1), (2) 3.9
65 . . . .   3.8
83 . . . .   3.10
(3) 3.10
99 . . . . 3.13, 3.14
(3), (4) 3.6
(5), (6) 3.12
Sch 1 . . . .   3.4
Sch 6
category 5 . . . .   3.13

Insolvency Act 1994 . . . .   3.13

Landlord and Tenant Act 1954 . .   14.17

Landlord and Tenant Act 1988 . .   8.25;
14.14

PARA

Landlord and Tenant (Coven-
    ants) Act 1995 ...8.25; 14.8, 14.14
    s 16 .... 14.8

Land Registration Act 1925 .... 14.2

Land Registration Act 2002 .... 14.2
    Sch 3 .... 14.9

Law of Property Act 1925 ..... 3.12
    s 141 .... 14.12

Law of Property (Miscellaneous
    Provisions) Act 1994
    Pt I (ss 1-13) 8.29

Local Land Charges Act 1975 .. 14.9
    s 10 .... 14.9

Misrepresentation Act 1967 .... 14.9
    s 3 .... 8.9

National Minimum Wage Act
    1998 .... 6.65

Pensions Act 1995 .... 9.17
    s 75 .... 9.2, 9.4, 9.7, 9.8, 9.13,
              9.16, 9.17, 9.24, 9.25

Pensions Act 2004 ..... 4.7; 6.37; 9.16,
              9.22, 9.33
    s 38-57 .... 9.23
    69 .... 9.5, 9.7, 9.28, 9.29
    96 .... 9.21

Planning (Hazardous Substances)
    Act 1990 .... 7.28, 7.48

Pollution Prevention and Control
    Act 1999 .... 7.23

Proceeds of Crime Act 2002 ... 7.47;
              8.22, 8.39
    Pt VII (ss 327-340) 8.13
    s 330, 335 .... 8.22
    340(3)(a) 8.13

Public Interest Disclosure Act
    1998
    s 5 .... 6.30

Radioactive Substances Act
    1993 .... 7.27
    s 6, 13, 16A 7.48

PARA

Restrictive Trade Practices Act
    1976 .... 6.10

Taxation of Chargeable Gains
    Act 1992 .... 13.5, 13.34
    s 29-34 .... 13.17
    48 .... 13.32
    49 .... 13.39
    116 .... 13.34
    117 .... 13.34
      (A1) 13.34
    135 .... 13.8, 13.15, 13.33,
              13.34, 13.35, 13.56
    136 .... 13.15, 13.54, 13.56
    137 .... 13.33, 13.34, 13.44
    138 .... 8.20, 8.31; 13.33,
              13.34, 13.43, 13.44,
              13.45, 13.53
    138A 13.35
    139 .... 13.54
    152 .... 13.5
    171 .... 13.18, 13.47
    176, 177 .... 13.17
    179 .... 13.8, 13.18, 13.19,
              13.40, 13.47,
              13.50
    190 .... 13.40
    280 .... 13.32
    Sch 5B 13.8
    Sch 7A 13.13
    Sch 7AC 13.10

Theft Act 1978 .... 8.30

Town and Country Planning Act
    1990
    s 106 .... 14.9

Trade Union and Labour
    Relations (Consolidation)
    Act 1992 .... 3.13; 6.31
    s 152 .... 6.30
    188 .... 6.54
      (2), (4) 6.54
    188A, 189 .... 6.54
    193 .... 6.31
    195 .... 6.54

Trade Union Reform and
    Employment Rights Act
    1993 .... 6.31

Unfair Contract Terms Act 1977: 6.12;
              15.37

PARA

Value Added Tax Act 1994
s 19, 49 . . . .   13.6

Water Act 2003 . . . .   7.26

Water Industry Act 1991 . . . 7.25; 11.59
s 6 . . . .   11.59

Water Resources Act 1991 . . 7.16, 7.17,
7.18, 7.26
s 24A, 59A 7.48
85 . . . .   7.24
87 . . . .   7.48
161 . . . .   7.17
Sch 10 . . . . 7.24, 7.48
para 11 . . . . 7.24, 7.48

CANADA
Companies Creditors Arrangement Act 1985 . . . 3.30, 3.31, 3.32,
3.33, 3.34

CZECH REPUBLIC
Act on the Protection of Economic Competition (1991) . 11.159

Act on the Protection of Economic Competition (143/
2001) 11.159, 11.160,
11.163
s 12 . . . .   11.161

Insolvency Act (182/2006) 3.36

FINLAND
Act on Competition Restrictions
(480/1992) 11.192, 11.194,
11.195, 11.196,
11.197, 11.198,
11.199

FRANCE
Code Géneral des Collectivités
Territoriales
art L1522-2 . . . .   11.81

Commercial Code
art L224-125
L233-7 . . . .   11.80
L233-10-1 . . . .   11.80
L233-32, L233-34 . . . .   11.80
L430-1, L430-3, L430-5,
L430-6, L430-8 . . . .   11.77

PARA

Employment Code 11.79

Monetary and Finance Code
art L151-3 . . . .   11.78
R153-7 . . . .   11.78

GERMANY
Act against Restraints of
Competition (ARC) 11.84,
11.85, 11.92
Pt I 11.84, 11.86
s 19(2) 11.96, 11.100
(3) 11.96
35 . . . .   11.86
(1) 11.93
(2) 11.94
36(1) 11.95, 11.98, 11.99,
11.100
(2) 11.89, 11.93, 11.94
37 . . . .   11.86
(1) 11.86, 11.87, 11.88,
11.89, 11.90, 11.93
(2) 11.91
(3) 11.92
38(2)-(5) 11.93
39(1) 11.102
(6) 11.105
40(1) 11.101
41(1), (2) 11.104
42 . . . .   11.101
43(3), (4) 11.106
54(2) 11.102
63(1) 11.106
81(1), (2) 11.106

Stock Corporation Act
s 17, 18 . . . . 11.89, 11.93
291, 292 . . . .   11.104

HUNGARY
Business Associations Act 11.182

Capital Market Act 11.182

Competition Act 11.166, 11.168,
11.170, 11.172,
11.175, 11.180
s 23(1) 11.167
(2) 11.169
26(3), (5) 11.171
28(2) 11.174
62 . . . .   11.177
63(3)(a) 11.176
68(2) 11.174

PARA

Competition Act – *contd*
s 74(1) 11.176
79 . . . . 11.178

Labour Code 11.182

Privatisation Act 11.182

Radio and Television Broad-
casting Act 11.182

IRELAND
Competition Act 2003 . . . . 11.137,
11.138, 11.145
Pt III 11.136
s 4, 5 . . . . 11.140
11 . . . . 11.146
16 . . . . 11.137
(2) 11.137
18(1) 11.147
(8) 11.139
19 . . . . 11.147
(1) 11.147
20(1)(a) 11.142
21(2) 11.147
22(3) 11.143
24(6) 11.145

ITALY
Rules on the Protection of
Competition and the Market
(Anti-trust Law) 1990 . . . . . 11.108,
11.115
art 5 . . . . 11.108, 11.110
6, 7 . . . . 11.108
10 . . . . 11.114
16 . . . . 11.108, 11.109
(2) 11.111
(7) 11.115
17-19 . . . . 11.108
20(3) 11.117

PARA

Law 1067/1936 . . . . 11.117

Law 576/1982 . . . . 11.117

Law 249/1997 . . . . 11.117

Law 262/2005 . . . . 11.117
art 19 . . . . 11.117
(12) 11.117

NETHERLANDS
Competition Act 1997 . . . . 11.71, 11.72

Works Council Act 11.75

POLAND
Act on the Protection of Competition and Consumers
2000 . . . . 11.127, 11.128,
11.129, 11.131,
11.134

SPAIN
Competition Act 1989 (Law
16/1989) 11.120, 11.125
art 14-18 . . . . 11.118

SWEDEN
Competition Act 1993 . . 11.148, 11.149
s 34 . . . . 11.149

Secrecy Act 1980 . . . . 11.153

UNITED STATES
Clayton Act 11.184
s 7 . . . . 11.183, 11.190

Hart-Scott-Rodino Antitrust
Improvements Act 1976 . . . 11.184,
11.187

Table of statutory instruments

PARA

Air Navigation (Environmental Standards) Order 2002, SI 2002/798 . . . . 7.2

Civil Procedure Rules 1998, SI 1998/3132
Pt 36 . . . . 6.11

Collective Redundancies and Transfer of Undertakings (Protection of Employment) (Amendment) Regulations 1995, SI 1995/2587 . . . . . . 6.31

Collective Redundancies and Transfer of Undertakings (Protection of Employment) (Amendment) Regulations 1999, SI 1999/1925 . . . 6.31, 6.54, 6.55, 6.60

Competition Act 2002 (Notification Fee) Regulations 2002, SI 623/2002 (Northern Ireland) 11.139

Control of Asbestos Regulations 2006, SI 2006/2739 . . . . . . 7.35

Control of Major Accident Hazards Regulations 1999, SI 1999/743 . . . . 7.29, 7.48
reg 6 . . . . 7.48

Control of Pollution (Oil Storage) (England) Regulations 2001, SI 2001/2954 . . . . . . 7.36

Corporation Tax (Treatment of Unrelieved Surplus Advance Corporation Tax) Regulations 1999, SI 1999/358 . . 13.8

Employment Act 2002 (Dispute Resolution) Regulations 2004, SI 2004/752 . . . . 6.42

PARA

Employment Equality (Age) Regulations 2006, SI 2006/1031 . . . . 9.3

Employment Tribunals Extension of Jurisdiction (England and Wales) Order 1994, SI 1994/1623
art 10 . . . . 6.22

Enterprise Act 2002 (Merger Fees and Determination of Turnover) Order 2003, SI 2003/1370 . . . . 11.68

Enterprise Act 2002 (Protection of Legitimate Interests) Order 2003, SI 2003/1592 . 11.56

Environmental Information Regulations 2004, SI 2004/3391 . . . . 7.10, 7.48

Environmental Protection (Prescribed Processes and Substances) Regulations 1991, SI 1991/472 . . . . 7.48

Financial Services and Markets Act 2000 (Financial Promotion) Order 2005, SI 2005/1529 . . . . 8.8
art 28, 28A 8.8
48, 49, 62 . . . . 8.8

Greenhouse Gas Emissions Trading Scheme Regulations 2005, SI 2005/925 . . 7.2, 7.32, 7.48

Groundwater Regulations 1998, SI 1998/2746 . . . . 7.23, 7.24

Income Tax (Employments) Regulations 1993, SI 1993/744
reg 55(2) 6.65

PARA

Information and Consultation of
Employees Regulations
2004, SI 2004/3426 ... 6.31, 6.54,
6.55, 6.61, 6.65

Insolvency Rules 1986, SI 1986/
1925
r 4.228 .... 3.10
4.229 .... 3.10, 6.16
4.230(b) 3.10

Money Laundering Regulations
2003, SI 2003/3075 ...... 7.47

Occupational Pension Schemes
(Deficiency on Winding Up
etc) Regulations 1996, SI
1996/3128
reg 16 .... 9.17

Occupational Pension Schemes
(Scheme Funding) Regu-
lations 2005, SI 2005/3377:   9.32

Pensions Regulator (Notifiable
Events) Regulations 2005,
SI 2005/900 ... 9.5, 9.7, 9.28, 9.29

Planning (Hazardous Substances)
Regulations 1992, SI 1992/
656 .... 7.48
reg 5(3) 7.48

Pollution Prevention and Control
(England and Wales} Regu-
lations 2000, SI 2000/1973:   7.23
reg 2(1) 7.23
18 .... 7.48

Producer Responsibility Obligations (Packaging Waste)
Regulations 2005, SI 2005/
3468 .... 7.31

Prospectus Regulations 2005, SI
2005/1433 .... 8.2

Regulatory Reform (Business
Tenancies) (England and
Wales) Order 2003, SI
2003/3096 .... 14.17

Regulatory Reform (Fire Safety)
Order 2005, SI 2005/1541 .   7.6

PARA

Restriction of the Use of Certain
Hazardous Substances in
Electrical and Electronic
Equipment Regulations
2005, SI 2005/2748 ......   7.40

Social Security (Contributions)
Regulations 1979, SI 1979/
591
Sch 1
para 32(1) 6.65

Takeovers Directive (Interim
Implementation) Regula-
tions 2006, SI 2006/1183 . 4.2; 8.53
Sch 2 ....   5.14

Transfer of Undertakings (Protection of Employment)
Regulations 1981, SI 1981/
1794 .... 3.13, 3.14, 3.15,
3.19; 5.15; 6.34, 6.35

Transfer of Undertakings (Protection of Employment)
Regulations 2006, SI 2006/
246 .... 3.14, 3.15, 3.17,
3.19; 6.10, 6.32,
6.34, 6.35, 6.36,
6.39, 6.42, 6.44,
6.50, 6.55, 6.62;
7.4; 8.3; 9.31
reg 2(1) 6.35, 6.36
3(1)(a), (b) 6.35
(4)(a) 6.35
(6)(a), (b) 6.35
4 ....   6.62
(1) 6.36, 6.40
(2) 6.37
(3) 6.38, 6.39
(4) 6.47
(5) 6.47
(a) 3.17
(7) 6.40, 6.43
(8) 6.43
(9) 6.40, 6.43
5 ....   6.37
(a), (b) 6.37
6 ....   6.37
7 .... 6.46, 6.62
(1) 6.39
8(3) 3.15
(7) 6.40, 6.62
9 ....   6.47

PARA

Transfer of Undertakings (Protection of Employment) Regulations 2006 – *contd*
reg 9(7)(b) 6.47
10(1) 6.37
(2) 6.37
(d) 6.65
(3) 6.37, 6.65
11 .... 6.65
13 .... 6.55
(6) 6.57
(9) 6.57, 6.62
15(7) 6.60
(9) 6.33, 6.59
16(3) 6.60
18 .... 6.40
19 .... 6.44

Unfair Dismissal and Statement of Reasons for Dismissal (Variation of Qualifying Period) Order 1999, SI 1999/1436 .... 6.18

PARA

Value Added Tax (Special Provisions) Order 1995, SI 1995/1268
art 5 .... 13.6

Waste Electrical and Electronic Equipment Regulations 2006, SI 2006/3289 ...... 7.39

Waste Management Licensing Regulations 1994, SI 1994/ 1056 .... 7.30, 7.34
Sch 2 .... 7.48

Working Time Regulations 1998, SI 1998/1833 .... 6.65

Table of cases

PARA

A

A & G Tuck Ltd v Bartlett [1994] IRLR 162 . . . . 6.41
ANC Ltd v Clark Golding & Page Ltd [2001] BCC 479 . . . . 8.50
Abbey National plc v HM Revenue and Customs (2006, unreported) 14.17
Abler and others v Sodexo Catering Gesellschaft mbH [2003] C-340/01 . . . . . 6.35
Abrahams v The Performing Rights Society [1995] IRLR 486, [1995] ICR
    1028 . . . . 6.11
Alamo Group (Europe) Ltd v Tucker [2003] IRLR 266 . . . . 6.33
Alamo Group (Europe) Ltd v Twose of Tiverton Ltd [2003] IRLR 266 . . . . . . 6.33
Allen and others v Amalgamated Construction Co Ltd (Case C-234/98) [2000]
    IRLR 119 . . . . 6.35
Alliance Paper Group plc v Prestwich [1996] IRLR 26 . . . . 6.10
Allders Department Stores Ltd, Re [2005] EWHC 172 (Ch), [2005] 2 All ER
    122 . . . . 3.13
Allied Dunbar (Frank Weisinger Ltd v Frank Weisinger [1988] IRLR 60 . . . . 6.10
Asko/Jacobs/Adia 16.5.91 OJ [1991] C132 (Merger Case No IV/M082) 11.15
Auborgine v Lakewood (2002, unreported) 14.14
Avesta 119.6.94 (Merger Case No IV/M452) 11.15

B

BASF/Shell OJ [1998] C81/5 (Merger Case No IV/M1041) 11.12
BAT and Reynolds v Commission and Philip Morris (Cases 142/84 and
    156/84) [1987] ECR 4487 . . . . 11.5
Babcock FATA Ltd v Addison [1987] IRLR 173 . . . . 6.23
Balfour Beatty Power Networks Ltd v Wilcox [2006] IRLR 258 . . . . 6.35
Bank of Ireland v Hollicourt (Contractors) Ltd [2001] Ch 555 . . . . 3.2
Banking Insurance and Finance Union v Barclays Bank plc [1987] ICR 495 . . 6.40
Barber v Guardian Royal Exchange Assurance Group [1990] IRLR 204 . . . . . 9.3
Baxendale v British Nuclear Fuels [1998[IRLR 706 . . . . 6.49, 6.62
Beazer Homes Ltd v Stroude [2005] EWCA Civ 265 . . . . 8.9
Beckman v Dynamco Whicheloe McFarlane Ltd [2002] IRLR 578, ECJ . . . 3.16, 6.37
Bernadone v Pall Mall Services Group [1999] IRLR 617 . . . . 6.37
Berriman v Delabole Slate Ltd [1985] IRLR 305 . . . . 6.44, 6.47
Betts v Brintel Helicopters Ltd [1997] IRLR 361 . . . . 6.3
Bibby Trade Finance Ltd v McKay [2006] EWHC 2936 (Ch), [2006] All ER
    (D) 266 (Jul) 3.6
Blokker/Toyr 'R' Us OJ [1998] L316/1 (Merger Case No IV/M890) 11.14
British Reinforced Concrete Engineering Co Ltd v Schelff [1921] 2 ChD 563: 8.26
Brookes v Borough Care Services [1998] IRLR 636 . . . . 6.16
Brook Lane Finance Co Ltd v Bradley [1988] IRLR 283 . . . . 6.41
Brown v Stockton-on-Tees Borough Council [1988] IRLR 263 . . . . 6.30
Buchanan-Smith v Schleicher & Co International Ltd [1996] ICR 613 . . . . . . 6.36
Buchler v Talbot [2004] UKHL 9, [2004] 2 AC 298 . . . . 3.6
Bushell v Faith [1970] AC 1099 . . . . 6.7
Business Seating (Renovations) Ltd v Broad [1989] ICR 729 . . . . 6.10

PARA

C

CWB/Goldman Sachs/Tarkett 21.2.94 OJ [1994] C67 (Merger Case No
IV/M395) 11.15
CWW Logistics Ltd v Digital Equipment (Scotland) Ltd (EAT 1.12.98) 6.35
CWW Logistics Ltd v Ronald (EAT 1.12.98) 6.35
Cabletel Installations Ltd, Re [2005] BPIR 28 .... 3.8
Carisway Cleaning Consultants Ltd v Richards & Coopers Cleaning Services
(unreported, 19 June 1998) 6.36
Casey v Texas Home Fires Ltd (1998 IDS Brief 376), EAT 6.12
Celtic Ltd v Astley and others [2005] IRLR 647 .... 6.35, 6.41
Cerberus Software Ltd v Rowley [2001] IRLR 160 .... 6.11
Chapman v Aberdeen Construction Group plc [1991] IRLR 505 .... 15.37
Chapman v CPS Computer Systems plc [1987] IRLR 462 .... 5.15
Cheeseman v R Brewer Contracts Ltd [2001] IRLR 144 .... 6.35
Chevron Petroleum (UK) Ltd v BP Petroleum Development Ltd [1981] STC
689 .... 13.32
Churchill v First Independent Factors & Finance Ltd [2006] EWCA Civ 1623: 3.10
Conegrade Ltd, Re [2002] EWHC 2411, [2002] All ER (D) 19 (Nov) 3.11
Conogna/Idea (Merger Case No IV/MOJO) 11.11
Continental Can v European Commission (Case C-6/72) (1973) ECR 215 ... 11.5
Cornwall County Care Ltd v Brightman [1998] IRLR 228 .... 6.47, 6.48
Courtney & Fairbairn Ltd v Tolaini Brothers (Hotels) Ltd [1975] 1 WLR 297: 8.17
Coutaulds Northern Spinning Ltd v Sibson and another [1988] IRLR 305 .... 6.26
Crawford v Swinton Insurance Brokers Ltd [1990] IRLR 42 .... 6.47
Credit Suisse Asset Management Ltd v Armstrong and others [1996] IRLR
450 .... 6.10
Credit Suisse First Boston (Europe) Ltd v Lister [1999] ICR 794 .... 6.47
Credit Suisse First Boston (Europe) Ltd v Padiachy & others [1998[IRLR 504: 6.47
Cross v British Airways plc [2006] EWCA Civ 549 .... 6.37

D

D v M [1996] IRLR 192 .... 6.10
DJM International Ltd v Nicholas [1996] IRLR 76 .... 6.37
Dr Sophie Redmond Stichting v Bartol [1992] IRLR 366 .... 6.35
Dabel v Vale Industrial Services (Nottingham) Ltd [1988] IRLR 127 .... 6.41
Daniel Reeds Ltd v Em-ess Chemists Ltd (unreported, 13 July 1995), CA . 8.30, 8.39
Darlington Borough Council v Wiltshier Northern Ltd [1995] 1 WLR 68 .... 8.50
Dawnay, Re; Day v De Braconier D'Alphen [1997[IRLR 285 .... 15.59
Demite Ltd v Protec Health Ltd [1998] BCC 638 .... 3.11
Dentmaster (UK) Ltd v Kent [1997] IRLR 636 .... 6.10
Derby Daily Telegraph Ltd v The Pensions Ombudsman [1999] IRLR 476 ... 6.22
Derby Daily Telegraph Ltd v Thompson [1999] IRLR 476 .... 6.22
Direct Radiators v Howse and Shepherd [1986] 315 IRLIB 17 .... 6.40
Drageri IBM/HMP (Merger Case No IV/MJ01) 11.11
Duncan Web Offset (Maidstone) Ltd v Cooper [1995] IRLR 633 .... 6.40
Dunnachie v Kingston upon Hull City Council [2004] EWCA Civ 6.23
Duomatic Ltd, Re [1969] 2 Ch 365 .... 3.11
Dylex Ltd, Re (1995) 31 CBR (3d) 105 (Ont Gen Div) 3.31

E

ECM (Vehicle Delivery Services) Ltd v Cox [1999] IRLR 559, CA 6.35
EMI Group Electronics v Coldicott [1999] STC 803 .... 13.30
ESS Production Ltd v Sully [2005] EWCA Civ 554, [2005] All ER (D) 158
(May) 3.10

PARA

Ellis v Torrington [1920] 1 KB 399, CA 8.50
Eridonia/ISI (Merger Case No IV/M062) 11.11
Eurocopy v Teesdale [1992] BCLC 1067 .... 9.30
Evening Standard Co Ltd v Henderson [1987] IRLR 64 .... 6.9

F
First Milk Ltd v Robert Wiseman Dairies (7 April 2005) 11.52
Footwear Corpn Ltd v Amplight Properties Ltd [1998] 3 All ER 52 .... 8.25
Foreningen af Arbejdsledere I Danmark v Daddy's Dance Hall A/S [1988[
    IRLR 315 .... 6.35
Fracmaster Ltd, Re (1999) 11 CBR (4th) 204 (Alta, QB) 3.34
Freakley v Centre Reinsurance International Co [2006] UKHL 45, [2006] All
    ER (D) 121 (Oct) 3.6, 3.8
Fulham Football Club Ltd and Others v Cabra Estates plc [1992] BCC 863 .. 8.31

G
G4S Justice Services (UK) Ltd v Anstey [2006] IRLR 588 .... 6.39
Gateway Hotels Ltd v Stewart [1988] IRLR 287 .... 6.46
General Billposting Co Ltd v Atkinson [1909] AC 118, HL 6.10; 15.59
Global Container Lines Ltd v Black Sea Shipping Co (unreported, 14 July
    1997)... 8.17
Government of Zanzibar v British Aerospace (Lancaster House) Ltd [2000]
    CLC 735 .... 8.7, 8.9
Go Ahead/VIA/Thameslink OJ [1997] C 253/2 (Merger Case No IV/M901) . 11.12
Go West Ltd v Spigarolo [2003] EWCA Civ 17 .... 8.25; 14.14
Gregory v Wallace [1998] IRLR 387 .... 6.11
Grimstead (EA) & Sons Ltd v McGarrigan (unreported, 27 October 1999) .. 8.7, 8.9

H
Hadley v Baxendale [1854] 9 Ex 341 .... 6.22
Hay v George Hanson (Building Contractors) Ltd [1996] IRLR 427 .... 6.43
Higher Education Statistics Agency Ltd v C & E Commrs [2000] STC 332 .. 13.6
Hill v CA Parsons & Co Ltd [1972] Ch 305, [1971] 3 All ER 1345 .... 6.6
Hinton v University of East London [2005] IRLR 552 .... 6.11
Homebase Ltd v Allied Dunbar Assurance plc [2002] EWCA Civ 666, [2002]
    L & TR 27 .... 14.6
Hope v PGS Engineering Ltd (in administration) (EAT 0267/04) [2005]
    UKEAT 0267 .... 6.43
Howard v Millrise Ltd t/a Colourflow (in liquidation) [2005] IRLR 84 ...... 6.55
Howard v SG Printers t/a Colourflow [2005] IRLR 84 .... 6.55
Huddersfield Fine Worsteds Ltd, Re [2005] EWCA Civ 1072. [2005] 4 All ER
    886 .... 3.13
Hutchings v Coinseed Ltd [1998] IRLR 190 .... 6.9

I
IBA Health Ltd v Office of Fair Trading [2003] CAT 28 .... 11.50, 11.70
ICI/Tioxide 28.11.90 (Merger Case No IV/M023) 11.15
IRC v Falkirk Ice Rink [1975] STC 434 .... 13.16
Infiniteland Ltd and JS Ariss v Artisan Contracting Ltd and Artisan (UK) plc
    [2004] All ER (D) 350 .... 8.30
Ingersol Rand/Dresner (Merger Case No IV/M121) 11.11
Investors Compensation Scheme Ltd v West Bromwich Building Society
    [1998] 1 WLR 896, HL 8.9

Table of cases

PARA

J

James Snook & Co Ltd v Blasdale (1932) 33 TC 244 .... 13.30
Jones v Darlows Estate Agency (CA LTL 6.7.98) 6.36
Jules Dethier Equipment SA v Dasey and Sovram Sprl (in liquidation) [1998]
    IRLR 266 .... 6.39, 6.44

K

Katsikas v Konstantinides [1993] IRLR 179 .... 6.43
Kerry Foods Ltd v Creber and others [2000] IRLR 10, EAT 6.33, 6.59
Kesko/Tuko OJ[1997[Ll10/53 (Merger Case No IV/M784) 11.14
Kwik Save Group plc, Re [1994] VATTR 457 .... 13.6

L

LTE Scientific Ltd v Thomas [2005] EWHC 7 .... 15.59
Langley and another v Burso [2006] ICR 850 .... 6.23
Lansing Linde Ltd v Kerr [1991] IRLR 80 .... 6.10
Ledernes Hoverdorganisation v Dansk Arbejdsgiverforening [1995] ECR I-
    2745 .... 6.35
Levett v Biotrace International plc [1999] IRLR 375 .... 6.22
Levison v Farin [1978] 2 All ER 1149 .... 8.30
Leyland Daf, Re [1994] 4 All ER 300; affd [1995] 2 AC 394 .... 3.13
Lightways (Contractors) Ltd v Associated Holdings Ltd (EAT 17.11.98) 6.35
Lightways (Contractors) Ltd v Hood and others (EAT 17.11.98) 6.35
Litster and others v Forth Dry Dock & Engineeing Co Ltd (in receivership) and
    another [1989] IRLR 161 .... 6.39, 6.40, 6.41, 6.46, 6.62
Little v Courage (The Times, 19 January 1994) 8.17
Living Design (Home Improvements) Ltd v Davidson [1994] IRLR 67 ...... 6.10
Lquitur Ltd, Re [2003] EWHC 999 .... 8.9
Lowe v Lombank Ltd [1960] 1 MR 196 .... 8.9
Lunt v Merseyside TEC [1999[IRLR 458 .... 6.11
Lyonnaise des Eate Dumz/Biochie (Merger Case No IV/M076) v 11.11

M

MAN Nutzfahrzeuge AG v Freighliner Ltd [2005] EWHC 2347 .... 8.30
MEI Computer Technology Group Inc, Re (2005) Can Lll 15656 (QC CS) ... 3.32
Macer v Abafast [1990] ICR 234 .... 6.41
Maggs v Marsh [2006] All ER (D) 95 .... 8.9
Magna Housing Association Ltd v Landscaping & Grounds Maintenance Ltd
    (unreported 21 October 1998), EAT 6.35
Magna Housing Association Ltd v Raison (unreported 21 October 1998), EAT: 6.35
Magna Housing Association Ltd v Turner (unreported 21 October 1998), EAT: 6.35
Mann v Secretary of State for Employment [1999] IRLR 566 .... 6.54
Marren v Ingles (1980) 54 TC 76 .... 13.35
Marshall v NM Financial Management Ltd [1996] IRLR 20 .... 6.10
Martin v Lancashire County Council [2000] IRLR 487, CA 6.37
Martin v South Bank University [2004] IRLR 74, ECJ 3.16
Meade v British Nuclear Fuels [1998[IRLR 706 .... 6.49, 6.62
Merckx v Ford Motors [1997] ICR 352 .... 6.43
Micklefield v SAC Technology Ltd [1990] IRLR 218 .... 6.12; 15.37
Morris v John Grose Group Ltd [1998] ICR 655 .... 6.44
Morris Angel & Son Ltd v Hollande [1993] RLR 169 .... 6.10
Morris (Herbert) Ltd v Saxelby [1916] 1 AC 688 .... 6.10
Murray v Foyle Meats Ltd [1999] IRLR 562 .... 6.30

PARA

N

National Bank of Sharjah v Delborg (unreported, 9 July 1997) 8.9
New Hearts v Cosmopolitan Investments Ltd [1997] 2 BCLC 249 .... 8.30, 8.39
New Skeema Forest Products Inc, Re 2005 BCCA 192 (Can Lll) 3.33
Nicholl v Cutts (1985) 1 BCC 99 .... 3.13
Nokes v Doncaster Amalgamated Collieries Ltd [1940] AC 1014 .... 6.25, 6.34
North East Lincolnshire Council v Beck and others (EAT 21.1.99) 6.35
Norton Tool Co Ltd v Tewson [1973] 1 WLR 4445 .... 6.23

O

OCS Cleaning Scotland Ltd v Olscot Ltd (EAT 29.6.99) 6.35
OCS Cleaning Scotland Ltd v Rudden (EAT 29.6.99) 6.35
Ontario Ltd (1078385), Re [2004] OJ No 6050 (QL) (CA) 3.34
Oxford University v Humphreys and another [2000] IRLR 183 .... 6.43

P

P & O Property Holdings Ltd v Allen [1997] ICR 436 .... 6.43
PR Consultants Scotland Ltd v Mann [1996] IRLR 188 .... 6.10
Paramount Airways Ltd (No 3), Re [1994] 2 All ER 513, CA; affd [1995] 2 AC
    394, HL 3.13, 3.14
Pearson & Son Ltd v Dublin Corpn [1907] AC 351 .... 8.9
Pechiney/ Ustinov-Sacllov (Merger Case No IV/M097) 11.11
Penrose v Official Receiver [1996] 2 All ER 96 .... 3.10
Photostatic Copiers (Southern) Ltd v Okuda and Japan Office Equipment
    [1995] IRLR 11 .... 6.40
Pitt v PHH Asset Management Ltd [1994] 1 WLR 327 .... 8.17
Polkey v AE Dayton Services Ltd [1987] IRLR 503 .... 6.30
Prestwick Circuits Ltd v McAndrew [1990] IRLR 911 .... 6.26
Provident Financial Group plc and Whitegates Estate Agency Ltd v Hayward
    [1989] IRLR 84 .... 6.9

Q

QR Sciences Ltd v BTG International Ltd [2005] EWHC 670 .... 8.17
Quality Kebab Ltd, Re [2006] EWHC 1764, [2006] All ER (D) 162 (June) ... 3.9

R

R v Panel on Takeovers and Mergers, ex p Guinness plc [1989] 1 All ER 509: 8.53
RCO Support Services Ltd, ex p Aintree Hospital Trust v Unison and others
    [2002[IRLR 401, CA 6.35
Rank Xerox Ltd v Chruchill [1988[IRLR 280 .... 6.26
Rao v Civil Aviation Authority [1992] IRLR 203 .... 6.30
Rask v ISS Kantineservice A/S [1993] IRLR 133 .... 6.35
Renault/Volvo (Merger ase No IV/M004) 11.9
Rendall v Morphew [1915] 112 LT 285 .... 8.51
Richardson (HM Inspector of Taxes) v Delaney [2001] IRLR 663 .... 13.30
Ricketts v Ad Valorem Factors Ltd [2003] EWCA Civ 1706, [2004] 1 All ER
    894 .... 3.10
Rock Refrigeration Ltd v Jones & Seward Refrigeration Ltd [1996] IRLR 675   6.10
Rossiter v Pendragon plc [2002] IRLR 483 .... 6.28
Rotsart De Hertaing v J Benoidt SA (in liquidation) and IGC Housing Service
    SA [1997] IRLR 127 .... 6.40, 6.41
Royal Oak Mines Inc, Re [1991] OJ No 709 (QL) (Ont Gen Div) 3.31
Russell v Northern Bank [1992] 3 All ER 161 .... 15.50

PARA

S

SBJ Stephenson Ltd v Mandy [2000] IRLR 233 .... 6.10
SE Services Ltd, Re (unreported) 3.8
St Martin's Property Corpn Ltd v Sir Robert McAlpine & Sons Ltd [1994] 1
   AC 85 .... 8.50
Sainsbury (J) plc v O'Connor [1991] STC 318 .... 13.21
Salomon v Salomon Co Ltd [1897] AC 22 .... 6.16
Samsung/AST 26.5.97 OJ [1997] C203/3 (Merger Case No IV/M920) 11.34
Sanofi/Synthelabo 17.5.99 (Merger Case No IV/M1397) 11.34
Scammell v Ouston [1941] AC 251 .... 8.17
Scully UK Ltd v Lee [1998[IRLR 259 .... 6.10
Secretary of State for Employment v Spence [1987] QB 179 .... 6.38
Secretary of State for Trade and Industry v Cook [1997] ICR 288 .... 6.40
Senate Electrical Wholesalers v Alcatel Submarine Networks [1999] 2 Lloyd's
   Rep 423 .... 8.29, 8.42
Senior Heat Treatment Ltd v Bell and others [1997] IRLR 614 .... 6.41, 6.43
Simmonds v Dowty Seals Ltd [1978] IRLR 211, EAT 6.2
Skydome Corpn, Re (1998) 16 CBR (4th) 118 (Ont Gen Div) 3.31
Snell v Revenue and Customs Commrs [2006] STC (SCD) 296 .... 13.53
Soveriegn Distribution Services Ltd v Transport and General Workers Union
   [1989] IRLR 334 .... 6.54
Spar/Dansk Supermarket OJ [1994] C132 (Merger Case No IV/M179) 11.12
Specialised Mouldings Ltd, Re (unreported, 13 February 1987) 3.13
Spectrum Plus, Re [2005] UKHL 41, [2005] 4 All ER 209 .... 3.6
Spencer v Marchington [1988[IRLR 392 .... 6.9
Spijkers v Gebroeders Benedik Abattoir CV [1986] 2 CMLR 296 .... 6.35
Susie Radin Ltd v GMB and others [2004] IRLR 400 .... 6.60
Süzen v Zehnacker Gebäudereinigung GmbH Krankenhausservice [1997]
   IRLR 255 .... 6.35
Sweetin v Coral Racing [2006] IRLR 252 .... 6.60
Symbian Ltd v Christensen [2000] UKCLR 879 .... 6.9
Systems Reliability Holdings plc v Smith [1990] IRLR 377 .... 15.59

T

T & D Industries plc, Re [2000] 1 All ER 333 .... 3.9
TGWU v Brauer Coley Ltd (in administration) UKEAT 3.13
TNT/Canada Post and others 2.12.91 (Merger Case No IV/M012) 11.15
TSC Europe (UK) Ltd v Massey [1999] IRLR 22 .... 6.10
Taylor v Connex South Eastern Ltd (unreported, 5 July 2000), EAT 6.47
Tetra Laval/Sidel (Merger Case COMP/M3255) 11.34
Thomas v Ewar Stud Farms Ltd and Lord Tyron [2002] All ER (D) 372 (Jan),
   EAT 6.43
Thomas Witter Ltd v TBP Industries [1996] 2 All ER 573 .... 8.7, 8.9
Thompson and others v Walon Car Delivery and BRS Automotive Ltd [1997]
   IRLR 343 .... 6.39, 6.50
Thompson v SCS Consulting Ltd [2001] IRLR 801 .... 6.62
Transbus International Ltd [2004] EWHC 932, [2004] 2 All ER 911 .... 3.9
Trego v Hunt [1896] AC 7 .... 8.26
Trendtex Trading Corpn v Credit Suisse [1981] 3 All ER 520, HL 8.50

U

Ultraframe (UK) Ltd v Fielding [2005] EWHC 1638, [2005] All ER (D) 397
   (Jul) 3.11
Unichem Ltd v Office of Fair Trading [2005] All ER (D) 51 (Sep) 11.50, 11.70

PARA

Unicorn Consultancy Services Ltd v Westbrook & others [2000] IRLR 80,
    EAT 6.37
United Bank Ltd v Akhtar [1989] IRLR 507 .... 6.26
United Used Auto & Truck Parts Ltd, Re (1999) Can Lll 5374 (BC SC) 3.31

V
Varta/Bosch (Merger Case No IV/M012) 11.11

W
Walford and others v Miles and another [1992] 1 All ER 453 .... 8.17
Walls Meat Co Ltd v Selby [1989] ICR 601 .... 6.30
Watford Electronics Ltd v Sanderson CFL Ltd [2001] All ER (D) 290 ..... 8.7, 8.9
Werhof v Freeway Traffic Systems [2006] IRLR 400 .... 6.37
Westar Mining Ltd, Re (1992) 14 CBR (3d) 88 (BC SC) 3.30
Western Excavating (ECC) Ltd v Sharp [1977] IRLR 25 .... 6.28
Western Wagon & Property Co v West [1892] 1 Ch 271 .... 8.50
Wheeler v Patel and another [1987] IRLR 211 .... 6.44
Whitehouse v Blatchford & Sons Ltd [1999] IRLR 492, CA 6.44, 6.46
William Hill Organisation Ltd v Tucker [1998] IRLR 313 .... 6.9
William West & Sons (Ilkeston) Ltd v EXEL/BRS Ltd (EAT 701/98) 6.10, 6.37
William West & Sons (Ilkeston) Ltd v Mr W Fairgieve and others (EAT
    701/98) 6.10, 6.37
Williams v Compare Maxam Ltd [1982] IRLR 83 .... 6.30
Williams v Natural Life Health Foods [1998] 1 WLR 830, HL 8.13
Wilson and others v St Helens BC [1998] IRLR 706 .... 6.36, 6.44, 6.47, 6.48
Wood Preservation v Prior [1969] 1 All ER 364 .... 13.21
Wren v Eastbourne Borough Council [1993] IRLR 425 .... 6.35

Z
Zim Properties Ltd v Proctor [1985] STC 90 .... 13.39

Chapter 1

Introduction

1.1 In the business press and in academic circles, acquisitions are as well known for destroying value as creating it. Successful value building buyers think, plan and execute acquisitions in quite a different way to those who are less successful. So what differentiates the value builders from the value destroyers?

Great judgment and superb execution are the hallmarks of the value-building buyer. They will also tend to apply the same principles to acquisitions as they do to organic growth. In the context of an acquisition these are:

- Clarity of purpose

  They know what they want to buy, why and what they are going to do with it.

- Best team for the job

  They assemble the right teams from within and outside the company to make the acquisition decision, to do the deal and then to maximise the value once the deal is done.

- Right processes

  They have a rigorous and very detailed set of processes for each stage of the acquisition from initial decision to post acquisition review. These processes are aimed at maximising value and minimising risk.

Value through an acquisition is generated by buying well and then increasing the value of what you have bought.

The commercial environment has a significant impact on the availability, pricing and risk of acquisition targets. By way of illustration, the chart below from Deallogic's Merger and Acquisitions review of 2006 showing announced deal volume and value for each quarter since 2000, reveals how activity was affected by the collapse in confidence in the capital markets which took place in the first few years of the decade and then recovered strongly from the middle of 2003.

Quarterly Global M&A Volume

Growth in the volume of M&A activity is driven by growth in the numbers of willing buyers and sellers. The increase in buyers is fuelled by greater confidence, a return to growth agendas following several years of battening down the hatches, and the combined forces of internationalisation and industry consolidation. These forces will increase the number of sellers, especially in continental Europe. Succession issues in private businesses provide another important source of supply. A further boost is provided when confidence in capital markets enables corporates to use their shares to do deals, something which only a few were able to do in the early part of the decade.

Another feature of the second half of the decade has been the increase in average size of transactions and the proportion of activity accounted for by Private Equity. The average deal size recorded in the Deallogic survey rose by 24% in 2006 to some $213m. The numbers of Billion dollar plus deals was a key factor in this. In 2006 there were over 650 $1bn deals compared to under 500 in 2005. Private Equity which accounted for 12% of total deal value in 2005 increased to 18% in 2006. Funds raised by Private Equity firms in 2006 of over $300bn suggest that there is the financial firepower to sustain this level of activity. In recognition of this trend we have added a specific chapter on Private Equity in this latest edition.

A consequence of increased M&A activity could be increased competition for your chosen target. Legendary management guru Warren Bennis once said that:

'Power is the ability to convert vision into reality.'

The powerful acquirer, therefore, needs to possess not just an eye for a great deal but the capability to turn it into a reality by beating the competition and avoiding the winner's curse of paying too high a price.

Highly effective operational CEOs don't necessarily make good buyers of businesses. Many of the most talented opportunity spotters and negotiators recognise that they need someone else to manage the acquisition, deliver the synergies and then grow the business once the deal has taken place. Value building buyers tend to have an accurate understanding of their own competence.

What about the mistakes? Why do so many acquisitions fail to deliver their value creating objectives? Overpaying and weak due diligence are the most obvious. Less obvious, but equally deadly, is to underestimate the management capacity required to effect a successful acquisition and, especially in bull markets or after a run of success, to overestimate our capability. Seasoned investor Warren Buffet's advice is especially worth bearing in mind in this respect:

> 'In a bull market one must avoid the error of the preening duck that quacks boastfully after a torrential rainstorm, thinking that its paddling skills have caused it to rise in the world. A right thinking duck would instead compare its position after the downpour to that of other ducks in the pond.'

Another critical sign that an acquisition is doomed is failure to establish the right board immediately post acquisition. Trade-offs over board seats in the middle of negotiations for all sorts of well-intentioned reasons frequently turn out to hinder the business post acquisition.

So, before even embarking on the acquisition search the top team should test whether they really do have the capacity and capability to make it a success.

A further important aspect to take into account is the balancing of business and financial risk. Value destroying boards appear happy to take on high levels of both.

Judging success in acquisitions needs to be viewed over a reasonably long period and also needs to take into account the economic and capital markets environment. So it is worth looking back at research from earlier years when different conditions prevailed. A report published by KPMG in 1999 Unlocking shareholder value: The keys to success, Mergers and Acquisitions A Global research report, which looked at 100 major cross-border deals in the previous few years in detail, contains the following paragraph.

How good are companies at mergers and acquisitions?

The survey found that 82% of respondents (the managers in the businesses) believed that the major deal that they had been involved in had been a success. However this was a subjective estimation of their success in achieving the deal objectives and less than half had carried out a formal review process. When we measured each one against our independent benchmark, based on comparative share performance one year after deal completion, the result was almost a mirror opposite. We found that only 17% of the deals had added value to the combined company. Thirty per cent produced no discernible difference, and as many as 53% actually destroyed value. In other words 83% of mergers were unsuccessful in producing any business benefits as regards shareholder value.

This is even more striking when you remember that this was in a healthy economic environment. So, when you hear a CEO utter the words '*this is a transformational acquisition*' he's likely to be right, but you should think hard about whether it will be for the best.

The merger of AOL, the internet service provider, and Time Warner, the publisher, in the United States in January 2000, a deal done at the peak of internet hubris, is an excellent example of a value destroyer. Pre-deal AOL was capitalised at around $136 billion and Time Warner $100bn. AOL employed around 12,000 people and Time Warner 70,000. The underlying logic for the deal was to marry Time Warner's content with AOL's distribution. Just two years later the combined business announced a loss of almost $100bn for the previous year and in early 2003, after much management change, the name AOL was dropped from the title. I'd say that was transformational.

Planning, logistics and sheer hard work in a deal are critical to making an excellent acquisition succeed, but '*a dog of a deal, is a dog of a deal*'. No doubt a huge amount of skill and effort was applied from some very talented people in putting together the AOL Time Warner deal but it was by any definition 'a dog of a deal' and value destroyer.

In recent years three factors have gained significantly higher prominence in acquisitions than was historically the case. These relate to increased scrutiny from independent directors, the media and regulatory authorities.

The collapse of Enron, Worldcom, Marconi, Vivendi and others at the beginning of this decade heightened the responsibility of independent directors and chairmen to ensure that there is good governance. Government reviews, and in some cases new laws such as Sarbannes Oxley in the US, may well have increased the power of independent directors but they have also significantly increased the risks. A consequence of this has been that they have needed to be surer than ever that the process for deciding and executing acquisitions is right. In my view this adds values except in cases where it has led to a risk averse board.

A supportive press can make an acquisition easier to achieve. If a company has developed a positive media profile over many years and on announcement the press report that the deal makes sense, the job of gaining buy in to the deal from many of the key audiences, including staff, will be much easier. If the company has a bad reputation and the press is hostile to the deal then it will prove harder to succeed. A major acquisition of a public or high-profile target requires a media savvy board and CEO who are also well advised.

Probably the two highest profile thwarted acquisitions this decade which collapsed due to competitive regulatory issues were General Electric's bid for Honeywell and the proposed purchase/ carve up of BOC Group by Air Products and L'Air Liquide. The chapter in Jack Welch's autobiography *Straight from the Gut* describing the process and the cultural clash between the driven CEO who is used to getting what he wants and the bureaucrat is most revealing and a salutatory lesson. Corporate Social Responsibility has also been high on the agenda in many European countries for a long time and has risen sharply up the agenda in many others. This is likely, and already has to some extent, lead to greater regulation.

The UK and the US have long been considered to be comparatively 'open' markets for bidders, local or foreign, friendly or hostile. This is still the case in the UK as the takeover of the UK airport's business BAA plc by Ferrovial from Spain in 2006 demonstrated. However there is a growing feeling that the US has become more sensitive to bids for US companies by foreign buyers as the acquisition by Dubai Ports World ('DP') of P&O, a UK company which owned a number of US ports revealed. In this case there was a significant amount of political activity and DP were not allowed to acquire the US activity. A thwarted Chinese bid for Unocal was also interesting in this regard.

In many other industrialised economies attitudes to M&A are to say the least less than friendly. One only has to look at the tremendous debate and opposition in the German press to Vodafone's takeover of Mannesman in 2000 and M&A activity levels in France and Germany compared with the US and UK to see this. The so called 'locust debate' in Germany in 2006 also highlighted the cultural differences in receptiveness to M&A activity and private equity in particular. In continental Europe acquisitions have tended to be friendly affairs and driven by natural extension of product or geography. The large-scale restructuring required in some of the continental European countries dealing with high costs and less flexibility in ever more competitive markets and falling working age populations inevitably drives increased M&A activity.

One very interesting trickle of activity which may well turn into a sustained trend is that of Asian companies becoming more significant international purchasers of businesses. It would seem entirely logical, especially for major Indian and Chinese corporates to use their increasing financial power to grow through acquisition as well as to develop their businesses organically. The £6.2bn takeover of UK steel business Corus by Tata of India is a very good example of this. Interestingly in this case the underbidder was Brazil's CSN Group, demonstrating that this trend will not be confined just to Asia but to other rapidly developing regions.

Summary

1.2   Success in acquisitions, whether you are buying or selling, is down to great judgement and superb execution. The pages which follow will provide some useful insights to inform the judgements and execution plans for those contemplating an acquisition.

Chapter 2

Accounting

At a glance

- Two different accounting frameworks may be applicable – UK GAAP and IFRSs – significant differences exist

- Merger relief may permit non-recognition of share premium on shares issued in connection with an acquisition

- Parent/subsidiary relationship is defined by ability to exercise control, rather than by shareholding

- Exemptions from preparing consolidated accounts are available for intermediate parent companies and parents of small and medium-sized groups

- UK GAAP permits two forms of accounting for business combinations – merger accounting (in limited circumstances) and acquisition accounting

- Merger accounting represents a combining of interests – but is not permitted under IFRSs

- Acquisition accounting involves determination of fair values of net assets acquired and of consideration given

- Under UK GAAP goodwill is capitalised and amortised over its useful economic life – under IFRSs goodwill is capitalised but subject to annual impairment review

- Choice of accounting framework may affect the view given by the balance sheet, borrowing covenants and distributable reserves

Introduction

2.1   This chapter considers some of the practical accounting implications of corporate acquisitions and mergers. It focuses primarily on accounting under UK GAAP but provides an insight into the principal differences between the UK's accounting framework and International Financial Reporting Standards which are becoming increasingly important both in terms of global financial reporting and in the development of the UK's own company law and standards.

The chapter is written primarily from the viewpoint of a UK company entering into a business combination by acquiring shares in another corporate vehicle. Many of the principles however apply to any business combination which is defined in UK Financial Reporting Standards as 'the bringing together of separate entities into one economic entity as a result of one entity uniting with, or obtaining control over the net assets and operations of, another'.

At the time of writing many parts of the *Companies Act 1985* are in the process of being replaced by equivalent provisions derived from the *Companies Act 2006* and Regulations to be made under it. However, the new provisions are not yet in force and this chapter therefore continues to refer to the 1985 Act. Other than removal of the exemption for medium sized groups from preparing consolidated accounts (see **2.8**) it is not expected that the 2006 Act will substantively change any of the principles or requirements set out here.

Accounting framework

2.2   Until recently all UK companies were required to prepare their annual financial statements in accordance with detailed accounting and disclosure requirements set out in the *Companies Act 1985 (CA 1985)*. In addition, companies (with the exception of small and medium-sized companies) were required to state whether the financial statements had been prepared in accordance with applicable accounting standards – which means Financial Reporting Standards ('FRSs') issued by the Accounting Standards Board ('ASB') together with Statements of Standard Accounting Practice ('SSAPs') adopted by the Board and authoritative interpretations of such standards issued by the ASB's Urgent Issues Task Force ('UITF').

Whether or not such a statement is required by the Act it is generally held that compliance with applicable standards is necessary for entities of all sizes in order for the financial statements to give a true and fair view – although departures are permitted in rare circumstances where compliance with the relevant standard would not result in a true and fair view.

This situation changed with effect from 1 January 2005. For accounting periods commencing on or after that date, Article 4 of EC Regulation No 1606/2002 of the European Parliament and of the Council requires all companies with securities traded on a recognised stock exchange within the EU to prepare their consolidated accounts in accordance with International Financial Reporting Standards (IFRSs). The Regulation effectively overrides previous requirements of the Act relating to the form and content of consolidated accounts for such companies but other requirements of the Act continue to apply.

At the same time the *Companies Act* was amended to permit the use of IFRSs as a basis for the preparation of financial statements by most unlisted companies and by listed companies preparing individual entity (as opposed to consolidated) accounts subject to certain conditions. As a result there are now two possible bases on which financial statements may be prepared:

- *Companies Act 1985* rules together with applicable UK accounting standards. This is known as UK Generally Accepted Accounting Principles (or Practice) ('UK GAAP'); or

- International Financial Reporting Standards ('IFRSs'), as adopted by the European Union.

Generally speaking a parent company (other than a listed company) may choose to use either framework for its consolidated accounts and may use either the same or a different framework for its individual accounts. Subsidiaries may use either framework, provided that all subsidiaries in the same group use the same framework. This need not be the framework used by the parent. Charities may not use IFRSs under any circumstances. However, once a company has switched to IFRSs as the basis for preparing its financial statements it may not switch back to UK GAAP unless there is a good reason to do so.

When considering the accounting implications of a business combination it is important to establish which framework will apply as there are a number of significant differences between them.

UK GAAP

2.3   Under UK GAAP accounting for acquisitions and mergers is largely governed by the *Companies Act 1985* and the following financial reporting standards:

- FRS 2 Accounting for subsidiary undertakings.

- FRS 6 Acquisitions and mergers.

- FRS 7 Fair values in acquisition accounting.

- FRS 10 Goodwill and intangible assets.

- FRS 11 Impairment of fixed assets and goodwill.

Parent company's individual accounts

2.4   In the parent entity's own accounts an investment in a subsidiary undertaking will initially be recognised at cost as required by the *Companies Act*. Subsequently the carrying amount may be determined on any basis that the directors consider to be appropriate providing that the carrying amount of the investment does not exceed its estimated recoverable amount.

Cost for this purpose will be the cost of the acquisition determined in accordance with FRS 7, ie cash paid together with the fair value of any other consideration and expenses incidental to the acquisition – subject to merger relief rules explained below.

As with any other asset, whenever there is an indication that an investment may be impaired FRS 11 Impairment of fixed assets and goodwill requires that the directors of the parent conduct an impairment review to determine the extent, if any, of the impairment. Impairment arises when the carrying value of the investment exceeds is recoverable amount, which in turn is measured as the higher of the amount that could be realised on a sale and the net present value of future cash flows expected to arise from it. Indications of impairment would include, for example, a failure by the acquired entity to achieve levels of performance anticipated at the time of the acquisition.

Share for share transactions and merger relief

2.5   Where part of the consideration for the acquisition of an interest in a subsidiary is satisfied by an issue of shares by the parent the 'cost' will include the fair value of the shares issued – with any excess of fair value over nominal value being recorded as share premium in accordance with *section 130* of *CA 1985*. However in certain circumstances the *Companies Act* provides an exemption from this requirement known as 'merger relief'.

Section 131 of *CA 1985* provides that where shares are issued by an entity under an arrangement whereby:

- the consideration for the shares allotted is the transfer, issue or cancellation of equity shares in another entity; and

- at least 90% of the nominal value of each class of the equity share capital of the acquired company is acquired as a result of the arrangement

then *section 130* does not apply and there is no requirement to credit any 'premium' arising on the issue of the shares to a share premium account. The Act does not specify what to do with any premium thus arising – generally it is credited to a separate reserve in the parent entity's balance sheet which may be called a 'merger reserve'; or something similar. This reserve is not subject to the same legal restrictions as a share premium account.

Where the conditions referred to above are met *section 131* applies to any shares issued as consideration for the acquisition regardless of what of the proportion of the total consideration they represent. It is also not necessary for the 90% threshold to be achieved in one transaction. So, for example, if company A already owned 50% of the equity shares of company B and issued shares to acquire an additional 40% then *section 131* would apply and no share premium need be recognised as a result of this transaction. It would not, however, have applied to A's earlier purchase of shares in B and could not be applied retrospectively.

The terms 'merger relief' and 'merger reserve' are slightly misleading in this context as the relief applies to any arrangement meeting the conditions described above – whether or not it qualifies, or is accounted for as a true merger. Merger relief thus commonly applies in business combinations accounted for as acquisitions – provided that the acquiring company acquires an interest of at least 90% in the acquiree.

However, *section 133* of *CA 1985* further permits the 'premium' to be disregarded in determining the amount at which the investment is to be included in the parent's balance sheet, effectively allowing the investment to be carried at the nominal value only of the shares issued.

There is therefore a range of possible accounting treatments:

(a) Include in cost of investment the fair value of shares issued, with the excess over nominal value being treated as share premium. This is not generally a popular option as legal restrictions on the use of a share premium account severely limit the entity's options in the future regarding distributions or recognition of impairment losses.

(b) Include in cost of investment the fair value of shares issued but take the 'premium' to a separate merger reserve. This has the advantage of better reflecting the true value of the investment in the parent's own balance sheet, but without the problems of a share premium account. Should the need arise in future to recognise an impairment write down this can be set against the merger reserve rather than the profit and loss account reserve. In addition the merger reserve may, in some circumstances, be regarded as realised – enhancing the parent company's ability to make distributions to shareholders.

(c) Record the investment initially at the nominal value of shares issued. This has the advantage of not creating a share premium – but does not generate the possibility of additional distributable reserves. This treatment would normally be applied where the combination is regarded as a merger rather than an acquisition but can also be legitimately applied in the case of an acquisition.

(d) Record the investment initially using one of the three methods above and subsequently revalue (for example to net asset value). Revaluation enables the parent to reflect value changes in its own balance sheet as well as in the consolidated balance sheet. Note however that any revaluation reserve created in this way will only become distributable on disposal of the investment – unlike the merger reserve referred to in (b) above.

Consolidated financial statements

2.6   Subject to certain exemptions mentioned below, where a company is, at the end of its financial year, a parent company, it is required by *section 227* of *CA 1985* to prepare group accounts as well as its individual accounts for the year. The group accounts required are consolidated accounts dealing with the state of affairs and profit or loss of the parent company and its subsidiary undertakings.

Section 258 of *CA 1985* defines parent and subsidiary undertakings. The definition is restated in paragraph 14 of FRS 2:

> 'An undertaking is the parent undertaking of another undertaking (a subsidiary undertaking) if any of the following apply.

(a)   It holds a majority of the voting rights in the undertaking.
(b)   It is a member of the undertaking and has the right to appoint or remove directors holding a majority of the voting rights at meetings of the board on all, or substantially all, matters.
(c)   It has the right to exercise a dominant influence over the undertaking:
   (i)   by virtue of provisions contained in the undertaking's memorandum or articles; or
   (ii) by virtue of a control contract. The control contract must be in writing and be of a kind authorised by the memorandum or articles of the controlled undertaking. It must also be permitted by the law under which that undertaking is established.
(d)   It is a member of the undertaking and controls alone, pursuant to an agreement with other shareholders or members, a majority of the voting rights in the undertaking;
(e)   (i)   it has power to exercise, or actually exercises, dominant influence or control over it, or
   (ii) it and the subsidiary undertaking are managed on a unified basis.
(f)   A parent undertaking is also treated as the parent undertaking of the subsidiary undertakings of its subsidiary undertakings.'

In this chapter, references to 'subsidiary' mean 'subsidiary undertaking' as defined above, and not 'subsidiary company' as defined in *section 736* of *CA 1985*. One difference is that the *section 258* definition includes the concepts of 'dominant influence' and 'control' and thereby includes a number of companies that would not meet the strictly objective definition of subsidiary company under *section 736*. Another significant difference is that the *section 258* definition includes undertakings such as partnerships, unincorporated bodies and overseas entities that would not be classified as subsidiary companies.

The *section 258* definition of subsidiary undertakings was changed with effect for years ending on or after 31 January 2005 to emphasise the importance of 'control' in the parent/subsidiary relationship and to bring it more closely into line with the definition used in International Financial Reporting Standards. In effect one entity is a subsidiary of another ('the parent') if the parent has the ability to exercise control over it – where control is the ability to direct the financial and operating policies of the entity with a view to gaining economic benefit from them. It does not matter whether the ability to exercise control derives from the parent's rights as a shareholder, its ability to control the composition of the board or from other factors. It also doesn't matter whether the parent actually exercises control – it is the ability to exercise control that counts.

FRS 5 'Reporting the substance of transactions' introduced the concept of the 'quasi-subsidiary' where the nature of the relationship between two entities was in substance indistinguishable from that of parent and subsidiary but the quasi subsidiary did not meet the legal definition of a subsidiary. Whilst FRS 5 retains the concept it would now appear to be largely redundant following the change to the definition referred to above, as this permits a parent/subsidiary relationship to be established even where the parent holds only a minority interest in the subsidiary, or even no shares at all.

Consolidation exemptions

Intermediate parent company exemptions

2.7   A parent company which is itself a subsidiary of a parent undertaking established under the law of a European Economic Area (EEA) state will generally be able to claim exemption from the requirement to prepare consolidated accounts by virtue of *section 228* of *CA 1985*. From 1 January 2005 *section 228A* of *CA 1985* introduced a similar exemption for subsidiaries of parent undertakings established outside the EEA. For this purpose the EEA comprises the member states of the European Union, Norway, Iceland and Liechtenstein.

For a company to take advantage of one of these exemptions the parent must hold more than 50% of the shares in the company and it must not have received notice from shareholders holding in aggregate more than half of the remaining shares or 5% of the total shares in the company, requesting the preparation of group accounts.

The exemptions are further conditional on compliance with all of the following conditions:

(a)   that the company and its subsidiaries are included in audited consolidated accounts for a larger group drawn up to the same date, or to an earlier date in the same financial year, by a parent undertaking;

(b)   in a case where that parent is incorporated under the law of an EEA state, that those accounts and the parent undertaking's annual report are drawn up, according to that law, in accordance with the provisions of the EU's Seventh Company Law Directive (83/349/EEC) or in accordance with international accounting standards;

(c)   in a case where that parent is not incorporated under the law of an EEA state, that those accounts, and where appropriate the group's annual report, are drawn up in accordance with the provisions of the EU's Seventh Company Law Directive (83/349/EEC) or in a manner equivalent to consolidated accounts and consolidated annual reports so drawn up;

(d)   that the company discloses in its individual accounts that it is exempt from the obligation to prepare and deliver group accounts;

(e)   that the company states in its individual accounts the name of the parent undertaking which draws up the group accounts referred to above; and

    (i)   if it is incorporated outside Great Britain, the country in which it is incorporated;

    (ii)   if it is unincorporated, the address of its principal place of business;

(f)   that the company delivers to the registrar, within the period allowed for delivering its individual accounts, copies of those group accounts and of the parent undertaking's annual report, together with the auditors' report on them; and

(g)   that if any document delivered to the registrar is in a language other than English (or Welsh), it is accompanied by a certified translation into English.

Small and medium-sized groups exemption

2.8   The other major exemption is that for small and medium-sized groups contained in *section 248* of *CA 1985*.

To be eligible for the exemption:

(a)   the parent company must itself qualify as a small or medium-sized company for the purposes of *section 246* or *section 246A* of *CA 1985*;

(b)   the group as a whole must satisfy two out of three of the size criteria set out in *section 248* of *CA 1985*; and

(c)   the group must not be an ineligible group.

The size criteria for small and medium-sized groups are currently:

Criteria	Small group	Medium-sized group
Aggregate turnover	Not more than £5.6 million net or £6.72 million gross	Not more than £22.8 million net or £27.36 million gross
Aggregate balance sheet total	Not more than £2.8 million net or £3.36 million gross	Not more than £11.4 million net or £13.68 million gross
Aggregate number of employees	Not more than 50	Not more than 250

The turnover limit must be adjusted proportionately if the accounting period is less than a year, and 'balance sheet total' is defined as the aggregate of the amounts shown as assets in the balance sheet (i.e. *before* making any deductions for liabilities). In this context, 'gross' means before the set-offs and other adjustments normally made in preparing consolidated accounts and 'net' means after making those adjustments. Use of gross figures means that a group does not have to go through the mechanics of consolidation in order to demonstrate that it is not required to prepare group accounts. There is no requirement for the turnover and balance sheet criteria to be considered on the same basis.

Generally speaking, in order to qualify as small or medium sized the group needs to satisfy the size criteria both in the current and previous financial years. However, the group will still be treated as qualifying as small or medium sized if it qualified in the previous financial year, regardless of its current size. There are also further complicated rules relating to borderline cases where groups satisfy the size criteria in some years but not in others. A group is ineligible for exemption if any of its members is:

(a)   a public company or other body corporate (such as an overseas company) which has power under its constitution to offer its shares or debentures to the public,

(b)   a person (other than a small company) who has permission under Part 4 of the Financial Services and Markets Act 2000 to carry on a regulated activity,

(c)   a small company that is an authorised insurance company, a banking company, an e-money issuer, an ISD investment firm or a UCITS management company, or

(d)   a person who carries on an insurance market activity (ie acts as a Lloyd's underwriter).

Once the *Companies Act 2006* is brought into force this exemption will apply only to small groups and will no longer be available to medium sized groups.

Excluded subsidiaries

2.9   Under *section 229* of *CA 1985* a subsidiary may be excluded if its inclusion is not material for the purpose of giving a true and fair view; but two or more subsidiary undertakings may be excluded only if they are not material taken together.

In addition, *section 229* of *CA 1985* sets out a number of circumstances in which a subsidiary undertaking may be excluded from consolidation. However, FRS 2 'Accounting for subsidiary undertakings' is rather less permissive and requires a subsidiary to be excluded where:

(a)   severe long-term restrictions substantially hinder the exercise of the rights of the parent undertaking over the assets or management of the subsidiary undertaking. The rights referred to are those by reason of which the parent undertaking is defined as such under *section 258* of *CA 1985* and in the absence of which it would not be the parent undertaking; or

(b)   the interest in the subsidiary undertaking is held exclusively with a view to subsequent resale and the subsidiary undertaking has not previously been consolidated in group accounts prepared by the parent undertaking.

Subsidiaries may no longer be excluded from consolidation on the grounds of dissimilar activities.

FRS 2 also makes it clear that neither disproportionate expense nor undue delay in obtaining the information necessary for the preparation of consolidated financial statements can justify excluding from consolidation subsidiary undertakings that are individually or collectively material in the context of the group.

Where all subsidiaries are required or permitted to be excluded from consolidation group accounts are not required.

Small companies and the FRSSE

2.10   The requirements of company law and accounting standards generally apply to all companies, irrespective of size. However, companies that qualify as small under *CA 1985* may adopt the Financial Reporting Standard for Smaller Entities (FRSSE) in place of other accounting standards. The contents of the FRSSE are based on other accounting standards, but definitions and accounting requirements are set out in a more straightforward manner, and more complex issues that are not expected to arise in smaller entities are omitted. Small companies are not generally required to prepare group accounts and the FRSSE therefore omits consideration of matters relating to business combinations and consolidated accounts.

However, where a small group voluntarily chooses to prepare consolidated financial statements the FRSSE requires that the reporting entity should regard as standard the accounting practices and disclosure requirements set out in FRSs 2, 6, 7 and, insofar as they relate to goodwill arising on consolidation, FRSs 10 and 11.

Acquisition or merger accounting?

2.11   Under UK GAAP there are two permitted methods of accounting for business combinations – acquisition accounting and merger accounting – although the circumstances in which merger accounting may be applied are strictly limited.

The major distinction between the two is that in an acquisition there is a transfer of ownership of at least one of the combining entities and substantial resources leave the group as consideration for that transfer; whereas in a merger only limited or no resources leave the combined group, and the voting rights and equity interests in the combined group are allocated to the former shareholders of the combining entities in such a way as to reflect the agreed values of their respective entities. Conceptually, therefore, a merger is a pooling of existing interests rather than the transfer of interests from one group of shareholders to another. Merger and acquisition accounting are conceived to reflect these different types of combination.

Acquisition accounting regards the business combination as the acquisition of one undertaking by another. The identifiable assets and liabilities of the acquired undertaking are included in the consolidated balance sheet at their fair value at the date of acquisition, and its results are included in the profit and loss account from the date of acquisition. The difference between the fair value of the consideration given and the fair values of the net assets of the entity acquired is accounted for as goodwill.

Merger accounting, on the other hand, treats two or more parties as combining on a more or less equal footing. It is normally applied without any restatement of net assets to fair value, and the consolidated profit and loss account reflects the results of all combining entities for the whole of the accounting period. Correspondingly, it does not reflect the issue of shares as an application of resources at fair value. The difference that arises on consolidation does not represent goodwill but is deducted from, or added to, reserves.

Acquisition accounting is by far the most common method used as the circumstances in which merger accounting is permitted are restricted by the *Companies Act* and by *FRS 6 'Acquisitions and mergers'*. The merger accounting method is not currently in favour with accounting standard setters around the world and it is likely that future accounting standards on the subject will further limit its use or ban it altogether. However, for the time being it remains a permitted option under UK GAAP in certain circumstances.

Merger accounting

Conditions

2.12   The conditions that must be met for a combination to be accounted for as a merger are contained in *paragraph 10* of *Schedule 4A* to *CA 1985* and in paragraphs 6 to 11 of FRS 6. Combining these gives the following conditions.

(a) At least 90% of the nominal value of the relevant shares in the undertaking acquired is held by or on behalf of the parent company and its subsidiary undertakings.

(b) That 90% was attained pursuant to an arrangement providing for the issue of equity shares by the parent company or one or more of its subsidiary undertakings.

(c) The fair value of any consideration other than the issue of equity shares given pursuant to the arrangement by the parent company and its subsidiary undertakings did not exceed 10% of the nominal value of the equity shares issued.

(d) No party to the combination is portrayed as either acquirer or acquired, either by its own board or management or by that of another party to the combination.

(e) All parties to the combination, as represented by the boards of directors or their appointees, participate in establishing the management structure for the combined entity and in selecting the management personnel, and such decisions are made on the basis of a consensus between the parties to the combination rather than purely by exercise of voting rights.

(f) The relative sizes of the combining entities are not so disparate that one party dominates the combined entity by virtue of its relative size.

(g) The consideration received by equity shareholders of each party to the combination, in relation to their equity shareholding, comprises primarily equity shares in the combined entity; and any non-equity consideration, or equity shares carrying substantially reduced voting or distribution rights, represents an immaterial proportion of the fair value of the consideration received by the equity shareholders of that party. Where one of the combining entities has, within the period of two years before the combination, acquired equity shares in another of the combining entities, the consideration for this acquisition should be taken into account in determining whether this criterion has been met.

For the purpose of the previous paragraph, the consideration should not be taken to include the distribution to shareholders of an interest in a peripheral part of the business of the entity in which they were shareholders; or the proceeds of the sale of such a business.

(h) No equity shareholders of any of the combining entities retain any material interest in the future performance of only part of the combined entity.

Many of the words or phrases used in the conditions above have defined meanings in either *CA 1985* or FRS 6. Readers needing to determine whether a particular combination meets the conditions should refer to the original sources for detail. Particular care needs to be taken in interpreting the phrase 'equity shares' as this is defined differently in the Act and the standard!

Acquisition accounting must be used for all business combinations that do not meet all of the above conditions, with limited exceptions in the case of group reconstructions.

The principle underlying the restrictive drafting of the conditions for merger accounting derives from one of the stated objectives of FRS 6, namely 'to ensure that merger accounting is used only for those business combinations that are not, in substance, the acquisition of one entity by another but the formation of a new reporting entity as a substantially equal partnership where no party is dominant'.

While the above is cast in terms of one company issuing shares in consideration for the transfer to it of shares in another company, the principles apply equally to other forms of combination, such as where a new parent company is formed to acquire all the combining parties, or other arrangements that achieve similar results.

Method

2.13 In presenting consolidated accounts using merger accounting the balances sheets of the combined entities are simply added together, after adjustment to align accounting policies where necessary – but with no adjustment to reflect assets or liabilities at fair value. The investment shown on the legal parent's books is eliminated against the share capital of the legal subsidiary with any difference being shown as a 'merger reserve'. Profit and loss accounts are also added together to present the combined results of the merged undertakings as if the merger had happened on the first day of the earliest period presented (ie the start of the comparative period).

Acquisition accounting

Principle

2.14 The basic principle of acquisition accounting is that the fair value of assets, liabilities and contingent liabilities acquired by the parent entity should be compared with the fair value of the consideration given – with any difference being accounted for as goodwill.

Date of acquisition

2.15   The date of acquisition, being the date from which the results of the acquired entity are brought into the consolidated profit and loss account, is the date on which the parent acquires control of the subsidiary, regardless of what is said in the purchase contract. It is quite common, for example, to see clauses in contracts along the lines of 'the transfer of the shares will take place on [date] but with effect from [some earlier date]' – the idea being that the purchaser will be entitled to the benefit of any profits earned after that earlier date. However, for acquisition accounting purposes the purchaser is only entitled to recognise profits arising after the date on which it gains control.

Fair value of assets, liabilities and contingent liabilities acquired

2.16   FRS 7 contains two basic principles of recognition and measurement on an acquisition:

(a)   the identifiable assets and liabilities to be recognised should be those of the acquired entity that existed at the date of the acquisition; and

(b)   the recognised assets and liabilities should be measured at fair values that reflect the conditions at the date of acquisition.

The notion of using the 'fair value' of assets, liabilities or consideration has been referred to before in this chapter, without a description of how it is determined. Whilst the term 'fair value' is used in the description of the acquisition method of accounting in *paragraph 9* of *Schedule 4A* to *CA 1985* it is not explained and it is therefore left to FRS 7 to define fair value as being 'the amount at which an asset or liability could be exchanged in an arm's-length transaction between informed and willing parties, other than in a forced or liquidation sale'.

These principles and definition have a number of important consequences.

Firstly, when determining which assets and liabilities have been acquired and should be recognised in the consolidated balance sheet, acquirers may only attribute values to 'identifiable assets and liabilities'. This means the assets and liabilities of the acquired entity that are capable of being disposed of or settled separately, without disposing of a business of the entity. Assets such as brand names that cannot effectively be sold separately from the business are considered to be part of the goodwill of the acquired business and are not recognised separately.

Another far-reaching effect of the principle that only assets and liabilities *of the acquired entity* may be recognised is that costs that will be incurred in reorganising the operations of the acquired entity or the acquirer so as to assimilate the acquired operations may not be recognised as liabilities in the fair value exercise, as they are not obligations of the acquired entity at acquisition. Indeed, the standard is explicit in saying that fair values at the date of acquisition are not affected by (amongst other things) 'provisions or accruals for future operating losses or for reorganisation and integration costs expected to be incurred as a result of the acquisition, whether they relate to the acquired entity or to the acquirer'.

19

FRS 7 specifies how fair values should normally be determined for specific classes of asset and liability, as follows:

Tangible fixed assets	Fair value is based on market values, where these are available. Where market values are not available fair value is represented by depreciated replacement cost – subject to any necessary write down for impairment
Intangible assets	Replacement cost, usually market value
Stocks and work-in-progress	For stocks purchased in a ready market (eg commodity stocks) fair value will be market value. Where there is no ready market the fair value is taken as the current cost of reproducing the stocks – ie replacement cost or manufacturing cost as appropriate – or net realisable value if lower
Quoted investments	Market price, adjusted if necessary for unusual price fluctuations or the size of the holding
Monetary assets and liabilities	For short-term items fair value will be the expected redemption/settlement amount. For longer term items it will be established by reference to market values or the present value of expected cash flows
Contingent assets and liabilities	Contingent assets and liabilities should be measured at fair values where these can be determined. For this purpose reasonable estimates of the expected outcome may be used
Business sold or held exclusively with a view to subsequent resale	Adjusted net proceeds of sale (but note there are severe restrictions on which businesses qualify for this treatment)
Pensions and other post-retirement benefits	The full actuarial value of any deficiency in the scheme (or the value of any surplus – to the extent that this can be recovered through reduced contributions or refunds from the scheme). Following the implementation of FRS 17 'Retirement benefits' this is less of an issue than it was previously when scheme liabilities were not reflected in the employers' accounts. However, it is worth noting that any liability or asset recognised on acquisition should be based on the pension arrangements of the acquired undertaking prior to the acquisition
Deferred taxation	Deferred tax on adjustments made to record assets and liabilities at fair values should be recognised in accordance with FRS 19 'Deferred tax'. Unrecognised deferred tax assets of the acquired entity that meet the recognition criteria of FRS 19 as a result of the acquisition should be recognised

It should be noted that FRS 7 requires that fair values be attributed to contingent assets and liabilities existing at the date of acquisition – even where they are not reflected in the acquired company's own financial statements. This creates the slightly anomalous situation in which some contingent liabilities of the subsidiary are recognised in the balance sheet whilst others, and those of the parent, are not.

For many assets and liabilities, in the absence of an active market or evidence of fair value from recent transactions in similar assets or liabilities the determination of fair values involves a significant degree of judgement. FRS 7 provides guidance on the application of that judgement and contains rules to prevent the use of excessive 'prudence' which, prior to FRS 7, had often been used as a justification for making significant acquisition provisions.

It is likely, of course, that it will take some time for an acquirer to estimate the fair value of assets and liabilities acquired with any degree of accuracy. Acquirers are therefore allowed a 'second bite' at the fair value exercise, adjusting earlier estimates and resulting in an adjustment to goodwill, in the year following the acquisition (but not after that – further adjustments would affect group profits).

Cost

2.17   Under FRS 7 the cost of acquisition comprises the amount of cash paid, the fair value of other purchase consideration, including shares, and the expenses of acquisition.

The 'cost' of an investment will include any expenses incidental to its acquisition. This will include fees and similar incremental costs incurred directly in making an acquisition, such as legal fees and reporting accountants' fees. Internal costs, and other expenses that cannot be directly attributed to the acquisition, should not be included in the 'cost' of an investment but should be charged to the profit and loss account. The question of which costs are directly attributable is considered further in **2.22** below.

Where consideration is contingent on future events, a reasonable estimate of the likely amount payable should be made. This estimate should be revised at each period end and where it is necessary to revise this will result in an adjustment to goodwill.

Any deferred element of consideration should be included in cost at its fair value. Arguably this means that discounting should be applied where the effect is material although FRS 7 is not explicit on that point.

The methods compared

2.18   The principal differences between the two methods of accounting are as follows:

	Acquisition accounting	*Merger accounting*
Inclusion of subsidiary's results	Group results include subsidiary's results from effective date of acquisition only	Results presented as if the companies had always been combined
Pre-combination results, including corresponding amounts	Those of subsidiary not included in consolidated profit and loss account	Restated on a combined basis
Treatment of combined assets and liabilities	Fair values of acquiree's assets and liabilities at date of acquisition regarded as cost to the group	Existing book values used (adjusted only to achieve consistency of accounting policies)
Goodwill	Almost invariably arises (either positive or negative)	Does not arise
Reserves	Acquiring company's reserves plus only the post-acquisition reserves of the subsidiary	Pre-merger reserves of both companies combined
Expenses of combination	Do not affect reported results	Charged against combined results

The following simple example illustrates the different results of accounting for the same combination under the principles of merger and acquisition accounting. Note that, given the relative sizes of the combining entities, merger accounting would probably not be allowed in practice. The same figures are used for both methods here merely for illustration.

A issues 100 10p nominal value shares, worth £1 each in the market, to acquire B's issued share capital.

Acquisition accounting: balance sheets

	A (before acquisition)	A (after acquisition)	B (at date of acquisition)	Elimination	Fair value adjustments	Group
	£	£	£			£
Goodwill	—	—	—	30	(10)	20
Investment in B	—	100	—	(100)		—
Other net assets	150	150	70		10	230
	150	250	70	(70)		250
Share capital	100	110	50	(50)		110
Other reserves	—	90	—			90
Profit and loss account	50	50	20	(20)		50
	150	250	70	(70)		250

Note: this assumes that A does not take advantage of *section 133 of CA 1985* and records the investment in B in its own books at full fair value, not just at the nominal value of the shares issued.

Merger accounting: balance sheets

	A (before acquisition)	A (after acquisition)	B	Group
	£	£	£	£
Investment in B	—	10	—	—
Other net assets	150	150	70	220
	150	160	70	220
Share capital	100	110	50	110
Other reserves	—	—	—	40
Profit and loss account	50	50	20	70
	150	160	70	220

As can be seen, the differences between the acquisition accounted and merger accounted consolidated balance sheets are as follows.

(a) Only the nominal value of the shares issued appears in the merger accounting group balance sheet. The amount by which the fair value of the shares exceeded the nominal value is not recognised – whereas under acquisition accounting it appears as 'other reserves'.

(b) The merger accounting balance sheet includes the pre-combination reserves of both companies (£50 + £20 = £70) whereas in the acquisition accounting balance sheet only A's reserves of £50 are included.

(c) The merger accounting balance sheet includes another reserve of £40 which represents the difference between the cost of the investment in B as recorded in A's books (£10) and the nominal value of the shares in B that have been transferred to A (£50). FRS 6 requires this difference to be shown as a movement on other reserves in the consolidated financial statements and included in the reconciliation of movements in shareholders' funds required by FRS 3 'Reporting financial performance'.

As a result, the total of the share capital and reserves of the two companies before the combination (£150 + £70 = £220) equals the share capital and reserves of the group (£230).

Note that where the carrying value of the investment is greater than the nominal value of the shares transferred, the difference is the extent to which reserves have, in effect, been capitalised as a result of the merger and should therefore be treated on consolidation as a reduction in reserves.

(d) Under acquisition accounting B's net assets are restated to fair value at the date of acquisition – increasing the carrying amounts of 'other net assets' by £10. Under merger accounting the carrying amounts attributed to B's net assets remain unchanged.

(e)   Goodwill of £20, being the difference between the fair value of A's investment in B (£100) and the fair value of B's net assets (£70+£10=£80), arises under acquisition accounting.

Intangible assets

2.19   Using the acquisition method under UK GAAP the cost of investment is attributed, on consolidation, to the identifiable assets and liabilities of the acquired company by stating them at their fair values.

FRS 10 'Intangible assets and goodwill' requires that an intangible asset acquired as part of the acquisition of a business should be capitalised separately from goodwill if its value can be measured reliably on initial recognition. It should initially be recorded at its fair value, subject to the constraint that, unless the asset has a readily ascertainable market value, the fair value should be limited to an amount that does not create or increase any negative goodwill arising on the acquisition.

FRS 7 requires that where an intangible asset is recognised, its fair value should be based on its replacement cost which will normally be the asset's estimated market value but may be estimated by other methods.

It is not possible to determine a market value for unique intangible assets such as brands and publishing titles. Replacement cost may be equally difficult to determine directly. However, certain entities that are regularly involved in the purchase and sale of unique intangible assets have developed techniques for estimating their values indirectly and these may be used for initial recognition of such assets at the time of purchase. Techniques used can be based, for example, on 'indicators of value' – such as multiples of turnover – or on estimating the present value of the royalties that would be payable to license the asset from a third party.

If its value cannot be measured reliably, an intangible asset purchased as part of the acquisition of a business should be subsumed within the amount of the purchase price attributed to goodwill.

Goodwill

2.20   Having established both the fair values of the assets, liabilities and contingent liabilities acquired and of the consideration any difference, positive or negative is deemed to represent purchased goodwill arising on consolidation. Positive goodwill (excess of consideration over net assets) appears on the balance sheet under the heading of intangible assets, as required by *Schedule 4* to *CA 1985*. Negative goodwill is placed in the same position, but is deducted from the total of other fixed assets, rather than added to it.

Purchased goodwill needs to be amortised each year on a systematic basis over its useful economic life. There is a rebuttable presumption that the useful economic life of purchased goodwill and other intangible assets acquired in a business combination will not exceed 20 years. A longer or indefinite useful economic life may only be attributed if:

(a) the durability of the acquired business or intangible asset can be demonstrated and justifies estimating the useful economic life to exceed 20 years; and

(b) the goodwill or intangible asset is capable of continued measurement (so that annual impairment reviews will be feasible).

Where it is considered that goodwill has a life in excess of 20 years an impairment review is needed every year to confirm that the assumptions about its life remain appropriate. Similarly, if it is considered that goodwill has an indefinite life no amortisation need be charged but again an annual impairment review will be required.

Negative goodwill is regarded in the first instance as representing a discount on the value of assets acquired and is therefore amortised over the lives of the non-monetary assets acquired in the combination (fixed assets and stock). If negative goodwill exceeds the value of non-monetary assets the balance is amortised over the period during which the entity is expected to benefit from the negative goodwill.

Impairment of goodwill and intangibles

2.21   Regardless of their estimated useful economic lives an impairment review must be carried out on goodwill and other acquired intangible assets at the end of the first full year following acquisition. Thereafter reviews will be required whenever there is an indication of impairment and at least annually in the case of goodwill or intangibles with an estimated remaining life of more than 20 years.

The impairment review requires a comparison of the carrying value of the goodwill with its recoverable amount. If the carrying amount exceeds the recoverable amount, goodwill is impaired and needs to be written down.

FRS 11 lists various indications of impairment. Those related to goodwill are as follows.

(a) A current period operating loss in the business in which the goodwill is involved or net cash outflow from the operating activities of that business, combined with either past operating losses or net cash outflows from such operating activities or an expectation of continuing operating losses or net cash outflows from such operating activities.

(b) A significant adverse change in:

   (i)   either the business or the market in which the goodwill is involved, such as the entrance of a major competitor; or

   (ii) the statutory or other regulatory environment in which the business operates.

(c) A commitment by management to undertake a significant reorganisation.

(d) A major loss of key employees.

This list is, however, not exhaustive and other indications of impairment may exist.

Impairment losses are recognised in the profit and loss account. Once an impairment loss has been recognised in respect of goodwill it may not be reversed, even if the circumstances giving rise to the impairment appear to have changed.

Acquisition costs

2.22   The term 'acquisition costs' can cover a variety of different types of costs, and even for a given type of cost, treatment may vary depending on the circumstances and the accounting method adopted.

One type of cost that may sometimes be included under this umbrella heading is share issue costs. FRS 25 and FRS 4 require these to be set against the proceeds of issue of the shares with the net proceeds reported in the reconciliation of movements in shareholders' funds required under FRS 3. Such costs would not therefore appear as a charge against profits or as a loss in the statement of total recognised gains and losses. Issue costs might include the cost of preparing listing particulars, for example, if the new shares are to be listed, as well as any underwriting commissions, etc.

Other costs may arise that may be properly treated as part of the cost of the investment by the acquiring company. For example, professional fees such as legal fees for the purchase and sale contract etc. and accountants' fees for carrying out a pre-acquisition investigation, in a private acquisition. Where these are treated as part of the cost of investment, they will be subsumed into the calculation of goodwill.

Under merger accounting, FRS 6 requires that the costs of the merger be charged to the profit and loss account of the combined entity at the effective date of the merger, as an exceptional item under the 'reorganisation or restructuring costs' heading in paragraph 20 of FRS 3.

The UITF has issued some clarification on takeover costs in Information Sheet 35. It notes that FRS 7 requires that:

> 'Fees and similar incremental costs incurred directly in making an acquisition should, except for the issue costs of shares or other securities that are required by FRS 4 "Capital Instruments" to be accounted for as a reduction in the proceeds of a capital instrument, be included in the cost of acquisition. Internal costs, and other expenses that cannot be directly attributed to the acquisition, should be charged to the profit and loss account.'

It also quotes the definition of issue costs from FRS 4 (paragraph 10):

> 'Issue costs are the costs that are incurred directly in connection with the issue of a capital instrument, that is, those costs that would not have been incurred had the specific instrument in question not been issued.'

The UITF concluded that:

> 'Incidental financial costs that do not themselves fall to be accounted for under FRS 4 are not incremental costs incurred directly in making an acquisition and therefore should not be included in the cost of the acquisition, but should be written off immediately.'

Whilst the reference in FRS 7 to FRS 4 has since been replaced with a reference to FRS 25 'Financial instruments: disclosure and presentation' the rationale for the UITF's conclusion remains the same.

Disclosure in accounts

2.23   The *Companies Act 1985* and FRS 6 both require specific disclosures to be made in the parent company's financial statements for the year in which an acquisition or merger occurs. The following disclosures must be made in respect of all business combinations, whether acquisition or merger accounted:

(a)   the names of the combining entities;

(b)   whether accounted for as an acquisition or a merger;

(c)   the date of the combination; and

(d)   where an undertaking has become a subsidiary other than by a purchase or exchange of shares, an explanation of the circumstances.

Mergers

2.24   The following must be disclosed in respect of combinations accounted for as mergers:

(a)   an analysis of the profit and loss account and statement of total recognised gains and losses ('STRGL') into:

  (i)   amounts relating to the merged entity for the period after the date of the merger; and

  (ii)   for each party to the merger, amounts relating to that party for the period up to the date of the merger;

(b)   an analysis of the previous year's profit and loss account and STRGL between the parties;

(c)   details of the consideration given;

(d)   the aggregate book value of the net assets of each party at the date of the merger;

(e)   details of accounting adjustments to the net assets of any party as a consequence of the merger; and

(f)   a statement of the adjustments to consolidated reserves resulting from the merger.

Acquisitions

2.25   The following must be disclosed in respect of combinations accounted for as acquisitions:

(a)   details of the consideration given, including extended details of deferred or contingent consideration;

(b)   a 'fair value' table showing the amount of goodwill arising and, for each class of assets and liabilities of the acquired entity:

  (i)   book values in the acquired entity's books immediately before the acquisition;

  (ii)   the fair value adjustments, analysed into:

    (A)   revaluations;

    (B)   adjustments to achieve consistency of accounting policies; and

    (C)   any other significant adjustments, giving the reasons for the adjustments; and

  (iii)   the fair values at the date of acquisition;

(c)   provisions for reorganisation included in the liabilities of the acquired entity, and related asset write-downs, made in the 12 months before acquisition;

(d)   a note of the fact that fair values are provisional, and, if so, the adjustments in following periods are to be disclosed in those accounts;

(e)   post-acquisition results of the acquired entity (as a component of continuing operations) and a note of any material impact on a business segment (where it is not possible to determine this, estimates must be made);

(f)   exceptional post-acquisition profits or losses determined using the fair values at acquisition;

(g)   post-acquisition costs of reorganising, restructuring and integrating the acquisition (strictly defined);

(h)   movements on provisions or accruals for costs related to the acquisition;

(i)   cash flow statement to show cash and cash equivalents paid as consideration, net of any cash and equivalents acquired;

(j)   material effects of the acquired entity on post-acquisition cash flows; and

(k)   profit after tax and minority interest of the acquired entity from the beginning of its financial year to the date of acquisition and for its previous financial year.

In the year of acquisition and all subsequent years, the cumulative amount of goodwill on acquisitions that has been written off other than through the profit and loss account must be given, net of goodwill attributable to subsidiaries or undertakings since disposed of.

In July 2001, the Financial Reporting Review Panel ('FRRP') published its findings following a review of the accounts of Avesco Plc for the year ended

31 March 2000. The company acquired an investment in an associate during the year and the financial statements stated that the cost of the investment was based on the book value of the assets acquired, together with associated acquisition costs. The directors confirmed to the FRRP that, in their view, the book value of the assets approximated their fair value and agreed to include a note in the 2001 accounts to clarify this. This highlights the importance of giving careful consideration to the wording of disclosures made in the financial statements, so that they demonstrate compliance with the appropriate standard as well as explaining the treatment adopted.

Cash flows

2.26 FRS 1 'Cash flow statements' requires entities to disclose acquisitions and disposals, insofar as they have an impact on group cash flows. Example 2 to the FRS considers a consolidated cash flow statement for a group, which includes details of the purchase of subsidiary undertakings and the sale of a business. These details are then broken down in the notes to the statement. It is therefore important when considering the disclosure of acquisitions in statutory accounts to be aware that the cash flows arising from these transactions will need to be shown in some detail in this statement.

Substantial acquisitions

2.27 For substantial acquisitions, as defined, the group accounts must also show the summarised profit and loss account and statement of total recognised gains and losses of the acquired entity from the beginning of its year to the date of acquisition, giving at least turnover, operating profit, exceptional items within paragraph 20 of FRS 3, profit before tax, tax and minority interests.

International Financial Reporting Standards

Introduction

2.28 Article 4 of EC Regulation No 1606/2002 of the European Parliament and of the Council requires all companies with securities traded on a recognised stock exchange within the EU to prepare their consolidated accounts in accordance with International Financial Reporting Standards (IFRSs). This Regulation has direct effect in all EU member states for accounting periods commencing on or after 1 January 2005.

In the UK the regulation applies to companies with a full listing. The alternative investment market (AIM) is not a recognised stock exchange for this purpose but the Stock Exchange has announced that a similar requirement will apply to the accounts of AIM listed companies for periods commencing on or after 1 January 2007.

Other companies in the UK may choose to use IFRSs for accounting periods commencing on or after 1 January 2005 subject to certain conditions. A parent company may choose to use IFRSs for its consolidated accounts but produce its own accounts on a *Companies Act 1985* basis. Subsidiaries may use either IFRSs or the *Companies Act* as the basis for preparing their accounts. All subsidiaries in the same group must use the same basis but this need not be the same basis as the parent uses for its own accounts or for the consolidated accounts. Charities may not use IFRSs under any circumstances.

Once a company has voluntarily adopted IFRSs as the basis for preparing its own accounts or consolidated accounts it may not change back to a *Companies Act* basis without good reason.

Accounting for business combinations under IFRSs is governed primarily by IFRS 3 'Business combinations' and IAS 27 'Separate and consolidated financial statements' and the detailed rules are significantly different from those applied under UK GAAP.

Overview

2.29   Key differences between IFRSs and UK GAAP are:

- Merger accounting is prohibited – all combinations are treated as acquisitions.

- Different rules for recognition of intangibles result in more separate intangibles than under UK GAAP.

- Goodwill must be allocated to cash generating units.

- Positive goodwill is not amortised but is subject to annual impairment review.

- Negative goodwill is taken immediately to profit and loss.

- Cost of investment in subsidiaries is stated in the parent entity balance sheet at fair value. Subsequent impairments will affect profit/loss.

- Dividends paid by subsidiaries from pre-acquisition reserves are treated in the parent entity as a reduction in the cost of investment – not as income.

- Transitional rules apply on first implementation of IFRSs – previous business combinations need not be restated and existing unamortised goodwill is retained.

IFRS 3

2.30   IFRS 3 defines a business combination as the bringing together of separate entities or businesses into one reporting entity. This may involve the purchase by one entity of another entity, the purchase of all the net assets of another entity, the assumption of the liabilities of another entity or the purchase of some of the net assets of another entity that together form one or more businesses.

Where a business combination involves one entity becoming a subsidiary of another entity (the parent) then IFRS 3 applies to the consolidated financial statements of the parent. In the parent's separate financial statement its investment in the subsidiary is accounted for in accordance with IAS 27 (see **2.36** below).

Under IFRS 3 all business combinations must be accounted for using the purchase method, under which one party must be identified as the acquirer. Merger accounting is not permitted. In order to apply the purchase method it is necessary first to identify the acquirer, then to establish the cost of the combination then to allocate the cost to the assets acquired and the liabilities and contingent liabilities assumed.

The acquirer is the entity that obtains control over the other entities involved in the combination where control is the power to govern the financial and operating policies of an entity or business so as to benefit from its activities. An entity is presumed to have control over another when it acquires more than half the voting rights in that other entity. Even if an entity does not acquire more than half the voting rights it may nevertheless have control when as a result of the combination it obtains:

- Power over more than half the voting rights by virtue of an agreement with other investors; or

- Power to govern the financial and operating policies of the other entity under statute or an agreement; or

- Power to appoint or remove a majority of the members of the board of directors or equivalent governing body; or

- Power to cast a majority of votes at meetings of the board of directors or equivalent governing body.

Reverse acquisition

2.31   Where a business combination is effected by an exchange of shares the company issuing shares is usually the acquirer. However, in identifying the acquirer all relevant facts and circumstances must be taken into account. For example it is not uncommon for a private company to arrange for itself to be taken over by a smaller public company as a means of achieving a stock exchange listing. In this situation, commonly referred to as a 'reverse acquisition', the private company becomes a legal subsidiary of the public company (the legal parent) but the former effectively gains power to govern its financial and operating policies. For the purposes of applying IFRS 3 therefore the legal subsidiary is treated as the acquirer and the legal parent as the acquired company.

Unlike UK GAAP, IFRS 3 deals explicitly with this situation and sets out in detail how the accounting works.

Cost of the combination

2.32   As under UK GAAP the cost of a business combination is the fair value, at the date of exchange, of assets given, liabilities incurred and equity instruments issued by the acquirer in exchange for control of the acquiree plus any costs directly attributable to the business combination.

Where control is achieved as a result of a series of transactions the cost of the business combination is the aggregate cost of the individual transactions.

IFRS 3 specifies that where settlement of any part of the consideration is deferred the fair value of the deferred component is determined by discounting the amounts payable to their present value.

It also makes clear that future losses of the acquiree or other costs expected to be incurred as a result of the business combination are not liabilities incurred or assumed by the acquirer in exchange for control of the acquiree and do not form part of the cost of the business combination.

As under UK, where adjustments to the consideration are contingent on future events, such as a achieving a certain level of profitability an initial estimate should be made of any likely adjustment to the cost and this would be included in the initial assessment of the overall cost of the combination. Should it be necessary to revise such estimates in the future, the cost of the business combination is adjusted accordingly.

Allocating costs

2.33   As under UK GAAP the cost of the business combination is allocated to the separate assets, liabilities and contingent liabilities acquired, based on their fair values at the time of acquisition – with any unallocated cost being classified as goodwill. Appendix B to IFRS 3 contains detailed rules on how to determine fair values for each separate class of assets and liabilities and contingent liabilities.

Unlike UK GAAP, IFRSs do not treat intangible assets and goodwill in the same way and it is therefore important that the acquirer identifies and attributes appropriate fair values to any intangible assets acquired, even where such assets were not previously recognised by the acquiree. Intangible assets, once recognised, will generally be carried at cost less amortisation calculated to write the asset down to its residual value over its useful economic life. Goodwill, on the other hand, is not amortised. Failure to identify all the intangible assets acquired in a business combination will overstate goodwill. This will in turn result in an understatement of amortisation and an overstatement of profit in future accounting periods.

An intangible asset is recognised separately from goodwill if it meets the definition of an intangible asset. IAS 38 'Intangible Assets' and its fair value can be measured reliably. IAS 38 provides guidance on determining whether the fair value of an intangible asset can be measured reliably but if an intangible asset acquired in a business combination has a finite useful life, there is a rebuttable presumption that its fair value can be measured reliably.

In order to meet the definition an intangible asset must be identifiable which means it must:

(a)   be separable, ie capable of being separated or divided from the entity and sold, transferred, licensed, rented or exchanged, either individually or together with a related contract, asset or liability; or

(b)   arise from contractual or other legal rights, regardless of whether those rights are transferable or separable from the entity or from other rights and obligations.

This means that an acquirer would recognise a separate intangible asset in respect of in-process research and development project of the acquiree although under IFRSs the acquiree would not have been permitted to recognise such an asset itself.

Illustrative examples attached to IFRS 3 give the following as examples of items acquired in a business combination that meet the definition of an intangible asset and are therefore separately from goodwill. The list is not intended to be exhaustive.

Marketing-related intangible assets

- Trademarks, trade names, service marks, collective marks and certification marks
- Internet domain names
- Trade dress (unique colour, shape or package design)
- Newspaper mastheads
- Non-competition agreements

Customer-related intangible assets

- Customer lists
- Order or production backlog
- Customer contracts and the related customer relationships
- Non-contractual customer relationships

Artistic-related intangible assets

- Plays, operas and ballets
- Books, magazines, newspapers and other literary works
- Musical works such as compositions, song lyrics and advertising jingles
- Pictures and photographs
- Video and audiovisual material, including films, music videos and television programmes

Contract-based intangible assets

- Licensing, royalty and standstill agreements
- Advertising, construction, management, service or supply contracts
- Lease agreements
- Construction permits
- Franchise agreements
- Operating and broadcasting rights
- Use rights such as drilling, water, air, mineral, timber-cutting and route authorities
- Servicing contracts such as mortgage servicing contracts

Technology-based intangible assets

- Patented technology

- Computer software and mask works

- Unpatented technology

- Databases

- Trade secrets such as secret formulas, processes or recipes

Goodwill

2.34   Goodwill is the difference between the cost of the combination and the amounts allocated to individual assets, liabilities and contingent liabilities as described above. As a result of separate identification of intangibles it is likely that goodwill measured under IFRS 3 will be significantly lower than it would have been under UK GAAP.

Where goodwill is a positive number it remains in the balance sheet until it becomes impaired. Goodwill is not amortised but is subject to an annual impairment review carried out on the cash-generating unit to which the good-will is allocated. For this reason it is necessary to attribute goodwill, as it arises, to the cash-generating unit expected to benefit from it.

Example

>   Company X has three cash generating units A, B and C. It acquires company Y in a business combination and transfers Y's business into cash generating unit C. In this case the goodwill relating to the business combination would be attached to unit C.
>
>   X then make a further purchase of company Z. The business of Z is retained in a separate cash-generating unit but units A and B are both expected to benefit from synergies arising from the acquisition of Z. In this case part of the goodwill arising on the business combination would be allocated to units A and B.

Where goodwill is a negative number the entity should first reassess the fair values given to the identifiable assets, liabilities and contingent liabilities acquired. If these are confirmed as appropriate any remaining negative good-will is taken immediately to the profit and loss account.

Business combinations involving entities under common control

2.35   IFRS 3 does not apply to business combinations where all the com-bining entities or businesses are ultimately controlled by the same party or parties both before and after the combination, and that control is not transi-tory. In these situations, unlike FRS 6, offers no guidance on the appropriate accounting treatment.

Parent company balance sheet and distributable reserves

2.36   IAS 27 requires investments in subsidiary companies to be stated at cost in the parent company's balance sheet. This means, in effect, that *section 133 of CA 1985* cannot be applied and that the cost of investments needs to include the full fair value of shares issued as consideration. *Section 133 of CA 1985* will however still apply in that the excess of fair value over nominal need not be taken to the share premium account.

Another area in which IAS 27 differs from UK GAAP is that dividends paid by subsidiaries from pre- acquisition profits must be credited directly against the cost of investment. In effect this means that pre-acquisition reserves of subsidiaries are not available for distribution by the parent.

Transitional rules

2.37   When first adopting IFRSs the general rule is that an entity should adopt standards that are extant at the reporting date, but backdate their application to the date of transition to IFRS. The date of transition is the start of the earliest period reported, ie the start of the comparative period. Thus an entity adopting IFRSs for the first time in its statutory accounts for the period ended 31 December 2007 would have a date of transition of 1 January 2006 – assuming accounting periods of 12 months. Business combinations taking place during the year to 31 December 2007 would be reported in accordance with IFRSs, as would combinations taking place in the comparative period to 31 December 2006.

Applying the general rule for transition to IFRSs the opening balance sheet at the transition date would also be drawn up as if IFRSs had been applied up to that point but IFRS 1 'First time adoption of International Financial Reporting Standards' contains a number of useful exceptions to this rule.

Firstly, business combinations that took place prior to the transition date need not be restated. It is not necessary therefore to attempt to recalculate goodwill using IFRS 3 principles for such combinations – nor is it necessary to unravel previous combinations accounted for using merger accounting under UK GAAP. Previous business combinations may be restated but where a combination occurring prior to the transition date is restated all business combinations after this date must also be restated.

Secondly, unamortised goodwill remaining in an entity's balance sheet at the transition date is effectively frozen and carried forward indefinitely, subject to annual tests for impairment. It is not necessary to attempt to separate out any intangible assets that would have been recognised separately had IFRS 3 been applied to the business combinations giving rise to the goodwill concerned.

Associates and joint ventures

2.38   Corporate acquisition activity is not confined to transactions involving acquisition of control and many companies choose to expand their business activities through investments in associates and joint ventures. For accounting purposes such investments are treated rather differently from investments in subsidiaries.

Under UK GAAP accounting for such investments is dealt with by FRS 9 'Associates and joint ventures'. Under IFRSs the relevant standards are IAS 28 'Investment in associates' and IAS 31 'Interests in joint ventures'.

Associates

2.39   FRS 9 defines an associate as 'An entity (other than a subsidiary) in which another entity (the investor) has a participating interest and over whose operating and financial policies the investor exercises a significant influence'. A participating interest is an interest held in the shares of another entity on a long-term basis for the purpose of securing a contribution to the investor's activities by the exercise of control or influence arising from or related to that interest. The investor's interest must, therefore, be a beneficial one and the benefits expected to arise must be linked to the exercise of its significant influence over the investee's operating and financial policies.

The exercise of significant influence means that the investor is actively involved and is influential in the direction of its investee through its participation in policy decisions covering aspects of policy relevant to the investor, including decisions on strategic issues such as:

(a)   the expansion or contraction of the business, participation in other entities or changes in products, markets and activities of its investee; and

(b)   determining the balance between dividend and reinvestment.

The *Companies Act* provides that an interest of 20% or more in the voting rights of another entity gives rise to presumptions both that the interest is a participating one and that the investor exercises significant influence – although this can be rebutted if the investor does not meet the criteria set out above.

Associates are included in consolidated financial statements using the equity method. This involves applying the same fair value principles to acquired assets, liabilities and contingent liabilities but only the investor's share is reflected in the consolidated balance sheet.

In its consolidated profit and loss account the investor includes its share of associates' operating result, immediately after the group operating result. From the level of profit before tax to the bottom of the profit and loss account the investor's share of the relevant amounts for associates is included within the amounts for the group. The investor's share of the total recognised gains and losses of its associates are included in the consolidated statement of total recognised gains and losses, shown separately under each heading, if material. In the balance sheet the investor's share of the net assets of its associates should be included and separately disclosed. The cash flow statement should include the cash flows between the investor and its associates. Goodwill aris-ing on the investor's acquisition of its associates, less any amortisation or write-down, should be included in the carrying amount for the associates but should be disclosed separately. In the profit and loss account the amortisation or write-down of such goodwill should be separately disclosed as part of the investor's share of its associates' results.

Under IFRSs the accounting for associates required by IAS 28 is not signifi-cantly different.

Joint ventures

2.40   A joint venture, on the other hand, is an entity in which two or more investors share control. That is no one investor has the ability to direct the financial and operating policies of the entity with a view to gaining economic benefit from them – but two or more investors acting together do have this ability. A common situation is where the voting rights are split 50/50 between two investors, neither of which has control over the Board. Acting together they control the entity but neither investor has control alone.

Under FRS 9 joint ventures are accounted for in a similar way to associates – except that FRS 9 prescribes a 'gross equity' method in which the investor's share of profits and share of net assets are presented in the con-solidated financial statements in a slightly more disaggregated way. For example, the venture's share of turnover is shown within the turnover line in the profit and loss account and the investor's share of assets and liabilities are shown separately.

IAS 31 is not significantly different in terms of how it defines a joint venture but does not permit a gross equity method of presentation. Instead it advo-cates proportionate consolidation in which the investor's share of profit, assets and liabilities is incorporated into the consolidated financial statements on a line-by-line basis (but not necessarily disclosed separately). As an alter-native it permits the use of the same equity method as is applied to associates – ie the investors share of operating profit appears as a single line item in the profit and loss account and the investor's share of net assets appears as a sin-gle line item on the balance sheet (with expansion in the notes).

Shares or assets?

2.41   As an alternative to purchasing shares in a company, an acquirer may purchase the assets of a business, either for cash or the issue of shares or other securities. With an assets purchase the acquirer can be clear as to exactly what assets have been acquired and what liabilities have been assumed as part of the transaction and can be relatively confident that there are no hidden or undisclosed liabilities, either actual or contingent.

However, if the acquirer issues shares at a premium in exchange for assets, *section 130* of *CA 1985* requires that any 'premium' associated with these shares be taken to the share premium account, as merger relief cannot be applied in this situation. Additionally, if the acquirer is a public limited company *section 103* of *CA 1985* applies and the assets acquired must be independently valued by a person qualified to be the company's auditor. One way of overcoming these issues is for the target company to first sell the assets and liabilities that are to be the subject of the transaction to an off-the-shelf private company, the latter in turn being sold to the acquirer. By this process, the acquirer can preserve the right to merger relief and avoid the requirements of *section 103*.

Possible future developments

2.42   When considering the extent to which UK GAAP should be converged with IFRSs the Accounting Standards Board decided not to change the basic principles of accounting for business combinations. This decision partly reflected the ASB's concerns at the time over some of the International Accounting Standards Board's (IASB) proposals – and partly reflected the fact that IFRS 3 only represented the completion of Phase I of much larger IASB project aimed at achieving convergence between IFRSs and US GAAP. It is unlikely therefore that there will be any significant changes to UK financial reporting standards in this area until the IASB's project reaches a conclusion.

The IASB and the US Financial Accounting Standards Board have meanwhile pressed on with Phase II of their project and a new IFRS is expected to be issued in the second half of 2007. The IASB has, however, announced that it will not require implementation of any substantive new standards until periods commencing on or after 1 January 2009 at the earliest.

Conclusion

2.43   Accounting for business combinations can be complex and there are a number of issues that should be thought about before the transaction takes place. For example, which accounting framework is applicable; what is the value of the intangible assets to be acquired; what is the estimated life of acquired goodwill and how will this impact on the profit and loss account; will additional liabilities need to be recognised in the balance sheet and how will this affect banking covenants and how will the acquisition affect distributable reserves? Prior consultation with the company's auditors and other accounting advisers may well pay dividends.

Corporate Rescue and Insolvency

At a glance

- The reforms introduced by the *Enterprise Act 2002* – in so far as intended to promote the survival of companies rather than their businesses – have proved to be more apparent than real

- This is largely due to the continued absence from English insolvency law of any means to secure 'super priority' for post-insolvency funding – in contrast to other common law jurisdictions such as Canada

- As a consequence, administration pre-packs are becoming ever more common, irrespective of the extent to which in any given case they address the legitimate interests and concerns of creditors

- Case law continues to throw up decisions likely to trip up practitioners

- *TUPE 2006* fails to tackle its insolvency subject clearly and is hedged about with official guidance that is both itself unclear (and in places plainly wrong) and which appears to conflict with the Regulations themselves

- Pension deficits continue to cause that sinking feeling

- The need for further reform is clear but the chances of further reform are remote

---

Introduction

3.1   In previous editions of this book, this chapter has opened by questioning, sotto voce, the need, in a work about the acquisition of companies, for a section on 'rescue' in the context of insolvency, but then has sought to show why analysis of the topic is nevertheless of value, with the parameters somewhat widely drawn.

The attempt was inevitably somewhat frustrated – as reflected by the use of the adjective rather than the noun in the chapter's title – by the consideration that where a company is insolvent, but has a viable business, any prospective purchaser is much more likely to make an offer for the assets and undertaking of the company than for its shares, for self-evident reasons (essentially, freedom from existing liabilities, accrued and contingent[1]).

The reforms made by the *Enterprise Act 2002* (*'EA'*) in the administration regime – with its principal aim now stated to be the rescue of the company itself – may in due course prove to be the first step towards making the attempt good and this chapter's parameters are accordingly now more narrowly drawn.

So far, however, the step has proved to be a small one.

1. Freedom only, of course, from some, but by no means all, liabilities: for examples of accrued and contingent liabilities that may be transferred/assumed notwithstanding any degree of legal ingenuity and associated cost, see the fields of employment and environmental law.

The scope of the chapter

3.2   This chapter does not attempt to provide an alternative to the mass of legal literature that exists for the various insolvency regimes, their detail, differences or respective histories. In particular, knowledge of the basic differences between liquidation and other insolvency regimes is assumed, as is knowledge of the scope of the moratorium on creditor action against companies in administration and of the two types of company voluntary arrangement ('CVA') – one (that applying to small companies[1]) with its own moratorium and one (that principally used as an exit mechanism from administration) without.

What this chapter does seek to do is to draw attention to some of those substantive and procedural features of insolvency law in England and Wales that are of particular relevance to parties addressing the question of what (if anything) may be bought and sold where the present operator of a business is so placed that insolvency law is engaged.

Accordingly, there are now excluded, as beyond the scope of the chapter, certain topics that were formerly covered: for example, wrongful[2] and fraudulent[3] trading; the adjustment of pre-insolvency transactions (for example, as preferences[4] or transactions at an undervalue[5] or by virtue of avoiding effect[6]); and matters of directors' disqualification[7].

Nor are there covered either those means of effecting compromises with creditors which are used where administration is not available[8] or the distribution in the context of winding up of a company's assets in consideration of shares or other membership entitlements in the purchaser[9].

Furthermore, although among the most dramatic effects of insolvency may be those upon existing rights and relationships, these are also excluded as either belonging, in conventional legal taxonomy, to other fields (for example, the effect of a tenant's insolvency upon its relationship with its landlord) or as being factually too diverse, although in a given case they may be critical (for example, the effect upon business licences and other permits and authorisations).

1. As defined by the *Companies Act 1985 ('CA') s 249*.
2. *Insolvency Act 1986 ('IA') s 214*.
3. *IA s 213*.
4. *IA s 239*.
5. *IA ss 238* and *423*.
6. Of floating charges under *IA s 245* and in respect of all property dispositions under *IA s 127* (presentation of a petition for winding up upon which an order is subsequently made) – in respect which latter provision see the general summary of its purpose and effect, with particular reference to the operation of bank accounts, in *Bank of Ireland v Hollicourt (Contractors) Ltd* [2001] Ch 555.
7. See *Company Directors Disqualification Act 1986 (as amended)*.
8. For example, *CA s 425* in respect of insurance companies.
9. Under *IA s 110*.

Matters considered, an absence regretted

3.3   The detailed reference made to procedural rules is now effectively limited to administration, as the most common of the relevant insolvency regimes, and space has been devoted instead to individual matters of concern and interest arising in the specific context of sale, such as:

- the concept and context of the 'pre-pack' (see **3.9**);

- an unexpected and unnecessary recent difficulty over names (see **3.10**);

- difficulty that can occur (and how it can be avoided) where company law provisions clearly designed for a solvent context, govern attempts to realise value upon insolvency (see **3.11**);

- the particular provisions now made for the protection of employee rights in the case of certain types of insolvency (see **3.12**);

- the problems over pensions and a potential, but expensive, solution (see **3.18**); and

- why hive downs now hardly happen (see **3.19**).

Of course, although treated discretely, these matters are not mutually exclusive and may often be encountered together – the first four in a typical case.

There remains a section (see **3.20**) dealing with 'work out' (notwithstanding the supposed depredations of the so-called 'vulture funds' on the requirement of consensus to the 'London Approach') because of the present continued absence from the structure of English insolvency law of any legally sanctioned, formal, way to obtain priority over existing debt (conventionally called 'super priority') for the funding required during the moratorium on creditor action that, in particular, administration brings.

This absence means that in many complex insolvencies, the larger (and not always secured) creditors may be inclined to take steps in their own interests (but sometimes with significant incidental benefits for the general body of unsecured creditors) to save a company through their collective agreement and action, in order to avoid any formal insolvency regime being engaged at all.

Although in a given case this may be necessary to avoid the adverse and potentially disastrous consequences that acknowledgement of, and publicity for, the insolvency may bring about, it is also very arguably in part because the administration regime still cannot achieve its apparent and restated purpose, because of the deficiencies in its provision.

Indeed, each (bar that involving pensions) of the specific items listed above as meriting particular attention, is encountered where the subject matter of the sale is necessarily not the company itself but, in one form or another, its undertaking.

This chapter concludes, therefore, in **3.30**, by considering 'super priority' further and what would need to be done to bring about a real change in the subject matter of rescue, by making particular comparison with the cognate jurisdiction(s) of Canada.

We start, however, with the recent reforms.

Administration – a new priority, on paper

3.4   The hierarchical requirement introduced into the *Insolvency Act 1986* (*'IA'*) by EA that an administrator must perform his functions with the object of:

- first and specifically, rescuing the company (note, not its business[1]) as a going concern: and only in default of that being, in a reasoned view which must be justified to the company's creditors, reasonably practicable;

- secondly, and rather more generally, achieving a better result for the creditors than would be likely if the company were wound up; with

- thirdly, the still further subordinated purpose of realising the company's property in order to make a distribution to secured or preferential creditors[2]

suggests that there has been a significant change of legislative and public policy aim in what administration, that form of insolvency process chosen to implement the 'rescue culture', is intended to achieve.

As will be seen, however, the legislative impetus behind *EA* was not as great as the bare words of the enactment suggest and any real attempt to bring about a change in what the rescue culture can actually rescue, namely the company rather than its business, will first need properly to address if and why such a change is felt to be desirable and then provide the means to achieve the end.

The significance of any such change would be shown by the following considerations.

Before *EA* came into effect, by amending *IA* with effect from 15 September 2003, the holder of a floating charge granted by a company which, with the other security granted to its holder, secured the whole or substantially the whole of that company's assets[3] could appoint a licensed insolvency practitioner to the office of administrative receiver over the assets so charged.

The administrative receiver could then, with a minimum of obligations owed to the unsecured creditors[4] exercise a comprehensive suite of powers, conferred by statute[5] and typically enlarged by the security, usually a debenture, securing a facility under which all monies were often repayable on demand, with more or less exclusive reference to the interests of his appointor, most frequently a bank.

Whether or not the appointor then sought financially to support the trade of the company's business, or even, infrequently, to secure the continued existence of the company itself (usually as a way of trying to preserve available tax losses as an additional saleable asset[6]), this was, inevitably and understandably, only ever with a view to the realisation, at a moment of its own choosing, of the value of the charged assets through sale (whether of a going concern or of assets or very occasionally of shares), its choice of action being determined by its view of its own interest.

However sophisticated the attitudes of appointing banks to borrower default, however successful the strategies deployed by administrative receivers for saving businesses and jobs, and whatever the costs savings derived from a largely unregulated and simple process – each of which assumed propositions excites lively debate – the process was controlled by that creditor likely to have, absolutely if not necessarily relatively to the eventuation of the risk of default, the greatest share of the debt, and in the premises secured debt with priority over all other creditors whose interests were not specifically protected by statute (eg the rights of preferential creditors in respect of floating charge realisations).

That any process under the control of such a person is unlikely to prove anything more economically sophisticated than single creditor enforcement – the realisation of the sale value of the assets already appropriated to identified debt and with both appointor and appointee to an office supplanting the directors and assuming their powers each free to act to the conscious detriment of other creditors, so long as each acts in good faith – is not to criticise it but to describe it.

The holder of such a floating charge could, furthermore, veto the appointment (by the Court) of an administrator whose function was (before *EA*) determined by the terms of his appointment, most frequently in the words of *IA* (as first enacted) 'the survival of the company, and the whole or any part of its undertaking, as a going concern'[7].

Thus the survival of the company itself as a trading entity, upon which the statute (at least as it was interpreted and applied[8]) itself conferred no greater importance than the survival of any part of its business, was something that the floating charge holder could, in practice, frustrate and would frustrate where it concluded that its own interests did not require that the company avoid liquidation and ultimate dissolution.

Now, that is in respect of security granted since 15 September 2003, the holder of such a charge, termed a 'qualifying floating charge' ('QFC')[9] exercises no veto over the appointment of an administrator, who may, as shall be seen below, now be appointed in one of several different ways (some of which do not require any substantive Court involvement): albeit the holder of a QFC may still control his identity.

So the holder of a QFC may determine who holds office, but – in theory if not yet in practice – the purposes, if not the powers, of the office have changed.

1. The attempts during the debates on *EA* as a bill to introduce a reference in the alternative to the whole or part of a company's business or undertaking were successfully resisted by the government: but see **3.8**.
2. See *IA Sch B1 para 3(1)*.
3. See the definition in *IA s 29(2)*.
4. Other than to employees and to preferential creditors as then constituted as a class, including, principally, the government for certain direct and indirect taxes.
5. *IA Sch 1*.
6. Usually achieved in any event through a hive down of assets to, and the sale of the shares in, a subsidiary: see *s 343 Taxes Act 1988*.
7. See *IA* (pre-*EA*) *s 8*: note that references to the company's undertaking in the equivalent part of Sch B1 have been omitted.
8. In practice, the conjunction between the company and its undertaking was always read as if it were disjunctive.
9. Defined by *IA Sch B1 para 14* in different words but to the same effect as *IA s 29(2)*.

A few figures illustrate[1]

3.5   In what follows, it should be borne in mind that the transitional provisions of *EA* permit the appointment of administrative receivers by holders of floating charges granted before 15 September 2003. The holder of such a security may no longer veto the appointment of an administrator but should it appoint an administrative receiver before the appointment of an administrator is sought, the appointment of the latter may generally then not be made and the 'old' regime still applies.

In 2003, the year in which *EA* came into effect, there were 1,261 administrative receiverships, 497 'old style' (under *IA* unamended by *EA*) administrations and 247 'new style' (under *IA* amended by *EA*) administrations.

In 2004, there were 864 administrative receiverships, there was 1 'old style' administration and there were 1,601 'new style' administrations.

In 2005, there were 590 administrative receiverships, 4 'old style' administrations and 2,257 'new style' administrations.

As time passes and as the number of available appointments of administrative receivers decreases (with appointments made, other forms of insolvency, including new style administrations, supervening sales and refinances[2]), the bare figures and the projections that might be made from them suggest that English insolvency law may be becoming more of a truly collective process.

Whether, as seems likely, the shift away from control by a single constituency proves more apparent than real, the tools of insolvency law are now to be wielded at least to a differently expressed purpose, albeit by largely the same engineers, the insolvency profession.

It is rather more accurate than it is kind to observe that the profession has shown no real enthusiasm for any change in its role: hardly, perhaps, surprising when the response of the British Bankers' Association to the proposals which gave rise to *EA* was open incredulity that it should be intended that the company, rather than its business, should be a fit object to try to save. It was even suggested that the reference to 'company' might be a typographical error[3].

1. Source: Insolvency Service website.
2. The various statutory exceptions from the new regime in favour of the old are not dealt with here but can be found in *IA ss 72A* to *72H*.
3. BBA Response to the Report by the Review Group on Company Rescue and Business Reconstruction Mechanisms.

Why, what and how?

3.6   But typographical error it is not, so the unavoidable questions are, why the apparent change and what the practical consequence?

The 'why' is no doubt philosophical. In theory at least, a move away from a secured creditor focussed perspective to one where the question has actually to be posed and answered: is it better, in the interests of all those with an economic interest in the company's fate (creditors, of all classes, employees and shareholders etc) that there be an arrangement or composition in which debt is postponed or foregone or swapped for equity, or equity diluted (etc), rather than that there should be a realisation of what is most easily sold indirectly by, and to satisfy, only one of those constituencies.

The 'what' is, of course, more difficult, a difficulty made no easier by the failure to address the 'how' – where, notwithstanding the moratorium against creditor action that administration brings, is the company to find the financial wherewithal to fund the period of trade to analyse the options and prepare any proposals? The stay on creditor action will itself rarely free enough cash for the purpose.

Although the administrator has the power to borrow against the security of assets the subject of a floating charge in priority to such security, as this is also in priority to his own remuneration[1] and affords no priority over fixed charges, the scope of this source of funding is likely in any given case to prove limited.

It is unlikely that the recharacterisation[2] in many cases of debts due to the company from being (a) assets subject to a fixed charge (appropriated first to the secured creditor's interest), to (b) assets subject to a floating charge (appropriated to the relevant insolvency expenses including loans to administrators, the remaining preferential creditors and the 'prescribed part'[3] of the claims of the unsecured creditors) will so swell the funds to which the administrator will have recourse that the question of funding will answer itself, not least if the banks' response is to encourage their customers to factor or discount debt.

Until the Companies Act 2006 reverses the effect of *Buchler v Talbot*[4], which held that the expenses of a liquidation do not rank in priority to the claims of the holder of a floating charge over the realisation proceeds of assets subject to such a charge, as the expenses in an administration equivalent to liquidation expenses do rank in priority to such claims[5], administration as a procedure has a relative funding advantage, viewed in terms of the availability of assets to meet expenses, over, say, a creditors' voluntary liquidation.

However, the advantage, while it lasts and which would exist in any event in the comparison given having regard to the respective functions of each insolvency regime[6], is illusory – it is derived from a rule about appropriating existing assets to liabilities and does nothing to generate new funds.

In the absence of funding from a party interested in making an acquisition, which is to beg the question of what there is to acquire, one of the effects of the law of unintended consequences may prove to be that *EA* has the effect of making funding more difficult to obtain where the secured creditor may be less inclined to advance funds into a process it controls to a lesser extent, and is less for its direct benefit, than that which it has superseded and where the other stakeholders in the debt may be disinclined to throw good money after what they fear may prove to be bad.

It may, therefore, simply mean that the number of cases where the phenomenon of the 'pre-pack' – dealt with below in **3.9** – is encountered, increases, which will have the effect of excluding the voice of the unsecured creditors even further than it is excluded now.

This may be no more than a reflection of commercial reality and accordingly in any given case objectionable neither in practice nor (less certainly) in principle. Nevertheless, it seems ironic that a measure one of the avowed purposes of which is to make the practice of insolvency law through the administration regime more of a truly collective process, may result in an increase in the number of those cases where the unsecured creditors are excluded from any participation in (and often any return from) that process.

Should this happen, it would largely be because, and only emphasise that, the most conspicuous feature missing from insolvency law in England and Wales is any attempt to meet the need for priority funding in insolvency ('super priority'). In many cases, the absence of such funding may mean that the benefits of the moratorium are discounted to nil and there is no real or effective choice of action open to any party.

1. *IA Sch B1 para 99(3), (4)* (formerly *IA ss 19(5)*: it is referred to as super-priority by Lord Hoffmann in *Freakley v Centre Reinsurance International Company* [2006] UKHL 45, [2006] All ER (D) 121 (Oct)): for an example in practice (where the fixed and floating charges were in favour of the party making the advance) see *Bibby Trade Finance Limited v McKay* [2006] EWHC 2836 (Ch), [2006] All ER (D) 266 (Jul).
2. Following the decision in *Re Spectrum Plus* [2005] UKHL 41, [2005] 4 All ER 209.
3. See *IA s 176A*.
4. [2004] UKHL 9, [2004] 2 AC 298, by inserting, some time in 2008, a new *s 176ZA* into *IA*: see *CA 2006 s 1282* – the difficulties with the decision include that the general rule of priority is that liquidation expenses rank before the claims of preferential creditors whose claims in turn rank before the claims of the holders of floating charges in respect of floating charge realisations: *IA ss 115* and *175(2)(a)*. Faced with the conundrum of how the claims of the floating charge holders could rank before those expenses themselves enjoying priority over the claims of preferential creditors to whose claims the claims of floating charge holders are themselves subordinated, the House of Lords effectively disapplied the rule by discovering the assets subject to the (crystallised) floating charge not to be assets of the company at all, although still subject to the same claims of the preferential creditors – a result that produced a reaction of something approaching derision from academia and practitioners alike.
5. *IA Sch B1 para 99(3)*.
6. A comparison with administrative receivership would involve different considerations, because the appointor is a potential source of funding: at present, floating charge holders enjoy the happy privilege, where able to appoint an administrative receiver, of being able to appropriate a class of the company's assets to their economic interest burdened only by the claims of the preferential creditors, free of the expenses of a concurrent or subsequent liquidation.

Administration – entry (and exit) routes

3.7   Before *EA*, an administration could only be brought about by the making of a court order, on the application of the company, its directors or a creditor, the order specifying one or more of a series of purposes, none of which had priority above the others[1].

After *EA*, an administration order may still be made in this way on the application of any of the same parties if the court is (a) (except in the case of an application by the holder of a QFC) satisfied that the company is or is likely to become unable to pay its debts within the meaning of *IA s 123* and (b) reasonably satisfied that one of the newly hierarchically ordered purposes will be achieved[2].

An application may under certain circumstances be made in respect of a company in liquidation and then the liquidation will be superseded by the administration[3].

What is new is that a company may enter administration without there being any court involvement (other than the receipt and checking as correct, and then the filing, of the relevant forms) by the company or its directors[4] or the holder of a QFC[5] applying to appoint (in reality, simply appointing) an administrator, in any case where the proposed appointee is willing to declare a belief that there is a reasonable likelihood of being able to achieve one of the purposes in the hierarchy.

The holder of a QFC[6] is the only person entitled to appoint an administrator – either itself or by persuading the court of the need to appoint, for which purpose it must prove its own right to appoint[7] – without having to establish that the company is or is likely to become unable to pay its debts. The company or the directors must still do so.

This fact may be thought to reflect that in some ways the right of the holder of a QFC to appoint is little different from the previous right to appoint an administrative receiver. Indeed, the holder of the QFC may be said now to be in a better position, as his appointee has the benefit of the moratorium[8] which the administrative receiver never enjoyed.

The rules contain, furthermore, a nod to what will surely continue to be the common situation of the holder of the QFC having a secured debt greater than the company's assets by providing that, save where creditors with more than 10% of the debts insist, the creditors' meeting can be foregone where the unsecured creditors will receive nothing[9].

This may, in a given case, be justifiable. The holder of the QFC will typically be a bank, with more knowledge than any other creditor of the company's financial position, whether derived from obligations imposed by loan documentation to provide financial information and/or from the company's spells in what is known as 'intensive care' – a term indicating increased stringency of bank control over credit and other financial limits and/or reports by bank appointed investigating accountants.

The bank may thus be best placed to decide when an appointment, imposing the moratorium, will crystallise and maximise value. But there is no reason why the bank should be considering the interests of any party but itself. What largely remains to be seen is how the administrator whose identity but not the fact of whose appointment the holder of the QFC now controls, will, upon the premise that he is appointed before the bank has had the chance to crystallise and prepare to extract value, approach his task under EA.

There would be few situations where the facts were such that proper valuations could not be obtained (in which respect the RICS 'Red Book', properly 'Appraisals and Valuation Standards' (fifth edition, 2003), expressly provides for alternative valuation bases respectively allowing for proper or insufficient to nil marketing because of 'constraints', according to circumstance) and the administrator articulates his thinking in writing and receives written valuation and legal advice.

In appropriate cases, those who might be aggrieved by a sale at the price for which the administrator has professional valuation input (for example, guarantors), might be given the opportunity to approve the sale or to better the price.

That the unsecured creditors may on the facts not be a constituency with any financial recovery interest in the outcome of a particular administration does not, however, mean that they should simply be told this, or indeed nothing at all.

That the means adopted to effect the sale without the statutory approval process being followed may be entirely proper, does not mean that the administrator should not answer to that constituency whose interests the discarded procedures were designed to protect – indeed, the purpose of EA means that the answer should be a full, reasoned and reasonable one.

But the rules seem to facilitate otherwise.

1. *IA* (pre-*EA*) *ss 8* and *9.*
2. See *IA Sch B1 paras 10* to *13.*
3. *Paras 37* to *38.*
4. *Paras 22* to *34.*
5. *Paras 14* to *21.*
6. Who is entitled to be notified of an application for an administration order and to written notice of an intended appointment by the company or the directors, in each case with the effective right to nominate who is appointed.
7. *See IA Sch B1 para 35.*
8. *Paras 42* to *44.*
9. *Para 52.*

Administration – a brief note on Chapter 11, the day before yesterday in Parliament and a conflict of roles

3.8   Administration is often compared to the Chapter 11 regime of the United States Code, where the concept is, for historically sound but presently misleading reasons, called 'bankruptcy'.

A brief summary of the Chapter 11 process is that the distressed company files a petition with the court. The act of filing imposes a moratorium on creditor (including secured creditor) action. The company then has 120 days to propose a plan of reorganisation designed to save the company itself as a trading entity. That plan is itself filed at court and must specify the different classes in which it is intended that the creditors will be asked to approve the plan. If satisfied with the process so far, the court will direct the holding of meetings of the respective classes of creditor and if the necessary majority of each (more than one half in number holding at least two thirds in value) votes in favour, the court will be asked to approve the plan (subject to dealing with any filed objections). If approved, the plan will reconstitute the debt nexus between company and creditors, usually in lesser amounts or over a longer payment period. Such a reconstitution may involve use of the feature of US law of the 'cram-down', whereby, for example, the rights of unsecured creditors can be crammed down into, which is to say limited to, the free equity of a company's secured assets.

However, a Chapter 11 plan may do significantly more than to provide for a binding rescheduling of debt – it may also be the opportunity to compromise and release claims by the debtor company and indeed even some of its creditors against certain other of its creditors and third parties, as the only practical alternative to litigation that would otherwise so distract management time and financial resource as to doom the debtor company to failure and thereby render the merits of the dispute moot.

For an example, see the legal notice published in The Times on 30 October 2006 in respect of Refco Inc[1], the plan for which provided for a complicated regime of claims release in respect of, among other things, 'piercing the corporate veil, alter ego, domination, constructive trust and similar principles of state or federal creditors' rights laws.'

What can be termed 'pre-packs', which appear as such a significant feature in the present practice of insolvency law in England and Wales, are also used under Chapter 11 – indeed the practice and the terminology originated in the US. The Chapter 11 process is simply accelerated by the plan being filed with the petition. If the creditors have voted upon the plan before filing, then they are bound by it (subject to savings for judicial rescission for misrepresentation or non-disclosure). Otherwise, they are asked to vote after filing in the normal way. The creditors may be crammed but they are not ignored.

In either situation, as is clear, the aim is to save the company, not its business.

That the government intended the same result for administrations under *EA* is obvious to anyone reading the relevant passages in Hansard.

> 'If the objective of administration were to rescue the company's business rather than the company itself, frankly there would be little incentive for directors of the company to enter into administration, which is one of the intentions of the Bill.'[2]

It is equally obvious to anyone familiar with practice in the field that this has not been the result of the reforms. However, this is in fact not the simple thwarting of the will of Parliament it might first seem.

In rejecting the amendments that would have expressly referred to the whole or any part of a company's business or undertaking as an alternative proper object for rescue, the Minister said that the amendments:

> 'would put the breaking-up of the company and rescue of its constituent businesses [sic] on a par with the rescue of the company. Clearly, there will be cases where the break-up and sale of some or all of a company's individual businesses as going concern would result in a better return to the creditors. Where that is the case, the duty of the administrator [in what is now IA Sch. B1 para. 3(2)] to act in the interests of the creditors as a whole will steer him towards that outcome. However, the amendments would go further than that; they would mean that in cases where all was equal, there would be no particular obligation on the administrator to rescue the company rather than breaking it up. That cannot be right... .'[3]

So, it would appear that the expectation has always been that in a given case, business rather then company rescue is a perfectly acceptable outcome and indeed the amendments proposed were withdrawn on the basis of this clarification.

So much may seem obvious. It is nevertheless to be regretted that to the attentive, never mind the casual, reader of the relevant provisions, it is far from obvious that the general obligations owed to creditors as a whole can be used to derogate from the primary statutory purpose quite so easily, not least where that general duty fails to distinguish between the different interests of the different classes of creditors that will exist. It is also far from obvious that such a general duty will in any event be the real reason to try to save the business rather than the company.

One consequence of this ability quickly to shift down from the primary obligation to save the company to the lesser but perhaps more realistic one of saving the business, is that it makes the pre-pack that much more attractive.

One issue that arises for the administrator to justify that tactic to the creditors at their meeting, summoned or convened (if it is held at all), is that the corollary of being able to do the deal immediately after appointment is that the underpinning work has to be done in advance of appointment.

Putting aside as beyond the scope of this chapter the questions that might arise as to the potential conflicts of interest for the insolvency practitioner who has worked hand in glove with bank and directors to set up a sale to the latter to the financial benefit of the former (which may indeed be rolling debt over into the new venture) then to present his work to an unconsulted constituency as the best that could have been done – who is to pay for this work?

Before *EA*, recovery of pre-appointment costs as expenses ranking ahead of the unsecured debts of the company was limited to the costs of preparing the statutory report that was a practical necessity for the grant of an administration order by the court[4] but which plays no part in the process after *EA*.

After *EA*[5] if costs incurred in the name of the company after administration pursuant to contracts entered into before administration cannot be recovered as administration expenses[6], it seems difficult to argue that the administrator's pre-appointment costs can be anything other than unsecured debts of the company ranking pari passu with the other unsecured creditors.

The administrator is thus placed in the somewhat invidious position in which he must either (a) take fees before appointment and then seek to defend a challenge to their legitimacy in the subsequent administration (the right to challenge those fees and relative cause of action being vested in him personally as administrator[7]) in practice by including his fees in the proposals for which he is going (if he is) to seek creditor sanction or (b) accept payment from bank or directors.

None of these choices does much for the transparency and independence of the process.

The unreported case of *Re SE Services Limited*[8] shows that it may be possible to persuade a court to order the recovery of pre-appointment costs in the exercise of its discretion[9], but the exercise of such discretion will always be fact sensitive[10] and invoking it would tend to promote court appointments or applications – which seems counter to the desire to simplify the administration process.

1. *United States Bankruptcy Court Southern District of New York case No 05-60006 (RDD).*
2. Douglas Alexander, Minister for E-Commerce and Competitiveness House of Common Standing Committee B (pt 3) Hansard, HC cols 548–549 (9 May 2002). One must understand the Minister to be referring to the rescue, and not the entry into administration, as the aim.
3. Col 556.
4. The report was that produced was under IR 2.2 (as enacted) and the limitation was imposed by *Re Cabletel Installations Limited* [2005] BPIR 28
5. Under which the general rules as to the priority of distributions have been incorporated from the field of liquidation: see *IA Sch B1 para 65* and *IA s 175*.
6. Cf *Freakley v Centre Reinsurance International Company* [2006] UKHL 45, [2006] All ER (D) 121 (Oct) in respect of a pre-EA appointment.
7. In an action for a preference under *IA s 239*.
8. Noted by Alistair Bacon in Insolvency Intelligence (Thomson Sweet & Maxwell) Vol 20 Number 1 p 1 (January 2007).
9. Under *IA Sch B1 para 13(i)(f)*, by effectively expanding upon the definition of 'administration expense' in IR r 2.67.
10. It appears that the judge drew a distinction between (a) situations where the creditors would benefit from the work done and (b) situations where the beneficiaries would be existing management in the guise of purchasers, the discretion being by far more likely to be exercised in the former case than in the latter.

Pre-packs – in administrations and otherwise

3.9   With the decline of the availability of administrative receivership and the consequent weakening of inclination on the part of a secured creditor to fund what it no longer controls, the role of the 'pre-pack' sale (although frequently encountered before *EA* in the context of both administrative receivership and 'old style' administration) has become more important, in part as a response to that lack of funding.

The essence of the pre-pack – an asset sale – is that before the administrator is appointed, the deal is done, the purchaser (very often a party associated with existing management) is identified, the price agreed, the sale documentation drafted, any corporate or other reorganisation primed and the funding lined up for the brave new world of post-administration business.

The administrator's role as such, although typically the practitioner involved will have been instrumental in the pre-pack being set up and its rationale, is to sign the papers and then discharge his other functions as such upon the basis of what to the creditors (and the court) is a fait accompli.

Before *EA*, there was what might be described (borrowing from a different legal context) as a wide margin of appreciation available to the administrator to decide whether to exercise, so long as consistently with the purposes set out in the order by which he was appointed, his statutory power of sale.

Although the administrator also had a statutory duty to put his proposals before the creditors (which he could hardly do if the business has already been sold), there was an acceptance that in an appropriate case and subject always to the terms of the order, sale before consultation would often be entirely proper and perhaps be the only means of extracting any value for creditors or some of them.

After *T&D Industries plc*[1] it was accepted that the urgency and importance of decisions might be such that the delay involved in the holding of the creditors' meeting might make choices moot and that where to seek directions from the court or to hold a meeting on abridged notice would advance matters no further, the sale opportunity could be seized. Indeed, in that case Neuberger J was at pains to point out that the sorts of issues that determined the need for early sale would often be commercial or administrative in nature and accordingly matters upon which judicial assistance would be limited (especially if applications were made on an ex parte basis, as the premised urgency would frequently require), an assistance that the court should, furthermore, be positively slow to give, where to give it would be simply to provide what he called a 'bomb shelter' for the administrator. The administrator was better placed to make the relevant sort of assessment, take, and stand by, his decision. He might, in a given case, where there were few, or few significant, creditors, seek to consult them as far as he felt circumstances permitted, but the decision should be his.

It appears from *Transbus International Limited*[2] that the position after *EA* will be the same.

Although neither case cited was a pre-pack and each involved a short period of trading, the principles hold for pre-packs proper.

The principal criticism that can be validly levelled at the pre-pack is that the alternatives have not been explored. But of course the validity of any such criticism must be fact specific and there is nothing about a pre-pack that prevents those alternatives being as fully explored as the circumstances realistically permit.

Marketing as extensive as the financial position allows may be possible to establish that the price proposed to be realised is the best available, but the process will inevitably be constrained by those factors that will, were the insolvency to become apparent or supervene, precipitate the need for prompt sale to avoid the loss of any substantive value – the termination of contracts or necessary licences, the loss of credit insurance or key personnel, the erosion of intellectual property rights, the dissipation of goodwill etc.

For the proposed administrator to take an informed decision in such circumstances to go for a pre-pack may not only be a perfectly proper decision for him to make, it may be the only proper decision for him to make in accordance with his obligations as prospective administrator and (when appointed) officer of the court, even though this may be to deprive the creditors of their right to be consulted as to his proposals in advance.

If it would have been possible before *EA* to have justified the decision to sell without consultation, it ought still to be possible to justify the same decision on similar facts, notwithstanding the enhanced justificatory obligation under *EA*, namely that saving the company was not reasonably practicable.

A higher hurdle perhaps, but frequently easily cleared nonetheless. As Lawrence Collins J pointed out in *Transbus*, where the facts are plain that the unsecured creditors must on any view receive nothing, this itself justifies foregoing their approval.

This is indeed one of the circumstances where the need for a creditors' meeting can be foregone, as is where the unsecured creditors will be paid in full or where neither of the purposes in the hierarchy above distributions to secured or preferential creditors can be achieved.[3]

The difficulty will be with the perception, where the only return is to the secured creditor funding a new business owned by the old management (which will not be the infrequent result), that reforms introduced to extinguish the secured creditor's veto have been hijacked to appropriate the available value to the secured debt effectively by ignoring the right of the creditors to have any say in the revised process at all, a process which will often result with the same assets in the hands of the same management but free of the unsecured creditors' claims, even trading with the same name if the administrator so allows under the statutory provisions as to the use of 'phoenix' names (but see **3.10**).

A notable example of the phenomenon nevertheless recently received judicial sanction in *Re Quality Kebab Limited*[4] where Kitchin J made an administration order on a directors' application in the teeth of the opposition of the principal creditor (which was petitioning for an order for the company's winding up) on the basis that the evidence before the court was that the interest expressed in the company's assets (at a fraction of their book value) from a party connected with the directors was the best offer likely to be achieved, even though it was plain that the relevant sale would be completed before the creditors' meeting and the judge was clearly concerned that the conduct of those same directors cried out for investigation.

The answer must surely be that while in a given case economic reality and the exigencies of realising value may forego the need to seek the approval of unsecured creditors, this does not justify failing to report to those same creditors the reasons and justifications for the choices made as well as their outcomes.

The rules do not, however, positively so require.

1. [2000] 1 All ER 333.
2. [2004] EWHC 932, [2004] 2 All ER 911.
3. *IA Sch B1 para 52(1)* excluding payments to which unsecured creditors may be entitled from the 'prescribed part' of floating charge realisations (see ibid. *s 176A*) and subject to the right of creditors to requisition meetings under *para 52(2)* at their own cost (see IR 2.37(3)).
4. [2006] EWHC 1764, [2006] All ER (D) 162 (June).

Phoenix companies – a ruse by any other name

3.10   One of the principal reasons for any pre-pack will be the preservation of goodwill, and a principal way in which goodwill is manifested is the corporate trading name. Insolvency legislation provides that where a company goes into insolvent liquidation and a person was a director of that company (the 'liquidating company') within the 12 months preceding liquidation, that person may not, save with leave of the Court or in one of the 'excepted cases', act in the period of 5 years following liquidation as a director or otherwise be involved in the management of, or form or promote, another company with a 'prohibited name' – a name by which the liquidating company was known at any time in the 12 months preceding its liquidation or a name so similar as to suggest an association.

Breach of the prohibition is a criminal offence and renders a person acting in contravention of the prohibition personally liable, jointly and severally with the company with the prohibited name, for the debts of that company[1].

In many cases, therefore, the rationale for the pre-pack will require the disapplication of this prohibition, as all or some of existing management will be involved with the company that will be buying the goodwill and with it the right to use a name which, where used in conjunction with their managerial role, will otherwise be prohibited.

Properly understood, the prohibition lies not in the use of the name, but in the managerial role of persons within the rule in a company using the name – the liability for breach of the rule is visited on the person, not on the company.

Among the 'excepted cases' is the 'first excepted case' of self-help, which provides that where a company – the 'successor company' – acquires the whole or substantially the whole of the business of an insolvent company, under arrangements made by an insolvency practitioner acting as liquidator, administrator, administrative receiver or supervisor of a CVA, the successor company may give notice, within 28 days of the completion of the arrangements, to the insolvent company's creditors of certain prescribed particulars, including the name of any person within the prohibition 'with a view to his being a director of the successor company'[2]. A person so named may then act as a director etc of the successor company without breach of the prohibition.

This rule clearly covers the case where the insolvent liquidation occurs subsequently to the completion arrangements in respect of which the notice is contemplated. The rule carefully does not describe the company whose assets are the subject of such arrangements as, at that stage, the 'liquidating company'. It would, furthermore, make no sense to have a rule that allowed, say, an administrative receivership containing a pre-pack immediately followed by a liquidation, to be outside the rule.

In *Churchill v First Independent Factors and Finance Limited*[3], the Court of Appeal interpreted the phrase 'with a view to', as referring to the future only and in such a way that any notice given in respect of a person who would otherwise be within the prohibition but who was already involved in the management of the successor company, would be invalid and that person remain in breach.

The practical effect of the decision is that many pre-packs may be put in peril where they are also purchases by phoenixes controlled by members of existing management. Although in theory other parties might be found to act as directors until the notice was given, this seems practically unlikely even if such an arrangement were not a sham and the prohibition found to have been breached whatever the guise given to the arrangements, as the successor company is unlikely to be able to arrange funding for the purchase when under the management of persons other than those contemplated as those who will be running its affairs, including repaying the funding – to say nothing of the lending bank's anti-money laundering regulatory requirements.

Although the circumstances of a pre-pack (or other) sale by an administrator followed by a liquidation will be fewer than such sales by an administrative receiver or supervisor (sales by a liquidator are by their very nature covered), since administrations are now prima facie to last only one year[4] and express provision is now made for there to be a conversion to a creditors' voluntary liquidation[5] – which is clearly an insolvent liquidation for this purpose – there is a real risk that those involved in such a sale may find themselves vulnerable to the risk of assuming personal liability for ongoing debts.

It is doubtful that this result, which exposes individual directors to the risk of personal liability[6] for the successor company's debts but which does nothing to assist the liquidating company's creditors, advances the rescue culture at all.

The response to it will have to be recourse to the 'second excepted case', application to the Court within seven days from the date on which the liquidating company goes into liquidation, which gives a grace period of six weeks' leave to act pending the determination of the application for leave to act[7].

About this may be said two things.

First, the individual in question may not know when liquidation is to supervene and thus when he has to make his application – a conversion from an administration to a creditors' voluntary liquidation, for example, is effected merely by notice filed with the Court and sent to creditors[8], not to the directors of the liquidating company.

Secondly, it is difficult to see easily upon what basis the Court should dispose of the application. The most obvious judicial reaction in the light of the evil against which the prohibition is aimed – that creditors of the liquidating company might be unaware that they are dealing with a new entity under the old management – would be to ask whether the creditor body has been informed of the position. One imagines a certain silence when the applicant's unhappy advocate has to explain that notice was indeed given but that one is there because the Court of Appeal has said that such notice was invalid, although fulfilling the very purpose just identified by the learned judge.

According to what criteria, therefore, is the judge to decide? If notice is not sufficient, what is? In the light of previous decisions that all that is required that leave be granted is that there should be no risk of the relevant confusion[9], the answer is not obvious. And if notice is what is required, why disqualify a notice that clearly has the effect of dispelling the ground for confusion?

The incorporation and stockpiling of companies with similar names as vehicles for bringing one within the 'third excepted case' (no leave required in respect of existing companies with names that would otherwise be prohibited) is blocked by the rules themselves[10].

1. *See IA ss 216, 217 and Insolvency Rules 1986 ('IR') r 4.228.*
2. R 4.228(3).
3. [2006] EWCA Civ 1623 (a case of a sale by a liquidator – which may explain why some of the unhappy consequences of the decision did not occur to the Court).
4. *IA Sch B1 para 6.*
5. Para 83.
6. Which is strict, as to both civil and criminal liability: *Ricketts v Ad Valorem Factors Limited* [2003] EWCA Civ 1706, [2004] 1 All ER 894.
7. IR r 4.229.
8. *IA Sch B1 para 83(3).*
9. For example *Penrose v Official Receiver* [1996] 2 All ER 96.
10. IR r 4.230(b). On the 'third excepted case' generally, see *ESS Production Limited v Sully* [2005] EWCA Civ 554, [2005] All ER (D) 158 (May).

A trap for the unwary

3.11   *Companies Act 1985 ('CA') s 320* ('substantial property transactions involving directors, etc') provides that with certain exceptions, a company may not enter into an arrangement whereby a director[1] or a person connected with such a director acquires one or more non-cash assets of the requisite value from the company, unless the arrangement is first approved by a resolution of the company in general meeting.

The 'requisite value' is not less than £2,000 but more than either £100,000 or 10% of the company's net asset value and 'connected' is defined[2] in such a way as to include the director's family, his partners and other companies with which he is 'associated', namely companies in which he and those connected with him have 20% of the shares or voting rights.

If the terms of the section are infringed, the transaction is voidable at the instance of the company unless[3]:

- restitution is impossible (which will be rare); or
- the company has been indemnified (which will be rarer); or
- the rights of a person – such as a mortgagee lending the money for the acquisition – who acquired those rights bona fide for value without actual notice of the infringement would be affected by its avoidance – notice is not easily avoided in the days of 'know your customer'; or
- the transaction is, within a reasonable period, affirmed by the company in general meeting.

In addition to the transaction being voidable, and whether or not it is set aside, the director and the connected persons involved are severally liable to account for any direct or indirect gain made by them and jointly and severally to indemnify the company against loss and damage suffered by it[4].

Among the exceptions is a transaction entered into by a company which is being wound up[5], that is, either compulsorily or in a creditors' voluntary liquidation.

It will be noted that there is no exception for transactions in either administrative receiverships or administrations, with the consequence that a typical insolvency sale in either situation to existing management or some of their number through a new company is vulnerable to being set aside, and the principal actors sued, by a liquidator subsequently appointed by aggrieved creditors.

The risk of a sale being avoided is real and not merely fanciful. In *Demite Limited v Protec Health Limited*[6], Park J set aside such a sale by an administrative receiver at the suit of a liquidator, holding that there was no implied insolvency exception for anything other than liquidation, even though he accepted that the section had been introduced to prevent sales instigated by directors of solvent companies – as he put it, 'statutory patches are commonly bigger than holes.'

Further, he held, obiter, that the common law principle of *Re Duomatic Limited*[7], namely that where it can be shown that all the shareholders who have a right to attend and vote at a general meeting of the company have assented to a matter which a general meeting could carry into effect, the assent is as binding as a resolution in general meeting would be, did not apply to *s 320* and so there could not be compliance absent a resolution duly passed.

However, in *Conegrade Limited*[8], Lloyd J took a different view of the applicability of the *Duomatic* principle and held that a board meeting of the directors, each of whom was a shareholder, at which they assented to the transaction, meant that it had been approved by the company and could not set aside in its subsequent liquidation.

In *Ultraframe (UK) Limited v Fielding*[9], faced with conflicting opinions of equal judicial status, Lewison J declined to decide between them but identified in the section's use of the word 'voidable' an indication that the general doctrine of election applied, so that the company could be found to have affirmed a voidable transaction it had entered by any means sufficient under that doctrine to constitute a bar to it then seeking to have it set aside. An example would be for the company, through a liquidator subsequently appointed, to demand payment of sums due under it – so this is not merely a case of *Duomatic* after the event.

The judge made plain that such affirmation could not be found in anything that the company had done through its directors (as, after all, it is as a protection against their participation in transactions unauthorised by the shareholders that the section was enacted) so seems to have contemplated that, for example, shareholders might collectively do something after the transaction sufficient to affirm it, whether or not the same something done at the time of the transaction would be sufficient to authorise it. The clear statutory reference to affirmation taking place in the context of a general meeting did not feature in his analysis.

The other relevant holding of significance was that where the sale was by an administrative receiver (and the logic extends to a sale by an administrator[10]), in order to decide whether the section is infringed, one must – because of the reference to 'net assets' – look at the value of the equity of redemption in the assets the subject of the transaction and either value that or compare it, as a percentage, with the total equity in the whole of the company's assets.

The judge reasoned as follows:

'Just as on the sale of an unencumbered asset the company's interest in the asset is exchanged for cash, so on the sale of a charged asset, the company's equity of redemption in the sold asset is exchanged for an equitable interest in any cash surplus after payment of the secured debt. Accordingly, the asset whose value must exceed the minima is the equity of redemption; and not the value that the charged asset would have had if unencumbered.

… One of the relevant comparators is the value of the company's net assets. This concentrates attention on the extent of the company's beneficial interest in the assets in question. In making any comparison, one would expect to be comparing like with like. Thus in comparing the value of an asset of which the company is disposing, one would expect the comparison to be one between the company's beneficial interest in the asset on the one hand, and its beneficial interest in the totality of its assets on the other.

… If the receiver wishes to sell charged assets, and the extent of the debt is such that there is no possibility of a surplus out of the proceeds of sale being available to the company, what is the point of requiring the shareholders to approve the sale? It would merely give disgruntled shareholders the ability to impede the orderly and speedy realisation of the company's assets towards the discharge of its debts. If, on the other hand, there is a prospect of a surplus which exceeds the requisite value, then there is every point in requiring the shareholders to approve the sale.'[11]

When the relevant part of the *Companies Act 2006* is brought into force[12], the exemption from *s 320* for transactions in liquidations will be extended to administrations[13]. Until then for administrators and until and after then for administrative receivers, because of the doubts as to whether the *Duomatic* principle applies to the actions of shareholders before the transactions, where the shareholders cannot be made to agree to a transaction covered by the section, either recourse must be had to the accounts or the purchaser must be invited to take the unwelcome risk of challenge within a 'reasonable time' (the length of which must be fact sensitive) and if nothing happens which amounts to affirmation.

The risk of challenge can of course be discounted if the price obtained was a proper one and less than the sum due to the charge holder, because then there is no point in the challenge: but of course there may in a given case be issues around the sufficiency of the price, not least if the purchasing vehicle is funded by the same charge holder, or about the validity of the charge itself.

A further difficulty with the *Ultraframe* analysis is that the accounts identified by the section are the last annual accounts laid before the company's general meeting and may, by virtue of the insolvency itself, bear little relevance to present value. The judgment does not deal with the point.[14]

The decision is therefore not without difficulty.

Ultimately, it may be necessary for the charge holder to exercise its power of sale, as then the transaction is not one by the company at all, which focuses any dispute in the field of charge validity and enforcement.

1. A term which is expressed to include a shadow director – a person in accordance with whose directions or instructions the directors of a company are accustomed to act: *CA s 741* – and thus must be taken to include a de facto director.
2. By *s 346*.
3. *Section 322(2)*.
4. *Section 322(3)*.
5. *Section 321(2)(b)*.
6. [1998] BCC 638.
7. [1969] 2 Ch 365.
8. [2002] EWHC 2411, [2002] All ER (D) 19 (Nov).
9. [2005] EWHC 1638, [2005] All ER (D) 397 (Jul).
10. Indeed there is nothing in the analysis that would suggest it should not apply to any sale by the company, whether informally insolvent or wholly solvent.
11. Paras 1408 and 1409: references are given in pity of the reader faced with a 487-page judgment. In rejecting leave to appeal (see [2006] EWCA Civ 1133), Jacob LJ referred to the dispute as having been one 'conducted by both sides as if a State trial'.
12. Probably in 2008.
13. *CA 2006 s 193*.
14. When the relevant provisions of *CA 2006* are brought into force, the relevant accounts will be the company's most recent statutory accounts, being those in relation to which the time for sending them to members is most recent (*s 191*): presumably, they will be the relevant accounts whether or not they have actually been sent to members. The problem as to their accuracy in the context of insolvency remains, emphasised by the fact that the section will provide that the question of whether an asset is a substantial asset is to be determined at the time that the arrangement in respect of it is entered into (*s 191(5)*). In the absence of there being any statutory accounts, asset value is determined by reference to the company's called-up share capital.

Employees and employment claims – Paramount lost, Huddersfield worsted

3.12   The interface between employment law and insolvency law (and in particular its history) is one for which only the word 'vexed' seems entirely apt.

In particular, the attempt to provide employee protection on an occasion of business transfer engages a tension between that aim and the reality that the employment costs may be a burden of which the business must be relieved if it is to be viable at all.

Upon appointment, an administrator[1] or receiver (administrative[2] or other[3]) has 14 days in which, in effect, either to dismiss employees or be deemed to

have adopted their contracts of employment should he by then not have suc-
ceeded in selling the business in which they work.

Should adoption occur, the appointee becomes the employer and personally
liable – but with recourse for indemnity to those assets to which his appointment extends – in most cases[4] for some but not all, of the liabilities which
accrue from adoption.

1. *IA Sch B1 paras 99(5)* and *(6)*.
2. *IA s 44.*
3. *IA s 37.*
4. The position of a non-administrative (or *Law of Property Act/'LPA'*) receiver is anomalous
   in that there is no limitation upon his liability.

How did we get here?

3.13   The short history of this present position of an adoption with only
limited consequence is as follows.

Before the insolvency legislation of 1986, such appointees owed no legal
obligation to see the employees paid for work done.

Accordingly, employees were exposed to a theoretical risk of being left
unpaid for their services. In practice, of course, employees would almost
always be paid for the period of the appointment – if only as otherwise they
might sue for breach of contract or for constructive unfair dismissal or lawfully strike or seek other employment, thereby bringing about the end of any
hope of selling a business as a going concern – and the State, in the guise of
the National Insurance Fund, would bear the bulk of their other accrued
statutory entitlements should the business not be sold and their jobs be
saved.

Nevertheless, the one reported case[1] of an employee not being paid for services rendered to a receiver[2] was reported during the passage of the insolvency legislation and was enough to bring about the introduction of the
adoption provision for receiverships and the then novel regime of administration.

Initially, this caused little change in practice, as both receivers and administrators, encouraged judicially to some extent from the sidelines[3] sidestepped
the consequences of adoption by a practice of writing to employees within 14
days of appointment supposedly to make clear that the continuance of their
contracts of employment beyond that period was not the adoption of those
contracts by the appointees but a continuation of those contracts with the
company – as if adoption was something that would only happen unless it
was forestalled and that it could be forestalled simply by a statement negat-
ing it.

Perhaps not altogether unsurprisingly, other judges were less than impressed
by accountants and solicitors selecting those parts of the legislation by which
they needed to abide and the decisions in *Re Paramount Airways Ltd (No 3)*[4]

(administration) and *Re Leyland Daf*[5] (receivership) asserted that the legislation meant what it said and that the appointees could not avoid the consequences of a more or less wholesale adoption of liability for the entire contractual relationship – including in respect of any contractual entitlements exceeding statutory minimum entitlements – after 14 days.

The decisions elevated employees to a unique position in corporate insolvency, that is of a statutory right of recourse without limit to a person other than the company, thereby in effect – because of the appointor's right of recourse to the assets to which his appointment extended – appropriating the whole of the value of the company's assets not the subject of security[6] to one class of unsecured creditor, a right quite separate from the preferential status that certain classes of employee claim in any event enjoy over all other unsecured claims and the rights of the holder of a floating charge[7].

The decisions also left appointees exposed to the risk of personal liability for accrued and accruing employee entitlements they might both before and upon appointment have difficulty in measuring, at a time when the possibility of saving the business and jobs could be uncertain, when time would be at a premium and with recourse to assets that might prove inadequate to cover the risk but no legal right to seek further support from their appointor. Furthermore, there were doubts as to whether appointees would be insured in respect of any shortfall in such recourse or support.

Extensive lobbying from the insolvency profession resulted in more less immediate legislation[8] which restricts the personal liability of appointees to one for wages or salary (including contributions to occupational pension schemes) incurred while in office and in respect of services rendered wholly or partly after adoption.

For these purposes, holiday pay (and sums payable in lieu of holiday) and payments for absence from work through sickness or other good cause, in each case where referable to the period from adoption, are included within the concept of 'wages' or 'salary'.

However, payments in lieu of notice (with the exception of payments during periods of garden leave) and protective awards under the *Trade Union and Labour Relations Act 1992*[9] (for a failure to consult with recognised trade unions or employee representatives in advance of redundancies) are excluded from the concept[10].

Some of the claims both included within, and excluded from, the scope of the 'wages' or 'salary' for which the appointee adopts liability may also be preferential and thus rank ahead of other unsecured claims and the rights of the holder of a floating charge[11].

But the principal relevance for employee claims in a rescue context is not the potential liability for the appointee (although of course most relevant to his likely choice of action) but the extent to which any purchaser of the business will be treated as assuming liability for those claims and liabilities.

Ever since the enactment of the *Transfer of Undertakings (Protection of Employment) Regulations 1981*[12] (*'TUPE 1981'*), when there has been a sale of the whole or part of an undertaking as a going concern, all material employment liabilities (bar some, but not all, pension entitlements) have passed with the employees from the seller (transferor) of such a going concern[13] to its purchaser (transferee).

Furthermore, after case law under *TUPE 1981*, any employee dismissed before the transfer of an undertaking for a reason connected with the transfer (otherwise than for an economic, technical or organisational reason entailing a change in the workforce ('ETO') – of which insolvency and its effect is of itself not one) was treated as automatically unfairly dismissed. The effect was that the employee's unfair dismissal claim would transfer in its entirety to the transferee. As there had in fact been a dismissal, this rule was effectively about claim and liability allocation and the employment of those whose dismissals were automatically unfair because of the transfer did not transfer.

In this way, a transferee would assume not only almost all accrued and continuing liabilities for those employees whose employment transferred but also accrued liabilities owed to those whose employment did not transfer but who were treated as if they had been dismissed unfairly because of the transfer.

This exposure to accrued and contingent employee liabilities would typically cause there to be applied a discount to the price paid for the concern. The uncertainty of the extent of the liabilities being assumed and the consequent discount to be applied would, it was said, often cause what might otherwise have been a viable transaction to be abandoned.

1. *Nicholl v Cutts (1985) 1 BCC 99, 427.*
2. Although to be accurate, the employee did not actively work during the period of the receivership, being ill in hospital – not, however, a circumstance likely to win favour for the receivers' position.
3. Cf *Re Specialised Mouldings Ltd* (unreported, 13th February 1987, Harman J (HC Ch)).
4. [1994] 2 All ER 513, CA affirmed by House of Lords [1995] 2 AC 394.
5. [1994] 4 All ER 300, Lightman J affirmed by House of Lords [1995] 2 AC 394.
6. And in the case of an administration even to assets the subject of what, as created, was a floating charge: see *IA* (pre-*EA*) *s 19(6)* – the equivalent provisions are now to be found in *IA Sch B1 para 99.*
7. See *IA Sch 6.*
8. *Insolvency Act 1994*, amending *IA s 19* (now *IA Sch B1 para 99*) and *s 44.*
9. Protective awards have odd incidents: where a union gets a protective award, which can then be enforced by those employees in respect of whom the union is recognised (whether or not those employees are members of the union), those employees for whom the union is not recognised (even if they are members of the union) cannot rely upon an employment tribunal's findings of fact as to the absence of consultation, even if those findings are equally applicable to all employees: see *TGWU v Brauer Coley Ltd (in administration)* UKEAT 0313_06_2710.
10. *Re Huddersfield Fine Worsteds Ltd* [2005] EWCA Civ 1072, [2005] 4 All ER 886: nor are redundancy payments or unfair dismissal payments included within the concept – *Re Allders Department Stores Ltd* [2005] EWHC 172 (Ch), [2005] 2 All ER 122.
11. See *IA Sch 6* category 5 for the detail.
12. SI 1981/1794 (now repealed).
13. The original employing company or any appointee to an office in which adoption of the contracts of employment and, as has been seen, certain of the liabilities arising under the contracts has occurred and who would of course in a typical case generally have conduct of the sale.

How did we get where?

3.14   The broad effect of the *Transfer of Undertakings (Protection of Employment) Regulations 2006*[1] (*'TUPE 2006'*) effective as of 6 April 2006, is to limit, in the context of certain types of formal insolvency, those liabilities which, on the transfer as a going concern of an undertaking or part of one having and retaining an identifiable economic entity[2], will themselves transfer with the employees to whom they relate, to the transferee of that undertaking.

There is also a limitation placed on what transfers of the liabilities owed to those employees who are deemed unfairly dismissed in advance, but because of, the transfer, the rule derived from case law under *TUPE 1981* having now been incorporated in *TUPE 2006*.

TUPE 2006 provides that for companies which have entered administration or a CVA and (probably) in respect of which an administrative receiver has been appointed (but not one in compulsory or creditors' or members' voluntary liquidation) certain statutory entitlements of transferring employees will not be transferred to such a transferee but will be met by the State (in the manifestation of the National Insurance Fund).

However, any contractual entitlement of the transferring employees in excess of the statutory entitlement (and therefore, for example, the bulk of the claims of the more senior employees) will continue to pass to the transferee.

The effect of this is to relieve the transferee only partly of obligations which formerly it would have assumed in full.

The twin qualifications for the application of the new Regulations are:

- that the employer and putative transferor should be the subject of 'insolvency proceedings' that do not have as their aim the 'liquidation' of the employer's assets; and

- that the proceedings should be under the control of an insolvency practitioner.

Even assuming that the 'liquidation' of assets can be limited to the formal process of that name and does not extend to any form of 'proceedings' (an undefined term) which may contemplate the liquidation of assets in the sense of reducing them to a cash fund with a view to distribution – because this would exclude some administrations and almost all CVAs, with arbitrary consequences – there are doubts whether the appointment out of court of an administrative receiver can be said to be 'proceedings', and thus whether the new regime will apply to that class of insolvency, at all.

The Insolvency Service guidance note 'Redundancy and Insolvency Payments'[3] simply states that administrative receiverships are subject to the same regime as administrations, without addressing the relevance and meaning of 'proceedings'.

It appears, therefore, that 'liquidation' is being given a formal and narrow meaning but 'proceedings' an expansive one.

Another person whose position must be addressed is the receiver who might have employees under his control but without satisfying the requirements for being an administrative receiver. For example, an appointee to one of a series of undertakings owned by the same company but which banks with different providers of credit in respect of each undertaking[4] may have under his control a discrete business with its own employees but without being appointed under any security containing a floating charge that would satisfy the definition of a QFC. Such a person need not be an insolvency practitioner at all and if he is not, then for that reason alone, the employees of the relevant undertaking will be outside the new Regulations whether or not one regards his appointment – which will not typically involve anything amounting to 'proceedings' conventionally understood – as one connected with insolvency. The statement in the Insolvency Service guidance that the appointment of such a receiver is not 'insolvency proceedings' (emphasis added) and that therefore the new Regulations as to insolvency do not apply, is, applied to many such receiverships, plainly incorrect.

But the Insolvency Service and the government seem always to have had difficulty with understanding what a non-administrative (or LPA) receivership can be. After the *Paramount* decision[5], the legislative limitation upon the personal liability assumed by administrative receivers and administrators was not extended to non-administrative receivers[6] for no good reason ever advanced or explained.

The position for such receivers thus appears to be both that they assume personal liability after adoption without limit but that on the transfer of a business as a going concern, they pass that liability on without limit (bar most but not all pensions rights). It seems hard to see what (if any) identifiable policy objective is being pursued here. The present position is inconsistent with limiting the liabilities respectively adopted and transferred.

1. SI 2006/246.
2. Or upon certain occasions of service provision change (whether outsourcing, retendering or insourcing).
3. http://www.dti.gov.uk/files/file30031.pdf
4. This scenario is not unduly rare – an operator of a chain of hotels comes to mind. The writer was involved in the receivership of the Scotch Corner Hotel in the early years of the last decade, which – whilst clearly an insolvency appointment – was not an *administrative* receivership for precisely this reason.
5. See **3.13**.
6. Compare *IA s 37* (non-administrative receivers) with *s 44* (administrative receivers) and *Sch B1 para 99* (administrators).

A State subsidy on/off transfer? Of what?

3.15   Where the relief for transferees applies, the extent of the relief includes:

- statutory redundancy pay (where redundancy is the cause of the dismissal);

- the basic award (but not the compensatory award) for unfair dismissal for other cause;

- notice pay to the statutory maximum, namely one week per year of service up to 12 weeks at a maximum weekly gross amount of £290;

- arrears of pay to the statutory maxima of 8 weeks and a weekly gross amount of £290;

- holiday pay to the statutory maxima of 6 weeks and a weekly gross amount of £290;

- guarantee payments; and

- protective awards.

Judging from the history of the DTI guidance, it was initially thought that this was so even though the employees transfer with continuity of employment rights.

Considerable support can be gained for this view by the fact that the Regulations refer[1] to the new scheme applying 'irrespective of the fact that the qualifying requirement that the employee's employment has been terminated is not met and … the date of the transfer shall be treated as the date of the termination….'; excluding, however, redundancy.

But for that rule, where there has been a transfer with continuity, there can in theory be no claim to redundancy, unfair dismissal or notice pay, in each case because there has been no dismissal and so it seems that the first three items on the above list would not in that case fall to be paid by anyone.

This indeed seems to be the present official view[2], notwithstanding that the wording of the Regulations would seem precisely to exclude that view, except in the case of redundancy.

It might plausibly be argued in a context in which the reforms were introduced to assist business rescue that there is no need that the State should assume any such liability after *TUPE 2006* that no-one would before *TUPE 2006* have been liable to pay.

What *TUPE 2006* seems designed – viewed narrowly – to do, in the context of the identified types of insolvency regime, is to prevent the transfer of those claims of employees which had accrued and were due but unpaid at the date that, but for the effect of *TUPE*, they would have been dismissed. This would cover the balance of the items on the list.

This is a partial subsidy to the transferee by relieving it of a more or less immediate cash requirement. The transferee still takes the accrued rights and liabilities not yet due (based on length of continuity of employment) of the employees where they are transferred by virtue of *TUPE 2006*.

The uncertainty of, and the possibility for a much broader, interpretation of the Regulations may lie in whether it is thought that by paying employees sums as if they were dismissed when they have not been dismissed, this would operate to make the contingent future costs associated with their dismissal sufficiently less – by effectively buying out their continuity – to cause transferees to be willing to take employees, and thus acquire businesses, that they would otherwise not acquire.

But there is nothing in *TUPE 2006* which says this and the logic of such analysis seems to apply to redundancy costs of notional dismissals with as much force as it does to the basic award of an unfair dismissal award – where the sum due will be much the same as a redundancy award – but the Regulations appear to exclude redundancy from this possible analysis.

Confusingly, as of the date of writing, the DTI online guidance still makes no distinction between the two[3].

The claims of an employee deemed unfairly dismissed (whose employment would not, and will not, transfer but whose claims formerly would transfer) now do not transfer to the purchaser in their entirety but the burden of his compensation package is shared – the State (the National Insurance Fund as the paying agency in the transferor's insolvency) will bear the basic unfair dismissal award (of up to £8,700) but the transferee will still be liable to bear the compensatory unfair dismissal award (of up to £58,400). As under *TUPE 1981*, as the employee has been dismissed, the rule is about claim and liability allocation, but a different allocation is now made.

Again, the relief of the transferee and thus the likely success of the stated aim of the measure, is only partial. Indeed, in a given case, it may be better for the transferee to take all the employees and then try make a proper redundancy selection and thereby seek to avoid an unfair dismissal claim (where it will have to pay a basic award equating to redundancy cost plus a compensatory award) than to be foist with the undiluted financial consequence of a dismissed and resentful cadre of senior staff.

In the types of insolvency regime to which the new rules do not apply, all of the liabilities are left with the insolvent employer (and thus the State) even where there may have been a transfer, for example, in a creditors' voluntary liquidation[4], of a business entity to which *TUPE 2006* might otherwise be thought to apply. Query, again, whether the State will (or ought) in practice accept a liability to pay claims where there has been, in practice, a transfer with continuity of employment.

1. *TUPE 2006 reg 8(3)*.
2. Letter from the Redundancy Payments Office of the Insolvency Service dated April 2006.
3. http://www.dti.gov.uk/files/file20761.pdf p30 as at November 2006.
4. cf http://www.dti.gov.uk/files/file30031.pdf passim.

Pensions and TUPE

3.16   Pension rights are not, as is commonly supposed, wholly excluded from the effect of *TUPE*. The Regulations are expressed not to apply only to so much of a contract of employment or collective agreement as relates to rights, powers, duties or liabilities arising under or in connection with an occupational pension scheme.

This means that certain other pensions related rights etc, such as a contractual obligation assumed by an employer to make a contribution into the employee's private pension provision, will transfer under *TUPE*, because not a right under an occupational scheme.

Furthermore, case law[1] has established that even within occupational schemes, only those benefits to which an employee is entitled because he has attained the age of retirement (old age, invalidity and survivor's benefits) are excluded from transferring under *TUPE*. Other rights, such as an enhanced redundancy entitlement, a right to early retirement on medical grounds and even enhanced pension rights triggered by something other than attaining retirement age itself (such as redundancy), transfer – even where contained in the occupational scheme documents.

1. *Beckmann v Dynamco Whicheloe McFarlane Ltd* [2002] IRLR 578 ECJ, *Martin v South Bank University* [2004] IRLR 74 ECJ.

Contractual variations under TUPE

3.17   One area where *TUPE 2006* may prove effective is where, again in the context of the designated types of insolvency, it allows either transferor (through the appointed insolvency practitioner) or transferee, before or after the transfer but in either case only for a reason designed to safeguard employment opportunities by ensuring the survival of the undertaking[1], to negotiate with the employees (through a recognised trade union or representatives appointed under a provided procedure) written variations in the terms of employment. Such a variation is expressed to be permitted only if the sole or principal reason for it is the transfer or reasons connected with it.

Such a variation may facilitate, without risk of lawful industrial action, the necessary restructuring in terms and conditions of employment that may otherwise prove a significant drag on the enterprise acquired. It remains to be seen whether the procedures, which are cumbersome, to bring this end about can be deployed in practice sufficiently quickly.

All in all, however, the jury is out on *TUPE 2006* as it applies to insolvency, both as to what it means and how it is to be applied. Clarification may come with case law. This is a thoroughly unsatisfactory state of affairs where employee related costs are such a significant feature in the context of, and often a perceived impediment to, rescue.

Parties (not least those whose rights are to be protected) should not be left guessing by reference to official guidance that does not even follow the language of that to which it purports to be a guide.

1. Not being an economic, technical or organisational reason entailing a change in the workforce – for which reasons variations are already permitted: see *TUPE 2006 reg 4(5)(a)*.

Pensions on insolvency – a very expensive problem, only expensively solved

3.18   As is generally recognised, a company in financial difficulty often enjoys the sort of relationship with its defined benefit (or 'final salary'[1]) pension scheme that recalls the fate of those condemned as felons by the fifteenth century Black Book of the Admiralty, namely that they be tied to a corpse and thrown in the sea.

Most defined benefit pension schemes – whether or not the company is otherwise insolvent or even in financial difficulty – will be in deficit, in an amount which, irrespective of the extent (if any) to which the previous assumptions and projections made as to funding requirements have been invalidated, will now be one that will be required to be (re)valued and accounted for according to Financial Reporting Standard 17[2].

The deficit will be shown as a debt in the company's balance sheet in an amount which may have little bearing on the actual cash requirements of the liabilities in, or in the near future coming into, payment.

The reasons for the change in the basis of the actuarial assumptions as to, and valuation of, pension liabilities and the relative consequent funding requirements, from a 'minimum funding requirement' to a 'scheme funding requirement' (the details of the distinction between the two being beyond the scope of this chapter) are largely political, although whether more damage was caused to the pensions industry and members' rights by matters such as the Maxwell scandal than by later tax changes is a topic worthy of debate elsewhere.

The practical effect of the changes is that the pension scheme's trustees, faced with an increase of the debt owed to that constituency whom they represent, are under an obligation to negotiate with the company for the reduction of the scheme shortfall and sooner rather than later.

This is an exercise in which they are encouraged by the Pensions Regulator, who applies that levy that is made of those employers operating defined benefit schemes and by the Board of the Pensions Protection Fund or 'PPF' which, applying the levy raised and ad hoc central governmental subventions, is the safeguard for members whose employers become insolvent.

The PPF is funded to provide benefits greater than at the level of the scheme funding requirement but at somewhat less than[3] the full 'buy-out' basis, the latter being the amount required to purchase annuities covering the full amount of the pension and other benefits provided by the scheme.

Upon certain qualifying types of insolvency (broadly, insolvent liquidation, administration, administrative receivership and entry into of a CVA), the PPF assumes the duties and rights of the scheme trustees and ranks as a creditor in the insolvency for the cost of providing benefits on the full buy-out basis, rather than on the lesser basis on which it is designed to provide benefits to members.

The control of the pensions sector that these changed expectations require comes not only in the trustees' more onerous obligations to negotiate short-fall reductions but also, and realistically rather more meaningfully, by the Pensions Regulator having the right (unexercised in fact at the time of writing) to issue to employers and their associates either:

- 'contribution notices' (which may be issued to companies and individuals), to forestall acts or omissions the apprehended effect of which is to prevent the full buy-out debt becoming due, being recovered or which are intended to compromise or reduce the debt – any such notice would require a payment into the scheme; or

- 'financial support directions' (which may be issued to companies), in respect of companies considered to be underfunded, that is (as a rule of thumb) to less than one half of the buy-out debt – requiring support from elsewhere within that company's group (eg a parent guarantee of the pension liability).

Further, the Pensions Regulator has the right to clear, often only upon condition, certain types of corporate transactions, including a change in control, an event which if it also means that a company is to leave a group of companies providing defined pension benefits to its employees, will require the company to pay up so much of the group's buy-out debt as is attributable to its own participating employees.

Accordingly, where a company in financial difficulty is the subject of interest in its shares, rather than its business, a critical issue arises as to the pension debt or the relevant part of the debt in a group situation.

Is this a liability that the purchaser can afford to assume, discounting the price accordingly, or (as surely will often prove the case) does the debt kill the deal?

If the deal is otherwise dead, what can be done? In practice, if otherwise faced with an inevitable insolvency and the entry of the scheme into PPF in any event, the Pensions Regulator may be prevailed upon to accept the scheme into the PPF with a view to the company surviving freed of the pension scheme, but only if its entry is funded at a level substantially greater than what the PPF would achieve if ranking as a creditor for the full buy-out debt in the premised insolvency.

This will have to involve a compelling case, a significant contribution of cash and/or assets and in most cases ongoing commitment, whether in the form of shares in the company so saved and/or restructured, a contribution to make further payments according to performance and security for it, or otherwise.

It will also require a formal insolvency event.

In 2005, the PPF assumed responsibility for the pension schemes of the Heath Lambert Group of companies (total deficit £210m) from administration, which allowed the companies' assets to be transferred to a new corporate vehicle in which the PPF took shares.

In 2006, Pittards plc successfully exited a CVA in which it paid all debts bar that attributable to its pension scheme (deficit £33m, liabilities £100m) which was left with the PPF, which was paid £1.6m cash, took a 18.5% equity stake in the company, a charge for a further £3m payable over five years and right to certain further sums in the eventuality of a sale of a specified asset above a specified profit.

In each case, the justification was that the alternative was worse – the companies in question would otherwise have failed fully and the PPF would have had to assume the same (or very similar) liabilities with a lesser, if in practice any, contribution to the same.

As is evident, recourse to the PPF is one of last resort: the formal insolvency may destroy much of the value that shedding the pensions liability may be intended to preserve (although where – as with Pittards – all other creditors are paid in full, the adverse effect on goodwill may be limited) and the route will not be open where the company cannot afford the present or future price for its burden to be lifted.

It seems that the sort of candidate best placed to try to use the PPF to loosen the ties that bind is one with a fundamentally sound business, weighed down by a pensions liability to which it can nevertheless make a significant contribution and which contribution would be lost, and the whole liability assumed by the PPF, were the liability left to drag the company under.

The regime is too new yet to know whether it is likely to be a frequent event that the PPF will assume a pensions liability in a context of the survival of the company freed of the pensions obligation, rather than on the company's failure and cessation of business.

1. The difficulties do not exist with defined contribution or 'money purchase' schemes.
2. Based on International Accounting Standard 19.
3. At the rate of 100% for pensions in payment but at 90% of deferred members' rights, subject to a 'cap' of £26,050 as at 65.

The 'hive down' – a moribund concept

3.19   This phenomenon existed for two reasons, the respective commercial justifications for each of which were rendered vestigial and for one of which has now been abolished altogether.

The phrase describes the process by which the assets and undertaking of a company were sold to a newly incorporated wholly-owned subsidiary, usually for a sum left outstanding on inter company account.

In the context of employees, the idea was that the shares in the new subsidiary could then be sold for a sum discounted by the amount of the unpaid transfer price or for that price (as the deal might be) with the employee related liabilities left in the parent, and thus not passing under *TUPE*.

Although *TUPE 1981* expressly provided for this stratagem (by postponing the date at which the undertaking was deemed transferred to the subsidiary to the date immediately before the subsequent sale of the subsidiary, shortly before which later date the employees would have been dismissed), case law rendered it ineffective (by holding that dismissals effected before a transfer of an undertaking or part – including postponed hive-down transfers – were almost always automatically unfair in terms which caused the relative liability to pass to the transferee) and *TUPE 2006* has now abolished the hive-down concept in context, by no longer acknowledging it.

In the context of tax, the subsidiary has assets but not liabilities (other than the outstanding sum for the assets transferred) but the unrelieved tax losses of the parent incurred in the hived-down trade can be carried forward against future profits earned by the hive-down subsidiary subsequently sold if arising from the same trade post sale.

However, financial legislation in the mid 1980s affected the extent to which the tax losses might be carried forward, materially by providing that the hive-down company's right to use the unused losses is reduced to the extent, in effect, that the liabilities of the parent were not assumed by it. This simplification of what is now to be found in *s 343* of the *Taxes Act 1988* is nevertheless sufficient to demonstrate why hive-downs are now rarely encountered.

Work outs

3.20   One of the continuing advantages of work outs to the directors of a company is that, generally speaking, the directors do not lose control. Further, unlike in an administrative receivership, administration or liquidation, there is no insolvency practitioner obliged to report upon the conduct of the directors and which might give rise to a threat of disqualification.

From the point of view of the participating creditors, the interest is more commercial.

Those creditors will value any security and reach a view, upon an individual basis, of its exposure. A work out provides, in particular, bank creditors with the opportunity of improving their security, subject to the risks of adjustment of prior transactions.

In the nature of work outs, there are no formal rules. In the more substantial work outs, however, the so-called 'London Approach' applies. The label simply signifies the market in which the practice first developed.

The general structure

3.21   The basis of all work outs is necessarily contractual. The advantages of this include flexibility and confidentiality but the disadvantages include the absence of any moratorium against the claims of those not participating in the arrangement and that if it fails and the company goes into liquidation, the full rigour of insolvency law, as to wrongful and fraudulent trading, preferences and transactions at an undervalue etc. applies.

The essence of work outs is that the company approaches its bankers and other providers of credit and, if appropriate, its major unsecured creditors, with the view to negotiating a 'standstill' on payments to ensure that it can still continue trading until current financial difficulty can be diagnosed and future viability assessed.

Where there is a need for further funds, these will generally speaking be provided by existing funders upon a syndicated basis in whatever proportion, whether or not related to existing exposure, can be negotiated. Those fresh funds may or may not, but usually will, enjoy priority over existing debt but this, subject to any existing priority arrangements that there may exist between lenders, can only be achieved by agreement.

The investigation

3.22   Another feature of work outs (realistically in all serious cases) is an investigation by accountants. The accountants will generally speaking be appointed by the creditors, or the lead creditor in a syndicate.

The terms of reference will generally be ones of analysis of the business, diagnosis of the current financial problems and prognosis according to a number of possible solutions. These matters will include a review of existing security and of existing management.

An agreement between the various lenders participating with the company in a work out as to a number of key issues is critical.

These will include:

- the funding of any new money;
- the security for that new money;
- any adjustment or regulation of existing debt and security priorities;
- the possibility of agreeing the proportions in which losses may be shared measured by reference to each lender's exposure upon a notional immediate liquidation;
- rescheduling of debt;
- subordination of debt; and
- debt/equity swaps.

In cases involving groups of companies, this review will need to assess the position of the group as a whole and each of the constituent members of the group, the position of each lender to the group and each constituent member and the possibility of a need to alter the structure within the group as well as the structure of the group's debt.

Intensive care

3.23   Work outs can, of course, take place between a company and a single creditor, usually its bank. Where a bank develops doubts about the viability of one of its customer's business, or the competence of management, it will frequently refer the account to what is often called 'intensive care'.

However, the principal feature of references to intensive care is the clear likelihood that the bank wishes to terminate the banking relationship with the customer and that it regards intensive care – a form of one-to-one work out – as an alternative or (as often) a preliminary to administrative receivership (where available) or a QFC holder appointed administration (where not).

As such, and subject to the risks of a finding of shadow directorship if the bank assumes too great a degree of control, this form of work out is really no more than a work out for one creditor. Indeed, such work outs often operate to the prejudice of other creditors. A bank deciding upon a series of reductions in overdraft facility will impose terms that, to be abided by, will frequently in practice oblige the directors of companies to 'rob Peter to pay Paul' and use moneys properly accountable in respect of PAYE, NIC and VAT to keep within reduced or reducing facilities.

This may be a perfectly acceptable result for the bank, but not for other creditors and not necessarily for the directors, who may by such a course of conduct be more exposed to the risk of an action in wrongful trading or to disqualification. The temptation for banks to impose this form of work out is great, as the risk to the bank is relatively small, as is the cost of monitoring the facilities when compared to an administrative receivership or administration.

Further, the risk of a bank being found to be a shadow director of a company is in most cases remote. Giving the directors no choice as to the terms upon which credit is to be provided is not the same thing as giving them directions in accordance with which they are accustomed to act, which is the definition of the concept.

Public companies

3.24   For public companies facing financial difficulties, the directors must be aware of the obligations imposed upon them by the rules of the Stock Exchange. Those rules are designed to ensure the making known of information which in its nature is likely to affect the price of listed securities. A company must notify new developments in its sphere of activity which are not public knowledge and which may by virtue of the effect of those developments on its assets and liabilities or financial position or on the general course of its business lead to substantial movement in the price of its listed securities. Although dispensations may be granted by the Stock Exchange, the Exchange's general approach is that once the negotiation of significant financial arrangements has been undertaken, an announcement should be made. An alternative, albeit a drastic one, is to seek a suspension of shares during such negotiations.

Further, there are potential criminal liabilities for directors who make misleading, false or deceptive statements, promises or forecasts, or who dishonestly conceal material facts for the purpose of inducing, or if the director is reckless as to whether they may induce, a person to make an investment decision.

Common features of work outs

3.25   Since larger work outs will generally be encountered in cases where there is some reason to avoid the disadvantages of the formal insolvency procedures, many work-out plans will necessarily involve contingency plans to avoid one of the other insolvency states being brought about. Work out participants may thus have to agree to pay off pressing non-participating creditors upon terms as to the assumption of additional liabilities reached between themselves.

In other cases, it may also be possible for the participants to reach agreement between themselves as to restructuring, further funding, further security, subordination, etc. as a necessary precondition to the company then seeking to put proposals to all its creditors, whether through an administration or a CVA.

Risks

3.26   Threats inherent in a work out to directors include:

- (for public companies) breach of the rules of the Stock Exchange;
- wrongful trading and fraudulent trading.

Directors must be astute to the risk that a work out may be being structured and run for the benefit of those participating in it but to the ultimate prejudice of other (unsecured) creditors from whom the companies continue to obtain credit in respect of supplies of goods and services. Whereas it is a key feature of a work out that the participant creditors expect to see their positions improve, it is not such an obvious hope of the participants that the positions of unsecured creditors might improve. Any such improvement may be incidental or designed to be temporary and such only to prevent creditors taking enforcement action or refusing further credit or supplies. This is relevant to the directors' position at common law generally, since directors owe fiduciary duties to their company, namely to act in good faith in the best interests of the company and to exercise their powers for proper purposes. Where a company is insolvent, however, the directors' obligations are in practice owed to the creditors, as the very notion of wrongful trading itself demonstrates. In considering whether, for example, to grant further security, particularly when no new money is involved, to participants in a work-out plan, the directors have to be particularly concerned that their actions are in accordance with the obligations owed to the correct constituency.

The risks to the lender participants in a work out are less obvious. Although there is a risk of shadow directorship, such a risk is more theoretical than real. Any properly advised, or commercially aware, lender will ensure that its participation in a work out is strictly upon the basis that the offered terms are precisely that, offered, even upon the basis that the only alternative is known to be insolvent liquidation. The terms will not take the form of instruction.

Further, although there is a risk that the participant benefiting from a work out might face a threat from a liquidator to return the value of that improvement based upon a knowing participation in a breach of trust (eg a breach of the directors' fiduciary duty owed in substance to the creditors of insolvent companies), liability under this form of restitutionary head appears to require actual knowledge of a breach of trust or a deliberate closing of the eyes to conduct so doubtful that the participant beneficiary is regarded as having actual knowledge.

Documents

3.27   Large work outs will involve at least two agreements, one between the company and its participating creditors and one between the various participants themselves.

The principal matters which can be expected to be found in each agreement are as follows.

The company/participants agreement

3.28   The principal feature of the agreement between the company and the participants would include:

- the terms of any moratorium on debt (the 'standstill');
- the nature and extent of the existing or new facilities to be made available during that standstill;
- the extent to which the participants waive any rights they may have arising out of existing defaults under facilities and financial covenants, and the circumstances which would once more give rise to the rights to enforce security. Typically all facilities are – to the extent not already so repayable – made repayable on demand;
- the provision of financial information on a periodic basis (budgets, cash flows, management accounts, aged debt analyses, the result of legal due diligence in connection with litigation etc);
- restrictions upon the company's ability to trade other than in the normal course of business;
- restrictions on the payment of dividends and inter-company transactions etc;
- the purposes for which new money is to be available, from whom, in what proportion, for what purpose, against what existing or new security, including cross guarantees.

The participants' agreement

3.29   The principal features of the agreement between participants in the work out would include:

- who is to be charged by the participants with the power to make decisions binding upon them and upon what terms, to determine what sums any participant is liable to contribute under a syndicated arrangement and to report to the participants;

- the basis upon which further moneys and new security (if any) is to be provided and employed;

- any basis for the sharing of recoveries over and above what the participants would recover upon immediate liquidation, and for the adjustment of actual or prospective losses, upon a pro-rated or other basis;

- the need for consequential new or revised priority agreements;

- providing for the costs of the work out;

- the basis upon which realisations across any group structure are to be credited amongst the various participants;

- the basis upon which decisions are to be taken by the participants;

- in what degrees participants are to be regarded as exposed to loss (eg actual exposure at standstill or the amount to which the lender participant could have been exposed had all granted facilities been fully drawn);

- the circumstances in which the new or revised facilities fall to be repaid/can be demanded with consequential provisions regulating the rights of participants to enforce security etc.

The aim of a work out may be trading out of difficulty with or without disposals, with a view to re-financing or with a view to subsequent appointments of administrators or administrative receivers.

Work outs thus provide flexibility, both as to purpose and as to form. Save in those cases of one-to-one work outs which generally involve the reference by a clearing bank of a corporate customer to intensive care, work outs are generally found – although the absence of publicity is one of their principal advantages – in circumstances where there are a number of institutional funders none of which is in a position to appoint an administrative receiver or administrator or in circumstances where such an appointment is judged by that creditor not to be to its advantage or where there may be existing priority arrangements that restrict the right to appoint.

It is said, but in the nature of the private structure of work outs it is difficult to know whether what is said is correct, that the 'vulture funds' (who would no doubt prefer to be thought of as players in the 'secondary' or 'distressed' debt markets) have made workouts significantly more difficult to arrange and work through, by taking up debt positions (acquired at heavy discount) in which they hold out for preferential treatment.

In an extreme case, it is said, the willingness of the fund to play its debt hand may threaten the whole arrangement.

Assuming that to be true, what it does is to emphasise once more the disadvantage of there being no means to combine a general moratorium on creditor action with the need for priority funding.

Lessons from America

3.30   In other jurisdictions, the need for sanctioned priority funding in insolvency, 'super priority', has been articulated and addressed.

In Canada, the Companies Creditors Arrangement Act ('CCAA'), originally passed in the 1930s, has been used by an active judiciary to sanction the creation of a range of fact-specific means by which it has proved possible to confer priority on several different classes of such funding, by the simple expedient of postponing the rights of existing secured creditors. This is a process made the more remarkable by the fact that the Act does not in terms provide for this.

The logic of a piece of legislation primarily addressed at the need for a moratorium on the rights of creditors of distressed companies pending proposals, has been extended to provide for the other need that prevails in such a situation.

What has been recognised is that not only is there a need for time, there is a need for money. The Canadian courts have taken the opportunity when asked to order a stay, often to order priority for funds advanced to the distressed company during the period of the stay, often referred to as 'debtor in possession' or 'DIP' finance.

The first case in which a court in Canada created a charge against the assets of a company in CCAA proceedings was *Re Westar Mining Ltd* in the early 1990s[1] where a charge was created against unencumbered assets.

1. (1992) 14 CBR (3d) 88 (BC SC).

Secured super priority – 'keeping the lights on'

3.31   It was but a short step to creating a charge that ranked ahead of existing security. In early days, the judicial power to do this was exercised with enthusiasm but in a relatively restricted compass.

In *Re Royal Oak Mines Inc*[1] and in the context of DIP financing restricted to what he called 'what is reasonably necessary to meet the debtor's urgent needs over the sorting-out period', Blair J observed that:

> 'such measures involve what may be a significant reordering of priorities from those in place before the application is made, not in the sense of altering the existing priorities as between the various secured creditors but in the sense of placing encumbrances ahead of those presently in existence. Such changes should not be imported lightly, if at all, into

the creditors' mix; and affected parties are entitled to a reasonable opportunity to think about their potential impact, and to consider such things as well as whether or not the CCAA approach to the insolvency is the appropriate one in the circumstances – as opposed, for instance, to a receivership or [liquidation] – and whether or not, and to what extent, they are prepared to have their positions affected by DIP or super priority financing. As [Counsel] noted, in the context of this case, the object should be to "keep the lights ... on" during the sorting out period, a power to be exercised "in a judicious and cautious matter"'.

But because the power is exercised in a context where the court acts in a supervisory role in the ongoing investigation – the length of which may be measured in months, if not years, and certainly not only the 30 days of the initial CCAA stay – of whether a compromise between company and creditors which will allow the former to continue trading is possible[2], the court has become increasingly willing not only to extend and refine such orders but also to make such new types of order as the circumstances require, a process in which the judicial attitude to the position of secured creditors has become more robust.

Seven years later the same judge could express the opinion[3], in respect of the judicial subordination of existing secured rights, that:

'this is not a situation where someone is being compelled to advance further credit. What is happening is that the creditor's security is being weakened to the extent of its reduction in value. It is not the first time in restructuring proceedings where secured creditors – in the exercise of balancing the prejudices which is inherent in these situations – have been asked to make such a sacrifice.'

The reference to the secured creditors being asked should not of course be understood to mean that they have a veto over the process. Although they have a right to be heard upon an application, so long as 'the benefit of DIP financing clearly outweighs the potential prejudice to the lenders whose security is being subordinated'[4], a process in which the exercise of balancing prejudice is carried out having regard to all the several different classes of all creditors and their different individual and class interests as well as the interests of others affected, the order will usually be made. 'Each subsequent DIP financing authorization and the priority to be attributed to it will have to be determined on the merits and circumstances then existing'[5]: which shows not only the possibility for successive applications for priority for DIP funding but also that the intended process is ongoing and dynamic, involving periodic reconsideration of the position of all the creditors and those others interested in the eventual outcome (eg shareholders and employees), not merely a simplistic comparison between the alternative outcomes of immediate realisation and further prima facie dilution of cover for the secured creditor.

1. [1991] OJ No 709 (QL) (Ont Gen Div).
2. For which court approval will ultimately be required in the context of the votes of the several different classes of creditors on the proposals and the court's view of the fairness of the proposals between the classes.
3. In *Re Skydome Corporation* (1998) 16 CBR (4th) 118 (Ont Gen Div).

4. Tysoe J in *Re United Used Auto & Truck Parts Ltd* (1999) Can LII 5374 (BC SC).
5. Holden JA in *Re Dylex Limited* (1995) 31 CBR (3d) 106 (Ont Ct (Gen Div)).

Classes of DIP funding

3.32   Charges ranking in priority to existing security have been granted not only for DIP financing for trading purposes (funds made available to allow the company to purchase goods and services, pay employees etc during the stay), but also for the remuneration and expenses of the court appointed monitor (who acts as the interface between company and creditors and who reports to the court), legal expenses for advice given to the company and the directors (who generally remain in office) and indeed by way of indemnification of the directors in respect of debt incurred during the stay and for which the directors may have a personal liability should no compromise or arrangement be possible.

An example of such a charge in favour of directors is *Re MEI Computer Technology Group Inc*[1] in which Gascon J stated that:

'it is now settled in Canadian jurisprudence that the CCAA is remedial legislation which is to be given a large interpretation to facilitate its objectives. The courts recognize that CCAA's effectiveness in achieving its objectives is indeed dependent on a broad and flexible exercise of the jurisdiction so as to facilitate a restructuring and continue the debtor as a going concern in the interim', and that for the purpose of 'giving to the CCAA such large and liberal interpretation and in facilitating the achievement of its objectives, courts … have relied on their inherent jurisdiction … as the source of judicial power to "fill in the gaps" or "put flesh on the bones" of the Act.'

1. 2005 CanLII 15656 (QC CS).

Some principles

3.33   That judge further stated that the principles guiding the Canadian courts in the exercise of their discretion as to the exercise of the power to confer super priority on DIP finance included the following:

- allowing DIP financing and creating a priority charge is an extraordinary measure to be used sparingly and only in clear cases – indeed the particular application for priority for further DIP finance in the case was refused;

- a court should be satisfied with proper evidence that the benefits to all creditors, shareholders and employees clearly outweigh the potential prejudice to some creditors, namely those whose existing priority of security will be weakened if super priority is ordered;

- it is not sufficient for the company to establish that the charge would be merely beneficial – it must establish that it is critical for the company to continue operating and to successfully restructure it affairs;

- the company should normally establish an urgent need for the creation of the charge in the context of a reasonable prospect of a successful restructuring;

- the charge should only be available for limited amounts, for a limited period and (by implication) for a limited period: reference was made once more to 'keeping the lights on';

- the exercise of the power should be just and equitable.

Although Gascon J's principles are no doubt a correct expression of Canadian legal orthodoxy, in practice the lights can be kept on in this way for a very long time. New Skeema Forest Productions Inc (as it became), one of the principal forestry businesses in British Columbia, went through a continuum of proceedings under CCAA, from 1997 to 2005 and traded with successive tranches of DIP funding for much of that time[1].

That ultimately no workable compromise or arrangement could be advanced and that New Skeema went into liquidation, demonstrates the self-evident truth that the making of an order for DIP finance will not always be blessed with the success of the company's survival. Equally, the availability of such finance is unlikely ever to make it less likely that a viable company can be saved.

1. See *Re New Skeema Forest Products Inc* 2005 BCCA 192 (Can LII).

And some differences

3.34   Because Canada has a federal court structure, different State courts have taken different approaches to the application of CCAA.

In Ontario, the moratorium on creditor action and the availability of DIP funding has been used to develop the 'liquidating CCAA', in which a business is kept together until its assets, rather than the company which owns the business, can be sold. The funds realised by asset sale are then paid to creditors in accordance with their rights. In this sort of CCAA, the avowed purpose is to make or maintain a market in the assets, not to save the company.

Indeed, there may even be no attempt to make a market. In *Re 1078385 Ontario Limited*, 'Bob-Lo Island'[1] proposals under CCAA for a plan of arrangement were promulgated only by the debtor company's secured creditors and excluded unsecured creditors even from any right to vote on the proposals advanced, proposals which amounted to little more than a foreclosure by those same secured creditors in a situation where, on the evidence, the debtor company's assets were worth less than the sums secured on them. Simmons JA in the Ontario Court of Appeal held that the exclusion in these circumstances of the voice and interests of the unsecured creditors did not of itself make the plan of arrangement unfair or unreasonable, notwithstanding that (to quote the judge's summary of the objections made to it) it was a 'secured-creditor-led plan that excludes the unsecured creditors … without requiring the secured creditors to go through the formal process of enforcing their security and without exposing the secured assets to the market … [A] shortcut for liquidating secured assets.' There was no equity in the assets and so the claims, and the views, of the unsecured creditors were irrelevant.

In Alberta, by contrast, it seems that to exclude the unsecured creditors is to invalidate the use of CCAA altogether and will result in the discharge of the moratorium on creditor action, leaving the secured creditors of a company with no equity in its charged assets to their remedy of enforcement[2].

Notwithstanding these differences in approach, the real issue is whether the availability of DIP finance under CCAA means that, in overall terms, a better result is achieved for those who might be described as all the stakeholders in the company and its debt than if it were not available and than if the test of viability was applied (in practice by the secured creditors and at a time of their choosing) only to the assets and business of the company rather than to the company itself.

1. [2004] OJ No 6050 (QL) (CA).
2. *Re Fracmaster Ltd* (1999) 11 CBR (4th) 204 (Alta, QB).

Some comparisons

3.35　　Canadian law seeks to identify those with interests in the outcome of corporate distress and to value those interests, in monetary terms where relevant, before posing a series of questions that seek to evaluate and balance the claims of those interested and determine which is the best viable outcome on the balance struck and in the light of the tools available, including DIP finance.

English law, for all of the supposed new emphasis on saving companies rather than their undertakings, simply does not address (and barely articulates) the difficulty that no realistic choice of action is available where there are no funds to allow the exercise of balance and determination to be undertaken.

This is not surprising – by tradition, English (property and insolvency) law has always favoured the secured debt interest, whose rights and priority, where not themselves colourable for any other reason, it has proved notably reluctant to erode.

A robust approach would conclude that this outcome, being the one that economic liberalism would determine, is the correct one and that all that social policy requires is the making of that protection for jobs and pensions that the law presently, in whatever inadequate and confused form, provides. But such an approach seems inconsistent with the words, and at least some of the spirit, of the principal recent reform.

For all the consultation and White Papers, for all the primary and secondary legislation of the last twenty years or so, there has simply not been a determined attempt to bring coherence to the composite question: do we want to save companies rather than businesses, why and at what cost (if any) to the vested rights of secured (and other) debt?

Some suggested answers

3.36　　Why, then, should it be thought that the proper aim should be to save the company rather than its business?

A conventional answer can be found in the words of The Law Reform Commission of Hong Kong[1]:

> 'it is beyond dispute that it is better for a viable business [sc in context, the company] to survive as a going concern, in whole or in part, than for it to be simply wound up and such assets as remain distributed. It benefits the company's shareholders, as if the company survives, their share holdings might become valuable, whereas if the company is insolvent and wound up they get nothing. It benefits the ordinary creditors of the company if they obtain more from a company reorganisation than from a dividend in a winding up, with the added benefit that they would keep a customer. It has become increasingly clear that secured creditors, usually banks, must look beyond the notion that being secured means that they are not affected by the winding up of a client company. Employment that would otherwise disappear would be preserved, at least to some extent. All of this has implications for government both in revenue and social terms.'

Furthermore, so this thinking goes, it should not be thought that the interests of secured creditors are wholly opposed to any alternative to an unrestricted freedom for them to enforce or indeed necessarily to DIP finance.

As the Commission continued[2]:

> 'why then should secured creditors have any interest in entering into a voluntary arrangement? On the face of it, they have security and the ability to realise it.....The reality, however, is that it is not unusual for there to be multiple secured creditors with varying securities and priorities over the assets of a company. Because of the nature of floating charges, in particular, which permit a company to deal with the assets covered by the floating charge in the ordinary course of business, and also because of what critics would say is the lack of caution in some lenders, the value of a company's assets can diminish, leaving some or all of the secured creditors under-secured. In such a situation, the secured creditors might conclude that a voluntary arrangement was an attractive proposition. It goes further than that however. Lenders, usually banks, are in a competitive business and realise that if a client company goes into liquidation they lose any prospect of new business with that company. Even if the gap left by a wound up company is filled by another entity there is no guarantee that the lender will get the business. If the lender can participate in a provisional supervision [the form of insolvency procedure the subject of the Report] leading to a voluntary arrangement..., the lender can retain a client which it understands much better and with which it can do business in the future.'

Similar policy considerations do not, however, lead to similar conclusions, even where a common law inheritance is more significant than geographical distance. The recommendation of the Hong Kong Commission was not to adopt a version of super priority of the sort developed in Canada, but[3] to make 'provision ... for a company to borrow during provisional supervision and that such borrowing should receive priority over all existing debts, with the exception of fixed charges' (emphasis added): a priority, furthermore, that it was envisaged should:

> 'where possible ... come from the existing lenders to the company. Existing lenders should be given a first refusal on any super priority lending the company may require. If existing lenders declined to provide the lending, the provisional supervisor should then be able to seek super priority lending from other sources. Super priority lending would, in any event, probably come from the company's bankers, who would have substantial security in respect of their existing lending, and who would [as a consequence of another of the Commission's recommendations] therefore have had the right of election to stay outside provisional supervision. Super priority lending by a secured creditor which had the right of election would be seen to be an act of faith by the principal lenders in the procedure.'

This view of super priority is obviously very different from the Canadian model.

Indeed, by giving a secured creditor not only an option not to participate in the process but then first refusal on a form of finance that will never in any event rank ahead of fixed charges, a secured creditor is put in a position where making further lending may improve the secured creditor's position[4] over other creditors, by giving the secured creditor enhanced quasi-security rights.

Every pound of super priority lending may not only be recouped in full but also increase the rate of return on existing priority debt, by giving the lender a greater degree of control, through the super priority of the further lending and the likely dependency of the company on that ongoing source of funds. This is very much a secured creditor's idea of super priority finance.[5]

Nevertheless, the point remains – the impact of a tool was never yet successfully assessed in its absence.

1. In their October 1996 Report on Corporate Rescue and Insolvent Trading para 1.18.
2. Paras 1.24 and 1.25.
3. Chapter 12 of the Commission's Report.
4. In cases where the security position may be doubtful, for example because the value of fixed charge assets may not be adequate and the creditor otherwise secured only by a floating charge vulnerable to super priority.
5. Of course, where there is no common legal inheritance, there is less reason to expect convergent thinking on the relevant policy issues. The *Czech Insolvency Act* 182/2006 Coll. which will come into force on 1 July 2007, will actually improve the position of secured creditors, by permitting full priority for secured debt (the limit has been 70% of the sale proceeds of the security) and providing for interest while security rights are subject to the moratorium imposed by the new restructuring regime of 'reorganizace'.

Some conclusions

3.37   For so long as English law proceeded on the basis that in an insolvency, creditors were to be left to their security and otherwise their own devices, employees were to be protected by limited preferential rights and the transfer of certain liabilities to others on business sale but that shareholders' rights were to be written off as their loss, there was no need for the tool of judicially sanctioned super priority finance.

If the increased sophistication of the rescue mechanisms (from the 1986 introduction of administration moratorium to the 2002 reformulation of purposes of administration) and the other reforms – expressly introduced because of dissatisfaction with the social and other outcomes under the pre-1986/2002 regimes – is to result in any real change in practice rather than only on the page, whether there is a need for such finance will have to be addressed.

Until it is, the apparent choices are largely illusory and those faced with the task of realising value from a company in financial crisis and those identifying value and an opportunity to buy it, will generally continue to deal with each other through the medium of asset sales.

At least to this writer, there appears to be a strong case for the consideration of judicially sanctioned super priority finance, to make the choices at least real ones where appropriate: that is, only where a powerful case for such finance can be made out.

It is not suggested that the availability of such finance (whether on the evolved Canadian, or proposed Hong Kong, or otherwise conceived, model) will result in more company rescues than business rescues or even a dramatic increase in the number of company rescues.

It is suggested that the example of Canada shows that a judicially overseen alternative to the present frequently encountered combination of financial paralysis and entrenched, mutually antipathetic, vested monetary interests is not beyond human devising.

Indeed, during the passage of *EA* as a bill, on an amendment moved in Committee in the House of Lords by Lord Hunt of Wirral, a section 57A was briefly canvassed, which would have provided that the court might order 'super-priority financing', being 'finance provided to a company in administration which shall rank as an expense in the administration with priority over the claims of existing secured and unsecured creditors', but only where the expenditure:

- was necessary to continue the operation of the business of the company to meet the administrator's objectives or otherwise to protect and preserve the business and assets of the company during the administration; and

- did not prejudice the position of secured creditors – presumably, what was contemplated was that the finance would have to be shown as likely to add value, so the overall position of secured creditors would not be adversely affected.

Even this modest proposal was rejected by the government, in a response that contradicted itself: having said that the question of funding in the context of insolvency was a commercial one for the lending market, Lord McIntosh of Haringey both rejected an analogy with US Chapter 11 (which analogy had not been advanced) by contrasting the availability of free assets in the US with their absence here ('where we have so many floating charges') but then suggested that:

'alternative sources of finance for companies and businesses have emerged. There is the growth of asset financing, factoring and discounting where funders may be more oriented towards the rescue environment and prepared to advance funding to companies in administration and subject to company voluntary arrangements.'[1]

The rather obvious point is that the assets premised as the subject of security for the further finance will in a typical case be the subject of security for existing finance – because of the floating charges to which reference had just been made – and thus not available at all.

When the matter was returned to in debate, Lord Hunt tried again, pointing out that 'if the new administration process does not allow a business properly to restructure and to be adequately financed while it does so, we risk making no real improvements to the rescue culture and nothing much will change.'[2]

Lord McIntosh was unmoved: 'it is a difficult and complicated issue … Legislative changes should be proposed only following extensive consideration and wide consultation. That is not something that should be dealt with in the Bill's progress.'[3]

The proposed amendment was withdrawn and there the matter rests.

The need for some version of super priority finance to be available (at least upon judicial sanction) is surely clear if work outs are being brought down or made unworkable by those who have bought debt cheap and seek to lever out dear or if all that in practice *EA* has caused is an increase in the number of pre-packs, irrespective of their individual merits.

However, the chances of further consideration and consultation of the sort Lord McIntosh had in mind presently seem remote. Certainly, nothing has happened in the years since his answer.

It seems it may take the next (and inevitable) recession to cause sufficient economic and social damage for the right question to be brought into proper focus.

1. Hansard, HL (series 6) Vol 638 cols 788-789 (Committee of the Whole House, 29 July 2002).
2. Hansard, HL (series 6) Vol 640 col 1114 (Consideration on Report, 21 October 2002).
3. Hansard, HL (series 6) Vol 640 cols 1115-1116 (Consideration on Report, 21 October 2002).

Chapter 4

Defence Tactics

At a glance

When considering the defence tactics as a public company, the following factors must be borne in mind:

- the regulatory environment

- the timetable for a hostile public offer

- measures that can be taken in preparation for a potential hostile bid

- measures to be taken during the bid process

Preparation and the taking of early expert advice is key to the successful defence of a hostile bid.

Introduction

4.1   Where a public company receives an unsolicited takeover bid from a third party, the directors of that company have a duty to consider that offer in the context of 'the interests of the company as a whole (The City Code on Takeovers and Mergers ('the Takeover Code'), General Principle 3) in recommending to shareholders the action they should take. Specifically, in formulating their advice, the directors are required by the Takeover Code to act 'only in their capacity as directors and not [to] have regard to their personal or family shareholdings or to their personal relationships with the companies'. It follows that the directors of a target company should only be seeking to oppose a bid where, in their opinion, and having received competent independent financial advice, the bid does not serve the best interests of the groups which they are required to consider. Usually, it is the interests of shareholders which will predominate, and, from their point of view, the critical question for the directors to ask will be: does the bid fairly value the company?

Clearly, it is seldom possible for the directors to measure the fairness of a bid by any objective criteria, apart from the share price of the company immediately before the announcement of the bid, knowledge of the terms of recent transactions involving similar companies and, sometimes, market valuations of the company's principal underlying assets. Directors must usually exercise their own judgement (after taking appropriate advice) in weighing the value of the bid now against the likely future value of the shares, taking into account trading prospects, the future financial position of the company, management strengths and weaknesses and the influence of economic factors on future market conditions.

The directors of the company making the hostile bid, for their part, also face uncertainty. They must rely, in the main, on published information about the target. They must anticipate that the defence tactics of the target's board will direct public scrutiny upon all aspects of the offeror company, including its management, particularly if offeror shares will form part or all of the offer consideration. Furthermore, failure may involve significant penalties for the offeror, not the greatest of which may be the high cost of mounting a hostile bid.

This chapter is concerned with the defence tactics which a quoted public company can employ to fight off a bid which its directors are unable to recommend or to force up the price which the offeror has to pay for his offer to succeed. The first part deals with the regulatory background to UK public takeovers. It is followed by a discussion of the pre-emptive measures that a company can employ to minimise the threat of takeover. Finally this chapter deals with the actual defence of a takeover and the regulation of defence tactics contained in the Takeover Code.

The regulatory environment

4.2   The regulations governing the conduct of takeovers limit the defensive measures which can be taken by a target company prior to, and during the course of, a bid. This body of regulation is principally set out in the Companies Act 1985 (as amended and restated in the *Companies Act 2006*), the Takeover Code, the UKLA Listing Rules, the *Financial Services and Markets Act 2000* and the *Financial Services Act 1986*. Consideration needs also to be given to Merger Regulation, insofar as the resulting merger may qualify for investigation by the Office of Fair Trading and the Competition Commission in the UK, or by the European competition authorities, respectively. In the case of takeovers affecting certain types of industries, such as television or newspaper companies, legislation affecting the control of companies within such industries might also have to be considered.

The principal body of rules governing the conduct of takeovers in the UK is the Takeover Code. The Panel is an independent body, established in 1968, whose main functions are to issue and administer the Takeover Code and to supervise and regulate takeovers and other matters to which the Code applies in accordance with the rules set out in the Takeover Code. It has been designated as the supervisory authority to carry out certain regulatory functions in relation to takeovers pursuant to the Directive on Takeover Bids (2004/25/EC) (the 'Directive'). Its Directive functions are set out in and under The Takeovers Directive (Interim Implementation) Regulations 2006 (the 'Regulations').

The conduct of both offeree and offeror during a takeover is circumscribed by the general principles and rules of the Takeover Code. The general principles set out the spirit of the Takeover Code and guide the Panel in making its decisions in situations where the rules of the Code are silent or where a point of interpretation is involved. The general principles seek to ensure, *inter alia*, that all shareholders are afforded equivalent treatment by the offeror; that sufficient information is made available to the shareholders of the target to enable them to reach a properly informed decision; that false markets are avoided; and that the board of the target company must act in the interests of the company as a whole.

The defences that a target can raise in the UK are therefore heavily limited by the Takeover Code, insofar as any attempt to create legal obstacles or impediments to the implementation of an offer are prohibited unless expressly sanctioned by shareholders. These issues will be further considered below.

The Takeover Code also sets out a precise timetable for the bid process (see below) thereby limiting the period of uncertainty faced by the offeree and its shareholders and employees.

Illustrative bid timetable

Timing	Event
Announcement ('A')	Announcement of offer by offeror.
A+1	Offeree sends copy of announcement to shareholders with a response setting out its initial views.
Posting ('P')	Posting of the offer document by offeree (within 28 days of A but normally much earlier).
By P+14	Posting of first response document of offeree.
P+20	Office of Fair Trading ('OFT') decision on referral expected.
P+21	Earliest first closing date for the offer.
P+22	Announcement of level of acceptances on first closing date.
P+39	No material new information may be disclosed by the offeree after this date without the consent of the Panel.
P+42	Shareholders may withdraw their acceptances after this date if the offer has not been declared unconditional as to acceptances.
P+46	Last day for revision to the offer.
P+60	1.00pm: Latest time and date for acceptances.
	5.00pm: Final time and date for announcement of results of the offer (in the absence of a competing offer). Offer to have been declared unconditional as to acceptances or to lapse.
P+81	Last day for satisfying all other conditions.

Defensive measures prior to a bid

At a glance

4.3   The following is a checklist of the defensive action that should be taken prior to a bid.

(a)   Conduct a comprehensive review of the market's perception of the company and its share price performance.

(b)   Conduct a 'dummy bid'.

(c)   Prepare 'defence bible'.

(d)   Devote resource to liaison with analysts, shareholders, potential shareholders and financial and trade press.

(e)   Monitor share price, trading volume and press comment.

(f)   Perform regular analysis of share register.

(g)   Prepare analysis of potential bidders.

(h)   Assess ability to fund an MBO defence.

(i)   Address issues highlighted in 'dummy bid' and other analyses.

(j)   Obtain maximum share buy-back authority.

(k)   Identify key advisers and potential conflicts of interest.

(l)   Identify any pension fund issues.

Defensive action prior to a bid

4.4   A company may be alerted to the possibility of a hostile bid in a number of ways, for example, by the occurrence of a sudden unexplained movement in the share price and/or press speculation. More dramatically, a target company may first become aware of its vulnerability to a bid by receiving a telephone call from the bidder very shortly before the announcement of the bid. However, a sophisticated board of directors should already be aware of the vulnerability of the company to a hostile bid through its own analysis of the situation and from discussions with its advisers. Given that a hostile bid timetable can be very condensed, advanced preparation is essential. Factors contributing to the conclusion that the company is vulnerable may include any of the following:

(a)   bid activity in the sector, particularly where there is a perception that the company concerned occupies a valuable strategic position or owns sought-after assets;

(b)   persistent underperformance in the company's share price compared to other companies in the sector, which is not justified on fundamentals and which may lead predators to the conclusion that there is a window of opportunity to acquire the company 'on the cheap';

(c)   criticism of the company's management by leading shareholders, or concerns about management succession becoming current; and

(d)   the need for a significant shareholder to dispose of its shares in order to generate cash.

The first objective of a company embarking on a pre-emptive defence strategy should be to conduct, as a matter of urgency, a comprehensive review of the market's perception of the value of the shares and of the performance of the businesses and assets within the group. Specifically, this review, which would be undertaken by, or in close consultation with, the company's advisers, should be aimed at answering the following questions:

(i)   Does the stock market value the company at a premium or discount to the sector in which it operates, and what factors underlie the market's valuation?

(ii)   If it is considered that the market currently underrates the shares, what steps should be taken to ensure that the market reflects this value more fairly?

(iii)   Is there a clear group strategy, and, if so, how successfully is this being implemented, and how well is it understood by key shareholders and by the market?

(iv)   Are there parts of the group that are underperforming, and if so how can the situation be improved?

(v)   Does the historic performance of the company reflect favourably on the management, and does the team require strengthening for the future?

The answers to each of these questions will provide the platform for the defence strategy and highlight specific areas to which the defence effort should be directed. Such a review might take the form of a 'dummy bid' whereby a hostile bid scenario is acted out to identify key areas of weakness on which a bidder might focus.

As opposed to financial markets in more litigious jurisdictions, the shareholders remain the deciding factor in nearly all UK takeover battles, whatever view the board may form about the value of the company's shares or however confident it may feel about the company's prospects. The communication of the offeree board's perception to the investment community is therefore all important. The management should therefore ensure that it is well acquainted not only with its major shareholders but also with managers of substantial institutional funds who are not yet large investors in the company. The management also needs to establish a relationship based on confidence with those groups which are most influential in forming investor opinion, key stockbrokers' analysts and financial journalists in the national press, and, where relevant, the local and trade press.

These objectives may be achieved by systematic programmes of company visits, presentations, financial analysts' briefings and carefully chosen press releases to announce significant achievements in trading, new products or research and development, which should be arranged by the company's stock-broker and/or public relations adviser. The investment community, being by nature conservative, generally fears the unknown quantity and the unexpected (particularly where it takes the form of an announcement of poor trading). The negative impact of the latter is therefore best mitigated in circumstances where the shareholders believe that they have been kept informed and have invested in a company with a clearly understood and believable strategy.

Before embarking on such an investor relations programme, it is important that management recognises any concerns which are being expressed by the investment community and the financial press and aims its effort at addressing these concerns. A company's reputation may be critically affected, for example, by factors which have no direct impact on the company's operational performances, such as concern about the appropriateness of its accounting policies or perceived shortcomings in its corporate governance arrangements. It would be an important part of the defence strategy to demonstrate that management took seriously the views of shareholders and outside critics alike and responded positively to well-founded concerns.

Equally important will be the measures the board takes either to improve financial performance or to show historical performance in the most favourable possible light. For example, if the board believes that the market value of the company's shares stands at a discount either to the net asset value or to the break-up value on disposal of the constituent businesses, it may be possible to demonstrate this by achieving a disposal of certain assets or businesses at a high value. Alternatively, the decision to sell, close or replace management at an underperforming subsidiary could help build investor confidence that problem areas were being addressed. In some cases, the board might decide to divest some businesses on the grounds that they were peripheral to the basic strategy of the group. Any such measures might have an immediately beneficial effect on the share price.

At the same time, it should be noted that large-scale restructurings undertaken as a defence measure once a bid has been made may lack credibility, if they are seen as a desperate resort to frustrate an otherwise unstoppable bid. Thus the planned restructuring announced by Hawker Siddeley as a defence against a hostile bid by BTR in November 1991 attracted little support from shareholders, and the extensive disposals made by Forte in defending the bid from Granada in late 1995 failed to swing the result in favour of the defence.

Before any decisions involving corporate restructuring are taken, however, the full implications of such measures in the context of a bid defence must be carefully thought through. For example, removal of a problem area may also address a point of concern to a bidder and remove an obstacle to his proceeding with a bid. The inflow of cash into the company from the disposal might also be attractive to a bidder.

Moving away from strategic to specifically tactical aspects of a defence strategy, one prudent step a vulnerable company may take is to ensure that it has powers under the relevant *Companies legislation* to repurchase the maximum allowed amount of its issued share capital. A repurchase may have the effect of boosting the company's earnings per share and reducing the number of shares in the hands of uncommitted shareholders and may be an attractive means by which to attempt to achieve an immediate boost to the share price. Whether or not a company wishes to take this option will depend on a number of technical considerations. These may include whether or not the company has sufficient distributable reserves to make the repurchase or if not, (whether the company is happy to fund a repurchase out of the proceeds of a fresh issue of shares), the relationship between the value at which the shares are being repurchased and the cost (if any) of borrowing funds. Unless the proposed purchase price of the shares is sufficiently low, the cost of borrowing may diminish the earnings per share boost intended to be achieved by reducing the number of shares in issue.

The repurchase route might also be attractive since it can absorb cash resources and may therefore make the balance sheet of the company less tempting to a bidder. However, the market may not welcome such a move if it suggests a lack of ambition and drive on behalf of management to grow the company by investment and acquisition, or if it results in the balance sheet becoming overgeared.

It is also worth noting that share repurchases have met with mixed success in a number of recent bid defences. In both the bid for Blue Circle Industries plc and the bid for Wickes plc in 2000, share repurchases were part of initial successful defences. However, both offerors were ultimately successful in acquiring the targets, having each acquired 29.9% of the offeree's issued share capital during the bid process (prior to the proposed repurchases) taking place. Following the failure of the first hostile offers for each of these companies, the respective repurchases led to the offerors significantly increasing their percentage stakes as neither offeror sold shares into the repurchase. A short while later, both offerors returned with slightly higher bids which were recommended by the target boards. In each case, the significant stake which the offeror then held was recognised as one of the key reasons for the subsequent recommendation.

Regular and detailed analyses of the share register are essential in any defence strategy. The directors should be aware of the identity of all significant shareholders. If they are not, they should consider making use of the power under *sections 793* and *803* of the *Companies Act 2006 (which came into force on 20 January 2007)* to require the disclosure by nominee shareholders of the identity of the persons beneficially interested in the shares. This power might also be used to monitor significant share transfers. However, the procedure should be used with discretion as the responses to enquiries must be made available for inspection at the company's registered office under *section 803* of the *Companies Act 2006* and are thereafter made available to inspection by the public. This information may subsequently also be useful to a predator.

The process of regularly monitoring significant sales and purchases has the additional benefit of identifying the stockbrokers which are most active in trading the shares and may thus help the company target its message to the stockholding community.

Once the identity of the potential predator has been discovered, through the section 793/803 route or otherwise, a detailed analysis should be prepared by the company and its advisers in order to identify information which could be used in an actual bid defence.

The directors should also carefully consider the appropriateness of the company's existing financial advisers, not only its corporate finance adviser and stockbroker, but also its accountants, solicitors, and public relations advisers. In considering this issue, the directors should also determine, so far as is possible, that none of their advisers have a conflict of interest which might require them to be replaced.

Choice of a suitable financial adviser is critical to the successful defence of a hostile takeover bid. The board of an offeree company is required, under Rule 3 of the Takeover Code, to obtain competent independent advice when recommending a course of action to shareholders in connection with a takeover. The financial adviser will not only give an independent view on the fairness of the offer, but also guide the company through the regulatory labyrinth and relationship with the Panel and advise on strategy and tactics, both before and after the bid is made.

During the stage of pre-emptive measures against a bid, the financial adviser will assist the board in drafting the defence plan and coordinating the defence work of other professionals. The defence plan will usually be in the form of a document conventionally known as a 'Defence Bible', which will contain both recommendations for action to forestall a bid, for example, in the area of investor relations, and draft press releases covering the initial response to an approach from a predator, a raid on the shares or an outright bid. The ability to respond promptly and decisively to the announcement of an offer can be critical to the market's perception of the target company board and ultimately to the outcome of the bid.

The financial adviser will also assist in identifying potential predators (or, if appropriate, white knights) and in analysing their strengths and weaknesses, particularly in relation to their capacity to finance a bid.

The stockbroker's role is crucial, too, not only in maintaining the relationship with the company's shareholders and investors generally through research and regular contact, but also in gathering market intelligence both on behaviour of shareholders and market perception of the company, its competitors and potential predators. The extent to which a stockbroker can effectively monitor market perception and activity in the company's shares will depend to a great extent on the proportion of the business in the shares transacted by the broker.

At a glance – defence bible contents

4.5   The defence bible should contain the following:

(a) List of parties: names, addresses and telephone numbers of:

    (i) board members;

    (ii) senior management; and

    (iii) key advisers.

(b) Administrative procedures, including draft announcements, to respond to:

    (i) press speculation;

    (ii) significant share price movement;

    (iii) dawn raid or announcement of a major shareholding;

    (iv) announcement by a third party of a possible bid; and

    (v) announcement of a hostile bid.

(c) Draft documentation, including:

    (i) outline announcements; and

    (ii) board minute appointing defence committee.

(d) Analysis of company's strengths and weaknesses (SWOT analysis).

(e) Updated budget and profit forecast.

(f) Valuation – sum-of-parts versus market capitalisation.

(g) Analysis of major shareholders.

(h) Outline advice on directors' responsibilities during the course of an offer.

(i) Analysis of potential predators and reasons for bidding.

(j) Information on potential white knights.

(k) Analysis of potential regulatory obstacles to a takeover.

Defensive measures following announcement of a bid

At a glance

4.6 The following defence measures should be considered following the announcement of a bid.

(a) Provide clear, unequivocal advice to shareholders immediately.

(b) Hold shareholder and press briefings.

(c) Attack the offeror and, where relevant, the value of its paper.

(d) Produce profit forecast.

(e) Produce asset valuation (if applicable).

(f) Assess ability for MBO defence.

(g)   Consider break-up defence.

(h)   Solicit white-knight bids.

(i)   Assess benefits of a demerger.

(j)   Consider share buy-back.

(k)   Lobby politicians and competition authorities (if applicable).

(l)   Purchase of blocking stake by a friendly party ('white squire').

(m)   Pac-man defence.

Defensive action following announcement of a bid

4.7   If its defence plan has been well prepared, then immediately on announcement of a bid the target company will be able to respond quickly with clear advice to its shareholders.

Assuming that the board has decided not to recommend acceptance, this should be followed as soon as possible by advice to shareholders that they should reject the offer and ignore all documents sent by the offeror. The purpose of the rapid response is above all to discourage shareholders from selling into the strengthening share price, and to set the tone of a united and confident board determined to pursue its chosen strategy of independence. The nature of this response will set the tone for the defence and give a signal to shareholders and to the market generally as to how the defence campaign will be conducted.

From the announcement of the offer, the offeror has four weeks to prepare and despatch an offer document to the shareholders of the target. In practice, a well-prepared offeror will frequently be in a position to post an offer document within a few days of announcement, reducing the time available to the offeree to compile their response document. During the time between announcement and posting the financial adviser and the directors of the target company should collate information about the offeror, further analyse the terms and conditions of the bid, and prepare a full defence strategy.

In some other jurisdictions a variety of tactics can be used to prevent the offeror from putting into effect its offer. These tactics, which may be put in place either before a bid or between announcement and posting, may include:

(a)   the 'scorched earth defence', whereby the company's assets are depleted through sale to a friendly party;

(b)   'poison pills' and 'shark repellents' which might involve inclusion in the Articles of Association of the company provisions for exceptional voting requirements for the implementation of mergers and removal of directors from office, or the issue of special shares to existing shareholders which carry extraordinary voting or dividend rights which only come into effect when a hostile bid is made for the company;

(c)   'capital restructuring' which involves the replacement of equity capital with debt through the repurchase of shares such that the acquisition becomes more expensive for the offeror; and

(d)   'golden parachutes' which provide the directors of the target with extraordinarily high severance pay or options over shares.

In the UK, however, the law and the Takeover Code require that the best interests of shareholders be the paramount consideration in guiding the directors as to how to respond to a hostile offer. Consequently, most of the above tactics are not permitted under UK rules unless expressly approved by the shareholders in general meeting. General Principle 3 of the Takeover Code requires that directors ignore their personal circumstances and only have regard to the interests of the company as a whole.

Rule 21 of the Takeover Code expands upon General Principle 3 and specifically prohibits, in the absence of shareholder approval, certain actions by the board of the target, either during the course of an offer, or where the board has reason to believe one might be imminent, which might have the effect of frustrating an offer. These include:

(i)   the issuing of shares;

(ii)   the granting of options over unissued shares;

(iii)   the creation or issue of securities carrying rights of conversion into shares;

(iv)   the sale or acquisition of assets of a material amount; and

(v)   entering into contracts outside the ordinary course of business, an example of which might be varying the terms of a director's service agreement where the change involves a significant increase in emoluments.

The effect of Rule 21 is to prevent the board of the target from adopting a strategy of evasion rather than addressing the merits or demerits of a particular offer. Issuing new shares and capital restructurings are unlikely to be sanctioned by shareholders during the course of an offer as such strategies will not be seen as necessarily aimed at improving the return on their investment. Furthermore, the notice period required to summon an extraordinary general meeting will provide a major opportunity for the offeror to study the evasive tactic proposed and to draw shareholders' attention to the actions of the board. In UK takeovers, defence tactics of this type may well rebound on the board of the target.

Although a number of the above defensive measures are feasible as pre-emptive measures, companies are rarely admitted to listing in the UK in circumstances where the Articles of Association or the capital structure are such as to favour certain shareholders over others, to restrict voting rights to certain categories of share, or in other ways to prevent the creation of a free market in the shares of the company.

4.7   Defence Tactics

In the vast majority of takeovers, the battle is primarily fought in the public arena in the form of documents sent to the shareholders of the target, public announcements and lobbying of major shareholders and financial commentators (primarily the press and financial analysts).

Following the publication of the offer document, the target company and its advisers will attempt to assemble cogent arguments suggesting, for example, that the offer undervalues the company and, if the offer consideration includes offeror securities, that the offeror company's own shares are a less attractive investment, that the offeror's management is weak, that the offeror's historic performance is less impressive than that of the target, and that the offeror's strategy is flawed and unlikely to improve the performance of the target company.

The first document issued by the target and its financial adviser (which must be published within 14 days of the offer document) will seek to repudiate the offeror's claim that its bid fully values the company and it may do this by comparison with the prevailing share price (if it is at a significant premium to the offer), by reference to the target's record of growth, profits and earnings per share, and by an analysis of the company's commercial strengths, be they products, market share, technological skills, key assets etc.

If an offer is made up of shares in the offeror company, this could be attacked on the basis that their longer-term value as an investment is open to question. This argument would need to be supported by analysis of the historic share price performance of the offeror compared with that of the target and/or that of the sector and the market as a whole. If the offeror has a track record of frequent share issues or existing convertible shares or loan stock, the target can raise the threat of dilution of earnings as a disincentive to accept the offeror's paper as an alternative investment.

Where the consideration offered includes securities of the offeror, the target will, in addition to comparing the growth in dividend payments and growth in earnings per share of the two companies, criticise the track record of the management of the offeror in terms of their investment decisions and past performance in managing acquisitions, as well as questioning any synergies the offeror alleges will be achieved by combining the two companies. The offeree might also seek to argue that the offer price provides that most of the value ascribed to these synergies is for the account of the offeror shareholders, therefore providing insufficient value to offeree shareholders.

The target will always seek to assert, whenever possible, that its business is unique, its strategy of independence is the best means to succeed in its markets, and that the offeror has failed to understand the target's business. Any evidence that past acquisitions by the offeror have failed to achieve anticipated returns or been subsequently sold at a net loss can be exploited to considerable advantage. The target may also seek to imply that the offeror's strategy is not to invest in the business for the long term but that it is attempting engage in an asset-stripping exercise for short-term gain. An analysis of the indebtedness of the enlarged group may enable the target to allege that the financing of the offer will require disposals of assets in order to reduce gearing to more acceptable levels.

Competition policy is too complex an area to deal with in detail in this context, but it is a potential defence tactic open to targets who are active in identifiable markets where they possess a significant share of the business and/or where a combination of the target and offeror may result in a monopoly situation. The advantage to a target in achieving a referral of the bid to the Competition Commission is not only the prospect of the merger being found by the Commission to be against the public interest, but the mere fact of a decision by the Secretary of State for Trade and Industry to refer a bid to the Commission can significantly improve a target's chances of successfully defending itself. Not only does the time taken by the Commission enable the target to marshal its defences more effectively, but the relative fortunes of both companies can change significantly over the period and in particular market perception of both companies may change. This process can be aided by a concerted and effective investor relations campaign. On the downside, the target's business can be damaged by such a protracted period of uncertainty.

Rule 12 of the Takeover Code requires that it be a term of every offer that the offer lapse if it is referred to the Competition Commission for investigation before the first closing date of the offer or, if later, the date on which the offer is declared unconditional as to acceptances. In practice, some offerors may be unwilling to undergo a full Competition Commission investigation and the bid lapses permanently upon a reference.

In deciding whether or not a merger is in the public interest, the Commission will take into account, *inter alia*, the promotion of effective competition in the provision of goods and services in the UK, the promotion of the interests of consumers of goods and services in respect of price, quality, and variety, and the promotion of the reduction of costs and the development of new techniques and new products through competition.

In the event that the Secretary of State accepts the recommendation of the Commission that the merger or aspects of it are against the public interest, he can block the merger or seek to obtain certain undertakings from the offeror relating to aspects of the offer which restrict competition. This might entail an undertaking by the offeror to dispose of certain businesses.

It is clear that a decision to refer a merger to the Commission is made only after extensive consultation which opens the door to considerable lobbying pressure from the opposing parties. The target's financial advisers, solicitors and public relations advisers (which may include a firm of political lobbyists) will need to coordinate a lobbying campaign to attempt to persuade civil servants, ministers and MPs that the resulting merger will be anti-competitive and against the public interest.

Where larger mergers are concerned, the competition issues are likely to be debated outside of the national forum. The European Commission is taking an increasingly active role in investigating major takeovers involving EU companies.

Competition issues can place one offeror at a disadvantage when compared to other offerors and this can be exacerbated by the actions of the offeree. Such a situation arose in the battle for More Group plc in 1998 following the announcement of a recommended cash offer by Clear Channel Communications Inc of the US. The Clear Channel proposal was countered by Decaux SA, a French company, which announced a higher cash offer that was not recommended by the offeree board who advised shareholders to take no action. Throughout the bid battle both More Group and Clear Channel expressed concern that the competition authorities would not clear a bid from Decaux. The battle reached a critical point when Clear Channel raised its offer, gaining a recommendation and the necessary competition clearances for the bid to proceed. By this point, the offer from Decaux had been referred to the Competition Commission and had lapsed in accordance with Rule 12 of the Takeover Code. However, Decaux then announced a further offer which was higher than the increased Clear Channel offer but pre-conditional on, *inter alia*, satisfactory clearances from the competition authorities. This higher offer was rejected by the board of More Group, principally on the basis that it was uncertain and likely to be blocked by the competition authorities. This ultimately led to Clear Channel winning the bid battle.

The cornerstone of most defence strategies is the publication of a formal profit forecast for the current financial year, or in the case of property investment companies or investment trusts, where market value is invariably related to underlying asset values, a revaluation of such assets. Given that the profit forecast or asset revaluation is likely to be the target's strongest weapon, the target will wait until most of the other available arguments have been presented and debated in documents to shareholders before announcing its forecast. Rule 31.9 of the Takeover Code prohibits targets from announcing any new information, trading results or profit forecasts and asset valuations following the 39th day of the offer period. Such profit forecasts and asset revaluations are normally made in this final defence or 'Day 39' document.

In the hostile offer by 3i plc for Electra Investment Trust plc in 1999, Electra constantly maintained that the 3i bid significantly undervalued the company and issued a number of asset revaluations. These revaluations were supported, not only by reports from financial advisers, but also by subsequent realisations of investments at above book value. Electra argued that this proved that shareholders would obtain better value from a gradual realisation of its entire portfolio. The 3i bid was eventually rejected by Electra shareholders in favour of winding up the trust and distributing the cash proceeds to shareholders.

The offeror has the right to revise its offer up to the 46th day (under Rule 32 of the Takeover Code), two weeks prior to the last day the offer is capable of becoming unconditional as to acceptances. As a result, one week before the offeror is obliged to make its final offer, the target is obliged to make a major strategic decision as to whether or not to publish a formal profit forecast.

The decision for the board of the target as to whether or not to make a profit forecast will be largely determined by the extent to which the level of profits that the directors can comfortably forecast is in excess, or at least in line with, what the market is currently expecting.

Rule 28 of the Takeover Code requires directors to compile profit forecasts with scrupulous care and objectivity, with a duty imposed on financial advisers to ensure that the forecast has been prepared with due care and consideration. The target's auditors will work closely with the directors to ensure that the forecast has been properly compiled in accordance with the company's accounting policies and will produce a report confirming this.

The Takeover Code's recognition of the profit forecast as the most formidable defensive measure available to the target necessitates that the directors and their advisers ensure that both the quality of information is sufficiently high and the margin of comfort sufficiently wide that the forecast will be met in the absence of extraordinary circumstances. The Panel sometimes follows up profit forecasts to establish whether or not they were achieved and ultimately the reasons for the failure to achieve the forecast. Therefore the ability to forecast accurately will be critical to the target's ability to use a profit forecast as a defence tactic. In addition, a forecast early in the target's financial year is likely to be less effective insofar as a wider margin of comfort will be required to ensure that the forecast is met. It is extremely rare for an offeree to issue a profit forecast for a period of more than 12 months from the date of publication as it is unlikely that such a forecast could be reported on to the appropriate Takeover Code standards.

The search for a 'white knight' or 'white squire' is a process that should be continually under review for any company that is under threat of possible takeover. As a pre-emptive measure the directors will maintain a list of possible offerors and identify those whom the board and its financial advisers believe would make a suitable alternative partner capable of mounting a competing offer. There are numerous examples of white knights 'rescuing' the offeree, normally with an offer at a significant premium to the original price of the hostile offeror.

In the event that a hostile offer is made for the company, dealings with white knights need to be conducted with considerable care and initial contacts are probably best made through the financial adviser. A company that is the subject of a hostile bid or bid rumour will be perceived to be vulnerable and negotiating from a standpoint of weakness. It is entirely possible that a potential white knight will, after a friendly approach, seize the opportunity to launch a competing bid on hostile terms. This was witnessed in the battle for National Westminster Bank ('NatWest'). Following the announcement of a hostile offer by Bank of Scotland, Royal Bank of Scotland was widely tipped as a white knight but then, when talks with NatWest broke down, it made an offer which, although initially rejected by the offeree, was ultimately successful.

4.7 *Defence Tactics*

An added complication in pursuing the white knight tactic lies in Rule 20.2 of the Takeover Code which, in elaborating the general principle of equality of information to all shareholders, requires that any information given to any offeror or potential offeror must, on request, be furnished as promptly to a less welcome offeror. The unwelcome offeror must specify what information it requires and cannot make a general request. However, an offeror faced with the announcement of a competing bid by a white knight will probably be best advised to compile a detailed shopping list of information it believes may have been provided to the white knight. In that way the offeror can attempt to alleviate the disadvantage stemming from its position as a hostile offeror.

Another defence tactic which may be available to a target is the purchase of a substantial share stake by a friendly, probably corporate, investor ('white squire'). This might involve the purchase by the white squire of a large share stake from a single shareholder who is looking for an opportunity to dispose of his investment. Alternatively the white squire may subscribe for new shares in the company, following approval of the transaction by shareholders in general meeting. The former route is designed to secure, in the hands of friendly shareholders, a large block of shares which might otherwise be acquired by a predator. However, it is clear a white squire is free to dispose of his stake and may be tempted to do so if a hostile bidder makes a sufficiently attractive offer. The Panel tightened its rules in this area and Rule 4.4 of the Takeover Code now prevents 'friendly' share purchases by certain 'associates' of the offeree as such action might distort the true democratic wishes of offeree shareholders as a whole.

Under the time pressure imposed by the normal timetable of a public takeover, a management buy-out may not always be a realistic option. However, it is one of the strategies likely to be considered by a management who believe the company is undervalued and vulnerable to a takeover. An example of management mounting a successful management buy-out in the face of a hostile bid was the buy-out of William Cook in 1996, at a time when it was subject to a bitterly fought hostile offer from Triplex Lloyd. Over the past decade, with low interest rates and the 'wall' of debt and private equity money available, MBOs have increasingly been seen as a realistic defensive measure.

Nevertheless, a management offer to buy out the share capital of a publicly quoted company immediately raises the issue of conflict of interests insofar as outside shareholders may wish to know why ownership is attractive to the management if satisfactory performance has not been achieved in the recent past under public ownership. As a result, the Takeover Code requires that only those independent directors of the offeree, being those unconnected with the management buy-out, join in giving the recommendation to offeree shareholders. The announcement of a management offer for the company puts a benchmark price on the shares which clearly opens the door to a higher competing offer. The resources available to a management buy-out team may not stretch to significantly higher levels than that which was originally offered, although it might have the benefit of creating an auction situation thereby maximising value to offeree shareholders.

Another defence tactic of an exotic variety is the so-called 'Pac-Man defence', whereby the target launches a retaliatory bid for the share capital of the offeror. Following the bid launched by Wolverhampton & Dudley Breweries for Marstons in 1998, the board of Marstons announced a counter bid for Wolverhampton & Dudley. As the offer consideration of each bid contained a significant proportion of offeror paper, the bid battle focussed on the strength of management in each company and their strategies for the enlarged group. Wolverhampton & Dudley eventually won the bid battle following an increase in its offer for Marstons.

With the increase of funding deficits in defined benefit pension funds of target companies, pension fund trustees are also increasingly being seen as having a key, and often deciding, role at the negotiating table in hostile bids. Their negotiating strength was increased following the introduction of the Pensions Act 2004 and the Pension Regulator. As the Takeover Panel will not allow public offers to be made conditional upon Pension Regulator clearance, pension fund deficits can often be seen as a key poison pill in any defence strategy. Specialist pension advisers are therefore key members of the defence teams for companies with defined benefit schemes.

Conclusion

4.8   The practice of public takeovers in the UK and the regulatory environment reflects a desire to focus shareholder attention on the merits of the offer as explained above. The Takeover Code reinforces this emphasis by prohibiting certain defence tactics designed to frustrate the ability of an offeror to implement its offer. The total effect of this is to create a takeover environment where attention is, to a large extent, focused on the shareholder's perception of the record and prospects of the target company in relation to their investment in that company. The task facing the target is to attempt to focus shareholders' attention on the inadequacy of the offer and force the offeror to pay the maximum price. In the case of a paper bid this will include analysis of the attractiveness of the offeror's shares as an investment. To that end the defence tactics that are likely to be most effective are those that involve effective communication with shareholders of the achievements of the target and its strategy for growth in the future.

Having faced the decision as to whether to accept the offer, to reject it or to find an alternative offeror, the directors of the target are locked into a 60-day offer timetable which is largely controlled by the offeror. The vast majority of shareholders (who tend to be institutional funds managed by professional fund managers) will not decide to accept or reject the offer until the final days. In the absence of an outright successful defence, experience suggests that the best price is achieved for target shareholders when the offer is vigorously defended throughout its currency by a united and determined board of directors.

The alternative tactics of disposals, buy-outs and recapitalisations are best viewed as pre-emptive defensive measures. Faced with an unsolicited offer for the shares, the target's shareholders are likely to view with suspicion such evasive measures as asset disposals and capital restructurings initiated by their directors and are unlikely to give them approval.

In the matter of takeovers, pre-emption is better than defence. A planned defence strategy put into place well ahead of any hostile approaches from predators is more likely to secure the target's independence than a desperate attempt to rally the support of shareholders at the eleventh hour.

Chapter 5

Employee Share Schemes

At a glance

- In the due diligence process, the purchaser should establish as early as possible the types of employee share schemes relevant to the target and the amount of shares subject to options and awards granted to the employees of the target.

- The impact the acquisition has on benefits under the employee share schemes should also be ascertained. In a company acquisition, the purchaser should ascertain, in particular, whether the scheme operates in such a way that there is a risk that the purchaser may not obtain 100% of the target. Any additional costs to the purchaser arising from such schemes should also be taken into account.

- The acquisition may result in employees in the target company or business becoming early leavers under the schemes. To avoid employee relations issues, the purchaser should seek the seller's co-operation to ensure (where possible) that such employees are not disadvantaged.

- Where the target operates share option schemes, the purchaser should consider whether alternative ways to deal with outstanding options (eg cash cancellation or exchange of options) should be offered to participants. The details of such alternative proposals have to be carefully communicated to the participants.

- Where the target operates an employee benefit trust in conjunction with its employee share schemes, the purchaser should be alert to issues arising from such trust which may affect the acquisition. The trustees' cooperation should be sought at an early stage to ensure that shares in the employee benefit trust can be dealt with in a way acceptable to both the purchaser and the seller.

- Consideration should also be given as to whether new arrangements should be put in place following the acquisition to harmonise employee benefits within the merged group.

Introduction

5.1   In recent years, more and more companies have introduced share schemes as part of the remuneration and incentive packages for employees. It is generally accepted that such schemes, if used effectively, can help to retain and motivate employees and generate a community of interest between employees and shareholders.

As share incentives are becoming increasingly important in the employees' remuneration and incentive packages, the purchaser of a target company or business should pay special attention to the operation of the target's share schemes and the impact the acquisition has on the employees' benefits under such schemes.

It is important that appropriate consideration is given at an early stage of the acquisition process to deal with issues arising from such schemes. Failure to address and resolve such issues may result in unexpected additional costs to the purchaser, dissatisfied employees following the acquisition and/or legal proceedings against the target.

In this chapter, issues relating to employee share schemes in the context of an acquisition are explored. Paragraphs **5.2–5.12** outline the principal features of the more common types of employee share schemes. Paragraph **5.13** describes some of the institutional investors' guidelines in relation to such schemes. Paragraphs **5.14–5.15** look at provisions governing such schemes which are particularly relevant in an acquisition, including the impact the change of ownership of the target has on share scheme benefits, the treatment of 'early leavers' and the operation of performance conditions (if any) in such schemes. Paragraph **5.16** looks at share options with emphasis on a public acquisition. Paragraph **5.17** looks at the position where the target operates its share schemes in conjunction with an employee trust. Paragraph **5.18** considers the importance of new share incentive arrangements following the acquisition.

Identifying the employee share schemes

5.2   In the due diligence process, it is important to identify as early as possible the different employee share schemes the target operates both for its general workforce and for its senior executives. Schemes will either be HM Revenue & Customs ('HMRC') approved or unapproved.

HMRC approved schemes

5.3   There are currently four types of HMRC approved schemes:

(a)   company share option scheme;

(b)   savings-related share option scheme;

(c)   share incentive plan;

(d)   enterprise management incentive ('EMI') scheme.

Their principal features are summarised below.

Company share option scheme

5.4   The company will grant selected employees a right (an 'option') to acquire shares at some future date at a price fixed at the date the option is granted. (The company's discretion over who may participate is a unique feature not found in other approved schemes except for the EMI.) For a scheme to be approved, its rules must provide (among other things) that:

(a)   options may only be granted to an employee or a full-time director of the company or, in the case of a group scheme, a participating company – directors who work less than 25 hours a week or self-employed consultants must be excluded. (Participation by persons who have a 'material interest' (as defined in the legislation) in the company is also prohibited);

(b)   the exercise price (the price payable by a participant to acquire shares on exercise of the option) of the option must be at least equal to the market value of the shares at the date of grant;

(c)   the total market value of shares, at the time when the options relating to them were granted, subject to outstanding options granted to a participant must not exceed £30,000.

Otherwise, the company has quite a lot of flexibility in the terms of the options. In particular, the rules can provide that options can only be exercised on the satisfaction of objective performance conditions.

To obtain income tax relief when the option is exercised, statutory time limits must be complied with. This provides that the option must be exercised between three to ten years of the date of grant. Early exercise may give rise to an income tax charge (and National Insurance contributions liability) in certain circumstances.

The £30,000 limit mentioned above was introduced in April 1996. Previously, the applicable limit was £100,000 or, if greater, four times the participant's 'relevant emoluments' (broadly, his earnings which were subject to PAYE). Historically, therefore, such schemes were usually used to incentivise the senior executives of the company.

Savings-related share option scheme ('SAYE Scheme')

5.5   The employee who wishes to participate enters into a savings contract with a building society or a bank nominated by the company to save for a fixed period. Currently, the minimum monthly saving is £5 and the maximum is £250. The savings period may be three or five years (as the company determines) at the end of which a bonus is payable by the building society or the bank. Where a five-year contract is available, the employee may leave his savings in the account for a further two years to earn a bigger bonus. In return, the company grants the employee an option to acquire shares in the company. The option is exercisable at the end of the savings period using the proceeds of the savings contract – these will be made up of the employee's savings and the bonus payable by the bank or building society at the end of the savings period. The option price is fixed at the date the option is granted and can be at a discount of up to 20% of the market value of the shares at the date of grant. All employees and full-time directors who have completed five years' service must be eligible to participate on similar terms.

No income tax charge will arise on the exercise of the option at the end of the savings period. Early exercise may give rise to an income tax charge (and National Insurance contributions liability) in certain circumstances.

Share incentive plan ('SIP')

5.6   Under the SIP, the company establishes a trust in which shares made available to employees will be held. Shares kept in the trust for five years or more can be transferred to employees free from income tax and national insurance. Shares taken out of the trust within five years will be subject to income tax and national insurance (except where the transfer out is as a result of the employee leaving the company for certain specified reasons). A company can give up to £3,000 worth of 'free shares' to each employee every year. An employee can buy 'partnership shares' from their pre-tax salary up to £1,500 a year. A company can give an employee up to two free 'matching shares' for each partnership share the employee buys. Free and matching shares must normally be held in the scheme for at least three years ('the holding period') (although an early transfer may be made if the employee leaves employment – alternatively, the scheme may provide for the free and matching shares to be forfeited in such circumstances). All employees who have completed a period of employment (defined as qualifying periods in the legislation) must be eligible to participate.

Enterprise management incentive ('EMI') scheme

5.7   This is an option arrangement which allows a qualifying company to grant options to selected employees. Each employee will be able to hold options over shares worth up to £100,000 at the time of grant. The total value of shares over which EMI options may be granted by a company must not exceed £3 million. To qualify, the company must be an independent company (quoted or unquoted) trading in the UK with gross assets not exceeding £30 million. Employees will be eligible for EMI options if they are employed by the company or group for at least 25 hours a week or, if less, for at least 75% of their working time.

Otherwise the company has quite a lot of flexibility in the terms of the options. In particular, the exercise of an option can be subject to objective performance conditions.

Provided that the exercise price is not less than the market value of the shares on the date the option is granted and provided that all the other qualifying conditions remain satisfied, there will be no income tax or National Insurance contributions liability arising on the exercise of the option. To qualify for favourable tax treatment, the options must also be exercised within ten years of the date of grant.

Unapproved share schemes

5.8   As unapproved share schemes are not subject to the constraints of HMRC, they can take numerous forms. The most common include:

(a)   unapproved share option scheme;

(b)   phantom share option scheme;

(c)   long-term incentive scheme;

(d)   restricted or convertible share scheme.

While the company usually has a relatively free hand in the design of such schemes, institutional investors have published guidelines relating to the terms and operation of employee share schemes which listed companies usually seek to comply with (see **5.13** below).

Unapproved share option scheme

5.9   Historically, the most common form of unapproved share scheme is the share option scheme. This operates in a similar way as the approved company share option scheme (see **5.4** above). No tax charge will generally arise on the grant of the option. An income tax charge will arise over the growth in the value of shares during the option period on exercise or where the option is released or exchanged for consideration. National Insurance contributions may also be payable (see **5.14** below).

Phantom share option scheme

5.10   Where the company does not want to grant share options but wishes to reward an employee by reference to the performance of the company's shares, a phantom share option scheme may be used. An employee will be granted an option to acquire a number of 'notional' shares during the option period at a price determined at the date of grant. On exercise, the employee will be paid a cash bonus based on the aggregate increase in the value of the notional shares under the option. The amount is taxable as emoluments and subject to National Insurance contributions.

Long-term incentive scheme

5.11   Long-term incentive schemes have a number of common themes:

(a)   the employee will be awarded shares on deferred terms;

(b)   the shares will generally be awarded free to the employee; and

(c)   the award will be subject to conditions, such as performance criteria and continued employment for a designated period.

It is not possible to list every structure but the following are some common permutations.

Contingent award: The employee receives a contingent award of shares which will vest when the applicable performance conditions are met. Where performance conditions fall short of the targets, the award will be scaled back. The employee will normally have no dividend or voting rights until vesting. Once the shares vest, the employee may receive the shares immediately or they may not be released for a further period, during which the shares will generally be held in a trust. The employee will have dividend and voting rights but will not be able to sell or otherwise deal with the shares.

Vested award: An award will be granted based on previous performance giving the employee an immediate vested interest in the shares. The shares will be held in trust and will not be released for, say, three or five years. The interest will be forfeited if the employee leaves employment during the restricted period, other than in specified circumstances, eg by reason of ill-health, retirement, or redundancy.

Matching award: The employee is invited to convert his potential bonus entitlement into a share award. The company will match the shares acquired with an award of equivalent value (or in whatever ratio it deems appropriate) at no cost to the employee. Both awards (or at least the matching element) will be forfeited if the employee leaves during the restricted period other than as a good leaver. The employee has to balance the risk of losing the bonus against the opportunity to acquire shares at a discount.

The tax treatment of the employee will depend on the actual terms of the arrangement. Generally, an income tax charge will arise when the employee obtains a vested interest in the shares. National Insurance contributions may also be payable (see **5.14** below).

Restricted or convertible share schemes

5.12   There are many variations on the basic theme as these arrangements are generally tailor made to suit the company's requirements. Typically, under a restricted share scheme, an employee acquires shares which are subject to restrictions (eg no voting or dividend rights) thus reducing their value. The restrictions will fall away on the attainment of performance targets. If the employee leaves in the meantime, he is normally bound to sell the shares at a reduced value. Alternatively, the acquisition right may be subject to performance conditions such that the employee has to satisfy two sets of performance targets before obtaining the full value of the shares. Under a typical convertible share scheme, an employee will acquire a special class of shares which will automatically convert into ordinary shares on the satisfaction of performance conditions.

The tax treatment of the employee will depend on the actual terms of the arrangement. Generally, an income tax charge will arise when the employee obtains a vested interest in the shares. A subsequent increase in the value of the shares due to the removal of restrictions or the conversion of the shares to a different class may give rise to a further income tax charge. National Insurance contributions may also be payable (see **5.14** below).

The purchaser should establish as early as possible the types of employee share schemes relevant to the target and the amount of shares subject to options and awards granted to the employees of the target. Depending on the terms of the schemes, such amount may be affected by the acquisition. The rules governing the schemes should be carefully considered to determine what impact (if any) the acquisition has on the share scheme benefits.

The following is a list of the documents and information which a purchaser should request from the seller in respect of each share incentive scheme relevant to the target:

(a)   rules governing the scheme, including any amendments;

(b)   documents sent to participants, eg explanatory notes, award/option certificates, notices of exercise;

(c)   ancillary documents relevant to the scheme, eg board or remuneration committee resolutions;

(d)   details of awards/options granted to each participant, eg dates of grant, exercise prices (if any), number of shares subject to the awards/options;

(e)   whether the awards/options are to be satisfied with new or existing shares;

(f)   details of any employee benefit trust operating in conjunction with the share scheme, eg trust deed and rules (including all amendments), ancillary agreements (if any) with the trustees, details of the current trustees, funding arrangement and details of shares held by the trust.

Institutional investors' guidelines

5.13   Listed companies generally take into account institutional investors' requirements or expectations in relation to the design and operation of employee share schemes. The Association of British Insurers have published guidelines which cover issues such as the eligibility of participants, the level of participation, the timing of awards, pricing and the imposition of performance conditions.

In addition, the guidelines also set out the dilution limits (ie the number of new shares which may be issued under the employee share schemes) which are acceptable to institutional shareholders. Broadly, no more than 10% of the issued share capital of the company in any rolling ten-year period can be used for all share schemes, of which no more than 5% can generally be used for discretionary schemes.

According to the guidelines, scheme rules should state that there will be no automatic waiving of performance conditions either in the event of a change of control or where subsisting options and awards are 'rolled over' in the event of a capital reconstruction, and/or early termination of the participant's employment. Also, where share incentive awards vest early as a result of change of control, awards should invest on a time pro-rata basis, ie taking into account the vesting period that has elapsed at the time of the change of control.

See **5.16** below on the relevance of these limits in an acquisition.

Impact of the acquisition

5.14   The rules of the schemes should be carefully reviewed. Obviously, as each scheme may contain different provisions governing the benefits in the event of an acquisition, it is not possible to list every possible permutation. The following sets out what is commonly found in typical schemes.

Where the acquisition relates to a business or a subsidiary participating in its parent company's scheme, the affected participants will typically be treated as 'early leavers' (see **5.15** below).

Where the parent company which operates the scheme is itself being acquired, share options will typically become exercisable (in some cases, in part) from the time when the control of the company passes to the purchaser ('the change of control') for a limited period, after which they will lapse. Awards under other share schemes will vest, in some cases, in part. Under an approved share incentive plan, the employees may direct the trustees to sell the shares held in the trust to the purchaser in such circumstances even if the holding period has not passed. Where the acquisition is on a share-for-share basis, the shares of the purchaser may be treated as the original shareholding under the share incentive plan and can be retained in the scheme in accordance with the terms of such scheme.

There are various issues which a purchaser should ascertain at an early stage of the acquisition process:

(a)   whether any performance conditions continue to apply to the exercise of options or vesting of awards (see **5.15** below);

(b)   whether new shares are to be issued for the satisfaction of the options or awards or whether shares already exist for the satisfaction of such options or awards. If options or awards are satisfied by existing shares, it is usual for a trust (an 'employee benefit trust') to be established to hold such shares until the options are exercised or the awards have vested. The existence of an employee benefit trust gives rise to further issues in the context of an acquisition (see **5.17** below);

(c)   the additional costs associated with the employee share schemes should be factored into the acquisition: where new shares are issued, these additional shares will have to be acquired; the transfer of shares will give rise to stamp duty charges; also the exercise of options or the vesting of awards may give rise to National Insurance contributions if the shares are 'readily convertible assets'. Broadly, shares will be regarded as 'readily convertible assets' if they are listed on a stock exchange or if 'trading arrangements' (which is widely defined) exist in relation to the shares as well as shares which do not qualify for the statutory corporation tax relief in the *Finance Act 2003, sch 23*. The employer National Insurance contributions can be substantial and, if payable by the target as the employer (rather than the seller), should be taken into account by the purchaser. It should also be ascertained whether the seller has entered into any agreements with optionholders that the optionholders will bear some or all of the cost of the employer's National Insurance contributions due on the exercise of an option; and

(d)   *section 429* of the *Companies Act 1985* and *schedule 2 of the Takeovers Directive (Interim Implementation) Regulations 2006* contain provisions which enable a purchaser to acquire compulsorily any minority shareholding at the price offered to other shareholders. The purchaser becomes entitled to trigger the compulsory acquisition procedure when it has obtained 90% of the shares to which the purchaser's offer relates. The purchaser has two months from the date on which it has achieved the 90% threshold to start the procedure. There are two traps to watch here:

   (i)   if 10% or more shares of the target are subject to options or awards under employee share schemes or held in an employee benefit trust, the purchaser will not be in a position to ensure that it will acquire the requisite 90% to trigger the compulsory acquisition procedure. This means there is a risk that the purchaser may not be in a position to acquire full control of the target. While in practice this risk may be considered small (since it is likely that the participants and the trustees should be prepared to sell the shares to the purchaser rather than become minority shareholders in a subsidiary of the purchaser), it is nevertheless a risk which the purchaser will need to take into account. If practicable, the purchaser may wish to seek assurance from the participants/trustees that they will accept the purchaser's offer for the shares (see **5.17** below), and

   (ii)   in some share option schemes, the rules are such that the options may continue to be exercisable after the compulsory acquisition period. This again means that there is a risk that the purchaser may not be able to compulsorily acquire the shares allotted on exercise of the options. Again, if practicable, the purchaser may wish to seek assurance from the participants that they will exercise their options early and accept the purchaser's offer in respect of the shares acquired (see **5.16** below on further issues relating to share option schemes).

Treatment of 'early leavers'

5.15   Generally, the design of an employee share scheme will ensure that a participant will get the full benefit under the scheme if he remains in employment throughout the whole incentive period. However, there are circumstances when it may be felt that a participant (an 'early leaver') who leaves the employ of the seller (or the seller's group of companies) to which the scheme relates should nevertheless get some (if not all) of the benefits.

Typically, a distinction will be drawn between 'good leavers' (i.e. those who leave through reasons beyond their control, eg redundancy, ill-health or sale of his employing company or business) and 'bad leavers' (i.e. those who voluntarily resign or are dismissed for, for example, incompetence or misconduct).

In the context of an acquisition of a business or a subsidiary company, the rules of the employee share schemes will often treat the affected participants as good leavers. In share option schemes, it is common for the exercise period for options (whether granted under an approved share option scheme or an unapproved share option scheme) to be accelerated for good leavers. In other words, their options are exercisable early but will subsequently lapse early, eg they may be able to exercise their options for a period of six months from cessation of employment with the seller (or the seller's group). In other share schemes, the awards will vest in part in good leavers. Bad leavers will get nothing – their options or awards will lapse immediately on cessation of employment with the seller or the seller's group.

In the approved share incentive plan, shares in the trust will have to be transferred to the employee on his leaving employment. The treatment of early leavers granted EMI options will depend on the terms of the options.

There are various issues relating to the treatment of early leavers which the purchaser will need to address:

(a)   In some schemes, the benefits (if any) which an early leaver (whether good or bad) will receive will depend on the board of directors (or remuneration committee) of the seller. If this is the case, the purchaser should ascertain and (if appropriate) seek assurance from the seller that the participants affected by the acquisition will be treated favourably. Otherwise, the purchaser may end up inheriting some disgruntled employees who feel that they have lost out as a result of the acquisition.

(b)   If the vesting of awards or exercise of options is dependent upon the satisfaction of performance conditions, it should be established whether such conditions will apply to the early leavers. Again, if the matter is at the seller's discretion, the purchaser may wish to seek assurance that the participants affected by the acquisition will not be adversely treated.

(c)   The early exercise of HMRC approved options may result in adverse tax consequences for the participants. As described at **5.4** above, in order to obtain income tax relief when the option granted under a company share option scheme is exercised, it must be exercised between three to ten years of the date of grant. Income tax relief will not be available on the exercise of an option granted under an SAYE scheme if it has been granted for less than three years. Various exceptions apply including where the exercise is as a result of a participant's redundancy. In *Chapman v CPS Computer Systems plc* [1987] IRLR 462 it was held that an exercise of options following a transfer of business (not a sale of shares) qualified for income tax relief even though the options were granted for less than three years. The participants were treated as having been made redundant even though the *Transfer of Undertakings (Protection of Employment) Regulations 1981 (SI 1981/1794)* applied to the transfer.

(d)   Where options under the SAYE scheme are exercised early, participants can only purchase the number of shares using the proceeds of the savings contracts up to the date of exercise. In other words, they will only be able to acquire a fraction of the original number of shares under the options. Similar principles apply to the early purchase of partnership shares by an employee under the approved share incentive plan.

Participants in employee share schemes may often be disadvantaged as a result of becoming early leavers following an acquisition. The purchaser should establish the impact the acquisition has on such participants and (where appropriate) seek the seller's cooperation to ensure that any adverse consequences are minimised. In some cases, it may also be appropriate to compensate such participants for their loss of share scheme benefits caused by the acquisition. Such costs should be factored into the price negotiation with the seller.

Share option schemes in acquisitions

5.16   As share option schemes are the most common type of employee share schemes, this section describes the arrangements which a purchaser may make in respect of the target's option schemes in an acquisition.

Where the acquisition is a public bid, the City Code on Take-overs and Mergers provides that the purchaser must make an 'appropriate offer or proposal' to option holders 'to ensure that their interests are safeguarded' on terms that ensure equality of treatment. Whenever practicable, this offer or proposal should be made at the same time as the offer document is posted. If this is not possible, the offer or proposal should be despatched as soon as possible thereafter. Change of control typically occurs when the purchaser's offer is declared or becomes unconditional.

As mentioned at **5.14** above, the rules of share option schemes typically provide that options become exercisable on a change of control for a limited period, after which they will lapse. The optionholders can then sell their shares to the purchaser on the same terms as those applicable to other shareholders. Early exercise of HMRC approved options may result in adverse tax consequences for the optionholders (see **5.15** above). For optionholders under an SAYE scheme, early exercise also means that they will only be able to acquire a fraction of the shares subject to the options (see **5.15** above). A purchaser should also ascertain whether the exercise period of the options may continue beyond the compulsory acquisition period (see **5.14** above).

Apart from the exercise of options on a change of control, the purchaser may wish to propose to the optionholders alternative ways to deal with their options. The common alternatives are:

(a)   the cancellation of options for cash; and

(b)   the exchange of options over the target's shares for new options over the purchaser's shares.

The purchaser may be prepared to offer optionholders cash in return for cancelling their options. This is often called the cash cancellation proposal. The amount of cash will typically be determined by multiplying the excess of the offer price over the exercise price by the number of shares subject to the options (or, in the case of an SAYE scheme, the number of shares optionholders may obtain using the proceeds of their savings contracts on the date of exercise). The cash payment will be subject to an income tax charge and may not, therefore, be attractive to optionholders who will obtain income tax relief on exercise of HMRC approved options. For other optionholders, accepting the cash cancellation proposal will mean that the optionholders will not need to fund the exercise costs. Optionholders under an SAYE scheme will also be able to continue saving in order to benefit from the tax-free bonuses payable on the maturity of their savings contracts.

As mentioned above, optionholders in HMRC approved option schemes are often disadvantaged on early exercise of options as a result of an acquisition. The adverse effects can be avoided if the rules of the schemes allow for (and the purchaser agrees to) the options over the target's shares being exchanged for new options over the purchaser's shares. This is often called a roll-over of the options. There are detailed HMRC requirements for a roll-over which will typically be set out in the rules of the approved schemes:

(a)   the exchange of options must take place within the 'appropriate period' meaning, broadly, six months after the change of control of the target and, if the compulsory acquisition procedure is triggered, the compulsory acquisition period;

(b)   the new options will remain governed by the rules of the target's schemes – they will be treated as if they were granted at the date the original options were granted and will be exercisable in accordance with the rules;

(c)   the shares used for the roll-over must satisfy various statutory conditions. Broadly:

(i)   the shares must comprise shares in the ordinary share capital of the purchaser (or its parent), and

(ii)   must be fully paid up, not redeemable and not subject to any restrictions (other than restrictions applicable to all shares of the same class), and

(iii)   the company whose shares are used must either be listed on a recognised stock exchange, an independent company or a subsidiary of a listed company. Also, unless there is only one class of ordinary shares, the shares must fulfil further conditions so that HMRC can be satisfied that they are not of an 'inferior' class to shares held by other shareholders.

It should be noted that the statutory conditions applicable to shares which can be used in an EMI scheme are less onerous. For example, the shares can be subject to restrictions such as limited voting rights or pre-emption rights requiring sale of the shares on termination of employment.

(d)   the bases of the roll-over will have to be agreed with HMRC. Broadly:

(i)   the total market value of the shares subject to the old option immediately before the exchange must be equal to the total market value of the shares subject to the new options immediately after the exchange,

(ii)   the total exercise price payable by the optionholder on the exercise of the new option must be equal to the total exercise price payable by the optionholder under the old option.

There are no income or capital gains tax consequences for the optionholders in a roll-over of HMRC approved options in accordance with the provisions of schemes. A roll-over may be attractive to optionholders as:

(i)   they will not need to exercise their options early and will be able to exercise the options in due course in a manner which attracts income tax relief;

(ii)   optionholders in an SAYE scheme will also be able to continue saving and exercise the options to the full extent on the maturity of the savings contracts.

While roll-over is most common in the context of approved options, there is no reason why the purchaser may not offer this in respect of unapproved options or awards under long-term incentive schemes. Before offering a roll-over, the purchaser may need to consider the impact this will have on the operation of its own share schemes. If it is a listed company, its share schemes may well contain various dilution limits to comply with institutional investors' guidelines (see **5.13** above). Allowing options over the target's shares to be exchanged for options over the purchaser's shares may restrict the number of shares which may be issued for options or awards granted in future under the purchaser's own share schemes.

Whatever proposals are made by the purchaser, they have to be carefully explained to the optionholders. In particular, the following issues (if relevant) will need to be pointed out:

(a)   the adverse tax consequence (if any) which may affect an optionholder if he accepts a cash cancellation instead of exercising an approved option;

(b)   if an optionholder accepts a roll-over, the 'value' of his option will depend on the share price of the purchaser (which could go down);

(c)   after a roll-over, the new option will not then be exercisable early other than in circumstances set out in the rules of the target's scheme. If the optionholder subsequently becomes a bad leaver, he may lose his option.

The optionholders should be encouraged to seek independent advice if they have any doubts or queries as to what action to take.

Employee benefit trust

5.17   The structure of an employee benefit trust usually takes the following form:

(a)   the company establishes a trust to purchase shares in the company from the market or from existing shareholders;

(b)   the trust will be funded by gifts by the company or by borrowings. The cost of those borrowings would be met either by regular contributions from the company or by dividends received by the trustees;

(c)   a share incentive scheme of some kind best suited to the company's objectives will be set up and the trust will provide shares for distribution to employees under that scheme.

Where a company uses existing shares for its share incentive schemes (because it does not want to issue new shares or cannot do so as it has already used up all the new shares available within the limits, for example, prescribed by institutional investors), it may wish to establish an employee benefit trust. The following are some of the advantages of an employee benefit trust:

(a)   historically, a company would not receive any tax deduction for the economic costs for issuing shares to employees at a discount to the market value. If, however, the company made contributions to the employee benefit trust which then used the funds to subscribe for shares from the company, the company's contributions would be tax deductible provided that they were revenue in nature and incurred wholly and exclusively for the purpose of the company's trade. This has now been changed. Contributions to the trust will be tax deductible provided, broadly, that qualifying benefits are provided. To be a qualifying benefit, a transfer of shares must give rise to a charge to both income tax and national insurance contributions. (In addition, most companies may also now claim corporation tax relief for the amounts on which employees are (or, but for the availability of a statutory relief from income tax, would be) charged to income tax on the acquisition of qualifying shares in the employing company or an associated company.

The use of an employee benefit trust to enable tax relief to be claimed is, therefore, no longer necessary);

(b)   an employee benefit trust can hold shares which have been allocated to employees where the terms of the allocation provide that the employees must retain the shares for a period;

(c)   an employee benefit trust provides a mechanism for the repurchase of shares held by employees who are leaving the company. This will enable the shares to be used again for allocation to other employees;

(d)   an employee benefit trust is sometimes regarded as a defence against a hostile takeover. The trustees (insofar as this is consistent with their duty to act in the best interests of the beneficiaries under the trust) will generally vote in accordance with the recommendations of the company's directors.

An employee benefit trust could be used in conjunction with any of the HMRC approved share schemes or with other forms of unapproved share schemes.

There are various issues which a purchaser will need to consider where the target operates such a trust in conjunction with its employee share schemes:

(a)   as mentioned at **5.14** above, if 10% or more of the target's shares are held by the trustees, the purchaser may not be able to operate the compulsory acquisition procedure;

(b)   while the purchaser may wish to seek assurance at an early stage from the trustees that they will accept the purchaser's offer in respect of shares held in the trust, the trustees may not be in a position to do so if the shares are designated for satisfaction of share options and awards granted to employees;

(c)   if the employee benefit trust operates in conjunction with a share option scheme, it will not be appropriate for the purchaser to offer a cash cancellation of such options. Otherwise, the purchaser will effectively be paying twice if it has to offer cash to cancel the options and then pay to acquire the shares held in the trust.

New employee share schemes after the acquisition

5.18   If the affected employees accept a roll-over of options or awards into the purchaser's shares, there may be no immediate need to set up new share schemes for them. In other cases, the purchaser may want to consider what (if any) new arrangements should be put in place following the acquisition. Alternatively, the purchaser may already have existing arrangements for its own employees which it may wish to extend to the employees in the target.

What arrangements are adopted going forward may depend on how important it is to harmonise benefits between the purchaser's employees and the target's employees. Harmonisation is important because:

5.18 *Employee Share Schemes*

(a)   it gives equal treatment to all employees;

(b)   the target's employees may want to have the same benefits as the pur-
       chaser's employees or vice versa (depending on which set of benefits is
       more generous)! Harmonising share schemes benefits can be seen as
       conferring benefits uniformly throughout the group;

(c)   a harmonised scheme will also widen corporate identity. Employees in
       the subsidiary may not identify with the parent company. In this case,
       share schemes can provide a link between the parent and its subsidiary.

Chapter 6

Employment Responsibilities and Objectives

At a glance

- It is vital that employment issues are addressed early.

- It should be established whether a transaction is a sale of shares, a transfer of a business/undertaking (governed by *TUPE*) or a transfer of assets alone (*Note:* impact of *TUPE* on contracting-out).

- If a TUPE transfer, it should be established whether employee representatives need to be elected prior to being informed and consulted and this may significantly affect the timetable of the transaction. (*Note:* the *ICE Regulations* may impose an additional duty on larger employers to inform and consult, and *TUPE* has introduced a duty on the transferor to provide 'employee liability information' to the transferee.)

- It is important to identify contractual documentation for key personnel and standard documentation for other employees (as part of due diligence).

- The apportionment of risk as between seller and purchaser should be agreed and appropriate warranty and indemnity protection negotiated to reflect this.

- It is essential to be open with persons affected and their representatives.

Introduction

6.1   Whatever type of acquisition it is contemplating the purchaser will require personnel. The purchaser has the option of relying either on the workforce being acquired, on its existing workforce or most probably on a combination of both.

Depending on commercial considerations, the purchaser will wish to determine the following before signing contracts (if information is available, and where appropriate):

6.1   *Employment Responsibilities and Objectives*

(a)   which *directors* it wishes to retain (and whether they are prepared to stay);

(b)   who are the key *managers* (and whether they are prepared to stay);

(c)   whether there are any *workers* providing services under a contract for services and if so, whether the purchaser wishes to retain them; and

(d)   in relation to *all personnel* (including the above), what special considerations apply.

The purchaser will need to be aware of any special terms in the employees' contracts of employment. It must establish whether any independent trade unions are recognised, whether collective bargaining arrangements exist, and whether arrangements have been formalised for redundancy procedures (including consultation) and payments. It must consider how the retained personnel of the target will integrate with any existing personnel. Furthermore, it must examine the state of industrial relations within the target and consider how this can be maintained or improved.

Having obtained all available information, the purchaser will wish to plan which directors, managers or employees are either to be dismissed (whether by reason of redundancy, business reorganisation or otherwise) or to be retained on similar or different terms and conditions by a process of integration with the purchaser's existing workforce.

Different considerations apply depending on whether the acquisition in question is a purchase of shares, of assets only (such as plant or machinery), or a purchase of a business or undertaking as a going concern.

For employment purposes there are important differences between each of these types of acquisition. In the case of a purchase of shares, employees remain employed after the acquisition by the same company as previously. Where there is a purchase of assets only, employees remain employed by their existing employer and their employment is unaffected by the acquisition itself; in other words they do not automatically become employees within the purchaser's organisation. In the case of a purchase of a business or undertaking, the employees' contracts of employment are transferred by operation of law to the purchaser. This means that the purchaser assumes all the transferor's responsibilities under the employees' respective contracts. (See **6.15–6.16** and **6.32–6.34** below for the considerations respectively affecting a purchase of shares, a purchase of assets only and a purchase of a business or undertaking.)

The purchaser must address personnel matters as early as possible before signing contracts. Where the target is a listed company, the purchaser must take account, where appropriate, of constraints imposed by the need for confidentiality under the City Code on Takeovers and Mergers (the Takeover Code) and the United Kingdom Listing Authority listing rules (the Listing Rules). Where the target is a private company, any confidentiality constraints will normally be set out in the confidentiality agreement between the parties. In particular, the purchaser must meet and consult with key personnel to be retained at all levels as early as possible to secure their support and goodwill.

Identifying the contract of employment

6.2   One of the first steps that a purchaser should take is to determine the nature of all contracts of employment held by employees in the target organisation. It should request copies of the written statements of employment (or, in a large acquisition, a specimen with a schedule of copies) which employees should have received from their employer. The employer is obliged by statute to provide each employee with a written statement containing certain particulars of employment within two months of the date that employment commences (in accordance with *section 1* of the *Employment Rights Act 1996* (*ERA 1996*)) and subsequently to notify each employee in writing of any changes in the terms of employment required to be included or referred to in the principal statement within one month of the change. [*ERA 1996, s 4*]. Note that further particulars may be contained in instalments issued separately from the principal statement. Although a written statement is not of itself a contract of employment, employers will often ask their employees to sign a copy of the statement and thereby agree that its terms constitute the terms of their contracts of employment.

The purchaser should note carefully that a written contract of employment is not necessarily the entire contract. There is no legal requirement that all the terms of a contract of employment or, indeed, that the contract itself, be in writing. Oral variations may be legally binding. (*Simmonds v Dowty Seals Ltd* [1978] IRLR 211 (EAT)). A written statement may therefore not contain all of the important terms of an employee's terms and conditions of employment.

Pre-contractual considerations

6.3   The purchaser should not seek to rely solely on the content of employment documentation made available by the seller unless suitable warranties are to be given by the seller confirming that the information in question is up to date and correct in all material respects. To ensure that it receives all the necessary information in relation to contracts of employment, the purchaser should request information with respect to each different category of employee in the target organisation in accordance with **6.5** and **6.13** below.

Directors (executive directors)

At a glance

6.4

(a)   If a director is to be retained, the purchaser will need to assess the cost of retaining him and other integration costs.

(b)   If a director is to be removed, the purchaser should establish the consequent costs.

(c)   In relation to each director, the purchaser needs to know the length of notice required to terminate the employment.

(d)   Where, as the result of a share acquisition, there is a change of control in the director's employing company, a 'golden parachute' clause in his service agreement can offer him additional protection.

(e)   The presence of a 'garden leave' clause in service agreements of departing directors may be of considerable assistance to a purchaser.

(f)   The purchaser should determine whether post-termination restrictive covenants in service agreements of departing directors will survive the termination of their employment and whether they are enforceable, in order to enable the purchaser to protect the goodwill of the target.

(g)   The purchaser should consider details of all remuneration arrangements and benefits, with information and details of each director's entitlement, including any share option schemes.

Directors – general considerations

6.5   Directors are possibly the most important personnel for the purchaser to consider when assessing a proposed acquisition and they therefore require special consideration. If a director is to be retained, the purchaser should establish that he supports the incoming management and is willing to stay. The purchaser will need to assess the cost of retaining him and the other costs of integration.

If a director is not to be retained, the purchaser should establish the cost of dismissing him. If there is a risk that the director will subsequently commence work for a competitor thereby constituting a threat to the new business, the purchaser should establish what steps, if any, may be taken to minimise this threat.

In relation to each director the purchaser should consider the following:

(a)   the director's service agreement; and

(b)   details of all benefits, contractual or discretionary, with information and details of each director's entitlement, for example any share option or other incentive schemes (see **6.12** below).

When the purchaser decides to remove a director there are a number of factors which should be borne in mind. Some of these will work in favour of the director, others in favour of the purchaser; this will depend on the particular type of agreement made between the target and the director.

Notice of termination

6.6   As with other employees, the purchaser needs to know the length of notice required to terminate a director's employment.

A director's service agreement will generally contain a fixed term of employment, a 'rolling' period of notice or a substantial minimum period of notice of termination from the company to the director. A limit is placed on the length of such periods of notice by *section 319* of the *Companies Act 1985* (*CA 1985*). (This section will be repealed by the *Companies Act 2006* – the repeal date is still to be appointed, but is expected during the course of 2007.) This provides that, in relation to any company other than a wholly-owned subsidiary of another company, any term in a director's service agreement which gives him the right to a notice period in excess of five years is void unless the term has been first approved by the shareholders of that company in general meeting. If the proper procedure has not been followed, the director will be deemed to be entitled to 'reasonable' notice of the termination of his employment.

The latest edition of the Combined Code on Corporate Governance (the Combined Code) was issued in June 2005, and gives principles and provisions that a company should abide by where it is listed or seeking a listing. Listed companies must comply with the Combined Code for financial years beginning on or after 1 November 2006. One of the provisions of the Combined Code is that a director's notice or contract periods should be set at one year or less, although it does make a concession where it is necessary to offer longer notice or contract periods to new directors recruited from outside. Even so, such periods should be reduced to one year or less after the initial period.

In the absence of any term, express or implied, as to notice, the director will be entitled to 'reasonable' notice of the termination of his employment. What is reasonable will depend on all the material circumstances of the case, including the director's age, length of service, position, responsibilities and any special circumstances such as whether the director relocated to take up the position.

Reasonable notice will not be less than the statutory minimum period of notice contained in *section 86* of *ERA 1996* (up to a maximum of 12 weeks' notice after 12 or more years of continuous employment), and may well be more. For directors and senior executives, it is unusual for reasonable notice to exceed twelve months and very often six or even three months will be appropriate. (*Hill v CA Parsons & Co Ltd* [1972] Ch 305, [1971] 3 All ER 1345).

Removal of directors

Statutory provisions: share purchase

6.7   Where the shares of the target are being acquired by the purchaser, there may be provisions in the Articles of Association of the target relating to the removal of directors; however, these will not often pose a problem to the purchaser for several reasons. Firstly, the vendor will usually procure the resignations of directors on whatever terms it can. If it is not successful, the deal will be unlikely to proceed. Secondly, a director will often also be a vendor, in which case he will usually resign of his own accord. Thirdly, if departing directors refuse to resign, *section 303* of *CA 1985* (this section will be repealed by the *Companies Act 2006* – the repeal date is still to be appointed, but is expected during the course of 2007) provides for their removal by ordinary resolution, of which special notice has been given, notwithstanding anything in the target company's Articles to the contrary. This procedure allows the director concerned to make representations opposing the resolution to the members of the company who are voting on the resolution and does not affect any right he may have for compensation or damages. Where, however, the Articles provide for weighted voting rights, a director may be able effectively to block any resolution to remove him (see *Bushell v Faith* [1970] AC 1099). However, in practice, weighted voting rights are only likely to be held by vendor directors and this is, therefore, unlikely to be an issue. A subsidiary company's Articles will usually contain a summary procedure for removal of directors which overrides *section 303* (see above).

It should be noted that a removed director should also be dismissed from employment.

'Golden parachute': share purchase

6.8   Where, as the result of a share acquisition, there is a change of control in the director's employing company, a 'golden parachute' clause in his service agreement can offer him additional protection. Typically such a clause will give the director the following benefits:

(a)   the right to resign with immediate effect and treat his employment as terminated without being in breach of contract; and

(b)   the right to receive a payment from the company. This payment would usually be taxable as an emolument under the normal PAYE rules.

Any sums payable on the exercise by a director of his rights under a golden parachute clause may be payable in addition to or, more often, in substitution for sums payable in lieu of notice or by way of damages for the termination in breach of the director's service contract.

The board of a company which proposes to grant a director a golden parachute must, of course, be satisfied that it is in the interests of the company to do so. In addition, the board of a company which is subject to the Takeover Code (including all public companies and certain private companies) must note the implications of the Takeover Code for service agreements of directors of an offeree company. General Principle 76 and Rule 21 (which restrict actions which would frustrate a takeover bid) can be relevant, but will not apply if no *bona fide* offer has been communicated to the board of directors and the board has no reason to believe that a *bona fide* offer may be imminent. Where an offer has been communicated or is believed to be imminent, the board will ordinarily need to consult with the Panel on Takeovers and Mergers on any proposed amendment to a director's service agreement which represents a significant improvement in his terms of service or an abnormal increase in his emoluments. The company is likely to be required to obtain approval of the proposal by the shareholders of the company in general meeting.

'Garden leave' clause

6.9 The presence of a 'garden leave' clause in the service agreements of departing directors may be of considerable assistance to a purchaser who needs to remove those directors quickly from their executive roles but wishes to hold them to certain obligations that they have to their employing company.

The purpose of a garden leave clause is to give an employer the right to hold a director (or sometimes another key employee) to his service agreement for all or part of the unexpired period of that agreement without having to offer him the work which he would otherwise be entitled to receive. This can be helpful either when the director wishes to leave early or when the employer no longer wishes to retain him. Where, for example, a key director resigns from his employment without giving due contractual notice (i.e. where he resigns in breach of contract), such a clause gives the employer the right to refuse to accept the director's breach, to hold the director to the terms of his contract, to relieve him of his duties and responsibilities and, effectively, to require him not to work for any employer for the remainder of his notice period. The employer will have to continue paying the director in accordance with his contractual obligations but it will not have to provide work for the director during this period (*Spencer v Marchington* [1988] IRLR 392; *Evening Standard Co Ltd v Henderson* [1987] IRLR 64). The director will continue to owe his obligations to his employer pursuant to his contract of employment; however the wider employer-employee relationship will cease (*Symbian Ltd v Christensen* [2000] UKCLR 879) and with it any general duties inherent in that relationship, such as not working for competitors of the employer, unless such duties are expressly incorporated in the service agreement. This is of particular importance to employers because of the difficulties of enforcing *post-termination* covenants against competition, dealt with below at **6.10**. Although the use of garden leave clauses is common, there is some doubt as to their enforceability and in particular the extent to which the employer must continue to provide work. (*Provident Financial Group plc and Whitegates Estate Agency Ltd v Hayward* [1989] IRLR 84; see also *William Hill Organisation Ltd v Tucker* [1998] IRLR 313 in which it was held that there was no implied right to impose garden leave in the absence of an express restraint; *Symbian* (see above); and *Hutchings v Coinseed Ltd* [1998] IRLR 190 in which it was held that exceptionally an employee on garden leave could work for a competitor without being in repudiatory breach of contract). The purchaser will need to consider each case on its merits.

Post-termination restrictive covenants

6.10 The ability to enforce post-termination restrictive covenants in the service agreements of departing directors may be of great importance to the purchaser in order to enable it to protect the goodwill of the target which it is acquiring.

Restrictive covenants will typically include:

(a)   a covenant by the director not to *solicit* the business of customers or clients of his employer with whom he dealt during a specified period prior to the termination of his employment for a period thereafter;

(b)   a covenant by the director similar to (*a*) but providing that the director may not *deal* with such customers or clients even if they wish him to do so (see *PR Consultants Scotland Limited v Mann* [1996] IRLR 188);

(c)   a covenant by the director not to *entice* away other employees of his employer whether or not they would leave in breach of contract;

(d)   a covenant by the director not to approach suppliers of his employer in certain circumstances;

(e)   a covenant by the director not to work in any business which competes with that of his employer for a stated period.

The scope of any of these covenants is commonly extended to cover other companies in the group of companies of which the employer is a member, although such extended covenants may be very difficult to enforce.

In each case the purchaser must determine firstly that the covenant will survive the termination of the director's employment, and secondly that the covenant is enforceable, for example that it does not constitute an unreasonable restraint of trade. Where the director is also a vendor, the purchaser can obtain new restrictive covenants from him as part of the sale terms.

When considering any restrictive covenant in a director's service agreement, the purchaser should consider in relation to such covenant whether the business has an interest meriting protection, whether the restraint is reasonable between the parties and whether the restraint is reasonable in the public interest. The reasonableness or otherwise of a covenant will depend upon many factors including: the nature and scope of the business or customer connection for which the employer seeks protection; the status or position of the employee; the geographical area of the restriction imposed; and the duration of the restraint. If the covenant fails on any of these counts, it is unlikely to be enforceable. The purchaser should also bear in mind the possible application (although only in limited circumstances) of the *Restrictive Trade Practices Act 1976* which stipulates that a previous failure to register service agreements containing restrictive covenants could render such covenants void. This will only apply to service agreements which should have been registered before the act was repealed.

Each of the covenants listed above may be *prima facie* enforceable as a matter of legal principle (depending of course on the particular circumstances) except, generally, the non-competition covenant (*e*). A covenant which restricts a director from competing in any way will often be void as an unreasonable restraint of trade (*Morris (Herbert) Ltd v Saxelby* [1916] 1 AC 688; *D v M* [1996] IRLR 192; *Scully UK Ltd v Lee* [1998] IRLR 259). However, it is sometimes possible to enforce a non-competition covenant contained in a service agreement where the scope of the covenant is narrowly defined and limited in relation to its duration and geographical area (see *Lansing Linde Ltd v Kerr* [1991] IRLR 80). Where an employer attempts to enforce a garden leave provision and restrictive covenant, a court will consider the reasonableness of the combined duration of the restraints in determining whether to enforce them (*Credit Suisse Asset Management Limited v Armstrong and others* [1996] IRLR 450). In appropriate circumstances, where departing directors are also proprietors of the target and are selling shares to the purchaser, the purchaser should seek to include appropriate restrictive covenants, particularly non-competition covenants, into the acquisition agreement. Where a non-competition covenant is given on the sale of goodwill it may well be enforceable against the covenantor (*Allied Dunbar (Frank Weisinger) Limited v Frank Weisinger* [1988] IRLR 60).

In *Dentmaster (UK) Ltd v Kent* [1997] IRLR 636 the Court of Appeal upheld the enforceability of a restraint which prevented solicitation ((*a*) above) for a period of six months after termination of any person or business who was a client of the employer during the six-month period prior to termination and with whom the employee had dealt in the course of employment.

A non-enticement covenant ((*c*) above), will need to be very narrowly drawn in order to give the greatest chance of being enforced by the courts. (See *Alliance Paper Group plc v Prestwich* [1996] IRLR 26 and *SBJ Stephenson Ltd v Mandy* [2000] IRLR 233 in which non-enticement covenants were upheld. However, the High Court in *TSC Europe (UK) Ltd v Massey* [1999] IRLR 22 (see above) held that a non-enticement covenant was unenforceable because it prohibited solicitation irrespective of seniority, technical knowledge or experience).

In considering the enforceability of restrictive covenants, the court may apply the 'blue pencil' rule by deleting words or phrases in the covenant if they are independent and the covenant remains meaningful thereafter. However, the court will not rewrite the covenant. (*Business Seating (Renovations) Ltd v Broad* [1989] ICR 729). The principles of severance were reiterated in the case of *Marshall v NM Financial Management Limited* [1996] IRLR 20.

The court at its discretion *may* also not enforce a provision seeking to save a covenant by diluting it, even where the contract of employment has been terminated unlawfully (see *Living Design (Home Improvements) Ltd v Davidson* [1994] IRLR 67).

The court will not grant an injunction which compels an employee to work in accordance with his contract of employment.

Note that on a transfer of an undertaking, the *Transfer of Undertakings (Protection of Employment) Regulations 2006* ('*TUPE*') (*SI 2006/246*) have the effect of transferring a restrictive covenant from the transferor to the purchaser, along with the business. However, the covenant can only be enforced by the purchaser in order to protect the business interests of the transferor, and (for example) a one-year covenant will cease to have effect one year after the transfer. (Note the possible implications for a transferee attempting to enforce restrictive covenants entered into by an employee with the transferor before the transfer (*William West & Sons (Ilkeston) Ltd v (1) Mr W Fairgieve & ors (2) EXEL/BRS Ltd* EAT/701/98).) It may be sensible for the purchaser to require the transferor to enter into new covenants with employees, ahead of the transfer (*Morris Angel & Son Ltd v Hollande* [1993] RLR 169).

A word of warning – where the purchaser dismisses a director in breach of contract, this will generally result in any continuing obligations of the director after his dismissal, including restrictive covenants, being terminated along with the contract (*General Billposting Co Ltd v Atkinson* [1909] AC 118 (HL)). However, an otherwise reasonable covenant which purports to remain binding in circumstances where the law will inevitably strike it down (i.e. if the employment is terminated unlawfully) should not on this account be held to be in unlawful restraint of trade and could be enforced (*Rock Refrigeration Limited v Jones & Seward Refrigeration Limited* [1996] IRLR 675, overruling the Court of Appeal's judgment in *D v M* (see above)).

Negotiations with departing directors

6.11   Although, in practice, the onus will usually be on the vendor to procure the resignation of the director, a director who feels that he has been unfairly treated or paid less than his contractual entitlement may decide to commence proceedings for unfair dismissal and/or wrongful dismissal against the purchaser. To minimise his exposure in this respect when negotiating terms with a departing director, and to ensure that the departure is handled lawfully and fairly, the purchaser should consider the following:

(a)   the director's age and prospects of obtaining alternative employment (applying an appropriate discount to any compensation payment on account of mitigation);

(b)   the need to be fair and the need to be seen to be fair by retained employees in the manner and terms of dismissal;

(c)   any previous practice in the business in relation to terminations and the risk of creating a precedent for the future;

(d)   the need to hold directors to their periods of notice and whether there is a discretion or right to payment in lieu of notice (see *Abrahams v The Performing Rights Society* [1995] IRLR 486; *Cerberus Software Limited v Rowley* [2001] IRLR 160; *Gregory v Wallace* [1998] IRLR 387);

(e)   the need to be able to enforce restrictive covenants against directors after the termination of their employment;

(f)   the availability of a tax-free lump sum for directors (currently a maximum of £30,000) by way of compensation for loss of office, depending on the circumstances; alternatively, in cases of early retirement, the availability of a tax-free lump sum where the director is able to commute part of his pension entitlement (but note that any *ex gratia* payment paid on or in anticipation of retirement is likely to be taxable in full);

(g)   the possibility of leaving directors on the payroll for a period to facilitate the exercise of options or other share incentives or the enhancement of pension benefits (and also to ease the company's disclosure
requirements in its annual report and accounts);

(h)   the need for a compromise agreement issued in compliance with *section 203(1)* of *ERA 1996* to prevent a director from subsequently pursuing a claim in an employment tribunal for compensation for unfair
dismissal (although a general 'blanket' agreement compromising all
possible claims, including contemporaneous claims and ones that have
not yet arisen, is not permitted (*Lunt v Merseyside TEC* [1999] IRLR
458), whereas an agreement which expressly gives the particulars of
any current or expected claims is permissible (*Hinton v University of
East London* [2005] IRLR 552)); or, alternatively, an ACAS form
COT3 (although ACAS will only provide such a form where there is a
dispute between the parties); and

(i)   as an alternative to (h), the withholding by the purchaser of a sufficient
amount of any compensation for the limitation period from the date of
termination of employment in which the employee/director would normally be required to commence tribunal proceedings, unless not reasonably practicable for him to do so (currently three months).

Should the purchaser be unable to reach satisfactory compensation arrangements with a departing director, there may be good tactical reasons for withdrawing from negotiations, prompting the director to issue proceedings in the
High Court or County Court for damages in wrongful dismissal. Under *Part
36* of the *Civil Procedure Rules 1998 (SI 1998/3132)* offers of settlement may
be made by the claimant director or by the defendant at any stage before or
after proceedings have been commenced.

If the claimant director fails to accept the defendant's Part 36 offer within the
period stated in the offer, but presses ahead with the proceedings, and he is
subsequently awarded by the court a sum less than that offered by the defendant, he will usually have to bear a substantial part of the defendant's legal
costs from the latest date on which the payment could have been accepted,
interest on those costs, together with his own costs. If he is awarded a greater
sum, the defendant will usually have to pay a substantial part of the claimant
director's costs as well as his own costs. If the claimant accepts the defendant's offer, the defendant must make the payment within 14 days or he will
lose the cost protection provided by Part 36.

If the claimant director makes a Part 36 offer and recovers as much or more
than he offered to accept, then he will usually get, from the latest date on
which his offer could have been accepted, indemnity costs (ie on a basis more
generous to the recipient) and a higher rate of interest on the amount awarded
and on the costs than he would otherwise receive.

Careful use of the Part 36 procedure will often help to promote settlements of
disputes of this nature.

The *Civil Procedure Rules 1998* also provide for the approval of 'pre-action protocols' ('PAPs'). The PAPs are designed to encourage settlement of claims by requiring the parties to follow a reasonable timetable in pre-action correspondence and to exchange information with each other. PAPs are approved in relation to particular types of claim, such as personal injury, construction and engineering disputes or medical negligence. None has yet been approved for wrongful dismissal claims in the High Court or county court. Nevertheless litigants are expected to apply the 'spirit' of the PAPs in pre-action dealings and to follow a reasonable pre-action procedure. In particular, claimants are expected to provide prospective defendants with a detailed letter of claim and to wait a reasonable period for the defendant to respond before issuing proceedings. If the parties fail to comply with the spirit of the protocols, they may be penalised in costs or be required to pay money into court. The court may also stay the proceedings for a month at a time to allow settlement negotiations or mediation to take place.

Although departing directors will often negotiate in the hope or expectation of being paid damages for the full unexpired period of their contracts, they will not necessarily be entitled to this. Damages payable to a director will be discounted by a court for a number of reasons, including most importantly mitigation (where the court must take account of any remuneration earned or likely to be earned by the director in reduction of his loss, bearing in mind his obligation to take reasonable steps to mitigate the same) and the accelerated receipt of the money in the director's hands. The Combined Code (which applies to listed companies) recommends that a 'robust line' should be taken on payment of compensation where performance has been unsatisfactory and on reducing compensation to reflect departing directors' obligations to mitigate loss. The purchaser should always consider applying such discounts in negotiations whilst bearing in mind the specific terms of the directors' contracts. In the event that agreement is reached with a director as to the terms of any payment for loss of office, consideration should be given to *sections 312, 313, 314* and *320* of CA 1985 (this section will be repealed by the *Companies Act 2006* – the repeal date is still to be appointed, but is expected during the course of 2007) which may require the payment to be approved by the company in general meeting (before it is paid). Such approval will not be necessary if the payment is a *bona fide* payment by way of damages for breach of contract or by way of pension in respect of past services. [*CA 1985, s 316(3)*] (see above).

Remuneration of directors

6.12   The purchaser must consider the remuneration arrangements of directors in the target because of the implications for directors being retained and for departing directors. These arrangements may be set out in the terms of directors' service agreements or may have come into being outside such agreements. In addition to salary, directors will often enjoy bonus or profit-sharing arrangements or be entitled to benefit under share incentive schemes.

Bonus or profit sharing arrangements or long-term incentive plans may exist where substantial sums may be payable as of right or merely on a discretionary basis, and where payment may be based on a formula which will need to be adjusted following the acquisition.

Share incentive arrangements may be a material consideration. In the event of an acquisition of shares, share incentive schemes often provide that options will become exercisable or awards of shares will vest immediately following the change of control. If the purchaser is unable to acquire the shares thus obtained by the employees, this may give rise to problems if those shares are held by departing directors or employees. The purchaser may wish to consider offering cash payments to option or award holders to buy out their rights at the time of the acquisition. Where the Takeover Code applies to a transaction, the purchaser must put appropriate proposals to all option-holders to ensure that their interests are safeguarded. In the case of retained directors, the purchaser may wish to take advantage of any provision in the scheme permitting participants to exchange their options or awards over shares in the vendor company for options or awards over shares in the purchaser's company (which is subject always to the purchaser's consent). In certain circumstances such a provision will maintain Her Majesty's Revenue and Customs' approval of share options, and may also help to secure the goodwill of the retained directors. (For further details see **Chapter 5 Employee Share Schemes**.)

Where as a result of a director's employment being terminated he loses the benefit of share incentive arrangements (eg where he has held options for an insufficient period to be able to exercise them as of right before such termination) there will often be a clause in the share incentive scheme disentitling him from the right to claim additional compensation in respect of the benefits under that scheme which he has lost as the result of his employment being terminated. In such circumstances, the director's rights differ depending on whether he is claiming unfair dismissal or wrongful dismissal. In the case of *Casey v Texas Home Fires Ltd* (1988 IDS Brief 376 EAT), an unfairly-dismissed employee was held to be entitled to compensation for loss of share options; however, in the case of *Micklefield v SAC Technology Ltd* [1990] IRLR 218, the court held that a wrongfully-dismissed employee could not recover damages for the lost opportunity to exercise share options where such a clause was present in the option scheme. (Note that the position is different in Scotland where the *Unfair Contract Terms Act 1977* may render the exclusion clause void.) Such a clause must be very clearly drafted as the court is likely to construe any ambiguity against the employer. In practice (where possible), employers may wish to procure that appropriate discretions are exercised to give departing directors the right to exercise options or receive shares at a later date, notwithstanding the termination of their employment, as this gives them valuable compensation without the need for a cash payment from the employing company.

Managers and all other employees

6.13   Just as it is important for the purchaser to familiarise itself with the matters discussed above in relation to directors, a similar exercise should be carried out in relation to managers and other employees. Particular emphasis should be placed on key managers who will often be prime candidates for future appointment as directors and should be identified immediately.

The purchaser should meet managers and, where appropriate, employees as early as it can to secure their goodwill. Their terms and conditions of employment should be analysed carefully to ensure that steps are taken to make the transition as trouble-free as possible.

The following information (*at least*) should be obtained by the purchaser:

(a)　a list of all employees (including key managers) identifying their date of birth, period of service, pay and notice entitlement (this will often be provided in the form of a schedule to the acquisition agreement which is warranted as correct by the seller) including details of employees who may not wish to transfer their employment to the purchaser;

(b)　a list of all workers providing services under a contract for services;

(c)　all available contracts of employment including any standard form contract of employment or statement of terms and conditions as required by *section 1* of *ERA 1996*;

(d)　any employee handbook and any employment-related policies and procedures not included in such a handbook;

(e)　details of additional benefits whether contractual or discretionary;

(f)　details of any option scheme rules and details of grants of options;

(g)　any pension scheme trust deed, rules and information booklet and any actuarial valuation;

(h)　details of company car arrangements;

(i)　a diagram of personnel structure by department or location;

(j)　details of health and safety policies and records, identifying any problems and including details of the extent to which health and safety regulations have been complied with;

(k)　details of any grievances, disputes, appeals, pending claims or litigation with employees or former employees;

(l)　details of any employees given notice or dismissals effected by the vendor within the previous six months;

(m)　details of any redundancy policies or procedures including arrangements for collective consultation on redundancies or transfer of a business;

(n)　(in a TUPE situation – 'employee liability information', which the vendor has an obligation to provide and which should include, inter alia, details of any grievance or disciplinary proceedings, information of any court or Tribunal case, claim or action brought within the previous two years, and information of any collective agreement which will continue to apply to transferring employees after the transfer);

(o) details of maternity policy and identification of pregnant employees;

(p) details of absenteeism, sickness policy and records and identification of employees absent due to sickness; and

(q) details of service occupancies.

All employees – the purchaser's legal obligations

6.14 The legal obligations of a purchaser making an acquisition vary depending on the nature of the acquisition. Different considerations apply to a purchase of shares (see **6.16**), a purchase of mere assets (see **6.32**) and a purchase of a business or undertaking (see **6.34**).

Share acquisition

At a glance

6.15

(a) Where a company's shares are sold there is no transfer of the company itself but merely a change of its ownership; *TUPE* does not apply.

(b) Subject to any change of control provisions or golden parachute clauses, the contracts of employment of the employees of the acquired company are unaffected by the sale of the company's shares (though see **6.16** below).

(c) If the purchaser dismisses an employee in breach of contract by failure to give him due notice of termination as specified in the employee's contract, the employee may be wrongfully dismissed and the purchaser liable to pay the employee damages.

(d) The purchaser may wish to reorganise the acquired company to suit his purposes.

(e) Where an employee's terms and conditions of employment specify that he is employed at a specific location and contain no mobility clause, the employer cannot require him to move to a different location without committing a repudiatory breach of contract.

(f) Where an employer varies the terms of an employee's contract of employment without his consent and the variation is sufficiently serious, the employee may resign and claim that he has been constructively dismissed.

(g) Where a purchaser wishes to effect redundancies, as the employer it must act with great care when selecting any particular employee for redundancy.

Share acquisition – general

6.16 A company is a legal person with a separate and distinct identity from its shareholders (*Salomon v Salomon Company Ltd* [1897] AC 22).

Where a company's shares are sold there is no transfer of the company itself but merely a change in its ownership. *TUPE (SI 2006/246)*, which applies to acquisitions of a business or undertaking where no transfer of share owner-ship is involved, does not apply. This was confirmed by the Employment Appeal Tribunal ('EAT') in *Brookes v Borough Care Services* [1998] IRLR 636. (*TUPE* is discussed at **6.34** below.)

On a share acquisition the employees of the acquired company remain employed by that company after the sale. Subject to any 'change of control' provisions or golden parachute clauses, their contracts of employment are unaffected by the sale (although note the possible impact on the scope and enforceability of post-termination restraint clauses which apply to group companies). The purchaser of shares must treat the employees of the acquired company as the seller should have treated them prior to the purchase. In other words it must have regard at all times (*inter alia*) to the law of unfair dis-missal and wrongful dismissal, particularly if it wishes to carry out any inter-nal reorganisation.

Unfair and wrongful dismissal

6.17   In dealing with the general question of the law concerning dismissal, it has been necessary for reasons of limited space to be very selective with legal material and only matters of particular relevance have been included in this text. Purchasers and sellers alike should be wary of relying too closely on the brief summary of the law of unfair dismissal and wrongful dismissal which follows; this is intended only to highlight some of the most important material considerations. Readers requiring further detail are advised to refer to *Tolley's Employment Law*.

Unfair dismissal

6.18   The *Employment Rights Act 1996* provides certain employees with a statutory right not to be unfairly dismissed. [*ERA 1996, s 94*]. To possess this right, the employee must show that he was employed by his employer under a contract of employment, that he was 'dismissed' within the meaning of 'dis-missal' in the statute (see below) and that he was employed by his employer (or has continuous employment) for the necessary qualifying period, which is normally one year at the effective date of dismissal. [*ERA 1996, s 108(1)*, as amended by the *Unfair Dismissal and Statement of Reasons for Dismissal (Variation of Qualifying Period) Order 1999 (SI 1999/1436)*]. Where the dis-missal is for a reason that is classed as 'automatically unfair', then the employee only needs to show that he was employed by his employer under a contract of employment and that he was 'dismissed' within the meaning of 'dismissal' in the statute (see below). [*ERA 1996, s 108(3)*.]

The term 'dismissal' is defined in *section 95* of *ERA 1996* as covering the fol-lowing circumstances:

(a)   where the contract under which the employee is employed by the employer is terminated by the latter with or without notice; or

(b)   where under that contract the employee is employed for a fixed term and that term expires without being renewed under the same contract; or

(c)   where the employee terminates that contract with or without notice in circumstances such that he is entitled to terminate it without notice by reason of the employer's conduct.

Fair dismissal

6.19   A dismissal under *section 95* of *ERA 1996* may be fair if the employer can show first that the reason for it is acceptable under the terms of *section 98* of *ERA 1996*. Acceptable reasons include:

(a)   redundancy (see **6.30** below) [*ERA 1996, s 98(2)(c)*];

(b)   some other substantial reason, which includes a dismissal following a reorganisation for a sound business reason and a dismissal for an economic, technical or organisational reason entailing changes in the workforce (see **6.44** below for further explanation of how the latter term applies in the context of a transfer of a business) [*ERA 1996, s 98(1)(b)*]; and

(c)   conduct, where, for example, an employee unreasonably refuses to comply with a reasonable instruction to accept lawfully justifiable changes in his terms and conditions of employment [*ERA 1996, s 98(2)(b)*].

To ensure that the dismissal is fair the employer must also show that it has acted reasonably in all the circumstances, having regard to equity and the substantial merits of the case. [*ERA 1996, s 98(4)*].

Unfair dismissal – remedies

6.20   The awards which an employment tribunal may make in favour of an unfairly-dismissed employee include: *[ERA 1996, s 118]* a *basic award*, which is calculated on the basis of the length of time the employee has been with his employer, his rate of pay and his age (the current maximum as at February 2007 is £9,300 (£8,700 if the effective date of termination fell prior to 1 February 2007)); *a compensatory award*, designed to compensate the employee for losses suffered as a result of the dismissal (the current maximum as at February 2007 is £60,600 where the effective date of termination falls on or after 1 February 2007, although there is no limit on compensation awarded to an employee who has been unfairly dismissed or selected for redundancy for health and safety or public interest disclosure (i.e. whistleblowing) reasons); and/or an *order for reinstatement or re-engagement*. Additional compensation, including an employee's full arrears of pay, is payable in the event of a failure to comply with a reinstatement or re-engagement order. Other substantial awards may be made in relation to union-related dismissals. Where the reason for the employee's dismissal is found to be redundancy, the tribunal will award him a statutory redundancy payment in place of any basic award, which is calculated with a similar formula.

Wrongful dismissal

6.21 If the purchaser dismisses an employee in breach of contract by failing to give him due notice of termination as specified in the employee's contract, the employee may be wrongfully dismissed and the purchaser liable to pay the employee damages for wrongful dismissal. The purchaser should have regard in this context to the entitlement of the employee to a statutory minimum period of notice based on his length of continuous employment, which overrides any lesser period specified in his contract. [*ERA 1996, s 86*].

Save where the reason for dismissal justifies a summary dismissal on grounds, for example, of gross misconduct, which would not normally be a dismissal in breach of contract and where the employee would have no cause of action in wrongful dismissal, the reason for dismissal is usually irrelevant in cases of wrongful dismissal, and the employee will have a cause of action no matter how fairly he has been treated if he has not been given proper notice or paid compensation in lieu.

Wrongful dismissal – damages

6.22 A claim for wrongful dismissal may be brought either in the employment tribunal or before a court. An employment tribunal can only make a maximum award of £25,000 for a wrongful dismissal claim. [*Employment Tribunals Extension of Jurisdiction (England and Wales) Order 1994, (SI 1994/1623), Art 10*]. In contrast, there is no limit to the amount of damages that a court can award for wrongful dismissal. In assessing damages for breach of contract, the court or tribunal will endeavour to place the employee in the position in which he would have found himself if the contract had been performed (*Hadley v Baxendale* [1854] 9 Ex 341). Damages will include compensation for the loss of any contractual benefits during the notice period such as pension benefits (see *Derby Daily Telegraph Ltd v (1) The Pensions Ombudsman (2) Thompson* [1999] IRLR 476) or the provision of a company car (but see *Micklefield v SAC Technology Ltd* [1990] IRLR 218 at **6.12** above). In *Levett v Biotrace International plc* [1999] IRLR 375, a director who was wrongfully dismissed was entitled to exercise his share options notwithstanding a provision in the share option scheme that options would lapse where an employee was dismissed following disciplinary proceedings. The employer could not rely on his own breach of contract to disentitle the director from exercising options after termination.

Unfair and wrongful dismissal – overlap

6.23 In assessing a compensatory award for unfair dismissal or damages for wrongful dismissal, the employment tribunal or court will deduct any amounts already paid to the employee by his employer (including pay in lieu of notice), insofar as those amounts have reduced any loss suffered by the employee (*Babcock FATA Ltd v Addison* [1987] IRLR 173). [*ERA 1996, s 123*]. This is to prevent the employee from effectively being paid twice for the same period by the same employer.

In the case of *Norton Tool Co Ltd v Tewson* [1973] 1 WLR 4445, it was held that an employee who is wrongfully dismissed without notice and without payment in lieu of notice, would normally be entitled to be awarded pay for his notice period if he finds a new job during that time because this accords with 'good industrial practice'. However this narrow principle has been discussed in subsequent cases and it is now undecided whether it is good law (*Dunnachie v Kingston upon Hull City Council* [2004] EWCA Civ and *Langley and Another v Burso* [2006] ICR 850), although the decision in the latter case did confirm that the principle in *Norton Tool* does not have wider application. In general, the purpose of the compensatory award for unfair dismissal is to compensate for loss actually suffered, not to provide a bonus or double recovery.

Internal reorganisation

6.24   Once the share acquisition has been completed, the purchaser may wish to reorganise the acquired company to suit his purposes. There are various steps that it may wish to take, each of which will require consideration of his legal position. Such steps may include:

(a)   a transfer of employees from one company to another (see **6.25**);

(b)   a change of the employees' place of work (see **6.26**);

(c)   a change in the terms and conditions of employment of employees either with or without their consent, and the dismissal of employees who refuse to accept such a change (see **6.27–6.29**);

(d)   the redundancy of certain employees (see **6.30**).

Transferring employees from one company to another

6.25   At common law, a contract of employment cannot be transferred between employing companies without the employee's consent (*Nokes v Doncaster Amalgamated Collieries Ltd* [1940] AC 1014). It is unusual in practice for a mere transfer without consent to give rise to a claim without other contributory factors, even though such a transfer does constitute a technical repudiatory breach of contract by the employer. This is largely because where an employee is moved from one 'associated employer' (as defined in *section 231* of *ERA 1996*) to another, his continuity of employment will not be broken.

The purchaser should note that it may be possible to 'second' employees within the scope of their existing terms and conditions of employment to other companies; however, careful consideration will need to be given to the employee's duties clause and whether, for example, the employer has the right to change the employee's place of work.

Changing the employee's place of work

6.26   Where an employee's terms and conditions of employment specify that he is employed at a specific location and contain no mobility clause, the employer cannot require him without his consent to move to a different location without committing a repudiatory breach of contract with the consequences outlined at **6.28** below.

In the absence of any specified place of work, the employee may be required to move provided that his new location is within reasonable daily travelling distance (*Rank Xerox Ltd v Churchill* [1988] IRLR 280; *Courtaulds Northern Spinning Ltd v Sibson and Another* [1988] IRLR 305). What is reasonable will depend, *inter alia*, on the particular circumstances of the employee in question. Reasonable notice of the requirement to move must be given (*Prestwick Circuits Ltd v McAndrew* [1990] IRLR 191).

Even where a contract contains an express mobility clause, there is an implied term that reasonable notice must be given before the employer exercises its power under the express clause (*United Bank Ltd v Akhtar* [1989] IRLR 507).

Closing down one place of work to transfer employees to another place of work will, in the absence of a mobility clause, involve redundancies entitling the employees to redundancy payments as appropriate. However, where an employee unreasonably refuses to accept an offer of suitable alternative employment at another location, his dismissal will be by reason of redundancy but he will not be entitled to a statutory redundancy payment by reason of that dismissal. [*ERA 1996, s 141*].

Changing terms and conditions of employment

6.27 It is necessary to examine briefly the concept of constructive dismissal which must be borne in mind where an employer is considering changing the existing terms and conditions of employment of its employees.

Constructive dismissal

6.28 Where (for example) an employer varies the terms of an employee's contract of employment without his consent and the variation is sufficiently serious, the employee may resign and claim that he has been constructively dismissed. In effect, the law regards such a variation of the terms of the employee's contract as an actual dismissal by the employer provided the employee brings his employment to an end in response to the employer's action (*Western Excavating (ECC) Ltd v Sharp* [1977] IRLR 25). Upon a transfer of an undertaking, an employee cannot establish a constructive dismissal by reason of a substantial change in his working conditions to his detriment unless there is a fundamental breach of contract by his employer (*Rossiter v Pendragon Plc* [2002] IRLR 483).

Any change in an employee's terms and conditions of employment without his consent is *prima facie* a breach of contract and may entitle the employee to bring an action for constructive dismissal. However, in practice it may still be possible for the purchaser to introduce some changes in terms and conditions without giving rise to successful claims of constructive dismissal. A business reorganisation constitutes 'some other substantial reason' for dismissing an employee (one of the permitted reasons under *section 98* of *ERA 1996*). Provided the employer can satisfy the usual test of reasonableness under *section 98(4)* of *ERA 1996*, the dismissal may be fair.

Some guidelines regarding reasonableness

6.29   Where the purchaser of a company decides that a reorganisation which necessitates a change in the terms and conditions of employment of the company's employees is necessary, it must ensure that such a change is undertaken for a sound business reason. Where employees are dismissed as a result of the reorganisation, the employer must be able to justify his actions and produce evidence of the reorganisation or the relevant economic reasons. It is not, however, necessary to establish that without the reorganisation total disaster would ensue. The employer will have to show that the dismissed employee's refusal to accept changed terms and conditions of employment is unreasonable.

While a change in hours of work will not necessarily be considered unfair where a genuine business reason can be shown, a reduction in pay will almost certainly be a fundamental breach of contract and unfair. It is important to note again that a constructive dismissal need not necessarily be an unfair dismissal if the employer has acted reasonably in all the circumstances.

In spite of these guidelines, the purchaser should recognise that the interests of the business will always be best served by his obtaining consent to any changes in terms and conditions which it wishes to implement. This may involve 'buying out' certain benefits enjoyed by employees or offering some other financial incentive. It is often thought sensible, on the first occasion after an acquisition that employees are offered pay increases, to seek to introduce changes in their terms and conditions of employment as a condition of their receiving such increases.

Redundancy

6.30   As noted at **6.19** above, redundancy is one of the permitted grounds for dismissing an employee fairly. [*ERA 1996, s 98(2)(c)*]. An employee's dismissal is by reason of redundancy if it is attributable wholly or mainly to:

(a)   the fact that his employer has ceased or intends to cease

   (i)   to carry on the business for the purposes of which the employee was employed by the employer, or

   (ii)   to carry on that business in the place where the employee was so employed; or

(b)   the fact that the requirements of that business

   (i)   for employees to carry out work of a particular kind, or

(ii)   for employees to carry out work of a particular kind in the place where the employee was employed by the employer,

have ceased or diminished or are expected to cease or diminish. [*ERA 1996, s 139(1),(2)*]. (See *Murray v Foyle Meats Ltd* [1999] IRLR 562.)

Where a purchaser has acquired a company and wishes to effect redundancies, as the employer it must act with great care when selecting any particular employee for redundancy. A redundancy dismissal will be automatically unfair where employees are selected on grounds of their:

(a)   pregnancy or maternity;

(b)   being a health and safety representative;

(c)   refusal to work on a Sunday;

(d)   having given (or proposed to give) the employer an opting-out notice in respect of Sunday work;

(e)   being a trustee of an occupational pension scheme;

(f)   activities as an employee representative;

(g)   having asserted a statutory right;

(h)   having made a protected disclosure under *sections 43A to 43L of ERA 1996* (inserted by the *Public Interest Disclosure Act 1998, s 5*) [*ERA 1996, s 105*]; or

(i)   trade union membership or activities. [*Trade Union and Labour Relations (Consolidation) Act 1992, s 152*].

Most importantly the dismissal for redundancy must be reasonable in all the circumstances. [*ERA 1996, s 98(4)*].

Provided the employer can show that the reason for dismissal is redundancy it should ask itself the following questions (with reference to the decision of the EAT in *Williams v Compair Maxam Ltd* [1982] IRLR 83):

(a)   *What is the basis of the selection?* Selection criteria should be objective (although there may be considerable flexibility in choosing them); where appropriate, trade unions or other appropriate representatives should be consulted about selection criteria.

(b)   *How are the selection criteria to be applied?* They must be applied consistently and fairly.

(c)   *Have reasonable efforts been made to find alternative employment for employees who are to be dismissed?*

(d)   *Has warning been given about the impending redundancy?* This is a separate requirement from the one which follows.

(e)   *Has there been consultation before the redundancy?* In all situations of redundancy the employer should (at least) *consider* consultation with *individual* employees *before* effecting redundancies. If, when considering the matter, it decides at that time that the process of consultation will be meaningless and may therefore be dispensed with, his action may or may not be unreasonable and therefore unfair, depending on all the circumstances. In this connection case law has established five principles of good industrial relations practice. The principles are:

(i)   as much warning as possible should be given by the employer of impending redundancies;

(ii)   consultation with appropriate trade union or employee representatives as to the best means by which employees should be selected for redundancy should take place so as to minimise hardship;

(iii) criteria for selection for redundancy should not depend solely on the opinion of the person making the selection. The criteria should be objectively checked. An employer is not entitled to make use of a redundancy situation 'to weed out his pregnant employees', according to the House of Lords in *Brown v Stockon-on-Tees Borough Council* [1988] IRLR 263. It does not follow, however, that an employer cannot dismiss a pregnant employee on the grounds of redundancy if, for example, her job has ceased to exist and there is no alternative employment;

(iv)   the employer should seek to ensure that the selection made for redundancy is in accordance with these criteria and should consider representations of any appropriate trade union or employee representative; and

(v)   the employer should investigate whether any alternative employment can be offered.

(For collective consultation obligations, which are *additional* to individual consultation obligations, see **6.54** below).

An employer who fails to consult an employee *before* making him redundant (or who fails to consider consultation at that time) cannot argue *after* effecting the dismissal that because consultation would not have made any difference (i.e. the employee would still have been made redundant), his failure to consult does not render the dismissal unfair. This was established in the case of *Polkey v AE Dayton Services Limited* [1987] IRLR 503 where the House of Lords held that it was up to the employer before or at the time of dismissing the employee (i.e. not afterwards when faced with a tribunal claim) to consider the consequence of not consulting or warning in accordance with the principles set out above. However, the House of Lords indicated that a failure to consult would not of itself necessarily render a dismissal unfair.

Where a dismissal is held to be unfair for procedural reasons, compensation may be reduced in the event that there is only a minimal chance that the employee would have continued in employment, even if a fair procedure had been adopted (*Rao v Civil Aviation Authority* [1992] IRLR 203).

The Court of Appeal has held that good industrial practice as adopted by a reasonable employer may require two-stage consultation: first, with any appropriate trade union or elected representatives; secondly, with those employees selected for redundancy in accordance with any agreement reached with the trade union or elected representatives (*Walls Meat Co Ltd v Selby* [1989] ICR 601). (See **6.31** below.)

Redundancy – other considerations

6.31   In the case of large-scale redundancies the purchaser must give due notification to the Secretary of State before giving notice to terminate an employee's contract of employment in respect of any proposed dismissals, which is normally done on a form HR1. [*Trade Union and Labour Relations (Consolidation) Act 1992* as amended (*TULRCA 1992), s 193*]. Broadly speaking, where: (i) 20 or more redundancies are to be effected at one establishment in a period of 90 days or less, then at least 30 days' notice must be given; or (ii) 100 or more redundancies are to be effected within a period of 90 days or less, then at least 90 days' notice must be given.

In such situations the purchaser will also have to consider his duty to consult appropriate representatives and the protective award legislation contained in *section 188 et seq.* of *TULRCA 1992*, as amended by the *Trade Union Reform and Employment Rights Act 1993* (*TURERA 1993*), the *Collective Redundancies and Transfer of Undertakings (Protection of Employment) (Amendment) Regulations 1995* (*SI 1995/2587*) and the *Collective Redundancies and Transfer of Undertakings (Protection of Employment) (Amendment) Regulations 1999* (*SI 1995/1925*). This is explained at **6.54** below where 'collective matters' generally are considered. The purchaser should note that consultation must be 'with a view to reaching agreement with the appropriate representatives'.

Furthermore, the vendor may need to bear in mind the *Information and Consultation of Employees Regulations 2004* (SI 2004/3426), which give employees in larger firms (those with 50 or more employees), rights to be informed and consulted about the business they work for. This is explained at **6.61** below, also under 'collective matters'.

Purchase of assets only

6.32   Where the purchaser is buying assets only (in other words where the acquisition does not constitute the transfer of an undertaking) the contractual position of employees working with those assets is unaffected by the disposal of the assets; they remain employed by their existing employer, the seller, who will doubtless find them alternative work or make them redundant. If the employees take up employment with the purchaser of the assets there will generally be a break in their continuity of employment (unless the combined effect of the transfer of assets and employees in fact constitutes a transfer of an undertaking under *TUPE (SI 2006/246)*) affecting, *inter alia*, their right to claim unfair dismissal, and their right to future redundancy payments which will be calculated by reference to the date upon which they commence employment with the purchaser.

Purchase of a business or undertaking

At a glance

6.33

(a) Employers should consider the following:

    (i)   the identity of the unit to be transferred as an undertaking;

    (ii)   which individuals work in the unit;

    (iii) whether those individuals are employees, secondees or independent contractors;

    (iv) whether the individuals will transfer;

    (v)   when the transaction will complete;

    (vi) whether there will be a series of transactions;

    (vii) whether it is accepted that *TUPE* applies.

(b) *TUPE* applies to the purchase of an undertaking, ie a transfer from one person to another of an undertaking or part of an undertaking situated immediately before the transfer in the UK.

(c) The transfer may be effected by a series of two or more transactions and may take place whether or not any property is transferred to the purchaser by the transferor.

(d) In order for there to be a transfer of an undertaking there must be an economic entity which transfers, which retains its identity and which is not limited to performing one specific works contract. It must refer to an organised group of persons and assets for the exercise of an economic activity which pursues a specific objective.

(e) *TUPE* provides for the automatic transfer of contracts of employment of persons employed by the transferor in the undertaking to the purchaser.

(f) The purchaser acquires all contractual liabilities and certain tortious liabilities in relation to transferring employees, but no criminal liabilities.

(g) The seller must provide the purchaser with certain specified 'employee liability information' in relation to any employee who is the subject of the transfer, no longer than 14 days before the transfer is to take place.

(h) Where there is a transfer of an undertaking, collective agreements and recognition of trade unions transfer in respect of any employee whose contract of employment is transferred with the undertaking.

(i) Employees employed immediately before the completion of the transfer will become the responsibility of the purchaser.

(j) The purchaser will inherit liabilities in relation to employees dismissed before the transfer where the transfer or a reason connected with it was the reason or principal reason for the dismissals.

(k)   Where an employee informs the transferor or the purchaser that he objects to becoming employed by the purchaser, the transfer will operate to terminate his employment with the transferor, but he shall not be treated for any purposes as having been dismissed and he cannot claim a redundancy payment.

(l)   The dismissal of an employee where the transfer, or a reason connected with it, is the reason or principal reason for the dismissal is automatically unfair unless there is an economic, technical or organisational reason entailing changes in the workforce.

(m)   Any change in the terms and conditions of newly-acquired employees will be ineffective if made for a reason connected with the transfer (even if the employees consent). There can be a valid variation for a reason other than because of the transfer.

(n)   There are obligations to inform or consult with appropriate representatives of 'affected employees' in relation to the transfer and the purchaser will inherit any liability in respect of the vendor's failure to do so. (*Kerry Foods Limited v Creber & Ors* [2000] IRLR 10 (EAT), see also *TUPE, SI 2006/246, Reg 15(9)* and *Alamo Group (Europe) Ltd v (1) Tucker (2) Twose of Tiverton Ltd* [2003] IRLR 266).

(o)   It is not possible to contract out of the effect of *TUPE*.

Purchase of a business or undertaking – general

6.34   It is critical to distinguish between a purchase of an undertaking and a sale of mere assets. This is because *TUPE (SI 2006/246)* applies to the purchase of an undertaking; however, it does not apply to a purchase of mere assets.

The distinction between the purchase of an undertaking, as opposed to mere assets, is a fine one governed by complex legal considerations referred to below.

The original *Transfer of Undertakings (Protection of Employment) Regulations 1981 (SI 1981/1794)* (the '*1981 Regulations*') were implemented to give effect to *Article 3(1)* of *EC Council Directive 77/187* which was intended to safeguard employees' rights on the occasion of transfers of undertakings, businesses and parts of businesses in Member States and which provided:

'the transferor's rights and obligations arising from a contract of employment or from an employment relationship existing on the date of a transfer shall by reason of such a transfer be transferred to the transferee'.

This contrasts with the position at common law decided in *Nokes v Doncaster Amalgamated Collieries Ltd* [1940] AC 1014 referred to at **6.25** above. In that case, it was held that such a transfer of a contract of employment could not be done without the employee's consent.

EC Council Directive 77/187, and *EC Council Directive 98/50* which amended it, have now been repealed by a new *Acquired Rights Directive 2001/23* (the '*Acquired Rights Directive*'), which came into force on 12 March 2001. The *Acquired Rights Directive* was enacted to codify the various amendments (contained in both case law and EC Council Directives) to *EC Council Directive 77/187*. Article *3(1)* of the *Acquired Rights Directive* is identical to that contained in *EC Council Directive 77/187*.

TUPE (SI 2006/246) was enacted to implement the *Acquired Rights Directive*, and replaces the *1981 Regulations* with effect from 6 April 2006. There are a number of material differences between the *1981 Regulations* and *TUPE (SI 2006/246)*, many of which are updates to reflect the existing legal position which has been established by the courts through case law. A small number of the changes to *TUPE (SI 2006/246)* do, however, represent a shift in approach to TUPE transfers.

When does TUPE apply?

6.35 *TUPE (SI 2006/246)* applies to 'a relevant transfer'. There are now two different tests to determine what is a 'relevant transfer' for the purpose of *TUPE (SI 2006/246)*. These two different tests are not mutually exclusive.

There will be a relevant transfer under *TUPE (SI 2006/246)* where there is a transfer from one person to another of an undertaking or part of an undertaking which was situated immediately before the transfer in the United Kingdom to another person where there is a transfer of an economic entity which retains its identity following the transfer [*TUPE, SI 2006/246, Regs 2(1) and 3(1)(a)*]. This test remains the same in substance as under the *1981 Regulations*, but has been reformulated to better reflect the tests actually utilised by the courts. 'Economic entity' is defined as an organised grouping of resources which has the objective of pursuing an economic activity, whether or not that activity is central or ancillary. As under the *1981 Regulations* the test of what constitutes a business transfer is heavily dependent on the facts of each case. Much of the case law in relation to what constitutes an undertaking and a relevant transfer for the purposes of the *1981 Regulations* will continue to be relevant in relation to *TUPE (SI 2006/246)* so far as a business transfer under *Reg 3(1)(a)* is concerned.

There will also be a relevant transfer under *TUPE (SI 2006/246)* where there is a service provision change as set out in *Reg 3(1)(b)* [*TUPE, SI 2006/246, Reg 2(1)*]. A service provision change under *TUPE (SI 2006/246)* covers outsourcing, insourcing or a change of contractor. However, the position reached due to case law prior to *TUPE (SI 2006/246)* was that most outsourcing situations would give rise to a transfer of an undertaking for the purposes of the *1981 Regulations*. These outsourcing situations will remain a business transfer covered by *Reg 3(1)(a)* of *TUPE (SI 2006/246)*. The precise detail relating to service provision changes is, however, outside the scope of this book.

A transfer of an undertaking under the *Acquired Rights Directive* (and *TUPE (SI 2006/246)*) can occur between two companies which belong to the same corporate group with common ownership, management and premises, and which are engaged in the same works (*Allen and others v Amalgamated Construction Co Ltd* ECJ C-234/98).

A series of transactions between more than two parties may constitute a relevant transfer. [*TUPE, SI 2006/246, Reg 3(6)(a)*]. Further, a relevant transfer may take place whether or not any property is transferred between the parties. [*TUPE, SI 2006/246, Reg 3(6)(b)*]. (*Magna Housing Association Limited v (1) Turner (2) Raison (3) Landscaping & Grounds Maintenance Limited* EAT 21.10.98 (198/98); *Lightways (Contractors) Limited v (1) Hood and ors (2) Associated Holdings Limited* EAT 17.11.98 (632/98); *CWW Logistics Ltd v (1) Ronald (2) Digital Equipment (Scotland) Ltd* EAT 1.12.98 (774/98)).

Previously there was an issue as to whether a transfer of an undertaking can take place over a period of time. This has now been resolved by the ECJ's decision in *Celtec Limited v Astley and others* [2005] IRLR 647. The ECJ held that the date of a transfer under the *Acquired Rights Directive* (and *TUPE (SI 2006/246)*) is a particular point in time which cannot be postponed to another date at the will of the transferor or transferee. The date of the transfer is the date on which the responsibility as an employer for carrying on the business of the unit transferred moves from the transferor to the transferee. Unfortunately, the ECJ did not go on to give any guidance on how the 'particular point' in time is to be identified.

'Undertaking' includes any trade or business. There is no requirement that the undertaking be 'in the nature of a commercial venture'. On the contrary, an undertaking may now include:

(a)   both public and private undertakings engaged in economic activities whether or not they are operating for gain [*TUPE, SI 2006/246, Reg 3(4)(a)*];

(b)   a contract for the supply of services ancillary to other economic activity such as the running of a staff canteen (*Rask v ISS Kantineservice A/S* [1993] IRLR 133);

(c)   the supply of services where the beneficiary of such services is seeking to contract them out (*Wren v Eastbourne Borough Council* [1993] IRLR 425);

(d)   a change of contractor for the supply of services (*ECM (Vehicle Delivery Services) Ltd v Cox* [1999] IRLR 559 (CA) *Abler and others v Sodexo Catering Gesellschaft mbH* [2003] C-340/01).

The grant or surrender of franchises, leases or licences may also constitute a relevant transfer of an undertaking. See for example, *Foreningen af Arbejdsledere i Danmark v Daddy's Dance Hall A/S* [1988] IRLR 315; but see *North East Lincolnshire Council v Beck and others* EAT 21.1.99 (1362/97).

Whether there is an economic entity which retains its identity may be indicated by the transferee continuing or resuming the same or similar economic activities. This will depend on an overall assessment of the facts characterising the transaction in question, including, *inter alia,* the type of business or undertaking concerned, whether or not tangible assets are transferred, the value of the intangible assets at the time of the transfer, whether there is continuity of the workforce and client-base, and the degree of similarity between activities carried on before and after the transfer and the period of suspension of any of those activities. (See *Spijkers v Gebroeders Benedik Abattoir CV* [1986] 2 CMLR 296; *Dr Sophie Redmond Stichting v Bartol* [1992] IRLR 366; *Ledernes Hovedorganisation v Dansk Arbejdsgiverforening* [1995] ECR I-2745; *Balfour Beatty Power Networks Ltd v Wilcox* [2006] IRLR 258; and *Allen* (see above)).

The transfer must relate to a stable economic entity which is not limited to performing one specific works contract. The entity will generally refer to an organised group of persons and assets for the exercise of an economic activity which pursues a specific objective but need not necessarily include significant numbers of people or tangible assets. For example, in *ECM (Vehicle Delivery Services) Ltd v Cox* [1999] IRLR 559 (CA) it was held that a single person was not precluded from being an economic entity capable of being transferred in appropriate circumstances.

The purchaser must consider:

(a)   the type of undertaking or business;

(b)   the transfer or otherwise of tangible assets such as buildings and stocks;

(c)   the value of intangible assets;

(d)   whether the majority of staff are to be taken over;

(e)   the transfer or otherwise of customers;

(f)   the degree of similarity between activities before and after the transfer; and

(g)   the duration of any interruption in the activities.

Each factor is only a part of the overall assessment required in each particular case. (See further *Cheesman v R Brewer Contracts Limited* [2001] IRLR 144.)

The European Court of Justice had previously considered these factors in the context of outsourcing. It held in *Süzen v Zehnacker Gebäudereinigung GmbH Krankenhausservice* [1997] IRLR 255 that an activity does not, in itself, constitute an economic entity. It did not follow that there was a transfer of an undertaking from the fact that a similar activity was carried out before and after the change of contractor. In *Süzen* it was held that in labour-intensive undertakings with no significant assets there would generally be no transfer unless a majority part of the outgoing contractor's workforce in terms of their numbers and skills assigned to the performance of the contract were taken on by the incoming contractor. (See also the Court of Appeal decision in *Betts v Brintel Helicopters Limited* [1997] IRLR 361). The EAT in *Lightways* (see above) went further, holding that only a material and identifiable number of employees had to be involved. However, the EAT in *Cheesman* (see above) distinguished *Süzen* and *Betts* from the later case of *ECM* (see above) and held that while the transfer of tangible assets will be a factor to be considered when deciding whether there has been a transfer of an undertaking it is not a prerequisite; in fact an undertaking need not necessarily have significant assets at all. Furthermore, in *RCO Support Services Ltd, Aintree Hospital Trust v Unison and others* [2002] IRLR 401 (CA), it was upheld that the fact that a majority of the workforce transferred was only one of a number of factors to be considered and was not in itself determinative.

It is unlikely that a transferee will be able to disapply *TUPE (SI 2006/246)* by deliberately refusing to take on the transferor's staff (*OCS Cleaning Scotland Ltd v (1) Rudden and (2) Olscot Ltd* EAT 29.6.99 (290/99); *Magna Housing*; *Lightways*; and *ECM* (see above)).

The effect of TUPE

6.36 *TUPE (SI 2006/246)* provides, broadly speaking, for the automatic transfer of contracts of employment of persons employed by the transferor and *assigned* to the organised grouping of resources or employees that is subject to the relevant transfer [*TUPE, SI 2006/246, Reg 4(1)*]. 'Assigned' under *TUPE (SI 2006/246)* means assigned other than on a temporary basis [*TUPE, SI 2006/246, Reg 2(1)*]. This test regarding which employees transfer is intended to reflect the current position under case law, which broadly is that an employee should spend a majority of their employment in the activity or undertaking in question. It is possible that an employee may be assigned to an employer's business, even though that employee spends time looking after another business (*Buchanan-Smith v Schleicher & Co International Limited* [1996] ICR 613; see also *Jones v Darlows Estate Agency* (CA LTL 6/7/98)). If the transferor wishes to retain in *his* employment certain employees employed in the undertaking to work in another part of his business, it may attempt to do so *with their consent* by transferring them to other duties within their existing terms of their contracts of employment or, if necessary, by seeking to vary the terms of such contracts of employment before the transfer is effected. Note that an attempt to transfer an employee to the part of the business being transferred may be ineffective (*Carisway Cleaning Consultants Ltd v Richards & Coopers Cleaning Services*, unreported, 19 June 1998). Although recent case law has held that even consensual variations of contracts of employment by reason of a transfer are ineffective, it may be thought that an employee who wishes to remain with the transferor may, in practice, be unlikely to claim subsequently that any variation was ineffective and that he had transferred to the purchaser (*Wilson & ors v St Helens BC* [1998] IRLR 706).

What liabilities does the purchaser acquire?

6.37 The purchaser acquires, broadly speaking, all contractual liabilities and certain tortious liabilities in relation to the employees but no criminal liabilities. [*TUPE, SI 2006/246, Reg 4(2)*]. It should be noted that:

(a) liability for redundancy payments or unfair dismissal generally (save, perhaps, for ETO dismissals – see **6.44** below) will pass to the purchaser;

(b) liability for contractual claims, for example for notice pay where notice was given by the transferor, will pass to the purchaser, and for profit-related pay in certain circumstances (see *Unicorn Consultancy Services Ltd v Westbrook & ors* unreported, 1999);

(c) continuity of employment will not be broken [*ERA 1996, s 218(2)*];

(d) collective agreements with a recognised trade union will pass to the purchaser [*TUPE, SI 2006/246, Reg 5*]. (See *Whent & ors v T Cartledge Limited* [1997] IRLR 153 in which, following the transfer, the transferred employees' pay continued to be fixed by national collective bargaining pursuant to their employment contracts; and *William West & Sons (Ilkeston) Ltd v (1) Fairgieve & ors (2) EXEL/BRS Ltd* EAT/701/98 mentioned at **6.10** above, but note *the case of Werhof v Freeway Traffic Systems* [2006] IRLR 400 where the ECJ decided that the transferor is not bound by collective agreements subsequent to the one in force at the time of transfer);

(e) the principal of automatic transfer does not apply to those parts of the transferring employees' contracts of employment or collective agreements that relate to occupational pension schemes or any rights, powers, duties or liabilities under or in connection with occupational pension schemes [*TUPE, SI 2006/246, Reg 10(1)*]. For these purposes, any provisions of an occupational pension scheme which do not relate to benefits for old age, invalidity or survivors, are not treated as being part of the scheme, and so pass to the purchaser [*TUPE, SI 2006/246, Reg 10(2)*]. Early retirement benefits, or at least those intended to enhance the conditions of such retirement, are not within this exclusion (*Beckmann v Dynamco Whicheloe Macfarlane Ltd [2000] IRLR 578, Martin and others v South Bank University* [2003] Pens L R 329). *TUPE (SI 2006/246)* prevents a transferred employee bringing a claim against the transferor for breach of contract or constructive unfair dismissal arising out of a loss or reduction in his/her rights under an occupational pension scheme as a result of the transfer unless the alleged breach of contract or dismissal occurred prior to the date *TUPE (SI 2006/246)* took effect (6 April 2006) [*TUPE, SI 2006/246, Reg 10(3)*]. *TUPE (SI 2006/246)* amends the *Pensions Act 2004* so as to give limited protection to an employee who, immediately prior to the transfer, is a member of an occupational pension scheme in relation to which the transferor is an employer. The precise detail of this protection is, however, outside the scope of this book;

(f) collective agreements relating to the transferring employees in existence immediately before the transfer will have effect after the transfer as if made by the transferee [*TUPE, SI 2006/246, Reg 5(a)*]. Anything done under or in connection with that agreement by or in relation to the transferor will be deemed after the transfer to have been done by the transfer [*TUPE, SI 2006/246, Reg 5(b)*];

(g)   any union voluntarily recognised to any extent by the transferor in respect of any of the transferred employees will be deemed to be recognised by the transferee to the same extent in respect of those employees, but only if the transferred organised grouping of employees or resources maintains an identity distinct from the remainder of the transferee's undertaking [*TUPE, SI 2006/246, Reg 6*]. According to the DTI's guidance, different arrangements are to be introduced in relation to unions recognised by the transferor via the statutory recognition procedure. Regulations are to be made in due course to ensure that declarations made by the CAC, and applications made to the CAC, are appropriately preserved in the event of a change in the identity of the employer;

(h)   the transferor and transferee will be jointly and severally liable for certain claims in respect of failures to inform, failures to consult with appropriate representatives of affected employees or failure to do both (see **6.59** below);

(i)   liability relates to the employee, not to a particular contract (*DJM International Limited v Nicholas* [1996] IRLR 76); and

(j)   a pre-transfer normal retirement age will not pass to the transferee (see the Court of Appeal decision in *Cross v British Airways Plc* [2006] EWCA Civ 549).

There has been some discussion as to whether liability for personal injury claims transfers with a transfer of an undertaking under *regulation 4(2)* of *TUPE (SI 2006/246)*. In *Bernadone v Pall Mall Services Group* [1999] IRLR 617 it was held that liability did transfer irrespective of whether the claim for personal injury was pleaded in contract, tort or breach of statutory duty. In addition, the transferor's right to an indemnity against an insurer in respect of the personal injury claim transferred to the transferee. This was upheld in *Martin v Lancashire County Council* [2000] IRLR 487 (CA).

At what point do the transferor's employees become the responsibility of the purchaser?

Employees employed 'immediately before' transfer

6.38   *First*, the purchaser will inherit liabilities in relation to employees employed and assigned to the organised grouping of resources or employees 'immediately before' the transfer. [*TUPE, SI 2006/246, Reg 4(3)*]. Many transactions take place in two stages involving the signing of the contract and the subsequent completion or closing of the transfer. Employees employed 'immediately before' the latter stage (i.e. completion) will become the responsibility of the purchaser.

In *Secretary of State for Employment v Spence* [1987] QB 179, the Court of Appeal decided that 'immediately before' means *at the time of the transfer*. (Note that the EC Directive refers to the 'date' of transfer so that there is some doubt as to whether liability passes in relation to employees dismissed on the date of transfer before the transfer is completed.)

Employees dismissed before time of transfer

6.39   *Secondly*, the purchaser will inherit liabilities in relation to employees dismissed *before* the time of the transfer where those employees were dismissed *by reason of* the transfer (i.e. where the transfer or a reason connected with it was the reason or principal reason for the dismissals). [*TUPE, SI 2006/246, Reg 4(3) and 7(1)*]. In its decision in the case of *Litster and Others v Forth Dry Dock & Engineering Company Ltd (In Receivership) and Another* [1989] IRLR 161, the House of Lords held that where employees had been dismissed by the seller by reason of the imminent transfer of the business to the purchaser, such dismissals were unfair, and ineffective, at least to the extent that liability for the dismissals still passed to the purchaser. (See also *Thompson & ors v Walon Car Delivery and BRS Automotive Ltd* [1997] IRLR 343). It is the claims arising from an unlawful dismissal which transfer to the transferee as opposed to the dismissal itself being a nullity (*Jules Dethier Equipement SA v Dassy and Sovram Sprl (in Liquidation)* [1998] IRLR 266).

In practice, the seller retains responsibility for his employees and may carry out effective dismissals until the time of the transfer, *provided* these are not by reason of the transfer. Dismissals by the seller or the purchaser for an 'economic, technical or organisational reason entailing changes in the workforce' may be fair and effective (see **6.44** below and the illustrations at **6.45** *et seq.* in which these principles are followed through).

Following the EAT decision in *G4S Justice Services (UK) Ltd v Anstey* [2006] IRLR 588, where an employee has been dismissed by the transferor prior to the transfer but whose internal appeal against that dismissal is pending at the time of a transfer to which *TUPE (SI 2006/246)* applies, that employee's employment will be treated as being preserved only for the purposes of determining his appeal. If the appeal is unsuccessful, the original dismissal stands and the employee will not be treated as having been employed by the transferor immediately before the transfer. However, if the appeal against the dismissal is successful and the dismissals are set aside, the dismissal 'vanishes' and the employees are treated as having been employed up until the transfer date and as continuing in employment with the transferee as a result of the transfer.

Exceptions from the automatic transfer effect of TUPE

6.40   The purchaser should note that employees will not be transferred under *regulation 4(1)* of *TUPE (SI 2006/246)* in the following circumstances:

(a)   where the employee exercises his right of objection under *regulation 4(7) of TUPE (SI 2006/246)* (see **6.62** below);

(b)   where the employee exercises his right under *regulation 4(9) of TUPE (SI 2006/246)* to treat his contract of employment as having been terminated where, due to the transfer, a substantial change is or will be made to his working conditions to his material detriment (see **6.43** below);

(c)   where employees are already employed by a separate service company which is not the subject of the transfer: *Banking Insurance and Finance Union v Barclays Bank plc* [1987] ICR 495 (although, following the approach of the court in *Litster and Others v Forth Dry Dock & Engineering Company Ltd (In Receivership) and Another* [1989] IRLR 161 where the court effectively amended *TUPE* in order to give effect to the EC Directive the position is not free from doubt; see also *Duncan Web Offset (Maidstone) Ltd v Cooper* [1995] IRLR 633 in which the EAT warned that tribunals must be astute to ensure that the Regulations are not to be evaded by devices such as service companies). It will not be possible for the transferor to move his employees into a service company before a transfer without their consent to avoid the impact of *TUPE*. Further, if a transfer is in contemplation any such consent may be invalid unless employees are informed of all the material facts;

(d)   where the transferor is an insolvent company to which regulation 8(7) of TUPE (SI 2006/246) applies (see **6.60** below); and

(e)   where the employees' employment will be maintained by the transferor after the transfer despite the sale by it of the business (*Direct Radiators v Howse and Shepherd* [1986] 315 IRLIB 17).

It is not possible for the parties to contract out of the effect of the transfer regulations. [*TUPE, SI 2006/246, Reg 18*]. Employees will be transferred under *regulation 4(1)* of *TUPE* (*SI 2006/246*) despite the fact that at the date of dismissal the employees did not know of the transfer or the identity of the transferee. (*Secretary of State for Trade and Industry v Cook* [1997] ICR 288, *disapproving* the EAT's decision to the contrary in *Photostatic Copiers (Southern) Ltd v Okuda and Japan Office Equipment* [1995] IRLR 11). Employees are automatically transferred by the mere contrary intention of the transferor or transferee and despite the latter's refusal to fulfil his obligations. (*Rotsart De Hertaing v J Benoidt SA (in liquidation) and IGC Housing Service SA* [1997] IRLR 127).

Transfers of employees before completion

6.41   Case law has been inconsistent when considering what point in time constitutes 'at the time of transfer' for the purposes of *TUPE* and the transfer of employees before completion. One approach has been a strict interpretation; that the time of transfer is a moment of time rather than a period (see *Spence* above, *Brook Lane Finance Co Limited v Bradley* [1988] IRLR 283 *and Senior Heat Treatment Ltd v Bell* [1997] IRLR 614). The other approach has been to give a broader understanding; that the machinery of a transfer may take place over a more extended period and that if an employee is transferred during this period, their continuity of employment will continue (see *Litster* above, *Macer v Abafast* [1990] ICR 234 and *A&G Tuck Ltd v Bartlett* [1994] IRLR 162).

However, in the light of the ECJ's decision in the case of *Celtec* (see **6.35** above), it would appear that the strict approach has prevailed, although it is again important to bear in mind that the ECJ did not deal with the issue of how to identify the particular point in time at which a transfer is deemed to be completed.

As the legal position is not entirely clear, the purchaser should proceed with caution and seek to avoid transferring employees across to the purchaser before completion. This is particularly important in transactions where completion of an acquisition is being staggered over a period (e.g. where different parts of the business are being transferred at different times) to ensure that employees are not transferred before actual completion. (*Dabell v Vale Industrial Services (Nottingham) Ltd* [1988] IRLR 439; see also *Rotsart De Hertaing v J Benoidt SA (in liquidation) and IGC Housing Service SA* [1997] IRLR 127).

'Employee liability information'

6.42   For relevant transfers that take place on or after 20 April 2006, *TUPE* (SI 2006/246) introduced a duty for the transferor to provide the transferee with certain specified 'employee liability information'. The information must be provided in relation to:

(a)   any person employed by the transferor who is assigned to the organised grouping of resources or employees that is the subject of a relevant transfer; and

(b)   any person who would have fallen into this category immediately before the transfer but for the fact that he was dismissed in circumstances in which the dismissal is automatically unfair (where the reason for the dismissal is the transfer itself or a reason connected with the transfer that is not an ETO reason).

The notification must be given not less than 14 days before the relevant transfer or, if special circumstances make this not reasonably practicable, as soon as reasonably practicable thereafter. If any of the information changes between the time when it is initially provided to the transferee and the completion of the transfer, the transferor must give the transferee written notification of the changes.

The transferor must provide the transferee with:

(a)   the identity and ages of the employees;

(b)   the key particulars of employment that an employer is obliged to give to an employee under *section 1* of the *Employment Rights Act 1996*;

(c)   information of any:

    (i)   disciplinary procedure taken against an employee;

    (ii)   grievance procedure taken by an employee;

    within the previous two years, in circumstances where the *Employment Act 2002 (Dispute Resolution) Regulations 2004* apply;

(d)   information of any court or Tribunal case, claim or action:

  (i)   brought by an employee against the transferor, within the previous two years;

  (ii)   that the transferor has reasonable grounds to believe that an employee may bring against the transferee, arising out of the employee's employment with the transferor; and

(e)   information of any collective agreement which will continue to apply to transferring employees after the transfer.

The information given must be as at a specified date not more than 14 days before the date on which the information is notified to the transferee.

If the transferor fails to comply with its duty, the transferee can bring a claim before a Tribunal. Where the Tribunal considers there has been a failure to comply with the requirement, it will make a declaration to that effect. In addition, the Tribunal may award compensation as it considers just and equitable subject to the transferee's duty to mitigate any losses.

The level of compensation is subject to a minimum of £500 for each employee for whom the information was not provided, or the information provided was defective but subject to the right of the Tribunal to determine that a lesser award would be 'just and equitable'.

The employee's position

6.43   From the employee's point of view he is employed by one company on day one and another company on day two, supposedly on the same terms and conditions of employment without any independent action by himself. Can he object?

(a)   Where the employee informs the transferor or the purchaser that he objects to becoming employed by the purchaser, the transfer will operate to terminate his contract of employment with the transferor, but he shall not be treated for any purposes as having been dismissed by the transferor. [*TUPE, SI 2006/246, Regs 4(7)* and *4(8)*]. (See *Katsikas v Konstantinides* [1993] IRLR 179 and *Hay v George Hanson (Building Contractors) Ltd* [1996] IRLR 427.) This objection does not need to be expressed in a particular way in order to be effective (see *Hope v PGS Engineering Ltd (in administration)* EAT 0267/04).

(b)   Where the transfer would, or does, involve a substantial change in the employee's working conditions to his material detriment, the employee may treat his contract of employment as having been terminated and he shall be treated for any purposes as having been dismissed by the employer (which may be the transferor or purchaser). A change in the identity of the employer as a result of the transfer will not constitute such a change unless the employee can show that it is a substantial change to his material detriment. [*TUPE, SI 2006/246, Reg 4(9)*].

Note that where an employee resigns prior to a transfer because the transferee refuses to guarantee his terms and conditions after the transfer, the employer may be treated as having dismissed him (*Merckx v Ford Motors* [1997] ICR 352*)*. Liability for such dismissal will fall to the transferee. (*P&O Property Holdings Ltd v Allen* [1997] ICR 436*)*. However, the Court of Appeal held that an employee's objection to the transfer of his employment under *regulation 4(7)* of *TUPE (SI 2006/246)* because it would involve a substantial and detrimental change in his terms and conditions of employment did not preclude him from bringing a constructive dismissal claim for which the transferor was liable. (*Oxford University v Humphreys and another* [2000] IRLR 183); see also *Thomas v (1) Ewar Stud Farms Ltd (2) The Lord Tyron* (EAT*)* where no statutory objection was raised but the common law right to claim constructive dismissal against a transferor in relation to a resignation before the transfer took place was preserved against the transferor and could never be asserted against the transferee). In *Senior Heat Treatment Limited v Bell and others* [1997] IRLR 614, the EAT held that an employee who opted out of the transfer and accepted a relocation severance payment did not object to the transfer under *regulation 5(4A) of the 1981 Regulations (now regulation (4(7)) of TUPE (SI 2006/246))*. It was relevant that he had entered into a contract of employment with the transferee before the transfer occurred.

Reorganisation

6.44   The purchaser of a business will often wish to reorganise the business in the same way as a purchaser of shares and carry out some or all of the steps referred to at **6.24** *et seq*. above. In addition to the general legal considerations on an internal reorganisation already considered above, there are certain particular matters that the purchaser of a business must bear in mind. Most importantly the purchaser must note that the dismissal of an employee where the transfer, or a reason connected with it, is the reason or principal reason for that dismissal is automatically unfair. However, where 'an economic, technical or organisational reason entailing changes in the workforce' ('an ETO') of either the transferor or the purchaser before or after the transfer is the reason or principal reason for dismissing an employee, the dismissal may be fair, *provided* the employer can satisfy the usual reasonableness test which applies in all cases of unfair dismissal (see **6.29** above). Both the transferor and purchaser can dismiss for an ETO reason (*Jules Dethier Equipement SA v Dassy and Sovram Sprl (in Liquidation)* [1998] IRLR 266). If an ETO dismissal is held unfair for, say, procedural reasons, it is generally thought that the resulting liability will remain with the transferor though the position is not free from doubt.

A dismissal of an employee for a reason connected with the transfer is effective (albeit automatically unfair unless there is an ETO reason). It is not a nullity. (*Wilson & ors v St Helens BC* [1998] IRLR 706, the House of Lords reversing the decision of the Court of Appeal). When considering whether a dismissal was connected with a transfer, it is relevant whether a transfer to any transferee who might appear, or a reason connected with such a transfer, was the reason or principal reason for the dismissal. In other words, it is not necessary for the employer to have in mind a specific purchaser at the time of dismissal (*Morris v John Grose Group Limited* [1998] ICR 655*).*

It is important to note the two parts of an ETO:

(a) an economic, technical or organisational reason;

(b) entailing changes in the workforce.

It is equally important not to overlook the requirement of 'reasonableness'.

An express requirement by a service user that an incoming contractor (transferee) reduce the number of employees assigned to the business could amount to an ETO reason. (*Whitehouse v Blatchford & Sons Limited* [1999] IRLR 492 (CA)*; Berriman v Delabole Slate Limited* [1985] IRLR 305; *Wheeler v Patel and another* [1987] IRLR 211).

TUPE (SI 2006/246) introduces a new protection for employees against dismissal that both the transferor and transferee should be aware of, particularly when selecting transferred employees for dismissal. It is now automatically unfair to dismiss an employee because he has brought proceedings under *TUPE (SI 2006/246)* or because he has alleged an infringement by his employer of his rights under *TUPE (SI 2006/246)* [*TUPE, SI 2006/246, Reg 19*, which amends *ERA 1996, s 104(4)*]. This may provide a way for employees to challenge dismissals that are otherwise sound under TUPE.

Illustrations and guidelines

6.45   In the following paragraphs a number of situations are considered which illustrate the application of these principles and, in particular, the extent to which the transferor and the purchaser can rely on an ETO to justify any reorganisation.

Where the purchaser requires that the transferor dismiss employees

6.46   If the purchaser insists that the transferor dismiss some or all of his employees prior to the transfer as a condition of the transfer, will the dismissals be fair?

In view of *Litster and Others v Forth Dry Dock & Engineering Company Ltd (In Receivership) and Another* [1989] IRLR 161 (see **6.39** above), it is difficult to carry out such dismissals fairly or, if the dismissals are unfair, to avoid a transfer of liability to the purchaser. The dismissals will only be potentially fair if the purchaser can show an ETO in relation to the business to be acquired such that the dismissals by the transferor are necessary [*TUPE (SI 2006/246), Reg 7*]. Given that the purchaser will almost certainly have a need for *some* employees after the transfer, it will be a very unusual case where requiring the transferor to dismiss *all* the employees can possibly be fair and effective. There may be scope for requiring the transferor to dismiss some of his employees where, in relation to those persons, an ETO can clearly be shown. However, it may be difficult to show that the reason for the dismissals is not the transfer or a reason connected with the transfer.

In endeavouring to show an ETO in the business to be acquired, the purchaser should have regard to the case of *Gateway Hotels Ltd v Stewart* [1988] IRLR 287 where it was held that the words 'economic, technical or organisational' should be restrictively construed and that their meaning should be interpreted by specific reference to the conduct of the business in question. If the reason for dismissals was simply a desire on the part of the transferor to obtain an enhanced price or to achieve a sale, it was said that this would not constitute an ETO and that the dismissals would be unfair. (See also *Whitehouse v Blatchford & Sons Limited* [1999] IRLR 492 (CA)).

A further consideration is whether the transferor will co-operate with any request by the purchaser that it dismiss any of its employees. Although commercial considerations will ultimately dictate the position, the transferor may be unwilling to effect dismissals before the transfer. If, nevertheless, it is prepared to contemplate such action, a prudent transferor should demand suitable indemnities from the purchaser. It should also request a satisfactory explanation as to the need for dismissals, which will need to be an ETO which has specific reference to the conduct of the business in question.

Recommended course of action: Because of the risks inherent in effecting dismissals before the transfer (see *Litster* above), it is considered that the most reliable and practicable solution for both transferors and purchasers on a transfer of a business will usually be for the employees in the business to be transferred to the purchaser who will then carry out such reorganisation as is necessary. This will involve a reduction in the price paid by the purchaser in many cases. If the purchaser prefers to insist on dismissals being effected prior to the transfer on the grounds of an ETO, the transferor should demand suitable indemnities from the purchaser.

Where the purchaser wishes to integrate new workforce with his existing one

6.47   Can the purchaser seek to change the terms and conditions of his newly-acquired employees and integrate them with those of his existing workforce?

Prima facie, any change to the terms and conditions of newly-acquired employees will be ineffective if made because of the transfer or for a reason connected with the transfer that is not an ETO [*TUPE (SI 2006/246), Reg 4(4)*]. In *Wilson & ors v St Helens BC* [1998] IRLR 706, however, the transfer of an undertaking did not constitute the reason for the variation. It was a variation to the 'same extent as it could have been with regard to the transferor'. There can be a valid variation for a reason other than because of the transfer or a reason connected with it that is an ETO [*TUPE (SI 2006/246), Reg 4(5)*]. (See also *Cornwall County Care Ltd v Brightman* [1998] IRLR 228). Changes to terms and conditions were found to be by reason of a transfer of an undertaking in *Credit Suisse First Boston (Europe) Limited v Padiachy & ors* [1998] IRLR 504 (HC) *and* by the Court of Appeal in *Credit Suisse First Boston (Europe) Limited v Lister* [1999] ICR 794. *In particular,* the Court of Appeal rejected the transferee's argument that the new terms and conditions were valid because the employee was better off overall.

Subject to *Wilson* (see above), the purchaser will need to show a change in the workforce when seeking to rely on an ETO when making changes to terms and conditions of employment after acquiring a business. A change in the workforce does not necessarily involve a change in the numbers or identity of the individuals who make up the workforce, provided that those persons are given different jobs to do (*Crawford v Swinton Insurance Brokers Ltd* [1990] IRLR 42).

In *Berriman v Delabole Slate Limited* [1985] IRLR 305, the employer merely attempted to reduce the pay of his newly-acquired employees to bring it into line with that of his existing employees. It was held that the newly-acquired employees had been constructively dismissed and the dismissals were automatically unfair.

Recommended course of action: In practice, a purchaser wishing to change the terms and conditions of his newly-acquired employees may find it simplest to 'red-circle' such employees for a period and then to implement changes at a later date as part of a general reorganisation, when it will argue that the principal reason for such changes (and for any constructive dismissal of an objecting employee) is no longer connected with the previous transfer of the business. Note, however, that it is still possible for dismissals to be held to be 'connected with the transfer' two years after the transfer in question. (*Taylor v Connex South Eastern Limited,* unreported, 5 July 2000 (EAT)).

Otherwise, the transferee may have to terminate the employment of such employees and re-engage them on new terms. This, of course, runs the risk of unfair dismissal claims, to defend which the transferee must be able to demonstrate an ETO reason. However, it is possible for parties to agree to variations which do not occur by reason of the transfer.

It should also be noted that *TUPE (SI 2006/246)* has introduced an ability, when the transferor is in an insolvency situation, for representatives of the transferred employees to make agreements with the transferor, purchaser or the persons exercising the transferor's powers, in prescribed circumstances, to change terms and conditions of their employment [*TUPE (SI 2006/246), Reg 9*]. The only variations permitted in these circumstances, however, are those designed to safeguard employment opportunities by ensuring the survival of the undertaking or business, or part of the undertaking or business, that has been transferred [*TUPE (SI 2006/246), Reg 9(7)(b)*].

Changes in terms and conditions prior to transfer

6.48   Can the purchaser insist as a condition of the acquisition that the transferor changes the terms and conditions of his employees *prior* to the transfer?

If the variations are by reason of the transfer as is likely to be the case, they will be ineffective (*Wilson & ors v St Helens BC* [1998] IRLR 706).

In an insolvency situation, see **6.47** above.

Re-employment of dismissed employees

6.49   Can the purchaser re-engage employees dismissed by the transferor selectively on new terms and conditions of employment?

The purchaser is free to re-employ employees dismissed by the transferor and to do so on new terms and conditions of employment. This is because the House of Lords in *(1) Meade (2) Baxendale v British Nuclear Fuels* [1998] IRLR 706 held that such dismissals were effective, even if unfair. (See also **6.47** above and *Cornwall County Care Ltd v Brightman* [1998] IRLR 228.) In practice, the purchaser is unlikely to wish to re-employ employees previously dismissed by the transferor by reason of an ETO. Further, liability for dismissals effected by the transferor by reason of the transfer will pass to the purchaser and generally the transferor will be reluctant to indemnify the purchaser in that respect.

Key points for the purchaser

6.50   If on a transfer of an undertaking the purchaser is accepting responsibility for the employees employed in the undertaking (as will normally be the case), it should consider negotiating a reduction in the purchase consideration and/or withholding part of such consideration pending the completion of any reorganisation of employees. Alternatively, it should endeavour to obtain an indemnity from the transferor in relation to claims by such employees and it should reserve to itself in the acquisition agreement the right to apply any sum withheld by it towards any claim by it under such indemnity. However, it will often be very difficult to assess the potential amount of compensation and it may therefore be wise to combine a retention with an indemnity. Note that a transferee can take advantage of a compromise of an employee's claim executed by the transferor, provided that such a compromise was effected before the date of the transfer (*Thompson & ors v Walon Car Delivery and BRS Automotive Ltd* [1997] IRLR 343.) The purchaser should also seek an indemnity in relation to claims by persons employed by the seller, other than employees whom the parties have agreed will transfer with the undertaking.

If, exceptionally, the purchaser requires the transferor to dismiss employees of the undertaking before the transfer, the purchaser must be sure that it can show that the reason (or the principal reason) for the dismissal is an ETO which has specific reference to the conduct of the undertaking in question. Should it be unable to do so, it will inherit liability for the employees whom the transferor has dismissed. Alternatively, where there is an ETO but the dismissals are unfair, where liability has not passed, it may have to satisfy any indemnity which it has given to the transferor in relation to claims by the employees against the transferor.

If changes are made to contractual terms, they should be attributed to a reason other than the transfer (eg costs, business needs etc.) or for an ETO reason. If the transferor is subject to insolvency proceedings at the time of the transfer, then contractual terms could be changed in prescribed circumstances (see **6.47** for further details).

Changes can be effected by serving contractual notice on transferred employees and offering re-employment on new terms to take effect immediately after termination of the original contract. The risk involved is that the dismissal will be almost certainly automatically unfair. In addition, such dismissals may trigger collective redundancy obligations (see **6.52** below).

A transferor may effect an internal reorganisation, hive the employees down to a company and sell the shares in the new company. Subsequent harmonisation of employees' terms by the purchaser of the company's shares may have nothing to do with the transfer. The danger, however, is that the hive-down and share sale could be considered as a series of transactions together constituting a transfer and attract the operation of *TUPE* (*SI 2006/246*).

The purchaser should seek appropriate warranty protection from the transferor in respect of all material employment matters. Warranties will offer the purchaser protection in the event that problems arise after completion of the transfer and will also force the transferor to make proper disclosure. The transferor may be asked to warrant (*inter alia*):

(a)   that full particulars of all material terms and conditions of employment and a list of names of all transferring employees have been disclosed;

(b)   that there will be no liabilities on completion in respect of employees other than in respect of remuneration and expenses;

(c)   that no employee has given or been given notice of termination of employment;

(d)   that no collective or individual disputes exist or are threatened;

(e)   that no contractual or non-contractual scheme or arrangement in relation to redundancy payments applies to any employees;

(f)   that all statutory obligations to inform and consult with appropriate representatives have been complied with;

(g)   that since a specified date no increases or improvement in emoluments or benefits have been given or proposed relating to any employees;

(h)   that all contracts of employment of employees are terminable on not more than four weeks' notice;

(i)   that no changes to the contracts of employees have been made by reason of the transfer; and

(j)   that no collective agreements or implied recognition arrangements (whether legally binding or not) exist with any trade union.

Appropriate indemnity protection should also be sought. See Precedents 2 and 3 at the end of this chapter.

Key points for the transferor

6.51 Provided commercial considerations permit, the transferor should endeavour to retain his employees on their existing terms and conditions of employment until the time of the transfer when they will be transferred to the purchaser. (This does not apply to employees whom the transferor wishes to dismiss independently of the transfer, eg for reasons of misconduct.) Alternatively, the transferor may be able to re-deploy certain of his employees away from the undertaking which is being transferred, in accordance with their terms and conditions or with their consent. In order to be effective, any such redeployment must be effected before the transfer and not be by reason of the transfer. Documentation relating to changes should not refer to the impending transfer and, if possible, should reflect other reasons.

If, exceptionally, the transferor is prepared to accept responsibility for dismissals or changes in terms and conditions of employment prior to the transfer, it should seek to negotiate an increase in price, obtain a suitable indemnity from the purchaser and satisfy itself that the reason for any dismissal (actual or constructive) is an ETO connected specifically with the conduct of the business being transferred.

The transferor must also provide the transferee with the necessary 'employment liability information', according to the guidelines outlined under **6.42** above.

Collective matters

Pre-acquisition investigation

6.52 The purchaser should make careful enquiries as to the nature of any trade union presence in the target and as to relationships between any trade union and senior management. Before formalising any arrangements for purchase, it should investigate the following:

(a)   any collective agreements with trade unions;

(b)   the details of relations with trade unions;

(c)   the company's history of industrial disputes;

(d)   the details of ongoing discussions and negotiations with trade unions or, if appropriate, elected representatives for information and consultation purposes;

(e)   any redundancy agreements, policy statements or particulars of custom and practice; and

(f)   the details of any lay-off and guarantee payment provisions.

In all cases, it is crucial that the purchaser should establish whether any recognition arrangements exist with trade unions which are not reduced to writing and then establish the nature of the relationship with any recognised trade unions. It is important to meet the officers of recognised unions as early as possible to try to secure their co-operation. The purchaser must consider whether to continue recognition arrangements is appropriate in all the circumstances.

Share purchases – post-acquisition changes

6.53 Following a purchase of shares the purchaser must have regard to arrangements with trade unions in the same way as for his existing workforce. An employer is obliged to recognise an independent trade union where the majority of the workforce so wish, and in any event, where the purchaser inherits well-established recognition arrangements it will often be in the interests of the business to maintain these.

Redundancies – duty to consult

6.54 Where the purchaser (as the employer) is proposing to dismiss as redundant 20 or more employees at one establishment within a period of 90 days or less, it should consult appropriate representatives. [*TULRCA 1992, s 188 et seq.*]. For these purposes redundancy means dismissal for a reason not related to the individual concerned. [*TULRCA 1992, s 195*]. In relation to collective redundancies effected on or after 1 November 1999 (and business transfers that complete on or after 1 November 1999) the *Collective Redundancies and Transfer of Undertakings (Protection of Employment) (Amendment) Regulations 1999* ('*1999 Regulations*') (*SI 1999/1925*) apply.

The *1999 Regulations* extend the duty to inform and consult so that it is no longer confined to the duty to consult with employees who may be dismissed but includes employees 'affected by the proposed dismissals or [who] may be affected by measures taken in connection with those dismissals'.

An employer must disclose in writing to the appropriate representatives:

(a)   the reasons for its proposals;

(b)   the numbers and descriptions of employees whom it proposes to dismiss as redundant;

(c)   the total number of employees of that description employed at the establishment in question;

(d)   the proposed method of selecting the employees who may be dismissed;

(e)   the proposed method of carrying out the dismissals, including the period over which the dismissals are to take effect; and

(f)   the proposed method of calculating redundancy payments, if it is to be otherwise than in compliance with the statutory payment regime.

The legislation does not expressly state when this information must be given but it must be disclosed before the consultations begin. The information provided must be sufficiently specific to enable meaningful consultation to take place.

Consultation must start at the earliest opportunity and must in any event begin:

(a)   where the employer is proposing to dismiss as redundant 100 or more employees at one establishment within a period of 90 days or less, at least 90 days before the first of those dismissals takes effect;

(b)   where the employer is proposing to dismiss as redundant 99 employees at one establishment within a period of 90 days or less, at least 30 days before the first of those dismissals takes effect.

The *1999 Regulations (SI 1999/1925)* changed the designation of the appropriate representatives for collective redundancies (and business transfers). Employers must consult representatives of recognised trade unions but, if no trade union is recognised, then employers must consult either existing employee representatives or specially-elected employee representatives. If an employer invites affected employees to elect representatives and they fail to do so within a reasonable time, the employer must give to each affected employee the information that would have been provided to the elected representatives.

In the event that elections are held for employee representatives (in relation to collective redundancies effected or business transfers completed on or after 1 November 1999), they must be held in accordance with the *1999 Regulations* (inserting s 188A into *TULCRA 1992)* which provide that:

(a)   the employer must make such arrangements as are reasonably practical to ensure that the election is fair;

(b)   the employer determines the number of representatives to be elected so that there are sufficient representatives to represent the interests of all the affected employees having regard to the number and classes of those employees;

(c)   the employer determines whether the affected employees should be represented either by representatives of all the affected employees or by representatives of particular classes of those employees;

(d)   before the election the employer determines the term of office as employee representatives so that it is of sufficient length to enable information to be given and consultations to be completed;

(e)   the candidates for election as employee representatives must be affected employees on the date of the election;

(fi)   no affected employee should be unreasonably excluded from standing for election;

(g)   all affected employees on the date of the election are entitled to vote for employee representatives;

(h)   the employees entitled to vote may vote for as many candidates as there are representatives to be elected to represent them or, if there are to be representatives for particular classes of employees, may vote for as many candidates as there are representatives to be elected to represent their particular class of employee; and

(i)   the election must be conducted so as to secure that so far as is reasonably practicable, those voting do so in secret, and the votes given at the election are accurately counted.

The provisions of *ERA 1996* relating to the right of employee representatives not to be dismissed or suffer detriment are extended to employees who participate in an election of employee representatives.

Consultation requires the employer, *inter alia*, to supply the written information prescribed in *section 188(4)* of *TULRCA 1992* (as amended) to the appropriate representatives, to consider their representations (if any) and to reply. Consultation shall be undertaken by the employer 'with a view to reaching agreement with the appropriate representatives'. [*TULRCA 1992, s 188(2)*, as amended].

The *1999 Regulations* [*Reg 5(1), (2)*] provide that a complaint may be brought:

(a)   in the case of a failure relating to the election of employee representatives, by any of the affected employees (or by any of the employees who have been dismissed as redundant in the case of collective redundancies);

(b)   in the case of any other failure relating to employee representatives, by any of the employee representatives to whom the failure related;

(c)   in the case of failure relating to representatives of a trade union, by the trade union; and

(d)   in any other case, by any of the affected employees (or by any of the employees who have been dismissed as redundant).

If a question arises as to whether or not any employee representative was an appropriate representative the employer must show that the employee representative had the authority to represent the affected employees.

If the complaint relates to the election requirements the employer must show that the requirements set out above have been satisfied.

If an employer can show special circumstances making it 'not reasonably practicable' for it to consult (which will be very hard for it to show), it must take all such steps to do so as are reasonably practicable. (As to whether the transferor or transferee will be liable for a failure to consult, see **6.59** below.) Failure to do so can lead to a 'protective award' being made against it in respect of such descriptions of employees as may be specified in the award (employees who have been or are to be dismissed for redundancy and in respect of whom the employer has failed to consult). The award requires the employer to pay remuneration to the employees for the 'protected period' which is subject to a ceiling of 90 days in respect of dismissals taking effect on or after 1 November 1999. [*TULRCA 1992, s 189*, as amended]. The maximum 30-day period which previously applied to between 20 and 99 redundancies is abolished.

In the case of *Sovereign Distribution Services Ltd v Transport and General Workers Union* [1989] IRLR 334, there was no meaningful consultation and a total failure to provide written information as required by what is now *section 188(4)* of *TULRCA 1992*. A protective award was made as it was held that the purpose of the legislation was to ensure that consultation took place even if the employer considered that consultation would achieve nothing. (As to whether an employer can set off against the protective award any other sums paid under the contract for that period see *Mann v Secretary of State for Employment* [1999] IRLR 566.)

Please note there may be an additional duty on employers to inform and consult under the *Information and Consultation of Employees Regulations 2004 (SI 2004/3426)* (the '*ICE Regulations*') which give employees in larger firms (those with 50 or more employees), rights to be informed and consulted about the business they work for (see **6.61** below).

Transfer of business – the duty to inform and consult

6.55   There are two separate and distinct duties imposed by *TUPE* (*SI 2006/246*) on the employer of employees (whether the transferor or the purchaser). They are the duty to inform and the duty to consult. [*TUPE, SI 2006/246, Reg 13*]. These duties are a legal requirement as opposed to merely recommendations of a Code of Practice (see **6.30** above in relation to consultation with individual employees). Note that the duty to inform and consult in the event of a business transfer is extended and the designation of appropriate representatives for this purpose is changed in accordance with the *1999 Regulations (SI 1999/1925)* (see **6.54** above). This means that the same requirements for the election of representatives apply. If affected employees fail to elect representatives within a reasonable time of being invited to do so, the employer must give the employees the required information individually. Employment protection against detriment or dismissal is extended to employees who participate in employee representative elections, and the right to time off work is extended to give employee representatives time off for training.

The case of *Howard v (1) Millrise Ltd t/a Colourflow (in Liquidation) (2) SG Printers t/a Colourflow* [2005] IRLR 84, *confirmed* the process of informing and consulting affected employees. It was held that if there is a TUPE transfer in prospect and no trade union is recognised, the employer is under a duty to choose between either dealing with representatives of the affected employees already in place that may have been appointed or elected for purposes other than *TUPE*, or inviting the affected employees to elect representatives and then informing and consulting with such elected representatives. If, after being invited to do so, affected employees fail to elect representatives within a reasonable time, the employer must then give the employees the required information individually.

Please note there may be an additional duty on employers to inform and consult under the *Information and Consultation of Employees Regulations 2004 (SI 2004/3426)* (the '*ICE Regulations*') which give employees in larger firms (those with 50 or more employees), rights to be informed and consulted about the business they work for (see **6.61** below).

The duty to inform

6.56   Certain information must be provided to the appropriate representatives long enough before the transfer to enable consultations to take place. The representatives must be informed about the transfer; the 'legal, social and economic' implications for affected employees (which will include the employees of both the target and the purchaser); the *measures* which the employer will be taking in relation to those employees, or if none, that must be stated; and in the case of the transferor, any measures which the purchaser envisages it will take in relation to the affected employees, or if none, that must be stated. Such information should be given in writing.

'Legal' implications include any changes in terms and conditions of employment which are envisaged and the effect of the transfer on other common law and statutory rights. 'Economic' implications seem to include the effects of the transfer on terms and conditions dealing with remuneration and benefits in kind as well as such consideration as future plans and prospects for the undertaking. 'Social' implications appear to include wider aspects of the employer's legal or voluntary responsibilities such as pension provision, training, communication policy, redundancy policy or welfare policy.

The duty to consult

6.57   The duty to consult, which is a separate duty, only arises where the employer of any affected employees envisages that it will be taking *measures* in connection with the transfer in relation to such employees. 'Measures' are likely to include any positive steps proposed to achieve a reduction in manpower but will not include manpower projections.

In the course of any consultations the employer should consider any representations made by the appropriate representatives; and it should reply to those representations stating his reasons if it rejects any of them. Consultation must be with a view to seeking the agreement of appropriate representatives to measures to be taken. [*TUPE, SI 2006/246, Reg 13(6)*].

If there are special circumstances which make it not reasonably practicable for an employer to comply with his duty to inform or consult, it is required to take all such steps towards performing that duty as are reasonably practicable in the circumstances. [*TUPE, SI 2006/246, Reg 13(9)*].

When must consultation begin?

6.58   Consultation should begin before an employer's proposals are at a definitive stage so as to enable the appropriate representatives to put forward matters which may influence the proposals. Consultation must commence in sufficient time to enable consultation to take place 'with a view to seeking agreement'. Where one of the parties is a listed company and consultation will involve a large number of people, that party's obligations as to the release of price-sensitive information under the Listing Rules should be considered at this stage. The employer should consider its obligations under the *Data Protection Act 1998* and the *Employment Practices Data Protection Code*. Each case will depend on its own facts.

A useful practice to reduce the risk of unwarranted disclosures is to require the purchaser to sign a confidentiality undertaking requiring it to destroy or return disclosed materials in the event that the sale does not proceed.

In the case of transactions involving publicly quoted companies, the usual reason why consultation may be thought impossible prior to the sale agreement being entered into is that the parties wish, or believe it is required, that the sale and purchase be kept confidential until it can be publicly announced, and that consulting the trade unions or employee representatives could require the making of a premature announcement. In fact, paragraph 9.4 of the Listing Rules does permit a listed company to give information in confidence to (*inter alia*) employee representatives and trade unions about an impending transaction, prior to publicly announcing it, but it is often feared that the confidence will not be respected by them and there will be a leak which will trigger the need to make an immediate announcement under the same rule. If a proper consultation is not possible, often the best thing is to telephone the employee representative or trade union officer slightly before the public announcement, so at least he is given some warning and is less likely to feel that the breach of the required consultation procedure should be challenged. The more consultation there is, the less likely it is that the maximum award of compensation will be made.

Liability for failure to consult

6.59   Whereas before liability for failure to consult would fall on the transferor, now both the transferor and transferee can be liable for a failure to inform and/or consult. Transferees are jointly and severally liable for awards for failure to inform and consult made against transferors. [*TUPE, SI 2006/246, Reg 15(9)*]. However, liability for failure to consult with regard to collective redundancies) transfers to the transferee as regards employees transferred and employees dismissed prior to the transfer by the transferor where the dismissal is automatically unfair (*Kerry Foods Limited v Creber & Ors* [2000] IRLR 10).

Remedy for failing to inform or consult

6.60   The provisions governing who may bring a complaint in respect of a failure to consult (under the *1999 Regulations (SI 1999/1925)* are set out at **6.54** above. The tribunal may make a declaration and order up to 13 weeks' pay to each affected employee [*TUPE, (SI 2006/246), Regs 15(7)and 16(3)*].

Provisions for offsetting any such award against payments made for failure to consult on redundancy have been abolished. [*TURERA 1993, s 33(7)*].

In *Sweetin v Coral Racing* [2006] IRLR 252, the EAT held that guidelines laid down in *Susie Radin Ltd v GMB & Ors* [2004] IRLR 400 in relation to awarding compensation payable by an employer for failure to consult in the context of collective redundancies were equally applicable in the context of TUPE. These guidelines suggested, *inter alia*, that the purpose of an award is penal as opposed to compensatory, that although the Tribunal has a wide discretion to do what is just and equitable it should focus on the seriousness of the employer's default, and that the best approach where there has been no consultation is to start with the maximum period and reduce it only if there are mitigating circumstances justifying a reduction to an extent which the Tribunal considers appropriate.

The EAT added the caveat that a Tribunal is also entitled to have regard to any actual loss that a claimant suffered as a result of the failure to consult, so long as it recognises that the purpose of any award is penal and that proof of loss is not necessary.

Additional legislation governing the duty to inform and consult

6.61   The *Information and Consultation of Employees Regulations 2004 (SI 2004/3426)* (the '*ICE Regulations*') give employees in larger firms – those with 50 or more employees – rights to be informed and consulted about the business they work for. The *ICE Regulations* implement EC Council Directive 2002/14, and are based on a framework for implementation agreed with the Confederation of British Industry and the Trades Union Congress. They apply to businesses with 150+ employees from 6 April 2005, to those with 100+ employees from 6 April 2007, and to those with 50+ employees from 6 April 2008. They will not apply to businesses with less than 50 employees.

The *ICE Regulations* apply to undertakings employing in the UK, whose registered office, head office or principal place of business is situated in Great Britain.

The requirement to inform and consult employees under the *ICE Regulations* does not operate automatically. It is triggered either by a formal request from the requisite number of employees for an information and consultation agreement, or by employers choosing to start the process themselves.

Whether an employer to whom the *ICE Regulations* apply has received a formal request from its employees to negotiate an agreement over the practical arrangements for information and consultation or has initiated the process itself, this will have resulted in either:

(a)   an individually negotiated agreement; or

(b)   the statutory provisions applying.

If the statutory provisions apply, an employer will have been required to set up an I&C committee representing all the employees in the undertaking. The duties to inform and consult with the I&C committee will arise before obligations to inform and consult under *TUPE* arise.

The employer must provide the I&C committee with information on:

(a)   the recent and probable development of the undertaking's activities and economic situation;

(b)   the situation, structure and probable development of employment within the undertaking and on any anticipatory measures envisaged, in particular where there is a threat to employment within the undertaking; and

(c)   decisions likely to lead to substantial changes in work organisation or in contractual relations, including business transfers.

Information must be given at such time, in such fashion and with such content as are appropriate to enable, in particular, the I&C committee to conduct an adequate study and, where necessary, to prepare for consultation.

The employer must consult the I&C committee on the matters in (b) and (c) above:

(a)   whilst ensuring that the timing, method and content of the consultation are appropriate;

(b)   on the basis of the information supplied by the employer to the I&C committee and of any opinion which those representatives express to the employer;

(c)   in such a way as to enable the I&C committee to meet the employer at the relevant level of management depending on the subject under discussion and to obtain a reasoned response from the employer to any such opinion.

In relation to decisions under (c), consultation must take place with a view to reaching agreement on decisions within the scope of the employer's powers.

An employer's duty to inform and consult the I&C committee in relation to transfers of undertakings will come to an end:

(a)   as soon as the obligation to consult collectively under *TUPE* is triggered; and

(b)   he has notified the I&C committee in writing that he will be complying with his duty under that legislation, instead of under the *ICE Regulations*;

provided that the notification is given on each occasion on which the employer has become or is about to become subject to the duty.

If an employer fails to comply with these provisions, a claim can be brought before the Central Arbitration Committee (CAC). If the CAC upholds the complaint it may make an order specifying the steps which the employer is required to take. Any order made by the CAC will not have the effect of suspending or altering the effect of any act done or of any agreement made by the employer or of preventing or delaying any act or agreement which the employer proposes to do or make.

If the CAC decides that the employer is at fault an application can be made to the Employment Appeal Tribunal for an order requiring the employer to pay a penalty to the Secretary of State. The amount of the penalty is subject to a maximum of £75,000.

Purchase from an insolvent company

6.62   Provisions have been included in *TUPE (SI 2006/246)* to encourage the sale of insolvent businesses as going concerns and the preservation of jobs on an insolvency; the new provisions reduce the liabilities which pass to a purchaser of an insolvent business and allow employers to negotiate changes to the terms of employment contracts which are to transfer under the Regulations.

The purchaser of a business from an insolvent company first needs to consider whether *TUPE (SI 2006/246)* applies. *Regulation 8(7)* provides that where the transferor is subject to bankruptcy proceedings or any analogous proceedings instituted with a view to the liquidation of the transferor's assets, and which are under the supervision of an insolvency practitioner, *regulations 4* and *7* of *TUPE (SI 2006/246)* will not apply; in those cases, liabilities under employment contracts will not transfer, and the termination of employment contracts will not be automatically unfair. *TUPE (SI 2006/246)* does not expressly state which corporate insolvency proceedings fall within the scope of *regulation 8(7)*, but the government's view is that it includes compulsory liquidations and possibly creditors' voluntary liquidations.

If the transferor is subject to insolvency proceedings which do not fall within the definition of *regulation 8(7)*, then *regulations 4* and *7* will apply. However, where the transferor is subject to 'relevant insolvency proceedings', the following special rules will also apply:

(a)   a transferee will not be liable for any debts due to employees which are guaranteed by the National Insurance Fund. These include pay arrears for up to eight weeks, holiday pay for up to six weeks, statutory notice entitlement, statutory redundancy pay and a basic award (but not a compensatory award) for unfair dismissal. In each case, pay is capped at £310 per week. Any other debts other than those guaranteed by the National Insurance Fund will still transfer to the transferee; and

(b)   changes to employees' terms and conditions may be made in the circumstances referred to in **6.47** above.

'Relevant insolvency proceedings' are collective proceedings which have been opened 'not with a view to liquidation of the assets of the transferor' and which are supervised by an insolvency practitioner. Again, *TUPE (SI 2006/246)* does not state which insolvency proceedings are included, but the government's view is that they are intended to cover administration, individual and company voluntary arrangements and possibly creditors' voluntary winding up, but that they do not cover administrative receivership or members' voluntary winding up. However, it is not clear whether it includes an administration which was opened with a view to liquidation of the assets, rather than a rescue of the company.

The purchaser of a business from a receiver or administrator (an 'officeholder') should note that dismissals by the officeholder made before the transfer will be automatically unfair if the reason or principal reason for the dismissals is the transfer itself (or a reason connected with it). Liability for such dismissals is transferred to the purchaser (see *Litster and Others v Forth Dry Dock & Engineering Company Ltd (In Receivership) and Another* [1989] IRLR 163, see **6.39** above). This decision effectively ended the practice of officeholders hiving down the business before selling it to a purchaser.

Although claims for unfair dismissal in connection with a transfer are transferred to the purchaser, the dismissals themselves will not be a nullity (see *(1) Meade (2) Baxendale v British Nuclear Fuels* [1998] IRLR 706).

The purchaser should enquire of the officeholder as to any dismissals made following his appointment and the circumstances surrounding them, since any dismissals effected by the officeholder in an effort to make the business more marketable, could be said to be connected to the ultimate transfer (see *Thompson v SCS Consulting Ltd* [2001] IRLR 801*)*.

When an officeholder is appointed with a view to a possible sale of the business, the obligation to inform (in relation to *TUPE (SI 2006/246))* arises on his appointment. The officeholder may be able to rely on *regulation 13(9)* which provides that where there are special circumstances which render it not reasonably practicable to comply with the consultation requirements, he is under a duty only to take all such steps as are reasonably practicable in the circumstances towards doing so. The purchaser will be jointly and severally liable with the transferor to pay compensation for failure to inform or consult under *TUPE (SI 2006/246)*. Where the transferor is insolvent, this means that liability will effectively fall on the transferee, and any risk to the purchaser should be reflected in the purchase price.

Recommended course of action

6.63   A purchaser buying from a receiver or other insolvency officeholder should be prepared to take over all the employees of the business in order to effect any necessary reorganisation subsequently. The price that it pays should be reduced to reflect the additional liabilities that it is acquiring in relation to employees. Note that the purchaser will not inherit liability for employees dismissed by the receiver/officeholder before the transfer for a reason wholly unconnected with the transfer, but the purchaser should make full enquiry of all dismissals.

Key points for the purchaser/transferee

6.64   The following steps should be taken by the purchaser/transferee:

(a)   Address personnel issues sooner rather than later.

(b)   Obtain documents and information as early as possible.

(c)   Establish personnel targets by identifying stayers and leavers.

(d)   Secure the co-operation of stayers by consultation and discussion.

(e)   If purchasing an undertaking, agree to accept a transfer of the employees of the undertaking. Consider negotiating an appropriate reduction in the purchase consideration. Alternatively, obtain indemnities from the transferor in relation to claims by the employees and in relation to claims by persons employed by the transferor other than those agreed to be transferred with the undertaking.

(f)   Establish procedures for dealing with redundancies and changes in terms and conditions of employment (if any).

(g)   Consider obligations to appropriate representatives early, and inform and consult as soon as possible.

(h)   Ensure the transferor provides the necessary 'employee liability information' in accordance with the time limits.

(i)   Obtain appropriate warranties as to employees, their terms and conditions of employment and such further indemnities as are available from the transferor. See the precedents at the end of this chapter.

(j)   Consider confidentiality arrangements, data protection and access to records, for example whether the transfer will release disciplinary records.

(k)   Notify the Secretary of State as early as possible about large-scale redundancies.

(l)   Maintain good industrial relations at all times by acting fairly and communicating in depth wherever possible.

Key points for the seller/transferor

6.65   The following steps should be taken by the seller/transferor:

(a)   If selling an undertaking, transfer all the employees of the business on their existing terms and conditions of employment to the purchaser.

(b)   If selling an undertaking, only dismiss employees before the transfer pursuant to a request by the purchaser after having obtained an indemnity from the purchaser in relation to potential claims in the event that the dismissals are found to be unfair. Negotiate an increase in price when accepting a liability for dismissing employees or changing terms and conditions of employment before the transfer.

(c)   Consider obligations to appropriate representatives early, and inform and consult as soon as possible.

(d)   Provide the necessary 'employee liability information' in accordance with the time limits.

(e)   Obtain suitable indemnities from the purchaser in relation to claims by employees after any transfer. See Precedent 3 at the end of this chapter.

(f)   Maintain good industrial relations by acting fairly and communicating in depth as much as possible.

The following pages contain precedents concerning employment warranties and indemnities.

Precedents – employment warranties and indemnities

Precedent 1 – Employment warranties given by the vendor/warrantor to the purchaser (share acquisition)

(A)   **[Directors]** – The particulars shown in [. . . . .] are true and complete and no person not named therein as a director is a director or shadow director of the Company.

(B)   **[Employees]**

(1)   The individuals listed in [. . . . .] ('the Employees') are all employed by the Company at the date of this Agreement [and will be employed by the Company at Completion]. There are no other individuals employed at the date of this Agreement by the Company. [There will be no other individuals employed at the date of Completion by the Company.] The further individuals, details of whom are annexed to [the Disclosure Letter] are all the individuals who are providing services to the Company in relation to the Business on a self-employed basis or are supplied by an agency ('the Workers').

(2)   All contracts of service of any of the Employees (including for these purposes the directors referred to in (A) above) and the Workers are terminable on three months' notice or less without compensation, (other than compensation payable in accordance with the Employment Rights Act 1996).

(3)   [The Disclosure Letter] gives true, accurate and complete details of ages and lengths of continuous service of all of the Employees and by reference to each of the Employees and Workers the remuneration payable and other benefits provided by or which the Company is bound to provide (whether now or in the future) to each Employee or Worker at [the date of this Agreement] or any person connected with any such person or the agency supplying him and (without limiting the generality of the foregoing) includes particulars of all profit sharing, incentive, bonus, commission arrangements and any other benefit to which each Employee or Worker is entitled or which is regularly provided or made available to [him/them] (including details of [his/their]

notice period and [his/their] entitlement to holiday) in any case whether legally binding on the Company or not.

(4) There are no subsisting contracts for the provision by any person of any consultancy services to the Company.

(5) No Employee or Worker has given notice terminating his contract of employment or has been or is to be withdrawn by the agency supplying him.

(6) No Employee is under notice of dismissal nor is there any liability outstanding to any Employee or former employee or any Worker or the agency supplying him except for remuneration or other benefits accruing due and no such remuneration or other benefit which has fallen due for payment has not been paid.

(7) During the period of six months ending with the date of this Agreement the Company has not terminated the employment of any person employed in or by the Company or who has been engaged by the Company on a self-employed basis to work in the Business.

(8) None of the Employees or Workers belongs or has belonged at any material time to an independent trade union recognised by the Company.

(9) There are no employee representatives representing all or any of the Employees.

(10) The Company has complied with all of its statutory obligations to inform and consult appropriate representatives as required by law, including obligations in relation to the election and treatment of employee representatives.

(11) The Company is not under any obligation to pay any Employee who is dismissed by reason of redundancy payments other than statutory redundancy payments and plan, scheme, arrangement, policy, custom or practice (whether legally binding or not) exists within the Company pursuant to which enhanced redundancy or equivalent payments have been paid to or are or may be payable to employees of the Company.

(12) All plans schemes, commitments, policies, customs or practices for the provision of benefits to Employees and Workers comply in all respects with all relevant statutes, regulations and other laws and all necessary consents in relation to such plans have been obtained and all governmental filings in relation to the same have been made.

(13) There are no loans owed by any of the Employees or Workers to the Company.

(14) Since [the last review date/the Balance Sheet Date,] no change has been made in (i) the rate of remuneration, or the emoluments or pension benefits or other contractual benefits of any of the Employees or Workers or the amount payable to any agency sup-

plying Workers or (ii) the terms and conditions of employment of the Employees or terms of engagement of the Workers nor has the Company entered into any informal or formal agreement to amend or change such terms and conditions.

(15) [Except for [*specify pension scheme[s]*] the Company is not under any present or future liability to pay to any Employee or Worker or to any other person who has been in any manner connected with the Company any pension, superannuation allowance, death benefit, retirement gratuity or like benefit or to contribute to any life assurance scheme, medical insurance scheme, or permanent health scheme and the Company has not made any such payments or contributions on a voluntary basis nor is it proposing to do so.

(16) There are no training schemes, arrangements or proposals whether past or present in respect of which a levy may henceforth become payable by the Company under the Industrial Training Act 1982 (as amended by the Employment Act 1989) and pending Completion no such schemes, arrangements or proposals will be established or undertaken.

(17) There is no outstanding undischarged liability to pay to any governmental or regulatory authority in any jurisdiction or any contribution, taxation or other duty arising in connection with the employment or engagement of any of the Employees or Workers.

(18) No Employee or Worker or any agency supplying Workers will become entitled by virtue of his contract of service or supply to any payment or enhancement in or improvement to his remuneration, benefits or terms and conditions of service or supply only by reason of the execution of this Agreement or completion of the sale and purchase under or pursuant to this Agreement.

(19) The Company has not entered into any informal or formal agreement to amend or change the terms and conditions of employment or engagement as required to be disclosed of the Employees or Workers or agency supplying Workers (whether such amendment or change is to take effect prior to or after Completion).

(20) There is no working arrangement, practice, policy or procedure operated by the Company in relation to the Business which contravenes the Working Time Regulations 1998 and the Company has kept all records required by those Regulations.

(21) There is no hourly paid Employee or Worker employed or engaged by the Company to work in the Business who is now paid less than the statutory minimum applicable under the National Minimum Wage Act 1998.

(22) [At the date of this Agreement] there is no:

(1) outstanding claim by any person who is now or has been an employee of the Company or was engaged by the Company on a self-employed basis or was supplied to the Company

by an agency to work in the Business, or any dispute with any of the said persons or any trade union or any other body representing all or any of such persons in relation to their employment by the Company or any circumstances likely to give rise to any such dispute;

(2) industrial action involving any employee, whether official or unofficial, currently occurring or threatened; or

(3) industrial relations matter which has been referred to ACAS or any other appropriate governmental agency for advice, conciliation or arbitration.

[(23) The warranties set out in paragraphs [insert appropriate numbers] above are and will be true and accurate as at Completion.]

Precedent 2 – Employment warranties given by the transferor of an undertaking (TUPE) (NB not applicable to a purchase from a receiver/administrator)

1.1 The individuals listed in [. . . . .] ('the Employees') are all employed by the Vendor in the Business at the date of this Agreement [and will be employed by the Vendor in the Business at the date of Transfer]. There are no other individuals employed at the date of this Agreement in the Business. [There will be no other individuals employed at the date of Transfer in the Business].

1.2 All contracts of service of any of the Employees are terminable on three months' notice or less without compensation, (other than compensation payable in accordance with the Employment Rights Act 1996).

1.3 [The Disclosure Letter] contains, in relation to each Employee entitled to a basic salary in excess of [£. . .] per annum or the equivalent in foreign currency (a 'Senior Employee'), true, accurate and complete details of ages and lengths of continuous service and remuneration payable and other benefits including (without limiting the generality of the foregoing) particulars of all profit sharing, incentive, bonus, commission arrangements and any other benefit to which any Senior Employee is entitled or which is regularly provided or made available to [him/them] (including details of [his/their] notice period and [his/their] entitlement to holiday) in any case whether legally binding on the Vendor or not.

1.4 The Vendor has disclosed all 'employee liability information' in accordance with *Regulation 11* of the *Transfer of Undertakings (Protection of Employment) Regulations 2006 (SI 2006/246)*.

1.5 There are no subsisting contracts for the provision by any specified individual of any consultancy services to the Business.

1.6 No Senior Employee has given notice terminating his contract of employment or is under notice of dismissal.

1.7 None of the Employees belongs or has belonged at any material time to an independent trade union recognised by the Vendor.

1.8　There are no employee representatives representing all or any of the Employees.

1.9　The Vendor is not under any obligation to pay any Employee who is dismissed by reason of redundancy payments other than statutory redundancy payments and no scheme, arrangement, policy, custom or practice (whether legally binding or not) exists within the Business pursuant to which enhanced redundancy or equivalent payments have been paid to or are or may be payable to employees in the Business.

1.10　All plans for the provision of benefits to Employees comply in all respects with all relevant statutes, regulations or other laws and all necessary consents in relation to such plans have been obtained and all governmental filings in relation to such plans have been made.

1.11　Since [the last review date/the Balance Sheet Date,] no change has been made in (i) the rate of remuneration, or the emoluments or pension benefits or other contractual benefits of the Employees or (ii) the terms and conditions of employment of any Senior Employees nor has the Vendor entered into any informal or formal agreement to amend or change such terms and conditions.

1.12　[Except for [*specify pension scheme[s]*] the Vendor is not under any present or future liability to pay to any Employee any pension, superannuation allowance, death benefit, retirement gratuity or like benefit or to contribute to any life assurance scheme, medical insurance scheme, or permanent health scheme and the Vendor has not, since the last Balance Sheet Date or in the twelve months prior thereto, made any such payments or contributions on a voluntary basis nor is it proposing to do so.]

1.13　None of the Employees or their representatives has attempted to make or made a valid request to establish an Information and Consultation body pursuant to the provisions of the *Information and Consultation of Employees Regulations 2004.*

1.14　There is no formal or informal understanding, agreement or commitment between the Vendor and any of the Employees or their representatives to establish on a statutory or voluntary basis an Information and Consultation body pursuant to the provisions of the *Information and Consultation of Employees Regulations 2004* or otherwise

1.15　[At the date of this Agreement] there is no:

(A)　outstanding claim by any Employee of the Vendor, or any material group of Employees, in relation to the Business or any dispute with any trade union or any other body representing all or any of such persons in relation to their employment in the Business and, so far as the Vendor is aware there are no, circumstances likely to give rise to any such dispute;

(B)　industrial action involving any Employee, whether official or unofficial, currently occurring or, so far as the Vendor is aware, threatened; or

(C) industrial relations matter which has been referred to ACAS or any other appropriate governmental agency for advice, conciliation or arbitration.

[1.16 The warranties set out in Paragraphs [insert appropriate numbers] above are and will be true and accurate as at the [Transfer Date].]

Precedent 3 – Employment indemnities (transfer of an undertaking (TUPE)) (NB vendor indemnities not applicable to purchase from a receiver/administrator)

1.1 The Vendor and the Purchaser agree and acknowledge that [the Regulations] shall at the [Transfer Date] be applicable in relation to the Employees. All wages, salaries and [other] benefits of the Employees and all PAYE, tax deductions and national insurance contributions relating thereto shall be the responsibility of and be discharged by the Vendor forthwith in respect of the period up to the Transfer Date and subject as provided below by the Purchaser thereafter.

1.2 The Vendor shall be responsible for and shall fully indemnify and keep indemnified the Purchaser from and against all and any costs (including legal costs on a full indemnity basis), claims, expenses, damages, demands, actions, losses and liabilities:

(A) arising, directly or indirectly, from any act omission obligation or liability of the Vendor in relation to the Employees prior to the [Transfer Date] including any act, omission, obligation or liability which is deemed by virtue of the Regulations to be the responsibility of the Purchaser after the [Transfer Date];

(B) arising from any claim in respect of any person engaged by the Vendor under a contract for services or any employee employed by the Vendor who is not an Employee prior to the [Transfer Date], (including, without limitation, the dismissal of such person or employee by the Purchaser or a change in his terms of employment) for which the Purchaser is liable by reason of the operation of [the Regulations];

(C) arising as a result of the Vendor's failure to comply with its obligations to inform and consult recognised trade unions or elected representatives of affected Employees as appropriate in respect of the business transfer contemplated by this Agreement; or collective redundancies relating to [the Business] and contemplated by the Vendor prior to the [Transfer Date]; and

(D) arising out of any claim made by any recognised trade union or any other body representing all or any of the Employees and which relates to facts or events occurring prior to the [Transfer Date] in relation to obligations to inform and/or consult on the part of the Vendor in respect of collective redundancies or business transfers other than pursuant to this Agreement.

[1.3 The Purchaser shall be responsible for and shall fully indemnify and keep indemnified the Vendor from and against all and any costs, claims, expenses, damages, demands, actions, losses and liabilities:

(A) arising, directly or indirectly, from any act, omission, obligation or liability of the Purchaser in relation to the Employees on or following the [Transfer Date]; and

(B) arising as a result of the Purchaser's failure to comply with its obligation to inform the Vendor of measures pursuant to Regulation 10(2)(d) and (3) of [the Regulations].]

1.4 The Vendor [and the Purchaser] shall notify the Purchaser [each other] on becoming aware of any claim by any of the Employees or any other person who is or has been, or purports to be or have been, employed in the Business, arising out of or in connection with the sale of the Business to the Purchaser, and the Vendor and the Purchaser shall [at their own respective expense] give each other such assistance and information which may reasonably be required in relation to the claim:

(A) to comply with [the Regulations] in relation to the Employees;

(B) in contesting any claim by any person engaged by the Vendor under a contract for services or any employee (including the Employees) of the Vendor resulting from or in connection with this Agreement or otherwise howsoever arising; and

(C) to comply with all applicable United Kingdom and European Union laws, statutes, regulations and directives in force as at the date hereof and relating to health and safety.

1.5 Where any such claim made against the Purchaser is one in respect of which the Vendor has agreed to indemnify the Purchaser under Paragraph 1.2, the Vendor shall have the conduct of the claim, at its own expense, and may institute or defend any proceedings and take such other action in relation thereto as it reasonably requires in the name of the purchaser.

FUTURE ARRANGEMENTS

1.1 On [ ] the Vendor and the Purchaser shall jointly communicate to the Employees a notice substantially in the agreed terms.

[1.2 As soon as practicable after [the Transfer], the Vendor shall deliver to the Purchaser either originals or copies of all PAYE and national insurance records and of any other documents or records (including, without limitation, personnel records and files) which are relevant to the Employees including, without limitation, those referred to in Regulation 55(2) of the Income Tax (Employments) Regulations 1993 and paragraph 32(1) Schedule 1 Social Security (Contributions) Regulations 1979) provided that:

(A) the Purchaser shall preserve the originals of such records or documents for a period of three years after the Transfer Date or until

Paragraph 1.2(D) is complied with and shall as and when requested by the Vendor to do so, produce the same to the relevant authorities;

(B)   the Vendor shall be entitled to retain a copy of any such record or document where the original is delivered to the Purchaser [or to retain the original of any such record or document where a copy is delivered to the Purchaser];

(C)   the Purchaser shall allow the Vendor access to any and all records and documents in its possession, at all reasonable times, to enable the Vendor to deal with any matters relating to the Employees retained by the Vendor or any claim by or against any Employee arising after the Transfer; and

(D)   in the event that the Purchaser intends prior to the expiration of three years after the Transfer Date to dispose of or destroy any such records or documents, the Purchaser shall not do so without first informing the Vendor of its intention and if the Vendor so requests the Purchaser shall as soon as practicable deliver such records or documents as the Vendor may request to the Purchaser.

Chapter 7

Environmental Responsibilities

At a glance

- Environmental liabilities and risks can be significant and therefore it is important that they should be addressed in corporate transactions. They can affect a wide range of business sectors.

- Such liabilities or risks may include: liabilities associated with contaminated land and water; the necessity to incur material capital expenditure; compliance and operational restrictions; permit breaches; and exposure to civil claims.

- It is important to conduct an appropriate level of due diligence to identify and assess the extent of any existing or potential liabilities of this nature.

- What is appropriate by way of due diligence will depend upon the nature of the business, the structure and size of the transaction and the jurisdiction involved.

- It may be necessary to involve environmental consultants (if technical input is required) and local lawyers (if the target has assets in overseas jurisdictions).

- Once the risks have been identified and are understood, the parties will be better able to negotiate and allocate these risks under the contract. There are a number of contractual solutions for apportioning liability.

Introduction and purpose of chapter

7.1 The purpose of this chapter is to consider environmental issues in England in corporate acquisitions. It describes the main types of legal environmental risk which can arise, how they can be investigated and assessed within the context of transactions, and the more typical contractual provisions for allocating and dealing with such risks as between seller and purchaser.

The concept of what is an environmental issue has broadened significantly over the last two decades and ranges from matters concerning releases to air, land and water, impacts on biodiversity, energy efficiency, the handling of waste and hazardous substances, packaging waste, asbestos in buildings, noise, climate change and sustainable development. Consequently, the number of business sectors affected by environmental issues has increased and ranges from the traditional power, mining, oil and gas, heavy manufacturing and chemicals sectors to retailers, hoteliers, hospitals and universities. Further, the amount of environmental regulation is growing at a rapid rate to be almost overwhelming. In the last three months from the time of writing, approximately 23 statutory instruments, two draft statutory instruments and 4 bills were issued in England and Wales; and the EU issued approximately 4 proposals for directives, 2 draft directives, 16 directives, 1 draft set of regulations, 6 sets of regulations, and 15 decisions which concerned environmental issues. This list does not even consider the consultation documents issued by these and other bodies such as regulators.

Although this chapter incorporates discussion of key pieces of environmental legislation, it is not a work on environmental law. Such legislation creates obligations and liabilities, however, the issue for this chapter is the types of environmental obligation and liability and their impact on transactions.

The structure of environmental liabilities

7.2   Environmental issues can be classed in a variety of ways, for example in terms of their environmental impact or the type of law which creates the relevant legal liability or obligation. However, in the context of a corporate transaction it is useful to class environmental liabilities in the following two ways:

(a)   Regulatory Liabilities: The cost of complying with regulation and statute. For example, the cost of meeting upgrade requirements in permits or of disposing of waste lawfully and costs for remediating contaminated land or remedying environmental damage (due to be implemented under EU law).

(b)   Penalties for Non-Compliance: Typically these are criminal penalties such as a fine or imprisonment for breaching environmental regulation, but recently civil penalties have been introduced – see the civil penalties for failing to surrender sufficient allowances under the *Greenhouse Gas Emissions Trading Scheme Regulations 2005*.

(c)   Civil Liabilities: These are liabilities relating to environmental matters arising under contract or tort between private parties. For example a liability to pay damages to a third party for pollution damage, or a liability to stop a polluting activity which adversely affects your neighbours, or a liability under a lease to comply with statutory notices.

OR

(a)   Historic Issues: Is there a potential for liabilities to arise from activities carried out in the past? These could relate to currently owned assets or to previously owned assets and could be liabilities arising under statute such as remediation of contaminated land or civil liabilities owed to third parties for damage caused by historic activity.

(b)   Current Issues: Is the business currently complying with all applicable law and regulation and does it hold all necessary permits? Are its activities causing any pollution damage to third parties which could lead to consequences? Are any works or costs required to maintain current compliance or to secure compliance?

(c)   Future Issues: Are there works or costs anticipated to deal with known legal changes? Are there any legislative proposals in the pipeline with consequences to the business? Does the purchaser have any future plans for developing, expanding or changing the business which could have environmental consequences and costs associated with them?

Key points to note when assessing environmental liabilities in the context of corporate transactions:

(a)   The Structure of the Transaction: This can significantly affect the types of liabilities which can be acquired. See the discussion below at paragraphs **7.3–7.5** on the differences between a purchase of shares and a purchase of assets.

(b)   The Jurisdictions Involved: It is important in the transaction to assess which jurisdictions are involved and make sure that all relevant jurisdictions are considered for the purposes of environmental risk. Some jurisdictions are more high risk than others and environmental liabilities can arise in different ways, for example in the US there is a risk of acquiring 'successor' liabilities on asset transactions.

(c)   Environmental Liabilities can be 'long-tailed': A long time can elapse between the polluting activity and the relevant liability. For example, in England there is the statutory contaminated land regime which imposes retrospective liability and in the USA the Superfund legislation which is also retrospective. The history of a business is relevant to assessing the risks – even if one of the risks ends up being the unknown.

(d)   Liabilities can arise Off Site as well as On Site: There is a tendency in transactions to concentrate on the liabilities associated with the current properties. This is understandable and sensible in that liabilities are likely to arise in relation to current manufacturing activities and in association with property holdings, but it is important to note that liabilities can arise in respect of offsite activities, for example the offsite disposal of waste, or an incident relating to an escape of fuel from a vehicle at someone else's site, and in the US liability can arise in respect of waste lawfully disposed at a third party site.

(e)   Law and Regulation can be Sector Specific: A lot of environmental law is of general application, but there is also a fair amount of regulation which is sector specific and can have material cost consequences. For example, the *Large Combustion Plants Directive* which regulates SO_2, NO_x and particulate emissions in the power generation sector and the *Air Navigation (Environmental Standards) Order 2002* which regulates noise and air emissions from aircraft. A purchaser who is not a trade buyer should specifically consider retaining specialist technical advice on such issues.

(f) Law and Regulation are Getting More Stringent: When assessing environmental costs associated with a business, it is important not just to think about current issues but, in so far as reasonably possible, to anticipate future costs, this may already be contained in existing or anticipated legislation. For example, the *Large Combustion Plants Directive* (2001/80/EC) which requires certain plant to reduce NO_x and SO_2 emissions in 2008 and NO_x further in 2016, or the long awaited REACH Regulation which was adopted in December 2006 and is due to enter into force on 1 June 2007.

The key differences between share and asset transactions

Purchase of shares

7.3   If the purchaser is buying shares (as opposed to the business owned by the company), it is buying the company and therefore buying the history of that company with all its consequences. This is significant in that due diligence cannot just be limited to the current assets and activities of the company but the purchaser will also need to consider the company's past. For example, in England, if the target company polluted a site 50 years ago which it no longer owns or occupies, by buying the company the purchaser is buying the potentially liable party to pay for remediation of that site.

If the company has committed criminal breaches of law (and a lot of breaches of environmental legislation are criminal), that potential criminal liability will travel on sale with the company. That said, a regulator may not necessarily prosecute a company where new management promptly institute changes to secure compliance. On an asset transaction, however, provided that the purchaser ensures that when it operates the business it does not breach any applicable law, it will not inherit any criminal liability. Similarly, by buying a company the purchaser is taking the company with all its contractual commitments and any related breaches of contract. These may extend to environmental obligations such as those which can arise under property leases or corporate sale contracts where it sold a previous business.

A prudent purchaser, buying a company which has low environmental risk now, would still raise enquiries about the company's past activities because the company may have done something different in the past which carries a greater risk. In a share purchase transaction which seemingly has no environmental issues, it is still worth asking some questions to establish the age of the company and whether it has always been in the same line of business.

Under English law, the advantage of a share purchase from an environmental viewpoint is that there is no need to secure the transfer of environmental permits as generally they do not contain change of control provisions (although it is prudent to check the position in each case). The position may vary in

other jurisdictions and although not an environmental permit it is worth noting that licences issued under the *Goods Vehicles (Licensing of Operations)
Act 1995* require a change in control to be notified to the regulator. That said,
it is important to check that the target company fulfils the requirements under
the relevant statutory regime entitling it to hold a permit, for example that the
company has sufficient control over operations to qualify as an 'operator'
under the PPC regime – see paragraph **7.23** below.

The above points will apply to each company in the target group that is being
acquired by the purchaser. Dormant subsidiaries may have also carried out
environmentally high-risk activities in the past.

Realistically, for companies with long and complex histories or substantial
and wide ranging operations it may not be possible (or cost-effective) to do
full due diligence on the history of that company or group of companies.
Historically, environmental issues will not have been important and companies may not be able to provide full information on all of their past activities,
all of their former ownership and occupation of sites, or the history of their
disposal of waste. This means that there will be an information 'black hole'.
It will be for the commercial negotiations as to where this risk sits between
the parties. The purchaser's assessment of this 'unknown' risk will depend on
the information it has gathered on the company (and its history) in question,
and the purchaser's view on the likelihood of certain types of risk coming
home to roost which will be affected by the type of business and the jurisdictions in which the target operates (or operated).

The example of Halliburton, who inherited enormous asbestos and silica liabilities through the acquisition of Dresser Industries, Inc in 1998, is a potent
reminder that lawyers' concerns about historic risks are not theoretical (a
BBC press report dated 4 December 2004 referred to a £2.1 billion settlement).

Purchase of assets

7.4   In an asset transaction, the purchaser, in some ways, is starting with
a clean slate in that it is not buying the company and will only be responsible
in its own right for its own activities when it operates the business going forward. However, there is still the potential to inherit environmental liabilities.
The purchaser will still need to assess whether the current assets and operations are legally compliant or are causing any damage which could lead to
civil claims or regulatory action. For example, if the purchaser acquires an
asset which is in breach of permit requirements, it may need to incur significant expenditure to install abatement equipment to achieve compliance.
Provided it achieves compliance it will not be criminally liable for breaches
of the law but it will still have to spend money to put things right. Also, if it
continues a damaging activity which affects third parties, it may be liable for
continuing and adopting a nuisance and as there is joint and several liability
it could end up (in theory at least) being 100% responsible for the loss.
Equally, if as part of acquiring the business, it takes assignment of relevant

contracts including leases it will need to assess the extent to which it may have environmental liabilities or obligations under those contracts. Further, to the extent that there are future changes in law the cost of complying with these obviously will be for the purchaser's account.

A key point on the purchase of assets is that steps will need to be put in hand to secure transfer of relevant environmental permits from the seller to the purchaser. The timetable for securing such transfer and the requirements on transfer (including whether any regulator's consent is needed) vary according to the particular legislative regime. A table is included at the back of this chapter setting out the main environmental permits in England and the requirements on transfer. In some cases the purchaser will need to ensure that when it operates the business it can meet the statutory criteria allowing it to hold the relevant permit, for example it is a 'fit and proper person' under the waste legislation contained in *Part 2* of the *Environmental Protection Act 1990*.

In asset transactions, in England, there is also a significant potential to acquire the seller's liability in respect of historically contaminated land in relation to properties which are forming part of the sale. For a more detailed discussion of this see the contaminated land section in paragraph **7.16** below. Also, it should be noted that the effect of the *Transfer of Undertakings (Protection of Employment) Regulations 2006* on asset transactions is that the purchaser will inherit the seller's industrial disease liabilities in relation to employees who transfer across on the sale of the business.

General

7.5   The rules on how liabilities transfer in asset and share transactions will vary in other jurisdictions. Transaction structure will have a direct impact on the structure of due diligence. Equally, the results of due diligence may affect transaction structure. If a purchaser is very concerned about historic environmental issues it may change a share purchase into an asset purchase, although often there are other reasons (such as tax) as to why this may not be desirable.

A question of semantics

7.6   On a transaction, it is important to ensure that all members of the due diligence team understand what is meant by 'environmental'. This is not an academic debate about semantics, but to ensure that no issues are neglected because different members of the team think someone else is dealing with them. The main area of overlap is between environmental, health and safety, food hygiene and industrial disease issues. In some cases environment and health and safety are a combined function in an organisation (SHE) and will be dealt with by the same team. Alternatively, they can be separate disciplines. The position will vary on a case-by-case basis. It does not matter who covers the areas as long as they have the relevant skills. The important point is to establish that those areas are being covered.

Traditionally, the law relating to the control and management of asbestos in buildings, although regulated by the Health and Safety Executive, is regarded as falling within the environmental area. Further, information relating to industrial disease or industrial injury claims may come through the employment due diligence but may need (for example, if they relate to large asbestos liabilities) to be investigated by environmental/health and safety specialists. Similarly, it is important that the need to carry out fire risk assessments and comply with the *Regulatory Reform (Fire Safety) Order 2005* is investigated but this may come through the property, health and safety or environmental due diligence.

Identifying and assessing environmental issues

7.7   Dealing with environmental risks and liabilities in any corporate transaction involves a two-stage process:

(a)   identifying and assessing those environmental liabilities and risks which are relevant or material within the context of the transaction (due diligence); and

(b)   the apportionment of these liabilities and risks between the parties (contractual allocation).

While these two stages might logically be expected to follow each other, in practice time constraints often mean that they develop in tandem in the course of most transactions.

Purchasers

7.8   The form of and costs allocated to environmental due diligence will be influenced by the nature (and history) of the target business or company, the structure of the transaction, the jurisdictions involved, the time available and the risk appetite of the purchaser.

In an ideal world, (subject to cost and time) a purchaser will want to know that it has purchased a legally compliant business which holds all relevant permits and which is not causing any potentially costly adverse impact on third parties. Equally it needs to establish whether there is anything lurking in the past which will come out at a later date or any anticipated future changes which could have a material cost.

Environmental law and regulation is constantly changing and is widening its scope. The concept of what is considered an environmental issue as compared to 20 years ago (for example contaminated land or air emissions from industrial processes) has been broadened significantly. For example, environmental issues include the obligations to reuse and recycle packaging, the EU Emissions Trading Scheme for greenhouse gases and the drive for energy efficiency. Clearly, some businesses such as manufacturers, electricity generators and mining carry more environmental issues and costs than others. That said, environmental issues increasingly touch a much wider range of businesses, for example, retail companies will be affected by laws in relation to packaging waste, litter and asbestos and large hospitals are required to hold greenhouse gas permits.

In exceptional situations, a view is sometimes taken that specific due diligence is not necessary, even though the business is inherently high risk, because the purchaser is in the same or a similar business and is willing to make a rough assessment of the likely problems. In small transactions, this is often because the purchaser believes that the likelihood of a significant environmental risk existing is negligible and does not justify the cost of an investigation to establish whether such a risk does exist. That said, there is no automatic correlation between the size of a transaction and the liabilities which may be associated with it. In the case of a major transaction involving lots of sites or companies, the purchaser may prefer to work out the likely level of overall risks on a statistical basis based on its understanding of the risks involved. It might be felt unnecessary to identify where the actual risks lie on a site or company basis.

The decision not to do due diligence is unusual and generally not advisable. Doing nothing will not protect a purchaser from the 'low risk high consequence' scenario. Moreover, we consider that such approaches are increasingly rare as a business is increasingly focused on its costs and responsibilities associated with environmental issues. It is difficult to see how a company could state that it takes environmental issues seriously and then not look at these issues as part of its corporate acquisitions.

Generally speaking, some form of due diligence should be undertaken even if, in its simplest form, it consists of a few basic questions to rule out environmental matters as an issue for the transaction or a questionnaire to identify high-level issues to be followed up. A trade buyer may need less assistance from external advisers than a financial buyer, but where environmental matters are a material business concern environmental due diligence can be a detailed exercise involving the combined skills of lawyers and consultants.

Sometimes the identity of the purchaser will increase the extent of due diligence required. A financial buyer is likely to be more cautious than an industry buyer because the former has less working familiarity with the risks associated with the industry. A financial buyer also seldom purchases as a long-term investment, and therefore will be more concerned to have a better assessment of the actual or potential risks with which it may be faced in the short term and which will impact on resale. A buyer who is financing the acquisition by way of external borrowing is likely to face the same approach from its lenders and lenders' requirements should be clarified early in the transaction.

Sellers

7.9   Sellers take varying attitudes towards environmental disclosure. Some provide a minimum amount of information and wait for the purchaser to ask questions. Others adopt a more proactive approach and provide a lot of information, having conducted an extensive information-gathering exercise as part of the pre-sale process. One reason for this is that they do not want environmental issues to delay the transaction later or to cause needless disputes in negotiations. Also, a seller may have decided that it wants to transfer all environmental liability as part of the transaction and a purchaser is unlikely to take this on without information to assess the risk. Sometimes a seller will commission environmental reports from independent consultants as part of disclosure. This is common in bid situations where the target is being offered to a number of potential purchasers. The seller wants to know that the bids it has received have taken into account all relevant issues and that once it has selected its preferred bidder the price will not be reduced at a late date for environmental reasons.

In England, full disclosure by the seller may have the additional advantage of enabling it to transfer certain contaminated land statutory liabilities to the purchaser. Also, if the seller identifies concerns it may be able to address them prior to sale. For example, it can commission missing asbestos surveys.

Environmental disclosure can be costly in terms of professional fees and management time, but it enables a seller to control the way in which information is disclosed and presented. Also, it should make dealing with environmental issues more predictable in the transaction. If both parties are better informed of the actual risks this will assist in their contractual negotiations. The purchaser is less likely to make unreasonable demands for indemnities if it understands the level of risk involved. A full understanding of the actual risks at the time of contract diminishes the likelihood of future disputes. Being properly informed before the sale will also give the parties an opportunity to restructure the transaction if a material liability has been identified. For example, if a particular problem site has been identified the seller may decide to retain the site thereby avoiding subsequent litigation and disputes over control of remediation.

Due diligence and disclosure

7.10   It is usual for a seller to provide the purchaser with some information about the business or company being sold. The quality of the information provided, however, is likely to vary. On the assumption that the seller is being reasonably co-operative and that there are no undue time difficulties, the environmental information sought by a purchaser or provided by a seller will typically include:

(a)   a list of current operating sites, (if relevant) closed sites and former sites, and their addresses;

(b)   breaches of consents, regulatory investigations, prosecutions or enforcement/prohibition notices and the relationship with the principal regulators;

(c)   confirmation that all requisite environmental licences and consents are held, that there are no material or persistent compliance problems, and that they will not be revoked or varied;

(d)   ongoing, anticipated and past civil liability problems (eg industrial diseases, complaints, disputes with or actions brought by employees, workers, neighbours or other third parties);

(e)   present or past uses of land, including by predecessors, particularly involving hazardous substances or activities;

(f)   any known or potential contamination problems and any migration issues whether onto the sites or from the sites;

(g)   exposure to offsite liabilities involving contamination or hazardous substances;

(h)   environmental harm caused by the company's products;

(i)   (if health and safety is being covered with environment) health and safety issues associated with the company's operations (eg principal risks to workers);

(j)   any known or anticipated material expenditure, whether because of licence reviews, improvement plans, pending or proposed legislation or otherwise;

(k)   information on environmental compliance and safety procedures and management systems, including whether these are accredited to international schemes such as ISO 14001;

(l)   provision of environmental consultants' reports on the sites to be acquired or for which the business or company could have responsibility;

(m)   details of relevant insurance cover and claims experience;

(n)   details of any environmental provisions in the accounts or approved capital expenditure plans;

(o)   details of any environmental liabilities or exposure under any contracts (such as under any warranties and indemnities given in previous transactions); and

(p)   details of any pressure group interest in or action against the company.

If the transaction is structured as a share sale then these issues should be addressed with reference to all members of the target group, whether active or not. Also, these issues need to be considered not only in relation to existing operations, facilities and sites but also in relation to the past, since the group could retain liabilities in this respect.

If, the transaction is structured as an asset purchase, it should be necessary only to look at the business being acquired, unless the intention is also to transfer, under the sale contract, any historic liabilities associated with that business, (which would then require due diligence into former sites and former offsite activities), or jurisdictional peculiarities require otherwise.

One of the most common ways of getting information is for the purchaser to submit a due diligence questionnaire to the seller. Responses normally comprise a mixture of replies in writing and the provision of relevant documents in a data room, to which the purchaser and its advisers are given access. Alternatively, but often in conjunction with the data room, the information may be provided during the course of meetings with representatives of the target who have responsibility for environmental management. In the case of such presentations it is sensible for both sides to make a record of the information disclosed.

This disclosure process has a dual purpose: first, to provide the purchaser with the information it is seeking, and secondly, to enable the seller to use the information provided as disclosure against any warranties it provides in the sale contract. Briefly, the seller will not be liable under environmental warranties if information concerning what would otherwise have been a breach of the warranties is included in the data room and is either specifically disclosed or deemed to be disclosed under the disclosure letter. If the purchaser identifies an important issue it should seek to address the matter by a price reduction or contractual solution.

The contents of the data room are only as good as the seller wishes them to be or is competent to provide. For commercial reasons, a seller may decide against including certain information. Whilst the purchaser may be able to bring a claim for breach of the warranties as a result, this is unlikely to result in it receiving full restitution for its losses and may be of very little benefit if a major unexpected liability has been inherited. If a purchaser receives limited environmental information in relation to a business which patently has environmental risks associated with it, this should sound a warning, particularly if the purchaser's environmental due diligence team is refused access to the sites, unless it is given convincing reasons by the seller for this position. It is not unusual to develop a cover story for investigations to avoid tipping off site staff and denting staff morale.

As part of its investigations, the purchaser may wish to obtain whatever information is publicly available concerning the company or its sites. For example, this could include visiting the target's website, making company searches and, where available, obtaining copies of the company's (or the group's) report and accounts (including any environmental reports published by the company or group). Also, more recently, it may be able to obtain information from the new business reviews. Various UK environmental periodicals and their websites can also be a useful source of information on prosecutions, pressure group activity and government or regulatory scrutiny of particular operations.

It is possible to do a computerised search of publicly available information. A due diligence investigation may also involve submitting enquiries for site-specific information from the regulators. This is not a particularly fruitful line of enquiry in the United Kingdom because of the pace at which regulators respond to questions and the fee levied. It is however useful in other jurisdictions. The *Environmental Information Regulations 2004* give the public wide rights to ask regulators for environmental information but the time for responding is long in the context of commercial transactions. Also, it is important to check whether the purchaser has signed any confidentiality letter which prevents it from raising such enquiries.

Using environmental consultants

7.11 Often, effective environmental due diligence requires both legal and technical input. Clients sometimes can be frustrated as to what they see as a doubling up of advisers. However, environmental liabilities can be a complex mixture of legal and technical issues. For example, a lawyer will advise on the requirements of the Large Combustion Plants Directive and the consequences of non-compliance, but a consultant will advise on the equipment required to abate NO_x emissions and potential costs involved. A consultant will say if ground contamination is likely to be present, a lawyer will conduct the legal analysis as to where liabilities are likely to fall. Often much of the environmental information available about a business is of a technical nature, for example, discharge and emissions data and technical investigations. This needs to be reviewed by someone suitably qualified, whether an in-house environmental manager or an environmental consultant.

It is usual practice (and advisable) to appoint environmental consultants under a written contract. Most environmental consultants have standard terms and conditions which are not overly client-friendly. Clients should not sign them without legal advice. Environmental lawyers usually negotiate separate terms and conditions. It is common for environmental consultants to cap their liability – this is usually agreed at a level between £1–5 million depending on the size of transaction, the size of fee and the relationship with the client. Higher caps are available for bigger deals and certain clients. The appointment should include obligations on the consultants to take out professional indemnity insurance which reflects the level of financial cap.

If the seller is commissioning the work, it will want to agree with the consultant that the purchaser and its lenders can rely on the work. This is usually done through the provision of deeds of collateral warranty (the form would be agreed as part of the original appointment document), but can be done by giving rights under the appointment pursuant to the *Contracts (Rights of Third Parties) Act 1999*. If a purchaser is commissioning the work it may also want reliance for its lenders and other group companies depending on its plans for the target companies or business.

If a purchaser asks to conduct environmental investigations a seller should think about the following:

(a)   asking for a copy of the reports;

(b)   requiring that they remain confidential until the transaction completes (this protects the seller should the transaction not proceed);

(c)   requiring that they form part of disclosure against the warranties; and

(d)   if intrusive investigations are undertaken, check that it is happy with the consultants and contractors used and it has appropriate contractual protection (if something goes wrong) whether from the purchaser or the consultants/contractors or both.

Usually a consultant's terms of reference will be contained in a proposal letter issued by the consultant. This is then incorporated into the contract and forms part of the consultant's appointment. The proposal may have been discussed and amended by the client and its lawyers to reflect the needs of the particular transaction. It is important when reviewing reports (especially when commissioned by other parties to the transaction) to consider the terms of reference. In particular, when looking at seller commissioned reports, purchasers should consider:

(a)   whether a materiality threshold has been set. For example, if a threshold of £25,000 per issue has been set there may be a large number of smaller issues not reported on, which, in the aggregate, are material;

(b)   whether assessments of contaminated land risks are based on the site remaining in its current use or do they take into account issues associated with redevelopment or expansion or other building works. The importance of this will depend on the purchaser's plans;

(c)   whether assessments of remediation costs include offsite liabilities;

(d)   if intrusive investigations were undertaken, the comprehensiveness of the sampling regime. Was it a quick 'look-see' or a more thorough investigation;

(e)   whether all the key issues been covered. 'Missing' issues may be difficult to identify as there may be no express reference to them; and

(f)   whether the report is factual only, with no commentary, conclusions, recommendations and accompanying cost estimates.

It should also be noted by both parties that although consultants may agree on whether a matter constitutes an environmental issue, estimates on likely costs can differ greatly.

There are a range of environmental reports which can be commissioned as part of the due diligence process:

(a)   Desktop review: A desktop review involves a review of publicly available electronic data sets including current and historic maps and information on registers of permits and prosecutions. Such reviews will not include a visit to the site. Environmental consultancy firms can carry out desktop reviews to provide an expert view on the potential issues on the site and they may make further enquires, if necessary, of regulators to ascertain further information which may close out or identify more fully any potential issues raised from the datasets reviewed. They can also review information provided by the seller. There are also a number of different types environmental searches and commoditised desktop reviews available in the market.

(b)   Phase I audit: These incorporate a desktop review, together with a site visit and, usually, interviews with site management. They do not involve intrusive investigations but generally (but not always) cover both compliance issues and consideration of whether the site has the potential to be contaminated or is already known to be contaminated. This is the most common form of consultant's report in corporate transactions.

(c)   Phase II (and subsequent phase) audits: These involve intrusive investigations and would normally involve soil, groundwater and gas sampling and a risk assessment. Further investigations and reports may be carried out if contamination is identified in the Phase II report. A remediation strategy may be written on the back of a Phase II report. It is important to understand the scope of any Phase II investigation.

A 'mix and match' approach can be taken to due diligence. A purchaser could choose to 'desktop' all sites but only carry out a Phase I at manufacturing sites. Alternatively a desktop review may be used to risk rank sites, in respect of contaminated land issues, and only those with a medium or high-risk allocation are subject to a more detailed review.

It should be noted that commoditised searches and desktop reviews are looking at environmental risk in relation to contamination, on the basis of publicly available data on the current and historic uses of the site and the surrounding area and the local geology and hydrogeology. A desktop review is only likely to produce hard data on contamination if a site has been classified as contaminated by the regulator, but even then there may be no information about likely remediation costs. A Phase I audit should produce concrete information on operational compliance and impacts on neighbours, but the contaminated land element of the audit will be a desktop assessment of risk (subject to information or reports provided by the site or visible evidence of staining, leaks and the like).

In some respects audits may be inconclusive or identify concerns which need further investigation. These may comprise enquiries as to the cost of the abatement equipment or discussions with regulators about permitting issues. If an intrusive Phase II audit is recommended, these take time and if they are to be undertaken prior to exchange of contracts may delay the transaction. Typically a Phase II investigation may take between two (very short) to five weeks depending on tests required, availability of drilling and other equipment and laboratory turnaround times.

Instructing local lawyers

7.12   If a transaction is multi-jurisdictional, then it may be necessary to instruct foreign lawyers, at least in the principal jurisdictions. This will be particularly likely if the subject matter of the sale is potentially environmentally high risk. Local lawyers will be better placed to assess the legal significance in their jurisdiction of matters arising out of due diligence and differences may exist under foreign laws which might not be anticipated. Where lawyers from other jurisdictions are involved in due diligence, they should also be asked to comment on contractual provisions so that any jurisdiction-specific amendments can be incorporated as appropriate. For example, in some regions in Belgium, the transfer of land can trigger a site audit and remediation obligations in certain circumstances and failure to comply with the relevant legislation may render a sale of land voidable.

Legal environmental issues

Introduction

7.13   The purpose of this chapter is not to provide a detailed treatise on environmental law, but to explain how environmental issues are assessed and then addressed within the context of corporate transactions. Also, as explained above, environmental regulation is a rapidly developing area and is often sector specific. That said, in this section (paragraphs **7.14–7.22**), we set out the general issues likely to arise in a transaction and then in paragraphs **7.23–7.32** and paragraphs **7.33–7.40** respectively an overview of general authorisations and notifications, and other general legislation applicable in this jurisdiction.

Environmental permits

7.14   Depending on the legislative regime an environmental permit may be referred to variously as a permit, consent, licence, permission or authorisation. Whether buying a company or assets, the main issues to consider when reviewing a business from a permitting perspective are as follows:

(a)   does the business have all the licences it requires under relevant legislation;

(b)   is the business complying with the provisions of all relevant licences, in particular the emission and discharge limits;

(c)   if there is a non-compliance, what is the position of the regulator and what are the costs of making the operations compliant;

(d)   if there is an improvement plan in any licence, have all relevant improvements been undertaken as required. Are any future improvements required? If not all improvements have been carried out what are the costs of carrying them out and is this included in the site budget;

(e)   how long is the licence valid for and when is the authorisation due for renewal or review? It is important to consider what modifications or further requirements may be anticipated and at what costs and in what timescale; and

(f)   the long-term costs and obligations associated with such a licence.

Additionally, as discussed in paragraphs **7.3** and **7.4** above:

(a)   on the sale of assets the transfer of permits from seller to purchaser needs to be addressed. Transfer may also trigger regulatory scrutiny of a permit and cause the regulator to consider whether any conditions should be changed; and

(b)   on the sale of a company, the purchaser should still ensure that the target company which holds the permit fulfils any relevant statutory criteria required for holding it.

Sometimes permitting can throw up more complex issues when the transaction involves part of a business or if the businesses of a company need to be separated before it is sold.

Splitting permits – transitional arrangements

7.15   Where the seller or target holds a licence which governs both operations which are being sold and operations which are being retained by the seller, then consideration needs to be given to how the licence can be 'split'. This may involve discussions with the regulator. Technically, some licences cannot be split and the regulator will need to cancel the old licence and issue two new ones. More modern licences such as PPC permits allow for partial transfer.

If separating the licence is not possible, or the joint arrangement is only short-term or the separation will take a long time to achieve, then the parties may have to enter into contractual arrangements governing the temporary or long-term 'sharing' of the licence. It may be that services (for example, drains) supplying the two operations are currently intertwined and will need to be separated out and the site divided. If so, this is an issue that should be considered as early as possible in the transaction since it can be complicated and expensive, and responsibility for liabilities and compliance will need to be contractually allocated.

Contaminated land

7.16   Onsite and migrating contamination (whether from existing or former sites) is one of the big environmental concerns in corporate acquisitions.

The UK regime for dealing with historically contaminated land is set out in *Part 2A* of the *Environmental Protection Act 1990* which came into force on

1 April 2000. The regime introduces strict retrospective liability for land contaminated by historic activities. In England, it applies where the contamination is causing a significant level of harm or significant pollution, or there is a significant possibility of such harm or pollution occurring (the significance threshold for water pollution is not in force at the time of writing). The regime is disapplied to the extent contamination can be addressed under other regimes like waste licensing.

The persons potentially liable for contaminated land under this regime are as follows:

(a)   The person who has 'caused' or 'knowingly permitted' the substances causing the contamination to be present in, on or under the land in question. In effect this will be the original polluter and/or any subsequent owner of the land who knew about the contamination, and was in a position to prevent the harm being caused by it, but who failed to do so. These persons are known as 'Class A' appropriate persons. If the contamination has migrated off the original site then remediation of neighbouring sites might be required.

(b)   If a Class A person cannot be found, the responsibility for remediation will fall on the owner or occupier for the time being of the affected land, regardless of whether it was aware of the existence of the contamination in, on or under its land. However, an owner or occupier has reduced liabilities and is not responsible for remediating offsite contamination (whether of land or water) or water pollution arising from the contamination. These persons are known as 'Class B' appropriate persons.

The government has published statutory guidance which sets out the detail of how the regime is to be applied (Defra Circular 01/2006 – replacing an earlier circular) by the regulatory authority. The main regulator is the local authority, but for certain 'special sites' it is the Environment Agency.

The statutory guidance contains certain provisions for the allocation and apportionment of liabilities. In relation to Class A liability groups it is worth noting the following:

(a)   Payment for Remediation Test: Briefly, where a seller who is a Class A person makes a payment to a purchaser who is also a Class A person (for example, by way of reduction in the purchase price) to enable the purchaser to remediate any identified contamination, and that payment was sufficient to deal with all such specified contamination, liability for that contamination passes to the purchaser who steps into the shoes of the seller for these purposes. The guidance requires that this arrangement is documented.

(b)   Sold with Information Test: Another way of transferring liability is where a Class A person sells the land and gives another Class A person, the buyer, sufficient information to enable it to be aware of the presence and extent of any contamination. In this case, the seller's liability may be transferred to the buyer. There is a presumption that in transactions since the beginning of 1990, where the buyer is a large commercial organisation or public body, permission from the seller to the buyer allowing the buyer to carry out his own investigations into the condition of the land should normally be taken as sufficient indication that the buyer falls within the sold with information test.

Points to note:

(a)   It is not clear at what stage the buyer becomes a Class A person – the above exclusion tests only apply as between Class A persons – for example, paragraph D.61 of the statutory guidance expressly states that receipt by the buyer of the information referred to in the sold with information test does not mean that it has caused or knowingly permitted the presence of the relevant pollutant.

(b)   *Part 2A* of the *Environmental Protection Act 1990* is not the only means by which liability for contaminated land (and associated water pollution) can be incurred. Hence, if a seller wants to transfer all such liability (not just under this regime) it should seek a contaminated land indemnity.

(c)   The statutory guidance requires that exclusion tests should not be applied so that there is no one left in the liability group to pay for the remediation.

(d)   Buyers should be aware that the risk of becoming a knowing permitter (which also applies to the *Water Resources Act 1991* discussed below) means that there is a strong potential to 'inherit' historically contaminated land liabilities on an asset transaction and for *Part* 2A this is exacerbated by the application of the tests described above.

(e)   The statutory guidance provides that regulators are required to have regard to contractual agreements on the sharing of liabilities, where a copy of the agreement is provided to the regulator and no party to the agreement tells the authority that it challenges the application of the agreement and provided that the person left to bear the costs can meet them.

Water pollution (arising from contaminated land)

7.17   There is some overlap between the statutory regimes which deal with water pollution and contaminated land. The initial legislation which regulated the remedying of water pollution was the *Water Resources Act 1991* (*WRA 1991*). Under *section 161* of *WRA 1991*, the Environment Agency is entitled to carry out preventive and remedial works if polluting matter has entered or is likely to enter controlled waters, and to recover its reasonable expenses from the polluter. The *Environment Act 1995* (*EA 1995*) amended *WRA 1991* giving the Environment Agency the right to serve a 'works notice' requiring the person who caused (or knowingly permitted) the pollution to remediate it.

If the water pollution is unconnected with any land contamination, the *WRA 1991* regime will apply. However, if the water pollution is being caused by the presence of substances on land, and this land contamination falls within the provisions of *Part 2A* of the *Environmental Protection Act 1990* then *Part 2A* and not the *WRA 1991* will be applied by the regulators.

Regulatory enforcement and prosecution

7.18   If a company fails to comply with its obligations imposed under legislation, then generally regulatory authorities will have powers of enforcement to secure compliance and to prosecute. Examples of enforcement actions include the withdrawal of an operational permit or service of a prohibition notice (with the potential consequence of closure), the service of an improvement notice (with potential cost consequences), the service of a works notice to remediate water pollution under the *Water Resources Act 1991*, and the service of an abatement notice in the case of a statutory nuisance (again with potential cost consequences or an adverse impact on operations). If the recipient of any such notice fails to comply with it, then it will be guilty of an offence. A discussion of penalties is included in later parts of this chapter discussing specific permits and legislation.

The fact that a company has been prosecuted or subject to regulatory enforcement action in the past is not necessarily indicative of a deep-seated problem. Not least, most breaches (including small ones) of environmental law are criminalised in this jurisdiction although a regulator is less likely to take formal action for small breaches. However, a pattern of persistent or serious breaches may reveal a serious problem or management failings which should be investigated further.

Directors' liability

7.19   It is also possible for directors and officers to be held personally criminally liable for the environmental offences of their company, with exposure to fines and the risk of imprisonment. For such liability to arise, the breach by the company must have been committed with the consent, connivance or neglect of the director or officer concerned.

Contract

7.20   Sale and purchase contracts relating to land or businesses and leases of land may expressly include specific provisions relating to environmental matters. If separate environmental provisions do not exist in a contract, unless the contract expressly excludes environment, some of the more routine contractual provisions may encompass environmental matters. A clause does not have to have the word 'environment' or 'contamination' in it to catch such matters.

A lot of leases are silent on environmental issues. A number of provisions typically included in English leases can catch environmental matters. The key issue is not just whether a tenant is responsible under the lease for the problems it creates but also whether it will pick up the landlord's liability. For example, some compliance with statutes and statutory notice clauses expressly provide that the tenant is responsible for complying even if the obligation falls on the landlord. The application of such a clause would result in a tenant paying to remediate historically contaminated land. On the other hand, the landlord has the problem of whether it can make the tenant clean up contamination which can impact on land value or the cost of redevelopment, but is not sufficiently bad to attract regulatory attention. In such circumstances, the landlord may be trying to stretch old-fashioned repairing, reinstatement and yielding-up covenants to cover the situation. Modern leases may have express provisions on apportioning liability for contaminated land or on environmental compliance, but they may not be comprehensive.

As it is apparent from the existence of this chapter, it is common for a separate set of specific contractual provisions, particularly environmental warranties, to govern environmental matters on corporate acquisitions. Sometimes these are subject to higher financial limits and longer time limits than other general warranties. Also many sale contracts will include an environmental indemnity. Claims under environmental warranties or indemnities or leases may result in significant liabilities. Conversely, if the target has inherited an environmental problem as a result of an acquisition, it is worth verifying whether there are any contractual rights under which it may seek contribution or compensation from the original seller (and whether such rights are transferable to the present purchaser).

Contracts for selling or purchasing allowances under the EU Emissions Trading Scheme are also relevant to contractual due diligence.

In short, potential liabilities under contract need to be considered as part of environmental due diligence.

Tort

7.21   It is important with the concern about increasing regulation, not to forget the risk of incurring liability in tort. Potential causes of action in tort are wide-ranging and could include actions in negligence (breach of a duty of care with resultant damage), nuisance, trespass, breach of a statutory duty, *Rylands v Fletcher* ((1868) LR 3 HL 330; (1866) LR 1 Ex 265) situations (an escape of a dangerous substance from a site upon which an unnatural use is taking place) and occupier's liability.

The following features of civil liability should be borne in mind:

(a)   the extent of losses recoverable can vary greatly and may include compensation for property damage, personal injury and death, and in some cases economic loss (such as losses of profits);

(b) liability may arise even where all relevant regulatory requirements under statute, regulations or permits have been observed;

(c) owners and occupiers of property may be liable even though the event causing the harm or nuisance started before their ownership or occupation, if the harm or nuisance continues to cause damage during their period of ownership or occupation;

(d) civil damages can be high, particularly if a large number of claimants are affected by an incident or circumstance. For example, industrial disease or injury claims such as asbestosis and vibration white finger can result in significant liabilities. They will also be higher in jurisdictions like the United States of America;

(e) tort law has been the basis of a lot of successful environmental or industrial disease claims to date, yet it is often overlooked as an area of possible concern. On any acquisition a purchaser should satisfy itself as to the absence of large tort claims for personal injury or property damage arising out of environmental or health and safety issues. It should also ensure that its environmental consultants have considered 'third party' impacts;

(f) some liabilities (particularly those relating to migrating pollution and industrial diseases) can be 'long-tailed' and rights of action in respect of these may arise years after the original polluting or damaging events. This is because such matters can take years to manifest themselves, and the time for bringing proceedings will not start to run until the individual becomes aware of his illness and the likely cause of it. In England, in respect of property damage, there is a longstop of 15 years from the date on which the damage occurred;

(g) in some cases, an injured third party may be able to bring a claim for an injunction to stop the damaging activity.

Pressure groups and corporate social responsibility

7.22 In the last edition of this book, a section was included on pressure groups and the impact they can have on business. Now, there are wider expectations from business in terms of CSR (corporate social responsibility) or CR (corporate responsibility). The impact of pressure groups is part of that broader CSR remit. In England there is no explicit statutory requirement stating that companies must behave in a socially responsible way, although laws on environmental protection, employee protection and health and safety contribute towards this. Further, the new codified duties requiring directors to have regard to such matters (*section 172* of the *Companies Act 2006* – not yet in force) and the requirements for a business review (*section 417* of the *Companies Act 2006*) to address such matters may result in companies assessing their environmental behaviour in a different way.

Public interest groups have been active for a number of years. Their actions on environmental and other CSR matters can result in businesses incurring significant costs and losses or a dent in their brand value. The overriding objective of environmental public interest groups is to prevent or minimise harm to the environment, and they seek to achieve this by a number of different approaches.

(a) In the absence of a prosecuting authority so doing, criminal law gives anyone the right to prosecute for any criminal offence, unless the offence expressly provides otherwise. Pressure groups in the UK have conducted private prosecutions for environmental breaches and statutory nuisances. However, these are rare. For example, see the actions of the Anglers Conservation Association.

(b) Any decision by a regulatory body is open to judicial review. Pressure groups may apply for judicial review of the decisions of environmental regulators if they grant licences for sites to which the group is opposed. Although applications are often unsuccessful, these cases can cause disruption and delay. For example, see the application for judicial review of the decisions to grant planning permission and hazardous substances consents to two LNG terminals at Milford Haven.

(c) Pressure groups have for some time been active at EU level, both generally (such as lobbying in connection with proposed legislation) and in a focused way (such as filing a formal complaint with the European Commission over the incorrect domestic application of EU legislation in connection with a specific site development).

(d) Pressure groups also take more direct action, such as targeting a particular site, company or industry. In so doing their actions may range from the unlawful (such as occupying an oil platform, as Greenpeace did with Shell's Brent Spar Platform in 1991) to a public relations campaign aimed at persuading consumers to boycott a product.

(e) Pressure groups sometimes also target lenders in order to discourage them from investing in particular companies, for example see CEE Bankwatch Network.

(f) Legislation also gives rights to pressure groups. Note the *Aarhus Convention* which (amongst other things) covers public participation in environmental decision-making and the *Environmental Liability Directive* which gives citizens and, in certain circumstances, NGOs the right to require competent authorities to act in respect of certain environmental damage.

CSR reports and related work may provide information on the management of environmental risk, how the business looks at these issues going forward and how it perceives the impact of external stakeholders such as pressure groups. However, it is important that the core parts of a business's operations are considered (such as key health and safety issues and process safety) and assessed fully within a due diligence exercise.

Overview of main authorisations

Pollution prevention and control and air pollution control

7.23   The *Pollution Prevention and Control (England and Wales) Regulations 2000* (the *PPC Regulations*) were introduced under the *Pollution Prevention and Control Act 1999*. The *PPC Regulations* transpose into national law the *Integrated Pollution Prevention Control Directive* (96/61/EC). The *PPC Regulations* control the environmental impacts of installations which carry out certain specified activities. They cover a wide range of industries and sectors. The *PPC Regulations* are gradually replacing the pollution control regime set up under *Part I* of the *Environmental Protection Act 1990* (known as Integrated Pollution Control or IPC). The transition period has been phased over eight years, being completed by 1 October 2007. It is important to check that an installation is permitted under the *PPC Regulations* if applicable and if the installation is due to transfer to PPC the application has been/can be submitted in the specified timeframe.

The *PPC Regulations* have introduced three separate but linked systems of pollution control:

(a)   Integrated pollution prevention and control which covers installations known as Part A(1) installations which are regulated by the Environment Agency.

(b)   Local Authority integrated pollution prevention and control which covers installations known as Part A(2) installations which are regulated by local authorities.

(c)   Local Authority pollution prevention and control which covers installations known as Part B installations, which are regulated by local authorities.

All three systems require the operators of certain industrial and other installations to obtain a permit to operate. A permit will include conditions aimed at reducing and preventing pollution to acceptable levels.

Points to note:

(a)   BAT: Permit conditions are based on the use of the 'best available techniques' (BAT) which balances the cost to the operator against benefits to the environment. Part A(1) and A(2) installations have permit conditions set for pollution to air, land and water and Part B installations have permit conditions only in relation to emissions to air. Part A installation permits also include provisions relating to energy efficiency, site restoration, noise, odour, waste minimisation, accident prevention and heat and vibrations.

(b)   Improvement conditions: The permit will have a set of improvement conditions attached to it. These will require the operator to carry out certain investigations, abatement activities and environmental improvements over a number of years. In some cases the conditions will have a price tag in the millions if not tens of millions of pounds. Understanding the costs associated with a permit is key for due diligence.

(c)   Legal requirement and offence: Failure to operate an installation or mobile plant after the prescribed date without a permit is a criminal offence. This is punishable on summary conviction by a fine not exceeding £20,000 or imprisonment for a term not exceeding six months, or both, and on indictment by an unlimited fine or imprisonment for a term not exceeding five years, or both.

(d)   Meaning of operator: The permit is granted to the 'operator'. *PPC Regulation 2(1)* defines an 'operator' as the person who has control over its 'operation'. It is most important to check that the person holding the permit falls within the definition of 'operator'. The Environment Agency has issued guidance, IPPC Regulatory Guidance Series No.3, indicating that in certain circumstances where a target company has outsourced its operations then the contractor rather than the owner of the installation should hold the permit. In most cases a single operator will have to obtain a single permit for a single installation. However, some sites involve more complex arrangements where different operators run different parts of a single installation. Where two or more operators run different parts of a single installation, they will each need a separate permit and be responsible for complying with its conditions.

(e)   Application for PPC permit and related documentation: During the due diligence process, if a target company holds a PPC permit it may be beneficial to obtain the application and other associated documentation. For example, Part A(1) permits require the preparation of a site report to enable appropriate permit conditions to be set to protect the land and to judge whether remedial action is required to make the land suitable for use. The site report in effect sets a baseline, as on surrender the operator will be required to put the site back in its original condition. Also, in many cases, the improvement conditions will require the operator to carry out further investigations and monitoring, and to prepare other reports. It is likely to be useful to review these as part of due diligence.

(f)   Site closure and surrender: Consideration should be given to what liabilities may arise for the holder of the PPC permit upon site closure or surrender of the permit. Under the *PPC Regulations*, a closure report is required to be carried out when an installation ceases to operate. A PPC permit can only be surrendered if the report satisfies the regulator that there is no ongoing pollution risk and that no steps are required to return the site to a satisfactory state. In certain circumstances, when dealing with a PPC permit for example to comply with the Landfill Directive, the regulator may require financial security from an operator to ensure that adequate provisions are available to comply with any after care provisions, including for any remediation which may be required upon site closure as a result of the operator's use of the site.

(g)   PPC activities involving waste. The *PPC Regulations* apply to major waste activities such as operating landfills. Prior to that they were governed under the waste management regime contained in *Part 2* of the *EPA 1990*, which is still the regime for licensing other 'smaller' waste management activities, for example storing oil drums, which is discussed at paragraph **7.30**. However, if a waste management activity is a secondary activity on a site which is permitted by the *PPC Regulations* for a different primary activity then the licensing of such waste management activity will be incorporated into the PPC permit.

(h)   Transfer of permits under PPC: Applications for transfer must be made jointly by the transferor and the transferee to the regulator. It is possible to have a partial transfer, where the operator retains part of the permit, which may be of use if the operator is retaining part of the operation. The regulator is obliged to effect the transfer unless it considers that the proposed transferee will not comply with the conditions of the transferred permit, or will not after the transfer be the person who will have control over the operation of the installation or plant covered by the transfer. In the case of a transfer of a permit which authorises the carrying out of a specified waste management activity, the regulator must also be satisfied that the proposed transferee is a fit and proper person in relation to carrying out that activity. Transfer will normally mean the permit is endorsed with the name or particulars of the transferee. The regulator is supposed to determine applications for transfer within two months of receiving an application, or a longer period if the regulator and the applicants have agreed in writing. If the relevant period is not complied with, then the joint applicants can treat this as a deemed refusal if they notify the regulator in writing of their position.

(i)   Links with other legislation: PPC permits contain conditions that implement a wide variety of other legislation such as the *Groundwater Regulations 1998*, the *Solvent Emissions Directive 1999/13/EC* and the *Large Combustion Plant Directive 2001/80/EC*.

Discharges to water (discharge consents)

7.24   Almost any solid, liquid or gaseous substance entering surface waters or groundwater could be a pollutant. This includes chemicals, salt, wash waters, waste products and trade effluents. Rainwater that runs across sites may be classed as a pollutant if it becomes contaminated from substances on the site. Consideration should be given to whether the target is discharging any effluent or contaminated run-off to surface waters or groundwater. If the target is discharging such substances then a discharge consent or other authorisation may be required.

Points to note:

(a)   Offences and penalties: Under the *Water Resources Act 1991, section 85*, it is a criminal offence for a person to cause or knowingly permit any polluting substance to enter controlled waters, or for a polluting substance to enter into controlled waters in contravention of a consent. Controlled waters include waters contained in underground strata, streams, lakes, rivers and groundwaters. The definition excludes water in mains and sewers which is dealt with under different legislation: see paragraph **7.25**. An offence is punishable on summary conviction by a fine up to £20,000 or a term of up to three months' imprisonment, or both. On conviction on indictment a person may be subject to a term of imprisonment of up to two years or an unlimited fine, or both.

(b)   Statutory permissions: A person is not guilty of an offence if the discharge into controlled waters occurs in accordance with statutory permissions. Such permissions include a discharge consent issued by the Environment Agency under *Schedule 10* of the *Water Resources Act 1991* or an authorisation under the *PPC Regulations*, a waste management or disposal licence, or any provision of a local act or statutory order which expressly confers power to discharge into water. Discharge consents normally contain conditions setting emission limits in relation to flow rates per day and the level of substances in the discharge and the like.

(c)   Transfer of discharge consents: A discharge consent issued under the *Water Resources Act 1991* may be transferred, under *Schedule 10 paragraph 11*, by the holder to another person who proposes to carry on the discharges in place of the holder. Joint notice to the Environment Agency must be given by the transferor and the transferee and may specify the date on which the transfer should take effect. The Environment Agency must give effect to the transfer within 21 days of receiving the joint notice.

(d)   Consultation: The Environment Agency has recently consulted on the way discharges to water are regulated based on the level of risk posed to the environment. The proposals for consultation looked at how to apply Operator and Pollution Risk Appraisal (OPRA) scheme to discharges and how OPRA scores could be used to assess compliance with discharge consents. The consultation period closes on 27 February 2007 and the response to the consultation is awaited.

(e)   Groundwater Regulations: The *Groundwater Regulations 1998* implement the *EC Groundwater Directive (80/68/EC)* and give the Environment Agency power to help prevent leaks and spillages from activities that may cause a direct or indirect discharge of List I (for example, hydrocarbons) or List II (for example, ammonia) substances into groundwater.

The Regulations require that any disposals of listed substances to land be authorised in advance by the Environment Agency. Such authorisation can only be given following a prior investigation into matters such as the hydrological conditions of the area concerned. Authorisation may be given subject to conditions, or withheld. An authorisation to discharge such substances is not required if the disposal is already covered by a discharge consent issued under the *Water Resources Act 1991*, a PPC permit or waste management licence.

If a disposal of either a List I or List II substance is made without an authorisation, then an offence will have been committed under *section 85* of the *Water Resources Act 1991*, such offences and the associated penalties are discussed at paragraph (a) above.

Discharges to sewers (trade effluent consents)

7.25   The control of discharges of industrial waste to the sewerage system is exercised by private sewerage undertakers within their areas of operation. The regulatory regime is set out in the *Water Industry Act 1991*. The basic legal requirement is that the occupier of trade premises may discharge trade effluent into a sewerage undertaker's public sewers only if he has the undertaker's consent.

Points to note:

(a)   Trade effluent: Trade effluent includes any effluent from trade premises other than domestic sewage or non contaminated surface water. It includes any liquid, either with or without particles of matter in aqueous suspension which is produced during the course of any trade carried on at the premises. Clean water is trade effluent, although the water undertaker may not consent to relatively small amounts of clean effluent on the grounds that the discharge is 'trivial'.

(b)   Offence: If trade effluent is discharged without a trade effluent consent or other authorisation, the occupier of the premises is guilty of an offence and liable on summary conviction to a fine not exceeding £20,000 and on indictment to an unlimited fine.

(c)   Occupier: The occupier means the person in occupation or having the charge, management or control of the premises, either on his own account or as the agent of another person. Therefore, in a commercial transaction, it is important to look at the precise contractual arrangements between the parties, especially where multiple parties have an interest in or share a drainage system.

(d)   Transfer of consent: The *Water Industry Act 1991* does not set out formal provisions for transferring a consent issued by a sewerage undertaker. Normally this can be dealt with by written notification to the relevant sewerage undertaker, alternatively contact the undertaker to ascertain the procedure to transfer the consent.

Abstraction of water (abstraction licence)

7.26   The legal framework for the abstraction of water for industrial processes is set out in the *Water Resources Act 1991*, which has been substantially amended by the *Water Act 2003*. It is important to consider the changes under the *Water Act 2003* especially if there is a licence issued prior to that Act. Although many existing licences will be unaffected by the changes there are several important issues resulting from the *Water Act 2003* which should be considered during due diligence.

Points to note:

(a) Revocation risk: If a licence has not been used for four years the Environment Agency can revoke it without paying compensation. This four-year period only applies for the period of non-use begun after 1 April 2004. Therefore, if the target has not been abstracting but it intends to do so at some point in the future, consideration should be given to the implications of the licence being revoked and whether a new licence will be granted.

(b) Third party damage: If an abstraction causes loss or damage to another person that person will have the legal right to claim damages against the abstractor. This provision only relates to loss or damage incurred after 1 April 2005 and removes the licence holder's existing defence provided by the abstraction licence. Therefore, it is important to ascertain whether any potential loss or damage has occurred, is occurring or has the potential to occur and what the financial implications may be.

(c) Offences and penalties: It is unlawful to abstract water without a licence, over the local exemption threshold, and it is also unlawful to extract in contravention of the conditions of a licence. If an offence is committed, a person may be subject to a fine on summary conviction of up to £20,000 and on indictment to an unlimited fine.

(d) Transfer of licence: Abstraction licences can be transferred by applying to the Environment Agency. The transferee must have a right of access from the date of the transfer, and such access must continue for one year, in relation to the abstraction point. However, an existing licence, which is not time limited, may become subject to the time limit of 12 years prescribed for new licences during the transfer process. Time-limted abstraction licences carry a presumption of renewal but licences will need to be reapplied for providing that the water is still required and that it has been used efficiently. Therefore, consideration should be given to the length of time left to run on an abstraction licence, the reliance of the business on the abstracted water and the consequences of operating either without a licence or operating with a different abstraction limit on the licence.

Radioactive substances

7.27 Radioactive material may not be kept or used or disposed of by any person on premises unless that person or company is registered under the *Radioactive Substances Act 1993* by the Environment Agency in respect of the presence and use on those premises of the material. There are certain statutory exemptions.

Points to note:

(a)   Offence and penalties: Failure to register or to comply with any registration or an exemption from registration leads to a criminal liability. A person guilty of an offence is liable on summary conviction to a fine not exceeding £20,000 or to imprisonment for a term exceeding six months, or both, and on conviction on indictment, to an unlimited fine or imprisonment for a term not exceeding five years, or both.

(b)   Transfer of registration: A registration for the disposal of radioactive material may be transferred by the transferor and transferee making a joint application to the Environment Agency with the appropriate fee. The transfer of a registration relating to only part of the premises can also be done. The Act does not specify transfer provisions for registrations which relate to keeping and using radioactive material, although this may be done by a joint application as above.

Planning and hazardous substances

7.28   A hazardous substance consent is required for the presence of a specific hazardous substance on, over or under land if the amount exceeds the relevant quantity under the *Planning (Hazardous Substances) Act 1990*. The temporary presence of a hazardous substance while it is being transported from one place to another will not require a hazardous substance consent, unless it is unloaded.

Points to note:

(a)   Benefit of consent: Any hazardous substance consent (unless the consent otherwise provides) is stated, in the *Planning (Hazardous Substances) Act 1990*, to run with the land and endure for the benefit of the land and all persons for the time being interested in the land to which it relates. A hazardous substance consent is generally not personal to the applicant.

(b)   Disposal of part of land: If there is a change in the person in control of part of the land to which the hazardous substance consent relates, then the consent is revoked unless an application for the continuation of the consent has previously been made to the planning authority. These provisions have been made to avoid the situation where the ownership of land and the keeping of hazardous substances becomes fragmented and thus the responsibility becomes unclear.

(c)   Offence and penalties: Failure to hold or comply with a hazardous substance consent is a criminal offence for which a person is liable on summary conviction to a fine not exceeding £20,000 and on indictment to an unlimited fine.

Control of Major Accident Hazards (COMAH)

7.29   The *Control of Major Accident Hazards Regulations 1999*, as amended, implement the EU Directive 96/82/EC known as the Seveso II Directive. *COMAH* applies mainly to the chemical industry, but also to some storage activities, explosives and nuclear sites, and other industries where threshold quantities of dangerous substances identified in the regulations are kept or used. The aim of *COMAH* is to prevent and mitigate the effects on people and the environment of major incidents involving dangerous substances. Therefore, it is important to consider whether a site falls within the obligations of the regulations and if so whether notification has been made and adequate measures have been put in place. The consequences of failing to take such steps may lead to the operation or installation being closed down.

Points to note:

(a)   Notification: Operators who will come within the scope of the regulations because dangerous substances will be present must submit a notification to the Health and Safety Executive before the start of construction and thereafter before operation. For operators who come within the scope for other reasons, such as a change in classification, or a change in the knowledge about a dangerous substance, they should submit a notification within three months.

(b)   Duties: Operators of sites that hold larger quantities of dangerous substances ('top tier' sites) are subject to more onerous requirements than those of 'lower tier' sites. The key duty for operators of lower tier sites is to notify the Health and Safety Executive, take all measures necessary to prevent major accidents and limit their consequences to people and the environment and prepare a major accident prevention policy. Top tier operators have to comply with the same duties as for lower tier sites and additionally, have to prepare a safety report, prepare and test an onsite emergency plan, supply information to local authorities for offsite emergency planning purposes and provide certain information to the public about their activities.

(c)   Prohibition of Operation: The Health and Safety Executive can prohibit the operation of any establishment, or any part thereof, where the measures taken by the operator for the prevention and mitigation of major accidents are not adequate. Additionally, if an operator has failed to submit any notification, safety report or other information required under the regulations within the relevant time period, the Health and Safety Executive may prohibit the operation of the establishment.

Waste management licence

7.30   A waste management licence is a licence granted by the Environment Agency, under *section 36* of the *Environmental Protection Act 1990* which authorises the treatment, keeping or disposal of any waste in or on land, or the treatment or disposal of any waste by means of a specified mobile plant. This regime applies to those waste activities which do not need a PPC permit, but if a site is permitted under the *PPC Regulations* due to other (non-waste) activities the waste management activities (even if they do not fall under PPC by themselves) will be included in the PPC permit.

There are two types of licence, one in relation to a specified area of land which is referred to as a site licence (for example landfills), and the other a mobile plant licence. The former is granted to the person who is in the occupation of the relevant land and the latter the person who operates the mobile plant.

Points to note:

(a)   Exclusions and exemptions: The *Waste Management Licensing Regulations 1994*, as amended, prescribe the operation of the licensing regime. They contain various exclusions and exemptions including, for example, a general exemption for the temporary storage of waste on the site where it is produced, pending its collection. If an exclusion or an exemption applies this should be registered with the Environment Agency.

(b)   Transfer: A waste management licence may be transferred upon a joint application to the Environment Agency by the transferor and transferee. The Environment Agency must grant the transfer unless it considers the proposed transferee is not a fit and proper person: see paragraph (c).

(c)   Fit and proper person: A person is not a fit and proper person if he has committed a relevant offence, for example a waste related offence, or the management of the site will not be in the hands of a technically competent person or the person cannot make adequate financial provision to discharge the obligations arising under the licence. Technical competence can be demonstrated by holding qualifications from the Waste Management Industry Training Advisory Board (WAMITAB).

(d)   Surrender: Mobile plant licences may be surrendered by the holder giving notice to the Environment Agency. However, a site licence may only be surrendered upon acceptance by the Environment Agency. Acceptance of the surrender is dependent upon whether the condition of the land is likely or unlikely to cause pollution of the environment or harm to human health.

(e)   Offences and penalties: It is a criminal offence to contravene the conditions of a waste management licence and to deposit, treat, keep or dispose of controlled waste unless a waste management licence is held. The maximum penalties for offences on summary conviction is six months imprisonment and/or a £40,000 fine, or both, and on conviction on indictment two years' imprisonment or an unlimited fine, or both.

Packaging waste

7.31   The *Producer Responsibility Obligations (Packaging Waste) Regulations 2005* implement the *Packaging and Packaging Waste Directive*

(94/62/EC) which seeks to reduce the impact of packaging and packaging waste on the environment by introducing recovery and recycling targets for packaging waste, and by encouraging minimisation and reuse of packaging. The Directive imposes national targets on the UK.

Points to note:

(a)   Handling packaging waste: A producer has obligations to recover and recycle packaging waste. A producer includes a manufacturer, converter, packer/filler, seller or service provider who 'handles' packaging or packaging materials. It is key to note that the regulations do not just apply to the manufacturers of packaging, but in simple terms catch all those in the supply chain apart from the end consumer (and in most cases the wholesaler).

(b)   Obligations: To be caught by the regulations a company must meet certain threshold tests. Obligations under the regulations are calculated on a yearly basis. A company satisfies the threshold tests if its turnover in the financial year was more than £2 million; and it handled in aggregate more than 50 tonnes of packaging or packaging material. The thresholds are assessed on a group basis, not an individual company basis. If a business is caught by the regulations, the obligations include registering on or before 7 April in the relevant year with the Environment Agency, to recover and recycle packaging waste and to furnish a certificate of compliance in respect of the recovery and recycling obligations. A company can register with a compliance scheme to fulfil its obligations.

(c)   Transfer: Consideration needs to be given as to how the target was registered, ie individually or as part of a group. This affects how registration will be affected post-completion. It is also dependent on whether the target is to register individually or as part of the purchaser's group. For example, if a subsidiary company ceases to belong to a group of companies for which there was a group registration, the target can register separately or as part of its new group with the Environment Agency or a compliance scheme.

(d)   Offences and penalties: There are a number of offences under the regulations including failure to register as a producer; failure to meet relevant recovery and recycling obligations; and failure to furnish a certificate of compliance. A person guilty of an offence is liable on summary conviction to a fine not exceeding £5,000 or on conviction on indictment to an unlimited fine.

Greenhouse gas emissions (EU ETS)

7.32   The EU ETS is a scheme introduced across Europe to control levels of carbon dioxide released into the atmosphere in order to combat climate change and help Europe meet its greenhouse gas emissions reduction target under the Kyoto Protocol. The *Climate Change Directive (2003/87/EC)* has been implemented into English Law through the *Greenhouse Gas Emissions*

Trading Scheme Regulations 2005. The English legislation only regulates the release of carbon dioxide although there is scope for extending the scheme to cover other greenhouse gases.

Points to note:

(a)   Operating Phases: The scheme is currently divided into two operating phases. The first phase runs from 1 January 2005 until 31 December 2007 and the second from 1 January 2008 until 31 December 2012. The scheme covers installations which carry out activities listed in Annex 1 of the Directive including energy activities, production and processing of ferrous metals, mineral industries, pulp and paper industries, and sectors with big combustion facilities such as hospitals and universities.

(b)   Permit: In order to emit carbon dioxide, the operator of an installation carrying out an Annex 1 activity is required to have a Greenhouse Gas Emissions Permit. Under the United Kingdom National Allocation Plan (UK NAP) the overall number of allowances is capped for all installations covered by the scheme and then allocated to the permit holders. One 'allowance' equates to an ability to emit one tonne of carbon dioxide and installations can sell allowances which are surplus to requirements and purchase additional allowances on the open market, if required.

(c)   Offences and Penalties: In order to demonstrate compliance with the EU ETS an installation must surrender allowances equivalent to the installation's verified CO_2 emissions by 30 April of each year. If this cannot be done the installation faces civil financial penalties. The penalty in Phase I for failing to surrender sufficient credits to match actual emissions is €40 per tonne of CO_2 increasing to €100 per tonne in Phase II. In addition, the offending operator still needs to surrender sufficient credits to cover any shortfall which will usually need to be purchased on the open market. Four UK companies were fined more than £750,000 in total for failing to account for their carbon emissions during the first year of the EU ETS.

(d)   Phase II: The UK Phase II NAP has been approved by the Commission and at the time of writing was being circulated together with a list of installation-level allocations to the stakeholders for comment prior to finalisation. The consultation period expired on 12 January 2007. The approach to the issuing of allocations set out in the UK Phase II NAP is a two-stage process. First, allowances are issued at sector level and then they are allocated to installations within that sector. The reduction in allowances against business is born entirely by the large electricity producers, as the UK's approach is that this sector is relatively insulated from international competition and can pass on the cost of carbon to consumers.

(e)   Changes: The *Greenhouse Gas Emissions Trading Scheme Regulations 2005* govern the process for obtaining a permit and also the process for obtaining a variation to a permit in the case of expansion or closure or any other change in operation at a particular installation. The UK NAP details how new entrants to the scheme are to be dealt with. A new entrant is an installation which either commences operation of an Annex 1 activity during the course of Phase II or extends its operation of an Annex 1 activity during Phase II. There are detailed rules set out in the UK NAP dealing with new entrant eligibility and treatment.

(f)   Transfer: A joint written application must be made to the Environment Agency from both the transferor and the transferee including the appropriate fee. Partial transfers are also allowed.

Overview of other general legislation

7.33   In addition to the various legislative regimes which require the holding of permits or the making of notifications for certain activities and environmental impacts, there is a swathe of further environmental legislation regulating business behaviour or which can impose potentially significant liabilities and costs. As discussed above, some of this is sector specific. We set out below some of the main areas of environmental legislation. Also, as stated above, this area is rapidly changing and new laws are being enacted or proposed on a frequent basis.

Waste

7.34   Points to note:

(a)   Duty of care: *Part 2* of the *Environmental Protection Act 1990* provides a wide-ranging system for controlling waste. All waste producers are subject to a duty of care under *section 33* of the Act to take reasonable and appropriate steps in their handling of waste. This duty involves preventing any escape of waste, and ensuring that the waste is transferred only to an authorised and competent person and that an adequate written description of the waste is given to the transferee. Wastes that are particularly hazardous are known as 'hazardous waste' and are subject to further controls. Hazardous waste requires greater care by those producing and handling it. For example, hazardous waste may be an issue where asbestos is being removed from a site or where contaminated soil is being removed because of building works.

(b)   Offences and penalties: It is a criminal offence to treat, keep or deposit waste unless a licence authorising its use is in place and complied with or the handling of such waste benefits from an exemption under the *Waste Management Licensing Regulations 1994*. If an offence is committed in relation to hazardous waste a person is liable on summary conviction to imprisonment for a term not exceeding 12 months or a fine not exceeding £40,000, or both, and on conviction on indictment to imprisonment for a term not exceeding five years or an unlimited fine, or both. A person who commits an offence, other than in relation to hazardous waste, is liable on summary conviction to imprisonment for a term not exceeding six months or a fine not exceeding £20,000, or both. On conviction on indictment to imprisonment for a term not exceeding two years or an unlimited fine, or both. Where waste has been deposited without a licence or in breach of a licence, the occupier of the land concerned can be made to remove the waste unless he neither deposited nor knowingly caused its deposit nor knowingly permitted it. In this case under *section 59* of the *Environmental Protection Act*, the regulator can remove the waste and recover the reasonable costs of so doing from the responsible person.

Asbestos

7.35   The *Control of Asbestos Regulations 2006* which implement The *Asbestos Worker Protection Directive 83/477/EEC*, as amended, impose duties to manage asbestos in non-domestic premises.

Points to note:

(a)   Duties: Under the regulations, the duty holder has an obligation to implement a regime to manage asbestos. This includes carrying out a survey to assess the presence of asbestos and to record the location and condition of asbestos, keeping the record up to date, assessing the risk of anyone being exposed to the asbestos and preparing a plan to manage that risk. The target should be asked for asbestos surveys and asbestos management plans and to confirm whether all necessary remedial and management works have been carried out.

(b)   Offences and penalties: A failure to comply with the regulations will lead to a fine on summary conviction of £5,000 per offence and on indictment to an unlimited fine.

Oil storage

7.36   The *Control of Pollution (Oil Storage) (England) Regulations 2001* apply to oil storage facilities on a site, which include tanks, intermediate bulk containers, oil drums and mobile bowsers, or an entity which has custody or control of such oil storage facilities. The regulations are mainly aimed at above-ground oil storage facilities which store more than 200 litres of oil on industrial, commercial and institutional premises. The Regulations set minimum design standards for all new and existing above-ground oil storage facilities, with certain exceptions. The key requirement is the provision of secondary containment, ie a bund or drip tray, to ensure that any leaking or spilt oil cannot enter controlled waters.

Offences and Penalties: A person with custody or control of any oil storage facility breaching the regulations will be guilty of a criminal offence. On summary conviction a person will be liable to a fine not exceeding £5,000. On conviction on indictment the penalty could be an unlimited fine.

Statutory nuisance

7.37   Every local authority has the power to control air emissions and other discharges or conditions that impact on the local environment under the statutory nuisance system pursuant to *Part III* of the *EPA 1990*. *Section 79* of *EPA 1990* provides that the following air-related matters constitute statutory nuisances:

(a)   smoke emitted from premises so as to be prejudicial to health or a nuisance;

(b)   fumes or gases emitted from premises so as to be prejudicial to health or nuisance; and

(c)   dust, steam, smells or other effluvia arising on industrial, trade or business premises and being prejudicial to health or a nuisance.

In addition to the air-related problems mentioned above, the following land-related issues may also constitute a statutory nuisance:

(a)   premises in such a state as to be prejudicial to health or a nuisance;

(b)   any accumulation or deposit which is prejudicial to health or a nuisance.

Offences and Penalties: If a local authority identifies that a statutory nuisance exists or is likely to occur or recur, it will serve an abatement notice on the occupier. The notice will require the nuisance to be stopped and will set out any works or other steps that may be necessary to achieve this. It is an offence not to comply with an abatement notice without reasonable excuse, and failure to do so will entitle the authority to take steps itself to abate the nuisance and recover the reasonable costs of so doing from the offender. It is open to anyone affected by a statutory nuisance to make a complaint to the Magistrates' Court. If the Magistrates' Court is satisfied that the alleged nuisance exists it can require the defendant to abate the nuisance and may also impose a fine.

Environmental Liability Directive

7.38   The *Environmental Liability Directive (2004/35/EC)* was adopted on 21 April 2004. It is required to be transposed into national law by 30 April 2007. In England, DEFRA is still consulting on policy options for implementing the Directive and at the time of writing it is not known how it will be implemented in England. The Directive is aimed at the prevention and remedying of environmental damage, specifically damage to habitats and species protected by EC law, damage to water resources and land contamination which presents a threat to human health. It would apply only to damage from incidents occurring after it comes into force.

The Directive is based on the polluter pays principle. It requires operators to inform the competent authority of environmental damage that has occurred and to take all reasonable steps to deal with it. Polluters would meet their liability by remediating the damaged environment directly, or by taking 'complementary' or 'compensatory' remediation. Competent authorities would be responsible for enforcing the regime in the public interest, including determining remediation standards, or taking action to remediate or prevent damage and recover the costs from the operator. Individuals and others who may be directly affected by actual or possible damage, and NGOs in certain circumstances may request action by a competent authority and seek judicial review of the authority's action or inaction.

Waste electrical and electronic equipment (WEEE)

7.39   The aim of the *WEEE Directive 2003/108/EC* is to require member states to encourage the separate collection of WEEE so that it can be recovered and recycled where possible rather than landfilled.

WEEE includes waste household appliances, computing and communications equipment, consumer equipment such as TVs, video players, audio equipment etc, light fittings and fluorescent lamps, electrical tools, toys, leisure and sports equipment, medical devices, monitoring and control equipment and various types of automatic dispensers for drinks, solid products, etc, but excludes high-voltage equipment, ie greater than 1,000 volts AC.

The *WEEE Regulations 2006* came into force on 5 January 2007. The marking of equipment requirements will come into force on 1 April 2007 and the distributor obligations on 1 July 2007. Once implemented in the UK, business users – any business that manufactures, brands or imports WEEE – will have a responsibility for financing the cost of collection, treatment, recovery and environmentally sound disposal of historic WEEE (ie products placed on the market before 13 August 2005), unless it is being replaced by a new product which is equivalent or fulfils the same function as the WEEE in which case the producer of the new product will meet those costs. For new equipment supplied by one business to another, there will also be collection, recovery and recycling targets and obligations. Businesses supplying electrical and electronic equipment to other business users will have to either register with a compliance scheme or directly register with the Environment Agency and provide evidence that they have met their obligations.

Restrictions on hazardous substances

7.40   The *Restriction of Hazardous Substances Directive (RoHS) (2002/95/EC)* was adopted in February 2003 by the European Union. The RoHS directive and the *Restriction of Hazardous Substances in Electrical and Electronic Equipment Regulations 2005* which implement the directive took effect on 1 July 2006. This directive restricts the use of six hazardous materials (lead, cadmium, mercury, hexavalent chromium, polybrominated biphenyl (PBB) and polybrominated diphenyl ether (PBDE) flame retardants) in the manufacture of various types of electronic and electrical equipment.

Allocating risks and liabilities between the parties

Relevant factors

7.41   In addition to doing disclosure and due diligence the parties will need to negotiate the allocation of environmental responsibility between them. It is self-evident that the relative bargaining strengths of the parties will be a significant factor in this process. Additional factors include:

(a)   Quality and availability of information: A purchaser may feel more comfortable taking on environmental risks associated with the target if the purchaser considers that it has obtained good quality information through due diligence which means that it fully understands the risks. Alternatively, the purchaser may have identified an issue which it finds unacceptable and for which it requires some contractual protection.

(b)   Unknown risks: If the speed of the transaction or the history and nature of the target means that there is an information 'black hole', the purchaser may be more nervous about accepting environmental risk as it is unable to quantify it. A typical 'black hole' in share acquisitions where the company has had a long history is the risk of contaminated land liability in association with former sites.

(c)   Desire for a clean break: Environmental liabilities can be 'long-tailed' with a long time elapsing between the relevant event and the claim arising, for example human exposure to asbestos and US superfund liabilities. A seller may want to secure the position that it has no residual liabilities once it has sold the target, for example if it is intending to wind itself up and return money to shareholders or if it is withdrawing from the market concerned. Purchasers may have similar views. A purchaser may only wish to be responsible for matters under its control, ie liabilities arising from operations carried out post-acquisition. A financial purchaser, who intends to restructure and then sell on in the short to medium term, will be more reluctant to assume liabilities on a long-term basis.

(d)   Transaction type: Broadly from an environmental perspective, in this jurisdiction, the purchaser of assets is in a better position than the purchaser of shares in that it can inspect the assets and operations which it is acquiring. Even if it is going to acquire liability for historically contaminated land this will relate to land being acquired which therefore can be investigated. A purchaser of a company (shares) at a practical level, may be unable to carry out full due diligence for environmental risk. That said, a company which has been incorporated recently or which is known to have only carried out one type of business at the same site, should present no more due diligence difficulties than those which arise on the acquisition of assets.

(e)   Desire for control: If a serious issue is revealed, a party may want to keep responsibility for it so it has the comfort of knowing that the liability is dealt with properly. For example, a seller of a severely contaminated site who is keeping the polluting company (and therefore liability) may wish to carry out remediation itself rather than give a price reduction and rely on the purchaser to do the works. Similarly, a purchaser may feel that as future owner of the site, it has a vested interest in doing the works because it has the long-term interest in the site and it may also have concerns about commercial confidentiality and potential disruption to operations by the seller.

Contractual provisions – general

7.42   Before asking lawyers to draft complex documentation, there should be a clear understanding between the parties and their lawyers as to the principles of allocation of environmental liability. A typical misunderstanding is where, in commercial negotiations, the parties agree that the seller shall provide the purchaser with an 'environmental indemnity' subject to certain financial and time limits. The seller believes it is giving a contaminated land indemnity, the purchaser believes that it is receiving a comprehensive environmental indemnity covering all contaminated land, regulatory and permitting liabilities and third party liabilities. Embarking straight into drafting where there are significant environmental issues to agree can be a waste of time and money.

The main types of contractual provisions are:

(a)   environmental warranties;

(b)   indemnities; and

(c)   bespoke contractual provisions.

Environmental warranties

7.43   Broadly, warranties are statements made concerning the veracity of particular states of affairs at a particular time (signing and usually again at completion). The scope of warranties is negotiated on a case-by-case basis. However, matters typically warranted included:

(a)   compliance with environmental laws;

(b)   no criminal, civil or administrative proceedings or investigations in respect of environmental matters and no notices or complaints;

(c)   the existence of all licences necessary for the operation of the business, compliance with these, and no knowledge of their likely revocation, amendment or breach;

(d)   that no contamination exists onsite or is migrating offsite, and no unpermitted discharges or emissions of hazardous substances have occurred at the current sites;

(e)   no contamination liability issues associated with former sites;

(f)   that no environmental expenditure is required or anticipated outside of the ordinary course of business;

(g)   that all environmental audits, impact assessments and other reviews have been disclosed;

(h)   other specific issues such as actions from NGOs, biodiversity impacts on sites, environmental contracts and asbestos.

If a warranty transpires to be untrue then the purchaser may be able to sue for damages. The calculation of damages for warranty claims is a complex topic but will not necessarily be the same as the amount it may cost the purchaser to put right the situation, and indeed the larger the overall value of the transaction, the less likely it is that the purchaser will make a full recovery of the expenditure required to rectify the situation. Also, if the breach is disclosed in the disclosure letter against the warranty, no liability will arise.

Warranties will also be subject to certain financial thresholds and caps, time limits and other exclusions which will be of general application to all warranties. Often a purchaser seeks a longer time limit for the environmental warranties as compared to the other warranties. Often a seller will want to 'ring fence' or 'box' environmental warranties to prevent the purchaser from using a general warranty such as a compliance with law or property warranty as a 'back door' to bring an environmental claim.

Indemnities

7.44   If a purchaser needs to know that certain types of environmental liabilities will be covered by the seller, it should not rely on warranties but seek an indemnity or other contractual protection. An indemnity is an agreement that the indemnifying party will satisfy any loss incurred by the beneficiary in connection with a specified matter or circumstance. Indemnities can be two-way, they are not always from seller to purchaser, it depends on who has agreed to take the risk. Generally, the negotiation of indemnities is tougher and more protracted than for warranties.

Whereas warranties are proffered as a matter of course, this is not the case with indemnities, which are tailored to the particular concerns of specific transactions and have to be sought and negotiated. The following are some examples of indemnities which may be given by the seller:

(a)   an indemnity for all liabilities which relate to pre-completion acts, omissions or states of affairs (unlikely);

(b)   an indemnity for all pre-completion matters relating to certain defined categories of risks (for example, contamination liabilities or industrial disease liabilities);

(c)   an indemnity relating to a specific risk or liability (such as contamination by a specific substance or a breach of a permit condition which can only be rectified by costly plant modifications);

If the seller gives the purchaser an indemnity, it is not unusual for the seller to seek a counter-indemnity back from the purchaser. For example, if the seller gives the purchaser an indemnity in relation to all liabilities which relate to pre-completion matters, the seller may seek a mirror image indemnity in respect of any liability which it may suffer relating to post-completion matters, or alternatively once its indemnity expires. If the purchaser agrees to bear a particular risk, then the seller may require to be indemnified for all losses suffered in connection with this.

It is important to consider who needs to benefit from the indemnity. For example, if the purchaser intends to move the business intra-group it is likely to want all of its group companies to have the benefit of the indemnity.

Scoping the indemnity – limitations and allowances

7.45   The beneficiary of the indemnity will want to know that it will get cover for the issues which it is concerned about. However, the indemnifier will want to know that it is not writing a blank cheque. The limitations and allowances in an indemnity can be complex to negotiate as they seek to reach a balance between these two drivers. Limitations and allowances might include:

(a)   requiring a trigger event, such as the commencement of legal or regulatory proceedings or receipt of written notification of an intention to commence such proceedings;

(b)   'stitch in time' measures – a purchaser may want the indemnity not only to be activated where there is a threat of legal action, it may also want to claim if it uncovers a problem which the authorities are not yet aware of but which may require immediate attention or constitutes a liability under law;

(c)   nature of recoverable loss – and whether it includes business interruption costs, loss of profit, consequential loss and losses under contract;

(d)   time limits – a requirement that in order for the indemnity to apply a claim must be lodged within a given timescale;

(e)   financial limits – there will usually be a financial cap on claims and generally the parties will also agree on individual and/or aggregate thresholds for environmental claims;

(f)   sharing the loss – another alternative is to provide for apportionment of loss between seller and purchaser. Sometimes this is on a sliding scale throughout the duration of the indemnity (eg 90:10 for the first two years, 80:20 for the next, and 60:40 for the final period); this has the benefit of encouraging the recipient of the indemnity to be cost-effective;

(g)   exclusion of liabilities to the extent caused or exacerbated by actions of the purchaser after completion; often this is qualified by negligence and/or if they fall outside the ordinary course of trading, although there will inevitably be argument as to what this term means;

(h)   exclusion of liabilities to the extent caused or triggered by changes of use or site closure, building demolition or redevelopment introducing pathways for contamination;

(i)   exclusion of liability triggered by voluntary admissions to third parties or regulators ('whistle blowing');

(j)   exclusion of liability for matters uncovered by voluntary site investigations by or for the purchaser ('no fishing');

(k)   no double recovery – inability to claim to the extent that the purchaser has compensated for the loss already (eg because of a provision in the accounts), or is able to recover for the same loss from insurance or from a third party; and

(l)   no cover for liabilities arising because of changes in the law or regulatory practice since completion.

In addition to provisions limiting liability, there will need to be other clauses addressing procedural matters such as notification and conduct of claims and litigation and conduct of remedial action where required. This area can take time to negotiate because both seller and purchaser may want to have control over claims or works (albeit for different reasons). A usual way of unblocking any impasse seems to be to provide for consultation and provision of information to the party who grants conduct to the other.

The party who has conduct may be put under certain obligations which help to comfort the other party, such as:

(a)   apportionment of reputable consultants and contractors;

(b)   requirements to try to ensure they fulfil the scope of work and comply with all applicable laws in doing so;

(c)   provision for the non-conduct party to receive a collateral warranty and notice of completion from the consultants and contractors; and

(d)   opportunity to inspect, attend site meetings etc.

In addition, expert determination clauses are often included to resolve technical disputes between the parties, as they will be quicker than litigation.

Bespoke contractual provisions

7.46   The parties can agree a wide range of solutions to meet the needs of a particular transaction. Common solutions include:

(a)   Purchase price reduction: A price reduction rather than an indemnity may be preferable. This avoids litigation risk and the cost and time of enforcing the indemnity. Also the beneficiary might have concerns about the indemnifier's solvency or continued existence. However, it is important to obtain an accurate assessment of the likely costs associated with the issue, and technical input from an environmental consultant is likely to be required.

(b)   Agreed programme of works: If issues have been identified, the parties may agree a programme of works to be carried out after completion. Drawing up the agreed programme will require technical input (whether from clients or consultants). This mechanism is often agreed for permit/regulatory compliance works. Sometimes the purchaser is given a short period after completion to check that the list is complete and to add to it if necessary. The seller is likely to want to impose a financial cap on the programme. Alternatively, a purchaser may require that the seller carries out the works between signing and completion and to make completion conditional on doing the works.

(c)   Post-completion audit or investigation: The parties might agree to conduct investigations either between contract and completion, or after completion. This could be for a number of reasons. Before the parties contract they should be clear about the scope of the proposed tests, who will conduct these, and what obligations or rights might flow dependent upon the results of the tests. For example, sometimes the tests are done solely for evidential purposes, ie to set a 'baseline'. This may lead to the purchaser requiring exhaustive investigations which may not be in the seller's interest. Alternatively, it may be agreed that all legal liability issues identified by the audit should be corrected and paid for by the seller, or their purpose may be to scope out remediation for a known problem. This may be dealt with by a joint appointment of an independent consultant. If time allows, it is better if the appointment is agreed before exchange of contracts rather than just the contractual provisions setting out its scope.

(d)   Buy-back provisions: Sometimes the seller will agree to take back a potential problem site. The triggers for this vary but will need to be set out in the contract, for example the purchaser may have a put option which gives it total discretion to 'put' the site back on the seller subject to a time limit. Alternatively, the seller may only be required to take the site if remediation costs exceed a certain amount, or a certain issue is identified.

(e)   Restructuring the transaction: In a share sale, if the concerns relate to previous businesses, it may be possible to restructure the deal as an asset sale or to leave behind certain subsidiaries in the vendor group. However, it would be necessary to consider the wider implications of this particularly as regards tax. In an assets sale, the purchaser may be able to leave the problem site behind.

(f)   Insurance: Often it is possible to obtain specialist insurance for environmental risks. There will be costs associated with reviewing (and to the extent possible) negotiating the policy wording on top of the premium which is often quite expensive. To reduce the premium, it is possible for one party to agree to bear the risk up to a fixed amount, and for any losses over and above the amount to be insured. This way the full potential of the loss will have been crystallised to a level which is acceptable. Before considering insurance it is important to understand that insurers may seek to claim a contribution under any existing policies (although the right to do so can be negotiated out of the policy wording). It is also possible to invalidate any cover you obtain if you do not make full disclosure of all relevant facts before the policy is issued and if you disclose it to a third party. Insurance policies also include a wide number of exclusions and exceptions and will be limited in duration. Whilst insurance has its uses, in particular to help unblock negotiations, parties who use it should make sure they fully appreciate the policy's limitations and that it is not necessarily the quick fix it is often thought to be.

(g)   Post-completion adjustments for carbon: In relevant sectors, contracts will contain provisions for a post-completion adjustment for a shortfall or excess in allowances under the EU Emissions Trading Scheme.

(h)   Transitional property arrangements: In some transactions the purchaser may not want to acquire a long-term interest in a site. It may only wish to occupy the site for a few months pending relocation. Also, it may only need part of a larger site owned by the seller and it has been agreed that it will take a lease from the seller. The allocation of environmental liability will need to be negotiated as part of such lease or licence documentation. In most cases, the purchaser will not want to take on historic liabilities and the seller will want to make sure that the purchaser does not cause any contamination and is obliged to remediate it if it does.

Money laundering

7.47   It may seem surprising that a chapter on environmental issues in corporate transactions would have a section on money laundering. The purpose here is to highlight the issue, as opposed to discuss it in detail. However, the language of the *Proceeds of Crime Act 2002* (*POCA*) is so broad that even 'passive' possession of criminal property is defined as money laundering. The purpose of *POCA* and the *Money Laundering Regulations* (the Regulations) is to maximise the difficulties criminals face when trying to launder money, including by disguising its origins and using it in lawful business activities. The legislation applies to a number of businesses and activities including the provision of legal services involving participation in a financial or real property transaction. The reason that it is relevant to environmental matters (as well as other matters such as data protection and health and safety) is that it applies to all criminal activity which results in financial advantage, rather than solely to the more usual types of crime associated with money laundering such as terrorism and drugs trafficking. Environmental and other regulatory lawyers advising in relation to a financial or real property transaction are obliged to report a knowledge or suspicion of money laundering. This means that when lawyers working on transactions come across breaches of environmental law which are criminal (however unintentional, technical or trivial) but have resulted in some financial advantage (for example, the saving of money by failing to carry out an asbestos survey), they have to report such matters to the Serious Organised Crime Agency (SOCA) for permission to continue to act. (There are exceptions for information subject to legal privilege.) Further, in many cases they will not be able to discuss this matter with their client as they then may commit a further offence of 'tipping off'. There are no minimum threshold provisions in *POCA* either in relation to the amount of the criminal property involved or the seriousness of the criminal offence. Clients in a regulated sector such as banks or private equity houses may also need to obtain consent to proceed. Breaches of the legislation can result in a fine or a custodial sentence.

Environmental Information Regulations

7.48   The *Environmental Information Regulations 2004* (*EIRs*) provide broad rights of access to environmental information. Although not directly relevant to transactions except possibly to gain information for due diligence (subject to any confidentiality letter), we have included this section as it is helpful to understand that most environmental information provided to regulatory bodies is accessible by the public if they ask for it.

The *EIRs* apply to all public authorities in England, Wales, and Northern Ireland. 'Public authority' means government departments and any other public authority as defined in the *Freedom of Information Act 2000*, which includes a local authority and the Environment Agency. Any person or organisation may apply for information. The applicant is not required to prove an interest, or to say why it wants the information.

The *EIRs* require proactive dissemination of information, including progressively making information available to the public by electronic means, in line with the *Freedom of Information Act 2000*. There is a 20 working day deadline for responding to requests. In the case of particularly complex requests involving a large volume of material, the time can be extended up to 40 working days.

There is a presumption in favour of disclosure. There are a number of exceptions to the public authority's obligations to disclose information if requested. However, in all cases the authority can only refuse the request if the exception is met and 'in all the circumstances of the case, the public interest in maintaining the exception outweighs the public interest in disclosing the information.' Additionally, certain exceptions cannot be relied on if they concern 'information on emissions'.

Environmental permits and the transfer process

Permit	Issued To/By	Transfer Process (Whole)	Transfer Process (Part)
Pollution Prevention and Control Permit – known as a PPC Permit	ISSUED TO The *operator* of an installation or mobile plant.	A joint application (including relevant fee) by the permit holder and purchaser to the relevant authority containing details as per *section 18 Pollution Prevention and Control (England and Wales) Regulations 2000.*	The same provisions for the partial transfer apply as that of a whole transfer but additionally it must identify the part of the installation; provide a map or plan identifying the part of the site used for the operation of that installation or mobile plant.
Pollution Prevention and Control (England and Wales) Regulations 2000	ISSUED BY Part A(1) Installations – Environment Agency (EA) Part A(2) Installations – the Local Authority (LA) Part B Installations – the LA	The EA or LA must effect the transfer unless it considers that the purchaser will not have control over the operation of the installation or will not ensure compliance with the permit. If the permit relates to a waste management activity, the EA or LA shall only effect the the transfer if it is satisfied that the proposed transferee is a fit and proper person to carry out that activity. The transfer takes effect from the date agreed with the applicants and endorsed on the permit. If two months has passed since the EA or LA received the application or such longer period as may be agreed in writing, and the transfer has not been effected nor notice of rejection given then the applicants can notify the EA or LA in writing that they are treating the application as having been refused. *Section 18 Pollution Prevention and Control (England and Wales) Regulations 2000*	The conditions included in the new permit and original permit after the transfer shall be the same as the original conditions immediately before the transfer in so far as they are relevant to any installation, site and mobile plant covered by the new permit or the original permit, subject to variations as the EA or LA see fit. The transfer takes effect from a date agreed between the applicants and specified in the new permit. *Section 18 Pollution Prevention and Control (England and Wales) Regulations 2000*

228

		Transfer (whole)	Transfer (partial)
1. Integrated Pollution Control (IPC) Permit 2. LA Air Pollution Consent (LAAPC) *Part I of the Environmental Protection Act 1990 (as amended)* *Environmental Protection (Prescribed Processes and Substances) Regulations 1991 (as amended)* These permits are being replaced by the Pollution Prevention and Control (PPC) Permit (see above). Transition period ends 1 October 2007.	**ISSUED TO** A person who carries on a *prescribed process* (either A or B). **ISSUED BY** 1. In relation to IPC permits relating to Part A processes – the EA 2. In relation to LAAPC relating to Part B processes – the LA	1. IPC Permits A purchaser must notify the EA of the transfer of the consent within 21 days of the transfer and enclose the relevant fee. The transfer takes effect from the date of transfer and is subject to the same conditions as before the transfer. *Section 6 Environmental Protection Act 1990* 2. LAAPC A purchaser must notify the LA of the transfer of the consent within 21 days of the transfer and enclose the relevant fee. The transfer takes effect from the date of transfer and is subject to the same conditions as before the transfer. *Section 6 Environmental Protection Act 1990*	No provision in the legislation for partial transfer of the IPC Permit or the LAAPC.
Greenhouse Gas Emissions Permit *Greenhouse Gas Emissions Trading Scheme Regulations 2005*	**ISSUED TO** The *operator* of an installation. **ISSUED BY**	Joint letter application (including relevant fee) to the EA from both the permit holder and purchaser containing the current permit holder's and purchaser's address and contact number; address of the site; and its national grid reference (or, for offshore installations, equivalent information identifying the installation and its location).	The same process for a transfer of the whole of the permit applies but the application must also identify the activity or part of Schedule 1 activity to which the transfer applies and identify the installation in which that transferred activity is carried out and information in respect of any applications for allowances from the new entrant reserve.

Permit	Issued To/By	Transfer Process (Whole)	Transfer Process (Part)
Greenhouse Gas Emissions Trading Scheme Regulations 2005 – contd	Environment Agency	The EA must effect the transfer unless it considers that the purchaser will not be the operator of the transferred unit after the transfer is effected; or the purchaser will not comply with any monitoring and reporting condition. The transfer takes effect from a date agreed between the applicants and specified in the updated permit. If two months has passed since the EA receives the application or such longer period as may be agreed in writing, and the transfer has not been effected nor notice of rejection given then the applicants can notify the EA in writing that they are treating the application as having been refused.	No provision in the legislation for partial transfer.
Discharge Consents *Water Resources Act 1991 – Schedule 10*	ISSUED TO A person or company which discharges into controlled waters (as defined in *section 104* of the *Water Resources Act 1991*). ISSUED BY Environment Agency	Joint notice is given to the EA by the purchaser and the consent holder of the transfer of the consent. The notice may specify a date on which the transfer should take effect. No fee is payable. The EA must give effect to the transfer within 21 days of receiving the joint notice. The transfer takes effect from the later of the date on which the EA amends the consent and the date (if any) specified in the joint notice. *Paragraph 11 of Schedule 10 Water Resources Act 1991.*	

Trade Effluent Consent *Water Resources Act 1991 – section 87*	ISSUED TO The occupier of trade premises who wishes to discharge effluent. ISSUED BY Statutory sewerage undertaker	No transfer provisions contained in the legislation. The purchaser should notify the undertaker in writing of the transfer and check whether the consent states how transfer is to be effected.	No provisions in the legislation for partial transfer.
Water Abstraction Licences *Water Resources Act 1991 – section 24A*	ISSUED TO A person or company which abstracts from any source of supply. ISSUED BY Environment Agency	Joint notice must be given to the EA from both the permit holder and a purchaser including the information required by *section 59A of the Water Resources Act 1991*. The notice may specify a date for the transfer to take place. If the notice complies with the requirements above the EA must effect the transfer by amending the licence to substitute the name of the purchaser as the holder of the licence. The transfer takes effect from the later of the date on which the EA amends the consent and the date (if any) specified in the joint notice. *Section 59A of the Water Resources Act 1991*	No provision in the legislation for partial transfer of a water abstraction licence.

Permit	Issued To/By	Transfer Process (Whole)	Transfer Process (Part)
Hazardous Substances Consent *Planning (Hazardous Substances) Act 1990* *Planning (Hazardous Substances) Regulations 1992*	ISSUED TO A hazardous substances consent (unless otherwise stipulated on the consent) is attached to and for the benefit of the land and all persons for the time being interested in the land. *s 6 of the Planning (Hazardous Substances) Act 1990* ISSED BY Hazardous Substances Authority.	Unless a condition is imposed limiting use of the consent to a specified person or company the consent will run with the land, rather than being personal to the applicant. This means that if the land is sold in its entirety, the new owner will be able to implement the consent.	A hazardous substances consent is revoked if there is a change in the person in control of part of the land to which it relates, unless an application for the continuation of the consent has previously been made to the hazardous substances authority. An application must be accompanied by the information required under *section 5(3) of the Planning (Hazardous Substances) Regulations 1992.* If an application relates to more than one consent/hazardous substance, the authority may make different determinations in relation to each consent/hazardous substance. Where the application is made for a continuation of a permit then, unless within such period as may be prescribed, or within such extended period as may be agreed upon in writing between the applicant and the hazardous substances authority, the hazardous substances authority either— (a) gives notice to the applicant of their decision on the application; or (b) gives notice to him that the application has been referred to the Secretary of State, the application shall be deemed to have been granted. *s 7 of the Planning (Hazardous Substances) Act 1990*

	ISSUED TO / ISSUED BY		See Transfer Process (Whole)
Control of Major Accidents Hazards (COMAH) *The Control of Major Accident Hazards Regulations 1999 (as amended)*	**ISSUED TO** The operator is the person who is in control of the operation of an establishment or installation. *Regulations 2(1); 3(1); 3(2) and Schedule 1* **ISSUED BY** The Health and Safety Executive and the EA jointly.	There is no permit to transfer however the operator must notify the competent authority when there is a significant change in any information notified to the competent authority under the Regulations in respect of the establishment. This would include the change of operator of the establishment or the modification of the establishment or an installation which could have significant repercussions with respect to the prevention of major accidents; or the permanent closure of an installation in the establishment. *Regulation 6 Control of Major Accident Hazards Regulations 1999 (as amended);*	See Transfer Process (Whole)
1. Radioactive Substance Authorisation 2. Use of Radioactive Material Registration *Radioactive Substances Act 1993*	**ISSUED TO** 1. A person who disposes of radioactive waste on or from premises used for the purposes of any undertaking carried on by him. *Section 13 of the Radioactive Substances Act 1993* 2. A person who keeps or uses, or causes or permits to be kept or used, radioactive material on premises which are used for the purposes of an undertaking carried on by him.	1. Joint application to the EA by permit holder and purchaser. A fee is payable. The EA must consult with local authorities, relevant water bodies or other public or local authorities. The EA may grant the application to transfer if it is satisfied that the purchaser will have operational control over the disposals; that he is able to ensure compliance with the limitations and conditions of the authorisation; and no other grounds exist on which to refuse to grant the application. Where the authorising authority grants the application, it must fix the date from which it is to have effect and furnish the transferee with a certificate. *Section 16A of the Radioactive Substances Act 1993*	1. The same process for the transfer in respect of the whole applies but where the application to transfer relates to part only of the premises, it must specify the part in question. *Section 16A of the Radioactive Substances Act 1993* 2. No transfer provisions contained in the legislation. The purchaser should notify the EA in writing of the transfer and check whether the registration under the *Radioactive Substances Act 1993* states how the transfer in respect of part is to be effected.

Permit	Issued To/By	Transfer Process (Whole)	Transfer Process (Part)
Radioactive Substances Act 1993 – contd	*Section 6 of the Radioactive Substances Act 1993*	2. No transfer provisions contained in the legislation.	No provision in the legislation for partial transfer.
	ISSUED BY Environment Agency	The purchaser should notify the EA in writing of the transfer and check whether the registration under the *Radioactive Substances Act 1993* states how the transfer is to be effected.	
Waste Management Licence (WML) 1. Site licence (authorising the deposit, recovery or disposal of controlled waste in or on land); and	ISSUED TO Site licences are granted to an occupier and mobile plant licences are granted to a person who deposits, recovers or disposes of controlled waste.	Joint application (including relevant fee) to the EA by the licence holder and a purchaser. The application must contain all of the required information set out in *Schedule 2 of the Waste Management Licensing Regulations 1994.*	
2. Mobile plant licence (authorising the recovery or disposal of controlled waste using certain types of mobile plant). *Environmental Protection Act 1990 – Part II section 29 – section 78* *Waste Management Licensing Regulations 1994*	ISSUED BY Environment Agency	If the EA is satisfied that the proposed transferee is a fit and proper person then it shall effect a transfer of the licence to the purchaser. If within the period of two months beginning with the date on which the authority received an application, or such longer period as agreed in writing, the authority has neither effected a transfer of the licence nor given notice to the applicants that the authority has rejected the application, the authority shall be deemed to have rejected the application. *Section 40 of the Environmental Protection Act 1990*	

Chapter 8

Legal Aspects of Acquisitions

At a glance

- A business may be acquired by purchasing either the entire issued share capital of a company or its business and assets.

- It is likely that, in addition to company law matters, specialist legal advice will be required in relation to: competition; pensions: employment; intellectual property; information technology; real property (and possibly environmental law); and tax.

- The basic stages of an acquisition are: due diligence; preparation of documents; negotiation; signing; completion.

- It is crucial to conduct an appropriate due diligence investigation in order to identify and analyse the commercial, legal and financial standing of the target company.

- Parties to contractual negotiations should avoid making false or misleading statements; these may lead to civil and/or criminal liability.

- In addition to the acquisition agreement, the following documents are usually required: tax covenant; disclosure letter; board minutes; powers of attorney; stock transfer forms; new articles of association and EGM documents; pensions documentation; resignation letters from target directors and company secretary; and service agreements.

- Whilst completion commonly occurs immediately after signing of the agreement, it is often delayed until a later date to deal with competition clearances (and other necessary consents).

- Post-completion formalities include the stamping and registration of the share transfers (if a share acquisition) and the filing of relevant returns with Companies House.

- The purchaser may use any combination of the three basic forms of consideration: shares; loan capital; and/or cash.

- The Prospectus Rules may apply if the purchaser is to issue shares as consideration.

- The City Code on Takeovers and Mergers can apply to the acquisition of certain private companies.

- The general prohibition on companies giving financial assistance (in *section 151* of the *Companies Act 1985*) for the purpose of the acquisition of their own shares, or shares in their parent company, may affect the financing of an acquisition. *Section 678* of the *Companies Act 2006* will remove the prohibition on a private company giving financial assistance for the purpose of the acquisition of its own shares. This change is expected to come into force in October 2008.

Introduction

8.1   In this chapter, the authors consider the legal structure of, and legal problems which arise on, the acquisition of private companies incorporated in England and Wales – that is, companies which are not designated as public under *section 1(3)* of the *Companies Act 1985* (*CA 1985*) and which, pursuant to *section 81* of *CA 1985*, cannot therefore issue shares or debentures to the public.

Private companies which are limited by shares or by guarantee must generally have the word 'Limited' or 'Ltd' at the end of their name. (*Section 30* of *CA 1985* allows certain very limited exceptions. The vast majority of private companies engaged in any form of trade or commerce will be limited by shares.) By contrast, the name of a public company must end in the words 'Public Limited Company' or 'PLC'.

Since, at the date of publication, most of the *Companies Act 2006* (*CA 2006*) is not in force, references to sections of *CA 1985* have not been updated unless *CA 2006* will amend the corresponding sections of *CA 1985* significantly.

A table has been included at the end of the chapter showing corresponding *CA 2006* references.

Sale or purchase of a private company

8.2   Any agreement for the sale or purchase of a private company is subject to normal principles of English law. Additional rules apply to certain other categories of company. The City Code on Takeovers and Mergers (the 'Takeover Code'), which is administered by the Panel on Takeovers and Mergers (the 'Panel') applies to acquisitions of companies which have their registered offices in the United Kingdom, the Channel Islands or the Isle of Man if any of their equity shares or other transferable voting securities

('securities') are admitted to trading on a regulated market in the United Kingdom, the Channel Islands or the Isle of Man. This will generally be limited to public, statutory and chartered companies. Certain parts of the Code also apply to acquisitions of companies which have their registered offices in one EEA member state and whose securities are admitted to trading on a regulated market in one or more other EEA member states (including, in each case, the United Kingdom). The Takeover Code also applies to acquisitions of certain private companies but only when they are considered by the Panel to have their central management and control in the United Kingdom and:

(a) any of their securities have been admitted to the Official List of the UK Listing Authority (the 'Official List') at any time during the 10 years prior to the relevant date; or

(b) dealings and/or prices at which persons were willing to deal in any of their securities have been published on a regular basis for a continuous period of at least six months in the 10 years prior to the relevant date; or

(c) any of their securities have been subject to a marketing arrangement as described in *section 163(2)(b) of CA 1985* at any time during the 10 years prior to the relevant date (eg there have been dealings in their shares on the Alternative Investment Market or OFEX); or

(d) the company was required to file a prospectus for the issue of securities with a relevant authority in the United Kingdom, the Channel Islands or the Isle of Man or to have a prospectus approved by the UKLA at any time during the 10 years prior to the relevant date.

(See paragraph 3 of the Introduction to the Code.)

Companies on the Official List (and their purchasers) are subject to the 'Listing Rules', published by the Financial Services Authority (the 'FSA') as UK Listing Authority (the 'UKLA'), the competent authority for listings in the UK. The Prospectus Rules ('PRs') implemented by the *Prospectus Regulations 2005* (SI 2005/1433), may be relevant to the acquisition of a private company where securities are issued as consideration.

The PRs apply to public offers of securities to 100 persons or more, other than qualifying investors, in each EEA member state where the offer is made, unless the minimum consideration payable, or the denomination of the securities offered exceeds 50,000 euros or the total consideration cannot exceed 100,000 euros. (See PR 1.2.1 and *section 86(1)* of the *Financial Services and Markets Act 2000 (FSMA)*.)

Companies which operate in regulated industries may also be subject to rules which impact on the sale and purchase of those companies. These are beyond the scope of this chapter.

At the end of the chapter, more detail will be given on acquisitions involving listed companies, public limited companies and, in relation to the Code, private companies to which it applies.

Purchase of shares or purchase of assets?

8.3   An acquisition may be undertaken either by purchasing the entire issued share capital of a target company or by purchasing the business from that company (which will normally involve the transfer of a range of individual business assets). There are differences in the results of these two types of takeover, but in both cases the purchaser will require extensive investigation of precisely what assets the target owns and of any problems which might arise in relation to them.

The choice of which type of acquisition to undertake will depend on a number of factors relevant to the purchaser and/or the seller. Often such a decision is tax-driven; the reasons for this are discussed in **Chapter 13 Tax Planning**.

Leaving aside taxation, which is normally the major consideration, the pluses and minuses of an assets purchase as opposed to a share purchase can be summarised as follows:

Benefits of assets purchase/disadvantages of share purchase	Benefits of share purchase/disadvantages of assets purchase
In an assets purchase there is scope for the parties to agree which assets and liabilities are to be acquired, whereas in a share purchase all of them would pass with the company.	In a share purchase it is easier to effect the transfer of title since only a stock transfer form is required, whereas the transfer of various assets may be complicated.
In a share purchase all shareholders must sign the sale agreement (or at least 90% by value must accept an offer for their shares, because at this level compulsory purchase of the remainder may be possible under *section 429* of *CA 1985*), but in an assets purchase only the selling company need sign.	In an assets sale the selling company must have power to sell its undertaking.
Security is more readily available over the assets acquired because the provisions of *section 151* of *CA 1985* only apply to financial assistance on share purchases.	An assets sale normally needs more consents and approvals from third parties such as landlords or licensors.
Trading arrangements already in place may terminate on an assets purchase (whilst existing arrangements will normally continue in a share purchase). This may be an advantage to the purchaser if there are liabilities and obligations of the target company which the buyer does not wish to inherit. The buyer may however agree to assume responsibility for certain liabilities in the acquisition agreement.	Existing arrangements will normally continue in a share purchase (although some important contracts and licences may be terminable on change of control). Continuation of these arrangements may influence the purchaser's view of the target and the desirability of the acquisition.

Benefits of assets purchase/disadvantages of share purchase	Benefits of share purchase/disadvantages of assets purchase
Where the purchase price represents a premium over book values, an assets purchase will often be more attractive to the purchaser, whilst a share purchase will often benefit the seller.	In an assets sale the seller may be obliged (under the *Transfer of Undertakings (Protection of Employment) Regulations 2006* (SI 2006/246)) to inform and consult with employee representatives before a binding agreement is made. This may be inconsistent with confidentiality obligations and UKLA Disclosure Rules and present practical difficulties if the workforce is not unionised.
Stamp duty is not payable on the transfer of assets but stamp duty land tax is payable at the rate of up to 4% on the transfer of real property.	Stamp duty is payable on the total consideration at 0.5%.

Areas of law involved

8.4 Various specialist areas of law will be relevant to a particular transaction, and experts will need to be consulted at an early stage regardless of the type of acquisition contemplated. The nature of advice needed will be dictated by the type of transaction concerned. Typically however, the following areas will be relevant: competition law, employment law, pensions and employee benefits, intellectual property, information technology, real property and tax.

Other areas may be relevant in particular circumstances, for example trust law where the seller is a trustee. Environmental law may be of major significance in certain industries and may need to be considered wherever the company owns or occupies (or has owned or occupied) land. Under *Part IIA* of the *Environmental Protection Act 1990*, the current owner or occupier of land may be liable for the contamination of that land where the polluter (including anyone who 'caused or knowingly permitted' the contamination) cannot be identified after reasonable enquiry.

The basic structure of a private acquisition

8.5 This section examines the relevant issues which arise when considering the purchase of shares (rather than assets) of a private company incorporated in England and Wales. They will be examined here as a series of discrete stages, although in practice the divisions will rarely be so clearly defined. (A checklist of steps to be taken at key stages is set out at **8.57** below.)

The objectives

8.6   The principal objectives of an acquisition by means of a purchase of shares are threefold:

(a)   to ensure that the purchaser receives the shares in the target, and any other assets which it is expecting to purchase, free from encumbrances;

(b)   to protect the purchaser against unforeseen liabilities; and

(c)   to ensure that the purchaser has adequate information in respect of the target to assess whether it can continue its affairs after the acquisition in the manner envisaged by the purchaser and (perhaps uppermost in the purchaser's mind) to give some indication as to the fairness of the price.

Obtaining information ('due diligence')

8.7   The first stage of a company acquisition includes the purchaser obtaining information relating to the target (often referred to as 'due diligence'). Some information can be obtained before negotiations have started; audited accounts and constitutional documents for the target and any subsidiaries are usually revealed by company searches, and other useful information may be gleaned from relevant publications, online information services and websites (including the company's own). Further public information will be available on a publicly listed company, from the London Stock Exchange and analysts reports. It is possible that such information may reveal important facts about a major business or subsidiary which is the subject of a private sale. Obtaining other documentation important to a purchaser in deciding whether to buy the target, such as contracts fundamental to the business of the target and details of its pension scheme, will almost certainly require an approach to the target. Before it is willing to provide such information, a well-advised seller will wish (and may be obliged – see **8.13** below) to impose a Confidentiality Undertaking on the potential purchaser. It will also wish to make it clear that information given is not to be relied upon except to the extent warranted in the formal agreement. (With regard to the exclusion of pre-contractual representations, see the discussion of *Thomas Witter Ltd v TBP Industries* [1996] 2 All ER 573; *E.A. Grimstead & Sons Ltd v McGarrigan* (unreported, CA, 27 October, 1999); *The Government of Zanzibar v British Aerospace (Lancaster House) Ltd* [2000] CLC 735 and *Watford Electronics Ltd v Sanderson CFL Ltd* [2001] All ER (D) 290, at **8.9** below.) If the seller is a listed company and the target is very significant to its business, it may also seek a 'standstill' agreement from the purchaser restraining the purchaser from using information it receives to launch a hostile takeover bid for the seller.

Preparing the documentation

8.8   The information-gathering process will be the first task, but will continue throughout the acquisition. The next step will be the preparation of the purchase documentation. This may begin with a letter of intent or heads of terms or may move straight to a draft sale and purchase agreement. Historically, preparing the sale and purchase agreement has been viewed as the purchaser's task as the party best placed to know which warranties it wishes to have in respect of the target, although the seller has always produced the 'disclosure letter' which lists certain matters which would otherwise be breaches of warranties, thus preventing the purchaser from suing on these disclosed matters.

However, particularly where the target is substantial and/or complex, it is common for potential purchasers to be approached by the seller with an information memorandum setting out details of the company and with a draft sale and purchase agreement. The sale may then take the form of a tender, the target being sold to the bidder offering the best terms. A well advised seller will take into account not only the price offered but also the effect of the purchaser's proposed amendments to the draft sale and purchase agreement. It should be mentioned at this stage that circularisation of prospective purchasers in this manner will be regulated by *section 21* of *FSMA*, and that a breach of the relevant provisions of *FSMA* would be a criminal offence. However, in many cases, the *Financial Services and Markets Act 2000 (Financial Promotion) Order 2005* (SI 2005/1529) (the '*Order*') will provide an exemption, in particular where:

(a)   the transaction relates to the acquisition or disposal of shares in a company and the shares consist of 50% or more of the voting shares (*Article 62* of the *Order*);

(b)   certain 'one-off' communications are made to a single recipient or group of recipients who are expected to act jointly (*Articles 28* and *28A* of the *Order*); or

(c)   communications are made to certain 'high net worth' individuals or companies (*Articles 48* and *49* of the *Order* respectively) meaning, in the latter case, companies with more than 20 members and share capital or net assets of £500,000 or more, or 20 members or less and share capital or net assets of £5 million or more (or any of whose subsidiaries or holding companies satisfy these tests).

If a particular communication does not fall within a relevant exemption, it will need to be made or approved by an 'authorised person' (such as an investment bank or similar institution).

Negotiation

8.9   Once the documentation has been prepared, it will usually be the subject of much negotiation. Whichever side has drafted the sale agreement will almost certainly have made it very much in its favour, so careful legal advice is crucial at this stage to ensure that a party is not exposed to an undesirable risk and to see that the negotiations proceed smoothly. All negotiations and documentation should be clearly expressed to be 'subject to contract'. The danger otherwise is that a binding agreement may inadvertently be brought into being by such documentation before the parties have completed negotiations.

Although the final documentation will normally contain an 'entire agreement' clause purporting to exclude claims for misrepresentations which are not included in the documents, *Thomas Witter Ltd v TBP Industries* [1996] 2 All ER 573 held that this is an exclusion clause which is subject to a 'reasonableness test' under *section 3* of the *Misrepresentation Act 1967*. Since the judgment in that case it has been customary to express 'entire agreement' clauses not to relate to fraudulent misrepresentations, as it was held that the entire agreement clause must otherwise be judged to be unreasonable. This view has been questioned in *The Government of Zanzibar v British Aerospace (Lancaster House) Ltd* [2000] CLC 735 which cited authority that clauses dealing with representations are taken not to apply to representations fraudulently made (see *Pearson & Son Ltd v Dublin Corporation* [1907] AC 351). Whether it is reasonable to exclude liability for innocent or negligent misrepresentation will depend upon the circumstances. Notwithstanding the Government of Zanzibar case, it is still prudent to include an express exception for fraudulent misrepresentations.

The Thomas Witter case also suggested that a statement that no pre-contractual representation had been relied on by the parties was an exclusion clause subject to the *Misrepresentation Act 1967*. This conclusion was rejected by the Court of Appeal in *Watford Electronics Ltd v Sanderson CFL Ltd* [2001] All ER (D) 290. In the unreported case of *E.A. Grimstead & Son Ltd v McGarrigan* (CA, 27 October, 1999), it was held that such a clause could operate as an evidential estoppel if the party seeking to raise the estoppel pleaded and proved all the necessary elements (see *Lowe v Lombank Ltd* [1960] 1 MR 196). For this reason, an 'entire agreement' clause should be accompanied by such an acknowledgement. However, discharging the burden of proof may be difficult. Where a seller has made a false statement intending that the purchaser should rely on it, that seller may face insuperable difficulties establishing that it entered into the contract in the belief that the purchaser had not relied on the statement.

In the light of these cases, the effective exclusion of pre-contractual misrepresentations should not be assumed and particular care should be taken over statements made in negotiations. False or misleading statements may give rise to other liabilities (see **8.13** below).

At this stage it is also worth noting the possible impact of the judgment in the case of *Investors Compensation Scheme Ltd v West Bromwich Building Society* [1998] 1 WLR 896 (HL). In that case, it was held that, while the negotiations and statements of subjective intention were not admissible in evidence when construing a contract, the entire factual matrix against which it was entered into was properly to be considered. If the document which the parties sign does not objectively convey the agreement which they reached (even if it is capable on its face of unambiguous construction), it may be open to them to adduce other evidence of the facts necessary to enable a proper interpretation to be made, including the background circumstances to the negotiations. This approach was criticised by the Court of Appeal in *National Bank of Sharjah v Dellborg*, (9 July 1997, unreported) shortly after the West Bromwich decision, and *Beazer Homes Limited v Stroude* [2005] EWCA Civ 265 held that evidence of the parties' intentions drawn from separate negotiations was inadmissible. However, the West Bromwich decision has been followed in *Re Loquitur Ltd* [2003] EWHC 999. Where an agreement is found to be partially oral, post-contractual conduct may be admissible as evidence of the parties' intentions (see *Maggs v Marsh* [2006] All ER (D) 95). This should rarely be the case where the contract includes an effective entire agreement clause.

Execution of the documents

8.10   Assuming that negotiations do lead to agreement, the parties will proceed to the execution of the agreement documents. Numerous documents will often be executed aside from the share purchase agreement itself. The following comprise the basic additional documentation usually required:

(a)   A tax covenant;

(b)   A disclosure letter;

(c)   Board minutes;

(d)   Powers of attorney;

(e)   Stock transfer forms;

(f)   New articles of association and EGM documentation;

(g)   Pensions documentation;

(h)   Resignation letters from (at least some) target directors and the company secretary; and

(i)   Service agreements.

Completion

8.11   The transaction will effectively terminate, in theory at least, at completion. Commonly this will take place concurrently with the signing of the contract, but in many circumstances it may be delayed. The reasons for, and legal implications of, a deferred completion will be considered later on in this chapter. (See **8.28** below.)

Certain legal steps will be necessary after completion. Amongst other things, the share transfers must be stamped and registered and appropriate returns must be filed at the Companies Registry.

Pre-contractual considerations

8.12   A more detailed examination of the structure of private company acquisitions follows.

Information-gathering

8.13   It is customary for the potential purchaser of a business to deliver a detailed information request to the seller. However, sellers are understandably irritated at receiving a pro forma list which might not be relevant to their business and which is not specifically designed to meet the purchaser's objectives. A purchaser should therefore consider what it really needs to know. The seller sometimes has an ambivalent attitude towards disclosure and fears that it might be providing information to a competitor who will be advantaged if the sale does not go ahead. If the seller's securities are listed on a regulated market it may have an obligation under the UKLA Disclosure Rules (DR) to ensure, 'under its own responsibility', that the prospective transaction is kept confidential (if it amounts to 'inside information') until it is publicly announced as required by DR 2.2.1 (see section 2.5 of DR); the seller may have difficulty in obtaining the information it would need to respond to the purchaser's request without news of the proposed sale leaking. It may also be concerned that the disclosure of any adverse information to the purchaser might be used by the purchaser, not unreasonably, to renegotiate the price. However, provided that the purchaser has signed a proper Confidentiality Undertaking (see **8.7** above), the seller must accept that it will be required to make extensive disclosures and should do so thoroughly and diligently. These are normally made in a disclosure letter, and on larger transactions, a data room will also be compiled (see **8.30** below). If the seller unreasonably refuses to supply information the purchaser might suspect that things are worse than they really are; if it conceals information, pretending to make full disclosure, or provides misleading information, not only will it in all probability face a warranty claim, but it may also face criminal prosecution, for example, for breach of *section 397* of *FSMA* or for common law or statutory fraud (under *section 2* or *3* of the *Fraud Act 2006*) or an offence under the *Theft Act 1978*. Any adviser who incites or connives in such action may also commit an offence. An adviser must also be aware of his duty, under *Part 7* of the *Proceeds of Crime Act 2002* ('*POCA 2002*'), to notify the Serious and Organised Crime Agency ('SOCA') of any known or suspected money laundering offence involving 'criminal property'. This is particularly important given the ever increasing body of statutes which provide for criminal sanctions on companies and their directors, and the very broad statutory definition of criminal property, encompassing anything which constitutes or represents (wholly or partly, directly or indirectly) a benefit from criminal conduct (*section 340(3)(a)* of the *POCA 2002*).

Representations which are made during the negotiations may become warranted information (see **8.9** above for a discussion of the exclusion of pre-contractual representations). It is therefore important that both parties ensure that the information that is intended to be warranted is clear to both as they go along. Maintaining detailed lists of all the information passed between them is fundamental. The purchaser may request the seller to warrant that all of the disclosed information is true, and in exchange the seller may want the purchaser to acknowledge all such information as 'disclosed' – therefore, if it is self-evident that there is in fact a breach of warranty (although the purchaser was not aware of it at the time), the purchaser will not be able to allege it had been misinformed. An alternative solution to the problems which arise with respect to warranties is for the seller to ask the purchaser to produce a shortlist of information on which it has relied and for the seller to warrant this shortlist only.

It is also noteworthy that an individual who gives assurances to a purchaser in the course of negotiations might, in certain circumstances, incur personal liability to the purchaser if he makes misrepresentations which the purchaser relies on (*Williams v Natural Life Health Foods* [1998] 1 WLR 830 (HL); *Ojjeh v Waller*; unreported, 14 December 1998).

It is also now a specific criminal offence under *section 2* of the *Fraud Act 2006* dishonestly to misrepresent the law or the state of mind of any person for gain, or to cause loss to, or impose risk on, another person.

The law relating to breach of warranty and misrepresentation in contract is complex, and it is beneficial to both parties to ensure that whatever information is passed is accurate and nothing of importance to the other party is withheld.

The most common sources of information are contained in **8.14–8.16** below.

Accounts and the accountants' report

8.14   Although the report and accounts of the target will be analysed by the purchaser and its accountant, the lawyer should also check the accounts to assist in drafting the sale and purchase agreement. For example, he should not ask for a warranty on the consolidated accounts if there are no subsidiaries. Further, it may be appropriate to address specific warranties to unusual items in the accounts, such as contingent liabilities, capital commitments or unusual reserves or provisions. He should also note intra-group liabilities and cross guarantees and consider with his client how these are to be dealt with.

A purchaser will usually instruct a firm of accountants to prepare a report on the business (unless there is a vendor due diligence report – see below). This will not usually be carried out until there is a firm agreement in principle, subject to contract, between the parties (to avoid wasting money). The purchaser's satisfaction with the report's results will often be crucial to its decision to proceed or may result in an adjustment to the price. The purchaser will also want to consider precisely what the accountants are to report on (eg the value of the net assets of the business, or a breakdown of its composition and its future prospects) and instruct them accordingly, preferably in writing.

Where the accountants' report reveals significant issues, the purchaser is likely to raise these in the negotiations. It will not usually wish to disclose the report to the seller (and it will be unable to do so without the consent of the accounts which, if given, is likely to involve the seller signing a letter agreeing not to rely on the report and to hold the accountants harmless against any consequences of the disclosure). However, the purchaser will need to be able to substantiate its arguments if it is claiming that the price should be reduced or it requires an indemnity or some other protection.

A seller will generally expect to limit the purchaser's right to bring claims under the warranties in relation to matters which are revealed by the accountants' report.

Increasingly, where a company is being sold as part of a divestment programme or in an auction process, the seller will procure the production of vendor due diligence reports by its accountants, lawyers and other relevant advisers, which will be made available to potential buyers during due diligence process and addressed to the ultimate purchaser. While these are not necessarily a substitute for the purchaser commissioning its own reports, they may help to limit the scope of the investigations it needs to undertake and speed the sale process.

Constitutional documents

8.15   The Memorandum and Articles of Association of the target will reveal additional information, such as whether the target is empowered to carry on its business as laid out in its objects clause.

It is necessary to check whether the directors of the seller or the purchaser have some interest in the transaction taking place (ie the sale/purchase of the company) since the Articles will usually govern whether they can vote or be counted in a quorum in relation to such a transaction. Thought must also be given to *section 320* of *CA 1985*, which governs property transactions with directors under these circumstances. An arrangement entered into in contravention of these rules may be voidable. In addition, the director may be liable to account to the company for any profit made or to indemnify the company for any resulting loss.

The constitutional documents of the purchasing company will also have to be read carefully to ensure that the purchaser has the power to enter into the transaction. For example, its objects clause may prevent it purchasing the target. Special issues arise with certain types of purchaser or seller, such as trusts, statutory companies, building societies, local authorities or overseas companies which will require separate investigation. The Memorandum and Articles of the target will also reveal how the shares are to be transferred; they may contain pre-emption provisions under which shares must be offered to existing shareholders prior to a transfer to third parties, or sometimes as soon as any seller 'wishes to sell'. In such a case, an agreement will be needed with the beneficiaries of such rights or the Articles will need to be altered at an early stage in order that the purchaser may acquire the shares. There might be similar provisions in a shareholders' agreement although these would be binding only on the shareholders (not the target itself). However, a purchaser who acquires shares knowing the seller has not complied with such (merely contractual) obligations may be liable to an action in tort by non-assenting shareholders.

A company search will establish details of the target's directors and share-holders so that the purchaser can ensure that it is dealing with the correct persons although shareholder information, in particular, will not necessarily be up to date. Problems may arise where the ownership of shares is vested in, for example, a trustee, a receiver, a minor or a deceased person. Most, but not all, charges or mortgages on the target's property will also be revealed by a company search.

It is also important to check immediately before signature and completion that the company has not commenced liquidation and that an administrator or receiver has not been appointed. If such is the case, the powers of the directors to manage the company are likely to have come to an end, and the purchaser may obviously need to reconsider its intention to proceed with the purchase. In addition to making a company search and/or a bankruptcy search at the Land Charges Registry, it is customary to make a telephone search at the Central Registry of Winding-Up and Administration Petitions, although this does not offer statutory protection.

Information relating to the business

8.16   The information to be requested in any particular case will depend upon the nature of the business of the target; for example, intellectual property rights are unlikely to be very important to a property development company but are probably critical to a computer software, pharmaceutical or biotechnology company. It will also depend upon the reasons why the purchaser is buying it and whether the purchaser is a competitor, in which case a detailed customer list might not be made available, but only statistics extracted from it, or may only be made available for a statistical report to the purchaser's reporting accountants and not directly to the purchaser. Also relevant is the identity of the seller (a listed company selling a subsidiary may not give such access to information as a company owned by individuals where that information cannot be relevant to the price of listed securities), how much the purchaser already knows about the business (possibly because it is a customer, competitor or supplier of the target or perhaps the sale is to the company's own management) and the respective bargaining positions of the parties. It is worth remembering therefore, as a purchaser, that any indication of a purchase price should be based on clear assumptions and coupled with a condition as to the level of information necessary to support that price and, as a seller, that limits on what it is willing to disclose should be signalled at an early stage.

When information about employees or other individuals is to be exchanged, due regard must be paid to the *Data Protection Act 1998* and published guidance from the Information Commissioner.

Contracts between the target or its subsidiaries and third parties will often be of the utmost significance to a purchaser and hence ought to be requested. First, all loan documentation (including all mortgages, charges and any debentures issued) will need to be carefully checked to discover what obligations the purchaser will be subject to once the acquisition has been completed. Secondly, it is quite likely that the target will have entered into a few contracts which are fundamental to its business – for instance, a large percentage of its turnover may be attributable to a single manufacturing or supply agreement. It will then be particularly important that these contracts continue in effect notwithstanding the acquisition. Normally, a change in control will not entitle a party to terminate a contract (although such a provision is nowadays more usual and is commonplace in, for example, financing arrangements and joint ventures). If a contract confers an express right to terminate or if a contract is only for a short term, but is renewed as a matter of practice, the purchaser may wish to be assured that the target will continue to enjoy the benefits of such contracts after the acquisition; therefore, either it or the seller may need to negotiate with the other parties to these fundamental contracts. The important contracts should be checked for compliance with applicable competition laws, otherwise there is a danger of invalidity and fines.

For many businesses, intellectual property rights will play a key role. The target may be dependent upon a patent licence or other licence from a third party, who may have a contractual right to terminate the licence in the event of a change in control. Alternatively, some of the value of the target may be attributable to the goodwill associated with its name, usually registered as a trade or service mark – hence, details of all intellectual property rights should always be obtained. A check can then be made that rights which the target owns are adequately protected (eg its patents and trademarks) and rights held by others upon which it depends will continue to be available to it on the same or similar terms after the acquisition. One should also check that renewal fees have been paid and, in the case of trademarks, there has been use by the registered proprietor in relation to the goods for which the trademarks are registered.

It is important to consider whether the acquisition will be subject to merger control review in one or more jurisdictions and, if so, whether it is necessary or advisable to make completion conditional upon receipt of the relevant clearances.

Where an acquisition involves companies which generate turnover (ie have customers) in the European Union, consideration should first be given to whether the turnover-based thresholds for EC merger control are satisfied (currently the primary thresholds are satisfied where the combined world-wide turnover of all undertakings concerned exceeds €5bn, at least two of the undertakings concerned generate turnover within the EU in excess of €250m and each of the undertakings concerned does not generate more than two thirds of EU turnover in one and the same Member State, however alternative thresholds may also apply). If the EC thresholds are met, the transaction must be notified to the European Commission for clearance which must generally be obtained prior to completion and an appropriate condition will therefore be required in the purchase agreement.

If the EC thresholds are not satisfied, it is necessary to consider whether merger clearance will need to be obtained from the relevant national authorities within the European Union. Different countries have different rules for this purpose. In the UK, an acquisition may be subject to merger control review where the target's UK turnover exceeds £70m or where the parties' combined share of supply exceeds 25%. Although there is no mandatory requirement to obtain clearance prior to completion, the UK authorities can investigate a merger which meets these thresholds regardless of whether the parties make a voluntary notification. Where significant competition concerns arise, the authorities may prohibit a proposed merger or, in the case of a completed acquisition, may require divestment of the acquired business. The purchaser will therefore need to consider whether to make a voluntary notification and include a relevant condition in the purchase agreement or whether to take the risk of an investigation following completion. This will depend on its assessment of the likelihood that the acquisition may give rise to material competition issues. A number of other European countries require merger control clearance to be obtained prior to completion. See **Chapter 11 Regulatory Aspects of Acquisitions in the EU**.

It is also necessary to consider whether merger clearance is required in countries outside the European Union. This typically requires an assessment of those countries where the parties have assets and/or generate turnover and an assessment of the applicable merger control rules.

The conduct of negotiations

8.17 As was discussed at some length in Chapter 1 Introduction – setting the scene, it is vital to the success of an acquisition that the parties involved are fully aware of their objectives. Bearing these in mind the negotiating teams (often including a lawyer from the outset) will set out to obtain as much information as possible before actually completing any contract with a target. The following procedure may be helpful to ensure that the negotiations are carried out with as little wasted time as possible.

- **Step 1: Preparation**

  The purchaser instructs its lawyers and accountants. A Confidentiality Undertaking is given. Information-gathering progresses and the purchaser's lawyers prepare the draft agreement, tax covenant and other documentation are prepared.

- **Step 2: Initial drafts**

  The purchaser and the purchaser's team meet and review the drafts. They are then revised and sent to the seller together with a covering letter explaining any points which might not be clear just from reading the drafts.

- **Step 3: Seller's comments and draft disclosure**

  The seller and its team meet, having read the drafts, and prepare a marked-up draft which is returned to the purchaser, again with a letter of explanation. Further, the seller's team commences preparation of a disclosure letter which should be sent as soon as practicable in draft to the purchaser. Thus, at this stage each of the two parties knows the other's full position.

(The drafting, review and commenting roles of the purchaser's and sellers' lawyers at Steps 1 to 3 may be reversed.)

- **Step 4: Assessment of positions**

   The purchaser and its lawyers should meet and decide how much of what the seller has changed is acceptable.

- **Step 5: Lawyer–only meeting(s)**

   The two sets of lawyers should meet, without principals, and in small groups (ie tax lawyer with tax lawyer etc.) to isolate those points which they can settle between them, and those which need a decision from the principals. Smaller groups and the absence of the client might lead to less posturing by the lawyers.

- **Step 6: Resolution of outstanding points**

   The parties should now have an agreed list of substantial outstanding points and, apart from these points, agreed drafts of all documents. There should now be an all-parties meeting to resolve these points. After hearing the arguments of the respective lawyers it is sometimes helpful if the two sides separate and consider what they feel they need to give up to complete the transaction. It may then be appropriate for the principals to meet, without advisers, and resolve the outstanding points.

All these stages will, of course, be subject to contract (but see **8.9** above).

While these steps outline the basic stages of a negotiation, in practice matters are rarely resolved in quite such an orderly fashion.

It is common for the parties at the outset to set out in a letter of intent or heads of agreement the broad principles which they have agreed. This should state the intention that there should be no binding agreement until the formal contract, and that until then each party is free to withdraw from the negotiations without liability. If accepted, all or most of the main terms of the transaction are then agreed in principle. This is not always advisable since there may be some uncertainty as to the legal effect of such a document even if the parties intend it to be legally binding (and unless it is expressly stated not to be legally binding it will generally be assumed by a court that it was intended to be legally binding). Under English law, a contract is void for uncertainty if any essential term is left unagreed (*Scammell v Ouston* [1941] AC 251). Thus, for example, if the price has not been decided upon, the contract will not be legally binding. The status of the agreement may be too uncertain – if it legally amounts to no more than an agreement to negotiate it will be unenforceable (as in *Courtney & Fairbairn Ltd v Tolaini Brothers (Hotels) Ltd* [1975] 1 WLR 297).

In some cases, preliminary contracts are entered into by the parties in which the seller agrees to grant a purchaser the exclusive right to negotiate for the sale of the target for a fixed period of time (an 'exclusivity period') and the parties undertake to use their best endeavours to negotiate an agreement. Such an agreement can be legally enforceable provided of course that the purchaser gives sufficient consideration in return for the seller's promise, such as a confidentiality undertaking, and the terms are sufficiently certain.

The House of Lords' decision in *Walford and others v Miles and another* [1992] 1 All ER 453 seems to suggest that such an agreement is enforceable while an agreement to negotiate in good faith is not. The decision in *Walford* has been considered in several further cases (*Pitt v PHH Asset Management Ltd* [1994] 1 WLR 327; *Little v Courage Ltd*, The Times, 19 January 1994; *Global Container Lines Ltd v Black Sea Shipping Co*, unreported, 14 July 1997 (Ch D) and *QR Sciences Ltd v BTG International Ltd* [2005] EWHC 670 (Ch)), which support the contention that such a 'lock out' agreement is enforceable while an agreement to negotiate is not. In English law, a promise is not generally binding unless it is made in the form of a deed or it is supported by some form of 'consideration' (ie something of value in the eye of the law must be given in return for the promise in order for it to be binding).

As a lesser protection, the seller will sometimes merely undertake to notify the purchaser immediately if the seller is approached by, or commences negotiations with, any other potential purchaser.

The purchase consideration

The form of consideration

8.18   The purchaser should consider three basic means of paying for the acquisition:

- shares;
- loan capital;
- cash.

Having completed its due diligence investigation, the purchaser should by now have a clear idea of the price it is willing to pay for the company. However, this price may well be adjusted by technical factors. For example, the parties may agree that the seller may take a dividend out of the target and reduce the price accordingly, thus reducing the seller's liability to capital gains tax and the stamp duty lost to the purchaser. Tax considerations may also dictate the choice in method of payment. It may be easier to persuade a seller to accept a lower price if the taxation treatment of it is attractive. If the seller receives a cash payment for its shares, it may find itself immediately liable to a capital gains tax charge (although it may benefit from a substantial shareholding exemption). On a 'share for share' or 'share for loan note' acquisition (where the purchasing company issues shares in itself or a loan note to the seller in exchange for shares in the target) the seller may, where certain conditions are satisfied, be able to roll over any gains made on the disposal of its shares in the target until it eventually sells the shares in the purchasing company which it received as consideration. The exchange of shares must have been made for bona fide commercial reasons and not mainly for tax avoidance purposes. (See **Chapter 13 Tax Planning**.)

Shares

8.19   A listed public company, in particular, might offer its own shares as consideration for the purchase. Technically, an unlisted company is also able to issue shares (or loan stock) for an acquisition, provided that (in the case of a private company) the sellers are not so numerous and diverse as to render the issue of shares an offer to the public. However, the seller may not be willing to accept such shares since there will be no ready market for them and furthermore the owners of the private company may not wish to dilute their controlling position in it. Where shares are to be issued as consideration, the PRs may require the publication of an approved prospectus, in particular if the shares are to be issued to 100 people or more or represent, over a period of 12 months, 10 per cent or more of the number of shares of the same class admitted to trading on the same regulated market (see sections 1.2.1 and 1.2.3 of PR).

Where it is agreed that a seller is to receive shares in the purchasing company it must be clear whether the seller ranks for the current dividend. Further, a seller may well be willing to accept a restriction on its right of disposal of such shares for a period of time. This could be particularly important if it is felt that the seller's holding might be sufficiently large to affect the market in the purchaser's shares if they were sold altogether.

One disadvantage of issuing shares as consideration arises if the purchaser, being a public company, wishes to take security over the consideration it pays for any breach of warranty, since *section 150* of *CA 1985* prohibits a public company from taking a charge over its own shares.

A further advantage in issuing shares is the potential availability of merger relief (see **Chapter 2 Accounting**).

Where a seller would prefer to receive cash whilst the purchaser wishes to pay in shares, a vendor placing or a cash placing may be the solution for a listed purchaser. In a vendor placing, the purchaser issues new shares to the seller but arranges with an investment bank or broker for the immediate resale of such shares in the market and guarantees in the sale and purchase agreement that the sale of the shares will yield the seller the right amount of the consideration. As a drafting matter, the right of the purchaser to use a vendor placing should always be left as an option and not an obligation. Additionally, the purchaser should arrange a loan facility to pay for the target in order to enable the purchase to proceed even if the purchaser's share price collapses (unless the issuing of shares as consideration is crucial to the Purchaser proceeding with the acquisition).

A cash placing merely involves the issuing of shares to investors for cash. The advantages of the vendor placing over a cash placing are that merger relief should be available and that the issue, being for shares rather than for cash, will only require directors' authority to allot shares under *section 80* of *CA 1985*, and not a disapplication of pre-emption rights under *section 95* of *CA 1985*. However, a cash placing does not require the co-operation of the seller which may be an advantage.

In order to protect the interests of a listed purchaser's existing shareholders, the Investment Committees of insurance and pension fund investors seek the imposition of a clawback offer upon those vendor or cash placings which exceed a certain proportion of the listed purchaser's share capital. Clawback offers give existing shareholders the right to call for the new shares in which case they are not delivered to the placees who originally agreed to take them, but are sold to the shareholders instead.

The use of shares as the consideration for the purchase by a public company of assets (other than shares in another company under a qualifying agreement) does give rise to an additional requirement of a valuation of the assets by the purchaser's accountants under *sections 103–108* of *CA 1985*, unless the purchaser is acquiring all of the assets and liabilities of the target.

Loan notes

8.20   A loan note (normally in registered form, repayable at the option of the holder semi-annually after the first year and with a final maturity on its fifth anniversary) is often included as an alternative to cash on the sale of a private company where the sellers include UK tax paying individuals. Capital gains tax will not be payable by the sellers provided (so far as holders of 5% or more of the target's shares are concerned) roll-over consent under *section 138* of the *Taxation of Chargeable Gains Act 1992* is obtained from HMRC (see **Chapter 13 Tax Planning**).

From the purchaser's point of view, a loan note may be advantageous if (as is common) the rate of interest to be attached to it is lower than the rate which would otherwise be payable on its banking facilities. Further, provided that it avoids the need for a bank guarantee of the loan note, the loan note will not absorb its bank credit facilities, though it will of course constitute a borrowing for most borrowing limits and will require a purchaser to retain sufficient credit facilities to repay all loan notes if presented for redemption on any periodic payment dates. Normally such loan notes, like most loan stock issued as consideration, have fairly weak events of default, undertakings and similar covenants.

If the loan notes are to be freely transferable, their issue may require the publication of a prospectus. It is therefore common to limit the transferability of loan notes so that they do not constitute 'transferable securities' within the meaning of *section 102A* of *FSMA*.

Cash

8.21   Perhaps the most frequently used consideration is cash, although cash may have been raised through borrowings, sales or other complex fund-raising schemes. There are circumstances where a purchaser has no choice other than to pay in cash. For example, in an acquisition of a public company or a private acquisition to which the Takeover Code applies, a mandatory bid required by Rule 9 of the Code must be made in cash or with a cash alternative. Additionally, Rule 11 of the Code requires cash or a cash alternative for any offer in connection with which there are purchases for cash during the offer period or where more than 10% of the shares have been purchased for cash during the offer period or the 12 months preceding it.

Whatever the consideration is to be, the lawyers will wish to ensure that the purchaser is able to pay it. In the case of cash consideration the purchaser's lawyers will need to ensure that there is no breach of the purchaser's borrowing limits or other covenants in raising such cash, even after allowing for the effect on its balance sheet of consolidating the target.

The financial assistance problem

8.22   Whilst it is for his client to decide which form of consideration to use to finance an acquisition, the lawyer will be concerned with certain legal restrictions which, if breached, will have serious repercussions for the client. *Section 151* of *CA 1985* prohibits a company (and its subsidiaries) from giving financial assistance for the purchase of its own shares. Financial assistance includes assistance by way of a gift, a loan, a guarantee, security or an indemnity. Thus, if the consideration money is borrowed, the assets of the target company itself cannot generally be charged to secure the borrowing (but see below). However, there are also numerous other cases in which unlawful financial assistance can arise, and considerable care must be taken in any case where, directly or indirectly, there can be any possibility of such assistance arising.

There are certain transactions which are not prohibited by *section 151*. If the net assets of the company are not materially reduced by the financial assistance and such assistance is not within any of the other parts of the definition of financial assistance, then the assistance may be lawfully given. Further, the payment of a lawful dividend by the target, either before or after it is sold, will not be unlawful financial assistance. The repayment to the seller of intragroup indebtedness would not normally constitute unlawful financial assistance if such indebtedness was, by its terms, repayable on demand, but may be unlawful (depending on the circumstances) if its contractual maturity had not been reached.

In the case of a private company, financial assistance may be given provided certain requirements are met, (*section 155* of *CA 1985*). The main ones which are generally relevant are as follows:

(a)   The financial assistance must be authorised by a special resolution, unless it is given by a wholly-owned subsidiary.

(b)   The company must be solvent, and any reduction in net assets resulting from the assistance must not exceed the company's 'distributable profits'.

This is defined in *section 263* of *CA 1985* as the accumulated realised profits of a company less accumulated realised losses.

(c)   The directors of the company must make a statutory declaration as to the company's solvency.

(d)   The auditors must sign a report supporting the directors' statutory declaration as to the solvency of the company.

It should be borne in mind that a breach of *section 151* of *CA 1985* is a criminal offence and actual or proposed non-compliance may give the parties' solicitors obligations under *POCA 2002* to report the matter privately to the SOCA and obtain clearance to continue acting (see *sections 330* and *335* of *POCA 2002*).

Section 678 of *CA 2006* will remove the prohibition on a private company giving financial assistance for the purpose of the acquisition of its own shares or shares in its parent company, so long as neither the company giving the assistance nor its parent company is a public company at the time the assistance is given. This amendment is not, however, expected to take effect until October 2008.

Delayed payment of the consideration

8.23   Delaying the payment of all or part of the consideration can be done for a variety of reasons. These may include the following:

(a)   to allow the production of completion accounts to verify the net assets or working capital of the business at completion;

(b)   awaiting the profits of the target, or its turnover or other relevant financial data, for a future period (a so-called 'earn-out') – arrangements of this nature give rise to difficult questions of definition and of the seller's protections to stop avoidance tactics by the purchaser;

(c)   as a cosmetic device to enable the seller to claim that he was paid more money than the purchaser was willing to pay – in this event interest is not paid (or not paid at a full commercial rate) on the outstanding consideration, and no payment on account is made, so the net present value of the consideration is less than its nominal value;

(d)   as a way of obtaining 'security' against breach of warranty or contingent liabilities – the purchaser will refuse to pay the deferred consideration, setting off against his obligation to do so the alleged breach of warranty or the amount of the liability; and

(e)   where the purchaser does not have adequate cash resources at the time of sale.

If the deferred payment is due to be satisfied in shares, a question arises as to the way in which the shares are to be valued. Should it be a number of shares fixed at completion or should the number depend upon the market value of the shares at, or over a period prior to, the payment date for the deferred consideration? If the latter route is to be adopted, the purchaser will have to consider how to obtain shareholders' approval to issue an unknown number of shares, and may wish to put a maximum on the number of shares which can be issued (as a trade-off against which the seller may insist upon a minimum). Depending on the number of shares to be issued, if the purchaser is a listed company, an obligation to issue an uncertain number of shares may result in a requirement to publish an approved prospectus before they can lawfully be issued.

There may be some tax complications in deferring payment. If the consideration ultimately payable is ascertainable, the full amount is taxable at the time of the disposal by the seller. (See **Chapter 13 Tax Planning**).

Commonly, the parties will agree that the purchase consideration is to be adjusted after completion to reflect (i) the difference between the amount of working capital which the company has at completion and the amount which the parties assumed it would have, or to reflect changes in the company's net assets since an agreed balance sheet date, and (ii) the net external debt of the company at completion (ie: debt less cash). It is also common to provide that inter-company indebtedness will be repaid (to avoid the financial assistance and other issues which would arise if debts are released) but that an equal and opposite adjustment will be made to the consideration, so the repayment and adjustment have no effect in cash terms.

The identity of the seller

8.24   The purchaser should establish who is entitled to sell it shares in the target. The relationship between the various sellers (if more than one) will also have some bearing upon the agreement (how the price is to be shared between them, whether they require different forms of consideration and who will bear liability in the event of a claim being made against them). The respective rights of different groups of shareholders may also need to be taken into account.

If the seller is an individual, a purchaser will need to know whether he is under a legal disability, for example because he is an infant, a bankrupt, or is of unsound mind. Where some of the sellers are trustees, it is sensible to examine the trust instrument to establish whether it confers a power to sell in accordance with the agreement. Similar issues arise in relation to building societies, local authorities and other special categories of seller.

There are disadvantages in buying from a receiver – not only is it necessary to check carefully the validity of the receiver's appointment and power to sell, but the receiver will be unwilling to give warranties and indemnities or covenants which could result in personal liability. Liquidators and trustees are also likely to give no, or only limited, warranties and to expect to limit that liability significantly.

Consents to the transaction may be required if the purchaser and seller are connected persons under *CA 1985*. Where a director or a person connected with him (defined in *section 346* of *CA 1985* to include close relatives and companies associated with the director) disposes to, or acquires from, a company assets the value of which exceeds a specified amount, the transaction must be approved by the shareholders of that company, (*section 320* of *CA 1985*). A similar obligation may exist in relation to a 'Related Party' transaction within Chapter 11 of the Listing Rules (that is, one which involves a director or substantial shareholder of a listed company or an associate of any such person) unless a relevant exemption applies. An example of such a transaction may be a management buy-out.

Additionally, if the seller or purchaser is a listed company, shareholder approval for the sale may be required if it amounts to a 'Class 1 transaction' within Chapter 10 of the Listing Rules.

Immovable property

8.25 Another area which may need detailed consideration at the pre-contractual stage is that of immovable or real property. Property interests may be important assets of a business and it is important, when looking at a prospective target, to bear the following factors in mind when dealing with real property:

(a)   the value of the property on the balance sheets may differ materially from its market value;

(b)   the relative value of the actual location of the property in question (ie would moving the business cause serious damage? Would it be too costly to move? If a move is contemplated, what sort of planning restrictions will the purchaser face in a new location? Are the employees subject to mobility clauses? etc.); and

(c)   the liabilities associated with the building (eg is it a leasehold, the terms of which require full repairs to be undertaken by the tenant or a contribution to a service charge including full repairs?).

The purchaser must first determine how the property is held, whether leasehold or freehold, and who actually holds the interest in it. Location plans should be requested and local searches should be made at the outset of discussions, since the results may take some weeks to arrive.

If a property is important to the target's business or value, or where a substantial liability may attach to it , the purchaser should have a full professional valuation and survey conducted. The results should be compared with the current book values of the property and with the purchaser's idea of the property's value, to assist in deciding what price might be offered for the business.

There are three possible ways of satisfying the purchaser that the target actually owns the property:

(i)   the purchaser's solicitors may conduct a full investigation of title;

(ii)   the seller's solicitors may supply a certificate of title; or

(iii) the purchaser may simply rely on warranties in the share purchase agreement (although these may be combined with the certificate of title).

The option taken will depend upon the time available, the importance of the properties to the target's business and the parties' relative bargaining power.

Option (iii) is likely to be adopted where the properties are not so important to the target. However, as damages for breach of warranty may not adequately compensate a purchaser, this route should be pursued with caution. In any event, a seller may disclose against the warranties, and to do so adequately may itself need to investigate title. A seller might resist giving warranties as these put the purchaser in a better position than it would have been in had it purchased the properties on their own.

If the transaction involves the transfer of leasehold property occupied by the target company, the consent of the landlord is likely to be required (and may be required before a change of control of the target's shares can occur). Landlord's consent may also be necessary if there is to be a change of use or if the purchaser envisages making alterations to the property following the acquisition. Although generally such consents cannot be unreasonably withheld by the landlord, either by statute or under the lease itself, obtaining them may cause delay. Hence this should be borne in mind when considering the timetable for the transaction. The Landlord and Tenant Act 1988 assists by imposing a strict duty on landlords to give a decision within a reasonable time where their consent cannot be unreasonably withheld, and by rendering them liable to pay damages for breach of this duty. The High Court has held, in *Footwear Corp Ltd v Amplight Properties Ltd* [1998] 3 All ER 52, that nine weeks was a reasonable period within which to give consent. Approving this judgment, the Court of Appeal held, in *Go West Ltd v Spigarolo* [2003] EWCA Civ 17, that a delay of eleven weeks was unreasonable.

The purchaser should also obtain confirmation that it has been told of all the properties used for the purpose of the business or in respect of which the target company may have a liability.

Previously under English law an original tenant under a lease or a subsequent assignee who has given a direct covenant to the landlord, which is invariably required nowadays in licences to assign, remained liable for payment of rent and performance of covenants even after assignment. It was not uncommon for a tenant to find himself liable for rent for years after assigning his lease because the assignee (or subsequent assignees) had become insolvent. This burden has been somewhat reduced by the introduction of the *Landlord and Tenant (Covenants) Act 1995*, which came into force on 1 January 1996. It abolished original tenant liability in respect of leases entered into after the commencement of the Act.

In practice it is often difficult for a seller to be able to produce lists of all leasehold properties previously owned by the company, particularly where the company has had a large number of properties over the years. Whilst it would assist the purchaser in quantifying its maximum exposure to possible leases, such a list (if produced) could not give any degree of probability to that exposure.

The target company may have obtained an environmental audit. The purchaser should ask to see this if one has been commissioned and, if not, should consider commissioning one. The audit could be either a desktop one or a physical investigation. The latter is both time-consuming and expensive but in certain geographical areas or certain types of business may be prudent. A target company may have environmental liabilities under statute in respect of land it no longer owns or occupies (see **8.4** above). It might also be exposed to environmental liability in respect of formerly occupied sites under contractual indemnities given on past disposals.

The law of real property varies greatly between different jurisdictions. Should the target occupy or own land outside England and Wales, entirely different considerations apply, and local legal advice should be taken.

Restrictive covenants

8.26   A seller will usually be expected to undertake in the sale and purchase agreement to refrain from competing in a business of the type he is selling, otherwise the value of the business he is selling may be substantially less than the purchaser expects. Such a restrictive covenant is prima facie in restraint of trade and unenforceable unless considered by the court to be reasonable for the protection of some legitimate interest. The covenant must be reasonable in geographical area, scope of its subject-matter and duration and will not be upheld if it purports to protect more than that which is being sold (*British Reinforced Concrete Engineering Co Ltd v Schelff* [1921] 2 ChD 563).

In the absence of any express restrictive covenants in the agreement, a purchaser of the goodwill of a business is entitled to minimal protection at common law. The seller cannot represent himself as the owner of the same business, cannot solicit customers of the business prior to the sale by direct means and cannot disclose information relating to the business (*Trego v Hunt* [1896] AC 7). However, this will usually prove inadequate protection.

The following covenants will usually be found in a sale and purchase agreement:

(a)   Not to compete in a business similar to that being sold.

(b)   Not to solicit existing or potential customers of the business.

(c)   Not to use the name of the business or any similar name.

(d)   Not to disclose any confidential information relating to the business, including trade secrets.

(e)   Not to solicit employees.

If the covenant is deemed too wide by the court, it will be of no relevance that the seller has agreed to the restriction and it will therefore be unenforceable. The English courts have so far proved reluctant to rewrite clauses in contracts in order that an excessive provision, instead of being declared void, is merely watered down into what the courts consider reasonable. It is therefore important to draft the restrictions very carefully and, in so doing, regard must be had to the relevant English (and, where relevant, EU) law on the subject.

If the agreement is found to be anti-competitive it might give rise to fines under the *Competition Act 1998*, as amended by the *Enterprise Act 2002*.

Continuation of services and intra-group relations

8.27   Many private acquisitions are of subsidiaries within a group of companies which may well be receiving services from other group companies (unlike a simple private company purchase from its owner/managers where the company is unlikely to be receiving any necessary services otherwise than from independent third parties which could be expected to continue on the same terms after acquisition). First, it may not be possible for the purchaser to replace these services at short notice and without disruption, so the purchaser needs a transitional period during which these services are continued. Secondly, the profitability of the target might historically have been exaggerated (or depressed) by undercharging (or overcharging) for services provided. It is therefore necessary to identify all such services (which may well include a common pension fund, central personnel and payroll services, seconded employees, a common insurance policy, treasury management, use of a computer system, supplies of raw materials, occupation of group properties and similar arrangements) and agree practical solutions to deal with each of them.

This problem can be exacerbated where the attribute in common is a trade name, trademark or other intellectual property right – even after a commercial solution to the problem has been found, detailed advice must be received to ensure that the value of such intellectual property is not inadvertently lost by such a solution.

A further problem can arise where the group has a common banking arrangement, possibly supported by cross-guarantees and secured upon the target's and other group companies' assets. There may also be intra-group indebtedness which will need repaying or capitalising.

These 'separation' issues need to be focussed on as early as possible in the sale process to avoid last minute delays, particularly in larger, more complex transactions, as there may be a great deal of detail to address and third party consents to obtain (for example, to share or separate real property, licensed software, etc.).

Gap between exchange and completion

8.28   A gap between exchange of contracts and completion of the sale and purchase is undesirable since it gives rise to at least four problems which can otherwise be avoided. However, where certain consents or approvals are required (see **8.31** below) such a gap may be unavoidable. The problems which arise are as follows:

(a)   Who is to bear the risk of the business during this period? Unless otherwise specified, risk, if the contract is unconditional, passes to the purchaser and the purchaser should insure its interest from exchange. (However, where there is a gap between signing and completion it will generally be because one or more conditions precedent to completion cannot be satisfied at the time of signing).

(b)   Who is to manage the business during this period and will that management be subject to restrictions?

(c)   Are the warranties to be repeated at completion or only to be given at the time of exchange of contracts, and what facts give rise to a right of rescission?

(d)   Is there a danger of lack of business direction, a loss of morale amongst employees, and a risk of losing customers?

These questions are interrelated; if a purchaser is given substantial freedom to manage the business from signing, it is more reasonable that there should be no repetition of the warranties and that risk should pass to it. How reasonable it is to give the purchaser substantial managerial control (which can never be total and must be subject to sensible limits) depends upon the likelihood of the consents and approvals on which completion is conditional being forthcoming. If these are mere formalities a seller should be more inclined to permit the purchaser greater managerial authority.

The sale and purchase agreement and disclosure letter

The sale and purchase agreement

8.29   This is the key document in a private acquisition. A common format would be as follows.

Date	
Parties	— Apart from the seller and the purchaser this could include guarantors of the obligations of the seller (eg under the warranties) and of the purchaser (eg for any deferred consideration). Under the *Contracts (Rights of Third Parties) Act 1999*, a contract can confer enforceable rights (but not obligations) on persons who are not parties to it. (See **8.52** below).
Recitals	— Describing the transaction in summary.

Clause 1   — Interpretation of the agreement, and the obligations of the sellers (which, as far as a purchaser is concerned, should be joint and several).

Clause 2   — The operative sale and purchase clause.

The sellers may sell with 'full title guarantee' or with 'limited title guarantee' in order to incorporate the covenants for title referred to in *Part I* of the *Law of Property (Miscellaneous Provisions) Act 1994* into the share purchase but care should be taken to ensure this does not cut across the agreed warranty position. If any rights of pre-emption exist, it is important to deal with them by insisting that the relevant articles are altered by special resolution so as to permit the sale or to obtain a waiver of them (particularly if they have already been triggered by any prior action).

Clause 3   — Conditions precedent.

Where Completion is to be delayed (eg for mandatory competition clearances, shareholder approvals etc (see **8.31** below)), this clause will set out the conditions which must be satisfied before Completion.

Clause 4   — The total consideration for the sale and the proportion to which each seller is entitled. Following the case of *Senate Electrical Wholesalers v Alcatel Submarine Networks* [1999] 2 Lloyd's Rep 423, a purchaser may wish to ensure that the agreement contains a clear record of the basis on which the parties have valued the target. A claim for breach of warranty made on the basis that the purchaser has valued a target on a multiple of its earnings is more likely to succeed if the contract clearly records that this was the basis of the sale.

Clause 5   — The completion procedure.

This will be set out in detail and will, for example, cover all the documents to be handed over by the sellers on completion. It is usual to require that board meetings of the company and of each subsidiary be held at completion. It is useful to check well in advance that there will be no difficulty in getting a quorum of directors to attend.

Clause 6   — Warranties and possibly indemnities or covenants (see **8.32–8.37** below).

Clause 7   — Restriction on seller's business activities (discussed at **8.26** above).

Clause 8   — Communication of know-how from the seller to the purchaser.

This is to ensure that the purchaser is informed of anything which may be necessary to enable him to continue to carry on the business in the same manner as it was carried on before the sale.

Clause 9   — Pensions.

Clause 10   — Intellectual property.

Clause 11   — Access to the premises and records etc.

Clause 12 — Effect of completion.

It is usual to provide that any warranties and indemnities or covenants and provisions capable of being performed after completion but which have not by then been performed shall continue in full force notwithstanding completion.

Clause 13 — Assignment.

Having bought the shares of the company, the purchaser may want to sell them on either to an outsider or to another company in his own group. The agreement should make it clear whether the purchaser can contractually pass on to a further purchaser the benefit of various terms in his favour in the agreement, in particular the warranties, tax covenant and the restrictions on competing activities. There will remain some legal difficulties in doing so, which are discussed below.

Clause 14 — Remedies for breach and waiver.

Clause 15 — Further assurance.

The seller undertakes to do all things necessary to enable the transaction to be carried out as intended and to vest in the purchaser all the benefits of the shares.

Clause 16 — Entire agreement.

A clause is usually included to the effect that no party has any right of action in respect of any pre-contractual statements other than those set out in the agreement, except in the case of fraud. This is to limit the possibility of a claim for misrepresentation. These clauses are discussed in **8.9** and **8.13** above.

Clause 17 — Release of sellers.

Any of the sellers may be released by the purchaser if it so wishes under a clause to that effect. It is also common for a seller to agree not to proceed against any of the personnel of the target on whom it may have relied when compiling the disclosures against the warranties.

Clause 18 — Governing law and jurisdiction, and appointment of agents for service of proceedings (if one of the parties has no address within the jurisdiction).

Clause 19 — Notices.

A clause governing the manner in which any necessary notices are to be given is useful in order to avoid uncertainty.

Clause 20 — Announcements.

It is usual to provide that no announcement may be made by either party concerning the transaction unless the other approves it in writing. This clause is qualified to allow announcements required by law, or the rules of the UKLA and other relevant regulators.

Clause 21 — Costs.

Clause 22 — Confidentiality.

Clause 23 — Exclusion of third party rights (under the *Contracts (Rights of Third Parties) Act 1999)*.

Schedule 1 — Definitions.

Schedule 2 — Completion arrangements.

Schedule 3 — Representations and warranties given by the sellers.

Schedule 4 — Limitations on the sellers' liability.

Schedule 5 — Tax covenant.

Schedule 6 — Environmental deed (if applicable).

Schedule 7 — Conduct of business before completion (if completion is delayed).

Schedule 8 — Details of sellers and their ownership of shares.

Schedule 9 — Basic information concerning the company.

Schedule 10 — Basic information concerning the subsidiaries.

Schedule 11 — Basic information concerning associated companies.

Schedule 12 — Diagrammatic representation of the company, its subsidiaries and associated companies.

Schedule 13 — Immovable property owned or used by members of the group.

Schedule 14 — Intellectual property owned or used by members of the group.

Schedule 15 — Action to be taken in respect of pension schemes.

Schedule 16 — Action to be taken concerning trademarks, names etc.

Schedule 17 — Action to be taken concerning distribution agreements, servicing obligations etc.

The disclosure letter

8.30   The purpose of the disclosure letter is to disclose specific items to the purchaser which would, if not so disclosed, result in a breach of warranty. Whilst information disclosed during the information-gathering exercise (see **8.13** above) will normally constitute the main part of the disclosure letter, it may need to be updated before the contract is signed. The purchaser should not object to this procedure if it is correctly done since it is telling the purchaser more about the target. For it to be correctly done, however, the disclosure letter should not constitute a further attempt to renegotiate the warranties – it should contain specific, factual disclosures with sufficient detail for the purchaser reasonably to be able to assess their impact on the target. It should be noted that any deliberately or recklessly misleading information given by the seller to the purchaser in connection with the transaction, whether in the disclosure letter or otherwise, might constitute a breach of *section 397* of the *FSMA*, an offence under the *Theft Act 1978*, the *Fraud Act 2006* and/or common law fraud and thus give rise to criminal liability.

It is common in the case of larger disposals (particularly where the sale is to take the form of an auction) for the seller to establish a data room (increasingly, by making documents available on a website) containing information about the target and copies of important documents. A seller will often then seek to disclose the entire contents (or perhaps selected sections) of the data room to a purchaser by way of limitation to all the warranties. Whether this is appropriate will depend on a number of factors including any agreed ground rules of the sale process, relative bargaining positions of the parties, size of the business being sold and quality of organisation of the data room. The efficacy of any general disclosure of the contents of a data room cannot be relied on where a standard of 'fair' disclosure is required (see below).

The disclosure letter, in draft, and the disclosure documents, should not be delivered to the purchaser for the first time at the signing of the sale and purchase contract, but sufficiently far in advance for the purchaser to be able to respond to the disclosures made. Its response may be to regard the matter as insignificant in the context of the acquisition in total; to ask for further information; to ask for an indemnity or covenant against the problem disclosed; to seek to renegotiate the purchase price or other terms of the purchase; or to withdraw from the proposed acquisition.

The final copy of the disclosure letter is delivered at exchange of contracts. Completion may occur later, with the warranties to be repeated at that time. If further disclosure is permitted in these circumstances, the purchaser would lose the benefit of having the warranties repeated since the purchaser could not refuse to proceed or decide to proceed only on different terms (unless the sale and purchase agreement permits the purchaser to terminate the contract for the breach so disclosed).

Sellers frequently seek to ensure that they can disclose not only against the warranties but also against the tax and other indemnities or covenants; a purchaser should resist this. It is also common for the disclosure letter (which mirrors in form the numerical order of the warranties) to provide that a disclosure against one warranty is a disclosure against them all.

On the basis of the Court of Appeal's interlocutory judgment in *Eurocopy v Teesdale* [1992] BCLC 1067, it had long been believed that a purchaser with actual knowledge of certain facts or circumstances not disclosed by the seller might be precluded from relying on them in an action for breach of warranty, despite a provision in the agreement stating that he should not be prejudiced by such knowledge. However, judicial commentary in *Infiniteland Ltd and J.S. Ariss v Artisan Contracting Ltd and Artisan (UK) plc* [2004] All ER(D) 350, suggests that a purchaser's right to claim for breach of warranty should not be qualified by his actual knowledge unless the contract provides so expressly. In *Levison v Farin* [1978] 2 All ER 1149, the Divisional Court held that the background knowledge which the purchaser obtained during negotiations indicating that a warranty might prove to be untrue was not sufficient to qualify the warranty. In any case, it would never be safe for a seller to rely on matters generally known to the purchaser as an alternative to making specific disclosures.

A purchaser will normally insist that disclosures will only be accepted if they are 'fair'. The judgments in *Infiniteland and MAN Nutzfahrzeuge AG v*

Freightliner Ltd [2005] EWHC 2347 confirm that there is no general principle requiring 'fair' disclosure in the absence of an express requirement in the contract and each contract must be considered on its own terms. The Scottish Court of Sessions commented on the meaning of 'fair disclosure' in *New Hearts v Cosmopolitan Investments Ltd* [1997] 2 BCLC 249, emphasising that, to be fair (and hence effective, where 'fair' disclosure is required) disclosures must be clear and specific and not merely provide the purchaser with a means to establish that the warranties may be untrue by making further investigations of materials which do not clearly show the manner in which particular warranties are to be qualified. By contrast, in *Infiniteland*, where the contract did not call for 'fair' disclosure, the court held that information supplied to the purchaser's accountants as disclosure validly limited its liability under the warranties. In *Daniel Reeds Ltd v Em-ess Chemists Limited* (unreported) CA 13 July, 1995, the Court of Appeal held that 'fair' disclosure requires some positive statement and cannot be inferred by the omission of information.

Consents

8.31   The consents which may be required on any private acquisition will of course depend upon the particular facts of the transaction. The following are some of the consents which might be relevant:

(a)   seller's shareholders' consent, for example because the corporate seller is listed and the transaction is Class 1, involves a Related Party (see **8.24** above) or requires shareholder approval for some statutory reason (eg *section 320* of *CA 1985*);

(b)   purchaser's shareholders' consent, eg:

    (i)   to increase its authorised share capital (where shares form part of the consideration);

    (ii)   to grant the directors authority to allot the consideration shares;

    (iii)   to disapply pre-emption rights to permit a cash placing;

    (iv)   to alter the borrowing limit in the Articles of Association; and

    (v)   any of the reasons applicable to the seller set out at (a) above;

(c)   consent of parties contracting with the target such as:

    (i)   customers;

    (ii)   suppliers;

    (iii)   licensors of software and intellectual property

    (iv)   joint venture partners;

    (v)   landlords; and

    (vi)   bankers;

(d)   regulatory consents in England and Wales, which may include:

    (i)   Secretary of State for Trade and Industry not to refer the acquisition to the Competition Commission;

    (ii)   UKLA agreement to admit the consideration shares to the Official List and London Stock Exchange agreement to admit those shares to trading;

    (iii) specific consents required because of the nature of the business (for example,

        (A)   the acquisition of a bank, insurance company or other financial services business will require the consent of the FSA under the FSMA – but note that companies which operate outside the insurance sector may nonetheless carry on regulated insurance related activities (for example, because they arrange insurance for other group companies) and failure to obtain the FSA's consent prior to a change of control of such a company is a criminal offence, so it is important to investigate this point during due diligence even where the company does not appear to carry on insurance business;

        (B)   the acquisition of a company with UK oil and gas interests or a UK utilities licence will often require the consent of the Department of Trade and Industry or the relevant industry regulator under the relevant legislation or licence);

    (iv) *section 138* of the *Taxation of Chargeable Gains Act 1992* consent if the consideration includes an issue of shares or debentures;

    (v) *section 707* of the *Income and Corporation Taxes Act 1988* consent, where there is a fear of HMRC contending that the sellers are deriving tax advantages, inherent generally in converting distributable income into capital gains proceeds; and

    (vi) Treasury consent under *section 765* of the *Income and Corporation Taxes Act 1988* for certain transactions where a UK-resident company causes or permits the issue or transfer of shares and/or debentures in a non-UK-resident company that it controls;

(e)   EC Merger Regulation clearance (if relevant turnover tests are met); and

(f)   overseas regulatory consents, such as Hart-Scott-Rodino in the USA. Many overseas territories will be concerned with overseas mergers which have an impact in their jurisdiction either because of sales in the territory or because of the indirect change of control in a subsidiary of the target. Local advice will be necessary.

Both parties usually undertake to use all reasonable endeavours (never best endeavours, as this is too burdensome) to fulfil the conditions to the agreement. However, neither party should undertake this obligation in respect of the consent of the shareholders of their company. The board of directors of a company should never give a commitment to recommend a course of action to shareholders for the future since, if there is a change of circumstances such that that course of action is no longer appropriate, they must obey their fiduciary duty to advise the shareholders of such circumstances and its effect upon their recommendation. Even though doubt has been cast on this position by the Court of Appeal in *Fulham Football Club Ltd and others v Cabra Estates plc* [1992] BCC 863, which held that the directors' duty to act bona fide in the interests of their company meant that the directors could make a contract binding themselves to the future exercise of their powers in a particular manner, directors should generally seek to avoid giving such a commitment. *Section 173(1)* of *CA 2006* provides that a director's duty to make independent judgements shall not be infringed if the company enters an agreement restricting the future exercise of discretion by that company's directors. However, at present, if any such commitment is given by the directors, it should be qualified by a requirement to act in the shareholders' best interests at the relevant time.

There should be a final date whereby, if the conditions have not been fulfilled, the contract is terminated but without prejudice to any prior breach.

Warranties, indemnities and covenants

8.32   It is principally by means of warranties, indemnities and covenants that a purchaser seeks to build into the contract legal protections relating to his acquisition. Such protections mainly take the form of assurances by the seller about the current state of the company and, in many cases, about future events as they might apply to the company or its business. If these statements prove untrue, the purchaser may be able to bring legal proceedings to recover any financial loss.

In effect, these assurances are a way of adjusting retrospectively the purchase price to what it should have been had the buyer and seller known all the relevant facts at the time of the sale. The knowledge, or otherwise, of the seller is not really relevant to this argument, except as regards the possibility of fraud and except for certain of the more judgmental warranties. The seller should not have an incentive to be ignorant, and therefore escape liability, and in any event proving that a seller was aware of a particular matter might be evidentially very difficult. The overriding point is, moreover, that if it had retained the business the seller would have suffered that loss in any event. The seller is not therefore being unfairly penalised in meeting a warranty claim, but having a windfall benefit removed, even if he did not know of the facts giving rise to the breach. This argument is only true, of course, if the warranties are sensibly based.

The differences between a warranty, an indemnity and a covenant

8.33   A warranty is intended to operate as an assurance that a particular state of affairs exists, and if the situation is not as stated the warrantor will be liable. The rationale lies in the contractual doctrine of caveat emptor. In the absence of misrepresentation on the part of the seller and contractual stipulations to the contrary, the purchaser has no remedy if the shares are less valuable than it believed. However, where there is a breach of warranty the purchaser is entitled to receive compensation for any loss of bargain suffered as a result of the breach.

An indemnity is a contractual obligation by which one party agrees to keep another protected from a specific loss.

There are some consequential differences which flow from whether a warranty or an indemnity is obtained. Normal rules of breach of contract apply to damages for breach of warranty, thus damages are only recoverable for loss reasonably foreseeable at the time of the contract as likely to flow from the breach. Thus damage which is remote or not reasonably foreseeable is probably not recoverable. An indemnity will typically provide a penny compensation for each penny lost. To take an example, if a person sold a ship knowing that it was to be used to perform a valuable long-term contract and warranted that the ship would not sink, and it does, that person could be sued for more than he received for the ship to account for the loss of the contract – something which was reasonably foreseeable at the time the seller sold the ship. An indemnity against that same ship sinking would, depending on how it is worded, probably only result in a reimbursement of the cost of the ship. However, not all lawyers would agree with this distinction and if it is intended to ensure that certain consequences do follow from a particular event, it is best to specify them explicitly.

A covenant is another protection which a purchaser might use in place of an indemnity for similar reasons. A covenant will provide penny for penny compensation since it is merely settlement of a liquidated demand, but will have the tax and contractual advantages outlined below.

In the past a purchaser would require an indemnity in favour of the target company (rather than the purchaser) in respect of any liabilities discharged by the target which are properly the liability of its past shareholders where certain taxes had not been paid by shareholders and HMRC had the right to recover the moneys due from the company instead. Little of this original function remains and tax indemnities have developed a much wider scope. For this reason, although the rationale is no longer so apt, indemnities, and more recently covenants, are given for taxation in addition to the tax warranties.

One advantage of a tax covenant is that while a payment to the purchaser under a warranty, covenant or indemnity is generally not subject to tax , a payment to the target directly under an indemnity or to the purchaser as trustee for the target is potentially chargeable to capital gains tax in the target's hands. To keep the purchaser whole, the seller would have to gross up for this. A direct payment to the purchaser under a covenant should fall within paragraph 13 of extra-statutory concession D33 and be exempt.

There may, however, be occasions where a payment to the purchaser under a warranty, covenant or indemnity is subject to tax. For example, if the amount paid under the tax covenant exceeds the original purchase price, the payment cannot be an adjustment to the purchase price and therefore arguably is taxable. This will rarely arise in practice as the amount which can be claimed is usually subject to a cap which is rarely more than the purchase price.

A warranty is a promise that a certain state of affairs exists. If this is untrue, and was known by the warrantor (ie in this case the seller) to be untrue, it could constitute fraud. This is not necessarily the case with an indemnity or a covenant.

Indemnities are also used where it is known that there is a contingent or actual liability or loss. For example, it would be customary for the seller to warrant that there are no bad or doubtful debts; if a major debtor is insolvent, the seller will seek to disclose the problem to the prospective purchaser. The purchaser may then seek to renegotiate the purchase price but the parties may have different views on the likely payment the target will receive in the liquidation of its debtor. In this case the seller may agree to give an indemnity to the target against non-payment by the debtor rather than accept a price reduction. A covenant may be used instead of this type of indemnity.

Covenants and indemnities

8.34 Why use a covenant rather than an indemnity? There are both contractual and tax advantages to using a covenant. The tax advantages have been outlined above (see **8.33**).

Amounts paid under a covenant are in the nature of a debt, not damages. They therefore cannot fall foul of the doctrine of penalties.

As a covenant creates a debt, the purchaser can be granted a right to claim by reference to a loss arising in the target.

Warranties

8.35 The warranties are normally found in a schedule to the sale and purchase agreement. The exact form such warranties will take is considered below. In essence the schedule is a list of important statements about the company and its affairs. Frequently, the warranties would not cover all taxation matters as these are the subject of a separate deed of covenant (see **8.33** above). The warranties are introduced by clauses in the main agreement which would typically govern the time when, and the manner in which, the purchaser may claim financial redress from the seller.

A secondary purpose of warranties

8.36 In addition to providing a means of redress, the warranties have a secondary purpose during negotiations in that they serve as an effective checklist of those matters that the purchaser ought to require the seller to check before signing a sale and purchase agreement. It is possible to provide a purchaser with adequate protection against unexpected liabilities in a business in a mere half dozen or so warranties on three or four pages. However, it is usual instead to ask for 50 or more warranties stretching over at least 30 pages, since this provides the checklist mentioned above and allows particular warranties to be better designed to suit the particular circumstances of the target. It also permits warranties to be focussed on specialist areas (such as, say, employment) so that the people responsible for negotiating those warranties do not need to involve themselves in discussions of the whole schedule. In this case, it is important for the seller to ensure that the fine-tuning of specific warranties is not overridden by more general warranties.

The nature of warranties

8.37   It is noted above that warranties are essentially promises. As with any promise, they may be absolute or qualified, that is to say they may apply in any circumstance or they may be conditional. A seller may, for example, only warrant that bad debts will not exceed 15% of turnover in the relevant period or may include limitations which bar a claim unless they exceed this amount. Typically also the period in which a purchaser may claim will be limited in time and other constraints will be imposed on suing on the warranties (see **8.40** and **8.41** below).

It should be remembered that claims for breach of warranty are based on contract. Under general contract law, as we have already seen, the purchaser must show that there has been a breach of warranty and that damage has flowed naturally from that breach or was within the reasonable contemplation of the parties at the time of entering into the agreement. In many cases, one or other of these elements will be difficult to prove and it is for this reason that indemnities or covenants are in some cases preferred by the purchaser and resisted by the seller.

In addition, the measure of damages recoverable for breach of warranty is based upon general contractual principles. Normally, the purchaser will be able to claim for the loss he has suffered compared with the position he would have been in had the statement made in the warranties been true provided, as already mentioned, that such loss is reasonably foreseeable.

If the purchaser were to bring a claim for misrepresentation then, under certain circumstances, it would be possible for him to seek to rescind the contract (ie to treat the contract as though it had never existed). Since this right depends upon it being possible to restore the parties to their original positions, it is almost never available after the purchase of a company in practice. Where there is an interval between contract and completion (see **8.28** above), rescission might be a useful remedy for the purchaser but the seller might try to exclude the right, especially after completion.

The purchaser may not wish to lose his right to rescission between contract and completion. However, the seller may demand this in exchange for allowing the purchaser managerial control during this period, arguing that managerial control is not compatible with a right to withdraw from the contract.

Sometimes a seller may also ask for a right to terminate the contract if a breach of warranty is discovered after exchange and before completion, since it would prefer to retain the company than sell it and face a sizeable damages claim.

A compromise sometimes arrived at is to allow the seller and the purchaser each to terminate the contract if a breach of more than a certain value is discovered between exchange and completion, but in the case of the seller only if the breach occurred prior to exchange or was otherwise caused by events outside its control (otherwise the seller can cause a breach and terminate the contract at will).

Warranties are given at the time the contract is signed and do not usually relate to future events (although there may be exceptions). It is inadvisable for a seller actually to repeat warranties at Completion (by reference to the facts then prevailing) as this may expose it to uncontrollable risk of liability unless it is entitled to limit its liability by making disclosure; this in turn removes the buyer's protection from having warranties repeated. This issue is might be addressed by using the warranties as a kind of condition (so that they must remain true in all material respects) at completion or the purchaser may withdraw.

Of course, the parties will usually seek to some degree,to vary the operation of the general law relating to breaches of warranty by providing specific terms of their own. One example might arise where the price is calculated as an exit price earnings ratio on prospective earnings. Assuming an exit price earnings ratio of ten times was agreed on prospective profits expected to be £1,000,000, there might be a warranty that 'profits' (a term which will need very careful definition) will be £1,000,000 and a liquidated damages clause requiring payment of £10 for each £1 by which profits are less than £1,000,000. This will be enforceable so long as the figure chosen is a genuine pre-estimate of loss and not a penalty (*Dunlop Pneumatic Tyre Co Ltd* [1915] AC 79). Clearly, in these circumstances, it is easy to quantify the purchaser's loss although, given the different ways which exist of measuring profit, careful drafting of the relevant contractual terms is required. However, in practice, such a provision would not normally take the form of a warranty.

In the majority of cases a purchaser is not simply relying on the legal protections set out in the contract. In many cases its commercial objectives will identify precisely where the real risks in acquiring the company lie and, depending upon the size and importance of the transaction, it will have already instructed accountants to investigate the business. Other experts will also have been consulted. By the time contracts are exchanged, a well prepared purchaser will know a great deal about the company it is buying and the warranties will be taken to underwrite the accuracy of the information it has obtained.

The matters covered by warranties

8.38   The following are examples of the most common areas covered by warranties.

- Ownership of shares.
- Capacity of the sellers and covenantors.

- Other interests of Sellers.
- Group structure and corporate matters.
- Arrangements between the target group and the companies retained in the selling group.
- Target group structure.
- Options, mortgages and other incumbrances.
- Accuracy and adequacy of information.
- Accounts.
- Management Accounts.
- Accounting Records.
- The Budget.
- Events since the last accounts date.
- Work in progress and stock-in-trade.
- Contracts and commitments.
- Powers of attorney.
- Grants and allowances.
- Trading.
- Substantial dependence.
- Licences.
- Working capital.
- Indebtedness.
- Litigation and claims.
- Product liability.
- Compliance with obligations.
- Ownership and condition of assets.
- Real property.
- Intellectual property.
- Information technology.
- Data protection.
- Competition and trade regulation.
- Insurance.
- Employment.
- Pensions.
- The Environment.

- Insolvency.

- Tax and duties.

Naturally, whether all of these areas are relevant depends upon the type of company being sold. For example, investment companies are unlikely to have large numbers of employees. In addition, much depends upon the commercial bargaining position of the two parties. On very rare occasions, and especially where 'a quick deal' is required, for example as a rescue operation where the consideration is very small, the parties will agree, even before the involvement of lawyers, that no substantial warranties will be given. One other area where this may occur is in a management buy-out because, in such cases, the management (eg of a subsidiary company being sold to them) will know at least as much about the factual position of the company as the seller and will have priced their offer accordingly. Aside from ownership and capacity, the warranties in such a case might therefore only deal with those matters covered at group level and, commonly, these would relate to tax, pensions, insurance and, possibly, litigation.

Protections and limitations for the seller

The disclosure letter

8.39   As we have seen, the disclosure letter provides protection from liability under the warranties for those matters properly disclosed (but see the discussion of the *New Hearts* and *Daniel* cases at **8.30** above). Such disclosure may lead to the purchaser attempting to renegotiate the terms of sale but it is far better to discover the actual worth of the business before it is sold than later when the warranty claims are made. Disclosure against matters intended to be protected by indemnities or covenants should not normally be accepted.

While disclosure protects a seller from claims for breach of warranty by a purchaser where the issues disclosed involve breaches of criminal law (such as the unauthorised use of a third party's copyright), the parties and their lawyers must give careful consideration to their obligations under *POCA 2002*.

Limitations

8.40   It has already been noted that the warranties will be given subject to a number of express limitations. Most firms of solicitors have a pro forma set of limitations which is used as indiscriminately as their standard form sale and purchase agreement. It will depend upon the circumstances which of these are appropriate to a particular transaction and a well-advised seller should agree the most important of these with the purchaser at the same time as the warranties and the price for the target are agreed. In any event the purchaser should ensure that none of these limitations apply if the breach arises from the wilful default or concealment of the seller.

It is usual for joint sellers to wish to limit their individual liability to the amount of consideration each is receiving. This may be reflected in the share purchase agreement or in a separate agreement between all the sellers. The purchaser will want the liability of the sellers to be joint and several.

'Several liability' arises when two or more persons each make separate promises to another third party. Each is separately liable, their promises are cumulative, and payment by one does not discharge the debt of the other. Joint liability, on the other hand, involves persons jointly promising to do the same thing. Since there is only one obligation, performance by one discharges the others. Where persons jointly promise to do the same thing and also severally make separate promises to do so, this gives rise to one joint obligation and to as many several obligations as there are promisers. Performance by one discharges all (giving the one who actually performs the obligation the right to sue each of the remaining obligors for his portion of the debt). *Section 3* of the *Civil Liability (Contribution) Act 1978 ('CLCA 1978')* provides that 'judgment recovered against any person liable in respect of any debt or damage shall not be a bar to an action, or to the continuance of an action, against any other person who is (apart from any such bar) jointly liable with him in respect of the same debt or damage'. Nevertheless, there are still a number of differences in legal effect between joint obligations and joint and several obligations.

A joint and several obligation enables the purchaser to recover all its damage from any one of the sellers, leaving that seller with the task of trying to obtain a contribution from the others. *Section 1* of *CLCA 1978* provides that any person liable in respect of any damage suffered by another may recover a contribution from any other person liable in respect of the same damage (whether jointly with him or otherwise). This section does not apply to liability for debt as opposed to liability for damage.

Section 2 of *CLCA 1978* provides, amongst other things, that in any proceedings for contribution under section 1, the amount of the contribution recoverable from any person shall be such as may be found by the court to be just and equitable having regard to the extent of the person's responsibility for the damage in question. Although it is by no means clear how the court would exercise its power in the case of warranties given by all the selling shareholders in a sale and purchase agreement, it is reasonable to suppose that, in the absence of any provision to the contrary, the court would rule that any seller who had paid up under the warranties would be entitled to a contribution from each of the other sellers in the proportion that the consideration receivable by each bore to the total consideration. It would be interesting to know whether the court might go further in cases where some of the persons giving the warranties were running the business whilst others were mere investors.

The following conclusions may be drawn from the above:

(a)   When acting for a purchaser of shares under an agreement where warranties are to be given by the sellers, it is obviously desirable to ask for joint and several warranties from each of the sellers.

275

(b)   When acting for sellers, it would be wise to state expressly how any lia-
        bility under the warranties should be borne as between each of the sell-
        ers. Unless the purchaser is expressly barred from claiming the whole
        amount of the damage from each seller, it is entitled to do so; each
        seller should therefore limit its individual liability.

Finally, it should be noted that the use of the word 'several' in relation to liability does not of itself place any limitation on the liability. The word is often
used loosely to imply some kind of limitation; that can normally be achieved
only by express words.

Specific limitations

Financial limitations

8.41   Normally, a seller would seek to limit the maximum claim for
breach of warranty. By doing so the purchaser would be restricted in the
amount of damages it could seek in the case of breach of warranty.

Often, the limit suggested is the amount of the consideration, on the grounds
that the seller is unwilling to lose the target for nil consideration and pay
money, in addition, to the purchaser. Increasingly, particularly in larger transactions, a lower limit might be appropriate, depending on the extent of the
claims which are likely to arise from the particular business. There may also
be circumstances where a limit in excess of the purchase price is appropriate.

The seller may ask for two de minimis limits. The first of these will be that no
claims may be made unless the aggregate of all claims exceeds a certain figure (generally between about 1% and 5% of the purchase price, although on
particularly high value deals this percentage is likely to drop below 1%). The
arguments for such a limit are that no purchase value of a company can be
fixed with absolute certainty so there must be some margin for flexibility, and
that the seller does not wish to set a minimum claims threshold at a level
which may encourage the purchaser to look for claims to bring after the sale
and burden the seller with the cost of defending claims for a relatively small
aggregate amount. This is a reasonable request for a seller to make provided
the figure is reasonable, but the purchaser should seek to ensure that once the
minimum figure has been exceeded he will be free to claim the total amount
of all claims, not just the excess over the minimum figure.

There is a second minimum figure that a seller may request. This is applied
not to the aggregate of all claims but to each claim individually and is normally fixed at a relatively low monetary value. The seller argues that the
transaction should be looked at in the round and the purchaser should not be
free to rake up individually insignificant claims to make up a total claim. A
purchaser should ensure that claims flowing from a common source or of a
similar nature are not each treated as individual claims below the minimum
figure. For example, if the individual limit is £1,000 and there is an arrears on
national insurance payments of £800 per employee and there are 15

employees, this should be treated as a single claim of £12,000 and not as 15 claims of less than £1,000.

Where a purchaser does accept such minimum limits on claims, it is less likely that it will be willing to accept individual qualifications of warranties as to the materiality of any breach, arguing that the minima on claims should provide adequate comfort to the seller.

Time limits

8.42   The seller will wish that claims for breach of the warranties are notified to him as promptly as possible, for such notification in any event to be made within a finite period and for legal proceedings to be commenced, if the purchaser is in earnest, within a specified period thereafter.

The seller may sometimes have taken out insurance against warranty claims and this may impose a time limit, but even where this is not the case the seller will wish to know at some stage that he has ceased to have any potential liability under the sale agreement. The length of the period for which the seller should remain liable depends upon the nature of the business and the warranties given, but it would be most unusual for the warranties not to survive at least one full accounting period.

The period in relation to tax covenants is traditionally fixed at seven years, since the tax legislation normally allows HMRC to reopen assessments for the last six complete tax years. For the same reason, the time limit for tax warranties is usually also seven years from the date of completion. Environmental indemnities may last longer.

In *Senate Electrical Wholesalers v Alcatel Submarine Networks* [1999] 2 Lloyd's Rep 423, the High Court construed a requirement to give notice of claims within a given time limit (as a pre-condition to the purchaser's right to recover for breach of warranty) strictly against the purchaser. Thus an obligation to notify claims within a short fixed period after becoming aware of them (rather than a general obligation to notify claims as soon as reasonably practicable and in any event before a final date for all claims) should be resisted.

Matters within the seller's knowledge

8.43   As discussed above, the seller may try to restrict warranties to matters of which it is aware. A seller's ignorance however, is no protection for a purchaser. In those few cases where this may be appropriate (perhaps on a management buy-out where the purchaser may be better informed than the seller) a question arises as to whether the seller should be asked to confirm that all reasonable enquiries have been made.

It is common, where certain warranties are given by reference to the state of a seller's knowledge, to seek to identify named individuals whose knowledge will be deemed to be that of the seller (or, where 'reasonable enquiries' are required, to identify their scope). Depending on who is named, and whether the list is expressed to be exclusive of any other person who might be regarded as part of the corporate 'mind' of the seller, this approach may benefit both the seller and the purchaser.

As the seller will not know of matters prior to its own period of ownership, it will not want the purchaser to sue for claims arising before the seller itself acquired the shares in the company, or its business, although the purchaser may point out that its loss is not affected by the time the seller acquired its interest.

No right of rescission

8.44   The seller may insist that a breach of warranty will not entitle the purchaser to rescind the contract, a remedy more relevant where there is a gap between contract and completion (see **8.28** and **8.37** above).

Future events

8.45   The seller will not wish to bear the risk of retrospective legislation which may give the purchaser cause to make a claim against it, for example, a future increase in rates of taxation which is given retrospective effect, or a future change in the laws of product liability which applies to products already manufactured by the target, on the grounds that if these altered in favour of the target the benefit would accrue to the purchaser.

More controversially, the seller may also wish to exclude liability where the damage from a breach of warranty only arises because of some voluntary act or omission of the purchaser after completion, for example selling one of the target's subsidiaries which could thus give rise to a loss of tax reliefs already obtained. The purchaser may feel that this is too great a restriction on its commercial freedom and may ask the seller to specify those things that a purchaser should not do after completion so that it can assess the impact of these constraints on the price it is willing to pay.

Insurance cover and other mitigation

8.46   Where the matter constituting a breach of warranty is also a loss to the target which would be covered by its insurance, there will usually be a term in the agreement preventing the purchaser from claiming against the seller where the target can recover its loss from the insurers. A seller may even go further than this and, where the target's insurance is on a 'claims made' as opposed to a 'loss incurred' basis (that is, where the insurance cover is in relation to the time when the claim is notified to the insurers ('claims made') and not when the liability first came into existence ('loss incurred')) and may seek to ensure that the purchaser retains at least the same level of insurance cover for the target under its new ownership. A purchaser will have to consider how practicable such an undertaking will be to perform.

Normal contractual principles require a person to mitigate his loss on a breach of contract. An explicit provision to this effect is usually found in share purchase agreements, not only requiring the purchaser to ensure that any third party claims which will be passed on to the seller are contested and minimised, but also ensuring that any third party rights (not just against the insurer but against any other party) are also first exhausted (or, at least, pursued). The purchaser should ensure that, where such a provision exists, the time limits referred to above during which it may bring an action against the seller are suspended until it has exhausted such third party claims (where requested to do so).

Provisions and reserves

8.47   A seller will quite reasonably request that where it has made a specific provision against a specific eventuality, for example a provision of £10,000 against a specific, known doubtful debtor which owes £10,000, that eventuality should not, to the extent of the provision, constitute a breach of warranty. Further, where a specific provision is made for an anticipated liability which never crystallises (eg a provision against a damages claim which is settled for a lower amount than anticipated) a seller will expect the release of the provision to act as a bar to claims for an amount equal to the amount released.

The seller may also request that general provisions made merely from prudence and not in respect of any particular event should also be utilised before any claim can be made.

Moreover some sellers argue that not only must any provision be exhausted before a claim arises, but also that any undervaluation in any assets in the accounts must be more than offset by the loss arising from a breach of warranty before a claim can be instituted. Unless the circumstances of the acquisition are unusual, this argument is unmeritorious; an undervaluation of, say, a freehold property in the accounts may have nothing to do with the price a purchaser is willing to pay (particularly, for example, where the price is calculated as a multiple of earnings) and should not be set against, for example, the loss of an important contract (which may be fundamental to the generation of those earnings).

Conduct of litigation

8.48   The seller will often suggest that, where there is a claim by a third party against the target which might result in the purchaser bringing an action against the seller, the seller should be the person who controls the litigation since it will be the seller who will pay if the third party claim is successful. The purchaser may be reluctant to deliver control of the litigation to the seller when the way in which the litigation is conducted can affect the reputation and goodwill of the business it has acquired. Sometimes, therefore, a compromise is reached so that whoever has control of the litigation has limits imposed on how it can conduct such litigation without the consent of the other party.

Purchaser's security for warranties

8.49   The seller's liability might contingently exist for some time, depending on the duration of the entitlement to claim under the warranties and indemnities. In the meantime, the purchaser remains exposed in respect of these unsecured liabilities. There is no commercial benefit in obtaining very full warranties from someone of no financial substance. The financial standing of the seller is thus of considerable importance to the purchaser. The purchaser should remember that the seller is the legal entity with which it is actually contracting and on which it is taking the credit risk, and that if it wishes to have the credit of the seller's parent company available it will need a guarantee.

Where the purchaser is not satisfied with the credit of the seller, it may take some security in the form of a charge over assets of the seller, or a guarantee from a third party. A more usual method of providing the purchaser with security is the retention by the purchaser of part of the consideration, often in a joint escrow account, in joint names, with the seller, with detailed provisions as to its release.

Insurance cover may also assist the purchaser (although warranty and indemnity insurance is more generally available to a seller).

Assignments of warranties and indemnities

Warranties

8.50   The purchaser may decide to sell the target shortly after the acquisition. The subsequent purchaser may request the benefit of certain warranties, indemnities and covenants as part of the sale. The original purchaser may refuse this request on the grounds that it is unfamiliar with the affairs of the company as it has had possession or control for such a short time and is not in a position to give them. It may, however, be prepared to assign the benefit of the warranties, indemnities and covenants it received from the original seller.

There are problems with such an assignment; there is no contractual relationship between the original seller and the subsequent purchaser. Furthermore, certain contracts cannot be assigned (eg where the assignment would result in the original party becoming compelled to perform something different from that which he had agreed to perform or where the contract was intended to be merely personal).

It is usual for the purchaser to attempt to take an express right to assign the benefit of warranties, indemnities and covenants and for the seller to try to prohibit such a right. A purchaser will probably feel that, at the minimum, he should have the right to assign the benefit of the warranties, indemnities and covenants to other members of his group. Certain purchasers will need the ability to assign these rights to providers of acquisition finance.

If a warranty is intended to operate in respect of a state of affairs said to exist at or prior to completion of the sale, one must determine whether the warranty was breached at the time of the contract or at the time of completion, as may be relevant. If it was not breached, the warranty has no significance and therefore there is nothing to assign (except in rare cases such as *St Martin's Property Corporation Ltd v Sir Robert McAlpine & Sons Ltd* [1994] 1 AC 85, in which the House of Lords held that the purchaser in the original sale may be regarded as having entered into the agreement on behalf of its successors; this decision has been applied by the Court of Appeal in subsequent cases including, *Darlington Borough Council v Wiltshier Northern Ltd* [1995] 1 WLR 68 and *ANC Ltd v Clark Golding & Page Ltd* [2001] BCC 479). It should also be borne in mind that contractual assurances can now be given for the benefit of third parties, such as any holder from time to time of the target's shares, by virtue of *section 1(1)* of the *Contracts (Rights of Third Parties) Act 1999*. If there was a breach, the cause of action which results from the breach, for loss suffered by the purchaser, would be the subject-matter of the assignment.

The general rule is that a cause of action is not assignable. There is an exception where the cause of action relates to rights attaching to property where the property is also transferred to the assignee or where the assignee has a genuine commercial interest in taking the assignment and enforcing it for his own benefit (*Trendtex Trading Corporation v Crédit Suisse* [1981] 3 All ER 520 (HL)). Provided the contract itself does not preclude the right of the assignment, it is probable that the exception which relates to property would be available if the cause of action was assigned to the subsequent purchaser at the same time as the on-sale of the shares (*Ellis v Torrington* [1920] 1 KB 399 (CA)).

If the cause of action is legally assigned, the assignee can enforce the rights of the assignor under the cause of action and obtain the damages which would have been payable to the assignor. The assignee's rights will depend upon the assignor's losses, not his own (*Western Wagon & Property Company v West* [1892] 1 Ch 271).

If a warranty is intended to operate in respect of a state of affairs in the future, one is not assigning a cause of action but the benefit of a term of the contract, as no cause of action will have yet arisen. Where a contract or a representation is personal and not for the benefit of others, the assignment is ineffective.

Indemnities

8.51　The obligation to indemnify is usually a continuing obligation to make good any losses sustained in relation to specific matters and thus should be capable of assignment as a matter of law in respect of future events. The amount payable may vary greatly with the identity of the person benefiting from the indemnity, for it is the fact and extent of such a person's loss which determines the extent to which the seller is liable (*Rendall v Morphew* [1915] 112 LT 285). Thus an indemnity may be held to be personal and therefore not assignable, unless the contract expressly permits assignment. Assignment of claims which have already arisen under an indemnity have the same legal consequences as an assignment of a claim arising from breach of warranty.

Other matters for the seller to consider

8.52 In addition to the points already discussed in this chapter, the seller may wish to obtain certain other promises or benefits from the purchaser. These could include:

(a) interest on the purchase moneys, possibly even from the date upon which the price was agreed in principle and before any documents were drafted;

(b) payment of a dividend;

(c) repayment of any intra-group debts and discharging of group guarantees;

(d) access to records for tax and other purposes – where the sale is by a large group of companies this might extend to an obligation to produce a 'de-consolidation pack' of accounting information in a prescribed format (to enable it to complete the consolidated accounts for the period in which the sale occurred);

(e) the right to complete and negotiate tax returns for periods prior to and including the disposal;

(f) payment of its costs;

(g) an obligation for the target to change its name or trading style and alter signage to avoid confusion with the selling group;

(h) a confidentiality undertaking about the target's affairs whilst in the ownership of the seller;

(i) protection of employees, either by general covenants, by service agreements or in other ways (and in this regard, the possibility of conferring directly enforceable rights on third parties – intentionally or otherwise – under the *Contracts (Rights of Third Parties) Act 1999* must now be considered. The contract must make it clear whether third parties are intended to have directly enforceable rights under it); and

(j) restrictions on future disposals (to stop the seller being embarrassed by a break-up of the target group at a higher price than the seller received) or a right to be paid a proportion of the proceeds of such a sale.

It is also common for a sale and purchase agreement to require the production of completion accounts and for the price to be adjusted by reference to the working capital and net debt, net assets or profits disclosed by those accounts.

Other regulations

The Takeover Code

8.53 The Takeover Code originated out of practice; it was not originally drawn up as a legal document. However, implementing the Takeovers

Directive (2004/25/EC), certain aspects of the Takeover Code have been given a statutory basis under the Takeovers Directive (Interim Implementation) Regulations 2006, pending the coming into force of *Part 28* of the *CA 2006*, (expected to be with effect from 6 April 2006). Amongst its powers to enforce the Takeover Code, the Panel may make directions restraining persons from breaching the Takeover Code, issue statements of censure, report the offending party to the FSA, order the breaching party to pay compensation to affected shareholders, or (in relation to Rule 11 only) seek enforcement by the courts. The Takeover Code applies to takeovers of all public companies, and to certain private companies (see **8.2** above).

In addition to the limited circumstances described at **8.2** above where the whole of the Takeover Code is applicable to a private company, there is one other Rule of the Code of which an acquirer of a private company needs to be aware. Where a purchaser holds shares in a company to which the Takeover Code applies and the target also has shares in the same company, and one of the important factors to the purchaser in purchasing the target is its holding in that other company, then if the combined stake comes to 30% or more of the equity of that other company (or if the purchaser and the target already together hold not less than 30%, but not more than 50%) the purchaser may, under the 'chain principle' in Rule 9 of the Takeover Code, be obliged to make a cash offer for all the equity of that other company.

The Takeover Code is made up of a set of general principles and a series of detailed rules. The principles provide guidance where the rules are silent, and lay down the spirit of the Takeover Code. The principles underline the importance attached to the concept of fairness. To give an example, the Takeover Code states that all shareholders of a particular class are to be treated equally.

More specifically, detailed rules cover various aspects of a transaction, such as the timing and content of announcements, dealings and restrictions on the acquisition of shares, valuations, profit forecasts, and so on. Perhaps the most important of these relates to the mandatory offer. The Takeover Code requires a person who has secured 30% or more of the voting rights to offer to acquire the balance of the relevant shares at a specified price; this is a price not less than the highest price paid by that person for such shares during the offer period and in the previous 12 months. The offer must be subject to the offeror securing shares in the offeree carrying over 50% of the voting rights. A financial advisor who breaches the Takeover Code or a Panel ruling may face disciplinary action from the Financial Services Authority. A failure to comply with, for example, the disclosure requirements of the Takeover Code may constitute market abuse under *section 118* of *FSMA*.

The Court of Appeal has ruled that determinations by the Panel are in principle susceptible to judicial review (*R v The Panel on Takeovers and Mergers, ex parte Datafin and Prudential Bache Securities Inc* [1987] 2 WLR 699 (CA); *R v Panel on Takeovers and Mergers, ex parte Guinness plc* [1989] 1 All ER 509).

SARs

8.54   The Rules Governing Substantial Acquisitions of Shares, introduced by the Panel in 1980, were abolished with effect from 20 May 2006.

The Listing Rules

8.55   The Listing Rules set out the obligations of companies listed on the Official List. The FSA acting as UK Listing Authority is the competent authority in the United Kingdom for admitting securities to the Official List; the London Stock Exchange is responsible for admission to trading. Private companies may not obtain a listing for their shares.

The Listing Rules impose on companies requirements relating to conduct and disclosure during takeovers and mergers of or involving listed companies. These vary according to the type of transaction in question.

Of particular relevance when dealing with a listed company are the 'Class tests' and 'Related Party' rules, which may require that the company publishes a circular and obtains the approval of its shareholders before proceeding with a transaction of a particular size or nature (see **8.24** and **8.31** above).

The Prospectus Rules

8.56   On 1 July 2005, the FSA published the Prospectus Rules (see **8.2**). The PRs may be relevant to the acquisition of a private company where securities are issued as consideration. The PRs apply to public offers of securities. Where transferable securities are offered to the public or application has been made for admission to trade on a regulated market (subject to certain exemptions), the PRs require the publication of a prospectus meeting detailed content requirements and containing all such information as investors would reasonably require and reasonably expect to find in order to make an informed assessment of the company and its securities.

Pursuant to Schedule 2 of the Prospectus Regulations, *section 86* of *FSMA 2000* details those offers to the public which are exempt from the requirement for a prospectus. These include offers made to no more than 100 persons and offers made to, or directed at, qualified investors only.

Practical steps – checklists

8.57   The following checklists may assist at the following stages of a share purchase transaction. References to the 'target' include any subsidiaries. The checklists which follow consider the steps which should be taken on behalf of the purchaser and assume there is a gap between signing and completion.

On taking instructions

8.58   When taking instructions the person acting on behalf of the purchaser should carry out the following steps:

(a) Ensure any necessary confidentiality undertakings have been obtained (if the purchaser is a listed company and the transaction is material).

(b) Make a company search against each company involved in the transaction.

(c) Make necessary property searches.

(d) Make patent and trademark searches if relevant.

(e) Obtain copies of the memorandum and articles of association of the target, seller(s) and purchaser. Check the seller(s) and purchaser have the necessary powers. Check for pre-emption rights etc. affecting the target.

(f) Issue an information request. Obtain copies of:

    (i) the target's latest accounts and accountants' report;

    (ii) the target's statutory books, certificate of incorporation and any certificate of incorporation on change of name;

    (iii) material contracts of the target;

    (iv) employment contracts and other documents relevant to the benefits of target employees (eg pension schemes, share schemes);

    (v) loan agreements;

    (vi) mortgages, charges, debentures;

    (vii) title deeds to relevant properties; and

    (viii) licences and intellectual property rights of the target.

(g) Apply for necessary tax clearances.

(h) Apply for necessary consents (eg from landlords) if possible at this stage – some consents cannot be applied for until signing.

(i) If any of the parties are listed, consider whether shareholders' approval is required (see **8.23**, **8.24**, **8.28** and **8.31** above). Note *section 320* of *CA 1985*, if directors or their associates are buying or selling shares or other non-cash assets.

(j) Consider whether *FSA* consent is required (see **8.31(d)(iii)** above).

(k) Check funding arrangements.

(l) Consider whether the target will be giving financial assistance (within the meaning of *section 151* of *CA 1985*). If so, check that it has net assets and arrange an auditors' report under *section 156(4)* of *CA 1985*. (See **8.22** above.)

(m) Organise any necessary environmental survey.

(n) Purchaser organises accountants' report on the target.

Immediately before signing

8.59   Immediately prior to signing the contract the person acting on behalf of the purchaser should carry out the following steps:

(a)   Check necessary survey/search results received, that all reports are satisfactory and that the disclosures are acceptable.

(b)   Make a bankruptcy search (against an individual seller) and/or a telephone search of the Central Registry of Winding-up and Administration Petitions (against a seller which is a company and against the target).

(c)   Make company searches against all relevant companies and check for changes since the initial searches.

(d)   Arrange board meetings of seller and purchaser to approve:

   (i)   sale and purchase agreement (for immediate execution);

   (ii)   disclosure letter and attachments (for immediate delivery);

   (iii)   tax covenant (agreed form for execution at completion);

   (iv)   environmental deed, if applicable (agreed form for execution at completion);

   (v)   any power of attorney under which the documents are to be executed;

   (vi)   any other relevant transaction documents (such as related financing agreements for the purchaser); and

   (vii) notice of extraordinary general meeting or form of written resolution (if shareholders' approval is required).

(e)   Arrange convening of any extraordinary general meeting necessary to approve the transaction.

(f)   Notify auditors under *section 381B* of *CA 1985* if a written resolution is to be used.

(g)   Consider need to effect insurance from signing.

(h)   Consider obligation to announce if seller or purchaser is listed and agree terms of announcement.

Immediately before completion

8.60   Immediately before completion the person acting on behalf of the purchaser should carry out the following steps:

(a)   Check all conditions precedent have been satisfied. Completion of the agreement might typically be subject to any of the following conditions:

   (i)   approval of the shareholders of the seller or purchaser (if required);

   (ii)   (as applicable) clearance under EC Merger Regulation or confirmation from the Office of Fair Trading that the transaction will not be referred to the Competition Commission (the latter is not mandatory but to include such a condition may be appropriate in some cases);

(iii)   relevant foreign competition clearances (for, example, under the Hart-Scott-Rodino Act in the United States);

(iv)   any regulatory consent necessary in the particular industry (eg from the Civil Aviation Authority, Department of Transport, FSA, etc.);

(v)   consent for the change of control under a material contract, lease or licence; and

(vi)   completion of any pre-sale reorganisation (where relevant).

Where such conditions apply, the agreement might also be conditional upon:

(vii)   no material adverse change having occurred in the financial position of the target and/or no material breach of warranty having occurred (if the warranties are repeated at completion) or come to light (if the warranties are not repeated); and

(viii)   no relevant authority having taken any action to restrain the parties from completing.

(b)   Check all necessary authorities have been obtained.

(c)   Repeat bankruptcy, winding-up and company searches.

(d)   Organise insurance cover from completion or check this has been done.

(e)   If the target (or any of its subsidiaries) is giving financial assistance, ensure a special resolution is passed if required by *section 155(4) or (5)* of *CA 1985* and have each director swear a statutory declaration as required by *section 156* of *CA 1985*.

(f)   Give notice to draw necessary funds.

At completion

8.61   At completion the following steps will occur:

(a)   Seller and purchaser exchange certified copies of board resolutions and (if relevant) powers of attorney.

(b)   Seller and purchaser execute and deliver:

(i)   tax covenant;

(ii)   environmental deed (if applicable); and

(iii)   other ancillary documents (as relevant; eg intellectual property licences).

(c)   Seller delivers:

(i)   executed stock transfer forms;

     (ii)   original share certificates;

     (iii)   any consents or waivers required (eg under the articles or a share-holders' agreement on a partial sale) to enable the purchaser to become registered as the holder of the shares;

     (iv)   title deeds to the immovable properties (unless these are charged, in which case the deeds will be held by the chargee);

     (v)   certificates of title to the properties (if applicable);

     (vi)   an auditor's resignation letter addressed to the target, confirming for the purposes of *section 394* of *CA 1985* that there are no circumstances connected with his ceasing to hold office which he considers ought to be brought to the attention of the members or creditors;

     (vii)   resignations under seal from directors and the company secretary confirming that they have no claims against the target (other than for accrued remuneration, where applicable);

     (viii) any relevant pension deeds or actuaries' letter (see Chapter 9 Pensions Aspects of Acquisitions);

     (ix)   statutory books and minute books written up to date; and

     (x)   original certificate of incorporation and certificates of incorporation on change of name.

(d)   Board meeting of target:

     (i)   convenes any necessary extraordinary general meeting on short notice (eg to amend the articles, if required); alternatively, a written resolution may be passed (in which case, the target's auditors must be notified – see *CA 1985, s 381B*);

     (ii)   approves the transfer of its shares (subject to stamping);

     (iii)   approves the issue of share certificates to the purchaser and/or its nominee(s);

     (iv)   approves the appointment of new directors and secretary;

     (v)   approves any new service contracts;

     (vi)   resolves to adopt a new registered office;

     (vii)   resolves to amend the accounting reference date; and

     (viii) approves new bank mandates.

(e)   Purchaser pays consideration.

After completion

8.62   After completion the person acting on behalf of the purchaser should carry out the following steps within the relevant statutory time limits, where appropriate (indicated in brackets after each item).

(a)   File necessary forms, as follows:

   (i)   Form 225(1) – change of accounting reference date (there is no time limit as such but the change will not take effect until the Registrar receives this notice);

   (ii)   Form 287 – change of registered office (as above);

   (iii) Forms 288a and b – appointment and removal of directors and secretary (within 14 days of the appointment or, as the case may be, the removal of the director or secretary);

   (iv)   Form 156 – directors' statutory declaration to approve financial assistance (if applicable) with auditors' report attached (within 15 days of the making of the declaration);

   (v)   Form 123 – for any company which has increased its authorised share capital in the transaction (within 15 days after the passing of the resolution authorising the increase);

   (vi)   Form 88(2) – if new shares have been allotted (within one month of the allotment); and

   (vii) Form 395 – if a relevant charge has been created (within 21 days after the date of the charge's creation).

(b)   File any relevant charge (with Form 395).

(c)   File copies of any special resolutions (within 15 days after they have been passed) (eg to amend the articles, disapply statutory pre-emption rights under *section 95* of *CA 1985* or approve financial assistance).

(d)   File amended articles (if applicable) (within 15 days after the special resolution has been passed to amend the articles).

(e)   Submit transfers for stamping.

Comparison of the Companies Act 1985 and the Companies Act 2006

8.63

Companies Act 1985	Companies Act 2006	Comments	Chapter 8 reference
Section 1(3)	*Section 4(1) to (3)*	The requirements for forming a public company have changed: the memorandum of association is no longer required to state the company is formed as a public company.	8.1
Section 30	*Sections 60 to 62*	Fewer exemptions from the requirement to use 'limited' as part of a private company's name.	8.1

Companies Act 1985	Companies Act 2006	Comments	Chapter 8 reference
Section 81	*Sections 755* and *760*	A public offer by a private company is no longer a criminal offence. Instead, *section 757* now enables the Secretary of State, or any member or creditor of the company, to apply for a court order restraining any proposed contravention of *section 755*. *Section 758* enables these parties to apply for the company's re-registration as a public company.	8.1
Section 88	*Sections 555, 557* and *597*	A statement of capital must now be filed together with the return of allotments. Previously, directors were liable to a fine for failure to file a return of allotments. Now, directors commit a criminal offence and, if convicted, are liable to a fine (*section 557, CA 2006*).	8.62
Section 95	*Sections 569* to *573*	The concept of 'relevant shares' (*section 94(5), CA 1985*) not retained. The Secretary of State may now reduce to 14 days (currently 21 days) the period for acceptance of pre-emption offers (*section 563(6), CA 2006*).	8.19, 8.62
Section 103	*Sections 593* to *595*	No material change.	8.19
Section 104	*Sections 598* to *604*	No material change.	8.19
Section 105	*Section 604*	No material change.	8.19
Section 106	*Section 584*	No material change.	8.19
Section 107	*Sections 592* and *609*	No material change.	8.19
Section 108	*Sections 596, 600* and *1150*	No material change.	8.19
Section 123	N/A	The current requirement for each company to have an authorised share capital is to be repealed. A company's articles of association should be amended to include any desired restriction on the number of shares which may be issued from time to time.	8.62

Companies Act 1985	Companies Act 2006	Comments	Chapter 8 reference
Section 150	*Section 670*	No material change.	**8.19**
Section 151	*Sections 678, 679* and *680*	The general prohibition now applies only to public companies and their subsidiaries.	**8.22**
Section 155	N/A	No special approval will be required for private companies unless they are subsidiaries of a public company).	**8.22**
Section 156	N/A	No special approval will be required for private companies unless they are subsidiaries of a public company).	**8.58, 8.62**
Section 163(2)	*Section 693(3)*	No material change.	**8.2**
Section 225	*Section 392*	No material change.	**8.62**
Section 263	*Sections 829, 830, 849* and *850*	No material change.	**8.22**
Section 287	*Sections 86* and *87*	There is no *CA 2006* provision comparable to *section 287(7)*, *CA 1985* (ie in proceedings for an offence of failing to comply with a duty under that section, burden of proof lies on the defendant).	**8.62**
Section 288	*Sections 162, 167, 275* and *276*	Non-compliance is a criminal offence under *CA 2006*.	**8.62**
Section 320	*Sections 190, 191* and *223*	It will be possible to make an agreement for a substantial property transaction specifically conditional on the receipt of shareholder approval for that transaction. Furthermore, the requisite value of non-cash assets will be increased from £2,000 to £5,000.	**8.24, 8.31**
Section 346	*Sections 252* to *255*	No material change.	**8.24**
Section 381B	*Section 502*	Auditors of a private company are entitled to receive the communications due to the members in relation to proposed written resolutions of that company.	**8.59**

Companies Act 1985	Companies Act 2006	Comments	Chapter 8 reference
Section 394	*Sections 519 to 521*	Addition of specific requirements applicable to auditors of quoted companies.	**8.61**
Section 395	*Sections 860(1), 861(5), 870(1), 874(1), (2)* and *(3)*	No material change.	**8.62**
Section 429	*Sections 977 to 980*	A 'dual threshold test' will be introduced. Under this, squeeze-out and sell-out rights will only be capable of exercise where a bidder holds both 90% of the shares to which the offer relates and 90% of the voting rights of those shares.

Squeeze-out and sell-out rights are exercisable within three months following the final date for acceptance of the offer. | **8.3** |

Chapter 9

Pensions Aspects of Acquisitions

At a glance

- Specialist actuarial and legal advice should be considered as early as possible, because the pension costs and risks may be material.

- It is crucial to consider the current funding position of any defined benefit scheme involved, and factor this into the acquisition price.

- The form, level and cost of future pension benefits provided to employees should be considered and, where appropriate, priced into the acquisition.

- Existing trustee valuations, accounting figures and contribution agreements are unlikely to provide a suitable basis for pricing an acquisition.

- Where defined benefits schemes are involved, it may be appropriate to seek clearance from the Pensions Regulator. Cash contributions or contingent security may be required to achieve this.

- If the acquisition involves an employer 'ceasing to participate' in a defined benefit scheme, a material debt (*section 75* debt) may be triggered against the exiting employer. Care should be taken to mitigate this risk or seek an appropriate indemnity from the vendor.

- In addition to any expected costs, there are material ongoing risks in running a defined benefit scheme. These risks need to be understood by a buyer and it may be appropriate to put a price on these risks in valuing the business.

Introduction

9.1   Over the last few years, the UK pension environment has changed substantially. Many of these changes impact directly on corporate transactions when defined benefit pension schemes are part of any deal.

When a company or business changes hands substantial amounts of pension scheme assets and liabilities may be involved. In many cases these sums are a significant part of the purchase price of the business, and so pensions can be a make or break factor.

Recent regulations have been designed to prevent companies 'abandoning' pension schemes. This means that a buyer who purchases a company with a defined benefit pension scheme often has to take on an extra level of unsecured debt. This debt can have unknown and volatile future financing requirements.

In addition to the direct financial implications, the pension benefits can be an emotive issue for the employees involved in an acquisition. Often pension is by far the most valuable and costly benefit provided by an employer.

The scale of the current challenge is such that some potential acquirers are walking away from deals that may involve defined benefits pension schemes. This can present an opportunity for other potential buyers as they may find themselves facing fewer competing bids and able to secure a better deal.

This chapter

9.2   The chapter deals with the main pension costs and challenges that may be faced as part of an acquisition.

Section **9.3** provides a brief overview of UK pension schemes, sections **9.4** to **9.15** cover the issues that may face the various parties involved and sections **9.16** to **9.34** discuss in some detail the key regulatory challenges. These significant regulatory challenges include: *section 75* debts, funding for pensions under the new regime and dealing with the Pensions Regulator and how companies can seek to limit some of the pension risks by agreeing withdrawal arrangements or clearance applications.

The particular features of a proposed transaction may give rise to non-standard issues and liabilities. It is therefore recommended that actuarial and legal advice is considered early in the process.

Pension benefits

9.3   Most companies provide some form of pension provision for their employees through either occupational or contract-based arrangements. The pension designs may be either defined contribution or defined benefit.

Occupational schemes normally have a formal trust which stands separate from the sponsoring employer(s). The scheme is governed by the trust deed and rules, and assets in the trust are held separate from those of the company. Trustees are appointed to administer the fund in accordance with the trust deed & rules and under trust law in general. An occupational scheme will have one or more employers of the company that participate in the scheme (the participating employers). Occupational schemes can be defined benefit or defined contribution in design.

Contract-based schemes are operated by insurance companies. The employer usually makes contributions to the scheme on behalf of the employees. Personal pension and Stakeholder schemes are both contract-based defined contribution arrangements.

Historically many UK employers provided 'final salary' occupational schemes. Under these schemes benefits are defined in terms of earnings and service, and are payable from retirement until the member dies. Final salary schemes are a form of defined benefit scheme. Through the scheme, the employer is liable to meet the future cost of the defined benefit promise. Benefits for members are defined and 'known', but the cost of providing them is unknown. The cost can only be estimated because the actual cost will depend on the future experience of the scheme, eg how long members actually live, and actual investment returns. Due to mounting costs and risks many UK final salary schemes are now closed to new entrants, and some are even closed to future accrual or are now providing lower levels of accrual.

Defined contribution schemes (or money purchase schemes) are increasingly common in the UK. The benefit provided to the member is directly related to contributions paid and the investment returns earned. The employer has limited risks beyond paying the agreed contributions and any expenses or insurance premiums.

Defined benefit schemes can include a range of designs other than just the traditional final salary scheme, eg CARE (career average revalued earnings) schemes which base benefits on average salary rather than final salary. Some scheme designs can superficially look like a defined contribution arrangement but if they have an element of benefit guarantee, they are really a defined benefit scheme. These alternative designs usually have lower risks and costs to the employer than a final salary scheme but the legal and funding requirements can be similar.

An employer with a defined benefit pension scheme can discharge its liabilities by buying annuities with an insurance company. The main difficulty with this is likely to be the cost. Insurance companies charge a premium significantly higher than the assets targeted by most pension schemes. The total cost could be easily 150% of the assets targeted by the scheme or more. The company would therefore normally need to inject a significant cash sum in order to buyout the benefits and most employers prefer to manage the pension risks rather than incur this upfront cost.

Pension arrangements may include a range of benefits, including: benefits on leaving the employer before retirement, spouses' pensions, lump sums on death in service or on reaching retirement, ill-health benefits, normal retirement pension, early or late retirement pensions and redundancy provisions.

Members leaving the scheme before retirement will be entitled to deferred pensions retained in the scheme or a transfer payment to another arrangement. In some cases, a refund of the member's contributions (less tax) may be paid as an alternative.

Pension arrangements may be contracted-out or contracted-in to the State Second Pension (S2P). Contracted-out employees accrue reduced benefits in S2P (and its predecessor SERPS). In return, both employee and employer receive a rebate in their National Insurance Contributions. Typically, final salary schemes tend to be contracted-out, and most other designs, especially defined contribution schemes, tend to be contracted-in.

Pension schemes are prohibited from unfairly discriminating between men and women in respect of service after 17 May 1990 (the date of the judgment in *Barber v Guardian Royal Exchange Assurance Group* [1990] IRLR 204). Age discrimination regulations apply to UK pension schemes from December 2006 (*The Employment Equality (Age) Regulations 2006*), but many common pension practices are exempt.

Pension schemes registered with HMRC enjoy considerable tax relief. Ordinary annual contributions paid by the employer are allowed as an expense against the company's liability to corporate tax and employee's contributions are allowable as a deduction for income tax purposes. Moreover, employer contributions to an approved scheme are not treated as benefits in kind for employees. Investments are free to UK tax apart from the liability to basic rate on UK equity dividends, and some tax advantages attach to benefits. As a result of this relief, HMRC seek to control the amount of money paid into funds and the level of benefits provided on favourable terms, contribution or benefits above a particular level attract tax penalties.

In addition to the main pension scheme benefits, some employees may have additional benefit provisions through direct company promises or Employer Financed Retirement Benefit Schemes (EFRBS – formerly known as unapproved arrangements).

The main focus in this chapter is on UK defined benefit occupational schemes because this is where the largest potential liabilities and risks often arise, although reference is also made to other arrangements.

An outline acquisition

9.4   When a buyer is considering a target, the pension issues will depend on a number of factors, including:

- the nature of the entity being purchased;

- the structure of the transaction;

- the target company's current pension arrangements;

- the buyer's existing pension provisions; and

- the buyer's intentions for both past and future service pension provisions.

The buyer may wish to adjust the potential purchase price to allow for the impact of pensions on the deal.

Where the target currently provides defined benefits there are three basic situations:

- The entity may have it own separate pension scheme. The whole scheme including all assets and liabilities will normally be part of the acquisition. The scheme would normally include both current employees and ex-employees of the target. The buyer will need to understand the: current funding position, the ongoing costs of the proposed future service benefits and the risks of running the scheme.

- The entity may be part of an employer, and may participate in the vendor's group pension arrangements. The buyer may need to use its own pension arrangements for future service or set up a new pension vehicle. The buyer may negotiate special transfer terms with the vendor and also offer members the choice of transferring their past service to the buyer's scheme. If no special terms are negotiated over the past service, then the transferring employees will become deferred pensioners in the vendor's scheme and lose the link in their benefits to future salary increases, which may create employee problems. The vendor may also wish to encourage a transfer of the past service rather than being left with the deferred pensioners. Normally only the current employees would be offered a transfer to the buyer's scheme.

- The entity may consist of one or more employers that participate in the vendor's group pension arrangements. The issues are similar to the part business above but in addition the *section 75* debt on the employer regulations will be triggered (see **9.17**). The exiting participating employers could be liable to pay a material debt to the vendor's scheme. The buyer may therefore seek indemnities from the vendor.

If the vendor currently provides a defined contribution scheme there are fewer issues for the buyer. The buyer will be mainly concerned with the level of future contributions it intends to provide, which may differ from the current provisions. The buyer may still need to set up a new scheme. A debt on the employer can arise even in respect of defined contribution schemes – see **9.19**.

Where the purchase, or any restructuring following the purchase, could adversely impact on the security provided to either the buyer's or the vendor's existing pension arrangements, the company should discuss the impact with the trustees and may also wish to seek clearance from the Pensions Regulator (see **9.27** and **9.30**). For example, the vendor may wish to seek clearance before agreeing to return the sale proceeds to its shareholders. If clearance is not obtained, and it is later determined that scheme members or the PPF suffered a loss, the Pensions Regulator has extensive powers to later impose additional costs on the parties involved.

Interested parties

Trustees of the vendor's pension scheme

9.5   Pension scheme trustees have a duty to safeguard the security of members' benefits. Broadly speaking, security is provided from three key areas: the assets of the scheme, contingent assets and the employer covenant. The employer covenant is both the ability and the willingness of the employer to finance the scheme and to correct deficits if and when they arise, including on wind-up.

If an acquisition target has a separate pension scheme that will transfer to the buyer, then the trustees will wish to understand any resulting reduction (or increase) in the employer covenant. For example, the buyer may intend to gear up the target to finance the deal. This may increase the risk of the scheme benefits not being paid, as the debt may rank higher than the pension scheme. The trustees may request additional funding or contingent assets to maintain the overall security.

Even if the scheme will remain with the vendor, the trustees will still need to consider the impact of the sale on scheme security. If the sale proceeds are retained within the business and reinvested, then there may be no net impact. However, if the vendor intends to return money to the shareholders or an overseas parent, then the trustees will need to consider whether this might materially reduce the employer covenant to their scheme. It may be that the employer covenant is strong enough for the reduced covenant to be sufficient but, if not, the trustees may request additional funding or contingent assets.

If as part of the acquisition a transfer payment is to be made from the vendor's scheme, the trustees will wish to ensure that the transfer value paid is:

- sufficient to allow reasonable security and benefits for the transferring members; and

- does not erode the security for the non-transferring members.

In doing so, they must abide by the provision of their trust deed & rules. The commercial sale agreement is not binding on the trustees and so the resulting transfer value released from the vendor's scheme might be higher or lower than that specified in the sale agreement. There may therefore need to be balancing payments from either the buyer or vendor as specified by any shortfall or excess clause of the sale agreement.

The trust deed & rules may also grant the trustees substantial powers such as to set contribution rates as they see fit.

The trustees may be required to notify the Pensions Regulator of certain events as part of the transaction under *section 69* of the *Pensions Act 2004* and *The Pensions Regulator (Notifiable Events) Regulations 2005*.

The trustees potentially have the power to make or break deals.

The buyer's trustees

9.6   The buyer's trustees have similar concerns to the vendor's trustees.

If the buyer already has a defined benefit plan, the trustees have a requirement to monitor the employer covenant of the buyer. An acquisition, with increased gearing or not, may initially be neutral to the covenant because additional assets have been acquired. However, if the trustees conclude differently, they may request additional funding or contingent assets. This can apply, even if the acquired business has no defined benefit arrangement.

If the buyer's trustees are asked to receive a transfer payment, they will need to ensure that the transfer is sufficient to purchase the promised benefits and to maintain the security of existing members. If not, they may request additional funding or contingent assets.

As with the vendor's trustees, the buyer's trustees must abide by the terms of their trust deed & rules and they may have substantial powers that could impact on the proposed transaction.

Vendor

9.7   Crudely, the vendor will want to transfer the maximum amount of pension liabilities for the lowest cost to itself. The cost to the vendor may arise through the transfer value to be paid from its pension scheme or through a pricing adjustment in the purchase price.

Conversely, the vendor may also wish to ensure that appropriate benefit provision and security are in place post-acquisition for its former employees.

If the sale involves a participating employer exiting its pension scheme, a *section 75* debt may be payable (see **9.17**) and the vendor may wish to minimise this. The debt actually falls to the departing employer (and therefore the buyer) but the vendor will normally be required to provide an indemnity.

Payment of the debt, in some circumstances, can be broadly cost neutral to the vendor because the payment will improve the overall funding position of its scheme and reduce future cash contributions. However, payment of the debt may represent a material cashflow strain to the vendor and limit other business plans. The vendor may therefore seek an approved withdrawal arrangement (see **9.20**) to modify the debt.

The vendor may also seek clearance from the Pensions Regulator over the sale and the use of the sale proceeds (see **9.27**). Whether or not the company seeks clearance, they may still be required to notify the Pensions Regulator and trustees of certain events as part of the transaction under *section 69* of the *Pensions Act 2004* and *The Pensions Regulator (Notifiable Events) Regulations 2005*.

The buyer

9.8   Crudely, the buyer will want to pay the lowest price for the assets and take on the lowest level of liabilities possible. For pensions this means either maximising the transfer payment, or limiting the liabilities taken on. In adjusting the purchase price to reflect the pension liabilities, the buyer will not want to understate the costs.

In practice, the buyer will also want to ensure that its new employees are suitably protected and avoid employee relationship problems. Plus the commercial reality may mean that the buyer must beat rival bids and therefore any additional pension costs may need to be met through reduced profit margins rather than an explicit price reduction.

The buyer would normally seek an indemnity against any *section 75* debt triggered in the vendor's schemes. If this is not available (or the vendor is not financially strong enough for the indemnity to be of value), the buyer may reflect this debt in the purchase price or seek to minimise the debt through an approved withdrawal arrangement.

A buyer may also seek clearance from the Regulator to avoid the risk of being subject to a future contribution notice.

Any actuarial valuations or accounting results available from the vendor will be helpful in assessing the pension liabilities but are unlikely to be directly suitable for placing a cost on the pension liabilities for pricing purposes or the buyer's accounts. Most sets of figures are out of date by the time a transaction is taking place, and many might have been calculated using inappropriate bases. For example, the trustee valuation might not be prudent enough when assessing future life expectancy.

The buyer should also be aware of the impact of the acquisition on any defined benefit scheme it already sponsors and may wish to discuss the acquisition with its own trustees as soon as possible. For example, if the members are to be offered service credits in exchange for the agreed transfer payment, additional funding may be required.

If the buyer is taking on a whole pension scheme from the vendor, then it must be aware that the trustees of this scheme may take a different view on funding and contributions post-acquisition. Where possible, the buyer should discuss this with the trustees before finalising the offer.

The buyer also needs to consider the level of post-acquisition benefits. These must generally be provided at a level no lower than specified by *TUPE* (see **9.31**). However, higher levels are generally granted based on satisfying the expectations of the transferring employees or harmonising benefits with the existing workforce. Depending on how the acquisition is being priced, the level of future benefits is often a relevant factor.

If the buyer intends to restructure the business post-acquisition, then it needs to investigate whether there are any special redundancy or early retirement terms hidden away in the rules of the scheme or within employees' contracts. These can often trigger significant additional liability. Sometimes 'change of control' or the acquisition itself can trigger additional pension liabilities, often for senior exectives.

Practical issues – establishing a new scheme

9.9   It may be necessary for the buyer to set up a new scheme because there is no suitable existing vehicle or to avoid complications of different benefit structures, different sponsorship companies, or particular provisions of the buyer's scheme trust deed and rules.

Registration of a new scheme with HMRC should be obtained and this will involve the preparation of deeds and making certain declarations to HMRC.

A newly contracted-out scheme will need to have undertaken procedures involving notification of the intention to contract out to employees and trade unions and the election to the Contributions Agency of HMRC for new contracting-out certificates.

The buyer should ensure that, if necessary, adequate arrangements for insurance of any death or ill-health benefits are in place when required. Problems may arise for schemes which were not previously insured as insurance companies are often reluctant to assume risk at short notice and on limited data.

The above tasks take time and an occupational defined benefit scheme will take several months to set up. In contrast, a contract defined contribution arrangement, eg Stakeholder, can be set up in around a month.

Benefits to be provided

9.10   The buyer will need to consider what benefits it proposes to offer for both past and future service and may treat these two quite differently.

The buyer's choices will be influenced by a number of factors including: whether a whole scheme is transferring, the buyer's existing pension provisions, the benefits currently being provided to the transferring employees, statutory minimums (see **9.31**), the likely reaction of the employees, cost budgets, appetite for risk, and the market practice for that sector. The vendor may also set conditions on the buyer, ie must offer the members a transfer to a similar final salary scheme for past service, and future service benefits of equivalent value to those currently being provided for at least the next 12 months.

Where a whole scheme is transferring, the buyer may prefer to simply continue with the existing benefits but could still review whether the level of benefits is appropriate for future service and build any changes into pricing the business.

Where a section of employees are transferring to the buyer's scheme and the vendor currently provides defined contributions, the buyer would typically (but not necessarily) retain this going forward. The buyer will still need to decide whether it wishes to accept a transfer of the funds accrued to date and the level of future contributions. The transfer of the accrued benefits will be largely cost neutral (minus any expenses) and the level of future service costs should be built into the business plans.

Where a section of employees are transferring to the buyer's scheme and the vendor currently provides defined benefits, the buyer needs to decide whether it wishes to continue this or switch to defined contributions.

The buyer will also need to negotiate on any special transfer terms (see **9.12**) on the past service. If the buyer offers a defined contribution scheme for past service, the transfer basis will impact on the benefit options facing the transferring members but not directly the buyer. If the buyer offers a mirror image of the existing benefits, or a service credit on a new defined benefit basis, the transfer terms will impact on the buyer's costs.

The transfer value basis is a commercial agreement between the vendor and buyer. It is possible that this transfer value may be insufficient to meet the cost of the agreed past service benefits in the buyer's scheme. The buyer would need to negotiate any additional funding requirements with the trustees of its scheme.

Whether or not the buyer offers defined benefits for past service, the buyer will need to consider the level and the nature of the future service benefits.

Transfer provisions of the seller's scheme

9.11   If the past service benefits are to transfer to the buyer's scheme, the basis of the transfer payment will be normally specified in the sale agreement. However, the transfer value payable from the vendor's pension scheme will depend on the provisions of its trust deed and not the sale agreement. The transfer value released from the vendor's scheme might therefore be higher or lower than that specified in the sale agreement and the sale agreement may specify a balancing payment from either the buyer or vendor is required (the shortfall or excess clauses).

The provisions in the trust governing the transfer payment may vary depending on whether the sale is of assets or shares, eg a sale of a business may fall to be treated as a collection of individual transfers that are based on the minimum early leaver benefits (see below), whereas the transfer of a participating employer may require the transfer of a proportionate share of the assets of the scheme.

The trust deed may define precisely how the transfer from the seller's scheme is to be calculated but most leave the calculations largely to the discretion of the actuary, the trustees, the employer, or a combination thereof.

Some deeds have clauses that 'trigger' special partial winding-up rules following a change of ownership and grant augmented benefits to the employees concerned.

Methods

9.12   There are three basic methods for calculating the transfer payment:

(a)   The sum of the normal leaving service transfer values. For current employee members the leaving service benefit only allows for increases to retirement linked to inflation rather than future salary increases. This is likely to be insufficient to allow the buyer to provide benefits linked to future salary in its scheme and the employees will normally remain in the vendor's scheme as deferred pensioners.

(b)   The sum of the past service funding reserves. This will make some allowance for future salary increases and may also use more prudent assumptions than the leaving service transfer values in other areas, eg longer life expectancy and lower assumed investment returns. The basis may be different to the funding basis adopted in the vendor's and buyer's scheme, which must be 'prudent' under the new funding legislation. In theory a past service reserve transfer value would allow the buyer to offer mirror image benefits or equivalent service credits in its scheme but there may still be additional funding requirements. The buyer may need to agree with the trustees how to finance this.

(c)   The share of fund attributable to the transferees. The assets are split amongst all of the existing members, usually in proportion to past service reserves. The transfer amount is the proportion of the fund attributable to the members transferring. If the fund is in surplus, a higher transfer is usually provided than in (b). Correspondingly, if the fund is in the deficit, the transfer amount will usually be less under this method than under (b).

Actuaries acting for the seller and the buyer can (and usually do) negotiate the assumptions used for the transfer payments, under instructions from their clients. However, the outcome may not be cost neutral either by design or outcome. The buyer's actuary can help the buyer assess whether there should be a deal-price adjustment because of the proposed transfer basis.

The participation period

9.13   To allow time for the future pension benefits to be agreed and, if necessary, a new scheme to be established, a participation period may be agreed between the vendor and the buyer. During the participation period, the employees would continue to accrue benefits through the vendor's scheme.

Although potentially useful and once common, legal advice should be taken before considering the use of a participation period.

The risks are twofold: firstly, even if the business acquired would not have previously triggered a *section 75* debt (see **9.17**) the participation period may lead to a debt on exiting and secondly, the buyer could become liable for any new debts arising from the vendor's other employers in the participation period.

Pension clauses of the sale agreement

9.14   For UK led sales there will normally be a separate schedule addressing pensions in some detail. For overseas based sales, the UK may not be sufficiently material (or appreciated to be material) to warrant this and it may be left to the wider principles of the deal and goodwill on both sides to reach a reasonable outcome.

The pension clauses of a UK sale agreement would typically:

(a)   cover who has to do what by when;

(b)   define the transferring employees;

(c)   define how the transfer payment, if any, is to be calculated. Usually this would be by reference to an Actuary's letter which would lay down the details of the calculations at the pension transfer date;

(d)   outline any continued participation within the seller's scheme, if necessary (see **9.13**), and the terms for the payment of contributions to the seller's scheme during this period;

(e)   outline the shortfall/excess clauses – if the seller's scheme pays a transfer amount below or above that specified in the sale agreement, a balancing payment less tax will be paid;

(f)   identify the actuaries involved, including reference to who is to calculate and who is to check the transfer amount, with procedures for dealing with disputes;

(g)   set out the timing adjustment – how will the transfer payment be adjusted in the period from the deal Completion date to the pension transfer date. The final agreement of the calculation will usually be some time after the employees have transferred for future service due to delays in collecting the necessary data and the time required to perform the calculations. Alternatively, the timing adjustment may be dealt with in the Actuary's letter;

(h)   include warranties by the seller concerning the reliability of information disclosed concerning pension arrangements (such information may include copies of latest actuarial valuation reports and audited accounts);

(i)   include warranties from the buyer concerning benefits for the transferring employees and the use of the transfer amount;

(j)   set terms for communicating to the employees;

(k)   include an indemnity by the seller should a debt on the buyer arise under the *section 75* debt on the employer legislation (see **9.17**);

(l)   discuss how the transfer payment is to be made, ie cash or the transfer of assets. An asset transfer is normally cheaper but a cash transfer may be appropriate in some circumstances, eg small amounts, or where the parties cannot agree on the assets to be transferred;

(m)   define how the calculations will be carried out;

(n)   provide for disputes, eg reference to an independent actuary.

Adjustment to the purchase price

9.15   If the buyer is taking on past service defined benefit liabilities, the proposed purchase price should be set with the knowledge of any net pension liabilities to be taken on. Whether these liabilities are directly reflected in the price will depend on how the deal is being structured. Rather than transferring to the buyer's scheme, the past service benefits may be retained in the vendor's plan as deferred pensions. In this case there would be no direct past service cost to the buyer but the buyer will need to consider the reaction of the employees.

If the purchase price is based on a multiple of future earnings, then as well as any net past service cost, it will also be important to allow for the expected future pension costs.

In pricing the pension costs, it should not be assumed that either the vendor's, or the buyer's accounting or funding valuations are a suitable basis for the pricing adjustment. For example, the existing valuations may not allow for: current market conditions, the latest view on life expectancy, the appropriate level of prudence for pricing purposes, or the correct allowance for tax. The pension costs may also depend on any restructuring plans, eg redundancies, expansion, or the eventual break-up of the acquired company. If the buyer intends to run a defined benefit scheme, it may also wish to include an additional cost for taking on these volatile liabilities from the vendor. This could be done by valuing the liabilities using prudent assumptions.

If the vendor currently provides defined contribution benefits, there is unlikely to be a past service cost but the buyer will still need to consider what level of future service costs should be built into pricing the business.

Pensions regulatory framework

The Pensions Regulator

9.16   The *Pension Act 2004* introduced the Pensions Regulator. The main objectives of the Regulator are:

● to protect the benefits of members of occupational pension schemes and personal pension schemes;

- to reduce the chances of a situation arising where compensation from the Pension Protection Fund (see **9.33**) would be payable;
- to promote the good administration of work-based pension schemes. This includes issuing codes of practice covering pension provision.

The Pensions Regulator has extensive powers and is changing the framework under which trustees and employers operate pension schemes. One significant desired change is that the Regulator wants trustees to negotiate with the employer in a similar way that a bank creditor would negotiate with that employer.

The Regulator has extensive powers including power to:

- issue 'improvements notices' to persons who contravene legislation, directing them to take specified remedial or preventative steps;
- issue 'third party notices', again giving directions as to what to do to a person whose failure to do something has led, wholly or partly, to someone else contravening legislation;
- ask the High Court or Court of Session to order any person knowingly involved in the misuse or misappropriation of the Scheme assets to take such steps as are necessary to restore the affected parties to the position they were in beforehand;
- impose a schedule of contributions, to modify future benefit accrual under the scheme, or to give directions regarding a recovery plan or the calculation of the technical provisions;
- recover any unpaid employer contributions (ie any that have not been paid on or before its due date) by exercising such powers as the trustees have to recover that contribution;
- require the trustees, employer or other person to provide the Regulator with a report from a suitable expert, to assist it in the exercise of its functions;
- wind up schemes and issue freezing orders and to combat 'Moral hazards' (see **9.23**);
- approve withdrawal arrangements (see **9.20**) to reduce the immediate payment of *section 75* debts (see **9.17**); and
- approve clearance procedures, protecting the buyer or vendor from future corrective action in respect of a transaction (see **9.27**).

The Regulator has issued a number of helpful guides and codes of practice on pension matters and these can be found at www.thepensionsregulator.gov.uk.

Debts on employers for defined benefit schemes (section 75 debt)

9.17   One of the most significant areas of legislation for corporate transactions involving defined benefits schemes is the *section 75* debt on the employer regulations. A debt can arise either when the scheme is wound-up, or an employer ceases to participate, or a relevant event occurs (eg an insolvency event, or voluntary winding-up). Crucially for the buyer and vendor, many acquisitions will lead to employer cessation events and trigger a potential debt. A typical situation would be the acquisition of an entire employer that currently participates in the vendor's group arrangement.

The debt is measured on the cost of buying out the liabilities through an insurance company, plus expenses, less the assets available in the scheme. This debt can be material even for relatively well-funded arrangements because the cost of buying out liabilities is typically much higher than the amount normally held within the scheme for going concern funding.

The debt covers current employees, ex-employees of the acquired employer and a proportion of ex-employees of other employers who no longer participate in the vendor's scheme. Depending on the past history of the scheme and the vendor, the latter group (orphan employees) can potentially lead to material debts for even relatively small employers.

The payment of a debt in respect of an exiting participating employer falls to the exiting employer but the vendor will normally indemnify the buyer. For the vendor, paying the debt to its ongoing scheme may simply impact on cashflow, because the debt can improve the overall funding position and hence reduce future contributions. The difficulty for the vendor is that it may be a material cashflow that impacts on short-term business plans.

It may be possible to reduce the debt via an approved withdrawal arrangement (see **9.20**).

The *section 75* position and calculations can be complex, particularly in multi-employer schemes. The impact and effects may not be easily foreseen by those involved. Expert legal and actuarial advice becomes almost essential to obtain. An example of how debt may be apportioned to an employer is set out below.

Apportionment of deficit relating to an employer who ceases to participate

Unless the scheme provides for the deficit to be apportioned in a different way, the amount of the debt in a multi-employer scheme is calculated for each leaving employer as (A divided by B) multiplied by (the deficit for the scheme as a whole plus the trustees' estimate of the expenses likely to be incurred in connection with the winding-up of the scheme) plus the cessation expenses where:

- A: represents the liabilities in respect of periods of employment with the leaving employer

- B: represents the liabilities in respect of periods of employment with any of the current participating employers (this serves to apportion the orphan liabilities across all current employers)

A and B both exclude expenses of winding-up.

Cessation expenses are all expenses which, in the opinion of the trustees or managers of the scheme, are likely to be incurred in connection with the employer-cessation event occurring in relation to that employer

If the scheme provides for the total amount of the deficit to be apportioned amongst the employers in a different way, the debt is calculated as the amount due from the employer under that provision.

The following points should be noted:

- If the statutory formula applies, then any deficit in respect of orphan liabilities (the liabilities in respect of employment with an employer that no longer participates in the scheme) is apportioned across the current employers. Note that the orphan liabilities can make a huge difference to the amount of the *section 75* debt.

- The amount of the scheme's liabilities attributable to 'employment with that employer' may be open to alternative interpretations, eg where an employee has been employed by more than one employer in the group, or where amounts are transferred in from other schemes.

- A special provision for determining employers' shares of the liability can be introduced by trustee resolution using the power in the *Pensions Act 1995* and *regulation 16* of the *Deficiency Regulations*.

- The 'cessation expenses' attributable to the employer are added to the debt. These are defined as 'all expenses which, in the opinion of the trustees or managers of the scheme, are likely to be incurred in connection with the employment-cessation event occurring in relation to the employer'.

- Where liabilities are being transferred out of the scheme as part of the same transaction, these liabilities can be excluded from the debt but only as part of a withdrawal arrangement (see **9.20**).

- Calculation and certification of a *section 75* debt can be a fairly lengthy process and is likely to require a full actuarial valuation, detailed investigation into employment history and discussions with the trustees.

Industry-wide schemes

9.18   An industry-wide scheme involves more than one non-associated employers participating in a scheme. Each section effectively operates as if it were a separate scheme with a specified proportion of scheme assets that cannot be used for the purposes of any other section.

In these circumstances, each section is treated as a separate scheme for the purposes of the debt.

Debts on defined contribution employers

9.19   A debt can arise on a defined contribution scheme if it suffers a loss through theft or fraud, or there are General Levies outstanding and the scheme's unallocated assets are less than the loss or outstanding levy.

A debt can also arise in respect of defined contribution employees, whose benefits happen to be provided through a section of a defined benefit scheme. Whether this applies will depend on how the defined contribution section was set up and legal advice would be required to assess this risk.

Approved withdrawal arrangements

9.20   A withdrawal arrangement sets out the proposals for the payment of a modified debt usually to permit the exiting employer to pay a lesser amount on exiting the scheme.

The modified debt will be made up of:

- Amount A – which is agreed with the trustees and must be equal to, or greater than, the MFR debt plus the cessation expenses.

- Amount B – which a guarantor agrees to pay in the event that the scheme is later wound-up or no longer has a solvent employer. Amount B may be either the shortfall in Amount A compared to full debt, or the actual shortfall at the point the debt is called.

The Regulator issued guidance on multi-employer withdrawal arrangements in November 2005.

The exiting employer can notify the Regulator that it wishes to enter into a withdrawal arrangement and apply for a direction to suspend the trustees' power to enforce the cessation debt which would otherwise be payable. The appropriate form is on the Regulator's website, and must be accompanied by a statement of the steps that have been taken to demonstrate that cessation has or is likely to occur. If the Regulator issues such a direction, it will specify a period during which the cessation debt is unenforceable. It is intended that this period will allow sufficient time for the parties to negotiate the withdrawal arrangement and obtain the approval of the Regulator.

The regulations stipulate that approval can only be given if the Regulator is satisfied that the guarantors have or will have sufficient resources that the debt is 'more likely to be met if the agreement is approved'. The Regulator is also likely to impose other conditions for approval. These are likely to be on a case-by-case basis, but will usually depend on the financial strength of the guarantor(s).

The arrangement may provide for the guarantors to be either jointly or jointly and severally liable for the debt. The guarantors (who may or may not include the cessation employer) pick up obligations to notify the Regulator on the occurrence of the same events that are 'Notifiable Events' for the employer or on an insolvency event.

Additionally:

- all expenses in connection with the agreement must be met by a party other than the trustees;

- it is possible for an arrangement to be approved before the relevant cessation of participation takes place;

- an approved arrangement may be amended (subject to Regulator approval) whilst it is in force, but this would not give rise to a further period of 'unenforceability';

- the Regulator may decide that an arrangement is no longer required, and bring it to an end.

Regulator's approval process

9.21 The application form on the Regulator's website should be completed and sent to the Regulator, together with copies of the following documents:

- the proposed withdrawal arrangement;

- minutes or resolutions of the relevant parties agreeing to the proposed arrangement;

- any additional documents required (eg certificates and other actuarial advice or supporting figures);

- independent financial advice obtained by the trustees (or reasons why they have not obtained such advice);

- legal advice obtained on any conflicts of interest (or a statement confirming that legal advice was taken – as this is subject to privilege).

The Regulator recognises that many withdrawal arrangements may also be a 'type A' clearance event (see **9.27**). The Regulator will therefore attempt to consider both matters simultaneously. However, as clearance is voluntary, and the triggering of a withdrawal debt is not, the approval of a withdrawal arrangement and giving clearance are entirely separate, ie a withdrawal arrangement may be approved but clearance may not be granted, and vice versa.

The Regulator will make a determination, following its standard procedure in *section 96* of the *Pensions Act*. Prior to issuing a determination, it will issue a warning notice to all 'directly affected parties' (which may include parties other than those who have agreed the withdrawal arrangement, eg other employers in the scheme), giving them a chance to make representations to the Regulator. The Regulator will then issue a determination notice:

- If the Regulator grants approval, a 'notice of approval' will accompany the determination notice, and (if applicable) a direction that modifies the withdrawal debt due from the cessation employer. These will take effect 28 days after the determination notice (during which time a directly affected party can make a reference to the Pensions Regulator Tribunal).

- If the Regulator does not grant approval, the determination will detail the decision and the cessation employer will remain liable for the unmodified withdrawal debt. The parties will also have a right to refer the decision to the Pensions Regulator Tribunal. The parties may alternatively submit an amended withdrawal arrangement for approval.

Effect on subsequent calculations and liabilities

9.22 Under the legislation in force since 1997, former employers remain 'on the hook' for a share of any subsequent debt calculation unless, at the time of ceasing to be an employer, the debt was paid (or it was confirmed there was no debt due, or the debt is regarded as irrecoverable). The amending regulations additionally exclude former employers from subsequent debt calculations if an approved withdrawal arrangement is in place and any 'Amount A' debt has been paid. Furthermore, in determining any deficit at a subsequent debt calculation, the liabilities in respect of the employer for whom an approved withdrawal arrangement was established are excluded, along with the 'debts treated as due' under the arrangement. (The intention here seems to be for the earlier debt to be assumed met in full and taken out of the equation at a later debt event, but it is unclear exactly how the legislation as drafted will work out here and whether it will have the intended effect, particularly if the alternative basis for Amount B has been adopted.)

Employers in respect of whom an approved withdrawal arrangement has been established and who have paid any Amount A debt due are also excluded from the definition of 'employer' for the purposes of the 'moral hazard' provisions of the *Pensions Act 2004* (see below).

Moral Hazard provisions

9.23 *Sections 38* to *57* of the *Pensions Act 2004* introduced (with effect from 6 April 2005) measures referred to throughout the pensions industry as 'Moral Hazard' provisions, as they are designed to prevent employers from taking 'immoral' action to avoid their pensions debts, resulting in their debts being transferred to the Pension Protection Fund. These provisions allow the Regulator to issue: contribution notices, financial support directions, and restoration orders.

The Regulator's powers to issue the above are not restricted to the current employer of an occupational pension scheme. There are therefore potential ongoing financial risks to both buyers and vendors if the pension issues are not properly addressed.

Contribution Notices (CNs)

9.24 The Regulator can determine that a company or individual has taken action (or refrained from taking action) with the main purpose of avoiding an obligation to meet a debt-on-the-employer under *section 75* of the *Pensions*

Act 1995. That person can then be required to pay a 'contribution' to the scheme (or Board of the PPF), essentially with the aim of recovering the money that would otherwise have come from the *section 75* debt. The types of action that it is envisaged could come under this power are corporate restructuring, asset stripping and artificially increasing the scheme asset value for a debt calculation.

Financial Support Directions

9.25   A second set of sections gives similar powers but applies where corporate structures exist for legitimate business reasons but where the effect is that the employer is 'insufficiently resourced' to deal with a potential *section 75* obligation. The Regulator can require the company group to put in place 'financial support' arrangements; permissible arrangements include an agreement from the parent company to assume responsibility, a 'joint and several liability' arrangement across a group, or an appropriate bank guarantee.

Restoration Orders

9.26   The third set of powers is less directly relevant to acquisitions. The Regulator can make 'restoration orders' where a 'transaction at an undervalue' has been made within two years of a subsequent employer insolvency event. Examples quoted in the Parliamentary debate included a company director being given a generous transfer value when his benefits would have been reduced by the compensation cap if the scheme fell into the PPF.

The Act also includes provisions for a clearance procedure, under which an application can be made to the Pensions Regulator to confirm that an act or failure to act would not give rise to a contribution notice, or a particular corporate structure would not give rise to a financial support direction. The decision is binding on the Regulator unless the circumstances have materially changed or were materially different from what was disclosed. Further details on the clearance process are given below.

Clearance

Guiding principles

9.27   Companies can apply for clearance to the Regulator to confirm that a particular action (eg acquisition of a business or return of money to shareholders) will not later give rise to a contribution notice or financial support directive (see **9.24** and **9.25**).

The Regulator has developed guiding principles which it expects to be observed. These are as follows:

(a)   A pension scheme in deficit should be treated like any other material unsecured creditor.

(b)   Trustees should have access to information and decision-makers and in return accept confidentiality responsibilities.

(c)   Conflicted trustees should act appropriately and use independent advice.

(d)   Clearance applications should contain concise, relevant and accurate information.

(e)   All parties to clearance should act in accordance with issued guidance.

(f)   The Regulator wishes to know about all events that could have a materially detrimental effect on a pension scheme's ability to meet liabilities.

The Pensions Regulator has classified three types of events depending on whether clearance may be appropriate. The most significant events (Type A) may often arise as part of a corporate transaction. Examples of type A events are:

- Changes in Priority. This covers changes in the level of security such that the pension creditor would be likely to receive a reduced dividend in the event of insolvency.

- Returns of capital. This covers actions, including paying dividends or buying back shares that reduce the overall assets available for a pension deficit.

- Changes in control structure. This covers changes or partial changes (including a change of principal employer) potentially reducing the employer covenant.

Role of trustees

9.28   The Regulator seeks to be a referee rather than a player in the transaction, and is looking to the trustees to play a key role:

- Where possible, applicants for clearance should have spoken to the relevant trustees.

- Trustees of schemes in deficit should generally act as any other material unsecured creditor (learning lessons from the way a bank would look to negotiate with a company).

- Trustees need therefore to monitor corporate activity and seek the employer's agreement to be given information at an early stage.

- With the above comes a confidentiality obligation – one way of formalising this is to have a confidentiality agreement that is arranged before a difficult issue crops up.

- Trustees and employers should plan in advance their approach to what happens when one or more of the trustees has a conflict of interest — trustees may need to get independent expert advice if the conflicted trustee is their main source of financial knowledge. The Regulator expects a Finance Director or Chief Executive who could be involved on both sides to ensure that all trustees receive information on a timely basis and to be absent from trustee meetings when the issue is discussed and decisions taken.

- The trustees may be required to notify the Pensions Regulator of certain events as part of the transaction under *section 69* of the *Pensions Act 2004* and *The Pensions Regulator (Notifiable Events) Regulations 2005*.

Role of directors

9.29   Directors are reminded of their duties to all creditors under the *Companies Act* and their fiduciary duty to act in the best interests of the shareholders, the company and its creditors, if there is any doubt over the business continuing as a 'going concern'.

The Regulator expects that employers will share independent reports on a transaction with the trustees, and if there is no such suitable report available to pay for the trustees to obtain one.

Whether or not the directors seek clearance, they may still be required to notify the Pensions Regulator and trustees of certain events as part of the transaction under *section 69* of the *Pensions Act 2004* and *The Pensions Regulator (Notifiable Events) Regulations 2005*.

Applications

9.30   Any party wishing to apply for clearance should involve the Regulator as early as possible.

A 'full and accurate disclosure' should accompany the application. Generally, the Regulator expects a similar amount of information to what would be provided to non-executive directors of a quoted company, and it can ask for further information if necessary. A pro-forma for the application is available on the Regulator's website. Each party seeking Clearance should apply separately, although multiple applications may be supported by the same information.

The Transfer of Undertakings (Protection of Employment) Regulations 2006 ('TUPE')

9.31   *TUPE* provides for the protection of the employment rights of employees following the transfer of a business. In cases where occupational pensions had been provided prior to the transfer, the new employer would be required, as a minimum, to offer a stakeholder scheme and to match employee contributions up to 6% of salary, regardless of the benefit currently provided.

Any rights established under contract (such as to contribute certain amounts to a personal pension) may also transfer in their current form.

Funding occupational defined benefit schemes

9.32 UK pensions have recently experienced some significant changes around scheme funding. The *Occupational Pension Schemes (Scheme Funding) Regulations 2005* came into force on 30 December 2005. The Pensions Regulator has also issued a Code of Practice (CoP) on funding defined benefits, an additional statement on funding defined benefits in May 2006, guidance on contingent assets and a discussion paper on abandoning defined benefit schemes.

For a going concern funding valuation, these include:

- the trustees will need to make an assessment on the security provided by the employer (the employer covenant) – the weaker the assessed covenant, the more prudent the basis the trustees are likely to adopt;

- transactions involving the employer may trigger a revision of the funding policy and existing contribution agreements;

- trustees, usually with the agreement of the employer, must develop and then follow their own scheme-specific approach to funding pension commitments and to correcting any deficits;

- if the scheme is in deficit, a 'Recovery Plan' must be prepared, setting out the steps to be taken to ensure that the shortfall is made up within a stated period;

- the Pensions Regulator has wide powers to intervene in the event of a failure in any part of the funding process, including the powers to modify future benefit accrual or to impose a schedule of contributions.

The Pension Protection Fund (PPF)

9.33 The PPF was established under the *Pensions Act 2004* to protect pension entitlements where a scheme's sponsoring employer becomes insolvent and commenced on 6 April 2005. It provides 'compensation payments' at a specified level, if on wind-up the scheme assets are insufficient to provide the scheme benefits.

Defined benefit arrangements need to pay a levy to the PPF based on the number of members, the assumed probability of insolvency (based on the Dun & Bradstreet 'failure score') and the funding level of the scheme. This is likely to be added to the contributions required from the employer. At the time of writing, the PPF Board is consulting on also making allowance for a scheme's investment strategy.

The size of the levy paid by an employer will materially depend on the number of claims from other unrelated employers falling on the PPF.

Accounting for pension costs

9.34 There are a number of accounting standards throughout the world but UK companies are most likely to come across:

- International Accounting Standard 19 (IAS19), applicable to companies accounting under IFRS.

- Financial Reporting Standard 17 (FRS17), applicable to companies accounting under UK GAAP.

- Financial Accounting Standard 87/132 (FAS87/132), applicable to companies accounting under US GAAP. (Some countries operate variations of this, eg the Japanese and Canadian accounting standards.)

These standards differ in many ways but also share several key features, for example:

- The assumptions underlying the reported figures should be a company's best estimate of likely future long-term experience.

- The key discount rate assumptions should be based on the market yields on long-dated, high quality (often AA corporate) bonds.

- The profit and loss charges are designed to reflect stable long-term costs (sometimes with spreading of historic gains and losses) and as such rarely coincide with cash contribution costs.

The pension aspects of any acquisitions (and associated events such as redundancy exercises) will need specialist accounting treatment and can lead to one-off recognition of gains or losses through the profit and loss account.

There is usually a range of acceptable assumptions that companies can use for calculating reported pension costs. Buyers should be aware that a target's pension liabilities, once restated on to assumptions appropriate for the buyer, may be materially different

Conclusion

9.35 Pension arrangements are currently having a significant impact on many corporate transactions. The critical issue for any buyer is to ensure they understand all of the costs and risks involved relating to pensions, and allow for pensions properly in any adjustment to purchase price. It is therefore essential that buyers seek appropriate actuarial and legal advice as soon as possible whenever pensions are involved in a transaction.

Chapter 10

Post-Acquisition Management

At a glance

- The objective of post acquisition management is to maximise the value created by the acquisition and achieve the specific objectives envisaged in the investment case.

- Pre-acquisition planning of post-acquisition management is critical to success. Every acquisition should have a 'Value Creation plan' consisting of a clear and detailed articulation of how value is to be created, timetables and responsibilities.

- The degree of integration should be considered in detail, planned comprehensively and involve key people from the acquired company.

- Awareness of the 'people' issues and an ability to give them sufficient priority throughout the process is critical to success.

- There should be a clear and well understood process for making decisions on the critical aspects of integration and key choices (eg which systems to use).

- Communication of the post-acquisition plan should be clear, honest and delivered energetically to employees of both companies.

- A rigorous process of review should be put in place to ensure that acquisition objectives are being achieved and that any learning from the process can be captured for subsequent acquisitions.

Introduction

10.1   In the introduction to this book, it was noted that value building buyers possess great judgement and superb execution skills. This chapter focuses on the execution aspects from the point at which the acquiring company takes legal control of the target. It is, therefore, assumed here that the buyer has made a good choice and that there is significant value to obtain from the transaction. If it hasn't, then approaching post-acquisition management in the way described will identify this early on and ought to provide the information to limit the damage.

So much thought and energy goes in to making an acquisition that sometimes the planning of post-acquisition management receives less attention than it deserves. Logistical constraints may also mean that the quality of information and access to senior management in the acquired business is less than ideal. Whatever the circumstances, a buyer needs to be ready not just to take control of the target on the duly appointed day, but also to ensure that the momentum of the target company's business hasn't suffered too much through the process of buying.

Good due diligence and investigation helps to inform the critical judgements that are made as part of preparing for post-acquisition management. The most important of these decisions relate to board composition and key management appointments.

Before looking at the integration subject in more detail, it is worth considering the key reasons why acquisitions fail or succeed in delivering their value creation objectives.

Why acquisitions fail

10.2   Surveys on post-acquisition success come to strikingly similar conclusions. These are that acquisition is a high-risk growth strategy and that many buyers fail to achieve their objectives. Failure rates quoted in surveys vary considerably but those quoted by KPMG in their 1999 global research report on Corporate Mergers and Acquisitions are dramatic. They studied over 100 of the top 700 cross-border transactions between 1996 and 1998:

> 'We found that only 17% of deals had added value to the combined company, 30% produced no discernible difference, and as many as 53% actually destroyed value.'

The nature of an acquisition will impact the risk. For example, one would expect the risk in a large complex cross-border deal to be higher than that in a small domestic infill acquisition. However, average failure rates quoted in other studies frequently exceed 50%. The definition of failure is failure to meet the acquirer's objectives for the acquisition.

However the Private Equity Industry over the last 25 years has had a somewhat different record. There is obviously a range of performance but industry statistics in Europe and the US show net positive returns of between 10 and 20% per annum with upper quartile performers regularly delivering high twenties.

For those acquisitions that prove not to be successful, the consequences of failure may vary from a minor reputational blemish with minimal financial impact to a fatal blow for the company and destroyed reputations for its directors.

A summary of the key reasons provided in the many surveys would be:

- absence of a valid strategic rationale for the acquisition;

- failure to identify a fatal flaw in the opportunity assessment and due diligence phases;

- overpaying;

- inappropriate financial structure;

- poor cultural fit;

- inadequate communication;

- lack of clarity over the degree of integration that was to take place;

- failure to conduct a post-acquisition review to confirm the true position of target and the validity of the post-acquisition plan;

- unanticipated market conditions;

- failure to adapt the post-acquisition plan in the light of the post-acquisition review;

- mismatch between the post-acquisition plan and the organisational competence to execute it; and

- the thrill of the deal preventing the acquirer from allowing sufficient priority to maintaining the momentum of the business and the planning and execution of the post-acquisition plan.

When an acquisition fails it is seldom due to just one of the above factors.

Why acquisitions succeed

10.3   Most of the literature on acquisition 'success' concentrates on 'avoiding failure'. The presumption no doubt being that avoiding the characteristics of failure will boost the chances of success. However, merely avoiding failure is not enough. To be truly successful and gain maximum value from an acquisition requires more than avoidance of the pitfalls listed above. Apart from making the right judgement in terms of target, price and financial structure, value building buyers tend to focus and execute energetically on all of the following issues in their value creation plans:

- people;

- communication;

- market;

- operations; and

- finance.

They ensure control is achieved in each of these areas as soon as is possible. With regard to people, they strike the right balance between speed and rigour when it comes to changes to board composition, organisational structure, human resource policies and key management appointments. The issues around this are covered in para **10.5**.

Value building buyers also take a balanced view to communication. They communicate vigorously in an open, consistent and honest way to a set of clearly identified internal and external audiences. Communication issues are covered in more detail in para **10.6**.

Considerable emphasis is placed on understanding, managing and maximising the market opportunities arising out of the transaction and protecting and enhancing brand reputation.

When it comes to merging operations this is planned and executed in a way that takes account of risk and disruption, but seizes the operational benefits outlined in the post-acquisition plan as rapidly as possible.

Financial control of the acquired company and post-acquisition processes will be tightly monitored and financial information to the key decision makers and leaders will be clear, timely and accurate.

A final point to make here is that in any acquisition there are a large number of decisions to make. So it is always worth stepping back at the start of the process and thinking about what will be the key decisions, what should be the process for taking these decisions and then agreeing a clear process for taking them.

Degree of integration

10.4   The degree of integration which is relevant in an acquisition varies considerably and is dependent upon the strategic rationale for the deal and the key drivers of value creation in the investment case. For example, if the whole rationale is to achieve an extension of distribution channels and cost savings then there is likely to be a high degree of integration. Conversely, if the acquisition is in a new area of activity for the buyer it may be less. However, the real way to determine the degree of integration that is appropriate is to take the investment case, consider each of the key activities in both businesses and then make some judgements. A good investigation and due diligence process should provide the information to inform these decisions.

The key principles in managing the integration process are to:

* decide what matters;
* do what matters; and
* do what matters at the right time and in the right way.

Generally the choice of what to integrate comes from the following menu:

* people and human resource management processes;
* brands;

- marketing;
- sales processes;
- distribution channels;
- products and services;
- operations;
- financial systems; and
- research and development activities.

From a target company employee's point of view, the actions of the buyer and their evident priorities make a big impression. There is an opportunity for the buyer to change negative perceptions, to impress and to motivate. However, there is also the danger of doing the opposite. Every buyer should be conscious that impressions created are magnified and, for some, any action will be viewed through the prism of suspicion.

There will be choices to make with regard to each of the items on the menu above. It is important for the buyer to have a clear and well understood process for making decisions on the critical aspects of integration. This is especially the case when it comes to board composition. This is covered in more detail in para **10.5**.

An example to illustrate an approach to decision making on another critical aspect could be the 'IT decision'. In almost every acquisition a decision needs to be taken with regard to this. A buyer who demonstrates a high level of professionalism in determining what will be the right choice will not only reduce a key area of risk in acquisition but will also increase its chances of impressing and motivating employees, customers, suppliers and others. So how might a company approach making a decision on systems?

There are normally five broad options to choose from, namely to install:

(i)   the buyer's systems in the target;

(ii)   the target's systems in the buyer;

(iii)   a new 'off the shelf' suite of systems in the integrated business;

(iv)   a new 'bespoke' system in the integrated business; or

(v)   do nothing, ie leave existing separate systems in place in both businesses.

Within these broad options it might be possible to mix and match, but apart from the decision as to the main approach, the timing of implementation also needs to be considered. For example, is the buyer going to implement changes in systems as soon as possible, in a phased way, or only after a post-acquisition probationary period?

In some cases this decision over options (i) to (v) above is simple. If the buyer is of a much greater scale than the acquired company, is a frequent acquirer and the target has a similar profile to an existing activity of the buyer then it is most likely that the buyer will choose option (i). Indeed, it may even have a formal policy to do this even if the target's systems are better.

However, sometimes the case is less clear and a more detailed analysis needs to be undertaken. The first step in such an analysis is to determine the criteria upon which a decision will be made. These are likely to include some of the following:

- total cost of new systems including implementation costs;

- future cost of maintenance and support;

- competitive advantage or market benefit from system choice;

- increased efficiency;

- elapsed time to implement;

- senior management time required;

- disruption effects;

- execution risk and organisational competence to implement; and

- time to obsolescence of systems.

Having chosen the criteria the buyer will need to prioritise and then benchmark each of the two companies' systems against each criteria to make an informed judgement. One challenge in this and in many other acquisition integration decisions is that although some of the criteria can be measured quantitatively, others are purely qualitative and even those that can be measured quantitatively may not be on the same measure. To illustrate this by example suppose a buyer was faced with the following analysis.

	(a) Buyer's	(b) Target's	(c) New off the shelf	(d) New bespoke
Cost £m	30	50	80	100
Elapsed time (months)	4	6	8	10
Senior management time (months)	0.1	0.3	1	1.5
Disruption (a ranking)	1	3	2	4
Competitive advantage (a ranking)	4	3	2	1
Execution risk (a ranking)	1	3	2	4
Time to obsolescence (months)	20	30	48	48

In summary, option (a) is the cheapest and easiest to implement but not only will the buyer be missing an opportunity to have a better system itself, but it will also reduce the quality of its target's systems. If this does turn out to be the right thing to do the buyer has to address the impression that will inevitably be created in the target company that 'the buyer is not as systems savvy as we are and we're taking a step backwards. They're also demonstrating that they have nothing to learn from us'. Communication issues are covered in more detail in para **10.6**.

Another issue is that rankings don't give a sense of scale. The execution risk between options may be marginally higher or considerable.

Classic decision theory suggests that there are a number of steps which can be taken to simplify the decision. The buyer can express all options as a ranking for each of the criteria. In the case above the table becomes:

	(a) *Buyer's*	*(b)* *Target's*	*(c)* *New off the shelf*	*(d)* *New bespoke*
Cost £m	1	2	3	4
Elapsed time (months)	1	2	3	4
Senior management time (months)	1	2	3	4
Disruption (a ranking)	1	3	2	4
Competitive advantage (a ranking)	4	3	2	1
Execution risk (a ranking)	1	3	2	4
Time to obsolescence	3	2	1	1

If the decision maker is fortunate then there will be a 'dominating choice', that is one option which ranks ahead of all others on every criteria. In the example above, option (a), to put the buyer's systems into the target, is almost a 'dominating choice'. It might be a very straightforward step from here to a decision if the competitive advantage differences are only marginal and the buyer believes it is worth the cost to put his systems in for now and decide on a new system for both companies later. Equally, there may be an inferior choice under all criteria enabling it to be eliminated.

However, what happens if it isn't that straightforward? One approach is to try to put a value on qualitative issues and then to simply add or subtract them to the cost. For example, if the competitive advantage is real then at some point it ought to convert into sales and profit. An extra week of senior management time at a point when there is so much to do may carry a high cost, etc.

Another way of simplifying the decision is to cancel out criteria of equal importance where they favour competing options. This is known as an 'even swaps trade'. It is often when trying to make such trade offs that the real strength of emotion on a point becomes more obvious or apparent.

Whatever way the acquirer chooses to make these sorts of key decisions, what matters most is that the acquirer makes the best decision, finds it easy to articulate why and gains the commitment of those required to execute the decision and deliver the benefits envisaged.

People issues

10.5 Awareness of the 'people issues', an ability to deal with them and the discipline to give them sufficient priority throughout the process is critical to the success of post-acquisition management. So is striving as hard as possible to ensure that there is a robust process for making decisions on 'people issues' and that it is seen to be appropriate.

The specific issues and their relative significance vary considerably from acquisition to acquisition. A small infill deal may have no impact in terms of the board composition of the acquirer or may involve few changes of reporting line or redundancies. A larger purchase of a company of similar size or a merger of equals is likely to involve a larger number of more significant issues.

In acquisition situations the key 'people issues' tend to be the following:

- board composition and composition of sub committees of the board;

- senior management positions;

- organisational structure and reporting lines;

- human resource policies in general;

- employee terms and conditions especially where there are wide differences between remuneration levels for the same roles between the acquirer and the target;

- the policy with regard to selection for specific roles;

- combining trade union arrangements;

- cultural differences between the companies involved;

- where relevant, issues arising out of downsizings; and

- whether the company needs external input to help manage the integration process, eg specialist human resource, remuneration or communication consultants.

Many of these issues arise when there is a divergence between personal and corporate objectives and this can happen for individuals on both sides of the deal. Sometimes the reputation of the acquirer's behaviour in previous purchases sets unhelpful expectations. A classic example of this latter point arose when the Royal Bank of Scotland (RBS) took over NatWest bank, widely regarded as a highly successful acquisition. The fact that the RBS Chief Executive was known by many in the industry as 'Fred the shred' undoubtedly set an expectation amongst staff in NatWest prior to the deal. RBS did indeed take out significant costs and did reduce the workforce considerably. It made no secret that this would happen if it was successful in its bid. However, the manner in which they achieved the savings and staff reductions was reported as highly professional and far from brutal.

With respect to board composition the roles to focus on first of all are those of the Chairman, Chief Executive, Finance Director and, if a public company, the Senior Independent Director. The decision-making process is normally a combination of the 'perfect world' and 'reality'. The 'perfect world' would be specifying the ideal board for the combined company and 'the reality', a deal struck between parties during the negotiation of the transaction. The balance of power in the negotiations will clearly impact the outcome.

The acquirer has to decide whether to have a 'best person for the job' policy for board and other senior appointments or not. It can be tough to do this if it means going outside to fill a position or if excellent people in the acquirer lose their positions to those in the target. Those in the target company tend to be pragmatic in takeover situations and expect to lose out in any competition with someone from the acquirer. Consequently, the acquirer can reap big motivational benefits if it does choose some of the target's people over its established staff. Whatever approach is taken it needs to be clearly understood and managed tightly. If the two companies have been in competition before it can prove to be even harder.

In a small private company where the Chairman is the major shareholder the decision process is usually very straightforward. The Chairman is the decision maker. However, in order to gain buy in from others they may decide to set up a brief consultation process or seek external advice. In a public company where the relative size of the acquirer and target are close, a small committee would be formed for the specific purpose. A very thorough assessment would be made of potential candidates for each role and external professional input would be sought.

If the board is to be restructured and as a result there are board members leaving it is generally best to deal with this as early as possible. Clarity about who is on the board, who is in what role and who has what authority is essential. The timespan of uncertainty and anxiety should be kept to the minimum. Some Chairmen see a significant acquisition as an opportunity to advance their own or others' retirement or perhaps to trade up the quality of the board. There are situations where the Chairman of the acquirer, though excellent for a company of its scale and complexity before the addition of the target, is not a natural fit for an enlarged group.

Differences in the composition, level and structure of remuneration between an acquirer and target may generate a number of other issues to deal with. Where the target and the acquirer are based in different countries this could simply be due to cultural differences. Many European businesses have found this on acquiring in the United States. The 'merger' of the automotive giants Daimler and Chrysler in 1998 is a dramatic example. It was reported that Daimler's Chief Executive, Jurgen Schremp, earnt around $2m in the year before the deal, about one eighth of that earnt by Robert Eaton, the head of Chrysler.

Whether it is the level of overall pay or the manner in which it is paid, the acquirer needs to have thought through how it is going to deal with these issues. For example, is it going to harmonise pay and conditions or not? It also needs to establish a clear process for decision making on remuneration issues and ensure that individual managers and, where relevant, union officials understand how decisions are to be made and communicated across the new organisation.

Pensions have become a growing challenge for corporations around the world and can turn out to be a 'deal breaker' in many potential deals. **Chapter 9 Pensions Aspects of Acquisitions** covers pensions issues in considerable detail. Suffice to say here that the buyer must recognise the anxiety and sensitivity of employees when it comes to pensions issues and understand properly the liabilities it is assuming upon a takeover. To be able to do this it will need to take professional advice.

Communication

10.6   The volume of work that is required to make any acquisition succeed is high. There are a large number of people involved and there is considerable potential for misunderstanding. It is, therefore, unsurprising that many of the studies on acquisitions highlight good communications as a key ingredient for success. The way that communications are managed is also an important component of corporate culture and has a significant bearing on the acquirer's ability to maintain the most important relationships. So the acquirer's approach to managing communications through the acquisition process and as part of post-acquisition management matters a great deal. This is especially the case if achieving a common culture as quickly as possible is an important objective.

If communication has been effective during the initial phases of the acquisition there should be a positive momentum and mood in the target company and a good platform from which to move forward as soon as the deal is announced. If, however, morale in the target is low and there is an air of deep suspicion or impending doom then unless the buyer plans to remove most of the staff in the target, they are likely to face a tough challenge implementing change.

In most acquisitions the buyer will need to communicate the following upon legal completion of the transaction:

- that the acquisition has taken place; and
- its intentions for reorganising the target and/or its existing business; and
- internally who needs to do what.

It may or may not want to, or be required to, communicate the terms upon which it has acquired the target.

Once the initial announcement has taken place the serious work of communicating in detail internally and externally to all the relevant audience groups begins.

In the pre-acquisition planning someone will have been given overall responsibility for planning internal and external communications and helping to organise and review them throughout the process. The leader of the communications function in the acquirer is the most likely candidate to be this person. If the deal is 'friendly' in nature then at the relevant point a senior person from the target company will be given a 'co-ordination' role.

When putting together the overall plan the 'communications' leader will have defined a series of key events. They will have prepared a list of key messages to be delivered to each of the audiences which need to be addressed, as well as ensuring that there is buy in from the relevant leaders. Questions will be anticipated and answers prepared to test whether the messages are robust and will bear scrutiny. They will be conscious that there is a wide range of channels through which they can communicate from direct face-to-face conversation to indirect communication via the press. The best will also be alive to the fact that communication is not a one-way exercise and ensure that there are good opportunities for feedback to acquisition activity leaders to enable them to refine their planning and actions.

Experienced communication professionals also have a good idea of the most efficient and cost effective processes and will be able to balance their objectives in terms of quality, speed and cost. Their overarching aim is to ensure that the acquiring company's communications are excellent in terms of clarity, relevance and style, reinforce the actions being taken and maximise the chances of the buyer achieving its strategic objectives for the acquisition. In addition, they will seek to minimise the chances of miscommunication or an error in communications which might undermine credibility.

Before looking at some of the key events and the issues surrounding them, it is worth considering the list of potential audiences or groups of people involved as a result of an acquisition:

- the acquisition leadership and integration teams themselves;
- shareholders;
- customers, including potential customers;
- employees, including potential former employees where relevant;
- unions;
- suppliers, including advisers and providers of finance;
- partnership or joint venture organisations;
- regulatory bodies and trade organisations;
- press and media;
- if public, analysts and other stock market audiences;
- government;
- non-governmental organisations;
- charities and organisations being sponsored; and
- organisations being sponsored.

The key events which will need to be communicated are:

- the initial announcement;

- each key integration activity;

- board, senior management or other key personnel changes;

- changes to organisational structure; and

- changes to employee terms and conditions.

It is also important to regularly communicate how the acquisition is progressing. The best way to do this is to publish a plan of key objectives and the steps planned along the way then to provide regular updates. This can be very helpful in building momentum and morale, especially if it is honest and recognises challenges and issues as well as successes. It is certainly more motivational to staff than silence or 'constant spin' and a failure to acknowledge any problems or issues which need to be dealt with. Doing this also provides a mechanism for setting and refining expectations. Many acquirers today use a 'first hundred days plan' as a simple way of achieving this.

For each audience and event it is likely that a simple matrix will be drawn up containing the following columns for each audience grouping:

- key messages;

- timing;

- method/s or channel/s to be used; and

- primary responsibility for managing communication to this group.

The 'communications' leader will then help the overall acquisition team leader to ensure that everybody involved in the communication process knows what they are expected to do and is equipped to do it. This may mean that some people need training or to visit other organisations who have been through the same process.

When it comes to methods or channels of communication it seems that today there is a bewildering array of choice. The speed and convenience of the internet have made it easier to communicate with large numbers of people in different locations with great speed either through text, voice or video. A consequence of this is that there is an expectation that communication will be rapid and if it is not then people can use the same technology to speculate. Any acquirer today must, therefore, be ready to communicate with great speed through its corporate website and additionally in a tailored way to specific audience groups through portals, intranets or other web-based systems. If the company is public a high-quality investor relations website makes the process so much easier.

In making full use of technology the acquirer must recognise that the most powerful communication is face-to-face contact. Powerful in a positive sense if it is done well and powerful in terms of potential damage if it appears rushed, insensitive or unprofessional in any other way. A cascade of personal briefings remains a popular choice for many acquirers, partly because it provides the opportunity to see reactions, take questions and deal with any potential misunderstandings as they arise. In order for a cascade approach to work there needs to be considerable effort put into preparing presentations and question and answer briefing sheets for those leading the briefings. Those giving briefings need to take ownership for what they are saying.

A final point with respect to methods of communication is an obvious one, but often forgotten. The acquirer should use methods which they are good at and avoid the desire to take big risks and experiment with a new approach unless they have prepared exhaustively and have taken full account of the systems capability of both companies.

Common communication issues which emerge during the post-acquisition phase include:

- overselling the benefits of the acquisition internally and externally;
- inconsistency in messages given to different audience groups;
- gaps between words and actions;
- over broadcast and under listening, which if combined with 'conquering hero syndrome' can quickly destroy morale amongst target company employees;
- not enough time is put into basic bonding communications;
- dominance of the acquirer inhibiting knowledge sharing behaviour;
- the cost and time involved in good communication is underestimated;
- underestimating the importance of logistics and timing in communication;
- in international acquisitions a lack of understanding of cultural differences;
- failure by key players to acknowledge and debate critical but sensitive issues; and
- over focus on internal issues at the expense of customers.

The best at the art of integration avoid these problems. They test how they are doing by making sure there are good feedback loops, they acknowledge challenges honestly and quickly and find and communicate ways to address them. They have a master plan and communicate superbly themselves but delegate to individual leaders, recognising that everyone will be very busy through the initial post-acquisition period. In their eyes, a fundamental element of leadership is to communicate and that goes for the leaders who work for them.

They also possess the ability to 'thought bubble' think, in that they have the sensitivity or antennae to hear what people are thinking as well as what they might say and are able to spot any anxieties or discomfort. Having spotted a potential conflict situation they then set about resolving it.

One aspect of communications which has grown in importance in acquisitions is that of public relations and the media. An acquisition should represent an item of positive news flow and if well handled can enhance a company's reputation. It is clear that General Electric under Jack Welch and his successor Jeff Immelt seeks to maximise the PR impact of acquisitions for the benefit of divisions and the group itself. It was also clear that the Royal Bank of Scotland's profile and reputation grew significantly as a result of the press coverage of its acquisition of National Westminster and it used this to position itself as a well run business in a broader sense.

In raising the profile of the company through an acquisition there is, however, the attendant risk of making people aware of failure if the company mishandles the communication or the acquisition is fundamentally flawed for some reason. There are numerous high-profile examples of this from every decade.

If an acquirer does want to maximise the press impact of a particular transaction to enhance its reputation, then it will need to have a clear set of messages it wants to get across and a limited and defined group of spokespeople who are well trained and prepared to deliver them. Uncertain spokespeople provide uncertain messages, so it is important that the company selects those who are best at communicating with the press. Although many business unit leaders possess excellent media skills, the acquirer should not assume that they do. It should in any event be training and preparing those it intends to put in front of the press.

However much planning and preparation takes place there are bound to be unforeseen issues emerging throughout the post-acquisition phase. It is important, therefore, that whoever is managing the overall communications process has a mechanism for gaining visibility of these issues early enough and the character to be able to act in a calm manner under pressure.

Chapter 11

Regulatory Aspects of Acquisitions in the EU

At a glance

- Concentrations which satisfy the turnover thresholds in the EU *Merger Regulation* must be pre-notified for clearance to the European Commission ('Commission').

- The notified transaction must be suspended until it has been cleared by the Commission except in certain defined circumstances.

- Following receipt of the notification, the Commission has an initial consideration period of 25 working days (which can be extended to 35 days in certain circumstances) to conduct an investigation. At the end of this initial period, known as Phase I, the Commission has the power to clear the transaction (with or without commitments) or initiate a more detailed second stage of investigation, known as Phase II, if it has 'serious doubts' as to the mergers' effect on competition in the common market. The standard Phase II investigation period is 90 working days (105 working days where the parties offer commitments). This can be extended by 20 working days in complex cases at the request of the parties. At the conclusion of the Phase II investigation the Commission may declare that the concentration is incompatible with the common market and prohibit the merger, grant conditional clearance subject to commitments or undertakings, or clear the merger proposal in its entirety.

- The substantive test is whether the concentration 'significantly impede(s) effective competition in the common market or in a substantial part of it, in particular as a result of the creation or strengthening of a dominant position' (*Article 2(2)*).

- Failure to comply with the provisions of the *Merger Regulation* can result in severe penalties including the imposition of substantial fines up to 10% of the worldwide turnover of the undertakings concerned. If the transaction has been put into effect it will be illegal and void.

- Mergers subject to the *Merger Regulation* are not subject to national merger control legislation of the individual EU Member States. Where a merger has a cross-border effect, clearance under the *Merger Regulation* operates as a 'one-stop-shop'.

- In the event that the *Merger Regulation* does not apply, the application of national merger control legislation of EU Member States needs to be assessed in those jurisdictions where the parties to the transaction have a presence.

- In the context of multinational merger transactions, the application of US anti-trust and merger control legislation needs to be considered by the parties at an early stage to assess any relevant filing requirements.

Introduction

11.1   Council Regulation (EC) No 139/2004 (*Merger Regulation*) was adopted on 20 January 2004 and replaces Regulation 4064/89 from 1 May 2004. The revised *Merger Regulation* has made changes both to the substantive and procedural provisions.

In this chapter we will look in detail at the mandatory pre-notification as required by EU law of 'concentrations having a Community Dimension'. We will also briefly describe the requirements under the European Area Agreement ('EEA'), though note that this currently only applies to Norway, Iceland and Liechtenstein.

Mergers falling outside the scope of the EU or EEA controls are still subject to national merger control legislation. Therefore, we provide a comparative analysis of national merger control laws of countries within the European Union, referring to the following countries: France, Finland, Germany, Italy, Spain, the Netherlands, Ireland, Sweden, Czech Republic, Hungary, Poland and the United Kingdom, but with particular reference to the UK. Given the importance of the US market, we have also supplied an outline of US merger control legislation. A review of the EFTA countries merger control legislation is outside the scope of this chapter.

EU merger control

11.2   In December 1989 the European Commission was granted exclusive competence to investigate large-scale mergers and takeovers under the previous *Merger Regulation*. Its provisions came into force on 21 September 1990 and were amended with effect from 1 March 1998. The new *Merger Regulation* was adopted on 29 January 2004 and came into force on 1 May 2004, timed to coincide with the enlargement of the European Union to 25

Member States. It was decided that rather than substantially amend the previous *Merger Regulation* it should be redrafted completely to aid clarity. It should be noted that special merger rules currently govern the Atomic Energy industry under the Euratom Treaty. The alternative regime for coal and steel products under the European Coal and Steel Treaty ended with the expiry of the Treaty on 23 November 2003. Concentrations in these industries are now covered by the *Merger Regulation*.

Since the *Merger Regulation*'s implementation, the European Commission has considered (as at 31 December 2006) a total of 3,266 merger cases, of which only 19 have been prohibited. It is interesting to track the increase in the number of cases notified under the *Merger Regulation*. In 1993, 58 cases were notified. This had risen to 131 cases in 1996, whilst 298 cases were notified in 1999. Merger activity seemed to reach a peak in 2001 with 335 cases notified. The number of cases notified changed in 2002 was 277, in 2003, 211, in 2004, 246, in 2005, 313. In 2006, the Commission reviewed an all-time record 356 cross-border merger cases.

Principal aims

11.3   The *Merger Regulation* was the first step towards the establishment of a broader European Union role in the policing of mergers. Although many commentators did caution against giving the Commission extensive powers in this area, wider EU controls were inevitable with the completion of the Single European Market. Without the uniform assessment of mergers having Union-wide implications, the regulation of mergers could vary between national markets with the various national authorities applying different criteria and taking account of different interests. The principal aims of the previous *Merger Regulation* which were continued into the current Merger Regulation therefore were to:

(a)   provide an end to the double jeopardy system to clearance by national as well as EU competition authorities and create a 'one-stop-shop';

(b)   lay down time limits for vetting mergers (these were made more flexible under the new *Merger Regulation* particularly in complex cases which go to a Phase II investigation in order to allow time for finding appropriate remedies); and

(c)   specify uniform criteria for the assessment of mergers.

General issues

11.4   The previous *Merger Regulation* was criticised on the basis that the high qualifying thresholds only gave limited scope for review. These thresholds were extended as part of the March 1998 amendments. The thresholds remain the same under the new *Merger Regulation*. In any event, as demonstrated by the increasing number of cases being notified to the Commission, many mergers do fall within the scope of the *Merger Regulation*.

The principle of 'one-stop-shopping' can be compromised to a certain extent by the ability of Member States to apply their own national procedures in certain cases subject to liaising with the Commission.

History

11.5   Unlike the former European Coal and Steel Community Treaty, there is no Article in the Treaty of Rome giving the Commission express power to vet mergers. In its judgment in the case of *Continental Can v European Commission*, Case 6/72 (1973) ECR 215, the European Court of Justice ('ECJ') decided that the Commission could deal with mergers under *Article 82* (*Article 86*) of the *Treaty of Rome* as a structural abuse of a dominant position. However, dominance was often difficult to prove and the Commission did not have power to review and condemn mergers prior to completion. In 1988 the judgment of the ECJ in the *Philip Morris* case (Cases 142 and 156/84 (1987) ECR 4487*) seemed* to open up the possibility of applying *Article 81(1)* (*Article 85(1)*) to mergers as well. The possible broadening of the Commission's merger powers after *Philip Morris* and their threat to put these powers into effect increased pressure on the Member States to act decisively on merger control and caused them to review the merger proposals previously blocked in the Council of Ministers since 1973. This resulted in the *Old Merger Regulation* being introduced in 1989.

The amendments effective from March 1998 were primarily aimed at addressing issues that had become apparent since the introduction of the *Merger Regulation*. The main change was to broaden the scope of the *Merger Regulation* to cover *all* full function joint ventures that attain a Community Dimension. This is different to the pre-amendment regime which distinguished between 'concentrative' and 'co-operative' joint ventures, with only the former falling within the previous *Merger Regulation*.

The new *Merger Regulation* affects both the substantive provisions and those dealing with procedure. Major changes include the following:

(a)   improved ability for firms who are a party to a merger which is not covered by the jurisdictional test and who would have to notify in three or more Member States to seek treatment under the 'one-stop-shop' principle before the Commission;

(b)   improved recourse to referral to national authorities in situations where competition will be significantly affected on a national market;

(c)   no requirement for binding merger agreement as a pre-condition of notification. It is sufficient for parties to demonstrate a genuine intention to form a concentration;

(d)   more flexible timetables for investigation, particularly in complex cases which go to a Phase II investigation in order to allow time for finding appropriate remedies; and

(e)   the Commission was given strengthened enforcement powers when carrying out investigations and to deal with cases where parties fail to meet the conditions of commitment given to the Commission, or where clearance is obtained by using false information.

The Merger Regulation

11.6   The *Merger Regulation* applies to 'concentrations with a Community dimension', the meaning of which will be analysed in the following sections. The new *Merger Regulation* is accompanied by an Implementing Regulation (Regulation EC 802/2004 (the '*Implementing Regulation*') and a number of Commission Notices (listed below) that explain various aspects of the European merger control regime The Commission launched, on 28 September 2006, a public consultation on a draft Commission Consolidated Jurisdictional Notice under the *Merger Regulation*).

The new consolidated Jurisdictional Notice is intended to replace the current four jurisdictional Notices, all adopted by the Commission in 1998 under the previous *Merger Regulation*: These are:

(a)   the Notice on the concept of concentration (OJ C 66, 02.03.1998, p. 5),

(b)   the Notice on the concept of full-function joint ventures (OJ C 66, 02.03.1998, p.1),

(c)   the Notice on the concept of undertakings concerned (OJ C 66, 02.03.1998, p.14); and

(d)   the Notice on calculation of turnover (OJ C 66, 02.03.1998, p.25).

The draft consolidated Notice therefore covers a wide range of issues of jurisdiction relevant for establishing the Commission's competence under the *Merger Regulation*. However, these four Notices will stay in force until the new Notice is adopted by the Commission and are therefore referred to accordingly in this chapter.

The proposed consolidated Notice has been undertaken for several reasons including to:

(a)   make the Notice more user-friendly and allow parties to establish more easily whether the Commission is competent for an envisaged transaction;

(b)   take into account the changes introduced by the new Merger Regulation in relation to jurisdictional issues, incorporate recent case-law and update Commission established practice on jurisdictional issues.

The draft Notice clarifies, for example, the conditions under which several transactions constitute a single notifiable concentration under the Merger Regulation. It also attempts to clarify the circumstances in which a concentration arises if a company outsources the provision of service or the production of goods to a third party.

Concentrations

11.7   The *Merger Regulation* applies to 'concentrations'. These are defined in *Article 3* of the *Merger Regulation* as existing where there is a 'change in control on a lasting basis'. This covers the following scenarios:

(a)   where two or more previously independent undertakings merge; or

(b)   either:

(i)   one or more persons already controlling at least one undertaking, or

(ii)   one or more undertakings,

acquire, whether by the purchase of shares or assets, by contract or by any other means direct or indirect control of the whole or part of any one or more other undertakings.

The creation of a joint venture, performing on a lasting basis all the functions of an autonomous economic entity, is also a 'concentration' under the *Merger Regulation*.

The Commission's *Notice on the Concept of a Concentration* (OJ CO66 02/03/99) ('Notice on Concentration') provides guidance as to how the Commission interprets the term 'concentration'.

The Notice on Concentration categorises concentrations using the two limbs in *Article 3* (as set out above).

Mergers between previously independent undertakings

11.8   This limb covers circumstances such as when two or more independent undertakings amalgamate into a new undertaking and cease to exist as separate legal entities, or where one undertaking is absorbed by another. A merger within this limb of the definition may also occur by the combining of the activities of independent undertakings to form a common economic unit, for example by way of contract. The prerequisite for the determination of a common economic unit is the existence of a permanent, single economic management. Other relevant factors may include internal profit and loss compensation as between the various undertakings within the group, and their joint liability externally.

Acquisition of control

11.9   Whether an operation gives rise to an acquisition of control depends on a number of legal and/or factual elements. There are extensive guidelines in the Notice on Concentration as to what constitutes 'control'. Control can be acquired by either one undertaking or by two or more acting jointly.

The taking of a minority shareholding in an undertaking may constitute a concentration for the purposes of the *Merger Regulation* if the new shareholder acquires a possibility of exercising a decisive influence on that company's activity. If the effect of acquiring a minority shareholding brings about a situation in which the company is jointly controlled by two or more persons then the *Merger Regulation* could apply.

Sometimes separate undertakings are brought closer together by exchanging shareholdings in each other. Such influences can secure industrial or commercial co-operation. They may also give rise to a merger. Since the implementation of the *Merger Regulation*, the subject of cross shareholding has arisen in several cases. In the *Renault/Volvo* case (Case No. IV/M004) each company took 25% and 45% stakes in the other's car, bus and truck businesses. The Commission considered that the high level of shareholding in the bus and truck link-up led to a concentration as the businesses could not operate independently of each other. Common membership of boards of directors of various undertakings can also be assessed in a like manner to cross shareholdings.

Article 3(5) sets out the three situations in which the acquisition of controlling interest does not constitute a concentration under the *Merger Regulation*. These are as follows:

(a)   financial institutions the normal activities of which include dealing in securities for their own account or for the account of others, where such holdings are temporary and held with a view to reselling;

(b)   where control is acquired by an office-holder under the laws of a Member State relating to liquidation, insolvency and the like; and

(c)   where a financial holding company within the meaning of the Fourth Council Directive (78/660/EEC) acquires control, provided the company only exercises its control to maintain the full value of its investment and not to otherwise determine directly or indirectly the strategic commercial conduct of the controlled undertaking.

Joint ventures

11.10   Until the 1998 amendments to the previous *Merger Regulation* a distinction was drawn between joint ventures that were 'co-operative' and those that were 'concentrative', with the former falling outside the *Merger Regulation* though still liable to be considered under *Articles 81* and *82* of the Treaty of Rome. However, the amendments ended this distinction, and now all joint ventures which 'perform on a lasting basis all the functions of an autonomous economic entity' will constitute a concentration. This was carried through into the new *Merger Regulation*. Note that the co-operative effects of such a joint venture will still be assessed under *Article 81(1)* (*Article 85(1)*), at the same time as the concentration is being assessed. This is discussed further at **11.13** below.

There are two essential characteristics of a joint venture which is deemed to be a 'concentration' and therefore to fall within the *Merger Regulation*. These characteristics are:

(a)   there is an acquisition of joint control by two or more undertakings; and

(b)   the joint venture must perform, on a lasting basis, all the functions of an autonomous economic entity.

These elements are discussed briefly below.

Joint control

11.11   The concept of 'control' is set out in *Article 3(3)*. This provides that control is based on the possibility of exercising decisive influence over an undertaking, and is usually determined by both legal and factual considerations. Joint ventures are generally controlled by two or more parent companies which set up the joint venture to pursue some defined economic activity on a lasting basis. The parents can exercise control over the joint venture in a number of ways. For example, the parents can exercise ownership rights over the joint venture's assets, exercise influence over the composition, voting or decisions of the joint venture's board of directors, or rely on the express provisions in the shareholders' agreement concerning the running of the joint venture.

Joint control is not deemed to exist where one of the parent companies is capable of determining the joint venture's commercial policy alone. This situation will arise where one party has a majority shareholding with the minority shareholder enjoying few rights. The Commission's Notice on Concentration details the factors to consider when determining whether or not joint control exists. For example, the Notice on Concentration sets out the type of minority protection rights which will allow minority shareholders to enjoy a position of joint control. These are the power to have an effective veto over important business decisions such as the joint venture's business plan and/or annual budget, major investments and/or the appointment of senior management. There also exist a number of other veto rights related to specific decisions which may be important in the context of the particular market of the joint venture (eg the type of technology to be used by the joint venture, when that may be a key feature of the joint venture's activities). By contrast, joint control will not be acquired by a minority shareholder if the rights he or she is given merely seek to protect the minority's financial investment (eg rights of pre-emption, non-dilution etc.).

The Commission's decisions under the *Merger Regulation* give some guidance as to what kind of minority shareholding rights are considered important enough to establish joint control:

(a)   approval of annual budgets (*Case No. IV/MOJO Conogna/Idea*);

(b)   middle and long-term strategy for the joint venture (*Case No. IV/M097 Pechiney/Ustinov-Sacllov*);

(c)   the development of new products and services and the entry into financially important contracts (*Case No. IV/M076 Lyonnaise des Eata Dumez/Biochiev*);

(d) approval of detailed budgets, appointment of members of the board and members of controlling bodies (*Case No. IV/M012 Varta/Bosch*);

(e) approval of, and material changes to, the long-term (three to five years) and annual business plans (*Case No. IV/M121 IngersollRand/Dresner*);

(f) approval of changes of a joint venture's corporate objectives, major capital investments or disposal of assets (*Case No. IV/MJO1 Drageri IBM/HMP*); and

(g) purchase and sale of plants and assumption of financial engagements (*Case No. IV/M062 Eridonia/ISI*).

Autonomous economic entity

11.12 This criterion essentially means that the joint venture must enter its relevant market on a lasting basis (eg for an unlimited period or for a long time) and be independent from its parents. Guidelines in relation to the interpretation of this requirement are set out in the *Commission Notice on the Concept of Full Function Joint Ventures* (OJ CO66 02/03/1998). The joint venture must have sufficient financial and other resources including finance, staff and assets in order to operate a business activity on a lasting basis. Therefore, the principal determining factors will be whether the parent companies transfer an existing undertaking or business to the joint venture or give it substantial technical or commercial know-how so that it can survive by its own means. Joint ventures which satisfy this requirement are commonly described as 'full function' joint ventures.

A joint venture is not a full function joint venture if it only takes over one specific function within the parent companies' business activities without access to the market. This may be the case where, for example, joint ventures are limited to R & D or manufacture. These joint ventures will be auxiliary to their parents' activities. This will also be the case where the joint venture is limited to distribution or sales of parent companies' products. However, the joint venture can still be regarded as full function if it uses its parent companies' distribution network or outlets for its products where they are acting as sales agents for the joint venture.

Where parent companies are active in upstream or downstream markets, this is a factor to be considered when assessing the full function character of the joint venture where this presence leads to substantial sales or purchases between parent companies and the joint venture. If a significant amount of sales are made to the parent companies by the joint venture in the initial start-up period, this will not prejudice its status as a full function joint venture, although the period should normally not exceed three years.

Where sales from the joint venture to the parents are intended to be made on a lasting basis, the essential question is whether, regardless of these sales, the joint venture is geared to play an active independent role on the market. Therefore the relative proportion of these sales compared with the total production of the joint venture is an important factor. Another consideration is whether the sales to the parent companies are made on the basis of normal commercial conditions. For example, in the *BASF/Shell* case (Case IV. M.1041, 23/12/97 – OJ [1998] C81/5) the parent companies entered into a joint venture to create a company to combine their polyethylene works. Whilst the joint venture company bought its raw products from the parents, and used premises and plant on their sites, the Commission still considered it to be autonomous as it had some of its own plant and 70% of its turnover came from sales to third parties. It was also free to source additional products from third parties.

To be a full function joint venture, the joint venture must add value to purchases made by it from its parents. The full function character is questionable if little or no value is added to the products or services concerned at the level of the joint venture itself. The joint venture in this case is closer to a joint sales agency.

However, if the joint venture is active in a market in which goods are commonly traded in this manner by other non-vertically integrated companies, and it acquires a substantial proportion of its supplies from other competing sources (*Spar/Dansk Supermarket* Case No. IV/M 179, 3/2/92 OJ [1994] C134), it will still constitute a full function joint venture.

Other factors to be borne in mind when assessing the lasting nature of a joint venture are dissolution provisions and specific contractual terms for the duration of the venture. The inclusion of terms in a joint venture agreement providing for certain contingencies (eg the failure of the joint venture or fundamental disagreement as between the parties) will not prevent the joint venture from being considered as operating on a lasting basis.

Where an agreement specifies that the joint venture will last for a definite duration, this will not undermine its claim to carry out its activities on a lasting basis as long as the period is sufficiently long to bring about a lasting change in the structure of the undertaking concerned. In *Go Ahead/VIA/Thameslink* (Case IV/M.901, 24/4/97 OJ [1997] C253/2) the Commission decided that even though the joint venture was to last for only seven years, it could still be regarded as an autonomous economic entity since it still possessed all of the resources needed to carry out its operations on a lasting operational basis.

Other aspects of joint ventures to consider

11.13   *Co-operative effects:* The creation of a full function joint venture may as a direct consequence lead to the co-ordination of the competitive behaviour of undertakings that remain independent. In such cases, *Article 2(4)* of the *Merger Regulation* provides that those co-operative effects will be assessed within the same procedure as the concentration. This assessment will be made in accordance with the criteria of *Article 81(1)* and *(3)* (*Article 85(1)* and *(3)*) of the Treaty, with a view to establishing whether or not the operation is compatible with the common market.

Ancillary restraints: Restrictions accepted by the parent companies of the joint venture that are directly related and necessary for the implementation of the concentration are known as ancillary restrictions and will be assessed together with the concentration itself. Ancillary restraints are discussed further at **11.35** below.

Community Dimension

11.14   As stated in the introduction, the *Merger Regulation* requires notification of concentrations having a 'Community Dimension'. These thresholds have not changed from the previous *Merger Regulation*.

Under *Article 1*, a concentration has a Community Dimension where:

(a)   the combined aggregate worldwide turnover of all the undertakings concerned is more than €5 billion (approximately £3.3 billion); and

(b)   each of at least two of the undertakings concerned has an overall EC turnover of more than €250 million (approximately £164 million),

unless each of the undertakings concerned achieves more than two thirds of its aggregate Community-wide turnover within one and the same Member State.

Article 1(3) goes on to provide circumstances in which a concentration has a Community Dimension, notwithstanding that it does not meet the thresholds described above. These additional circumstances are as follows:

(i)   the combined aggregate worldwide turnover of all the undertakings concerned is more than €2.5 billion (approximately £1.65 billion);

(ii)   in each of at least three Member States, the combined aggregate turnover of all the undertakings concerned is more than €100 million (approximately £67 million);

(iii)   in each of at least three Member States included for the purpose of point (*b*), the aggregate turnover of each of at least two of the undertakings concerned is more than €25 million (approximately £16 million); and

(iv)   the aggregate Community-wide turnover of at least two of the undertakings concerned is more than €100 million (approximately £67 million),

unless each of the undertakings concerned achieves more than two-thirds of its aggregate Community-wide turnover within one and the same Member State.

When the turnover test is met, the Commission has jurisdiction over the transaction, save in the following situations:

(A)   A national competition authority of a Member State makes a request to the Commission that the whole or part of the notified transaction is referred.

(B)   The parties make a request to the Commission (during the pre-notification stage explained below at **11.18**) that a national competition authority of a Member State has jurisdiction in a situation where the
concentration may significantly affect competition in a distinct market
within that member State (and does not have significant cross-border
effects in other Member States)

The transaction raises certain national public policy issues.

Where the turnover test is not met, the national competition authority will
have jurisdiction. However there are some exceptions to the rule. The
Commission may still exercise jurisdiction in the following situations:

- *Article 22* of the *Merger Regulation* allows the Commission to act upon
  a concentration (even in the absence of a 'Community Dimension')
  when requested to do so by a Member State. This clause was inserted
  into the *Old Merger Regulation* because at the time it was adopted
  some national authorities did not have the power to investigate concentrations. In addition, the clause is sometimes used where there are significant cross-border aspects which the Commission is in a better
  position to assess.

  By way of example, two cases from 1997 – *Kesko/Tuko* (Case IV/M
  784, 20/11/96 – OJ [1997] LI10/53) concerning two retail chains in
  Finland and *Blokker/Toys 'R' Us (Case IV/M.890, 26/6/97 – OJ [1998]
  L316/1*) concerning the Dutch toy market – did not have a Community
  Dimension yet they were considered by the Commission following
  requests by (respectively) the Finnish and Dutch authorities.

- *Article 4(5)* allows the parties to make a request to the Commission in
  a situation where the transaction would otherwise have to be notified in
  at least three member States and upon approval by the relevant national
  competition authorities. This was not possible under the previous
  Merger Regulation.

'Undertaking concerned'

11.15   Further guidance on what constitutes an 'undertaking concerned' is
set out in the Commission's *Notice on the Concept of Undertakings
Concerned* (OJ C66, 02/03/98). The Notice deals with a number of situations
relating to mergers and acquisition of sole control and joint control, and elab-
orates upon the general guidance set out in the *Merger Regulation* itself. The
situation in each of these transactions is as follows.

(a)   *Mergers:* Where several previously independent companies combine to
create a new company or, while remaining separate, create a single economic unit, the undertakings concerned will be each of the merging
entities.

(b)   *Acquisition of sole control of whole company:* The undertakings concerned will be the acquiring company and the acquired or target company.

(c) *Acquisition of sole control of part of a company:* Where an undertaking buys part of a business, the undertakings concerned will be the acquirer and the acquired part of the target company. There is also a creeping control provision which provides that where several acquisitions of parts by the same purchaser from the same seller occur within a two-year period, these transactions shall be treated as one and the same operation. In that event, the undertakings concerned are the acquirer and the different acquired part of the target company taken as a whole.

(d) *Acquisition of sole control through a subsidiary of a group:* Where a target company is acquired by a group through one of its subsidiaries, the undertakings concerned will be the target company and the acquiring group.

(e) *Acquisition of joint control of a newly created company:* In this case the undertakings concerned are each of the companies acquiring control of the new joint venture. As the joint venture does not yet exist and has no turnover, it cannot be considered as an undertaking concerned.

(f) *Acquisition of joint control of a pre-existing company:* Where there is acquisition of joint control of a pre-existing company or business, the undertakings concerned are each of the companies acquiring control on the one hand, and the acquired company on the other hand. Where the existing company was under the sole control of one company, and then one or several shareholders acquire joint control although the initial parent remains, the undertakings concerned are the jointly controlling companies (including the initial shareholder) and the target company.

(g) *Acquisition of joint control to split assets:* If several undertakings come together solely for the purpose of acquiring another company and agree to divide it up according to a pre-existing plan immediately on completion, there is no effective concentration of economic power between the acquiring companies and the target company. This involves a number of operations for the purposes of the *Merger Regulation*. For each of them the undertakings concerned will be the acquiring company and that part of the target being acquired.

(h) *Acquisition of control by a joint venture:* Where a joint venture acquires control of another company, there are two possible interpretations. The undertakings concerned could be the joint venture as a single body and the target. This will be the case where the joint venture is a full function joint venture as described at **11.10** above. However, where the joint venture is no more than an acquisition vehicle, each of the parents of the joint venture will be undertakings concerned. (*Case No. IV/M102 TNT/Canada Post and Others 2/12/91*).

(i) *Passage from joint control to sole control:* In the event of passage from joint control to sole control, one shareholder acquires the stake previously held by the other shareholders. Where there were two shareholders with joint control, each having 50%, but the transaction leads to sole control (100%), then the undertakings concerned will be the acquiring shareholder and the joint venture. (*Case No. IV/M023 ICI/Tioxide 28/11/90*). In that notified concentration, ICI acquired the shareholding in Tioxide which it did not own from its joint venture partner Cookson. In that case, ICI and Tioxide were treated as the relevant companies but not Cookson.

(j)   *Change of shareholdings in an existing joint venture:* Where there is a situation of joint control in an existing joint venture, the *Merger Regulation* can apply to certain changes in shareholdings of the parents. One or more existing shareholders can exit, additional shareholders can enter and one or more existing shareholders can be replaced by one or more new shareholders. Each can have *Merger Regulation* consequences.

A reduction in the number of shareholders can lead to sole control from joint control of a joint venture. In this situation the undertakings concerned will be the remaining shareholder and the acquired company (previously the joint venture). This analysis is not affected by the fact that there may be other shareholders with minority stakes who do not have a controlling interest in the company. These shareholders are not undertakings concerned.

Where the number of shareholders is reduced, but does not affect the position of joint control of a joint venture, this is not likely to be a notifiable transaction. This is so because it does not affect the quality of control.

If an increase in shareholding leads to the creation of additional veto rights and other increased rights, then there may be a notifiable concentration. In this case the undertakings concerned will be each of the remaining shareholders which exercise joint control and the joint venture itself. (*Case No. IV/M452 Avesta 119/6/94*).

In the situation where new shareholders are added, and existing shareholders move from sole to joint control, or where a minority shareholder acquires a controlling interest, the Commission will consider the undertakings concerned to be the existing and, if relevant, new shareholders which exercise joint control and the joint venture itself.

(k)   *Demergers:* In situations when two undertakings merge or set up a joint venture, and then subsequently demerge or break up the joint venture, and the assets are split between the demerging parties differently from the assets originally put into the joint venture, there will normally be more than one acquisition of control.

In the case of a demerger the undertakings concerned will be the original parties to the merger and the assets that each original party is acquiring. In respect of the break up of a joint venture, the undertakings concerned for each break up operation will be each of the original parties to the joint venture plus that part of the joint venture which each original party is acquiring.

(l)   *Swap of asset:* Where two or more companies exchange assets, each acquisition of control will constitute an independent concentration, even if the transactions are regarded by the parties as interdependent. The undertakings concerned will be, for each property transfer, the acquiring companies and the acquired companies or assets.

(m) *Acquisition of control by individual persons:* The *Merger Regulation* will apply only if an individual acquirer of a company carries on economic activities in his own right. In this case the Commission regards the undertakings concerned to be the target company and the individual acquirer, the turnover of the undertaking controlled by that individual being taken into account in the calculation of turnover. (*Case No. IV/M082 Asko/Jacobs/Adia 16/5/91 – OJ [1991] C132*).

(n) *Management buy-out:* An acquisition of control of a company by its own managers is an acquisition by individuals (see above). The management may form a vehicle company for the acquisition and it can be an undertaking concerned. However, if it was specifically set up for the task it is likely that it would be disregarded and the individuals themselves will be undertakings concerned.

In many cases, whether there is a vehicle company or not, investment funds, and all investment funds companies it controls, may be given control within the meaning of the *Merger Regulation* in return for their investment. In these cases the investment funds would be an undertaking concerned and not the managers. (*Case No. IV M395 CWB/Goldman Sachs/Tarkett 21/2/94 OJ [1994] C67*).

Turnover

11.16 *Article 5 of the Merger Regulation* sets out details provisions in relation to the calculation of turnover. These are further expanded by the *Commission Notice on Calculation of Turnover (OJ C66, 02/03/98)*.

For the purpose of calculating turnover under the *Merger Regulation*, not only the particular companies involved in the transaction but also the groups to which they belong must be included. However, where the merger involves the acquisition of only part of a business, the seller's turnover to be taken into account is the turnover of the part of the business which is the subject of the transaction. According to the *Merger Regulation*, the turnover of the particular undertakings concerned is to be calculated by aggregating that particular undertakings turnover with any subsidiary parent, collateral undertaking or other undertaking in which any of the above undertakings together have rights or powers which give them effective control.

Note that special rules exist for credit institutions and other financial institutions.

Procedure

11.17 Under *Article 4*, a concentration with a Community Dimension must be notified to the Commission. The Commission's 2004 *Implementing Regulation* includes (as annexes) the forms to be used when notifying deals to the Commission. These are:

(a) Form CO: This requires notifying parties to answer a very detailed list of questions about the parties, the transaction and the affected markets.

(b)   Short Form: This may be used to notify concentrations that are unlikely to raise competition concerns, ie those that qualify for the Commission's simplified procedure (see below at **11.32** for more details on the simplified procedure).

(c)   Form RS (standing for Reasoned Submissions): This is to be used by parties making reasoned submissions in support of a pre-notification referral. It requires details on parties, the transaction and the affected markets.

Under the *Old Merger Regulation*, parties had a legal obligation to notify eligible concentrations within one week after the conclusion of the agreement, the announcement of the public bid, or the acquisition of a controlling interest.

However, the new *Merger Regulation* has abolished the requirement of a binding merger agreement as a pre-condition of notification. It will be sufficient for parties to demonstrate a genuine intention to form a concentration. The one-week deadline no longer applies and parties can now notify before a binding agreement is entered into, or some time afterwards, provided that they respect the rule on suspension of completion until clearance.

The new *Merger Regulation* introduces the possibility of notifying the Commission at an earlier stage, where the parties can show a good faith intention to conclude an agreement or have publicly announced their intention to make a public bid. It is important to note that the transaction may not be completed until clearance has been obtained or the relevant deadline has passed, although the Commission may grant a derogation in exceptional circumstances.

Pre-notification

11.18   Because of the time pressure created by the tight time limits imposed by the *Merger Regulation*, the Commission encourages parties to consult with them and in most cases, to submit a draft notification to them beforehand. Pre-notification is usually beneficial for the parties concerned because it provides them with the opportunity to verify the application of the *Merger Regulation* to their transaction and, sometimes to ask for dispensation from the obligation to provide all the information requested in the Form CO in cases where it would be irrelevant to the case in question.

The importance of clarifying before notification what information will be required should not be underestimated. If the Commission considers that the information provided is inadequate, they can delay the acceptance of the notification so that the time periods allowed for will not begin to run until full notification is made. This may adversely affect the timing of the transaction itself. In addition, the Commission can impose fines for incorrect or misleading information supplied intentionally or negligently by the parties (see **11.33** below).

DG Competition's 2003 Best Practice Guidelines on the conduct of EC merger proceedings suggest that the pre-notification phase of the procedure is an important part of the whole review process.

Pre-notification contacts provide DG Competition and the notifying parties with the possibility, prior to notification, to discuss jurisdictional and other legal issues. They also serve to discuss issues such as the scope of the information to be submitted and to prepare for the upcoming investigation by identifying key issues and possible competition concerns at an early stage.

DG Competition stresses the importance of ensuring that notification forms are complete from the outset so that declarations of incompleteness are avoided as far as possible. In DG Competition's experience, in cases in which notifications have been declared incomplete, usually there were no or very limited pre-notification contacts. Accordingly, it is recommended that notifying parties contact DG Competition prior to notification.

Pre-notification discussions are held in strict confidence. The Best Practice Guidelines state that the discussions are a voluntary part of the process and remain without prejudice to the handling and investigation of the case following formal notification. However, the mutual benefits for DG Competition and the parties of a fruitful pre-notification phase can only materialise if discussions are held in an open and co-operative atmosphere, where all potential issues are addressed in a constructive way.

Even in straightforward cases DG Competition finds it appropriate to have pre-notification contact with the notifying parties.

Pre-notification contacts should preferably be initiated at least two weeks before the expected date of notification. The extent and format of the contact required will however be linked to the complexity of the individual case in question.

Pre-notification contacts should be started with a submission that allows the selection of an appropriate DG competition case team. After initial contact DG Competition may choose to make oral comments in straightforward cases. In more complex cases and cases that raise jurisdictional or other procedural issues, one or more pre-notification meetings are appropriate.

The first pre-notification meeting is usually held on the basis of a first draft Form CO or a more substantial submission. Any submission sent to DG Competition should be done so well in advance of any meeting in order to allow for discussion. Briefing memos/draft Form COs should be sent to DG Competition in good time before meeting (at least three working days).

In DG Competition's experience it is generally preferable that both legal advisors and representatives of the businesses concerned, who have a good understanding of the relevant markets, are available for pre-notification discussions with the case team.

Who must notify?

11.19   If there is an agreement for a full-scale merger of two businesses or joint control of a company is acquired, notification must be made by both parties to the merger or those acquiring joint control. In the case of acquisition of the controlling interest in the company by another, only the acquirer (or the bidder in the case of a public bid) need complete the form. In each case, the notifying parties must appoint an authorised representative or, if a joint notification, a joint representative to act on their behalf to receive correspondence and to accept the service of the documents.

How to notify

11.20   The notification must be completed in one of the official languages of the European Community. Notification is made by means of completion of the Form CO. It is necessary to provide 35 copies of the completed Form CO and supporting documentation (plus an electronic version) because a copy will be sent to the competition authorities of each of the national competition authorities within the EEA. A recent Communication (2006/C 251/02) sets out the prescribed format in which the notification and the 35 copies should be delivered to the Commission. The Commission requires:

(a)   One signed original on paper.

(b)   Five paper copies of the entire form and its annexes.

(c)   Thirty copies of the notification in CD or DVD ROM format. There are specific specifications that must be adhered to when supplying the CD/DVD.

As mentioned above, a simplified procedure exists for concentrations that do not raise serious competition concerns and a short form can be submitted instead of the full Form CO. The notifying parties must get the agreement of the Commission at pre-notification stage before using the short form. The Commission will issue a short form decision within 25 days.

Irrespective of whether pre-notification meetings have taken place or not, the Best Practice Guidelines state that it is advisable that the notifying parties systematically provide a substantially complete draft Form CO before filing a formal notification. DG Competition would thereafter usually require five working days to review the draft before being asked to comment, at a meeting or by telephone, on the adequacy of the draft. This time period would be extended for larger submissions.

Information required under Form CO

11.21   The information requested in Form CO is extremely complex and its completion is likely to place a costly burden on the notifying parties. Given the very tight timetable for notification, companies will need to have the majority of the information collated well before the signature of the deal or announcement of the bid.

A notification is not considered effective until the information to be submitted in Form CO is complete in all material respects. The notifying parties should ensure that the information contained in Form CO has been carefully prepared and verified: incorrect and misleading information is considered incomplete under DG Competition's Best Practice Guidelines.

The main areas of information required by the form are set out below:

The parties and the transaction

11.22   Form CO requires detailed information on the parties to the merger transaction and the nomination of representatives. Details of the merger transaction, including its legal nature, are also requested. For example, is the proposed merger a full legal merger or an acquisition, a full-function joint venture or a 'control' contract? Full financial and economic details of the transaction will need to be given. In line with the emphasis placed by the Commission recently on state aids, all public authority aid or funding must be fully disclosed.

A complete record of the parties' worldwide, EFTA, European Community and Member State's turnover is also important. Accuracy in calculation is essential as this can give or remove the Commission's jurisdiction to vet the transaction.

Specific rules exist for credit, insurance, other financial institutions and joint undertakings companies and these are set out in the *Merger Regulation* at *Articles 5(3)* to *5(5)*.

Ownership and control

11.23   A comprehensive list of each of the merging parties' ownership and control (direct or indirect) of other undertakings including details of acquisitions made by the parties within the last three years in markets affected by the merger needs to be provided. All companies in which the parties have an interest of 10% or more of voting rights or share capital must be disclosed. In certain other cases, further detailed investigation of the board representation is also relevant where the merging parties' designees hold multiple directorships.

Market information

11.24   In any competition law analysis, the definition of the relevant market (both the product and geographic elements) will have a profound effect on the assessment of the case. The narrower the definition of the market drawn, the higher the resulting market share of the participants in the market. The higher the combined market share enjoyed by the merging parties the more likely the Commission will be concerned with the effects of a merger.

Form CO sets out guidelines as to how to define the relevant product market and relevant geographic market. The relevant product market comprises 'those products and/or services which are regarded as interchangeable or substantially substitutable by the consumer by reason of the products' characteristics, price and intended use'. The relevant geographic market is assessed by reference to 'an area in which the undertakings concerned are involved in the supply of products or services in which the conditions of competition are sufficiently similar'. Clearly the market definition will depend on the products or services under consideration but the party or parties making the notification will be expected to justify and explain the chosen definition.

For further guidance in relation to the definition of the market, the Commission has published a *Commission Notice on the Definition of the Relevant Market for the Purposes of Community Competition Law* (OJ C372 (09/12/1997)). In this Notice, the Commission sets out one way of making a determination as to the range of products that consumers view as substitutes. This is known as the SSNIP test, and involves postulating a hypothetical small (in the range of 5% to 10%), non-transitory change in relative prices and evaluating the likely reactions of customers to that increase. If substitution by customers would be enough to make the price increase unprofitable because of the resulting loss of sales, then the substitutes are included within the relevant market.

The Commission is interested in the 'affected markets' which are defined as those in which the merger will result in the parties having a combined market share of 10% or more in the relevant market. Form CO asks for data for the relevant markets in each Member State, the EEA territory and the European Community as a whole; in particular the volume and value of each market, the parties' main competitors, price comparisons for the products sold in different markets (eg USA, Japan and EFTA) and estimates of imports into and exports from the EEA, the EU and each of the Member States.

Parties will also be required to give information on any markets in which, prior to the merger, they held 25% or more in any product market or individual product groups whether or not the merger will provide any aggregation in market share.

Market conditions

11.25   There are a number of market factors which may favourably influence the Commission in its assessment of the merger. The two most important are the existence of effective competition on and the ease of entering the relevant product market. The Commission is concerned to find out whether sizeable competitors exist in the affected market to challenge the merged enterprises. The Commission has, therefore, requested information on competitors, their market shares and the structure of supply and demand (ie who buys or sells the product). Low barriers to entry are pro-competitive. Where the capital cost and the level of technology required to enter the market is low, and the customer base is relatively free from long-term supply contracts, the ability of new competitors to enter that market is greatly increased and new entrants will act as a countervailing balance to any market leading producer.

Suspension of concentrations

11.26 Under Article 7, a merger that falls under the new *Merger Regulation* cannot be implemented unless it has been cleared by the Commission except:

(a) in the case of a public bid provided the concentration is notified to the Commission without delay and the acquirer only exercises voting rights attached to the securities in order to maintain the full value of its investment; or

(b) where the Commission grants a derogation following a reasoned request from the parties.

Substantial financial penalties may be imposed on companies that fail to suspend their merger transaction. It is also possible to apply to the Commission to be released from this undertaking sooner if necessary.

Main stages in the Commission's investigation and time limits

11.27 Following receipt of the formal Form CO notification, the Commission will commence its investigation. It will publish a summary of the transaction in the Official Journal and on its website and invite third parties to make submissions on the transaction within 10 days.

There are two potential formal stages to any Commission investigation. The initial consideration of the merger following notification is called Phase I. Any further in-depth analysis due to the Commission having 'serious doubts' as to the compatibility of the deal with the common market is known as Phase II.

Phase I

11.28 The majority of transactions are cleared within a Phase I investigation. The timetable for investigation is as follows:

(a) 25 working days starting from the day following receipt of the notification; or

(b) 35 working days if undertakings are offered or a request for referral to one or more national competition authorities is received.

The Commission's review in Phase I involves sending detailed requests/questionnaires, called 'Article 11 letters', to parties including principal competitors, customers and suppliers for their comments.

DG Competition's Best Practice Guidelines provide for a 'state of play' meeting with the parties if the Commission thinks that 'serious doubts' may exist following the initial investigation.

At the end of Phase I, the Commission will make one of the following decisions:

(i)   **Clearance:** the concentration does not raise serious competition concerns, and therefore is cleared unconditionally. The majority of Phase I investigations result in this outcome. The Commission has made this decision in 2797 transactions as at 31 December 2006;

(ii)   **Clearance with commitments:** the merger raises competition concerns but the Commission is happy that these can be addressed by conditions attached to the merger. As at 31 December 2006, 140 mergers have been cleared with commitments;

(iii)   **Phase II:** the Commission believes the merger raises 'serious doubts' as to its compatibility with the common market and a more detailed investigation is necessary. There were 10 Phase II proceedings launched in 2005 and 13 in 2006. The highest yearly total of second stage investigations initiated was 21 in 2001.

(iv)   **No Jurisdiction:** the merger does not fall within the Merger Regulation as it is not a concentration or does not have Community dimension. 52 decisions have been made under this heading. None have been made under the new Merger Regulation.

(v)   **Article 9 referral:** the deal would more appropriately be dealt with at national level and a referral to the relevant national competition authority will be made if an NCA has made a formal request. 75 Article 9 requests have been made in the history of the merger regulation resulting in 35 Article 9.2 partial referrals to a member state and 30 full referrals. Only 3 such referrals were refused by the Commission.

Phase II

11.29   Phase II investigations involve a detailed enquiry into the markets in which the parties operate. During this time, the parties (and third parties) can make further submissions both oral and written.

The timetable for a Phase II investigation is as follows:

(a)   90 working days from the day following the decision to carry out an in-depth inquiry;

(b)   plus 15 working days if the parties offer remedies 55 days or more after the initiation of the in-depth inquiry; or

(c)   plus 20 days upon request of the notifying parties or by the Commission with the Agreement of the parties.

The timetable of 90 days is tight, given that the investigation is in-depth. During this period there will normally be a number of steps carried out such as:

(i)   a statement of objections sent by the Commission to undertakings concerned;

(ii)   a period for them to reply;

(iii)   access for the parties to the files of the Commission;

(iv)   an oral hearing which may last for 1 or 2 days;

(v)   a meeting (or meetings) of the Advisory Committee on Concentrations;

(vi)   a period in which commitments can be discussed and an opportunity for interested third parties to comment on commitments;

(vii) consultation of other Directorates General;

(viii) preparation of a draft decision for the College of Commissioners to consider; adoption by the full Commission of the final decision.

The Commission blocks very few transactions as generally where competition concerns arise, the parties will make changes to the arrangements or make commitments to meet these concerns. Since 2000, only 8 Phase II cases have been blocked.

Commitments

11.30   Where competition concerns arise as discussed above, the parties can seek to remedy the situation by offering commitments to the Commission. In general the Commission prefers a structural solution (eg the divestiture of a business) as it does not have to continually monitor this, although in some situations it may accept other forms of behavioural remedy.

Commitments can be offered during both Phase I and II of the investigation. The Commission has set the following timetable for offering commitments:

(a)   commitments offered by the undertakings during the Phase I investigation must be submitted not more than 20 working days from the receipt of the notification;

(b)   commitments offered by the undertakings during the Phase II investigation must be submitted not more than 65 working days from the date on which proceedings were initiated; however

(c)   where the time limit is extended during Phase II the 65-day limit is also extended by the agreed period.

Substantive assessment

11.31   The new *Merger Regulation* has introduced a new substantive test under which the Commission will assess the merger. The test is whether the concentration '*significantly impede(s) effective competition in the common market or in a substantial part of it, in particular as a result of the creation or strengthening of a dominant position*' (Article 2(2)).

The test is sometimes referred to as the 'SIEC' test to distinguish it from the 'dominance' test that existed under the *Old Merger Regulation*. The SIEC test was developed to take advantage of the principles developed under old case law.

The Commission will look at a range of factors in coming to its decision. The Commission has issued Guidelines on the assessment of horizontal mergers (2004/C 31/03) ('Horizontal Merger Guidelines'), which set out the factors that the Commission considers when looking at a merger. The Commission will analyse the possible anti-competitive effects and will compare the post-merger market structure with the counterfactual, ie the market structure that would be likely to develop if the merger did not take place.

The Guidelines focus on the two main ways in which horizontal mergers may significantly impede effective competition, in particular by creating or strengthening a dominant position:

(a) by eliminating important competitive constraints between the parties, a horizontal merger may allow the merged firm to increase its prices regardless of the response of its remaining competitors. A merger that has these characteristics is said to give rise to unilateral effects, although the Commission in the Horizontal Merger Guidelines have chosen to use the tern **non-coordinated effects** to describe this effect.

The Horizontal Merger Guidelines set out a number of factors that may influence whether significant non-coordinated effects are likely to result from a merger. These include the following:

(i) **Market shares:** the Commission places a great deal of emphasis on the parties' market shares affected by the merger. The larger the market share the more likely a firm is to possess market power. Market share figures of more than 40% and the firm may be considered in a dominant position.

(ii) **Whether the merging firms are close competitors**: The Commission takes the view that the closer the substitute between the merging firms' products, the more likely it is that that merging firms will raise prices significantly.

(iii) **Barriers to entry:** there could be competition concerns if there are few alternatives to the merging firms and switching is difficult/high cost.

(b) by creating an environment more favourable to sustainable tacit collusion a merger could reduce the effectiveness of competition and lead to price rises. A merger with these characteristics will have **coordinated effects**:

(i) The situation of joint dominance may occur where there are economic links, in a market with the appropriate characteristics, which create interdependence between parties in a tight oligopoly in which they are able to anticipate one another's behaviour and are strongly encouraged to align themselves in the market.

(ii) An oligopolistic market will therefore provide opportunities for 'tacit collusion' by the players in the market. The Commission will try to establish in its investigation whether the concentration will result in a market structure which would create incentives for the remaining major players on the relevant markets to discourage market entry or otherwise distort competition to the detriment of consumers or of smaller companies outside the market.

Notice on a simplified procedure

11.32   The Commission published a *Notice on a Simplified Procedure for Treatment of Certain Concentrations* (2005/C 56/04) under the *Merger Regulation* relating to certain concentrations that do not raise competition concerns. By following the simplified procedure the Commission aims to make Community merger control more focused and effective.

The simplified procedure applies to the following categories of concentrations:

(a)   two or more undertakings acquiring joint control of a joint venture, provided that the joint venture has no, or negligible, actual or foreseen activities within the territory of the EEA. Such cases occur where:

    (i)   the turnover of the joint venture and/or the turnover of the contributed activities is less than €100 million in the EEA territory; and

    (ii)   the total value of assets transferred to the joint venture is less than €100 million in the EEA territory;

(b)   two or more undertakings merging, or one or more undertakings acquiring sole or joint control of another undertaking, provided that none of the parties to the concentration are engaged in business activities in the same product and geographical market, or in a product market which is upstream or downstream of a product market in which any other party to the concentration is engaged;

(c)   two or more undertakings merging, or one or more undertakings acquiring sole or joint control of another undertaking:

    (i)   and two or more of the parties to the concentration are engaged in business activities in the same product and geographical market (horizontal relationships); or

    (ii)   one or more of the parties to the concentration are engaged in business activities in a product market which is upstream or downstream of a product market in which any other party to the concentration is engaged (vertical relationships), provided that their combined market share is not 15% or more for horizontal and 25% or more for vertical relationships.

Essentially the simplified procedure is such that when a concentration falls within the categories, and provided there are no special circumstances, the Commission will normally issue a short form decision clearing the merger This includes appropriate cases not giving rise to any competition concerns where it receives a full form notification, The concentration will therefore be declared compatible with the common market, within 25 working days from the date of notification. The Commission will endeavour to issue a short form decision as soon as practicable following expiry of the 15-day working period during which Member States may request referral of a notified concentration.

Penalties

11.33   The *Merger Regulation* also provides for a scale of fines in *Article 14*. For example, for:

(a)   Supplying incorrect or misleading information in a notification, or for failing to comply with requests or decisions of the Commission: up to 1% of the aggregate turnover of the offending undertakings.

(b)   Failing to notify a relevant merger prior to its implementation, failing to comply with the Commission's decision prohibiting a merger: up to 10% of the aggregate turnover of the offending undertakings.

The ultimate sanction the Commission has is the power of divestiture, and it may require an unlawful merger to be broken up.

Examples

11.34

> *Case IV/M.920 – Samsung/AST (26/5/97 – OJ [1997] C203/3):* This case concerned the late notification of a concentration, resulting in a €33,000 fine. This was the first fine to be levied since the *Merger Regulation* came into force.
>
> *Case IV/M.1397 – Sanofi/Synthelabo (17/5/99):* The parties provided incomplete information to the Commission and this resulted in the Commission having to annul its approval. The parties failed to notify the Commission that they were both involved in the same market (namely morphine and morphine derivatives). The Commission later approved the merger subject to conditions. Each party was fined €50,000 – the first time such a penalty had been given for inducing the Commission to make an erroneous decision.
>
> *COMP/M.3255 Tetra Laval / Sidel.* There have only been three decisions imposing fines since 1999. The most recent decision was *Tetra Lavel/Sidel* in 2004, under the Old *Merger Regulation*, where a fine of €90,000 was imposed.
>
> In this case, the Commission discovered that during its examination of Tetra Laval's acquisition of Sidel in 2001, the Swiss-Swedish company had failed to fully disclose relevant R & D and IP rights by not providing information about Tetra Fast technology both in the Form CO and in response to a letter in which the Commission asked for information.

Ancillary restrictions

11.35   Under *Article 6(1)(b)* and *Article 8(2)* of the *Merger Regulation*, the acceptance of restrictions which are ancillary ie 'directly related and necessary for the implementation of a merger' will be covered by any clearance given by the Commission under the *Merger Regulation.*

The Commission Notice on restrictions directly related and necessary to concentrations 2005/C 56/03 which came into force on 5 March 2006, replaced the 2001 version of the notice with the same title (the Ancillary Notice).

In the 2001 Ancillary Notice the Commission declared its intention no longer to explicitly assess such restrictions in its merger decisions. Any restriction which is not deemed to be strictly ancillary to the merger or where the duration of that restriction goes beyond that which the Commission indicates is generally acceptable, will fall to be considered independently under *Articles 81* and *82* of the *Treaty of Rome.*

For agreements to be considered *directly related and necessary to the implementation of a concentration*, the concentration could not have been implemented without those agreements or only under much less favourable conditions, substantially higher costs, with greater difficulty or be intrinsically necessary (eg to maintain continuity of supply).

An exception to the principle of self-assessment exists in cases which present 'novel and unresolved questions giving rise to genuine uncertainty', where the Commission should, at the request of the undertakings concerned, expressly assess whether or not the restriction is directly related to, and necessary for, the implementation of the concentration.

The 2005 Ancillary Notice introduces some changes in the Commission's policy approach in respect of the ancillary restraints in relation to concentrations regarding non-competition and confidentiality clauses and purchase and supply obligations.

Non-compete clauses in relation to a merger or acquisition

11.36   A contractual prohibition on competition may be imposed on the seller in the context of a merger transaction, as it is essential to guarantee to the purchasers the full value of the assets and goodwill transferred. Such restrictions are generally recognised as being necessary to the implementation of the transaction, since without them it would be unreasonable to expect the completion of the sale of the undertaking. However, such clauses are only considered justified when their duration, geographic scope and subject matter do not exceed what is reasonably needed for completion.

As a general rule, where the transfer of the undertaking includes both goodwill and know-how, non-competition clauses are generally justified for a period of up to three years. In cases where only goodwill is transferred the acceptable duration is normally two years. A longer duration may be justified in exceptional circumstances (eg where the nature of the know-how transferred justifies an additional period of protection).

The geographic scope of the non-competition clauses should generally be limited to the area where the seller established his products or services before the transfer. Similarly, the clause can only relate to the products (or improved versions) and/or services which formed part of the business activities of the vendor. A non-compete clause which binds not only the vendor but also members of the same corporate group and its commercial agents can still be considered ancillary, but this is not the case in relation to clauses which restrict third parties (eg resellers).

Commonly, merger agreements will also contain non-solicitation and confidentiality clauses. Generally these would be treated in much the same way as non-compete clauses in terms of duration and scope.

The 2005 Ancillary Notice deems non-competition causes between a joint venture and its parent company ancillary for the lifetime of the joint venture.

Intellectual property licences in the context of a merger or acquisition

11.37   Where a seller retains certain intellectual property rights but transfers the assets of a business, it is sometimes necessary to give the purchaser a licence of those rights to ensure that he can fully exploit the assets transferred. Such licences may be exclusive or non-exclusive and may be limited to the field of use corresponding to the activities of the business being acquired. Such provisions are considered ancillary.

Generally speaking, the Commission considers that territorial limitations on manufacture are not considered *necessary to the implementation of the operation*. Other restrictions in a licence (particularly those intended to protect the licensor rather than the licensee) are usually not considered ancillary and have to be assessed under *Article 81* of the *Treaty of Rome*.

Purchase and supply obligations in the context of a merger or acquisition

11.38   To make possible the break-up of the seller's business or the partial transfer of assets to a purchaser, it is often necessary to maintain similar supply arrangements between the seller and the purchaser for a transitional period to ensure security of supply.

Supply and purchase obligations which provide for fixed quantities (possibly with a variation clause) may be considered directly related and necessary to the implementation of the merger. However, an obligation for unlimited quantities or conferring preferred status on the supplier or purchaser would not be considered directly necessary and would have to be justified in the particular circumstances of the case. Similarly there is no general justification for exclusive purchase and supply agreements, although they may be considered necessary in exceptional circumstances (eg relating to the specificity of the product in question). Service agreements are likely to be treated in a manner analogous to supply agreements.

For such clauses to be regarded as ancillary they *must be limited to a period necessary for the replacement of the relationship of dependency by autonomy in the market.* The 2005 Ancillary Notice indicates that the duration of purchase and supply contracts for complex industrial products is normally justified for a transitional period of up to five years depending on the circumstances (this was previously three years under the 2001 Ancillary Notice). It is inferred that with less complex products a shorter period only is justified.

Joint venture restrictions

11.39   The *Merger Regulation* applies not only to acquisition and mergers but also to certain forms of concentrative joint ventures. As with mergers and acquisitions, common forms of restrictions include non-compete clauses, intellectual property licences and purchase and supply obligations (see **11.36** to **11.38**). In addition, there are certain types of restrictions which may be necessary to achieve the creation of a joint venture and which are generally treated as ancillary. For instance, a restriction on each of the joint acquirers from making separate competing offers where two or more companies make a joint bid to acquire a third company.

Non-compete clause in a joint venture

11.40   Generally speaking, non-compete obligations between each of the parent undertakings and the joint venture will be treated as ancillary for a period of three years. A period of up to five years may be justified by the particular circumstances of the case. However, a restriction upon competing which goes beyond the lifetime of the joint venture will never be considered ancillary. The geographic scope of the non-compete clause must be limited to the area where the parents were active before establishing the joint venture. Similarly, the non-compete clause must relate to the products and services which constitute the economic activity of the joint venture, although this may be extended to cover products and services which at the time were at an advanced stage of development, even if not yet marketed. In the case of a joint venture established in order to enter a new market, it is possible to restrict competition in respect of the anticipated products, services and territory of the joint venture. By analogy, similar rules would apply to non-solicitation and confidentiality clauses.

Restrictions which protect one parent company from competition from the other are not generally considered necessary to the creation of the joint venture and are not ancillary.

Intellectual property agreements and joint ventures

11.41   The general rule is that a licence granted by the parents to the joint venture is considered ancillary, whether it is exclusive or non-exclusive and whether or not it is limited in time. The licence can be limited to a particular field of use which relates to the activities which the joint venture is established to perform. Similarly, a licence granted by the joint venture to one parent or a cross licence between parent and joint venture may be considered ancillary. However, licence agreements between the parents are not generally considered directly necessary and related to the implementation of the joint venture. Where a licence agreement is not ancillary, consideration should be give as to whether it may benefit from the exemption granted under the *Transfer of Technology Block Exemption Regulation* (*Commission Regulation No. 240/96* or its anticipated successor).

Purchase and supply obligations and joint ventures

11.42   Where a parent company continues to operate in a market upstream or downstream to that of the joint venture, a purchase, supply or distribution agreement may be treated as ancillary under the same terms and conditions as described above in **11.38** in relation to mergers and acquisitions.

EEA Agreement merger control rules

11.43   The EEA Agreement provides for the control by the European Commission and the EFTA Surveillance Authority of mergers with a Community or EFTA dimension. The Agreement extended European merger control powers for bringing within their ambit mergers having an EFTA dimension. Mergers subject to vetting under the EEA Agreement need prior notification and clearance. Mergers will only be allowed if they are not incompatible with the EEA Agreement. Therefore, if any merger could create or strengthen a dominant position as a result of which effective competition would be significantly impeded within the territory covered by the Agreement or a substantial part of it (*Article 57* of the EEA Agreement) will be prohibited.

With mergers having a Community and an EFTA dimension capable of being covered by both the *Merger Regulation* and the EEA Agreement, there are special rules as to the division of the jurisdiction of the European Commission and the EFTA Surveillance Authority (see *Article 57(2)* of the EEA Agreement). The importance of the EFTA dimension has, however, been reduced considerably following the accession of Finland, Sweden and Austria to the EU at the beginning of 1995. The EFTA members of the EEA are now only Norway and Iceland.

We have already considered what mergers have a Community Dimension under the *Merger Regulation*. The EEA Treaty will only apply where there is an effect on trade between the 'Contracting Parties' (ie the Union and EFTA). Mergers will be subject to EEA rules on the basis set out below.

A merger will have an EFTA/EEA dimension where the aggregate worldwide turnover of the parties exceeds €5,000 million (approximately £3.45 billion) and the EFTA-wide turnover of each of at least two of the parties exceeds €250 million (approximately £172 million) unless each of the parties has more than two-thirds of its EFTA turnover in the same EFTA state.

Under the jurisdictional rules set out in *Article 57(2)* of the EFTA Agreement the following institutions have competence to investigate the following mergers:

(a) the European Commission has exclusive competence over all mergers which fall within the thresholds of the *Merger Regulation* whether or not they also have an EFTA dimension; and

(b) mergers which have an EFTA dimension but not a Community Dimension will be investigated by the EFTA Surveillance Authority.

Mergers which have neither a Community nor EFTA dimension come within the jurisdiction of national competition authorities of EU and EFTA Member States to apply their own national merger control laws.

The EFTA Surveillance Authority and the European Commission have the same powers and functions for the application and enforcement of the EEA Agreement merger control rules as the European Commission does under the *Merger Regulation.*

United Kingdom

11.44 As a general rule UK merger control only applies if the EU and EEA merger rules do not apply. There are however a number of very limited exceptions where the European Commission and/or the EFTA Surveillance Authority have the power to refer back a particular case which has a specific effect on a distinct national market. Note that *Article 21(2)* of the *Merger Regulation* specifically states that no Member State may apply the provisions of its national legislation on competition to a merger, which has a Community Dimension.

Enterprise Act 2002

Introduction

11.45 The legislation governing merger control in the UK is contained in the *Enterprise Act 2002 (EA 2002)*. The enactment of the *Competition Act 1998* does not affect the operation of the merger control provisions of the *EA 2002.*

The merger provisions of the *EA 2002* came into force on 20 June 2003, and replace the previous regime for the control of UK mergers and acquisitions contained in the *Fair Trading Act 1973 (FTA 1973)*.

The *EA 2002* makes significant changes to the merger control regime. First of all, it establishes the Office of Fair Trading (OFT) on a statutory basis as a corporate body and abolishes the position of the Director General of Fair Trading. Under the old law the OFT did not exist as a legal entity, but was merely the administrative support for the Director General of Fair Trading. The *EA 2002* also establishes an independent appeals tribunal – the Competition Appeals Tribunal (CAT), replacing the Appeals Tribunal of the Competition Commission. In the context of mergers this body will hear appeals from aggrieved parties in relation to merger decisions of the OFT, the Competition Commission or the Secretary of State. The Secretary of State for Trade and Industry ('Secretary of State') will not now take most decisions on merger control. Instead, most decisions will be taken by the OFT and the Competition Commission (CC) as specialist independent competition authorities. Only in limited public interest cases can the Secretary of State intervene. The Act also introduces a new assessment test for mergers. Instead of the wider public interest test set out in the *FTA 1973*, mergers will be prohibited or undertakings sought in situations where there is realistic prospect of a substantial lessening of competition on the relevant market or markets concerned.

The institutions

11.46   Before considering the UK merger control provisions, it is helpful to review the functions of each of the institutions involved in the merger control process.

The Office of Fair Trading

11.47   The OFT was established as a corporate body on 1 April 2003. Under the *EA 2002,* the OFT has the function to obtain and review information relating to merger situations and a duty to refer to the CC for further investigation mergers covered by the Act where it believes that they may result in a substantial lessening of competition in a UK market. The Secretary of State retains a role in relation to public interest mergers described in more detail in **11.49** below. The OFT also advises the Secretary of State on these. The OFT may also be asked by the CC to negotiate undertakings with the parties if a merger is prohibited or cleared subject to the giving of certain undertakings.

The Competition Commission

11.48   The CC is an independent non-governmental body. It investigates mergers referred to it by the OFT and/or the Secretary of State to determine whether the merger should be cleared or alternatively prohibited on the basis that it may be expected to result in a substantial lessening of competition or in the case of public interest cases, mergers may be expected to operate against the public interest. It proposes remedies where there is a negative finding and can ask the OFT to negotiate undertakings with the relevant parties to give effect to its conclusions, or can issue orders prohibiting the merger in default.

Secretary of State

11.49   The Secretary of State has retained a role in merger decisions which involve certain public interest issues such as national security, defence and now, with the passage of the *Communications Act 2003 (CA 2003)*, media mergers (in particular those involving newspapers). The Secretary of State is also able to modify certain provisions of the Act, such as those relating to which type and size of mergers are capable of being investigated under the Act and also the level of merger control fees.

The Act also allows the Secretary of State to intervene in mergers that do not meet the jurisdictional thresholds where one of the companies concerned is a relevant government contractor. These mergers are considered under the special merger situations regime in **11.57** below.

Challenges and appeals process: the role of the Competition Appeals Tribunal

11.50   The *EA 2002* establishes an independent tribunal to hear appeals from aggrieved parties under the *Competition Act 1998* and the *EA 2002*. In relation to mergers, its role is to review decisions on relevant mergers, public interest mergers or special merger situations taken by the OFT, CC or Secretary of State.

Parties to a merger or other persons sufficiently affected by the decision may apply to the CAT for a review. The CAT cannot substitute its own decision on the merits of a case, but it can review the reasonableness, lawfulness and fairness of the decision and, if necessary, require it to be reconsidered by the relevant authorities (See *EA 2002 s 120*).

In *IBA Health Limited v Office of Fair Trading* [2003] All ER, the CAT considered an application by a competitor of Torex plc and iSoft plc, called IBA Health Limited, to have the OFT decision to clear the merger between Torex plc and iSoft plc set aside. The CAT considered that the OFT applied the wrong competition test and quashed the OFT's decision to clear the merger. It stated that the relevant test the OFT should use was 'whether there was any significant prospect that the Competition Commission ('CC') would find there to be a substantial lessening of competition'. The OFT then appealed to the Court of Appeal ('CA') which overturned the CAT's decision stating that the test formulated by the CAT could not be justified. The CA explained that the relevant belief as to whether there was a substantial lessening of competition should not be that held by the CC but should be the relevant belief held by the OFT.

The CA considered that the OFT had interpreted their duty to refer a merger to the CC only if there was a greater than 50% chance that the merger concerned may be expected to result in a substantial lessening of competition. However, the CA disagreed with the OFT's interpretation. It said that on the correct construction of the OFT's duty (as set out in the *Enterprise Act 2002 section 33(1))* the OFT has a lower threshold to refer. The CA held that there was a wider margin in which the OFT is required to exercise its judgement to refer which was 'higher than fanciful, but lower than 50%'. This amounted on a substantial extension of the OFT's duty to refer mergers to the CC and is reflected in the much higher number of cases which are being now referred to the Commission. It is not at all clear that Parliament intended such a liberal construction to be placed in the OFT's duty to refer. Despite the fact the CAT used the wrong test, the CA decided that the CAT's decision was correct and should be upheld. The CA therefore dismissed the appeal and the matter was referred back to the OFT which reapproved the merger.

Even though the case produced the same result in terms of the approval of the merger, it has dramatically changed the way in which the OFT interprets its statutory duties and has lowered the threshold for CC referral. This has meant that more cases are considered in greater details and it has caused great pressure on OFT resources.

The decision in *Unichem Ltd v Office of Fair Trading* [2005] All ER (D), 51 (Sep) has further highlighted the fact that the OFT's decisions can be challenged and overturned by the CAT. In Unichem, the OFT was found not to have taken into account competitor's (Unichem's) evidence before deciding not to refer a merger to the CC. Instead it placed reliance of the merging parties' evidence in relation to their competitors without corroborating that evidence by reference to the actual evidence submitted by those competitors themselves. Because of this the CAT felt it had no choice but to quash the decision and resubmit the matter to the OFT for reconsideration in order to take into account what Unichem said in the proceedings.

The above decisions mean that the OFT's every move is now being scrutinised in greater depth and its decisions can be challenged and overturned. The OFT is keen to ensure that its future published decisions are not overturned. With this in mind, it has decided to focus its resources on public merger applications at the cost of informal and confidential guidance (discussed in **11.61** and **11.62**).

Relevant mergers

11.51   The *EA 2002* applies to mergers qualifying for investigation. These occur where:

(a)   two or more enterprises cease to be distinct;

(b)   at least one of the enterprises is carried on in the UK by or under the control of a company incorporated in the UK;

(c)   the merger has taken place within the last four months (unless it has taken place in secret); and

(d)   either:

    (i)   *Market share test:* the enterprises are both engaged in supplying or consuming goods or services of the same description and have between them at least 25% of the market for the supply of those goods or services in the UK, or a substantial part of it. The regulatory authorities have a wide discretion on how to define the relevant goods or services. The market share test is only satisfied if a monopoly share is created or enhanced, or

(ii) *Turnover test:* the UK turnover associated with the enterprise, which is being acquired, exceeds £70 million.

Ceasing to be distinct

11.52 Enterprises cease to be distinct when they are brought under common control or ownership or where there is an arrangement whereby one of the enterprises ceases to be carried on so as to prevent competition. There are complex provisions governing 'common control' to cover acquisitions falling short of a complete takeover. Enterprises come under common control where:

(a) the acquiring company becomes able to materially influence policy of the target. This can be done by way of shareholdings, board representation, management contract or acquisition of secured or unsecured loan stock or a combination of those factors. Whether material influence exists is a question of fact in each case. A shareholding of 25% or more generally enables the holder to block special resolutions, and this is seen as automatically conferring the ability materially to influence the policy of the company concerned. The Office of Fair Trading (OFT) usually examines cases where there is a shareholding of 15% or more to see if the holder is able to materially influence the company. In the OFT decision *First Milk Limited/Robert Wiseman Dairies PLC*, 7 April 2005 the OFT said that First Milk's 15% stake in Wiseman may be able to materially influence Wiseman's policy. However, the OFT only came to this conclusion when taking into consideration the fact that the First Milk board appointee could have considerable influence at board meetings. In exceptional cases material influence can be exercised by any company holding over 10% (Kuwait Investment Office/BP). However, it is reasonable to assume that material influence is unlikely to arise if a company holds less than 15% and does not have board representation;

(b) the acquiring company becomes able to control the policy of the target; or

(c) the acquiring company gains a controlling interest in the target.

The merger clearance process

Office of Fair Trading's duties

11.53 The *EA 2002* imposes a duty on the OFT to refer completed or anticipated mergers to the CC for further investigation if it believes that:

(a) a relevant merger situation has been or will be created; and

(b)   the creation of that situation has resulted, or may be expected to result, in a substantial lessening of competition within any market or markets for goods or services in the UK.

However, the OFT may not proceed with a reference if it believes that:

(a)   the market concerned is of insufficient importance to justify a reference; or

(b)   customer benefits created by the merger outweigh any substantial lessening of competition the merger may cause; or

(c)   in the case of a contemplated merger, the terms are not sufficiently advanced to justify the making of a reference to the CC.

In circumstances where a loss of competition is identified which would otherwise merit a reference to the CC, the OFT is empowered under the Act to accept binding undertakings from the merged business as an alternative to making a reference to the CC. Any undertakings must be for the purpose of remedying the adverse effects identified. There are two types of undertakings, structural and behavioural. Structural undertakings involve the merged company agreeing to divest itself of part of the merged business. Behavioural undertakings focus on the parties giving a formal commitment about their future conduct in the market, such as restrictions on raising prices or withdrawing product lines.

To prevent the parties to a relevant merger situation taking any action which might prejudice the OFT's initial enquiry or, following a reference to the CC's further investigation, both are empowered under the *EA 2002* to make orders restraining the parties from putting the merger into effect or taking other pre-emptive action which might frustrate the regulatory process.

Competition Commission's duties

11.54   If referred, the CC must decide whether a relevant merger situation is created or would be created by the transaction and, if so, whether it is reasonably believed that there is a realistic prospect that the merger will result in a substantial lessening of competition in any market or markets in the UK for jobs or services.

If the CC finds that a transaction will result in a substantial lessening of competition, it will decide what remedies are available to mitigate or prevent the substantial lessening of competition or any adverse effect resulting from it and what action should be taken in that particular case. The CC will publish its report upon the conclusion of its investigation. If the CC makes a negative finding it can prohibit the merger outright, impose conditions on any clearance and ask the OFT to seek appropriate undertakings from the parties. In default of those undertakings it will make necessary orders under the Act to enforce its decision.

Public Interest Mergers

11.55   In the vast majority of merger cases the *EA 2002* removes the political interference of the Secretary of State from the merger control process. There are, however, a number of situations in which the Secretary of State still retains his role in the merger control process. These are referred to in the *EA 2002* as Public Interest Mergers and Special Merger Situations.

Under the *EA 2002* the Secretary of State can issue an intervention notice in cases where mergers have public interest implications. This covers mergers which relate to national security (*EA 2002, s 58*). Now, following the passage of the *Communications Act 2003*, the Secretary of State has the power to intervene in a merger which satisfies the criteria for a 'relevant merger' (as defined in **11.49** above) where media and public interest issues may be present.

The procedures in respect of national security and media mergers are considered in **11.56** and **11.58** below.

NATIONAL SECURITY MERGERS

11.56   Mergers having national security implications will be considered on the following basis.

If the Secretary of State does not issue an intervention notice in respect of a transaction the OFT will review the case under the rules set out in the *EA 2002*, as if it were any other merger case.

If an intervention notice is issued, the OFT provides advice to the Secretary of State on whether the merger constitutes a merger qualifying for investigation under the Act and on its competition analysis of the transaction. The Secretary of State must accept this advice. The OFT will also provide advice on the public interest considerations which the Secretary of State must consider when making his decision whether or not to refer the matter to the CC. The Secretary of State can make a reference if either:

(a)   the merger results in a substantial lessening of competition and combined with the public interest issues will operate or is likely to operate against the public interest; or

(b)   the merger raises public interest issues which are likely to operate against the public interest not withholding the fact that the merger will not result in a substantial lessening of competition.

As an alternative to making a reference, the Secretary of State can consider whether undertakings from the parties are acceptable to remedy any perceived competition or national interest issues.

If a reference is made on public interest grounds (with or without competition grounds as well) the CC will report their findings to the Secretary of State who will take the final decision on the merger.

If, after the issue of an intervention notice, the Secretary of State concludes that no public interest issues do in fact exist, the OFT will be instructed to deal with the merger as an ordinary merger case.

The Secretary of State may also intervene on public interest grounds in cases falling for consideration under the Council Regulation 139/2004 (the *EC Merger Regulation (ECMR))* through the use of *Article 21(4)* of the *ECMR*. Where *Article 21* is relied upon the OFT will advise the Secretary of State on the considerations relevant to making a reference under *EA 2002 s 22* or *s 33* and the *Enterprise Act 2002 (Protection of Legitimate Interests) Order 2003*. This will relate to the public interest considerations alone and will not contain a competition law assessment. Under these provisions, the Secretary of State can make a reference to the CC if it is believed that taking account only of the public interest considerations, the creation of the European relevant merger situation operates or may be expected to operate against the public interest.

SPECIAL MERGER SITUATIONS

11.57   The Secretary of State can also intervene in defence industry mergers even if they do not qualify under the general merger regime. These are called special merger situations and they arise if at least one of the enterprises concerned is a relevant government contractor. These mergers will be assessed on public interest grounds alone and there will be no competition assessment. The OFT will advise the Secretary of State on the public interest issues but the decision to refer special merger situations to the CC for further investigation and ultimately whether to accept the CC's recommendations falls to the Secretary of State.

MEDIA MERGERS

11.58   The amendment of the *EA 2002* by the *Communications Act 2003* conferred certain public interest powers on the Secretary of State in relation to media mergers. This includes powers to intervene in relation to broadcasting and newspaper mergers. Under the *FTA 1973* there were special rules for newspaper mergers. These were abolished by *section 373* of the *Communications Act 2003*.

Under the *EA 2002*, newspaper mergers which qualify for investigation will be subject to the general merger regime. However, the Secretary of State can intervene if he believes that a public interest consideration as specified in the *EA 2002, s 58 is* present.

Section 375 of the *Communications Act 2003* amends *section 58* of the *EA 2002* to provide for the Secretary of State's intervention on the grounds of certain media public interest considerations as set out in the *EA 2002, s 58(2A) to (2C)*. These are as follows:

(a)   freedom of expression in newspapers: the need for accurate presentation of news and freedom of expression of opinion in newspapers. This car-

ried forward the specific reference to these two factors in the public interest test that was applied by the CC when considering newspaper transfers
under the *FTA 1973* newspaper merger regime (*EA 2002, s 58 (2A)*);

(b)   plurality of views in newspapers: the need for, to the extent that it is
reasonable and practicable, a sufficient plurality of views in newspapers in each market for newspapers in the UK or part thereof (*section
58 (2B)* of the *EA 2002*); and

(c)   broadcasting standards: the need for persons carrying on media enterprises (defined as those enterprises involved in broadcasting) and for
those with control of such enterprises to have a genuine commitment to
the attainment in relation to broadcasting of the standards and objectives
set out in *section 319* of the *CA 2003* (*section 58 (2C)* of the *EA 2002*).

Water and sewerage mergers

11.59   In certain circumstances mergers of water or sewerage undertakings
are subject to mandatory reference to the CC. Under the *Water Industry Act
1991* as amended by *section 70* of the *EA 2002*, the OFT must refer any
merger involving two or more water enterprises to the CC for further investigation. A water enterprise is an enterprise carried on by a water or sewerage
undertaker appointed under *section 6* of the *Water Industry Act 1991*.
However, the OFT shall not make a reference if it appears that:

(a)   the value of the turnover of the water enterprise being taken over does
not exceed £10 million; or

(b)   the only water enterprises already belonging to the person making the
takeover are enterprises each of which has a turnover of the value of
which does not exceed or would not exceed £10 million.

Notifying mergers to the Office of Fair Trading

11.60   Although not obligatory under *EA 2002*, it is usual to seek prior
clearance for a 'qualifying merger' particularly where the market share test is
satisfied or other significant public interest issues arise. A merger can be
referred to the CC up to four months after it has been put into effect and the
regulatory authorities can, in certain circumstances, order divestiture.

To obtain clearance of the completed transaction the parties approach the
OFT and provide details on the transaction and any possible effects on competition.

There are a number of ways of obtaining merger clearance from the OFT, as
discussed in **11.61** TO **11.63**.

Informal advice

11.61   Originally under the *EA 2002* the OFT could be approached to give
advice on an informal basis as to the likely competition issues associated with

a prospective merger situation which has not yet been made public. However in November 2005 the OFT withdrew this provision of informal advice citing lack of resources.

In April 2006 the OFT published a notice of interim arrangements for informal advice and pre-notification which reinstated the possibility of obtaining informal advice, subject to certain restrictions. The OFT considered these changes necessary as they considered the routine provision of this non-statutory service was detracting from their ability to conduct high quality reviews of public-domain merger cases.

The interim practice provides that the OFT will consider applications for informal advice for confidential transactions where there is a good faith intention to proceed, and where the OFT's duty to refer to the CC is a 'genuine issue'. The OFT is seeking to encourage the reliance on parties' external advisers rather than approaching the OFT for assurance. The OFT has stated that it sees 'no value to business or the taxpayer in accepting invitations to endorse the propositions of advisers that a transaction raises no issues'. The OFT states that parties are well-placed to rely on proper external advice for such cases. In practical terms, a genuine issue will only arise if the merger is a 'credible candidate for reference' to the CC. To qualify for informal advice the parties will therefore be expected to present reasons why the OFT might consider a reference to the CC – ie a case against the merger. There may be unique issues creating a genuine issue, for example, there may be a concurrent Competition Commission Inquiry in the market in which the merging parties are active. The OFT has however stated that the requirement for a genuine issue will not be met through claims that the client is 'very risk averse' or that 'third parties might complain'. Due to the strict criteria for the use of the procedure, few cases are likely to qualify for informal advice.

The OFT has stated that the application for informal advice should be an executive summary of no more than five pages in length. The OFT have said they will endeavour to indicate within five working days of receipt of the application whether it will accept or reject the application. Where informal advice is only given at the end of a meeting, the OFT will endeavour to schedule that meeting within 10-15 working days of receipt.

As this is an interim arrangement further clarification of the long-term procedure is expected by April 2007.

Confidential guidance

11.62   Under the *EA 2002* in certain merger cases the OFT was originally prepared to give confidential guidance before any public announcement was made. However in November 2005 the OFT withdrew the provision of confidential guidance. This suspension was continued in a further OFT notice published in April 2006, in which confidential guidance was asserted to be an unjustifiable call on OFT resources given the few additional benefits it may provide. Again this is an interim procedure and clarification of the long-term procedure is expected by April 2007.

Statutory voluntary pre-notification process

11.63   To improve efficiency, the government introduced a new 'fast-track' merger clearance procedure under the *Companies Act 1989*. Under the new procedure the OFT have 20 business days (subject to a standard ten-day extension and the potential for an additional ten-day extension if the Secretary of State has issued an intervention notice in respect of the case) from notification using the Official Merger Notice Form ('the Merger Notice') to raise objections to the merger proposals. If no action is taken within that period the merger may usually proceed without risk of a reference to the Competition Commission. The only exception is where either inadequate or misleading information has been supplied. To benefit from the fast-track procedure, the merger must be completed within four months of approval being given.

The Merger Notice consists of three sections. Parts 1 and 3 are formal sections requiring the details of the parties and a declaratory undertaking, and Part 2 requires the notifier to answer 18 standard questions on the merger proposals, their effect on competition and the barriers to entry onto the market in question. These questions have to be replied to in the form in which they appear on the form to qualify for this procedure. [Filing a submission covering the areas relevant to the questions will not be allowed under this procedure?]. The Merger Notice is usually filed on or several days after the public announcement of the transaction.

Merger control fees are payable for the use of the 'fast-track' procedure at the time of the application.

Although it was desired to give parties the comfort of knowing that they would receive a decision in a set statutory period, in practice it has not been particularly well received. The use of extension periods in complex cases, the prohibition of completing the merger within the consideration period and the adherence to a set timetable within the OFT when dealing with these cases, has created a perception that the old regular merger clearance procedure is quicker, more flexible and less bureaucratic. Therefore, most practitioners still prefer the old regular merger clearance procedure unless there are very good grounds to the contrary in any specific case.

Regular merger clearance procedure

11.64   Merger clearance applications not using the *Companies Act 1989* are very popular. The OFT is under no duty to announce its decision within any predetermined period. Such a fixed period is the advantage of the 'fast-track' procedure, described above in **11.63**. However, the OFT are usually able to process these applications within one month. Although recent guidelines issued stipulate that the OFT will handle these cases within 40 working days.

This again is taken to be as a maximum target. No merger control fees are payable under this system until the merger is referred to the Competition Commission or cleared by the OFT, in which case the scale of charges referred to below will apply. However, the government has now passed regulations exempting certain small and medium-sized enterprises from the payment of fees as detailed in **11.68** below.

OFT's assessment process

11.65   Once an application for merger clearance has been filed by the parties, or alternatively the OFT becomes aware through publicly available information of a qualifying merger situation, it will use its information gathering powers under the *EA 2002, s 31* or *99*. It may ask the parties to provide information on the merger situation in so far as they have not received such information in the parties' submission. It may, for example, ask for pre-merger strategic or marketing plans.

The OFT will also invite comments on any public merger situation from interested third parties by means of an invitation to comment notice published through the Regulatory News Service and on its website at www.oft.gov.uk. It may also seek the views of individuals or types of third parties (eg customers, suppliers and competitors). The OFT will usually give more weight to the views of customers than competitors. Where comments demonstrate that significant competition concern may be present, the parties proposing the merger are told of the nature of the concerns expressed and are given the opportunity to respond to them. The OFT will also contact other government departments and sectional regulators for their views.

False or misleading information

11.66   Parties or third parties supplying false or misleading information to the competition authorities may commit an offence under the *EA 2002, s 117* of knowingly or recklessly supplying false or misleading information to the OFT, Secretary of State or the CC. The penalty for a breach is a fine or a maximum of two years' imprisonment or both.

Decision-making process

11.67   The OFT case team dealing with a merger clearance application will prepare a clearance decision paper and circulate it to an OFT review group which includes the Chairman, Executive Director of Competition Enforcement Division, a representative of Competition Policy Co-ordination Branch, OFT Chief Economist, a representative of OFT Legal Division, representatives of the case team and the director of the relevant OFT sectional branch. Members of this review group who disagree with the decision can call for a case review meeting. If there are no dissenting voices, the decision will be finalised and publicly announced and relayed to the parties or their advisers.

In cases which give rise to material competition issues, a different process is followed. The parties will be invited to attend an 'Issues Meeting' with the OFT case team. To assist the parties in preparing for the meeting, the case officer will send an 'Issues Letter' to the parties. This will set out the core arguments and evidence in the case. The Issues Letter will also set out arguments in favour of a reference so that the parties have an opportunity to respond.

Parties to a merger may either comment on the Issues Letter in writing or orally at an Issues Meeting or both. The OFT usually allows an interval of around two days between receipt of the Issues Letter and the date of the Issues Meeting.

Following the Issues Meeting, an outline decision containing arguments for and against a reference will be circulated with the Case Team, internal economic analysis, Issues Letter and written response by the parties to members of the review group in advance of a case review meeting. This meeting will usually be chaired by the Director Competition Enforcement Division and attended by the case team, Director of the OFT branch and senior mergers economist. It may also be attended by OFT Board Members, the OFT Chief Economist and a representative from the OFT's Legal Division.

Following the case review meeting, there will be a separate decision meeting chaired by the 'decision maker', who may be the chairman, another member of the OFT Board or a duly authorised officer acting on behalf of the OFT and attended by the chair of the case review meeting, the case team, the devil's advocate and others from the case review meeting. A decision is then taken as a result of this meeting. The case officer will then draft the decision and the final version will be signed and the decision announced (in public cases) and communicated to the parties and their advisers.

Merger control fees

11.68   Merger control fees are payable in respect of qualifying merger situations which are either referred to the CC or cleared by the OFT (*Enterprise Act 2002 (Merger Fees and Determination of Turnover) Order 2003*). If a merger is pre-notified under the *Companies Act 1989* procedure, the relevant fee must accompany the application. In all other cases merger control fees are payable when a merger is cleared by the OFT or referred to the CC for further investigation.

Fees vary according to the type and size of the merger, but as at 6 April 2006, the fees in force were as follows:

(a)   value of the UK turnover of the enterprises being acquired is £20 million or less: £15,000;

(b)   value of the UK turnover of the enterprises being acquired is over £20 million, but not over £70 million: £30,000; and

(c)   value of the UK turnover of the enterprises being acquired exceeds £70 million: £45,000.

Small and medium-sized enterprises (SMEs) (as defined by the *Companies Act 1985*), are exempt from paying the above fees. SMEs are those companies which satisfy two of the following three criteria:

(a)   turnover: not more than £22.8 million;

(b)   balance sheet total: not more than £11.4 million; and

(c)   employees: not more than 250.

Undertakings In lieu of reference

11.69   Where competition problems are identified by the OFT, remedies in the form of structural and/or behavioural undertakings may be negotiated with the parties.

The OFT's guidance states that in order to accept undertakings they must be 'clear-cut' and 'capable of ready implementation'. Structural remedies, in particular divestements, are likely to be considered more suitable than behavioural undertakings.

The parties can propose undertakings at any stage in the OFT investigation. The latest point at which the parties can suggest undertakings is at the issues meeting or shortly after.

Where the OFT concludes undertakings are a suitable remedy to the identified adverse effects of a merger, it will normally issue a public announcement saying the merger will be referred to the CC unless satisfactory undertakings in lieu of reference can be obtained. The detailed terms and conditions of the undertakings will be negotiated with the parties after the final decision is announced.

Once the form of undertakings are agreed the OFT will consult on the undertakings. Following a press release, the OFT will ask parties to respond within 15 days on the purpose and effect of the proposed undertakings. This may be at the time of the decision or, more likely, a short period afterwards. If the original proposed undertakings are modified by the consultation process in any material way, a second consultation period of seven days will be required.

Until negotiations with the parties are concluded and the final undertakings accepted by the OFT, the normal statutory timetable for considering a merger may be extended to allow for the negotiation process. This is to avoid the situation where parties may be deprived of the right to negotiate undertakings because there is insufficient time to do so before the expiry of the statutory deadlines. The aim is to negotiate the undertakings as quickly as possible and a reference may still be made if agreement on undertakings cannot be agreed in a reasonable timescale.

The undertakings will then be signed by the parties and published in the OFT's Register of Undertakings and Orders. The OFT has the power to issue orders to require the parties to fulfil their undertakings. In addition third parties have rights under the *Enterprise Act* to bring an action for breach of statutory duty should a party not comply with an undertaking.

Appeals process

11.70   Under *the EA 2002 s 120*, the CAT has the power to review any relevant decision of the OFT, Secretary of State or the CC in connection with a reference or possible reference in relation to a relevant merger situation or a special merger situation.

For the purposes of *section 120* a decision means any decision in relation to mergers including a decision to clear or refer a merger, to impose undertakings or to prohibit the merger outright. It does not include a decision to impose a penalty under *sections 110(1)* or *(3)* in relation to the production of documents or attendance of witnesses, but does include a failure to take a decision permitted or required in connection with a merger reference or possible merger reference under *Part 3* of the Act.

Persons having a sufficient interest can apply for the review of the decision. These are the merger parties themselves or other persons having interest in the outcome of the case, such as competitors.

The review powers of the CAT do not entitle it to vary the relevant decision or substitute its own decision, but the CAT can quash the decision on grounds of procedural unfairness, illegality or unreasonableness as has been seen in the *IBA Health* and *Unichem* cases discussed at **11.50** above.

The Netherlands

The Competition Act

11.71   The Dutch Competition Act (Mededingingswet, Wet van 22 mei 1997, Stb 1997, 242) provides, amongst other things, for concentration control (**Chapter 5 Employee Share Schemes**). Dutch concentration control is largely based on the Merger Regulation. In addition, the principle of subsidiarity applies. In absence of the applicability of the Merger Regulation Dutch merger control will apply to each and every concentration whereby the aggregate turnover of all companies concerned in the previous calendar year was more than €113.45 million provided however that at least two of such companies concerned each achieves in the Netherlands a turnover of €30 million (Article 29).

A concentration is:

(a)   the merger of two or more previously independent undertakings;

(b)   direct or indirect acquisition by:

   (i)   one or more persons or legal entities who already have control over at least one undertaking; or

(ii)   one or more undertakings.

over one or more other undertakings or parts therefore through the acquisition of share capital or of assets, pursuant to an agreement or in any other way; or

(c)   the establishment of a joint venture that fulfils all functions of an independent economic entity without such establishment leading to a coordination of market behaviour.

Procedure

11.72   It is prohibited to carry out a concentration before the intention to do so has been notified to the Board ('Raad van Bestuur') of the Dutch Competition Authority (Nederlandse Mededingingsautoriteit) and four weeks having passed since the date of notification ('the notification stage'). The notification must provide detailed information so as to allow the Board to assess the application on its merits. If the undertakings concerned have not provided all the information which has been requested or if the information provided is clearly insufficient for giving a sound judgement on the notification, the Board may ask the notifying party for additional information. A request for additional information will lead to a suspension of the four-week period as from the date of the request. Such suspension will end on the date the Board has been provided with adequate information. All undertakings concerned are obliged to notify the concentration. Notification by one of the undertakings concerned, however, relieves the other undertaking(s) from the obligation to do so.

During the notification stage the Board of the Dutch Competition Authority will inform the undertakings concerned whether the concentration is subject to a licence. The Board may decide that a licence is required for a concentration if it presumes that the concentration will create a dominant position or if it will strengthen such dominant position, this resulting in a restriction of effective competition on the Dutch market or on a significant part thereof. Should the Board however not make a decision during the notification stage (ie within four weeks after receipt of the notification), no licence will be required and the concentration may be carried out freely. Should the Board however decide that the acquisition is subject to a licence, a second stage ('the licence stage') will apply, becoming effective at the date of application for such licence. A concentration for which a licence is required may not be carried out without such licence having been granted. The Board will decide within 13 weeks after receipt of the application for a licence. Should the Board not have decided within that period, the licence is deemed having been granted, and the concentration may be carried out freely. A licence may be granted subject to limitations or conditions. The Board will refuse to grant a licence in cases where the envisaged concentration will create a dominant position or will strengthen a dominant position, resulting in the actual competition on the Dutch market or a significant part thereof being significantly impeded.

The Competition Act provides for a specific exemption of the prohibition in case the concentration is effected through a public takeover bid. The prohibition to establish a concentration before notification and prior to a four-week period after the date of notification will not apply in the event of a public offer, provided that (i) the takeover bid is immediately notified to the Board of the Dutch Competition Authority, and (ii) the bidder will not exercise any voting rights in respect of his acquisition in the share capital of the target company. At the request of the notifying party (usually the bidder) the Board may, however, allow the bidder to exercise its voting rights in the target so as to maintain the full value of the participation.

Other legislation

11.73   In the Netherlands there is particular legislation with regard to the protection of rights of employees in a proposed merger. In addition, collective labour agreements may provide for rules relating to the protection of employees involved in a merger. These considerations are still relevant if a concentration is being considered under the *Merger Regulation* or Dutch law.

Merger Code (SER Fusiegedragsregels 2000)

11.74   The Merger Code provides for rules to be observed in relation to mergers, so as to protect the employees' interests. These rules will apply provided at least one enterprise located in the Netherlands employing at least 50 employees regularly, is involved in an envisaged merger. The Merger Code imposes a duty on the management of each enterprise that is involved in the envisaged merger to notify the trade unions of preparations taking place to effect such an envisaged merger (Article 4 paragraph 1 of the Merger Code). The management will have to provide the trade unions with (i) a motivation on the envisaged merger, (ii) the intentions as to the company policy to be pursued as a result of the merger and (iii) the social consequences of the merger. Subsequently, the trade unions should be given the opportunity to express the employees' viewpoint on the merger (Article 4 paragraphs 2 and 3 of the Merger Code). The unions will have to treat the information they have gained from the management in the context of the notification confidentially, unless the management has advised otherwise (Article 7 paragraph 1 of the Merger Code). The same notification shall be made to the secretariat of the Social Economic Council (Sociaal Economische Raad) (Article 8 of the Merger Code).

In the event of an alleged infringement of the Merger Code by a party to the envisaged merger or by the trade union concerned, the trade union concerned, respectively a party to the envisaged merger, can initiate party proceedings before a complaints commission (Geschillencommissie Fusiegedragsregels). As a result of these proceedings, the complaints commission can decide that a party to the envisaged merger or the trade union concerned has not (fully) observed the Merger Code. The complaints commission can add to the decision that the non-observance of the Merger Code is of a serious nature and highly imputable. The decision is made public. It should be noted that the Merger Code is generally well observed in the Netherlands. The Merger Code applies only to mergers involving at least one enterprise established in the Netherlands that regularly employs at least 50 employees.

The Merger Code will not apply in cases where the merger is effected outside the jurisdiction of the Netherlands. This is, for example, the case where two foreign companies located outside the Netherlands merge, while one of them has a subsidiary in the Netherlands, employing at least 50 employees. However, should the merger between two or more foreign companies indirectly involve a Dutch company and should the sole or the main purpose of such merger be the obtaining of the control of such Dutch company, the Merger Code will apply. This will be the case, for example, where a foreign entity, having no operational activities, acquires control over a foreign holding company holding the shares in a Dutch subsidiary (employing at least 50 employees).

Works Council Act (Wet op de Ondernemingsraden)

11.75   In the Netherlands a company employing in general at least 50 employees is obliged to establish a works council (ondernerningsraad). According to the Dutch *Works Council Act* (Wet op de Ondernemingsraden) the management must give the Works Council the opportunity to render its advice on any proposed action involving (i) the transfer of control over the enterprise or any part thereof or (ii) the acquisition of control over another company. Any request for advice must be made at such stage that the advice will be able to exercise significant influence over the envisaged merger. Jointly with the request for advice, the management should provide information on (a) the reasons for the proposed merger, (b) the consequences to be expected therefore for the employees as a result of the merger and (c) the proposed measures to be taken in relation to the merger.

Within a reasonable time after the notification, the Works Council will have to render its advice. Should the management decide to go ahead with the merger contrary to the Works Council's advice, it shall have to notify the Works Council accordingly, supplying the Works Council with a motivation for its decision to do so. Subsequently, the management must suspend the implementation of the envisaged merger for a period of one month, beginning as of the date of notification of the management decision. The Works Council may subsequently decide to lodge appeal with the Enterprise Chamber (Ondernemingskamer) of the Court of Appeals at Amsterdam against the management decision within this one-month period.

Should the Enterprise Chamber sustain the Works Council's claim, it may order the management to unwind the transaction wholly or partly.

Collective labour agreements

11.76   Finally, collective labour agreements may also provide for consultation with the trade unions in case of a transfer of control over the company or in case of transfer of (a part of) a business.

France

Competition issues

11.77   The French Finance Minister through the Competition Directorate (DGCCRF – *Direction Générale de la Concurrence, de la Consommation et de la Répression des Fraudes*), after consulting the Competition Council (*Conseil de la Concurrence*), has power under articles L430-1 et seq of the French Commercial Code to disallow qualifying mergers (including acquisitions) on competition grounds. French competition law was significantly modified in 2001 with further amendments in 2004 and 2005.

Qualifying Transactions: The definition of 'concentration' under French competition law has now been harmonised with the same term under EU Council Regulation no 139/2004 which has replaced the EU Council Regulation no 4046/89 since 1 April 2004 (*EU Merger Regulation*) and covers:

(a)   mergers between two or more independent undertakings;

(b)   acquisitions of direct or indirect control by one or more undertakings of one or more other undertakings; or

(c)   the creation of joint ventures performing all the functions of an autonomous economic entity on a lasting basis.

'Control' is the exercise of a decisive influence over another undertaking through the transfer of ownership or the benefit of all or part of the assets of an undertaking or through the exercise of rights or contracts which confer a decisive influence over the management of an undertaking. To assess the existence of 'decisive influence', French competition authorities review factual circumstances such as the exercise of voting rights, minority veto rights, shareholders' agreements providing for voting coordination or entrenching rights to appoint managers, the existence of privileged commercial relationships accounting for a significant part of the turnover of the target or a substantial role as lender to the undertaking[1].

The definition of 'concentration' now includes the creation of 'full function' joint ventures as provided in EU Merger Regulation and are subject to the same threshold tests.

The French competition authorities have suggested that they will refer to DGCCRF and European Commission precedents as well as the interpretation of the European Commission for the definition of 'concentration' (section 2 of Guidelines dated 20 October 2005 issued by DGCCRF relating to the analysis of concentration and control procedures – *DGCCRF Guidelines*).

A merger transaction, which falls out of the scope of the EU Merger Regulation, will qualify for review by the French competition authorities if certain turnover thresholds are met:

(a)   the parties concerned (including their respective groups) have a combined worldwide turnover (excluding taxes) of more than €150 million; and

(b)   the domestic turnover (excluding taxes) in France of at least two of the parties to the transaction is greater than €50 million (increased in 2004 from €15 million) each (and not combined together as confirmed by DGCCRF Guidelines section 31).

Under the 2001 legislation, the turnover thresholds were significantly reduced (previously, the thresholds were a combined turnover of more than FF7 billion/€1.07 billion with two or more of the parties concerned having a turnover of at least FF2 billion/€305 million) and there is no market share test (the 25% market share test under the former regime was abandoned). As a consequence, transactions where the turnover thresholds are met but which do not have significant impact on a relevant market, are required to be notified to the French competition authorities.

Once the turnover thresholds are met, notification to French competition authorities becomes compulsory. Merger transactions between foreign companies which do not have any asset, subsidiary or branch in France can be brought within the ambit of French merger control rules if such companies realise a turnover in France exceeding the thresholds mentioned above (*Boeing/Jeppesen* case). However the enforcement of any French decision against such non-French concentrations would seem to be problematic for the French State (in *Boeing*, the merger was cleared).

Guidance for the calculation of qualifying turnover is provided by decree no 2002–689 of 30 April 2002 (which refers to Article 5 of EU Merger Regulation) and in sections 33–41 of DGCCRF Guidelines. Generally speaking, the turnover to be taken into consideration is the turnover realised by the group to which the parties belong, except in certain cases such as:

(a)   Acquisition of a target: turnover of the target and that of the group to which the purchaser belongs (but not that of the seller's group other than the target);

(b)   Sale of assets such as trademarks: turnover from products sold under such trademarks (even though the production sites are not acquired);

(c)   Transfer of real properties: turnover from rental income.

Notification Requirement: The 2001 rules replace the previous voluntary notification regime by an obligation to notify any qualifying mergers prior to implementation (Article L430–3 of the French Commercial Code).

No qualifying transaction may be completed without the Finance Minister's clearance and, if relevant, clearance from the Minister for the relevant sector. However, in certain limited circumstances, a qualifying transaction may be completed without clearance (eg in certain insolvency buy-outs or public takeover bids, although voting rights are suspended until a decision on competition grounds from the Finance Minister or acquisitions by investment funds in sectors where such funds do not have holdings (DGCCRF Guidelines – Summary 2.2.1 section 3)).

The person in charge of notifying a qualifying transaction to the Ministry is the purchaser and in the case of a merger or the setting up of a joint venture, all parties are jointly responsible for filing (Article L 430–3 of the French Commercial Code).

Penalties may be imposed for failure to notify and/or for completing a transaction without prior approval being granted (or being deemed to be granted), up to €1.5 million for individuals and up to a maximum of 5% of the pre-tax annual turnover in France of the companies responsible for the filing and, if applicable, that of the target (Article L430–8 of the French Commercial Code). In addition, the Finance Minister may refer a matter to the Competition Council even absent a notification (Article L 430–8 I of the French Commercial Code).

Under the 2001 law, a binding agreement, subject to merger clearance, was required for the notification to be admitted for review. However, since December 2004, notification can be filed where the transaction has reached a sufficiently advanced stage of negotiation (*un projet suffisamment abouti*), the parties evidencing an intention to enter into a binding agreement (such as a letter of intent, exclusivity right granted to the purchaser or where the arrangement provides for a significant breakage fee etc). The new rules enable parties to clear the competition hurdle at an early stage.

It is also possible to consult the DGCCRF on an informal basis as to whether a notification is necessary or for the calculation of turnover or for assessing any anti-competitive effects of a particular transaction (DGCCRF Guidelines section 96).

Form of notification: the notification of mergers was formalised by Decree no. 2002–689 of 30 April 2002 (as modified in 2005) setting out the information to be provided, including a description of the transaction, the parties and their groups, 'relevant' market(s) involved (ie markets on which the qualifying transaction has a direct or indirect effect) and the 'affected' market(s). Although the 25% market share test is no longer applicable in determining if a merger qualifies for review, market share is still used in assessing how the market is 'affected'. Pursuant to Decree no. 2002–689, a market is 'affected':

(a) if the accumulated market share of the parties is equal to or exceeds 25%; or

(b) if one of the parties is active in the affected market and another of the parties is active in a market which is in a vertical relationship to such affected market and the market share of the parties involved in either of such markets equals or exceeds 25%; or

(c) if the transaction will lead to the disappearance of a potential competitor on a market where the parties are active.

If market share falls below 25%, a shorter form of notification should be acceptable (ie without the information on affected market(s)).

The information to be filed is similar to Form CO used in EU merger notifications but with less detail. Further, unlike Form CO, the Decree does not mention providing details of the pro-competitive aspects of the proposed merger although, in practice, these should be provided.

The DGCRFF Guidelines contemplate simplifying notifications filed by investment funds which realise a large number of transactions each year. After closing their accounts each year, such investment funds may make an electronic filing which constitutes core information for the following year. Each transaction will then be subject to a short form of notification and notification will be limited to information regarding the target, relevant and affected markets (if any) as well as updating the core information (if necessary) (DGCCRF Guidelines Annex 1 – section 512).

Review Timetable and Decision Making: The Finance Minister's initial review period is five weeks (as opposed to two months under the former regime) from receipt of a notification (provided information filed is considered to be complete – and the Ministry has been known to postpone the start date of the five-week period until the information is collated). This can be extended by up to three weeks if undertakings to cure any anti-competitive effects are submitted (Article 430–5 of the French Commercial Code). Parties may submit their undertakings at the same time as the notification or during the initial review period. The Minister will then:

(a)   decide that the merger falls outside of the scope of the regulations;

(b)   approve the merger (with or without the offered undertakings); or

(c)   refer the merger to the Competition Council for a detailed investigation.

Failure by the Minister to respond during the initial review period is deemed approval. The approval given by the Finance Minister is valid for an unlimited period of time provided that the *de facto* and *de jure* circumstances remain the same. Any substantial changes to the proposed transaction will qualify for a new review.

Where there is a referral to the Competition Council, the parties are given three weeks to provide their observations, as opposed to one month previously (Article 430–6 of the French Commercial Code). The Competition Council must report back within three months and the Minister's decision to approve or disallow the merger must be rendered within a further four weeks from the date of receipt of the findings of the Competition Council (again extendable by up to three weeks if the parties submit further undertakings). The new regime shortens considerably the overall merger control timetable where there is a referral to the Competition Council, from six months to four months from the initial notification.

Grounds for Disallowing Qualifying Transactions: The Finance Minister will refer a matter to the Competition Council if, in his view, such transaction is 'likely to undermine competition' and/or if the undertakings of the parties are not sufficient to cure any anti-competitive effects.

The Competition Council will review if a transaction is likely to undermine competition, in particular 'by the creation or strengthening of a dominant position' and, under the new law, if the transaction 'creates or strengthens buying power on the part of the merged entity which places suppliers in a position of economic dependency'.

Substantive Assessment: Generally speaking, in the case of horizontal mergers, French competition authorities examine if the transaction produces non-coordinated or unilateral effects (ie enabling the combined/new entity to increase its prices or determine the quality or quantity of production unilaterally without being subject to any pressure from competitors) or coordinated effects (undermining competitivity by creating or enhancing tacit collusion or a collective dominant position whereby the companies refrain from competing with each other). The review for non-coordinated effects will include various facets of the relevant market including market share of the parties involved and that of other national players, ease of entry of equivalent foreign imports, supply difficulties, importance of economies of scale or working capital requirements in the industry, cost of marketing to penetrate or stay in the market and the existence of manufacturing patents protecting the parties to the merger. The review for coordinated effects will be to assess if the structure of the relevant market is likely to create or enhance tacit collusion using the tests applied by the Court of First Instance of the European Communities in the Airtours case – for a collective dominance to be identified, there must be (i) sufficient market transparency leading to a tacit coordination amongst oligopolists to align their behaviour in the market; (ii) potential retaliation for departing from a common policy; and (iii) absence of reaction from competitors or consumers calling into question the coordination. The French competition authorities will also examine if the contemplated horizontal merger will cause a potential competitor (one of the entities involved in the merger) to disappear or will increase the buying power of the combined/new entity thereby placing suppliers in an economically dependent situation.

In the case of conglomerate mergers between firms in different markets, French competition authorities take into consideration the impact of the transaction in terms of its 'range effect' (addition of different types of products) or its 'portfolio effect' (addition of trademarks). Product extension may produce a 'range effect' undermining competition if a widened range of products will provide the combined/new entity with leverage, competitors being unable to propose such a complete range of products, a determining factor in the customer's mind. The acquisition of renowned or notorious trademarks can produce a 'portfolio effect' if the combined/new entity can gain market power deriving from a portfolio of notorious trademarks, thereby strengthening its position on the market. The analysis by the French competition authorities will include identifying the leading trademark holder on the relevant market, the market share of each trademark covered by the portfolio, the extent of market shares and trademarks held by each party to the merger and the relative importance of competing trademarks.

As to vertical mergers, French competition authorities will examine if the transactions will render competitors dependent on the supplies of the parties involved in the mergers and may, in certain cases, create risks of closing off a substantial part of the market to competition. French competition authorities may also use the 'failing firm' doctrine (the merger review taking into account what might happen to a target in difficulty if the merger is blocked) or market entry barriers to clear or prohibit proposed transactions.

Even if a qualifying merger is likely to undermine competition, the Competition Council may recommend it go through on the grounds that it contributes sufficiently to economic progress to outweigh the harmful effects on competition. Such appraisal will take into account the competitiveness of the companies involved in the light of the international market and the number of jobs to be created or maintained (article L430–6 section 1 *in fine* as modified in 2005).

Although the Finance Minister is required to consult the Competition Council if he or she considers there is a risk the qualifying transaction may undermine competition, he or she is not bound by the opinion of the Competition Council and may take a contrary view in giving the decision.

The decisions of the Finance Minister may be contested before the French administrative court (*Conseil d'État*) – such challenge to be notified within two months of notice of the decision.

1. In *Gillette/Wilkinson-Eemland* case, Gillette was found to have exercised a determining influence over the management and the commercial strategy of Eemland even though it held only bonds convertible into shares in Eemland.

Non-resident investment issues

11.78   Up to February 1996, in addition to merger control issues, non-EU investors had to obtain French Finance Ministry approval to a French investment, whilst EU investors would demonstrate their EU credentials by filing a notice before completion of a French acquisition.

Under the Law, Decree and Ministerial Order, all dated 14 February 1996 (and amended in 2003), the EU/non-EU distinction was removed and the acquisition (or disposal) of control of a going concern in France by a non-resident person is subject to filings with the Finance Ministry or, in limited cases, approval by it. However, decree 2005–1739 of 30 December 2005 (the '2005 Decree') tightened the existing regulatory framework for foreign investment and introduced once again the EU/non-EU distinction as far as investments requiring prior approval are concerned, non-EU investments being subject to more restrictive rules.

The Ministry's prior approval (*autorisation préalable*) is required for 'sensitive' investments by foreign investors which may affect the exercise of public authority, or which could undermine public order, public security or national defence or which are related to research, production or trade in arms, munitions, explosives or other military equipment (Article L151–3 of the French Monetary and Finance Code). The 2005 Decree (introducing articles

R 153-1 *et seq* of French Monetary and Financial Code) specified this list which can be subdivided into 'sensitive' and 'extra-sensitive' sectors.

The 'sensitive' sectors include gambling; private security services; research, development or production of antidotes; activities regarding equipment for intercepting communications or eavesdropping; services related to the security assessment and certification of IT systems and products; provision of goods or services relating to the IT security of companies managing facilities of vital importance to the nation; provision of goods or services related to dual use (civil and military) technologies set out in Annex IV of Council Regulation (EC) no 1334/2000. The 'extra-sensitive' sectors include certain types of cryptology activities; investments in entities having access to national defence secrets; research, manufacture and sale of arms, munitions, powder and explosive substance for military use or war equipment; and provision (direct or indirect) of goods or services to the defence ministry in relation to cryptology and extra-sensitive sectors.

Non-EU investments in both sensitive and extra-sensitive sectors are subject to prior authorisation if such investments concern the acquisition of a controlling stake in a French company, or the purchase (direct or indirect) of all or part of a branch of activities based in France or obtaining more than 33.33% of the share capital or voting rights of a French company.

This restriction is applied in a less stringent manner to EU investors – contrary to the case for non-EU investors, the acquisition of 33.33%–49.9% of the share capital of a French company active in a sensitive or extra-sensitive sector by EU investors does not require prior authorisation as above. In the case of the acquisition by a EU investor of a controlling stake, prior authorisation is required where the investment is made in an 'extra-sensitive' sector but not in a 'sensitive' sector. As to the acquisition of a branch of activities in whole or in part, prior authorisation is required in both 'extra-sensitive' and 'sensitive' sectors. Further, the scope of control in the 'sensitive' sectors is reduced and in certain cases, the review is only to the extent required for anti-terrorism or money laundering or for national defence purposes[1].

The 2005 Decree is seen as a revival of French protectionism to vet foreign takeovers in strategic sectors[2]. As of October 2006, the European Commission requested France to review the consistency of these rules with the EC Treaty on the free movement of capital and the right of establishment.

Failure to respond by the Finance Minister within two months of the application for authorisation will be deemed approval. Failure to file such application could lead to a fine equal to twice the investment amount (Article L151–3 of the French Monetary and Finance Code) and the investor can be ordered to establish at its own cost the status quo ante. Any undertaking or contractual provisions in view of implementing the foreign investment will be considered as void and therefore unenforceable.

Prior to investment, it is possible to consult the Finance Ministry to see if the contemplated investment is subject to the procedure of prior authorisation.

However, the absence of a reply will not be deemed to be an exemption (article R 153–7 of the French Monetary and Financial Code).

Since the 2005 Decree, the Finance Minister may also subject an authorisation to certain conditions: obligation to continue the target's business operations in the future; undertaking to protect the target's industrial, research and development capacities, know-how or to preserve its supply chain and obligation to perform contracts (procurement, public security, national defence or armament). If the activity subject to prior authorisation is an ancillary activity of the target, the government may demand the divestment of the ancillary activity to a third party company. The conditions imposed must be in proportion to the objective of safeguarding France's national interest.

The Finance Minister is entitled to refuse an application if he or she is convinced that the investor is likely to commit certain crimes (terrorism, corruption, money laundering etc) or unlikely to carry out the conditions mentioned above to safeguard France's national interest.

Administrative Filing – In all other (non-sensitive sector) cases, the following types of inward investment carried out by a non-resident (EU and non-EU) are subject to the filing of a declaration (déclaration administrative) upon exchange of contracts or upon the transaction occurring: establishment of a company in France, acquisition of a branch of activity of a French company, acquisition either directly or indirectly of more than 1/3 of the share capital or voting rights of a French company (20% of a listed or 1/3 of an unlisted French company under the former regime). A filing must also be made where a transaction entered into by a non-resident investor such as the grant of a loan, guarantee or acquisition of patents or licences, commercial contracts or the provision of technical assistance results in the gaining of de facto control of a French company. The same applies where the transaction is effected by a French company of which a foreign entity holds more than 1/3 of the share capital or voting rights.

Failure to file the 'déclaration administrative' can lead to a fine of €750. Certain non-resident investments are expressly exempted from the filing obligation. For example, extensions valued under €1.5 million of existing French businesses held by non-residents, increases in shareholding where 50% is already held by the non-resident investor (the threshold was 66.66% prior to the 2003 amendment), direct investment under €1.5 million in specific sectors such as the hotel, retail or restaurant sectors (Article R152–5 of the French Monetary and Financial Code).

Certain additional rules on foreign ownership exist depending on the sector concerned (eg audiovisual – see **11.82** below).

1. Gambling industry – investment control is limited to investments in casinos and only to the extent that the investment control is required for anti-money laundering;

   Private security services – only to the extent that the businesses provide (i) such services to entities in the public or private sector operating facilities and equipment which are of vital importance to national defence; (ii) airport and harbour security services; or (iii) services in relation to the protection of facilities and premises or information vital to national defence;

Research, development or production of antidotes – investment control is limited to investments in activities which are related to certain biological agents or toxic substances or chemical agents and only to the extent that such control is necessary to anti-terrorism and to avoid adverse impact of terrorism on health;

Activities regarding equipment for intercepting communications or eavesdropping only to the extent that investment control is necessary to anti-terrorism;

Services related to the security assessment and certification of IT systems and products only to the extent that investment control is necessary to anti-terrorism;

Provision of goods or services relating to the IT security of companies managing facilities of vital importance to the nation only to the extent that such supply is necessary for the protection of the facilities;

Provision of goods or services related to dual use (civil and military) technologies only to the extent that they are supplied to companies involved in national defence.

2. Examples of foreign purchase/takeover of French crown jewels in sensitive sectors: Alcatel's sale of Saft batteries to Doughty Hanson in 2004; takeover offer to acquire Arisem in the economic intelligence sector by a Canadian investment fund in 2003 and thwarted by French governmental intervention; acquisition of 26% of share capital of Gemplus, French smart card producer, by Texas Pacific Group in 2000.

Employee consultation

11.79   Changes of controlling shareholders or business transfers in companies where there is employee representation in the form of a works council (*comité d'entreprise*) will, under the French Employment Code, require, prior to signing an acquisition agreement or upon filing of a public takeover bid, consultation of the works council. There have been numerous French court decisions as to what constitutes appropriate consultation and, whilst a negative opinion from the works council need not prevent the transfer of shares or assets, transactions have been delayed because of inappropriate or insufficient information to the works council. Under 2001 legislation, a bidder in a takeover bid which fails to attend meetings organised by the workers' council of the target company could be deprived of its voting rights over the shares acquired in the target company until it has heard the target's works council. Since March 2006, the information obligation of a bidder is extended by requiring the purchaser to disclose its industrial and financial policy and strategic plans in respect of the target and the effects of the offer on the target. In companies where no works council exists, such information will be given directly to employees or employee representatives. Since 2006, the bidder must also provide information to its own personnel regarding the offer and the consequences it may have on employment.

Quoted companies

11.80   *Thresholds*: Under Article L233-7 of the French Commercial Code (as amended in 2005), any person or persons acting in concert acquiring a number of shares representing more than 1/20, 1/10, 3/20, 1/5, 1/4, 1/3, 1/2, 2/3, 18/20 or 19/20 of the share capital or voting rights of a French registered company[1] whose shares are quoted on a regulated exchange or the OTC market must notify the company within 5 days of passing through such thresholds (15 days under the old law). The acquirer must also inform the Autorité des Marchés Financiers ('AMF') (the market authority) within the same time limit. This requirement to notify also applies when the holding falls below the above thresholds. In addition, the acquirer whose holding passes through the thresholds of 1/10 or 1/5 of the share capital or voting rights of the company is required to notify the company and the AMF of the objectives it intends to pursue over the next 12 months with regard to the investment (eg acquiring control of the company, nomination of any person to the management of the company etc.) within 10 days of passing the relevant threshold (previously 15 days). Information provided to the AMF will then be made public as provided by the General Regulations of the AMF.

Any failure to notify will automatically result in a suspension of voting rights in any shareholders' meeting with regard to the portion of shares or voting rights exceeding the thresholds.

Takeovers: France adopted a new law on takeover bids – Law no 2006–387 of 31 March 2006 (the '2006 Law') and amended the AMF takeover regulations in September 2006, principally to implement the European Takeover Directive.

Persons acting in concert – Article 233–10–1 of the French Commercial Code as introduced by the 2006 Law distinguishes two cases of persons acting in concert in a takeover. A person is considered to be acting in concert when it has entered into an agreement (i) with an offeror to obtain the control of a target company or (ii) with the target company with a view to taking frustrating action.

Triggers for a compulsory takeover – A compulsory takeover offer will be required when the acquirer, acting alone or in concert, purchases over one-third of the shares of a company quoted on a regulated market (Article 234–2 of the AMF General Regulation) or when there is a change of control in such shareholder (Article 234–3 of the AMF General Regulation). Since July 2005, an offer for a French company triggers an obligation to offer to purchase not only a French but also a foreign subsidiary held over one-third by the French target and listed on an EEA or foreign regulated market, if such subsidiary constitutes a substantial asset of the target[2]. It will also be required when a shareholder (alone or in concert) holding directly or indirectly 1/3 or 1/2 of the share capital or voting right of a company increases his participation by 2% or more in a 12-month period (Article 234–5 of the AMF General Regulation). In all of the above cases, the 2006 Law requires the price proposed to target shareholders to be at least the highest price paid for any target company's shares acquired by the offeror acting alone or in concert over a period of 12 months prior to the offer. However, the AMF General Regulation (article 234–6) allows three exceptions: intervening events significantly affecting the market value of the target company over the 12-month period prior to the offer; intervening financial difficulties of the target company; the highest price paid by the offeror over the 12-month period was due to a connected transaction between the offeror (acting alone or in concert) and the vendor during this period. In such cases or in the absence of any acquisition by the offeror of the target's shares during the 12-month period prior to the offer, the minimum offer price will be fixed in accordance with a 'multicriteria' method taking into consideration generally applied 'objective' valuation methods, the characteristics of the target and the market price of the shares.

Minority squeeze-out – Since 1994, offerors may carry out a squeeze-out of minority holdings by initiating a buy-out offer (offre publique de retrait) providing that they have acquired over 95% of the shares of the target company. Further, a minority shareholder may request the market authorities to require majority shareholder(s) holding alone or in concert more than 95% of the voting rights of a company to buy out his or her holding (Article 236–1 to article 236–4 of the AMF General Regulation). The 2006 Law introduces a new type of procedure permitting a minority squeeze-out to be implemented within three months of the end of the main public offer without the need for an *offre publique de retrait* procedure. In all cases, provisions apply regarding the valuation of the company and the price to be offered or paid to the minority shareholders.

Neutrality Obligation of the Board – The restrictions on taking frustrating action under article 9 of the European Takeover Directive are transposed into the French rules (article L233–32 of the French Commercial Code). Apart from seeking a 'white knight', the board of the target company is prohibited from taking any frustrating action without prior shareholder approval during the offer period. However, there is a carve-out based on reciprocity: the restrictions do not apply (ie actions which may be frustrating of an offer may be taken) if the offer is made by an entity (or one of its parent companies or parties in concert) which is not (in view of its country of origin) itself subject to such restrictions or equivalent measures (article L233–33 of the French Commercial Code). The target company can apply reciprocity carve-out to any offeror including non-EEA companies. Any action proposed to be taken by the management of the target company which may be frustrating must have been approved by the shareholders during the 18-month period preceding the offer.

New type of poison pill – The 2006 Law allows expressly shareholders to issue under preferred warrants (*bons d'offre*) which can dilute the share capital and voting rights acquired by the offeror. They are required (i) to have been approved by shareholders of the target 18 months prior to the takeover bid and can only be used by the management in the case of reciprocity carve-out (ie frustrating action may be taken) or (ii) to be approved by shareholders during the offer period, whether the reciprocity carve-out applies or not (same principle as above).

Breakthrough provisions (unenforceability of restrictions on share transfers (vis-à-vis the offeror) and voting rights and suspension of certain other shareholder rights when a bid has been made public) – France has opted out of the breakthrough provisions under article 11 of the Takeover Directive except two which were adopted by AMF in practice: (i) limitations on voting rights provided in the by-laws of a target company will not be applicable in the first shareholder meeting following a public offer whereby the acquirer acting alone or in concert holds more than 2/3 of the share capital or voting rights of the target (article L225–125 of the French Commercial Code; article 231–43 of the AMF General Regulation); (ii) unless required by applicable law, any clauses restricting the transfer of shares in the by-laws of a quoted company will not be applicable to an offeror during the offer period (article L233–34 of the French Commercial Code; formerly article 231–6 of the AMF General Regulation). All the other provisions of article 11 of the Takeover Directive may be adopted voluntarily by quoted companies (suspension of restrictions on voting rights etc).

Put-up or shut up – In response to the market speculation on the persistent rumour that Pepisco would launch a takeover bid for Danone in 2005, the 2006 Law gives power to AMF to require any person acting alone or in concert to disclose its intentions with regard to the target company if the AMF has reasonable grounds (based on, for example, discussions between the issuers and advisers being appointed) to believe that it is preparing a public offer, in particular when a financial instrument of the target is subject to significant fluctuations in terms of price and volume of transactions. If the potential bidder discloses its intention to launch a public offer, the AMF will then set a timetable to file the offer or a press release on the characteristics of the offer (financial conditions, shareholding of the bidder, contemplated timetable etc). If the potential acquirer indicates its intention not to launch a public offer or is deemed not to have any such intention, it will be (i) prohibited from making any offer for six months; and (ii) required to disclose every 2% increase in shareholding and voting rights.

1. The application by the French court is restrictive and the passing of each threshold should be notified. In the CNIM case, certain minority shareholders acting in concert notified the passing of 20% but had failed to notify the company for passing through 10% threshold. As a result, they were permitted by the company to exercise only 10% (instead of 20%) of the voting rights in a general meeting. The French Supreme Court in May 2006 confirmed that (i) the notification concerns the number of shares and voting rights on the date the relevant threshold is exceeded and not that on the date of notification; and (ii) a notification concerning the passing of a higher threshold will not regularise the failure to notify the passing of a lower threshold.
2. This provision known as 'Nissan Amendment' is seen to be tailor made to protect the interest of Renault as this will render onerous a takeover bid for Renault: Nissan, in which Renault holds a 44.4% stake, has a market capitalisation significantly higher than that of Renault.

Mixed economy companies/privatisations

11.81   Mixed economy companies are private limited companies with private and French State shareholders. In certain cases, the State will have the right to nominate members to the board of the company and even to approve changes of private shareholding blocks. Air France was one such company when it was set up in 1932.

Local mixed economy companies (with private and local authority shareholders) are generally set up for the purpose of combining private finance and/or expertise with a project with a local public interest (eg road construction or a bus service). In general, the local authority will hold a majority of the shares and control the board of directors and there are rules for the private shareholders to hold a minimum number of shares each, which has been lowered from 20% to 15% (Article L 1522–2 *Code Général des Collectivités*

Territoriales as modified by the Law no 2002–1 of 2 January 2002). Since 2002, foreign mixed economy companies have been allowed to take a participating interest in French mixed economy companies; but, in the case of such entity being non-EU, provided that a bilateral treaty has been entered into between France and the relevant foreign country. Non-EU mixed economy companies may not hold more than 50% of the share capital and voting rights of shareholders.

The state has reserved a right to create and retain a golden share (*action spécifique*) in privatised companies where it is 'for the protection of the national interest'. The golden share, for example, in TotalFinaElf (formerly Elf-Acquitaine) provided the government with veto rights on transfers of a certain percentage of the shares, rights to nominate observers to the board and the right to veto the disposal or pledge of certain assets where the same could be detrimental to the national interest. As such privileged share was found by the European Court of Justice to be incompatible with the EU Treaty on the free movement of capital in June 2002, the decree granting the French state's rights in Elf-Acquitaine was repealed. The European Court has not, however, fully prohibited golden share schemes if the state control is justified by overriding requirements of the general interest and qualified by stable, objective criteria which have been made public so as to restrict to a minimum the discretionary power of the national authorities. Further, the means employed must be proportionate to the objective pursued.

Special regulations for certain sectors

11.82   Notwithstanding the nationality of the acquirer, regulatory approvals are imposed on acquisitions in certain sectors. These include the following sectors.

Banking: the French *Comité des établissements de crédit et des entreprises d'investissement* (CECEI), a body composed of *Banque de France*, French Treasury and other officials and ministerial appointees) must give its prior authorisation to changes affecting the situation of a French credit establishment including appointments to the board (whether new directors are fit and proper) or the acquisition or disposal of (i) the effective management control or (ii) 1/3, 1/5, or 1/10 of the voting rights. The Committee will usually seek comfort letters regarding the support a new controlling shareholder will give to its French subsidiary. Since legislation in 2001, the Governor of the Banque de France must be informed of a takeover at least eight days prior to submission to the CECEI.

Newspapers: Regulations have been put in place for newspaper publications with a view to protecting 'pluralism' in the media. Under Article 11 of the Law of 1 August 1986, no person may acquire control directly or indirectly of, or take over, under a business lease, the publication of daily printed newspapers with a circulation exceeding 30% of the total national circulation of similar publications over a period of 12 months preceding the date of acquisition or takeover or business lease. Any transaction which would exceed this threshold would be null and void. In addition, the regulations restrict the number of television and radio licences which may be held by a person or group which already publishes newspapers. Further, under Article 7 of the 1986 Law and subject to France's 'international undertakings' (eg the EU non-discrimination principles), no foreign person may hold more than 20% of the share capital or voting rights of a French-language publishing house.

Audiovisual: the audiovisual sector is the subject of complex regulation designed to promote pluralism in the various media. Thus, for example, no person may hold more than one hertzian national television licence or hold more than one licence to operate a television channel broadcasted by satellite (Article 41 of the law no 86–1067 of 30 September 1986). Moreover, under legislation adopted in 2001, no shareholder may hold more than 49% of a terrestrial national television channel with at least 2.5% of the national audience for television services (and no more than 50% in the case of a television channel broadcasted by satellite). The acquisition of a stake in a television company is restricted (to 15% of the share capital and voting rights of the target if the purchaser holds a licence to operate a national terrestrial hertzian channel or 1/3 of share capital and voting rights of the target if the purchaser holds a licence to operate a television channel broadcasted by satellite) where the acquirer already has interests (exceeding 15% or 1/3 of share capital and voting rights) in television companies with such licences. Such restriction is reduced to 5% if the investor already has interests in two television companies exceeding 5%. Further, subject to France's 'international undertakings' (eg the EU non-discrimination principles), no foreign person may hold more than 20% of the share capital or voting rights of a company with a French language radio or hertzian television licence. In the event of a referral of a qualifying transaction in the audiovisual sector to the French Competition Council, the latter will consult the CSA (*Conseil Supérieur de l'Audiovisuel*) which will transmit its advice to the French Competition Council within one month.

Regulated professions

11.83   Each profession in France is the subject of its own specific regulation imposed by law and/or its professional body (which usually cover issues such as training, specific authorisations or licences, the method of offering services to the public, the use of a professional title, professional indemnity insurance and financial guarantees). Where the practitioners are able to practise their profession in the form of companies, specific rules exist with regard to the composition of the board of such companies, the ownership of shares, the location of the registered office and even the form of borrowings of such companies. As examples:

(a)   only pharmacists may hold shares in and manage a company exploiting a pharmacy;

(b)   industrial/intellectual property advisors (*conseils en propriété industrielle*) who represent their clients before the patent office must hold more than 50% of the shares of their companies and be in the majority on the board;

(c)   lawyers (avocats) may exercise their profession in the form of a professional company in which French qualified lawyers (practising within or
without the company) or their investment vehicle hold more than 50%
of the shares. Up to 49% of the shares can be held by non-avocats who
exercise one of the legal profession (ie notaries, bailiffs, specialist
counsels) or, for a limited time, former French lawyers or their successors. The manager of such company or at least two-thirds of the board
members must be lawyers practising within the company. Transfers of
shares must be subject to the prior approval of at least two-thirds of the
lawyer shareholders or two-thirds of the lawyers on the board.

Germany

11.84   The statutory basis for merger control in Germany is the Act against
Restraints of Competition ('ARC') (Gesetz gegen Wettbewerbsbeschraen-
kungen). Part 1 of the ARC ('Restraints of Competition') is divided into several chapters of which Chapter VII is, in particular, concerned with control of
concentrations. German merger control, therefore, has to be seen in context
with and in the light of German control of competition.

The latest major amendment to the ARC merger control provisions came into
effect on 1 July 2005. Following a line of previous amendments, the general
purpose of the amendment of 1 July 2005 is to align German anti-trust and
merger control laws with the respective European laws, in particular with the
European Antitrust Regulation 1/2003. As regards merger control, the amendment introduces several minor changes, which largely concern the procedure
of merger control by the Federal Cartel Office.

Concentrations which are subject to control

Domestic effects

11.85   The Federal Cartel Office (Bundeskartellamt) only examines mergers in the geographic area of application of the ARC. The ARC applies to all
constraints of competition having a noticeable effect within Germany.
Transactions will be regarded as having a domestic effect if:

(a)   a foreign undertaking acquires shares of a domestic undertaking;

(b)   foreign undertakings participate in a domestic joint venture; or

(c)   the undertaking, the shares in which are acquired in the transaction, has
subsidiaries or affiliated companies in Germany.

Domestic effects will also have to be considered if the transaction is put into
effect outside of Germany, but nevertheless influences the structural conditions for competition within Germany. Pursuant to the current practice of the
Federal Cartel Office such influence is to be assumed in the following cases:

(a)   At least two of the participating undertakings (see below for meaning
of this term) have been operating on the same domestic market.

(b)   Only one of the participating undertakings has been operating on a domestic market and, as a consequence of the merger, future deliveries into Germany by other participating undertakings are deemed likely. For the purpose of this rule, deliveries into Germany will be deemed likely if there are already existing relations between the participating undertakings with respect to production (eg the participating undertakings are operating each on different stages of production) and assortment.

(c)   The merger leads to an increase of financial or technical resources, to an enhancement of know-how, or to the availability of industrial intellectual property rights for a participating undertaking which has been operating on a domestic market.

In the above cases, the operation on a domestic market required respectively may be effected through subsidiaries, affiliated companies, branches or importers. A merger between undertakings which do not have any relation of such kind to the German market nevertheless falls within the scope of control by the Federal Cartel Office if it leads to alterations of the German market structure. This may be the case, for example, if two airlines merge, none of which has subsidiaries or affiliated companies in Germany and at least one of the airlines is flying German air routes. The same applies to international joint ventures which intend to enter the German market or which operate in an overall European or worldwide market.

Types of transactions subject to control/turnover thresholds

11.86   Transactions having domestic effects as described above are subject to the provisions on merger control in Part 1, chapter 7 of the ARC, if:

(a)   they form a concentration within the meaning of ARC, s 37 (see further below in this section and **11.87** through **11.90** below); and

(b)   the participating undertakings reach or exceed the turnover threshold values in ARC, s 35 (see **11.93** below for threshold values).

The provisions of the ARC on merger control do not apply to the extent the Commission of the European Communities has exclusive jurisdiction pursuant to sections 1 and 3 of the Merger Control Regulation, as amended [see ARC, s 35(3)].

There are four kinds of transactions that can constitute a concentration:

(i)   acquisition of assets [ARC, s 37(1) No. 1], (see **11.87** below);

(ii)   acquisition of control [ARC, s 37(1) No. 2], (see **11.88** below);

(iii)   acquisition of shares [ARC, s 37(1) No. 3], (see **11.89** below); and

(iv)   transactions which enable one or several undertakings to exert a significant influence on another undertaking [ARC, s 37(1) No. 4], (see **11.90** below).

In practice, ARC, s 37(1) Nos. 1 to 3 are most significant. ARC, s 37(1) No. 4 serves as gap-filler.

The ARC does not define the term 'participating undertakings'. However, it is settled that the term varies with the different types of transactions. The respective meaning of the term in the context of the different types of concentrations is specified in **11.87** to **11.90** below. The term, moreover, has particular importance for determining the turnover relevant for the turnover thresholds (see **11.93** below).

Acquisition of assets

11.87   The acquisition of all or of a substantial part of another undertaking's assets is deemed to be a concentration [ARC, s 37(1) No 1]. An acquisition of assets is substantial if, in relation to the total assets of the seller, the relevant assets are of a sufficient quantity or if they have significance in their own right with regard to production, distribution targets and current market conditions and accordingly appear to be a unit that can be separated from the seller's other assets. Such a unit may be, for example, a branch, a division, a trademark, a real property or a newspaper's right of publication.

In the case of an acquisition of assets, both the acquiring undertaking and the selling undertaking which sells all or a substantial part of its assets are considered to be participating in the merger. However, in particular with regard to computing the relevant turnover thresholds, the selling undertaking is only considered to be participating to the extent its assets are sold. This means that the relevant asset's turnover has to be singled out.

Acquisition of control

11.88   The acquisition of direct or indirect control over the whole or parts of one or more other undertakings is the second kind of transaction which is deemed to be a concentration [ARC, s 37(1) No 2]. Control can be exercised by way of rights, contracts or any other means which, either separately or in combination, and having regard to the considerations of fact or law involved, confer the possibility of exercising decisive influence on an undertaking. Control can be created in particular through:

(a)   ownership or rights of usage regarding all or part of the undertaking's assets; and

(b)   rights or contracts which confer decisive influence on the composition, voting or strategic decisions of the undertaking's corporate bodies.

An acquisition of control can only be assumed if the possibility of exercising influence is permanent and comprehensive. The most important case of an acquisition of control is the acquisition of the majority of voting capital in the target undertaking. Further examples are the conclusion of a company lease agreement or of a domination agreement, permitting one undertaking to give instructions to the corporate bodies of another undertaking.

Control within the meaning of ARC, s 37(1) No 2 can also be acquired and exercised jointly by several undertakings. Such undertakings do not have to be affiliated companies. It is sufficient, if the undertakings are in the position to coordinate their competitive conduct vis-à-vis the controlled undertaking on the basis of a common strategy, eg on the basis of pool treaties or increased majority thresholds in the shareholder's meeting of the controlled undertaking.

The above concept of acquisition of control is similar to the concepts of sole and joint control under the Merger Control Regulation. It therefore has to be interpreted in the light of the practice of the European Commission and the rulings of the European Court of Justice.

In the case of an acquisition of control, both the acquiring undertakings and the controlled undertaking are considered to be participating in the merger. Depending on the circumstances, the undertaking transferring control of another undertaking may also be considered to be participating.

Acquisition of shares

11.89   The acquisition of shares in another undertaking (target undertaking) is deemed to be a concentration if the shares, either separately or together with other shares already held by the acquiring undertaking, reach or exceed:

(a)   50%; or

(b)   25%,

of the voting capital or the voting rights of the target undertaking [ARC, s 37(1) No 3].

It is significant to note that to reach or exceed each of the above threshold values is deemed a concentration which can trigger a merger control procedure (ie if the second threshold value of 50% is reached after prior acquisition of 25% or more of the shares, each acquisition constitutes a separate concentration).

Shares held by an undertaking include the shares held by a third party for the account of this undertaking and, if the owner of the undertaking is a sole proprietor, also any other shares held by him outside of the undertaking which he runs as sole proprietor. If several undertakings simultaneously or successively acquire shares in the target undertaking and each of them thereby reaches or exceeds one of the thresholds above, this is deemed not only a concentration in relation to the target undertaking. It is further deemed a concentration among the acquiring undertakings with respect to those markets on which the target undertaking operates.

Further, if an acquiring undertaking is affiliated with other undertakings (as a controlling or controlled undertaking or as a group undertaking within the meaning of the Stock Corporation Act [Aktiengesetz] s 17 and 18), then the acquiring undertaking and all affiliated undertakings are regarded as one undertaking [see ARC, s 36 (2)]. As a result, the shares held by the acquiring undertaking and by its affiliated undertakings in the target undertaking will be considered in the aggregate for the purpose of computing the above thresholds of 25% and/or 50%.

In the case of an acquisition of shares in the target undertaking, both the acquiring undertaking and the target undertaking (as well as their respective affiliates) are considered to be participating in the merger. The undertaking selling the shares is considered to be participating only if it retains 25% or more of the capital or the voting rights of, or a material competitive influence on, the target undertaking. Only in this case will the turnover of the selling undertaking be taken into account in the computation of the turnover thresholds (see **11.93** below).

Transactions which enable undertakings to exert a significant influence on another undertaking

11.90   Finally, any other combination of undertakings enabling one or several undertakings to directly or indirectly exert a competitively significant influence on another undertaking is deemed to be a concentration [ARC, s 37(1) No 4]. The ability to exert a competitively significant influence must arise under corporate law. Mere commercial influence will not suffice. The exercise of a competitively significant influence will have to be considered in instances where the relationship between the participating undertakings gives reason to expect that the competition between them is restricted to such a significant extent that they cannot act independently in the market.

The ARC, s 37(1) No. 4 has practical relevance in acquisitions of shares below 25% (ie where ARC, s 37(1) No. 3 does not apply), if the purchasing undertaking additionally gains direct influence on the corporate bodies of the target undertaking, eg by way of special voting rights or any agreement having effect on voting results, or in the case of a publicly listed undertaking, because of the low presence of shareholders in shareholders' meetings, a shareholding of less than 25% practically confers substantial influence.

In the case of transactions, which enable undertakings to exert a significant influence on a target undertaking, the undertaking acquiring a significant influence and the target undertaking subject to such influence are considered to be participating in the merger.

Gradual increase of concentration

11.91   In the above cases, a concentration may also arise if the participating undertakings had already merged previously, unless the intensification of the concentration does not result in a substantial strengthening of the existing affiliation between the undertakings [ARC, s 37(2)].

Thus, eg if an undertaking which already holds 25% or 50% of the shares in another undertaking acquires a further interest in such undertaking or enters into a control (domination) agreement with such undertaking, such transaction will be deemed an increase of concentration, if it strengthens the acquiring undertaking's influence on the other undertaking.

In contrast, eg if a group holding company transfers its shares in a second-tier subsidiary to a first-tier subsidiary, such transaction will usually not be considered as an increase of concentration.

Therefore, unlike under Article 3 of the Merger Control Regulation, a concentration may be subject to German merger control even if the merging undertakings previously were not independent.

Exemptions for certain transactions by banks and insurances

11.92   Similarly to the Merger Control Regulation, the ARC contains a banking clause according to which the acquisition of shares through credit institutions, financial institutions or insurance undertakings for the purpose of a subsequent divestment shall not be deemed to constitute a concentration as long as they do not exercise the voting rights attached to the shares and provided the divestment occurs within one year [ARC, s 37(3)]. This time limit might, upon application, be extended by the Federal Cartel Office if it is substantiated that the divestment was not reasonably possible within this period.

Turnover threshold values

11.93   Concentrations are only subject to control if, in the *last business year preceding the concentration*, the turnover threshold values as listed in ARC, s 35(1) are reached or exceeded by the participating undertakings.

Accordingly, German merger control will apply if in the last business year prior to the merger:

(a)   the combined aggregate worldwide turnover of all participating undertakings was more than €500 million; and

(b)   the domestic turnover (in Germany) of at least one participating undertaking was more than €25 million.

Whether an undertaking is a participating undertaking for the purpose of computing the thresholds depends on the respective type of concentration (see **11.87** to **11.90** above). In particular, the following applies:

(a)   in the case of an acquisition of assets of another undertaking [ARC, s37(1)], the calculation of the turnover of the selling undertaking has to take into account only the turnover achieved with the assets sold (eg the rental income of a real property sold) [ARC, s 38 (5)];

(b)   in the event of a sale of shares the turnover of the selling undertaking will be included only if it retains 25% or more of the shares in, or a material competitive influence on, the target undertaking (see **11.89** above);

(c)   finally, if a participating undertaking is a group undertaking or an affiliated undertaking within the meaning of Stock Corporation Act s 17 and s 18, then the affiliated and group undertakings shall be treated as one undertaking according to ARC, s 36(2). As a consequence the turnover of the so affiliated undertakings or the group undertakings will be combined for the purpose of computing the above thresholds.

The ARC further contains specific rules for determining the turnover of certain business branches:

(a)   in the case of concentrations involving undertakings trading in merchandise, only three quarters of the respective turnover has to be taken into account [ARC, s 38(2)];

(b)   for the publication, production and distribution of newspapers and magazines, the production, distribution and broadcasting of radio and television programmes, and the sale of radio and television advertising time, 20 times the amount of the turnover shall be taken into account [ARC, s 38(3)];

(c)   in the case of financial institutions (notably banks) the turnover shall be replaced by the aggregate amount of interest earned, net income from securities, commission earned, income from financial transactions and other commercial income, minus value added tax [ARC, s 38(4)]; and

(d)   in the case of insurance undertakings the premium income in the last business year shall be relevant. Premium income shall be income from insurance and reinsurance business [ARC, s 38(4)].

Concentrations not subject to control

11.94   De minimis clause [ARC, s 35 (2) No 1]: Concentrations are not subject to German merger control where an undertaking that merges with another undertaking is not a controlled undertaking within the meaning of the ARC, s 36(2) – see **11.89** above) and generated a worldwide turnover of less than €10 million in the last business year. This rule, however, is not applicable to the press market, as this market is typically characterised by relatively low turnover figures.

Minor market clause [ARC, s 35 (2) No. 2]: In addition, there is a so-called 'minor market clause' which rules that there will be no merger control with regard to a market in which goods or commercial services have been offered for at least five years, and which had a sales volume of less than €15 million in the last calendar year.

Criteria for instituting merger control proceedings

11.95   If a concentration is subject to merger control under the above criteria, the Federal Cartel Office will prohibit the concentration if it is expected to create or strengthen a dominant market position, unless the participating undertakings prove that the concentration will also lead to improvements of the conditions of competition, and that these improvements will outweigh the disadvantages of the market dominance [ARC, s 36(1)].

Dominant position

11.96   According to ARC, s 19(2), an undertaking is market dominant where, as a supplier or purchaser of certain kinds of goods or commercial services, it:

(a)   has no competitor or is not exposed to any substantial competition; or

(b)   has a paramount market position in relation to its competitors; for this purpose, account has to be taken in particular of the following market structure elements:

   (i)   the undertaking's market share;

   (ii)   its financial power;

   (iii)   its access to supplies or markets;

   (iv)   its links with other undertakings;

   (v)   legal or factual barriers to market entry by other undertakings;

   (vi)   actual or potential competition by undertakings established within or outside Germany;

   (vii)   its ability to shift its supply or demand to other goods or commercial services;

   (viii) the ability of the opposite market side to resort to other undertakings.

Two or more undertakings are dominant to the extent that no substantial competition exists between them with respect to certain kinds of goods or commercial services and that they jointly satisfy the conditions listed above.

A single undertaking is presumed to be dominant if it has a market share of at least one-third. Several undertakings are presumed to be dominant if they:

(a)   consist of three or fewer undertakings reaching a combined market share of 50%; or

(b)   consist of five or fewer undertakings reaching a combined market share of two-thirds,

unless the undertakings demonstrate that the conditions of competition may be expected to maintain substantial competition between them, or that they jointly have no paramount market position in relation to the remaining competitors [ARC, s 19(2), (3)].

Relevant market: In defining the relevant market, criteria relating to product, time and place should be considered. All products or services which are – from the point of view of an average (private or commercial) consumer – substitutable to cover his same needs, belong to one market.

Market dominance: To determine a market dominance, initially only the market structure elements listed in ARC, s 19(2) have to be taken into consideration. The most important will be the market share of the concentration as well as the financial strength, as it implies potential barriers for competitors to entry into the relevant market (existing competitors might refrain from making investments in innovative market technology or approaches and potential new competitors might be discouraged from competing with a financially powerful competitor). If the market structure elements listed in ARC, s 19(2) do not suffice to prove a significant market dominance, market behaviour can be taken into account additionally. Other criteria, such as public interests, will not be taken into consideration.

Creation or strengthening of a dominant position

11.97   A dominant position will be created or strengthened if the market structure has deteriorated to such an extent that the concentrated undertakings gain or extend an uncontrolled scope of economical behaviour (eg the financial strength of the newly formed concentration has a deterrent effect on existing or potential competitors). Furthermore, the change of the relevant market structure elements must be noticeable.

Causal connection

11.98   ARC, s 36(1) requires a causal connection between the concentration and the change of market structure (eg the conditions of competition). There will be a lack of causal connection if the concentration leads to a deterioration of competitive market conditions which would have occurred even without the concentration.

Prediction

11.99   ARC, s 36(1) implies a prediction regarding the expected consequences of a concentration. There are two aspects to consider: changes regarding the market structure resulting immediately when the transaction takes effect; and long-term consequences for the conditions of competition. The prediction will take into account a period of three to five years following the concentration.

Consideration clause

11.100   A concentration cannot be prohibited if the participating undertakings manage to prove that the concentration will simultaneously lead to an improvement of conditions of competition and that these improvements will outweigh the disadvantages of dominance [ARC, s 36(1)]. However, aspects to be considered in determining improvements of the conditions of competition are restricted to those aspects which define the market structure, as listed in ARC, s 19(2). Aspects such as job protection, macroeconomic advantages or the sustainment of an undertaking will not be taken into consideration.

Procedure regarding control of concentrations

Competence

11.101   The Federal Cartel Office has the exclusive authority with regard to the control of concentrations [ARC, s 40 (1)]. Notifications must be sent to the following address: Bundeskartellamt, Kaiser-Friedrich-Str.16, D-53113 Bonn, Germany. Tel: +49 228 9499 0. Fax: +49 228 9499 400. Email-address: info@bundeskartellamt.bund.de. Website: www.bundeskartellamt.de.

However, in certain circumstances the Federal Minister of Economics has authority to approve, upon application, a concentration prohibited by the Federal Cartel Office, if, in the particular case, the restraint of competition is outweighed by an overriding public interest or by overweighing macroeconomic reasons [ARC, s 42].

Pre-merger notification

11.102   The Federal Cartel Office always has to be notified of concentrations which are subject to control prior to putting the concentration into effect [ARC, s 39(1)]. The obligation is, in principle, imposed on the participating undertakings (see **11.85** to **11.90** above).

The notification must be filed before the concentration takes effect. In practice, the notification will be filed after signing of the relevant transaction but prior to the consummation/closing of the respective transaction (eg by transfer of shares or assets, etc.) (see **11.104** below).

The notification must specify the type of concentration and identify each of the participating undertakings and the seller of shares in, or assets of, the target undertaking by indicating their name or other designation and place of business or registered domicile. In addition, the notification must indicate the business and detail the turnover of each participating undertakings in Germany, in the EU and worldwide for the last business year preceding the transaction. The notification also has to set out the market shares and the relevant calculation basis of each participating undertaking, including its affiliated undertakings, if the combined market shares of all participating undertakings amount to at least 20% within Germany or a substantial part thereof. In the case of a share acquisition, the notification should indicate the size of the interest acquired as well as the total interest held. Furthermore, the notification should clarify the interlinkage between the participating undertakings.

If the registered domicile of a participating undertaking is not located in Germany, a person authorised to accept service of process in Germany must be named in the notification. The same applies if the seller of shares in, or assets of, the target undertaking is not located in Germany.

Third parties (eg competitors, customers or suppliers) whose interests will be materially affected by the decision of the Federal Cartel Office to clear or prohibit a concentration will, upon application, be admitted to the proceedings as interveners [ARC, s 54 (2), No. 3].

In practice, the Federal Cartel Office requires the identification of other countries in which the transaction is intended to be notified or has already been notified (multiple filings).

An application form based on the above requirements can be obtained as a download at www.Bundeskartellamt.de.

Clearance and prohibition of the concentration

11.103   If the Federal Cartel Office decides within one month after filing of the complete notification that the concentration does not raise any concern, it will clear the concentration. In practice, it will then inform the participating undertakings about the clearance in writing.

If the authority, however, decides within this one-month period to initiate main examination proceedings [Hauptprüfungsverfahren], the Federal Cartel Office will inform the participating undertakings, by a so-called one-month letter [Monatsbrief], that it will proceed with further examinations.

In the main examination, the Federal Cartel Office decides by way of formal decision whether the concentration is prohibited or cleared. Clearance can be subject to conditions and obligations and will be published in the Federal Gazette.

If the Federal Cartel Office does not react within one month by issuing a one-month letter the concentration is deemed to be cleared. The same applies if, in the event of a one month letter within four months after filing of the complete notification, the Federal Cartel Office does not deliver its decision to the undertakings which have filed the application.

The four-month period can be prolonged with the consent of the undertakings which have filed the application. Without such consent, it can be prolonged if the Federal Cartel Office has refrained from issuing a one-month letter by reason of untrue or delayed information by the applicants. The same applies if a person authorised to accept service in Germany cannot be identified with respect to any participating undertaking the registered domicile of which is located outside Germany.

The Federal Cartel Office can prohibit foreign concentrations to the extent that such concentrations result in or strengthen a dominant position of one of the participating undertakings in the domestic market. As it is not competent to prohibit foreign concentrations altogether, such prohibitions may only relate to their effects on the domestic market (eg the concentration of domestic subsidiaries).

The notification of clearance may be withdrawn or amended by the Federal Cartel Office if it is based on incorrect information provided by the applicants or if it results from fraudulent conduct. The same applies if the participating undertakings do not comply with obligations and conditions contained in the notice of clearance.

Prohibition of putting a concentration into effect

11.104   It is unlawful to put a concentration into effect (or to participate in it being put into effect), unless the concentration is cleared or deemed to be cleared [ARC, s 41(1)]. Legal acts regarding the consummation of a concentration (eg transfer of shares or assets) prior to clearance are null and void. However, it is lawful to sign an agreement on the contemplated transaction, provided that it is consummated/closed by the parties only after notification to and clearance by the Federal Cartel Office. Legal Acts that are null and void pursuant to ARC, s 41(1) will be cured upon clearance by the Federal Cartel Office.

According to ARC, s 41 (1) the prohibition to put a concentration into effect does not affect the legal effectiveness of the following types of agreements:

(a)   Agreements for the sale and purchase of real estate provided that such agreements have become legally effective by way of entry into the land register.

(b)   Agreements on the foundation of a company, the change of the corporate form (Umwandlung) or the merger of a company into another undertaking provided that such agreements have become legally effective by way of registration with the commercial register.

(c)   Agreements pursuant to the Stock Corporation Act s 291 (agreements of domination and profit transfer agreements) and s 292 (profit pooling agreements, limited profit transfer agreements and company leasehold agreements) provided that such agreements have become legally effective by way of registration with the commercial register.

Further, upon application, the Federal Cartel Office may grant exemptions from the prohibition of putting a concentration into effect, if the participating undertakings put forward important reasons for this, in particular, the need to prevent serious damage to a participating undertaking or to a third party [ARC, s 41(2)].

Post-merger notification

11.105   The Federal Cartel Office must be notified of the consummation of concentrations that are subject to control and have been examined according to the merger control procedure [ARC, s 39(6)].

Administrative offences

11.106   A violation of the prohibition to put a concentration into effect prior to clearance constitutes an administrative offence and may be punished by a fine of up to €1,000,000 [ARC, s 81(1)]. With respect to each undertaking participating in the merger the fine may, however, not exceed 10% of the turnover which has been generated in the business year preceding the merger. Furthermore, legal transactions violating this prohibition are of no effect and the Federal Cartel Office can dissolve the concentration [ARC, ss 41(3), (4), 63(1)].

If the obligation to correctly and completely submit pre- and post-merger notification is wilfully or negligently unfulfilled, then this constitutes an administrative offence and may be punished by a fine of up to €100,000 [ARC, s 81(2)].

Right of appeal

11.107   Decisions of the Federal Cartel Office may be appealed, not only by the participating undertakings but also by third parties who are admitted to the proceedings as interveners (see **11.102** above). Third party appeals do not suspend the clearance of the merger unless the third party can substantiate that the merger violates any of its rights. The Court of Appeal responsible for the Federal Cartel Office in Bonn is currently the Düsseldorf Court of Appeal.

Italy

Applicable rules

11.108   A comprehensive competition law was introduced in Italy with an Act entitled Rules on the Protection of Competition and the Market (the so-called 'Antitrust Law', no. 287 of October 10, 1990, as amended). The procedural rules applicable in competition law cases are set forth in Presidential Decree no. 217 of April 30 1998.

The rules regarding merger control are contained in articles 5, 6, 7, 16, 17, 18 and 19 of the Antitrust Law.

Competition authority

11.109   According to article 16 of the Antitrust law, concentrations are assessed by the 'Autorità Garante della Concorrenza e del Mercato' (hereinafter the 'Authority' or the 'IAA' – see www.agcm.it) which has its offices in Rome.

Definition of concentration

11.110   According to Article 5 of the Antitrust Law, a concentration arises when:

(a)   two or more undertakings merge;

(b)   one or more persons controlling at least one undertaking, or one or more undertakings, acquire direct or indirect control of the whole or parts of one or more undertakings, whether through the acquisition of shares or assets, by contract or by any other means; or

(c)   two or more undertakings create a joint venture by setting up a new company.

The following situations are not considered to be concentrations:

(a)   the acquisition by a bank or by a financial institution of shares in an undertaking, provided the shareholding is resold on the market within 24 months and voting rights are not exercised;

(b)   co-operative joint ventures;

(c)   intra-group transactions; and

(d)   merger and acquisitions of undertakings that do not carry out economic activities and do not control any undertaking carrying out economic activities.

General guidance is provided in the notification form, which can be downloaded from the Authority's website. The interpretative criteria set out in the European Commission's relevant notices also provide useful guidance (pursuant to article 1, last paragraph, of the Antitrust Law, the IAA applies the Antitrust Law in accordance with the principles of EC competition law).

Jurisdiction and thresholds

11.111   A concentration is not to be notified at national level if it falls within the scope of the EC Merger Regulation.

The obligation to notify a concentration to the Authority is subject to the following turnover thresholds:

(a)   the combined aggregate gross turnover in Italy of all the companies involved exceeds €432 million; or

(b)   the gross aggregate turnover in Italy of the acquired company exceeds €43 million.

The thresholds are updated each year to take account of inflation (the above thresholds were established in June 2006).

Special rules exist under Article 16(2) of the Antitrust Law for the calculation of banks and insurance companies' turnover. For banks, the relevant turnover equals the value of 1/10 of their total assets excluding 'memorandum accounts'. For insurance companies, their turnover will be equal to the value of the premiums collected.

A concentration that falls within the thresholds does not need to be notified if it does not affect national market(s). This exception applies to:

(i)   mergers by incorporation and acquisitions, when all the parties are foreign, they have not generated any turnover in Italy in the three years preceding the proposed concentration and the resulting company will not generate any turnover in Italy; and

(ii) joint ventures or mergers, when one of the parties is foreign and has not generated any turnover in Italy in the three years preceding the proposed concentration and the resulting company will not perform any economic activity in Italy after the concentration.

Notification

11.112   If the statutory turnover thresholds (see **11.111**) are met, notification to the Authority is mandatory unless an exception applies.

Notification must be made before the concentration is implemented. In cases of merger transactions, the notification has to take place before the merger deed is executed. If control is acquired through a share purchase, the prior notification obligation is considered complied with if the effectiveness of the agreements transferring the control is subject to the IAA's clearance. Where a joint venture is created by establishing a new company, the notification must be filed before the deed of incorporation is filed with the Companies Register.

The notification must be drafted in Italian using the official form, which is downloadable from the Authority's website (see **11.109**) and which details the information to be provided. Supporting documents to be attached to the form include the undertaking's representative(s)' relevant power of attorney, copies of the most recent version of the agreements between the parties, annual reports and balance sheets of the parties for the three financial years preceding the concentration, studies, surveys and any additional documents that might be useful for the assessment of the deal.

Pre-notification contacts and calls for market comments

11.113   If both the statutory thresholds (see **11.111** lett. a/b) or if only the second threshold (ie if the 'target' undertaking's turnover exceeds €43 million) are met, the undertakings concerned may submit to the Authority's competent Office an informal memorandum describing the essential terms of the transaction – and in particular the aspects which are relevant for its competition law assessment – at least 15 days before the formal notification, in order to obtain pre-notification guidance on the proposed transaction.

The scope of this practice is to detect and discuss ex ante the potential competition concerns which may arise in connection with the proposed concentration and to identify the relevant information to be submitted with the notification, in order to prevent the interruption of the proceedings due to requests of additional information by the Authority (see in this regard infra **11.115**).

When a concentration meets both the statutory thresholds, the Authority (if the party(ies) concerned have given their consent) publishes a 'notice of merger submission' on its website, inviting any interested party, including customers and competitors, to submit observations concerning the notified concentration. The deadline to make any comment is five business days from the publication of the notice on the website.

Filing fees

11.114 As of 1 January 2006 undertakings who have the obligation to notify a concentration are obliged to pay filing fees covering merger control costs.

For the year 2006, the amount of this fee is equal to 1% of the total value of the transaction, with a minimum contribution of €3.000 and a cap of €50.000. Specific guidance concerning the method to calculate the due filing fee is provided by the Authority on its website.

The filing fee must be paid (by bank transfer) on the date of the formal notification by the interested party(ies).

Instructions relating to filing fees and the payment thereof are published on the Authority's Bulletin and on its website (Article 10 (7 bis) of the Antitrust Law).

Procedure and timetable

11.115 Once it has received a notification of a concentration, the Authority has a 30 calendar days term (15 for public takeover bids) to adopt a clearance decision or to start an in-depth (phase II) investigation. With respect to the substantial test applied to merger control, the Antitrust Law mirrors the former ECMR n. 4064/89, relying on the dominance test. Under the Antitrust Law, clearance may be denied if the Authority has reasons to believe that the notified transaction may result in the creation or strengthening of a dominant position in the Italian market which could eliminate or significantly reduce effective competition on a lasting basis.

In its assessment the Authority takes into account:

(a)   substitution possibilities available to suppliers and users;

(b)   market position of all parties;

(c)   access conditions and entry barriers to market and sources of supply;

(d)   structure of the relevant geographic and product markets;

(e)   the overall competitive scenario in the domestic industry; and

(f)   demand for the relevant goods or services.

If the documents and information submitted by the party(ies) contain serious inaccuracies, omissions or misrepresentations the Authority may:

(i)   notify the parties of the said inaccuracies, omissions or misrepresenta-
       tions and subsequently interrupt the 30 days term. The 30 days term
       will start again from the date on which the complete information is
       received by the Authority (Article 5.3 of Presidential Decree No.
       217/1998); or

(ii)   start the investigation once the 30 days deadline has expired (Article
       16.7 of the Antitrust Law).

Once the in-depth investigation is launched, there is no automatic obligation
to suspend the implementation of the transaction pending the Authority's
decision. In any event, the Authority may expressly order the parties to suspend the transaction until the end of the investigation. This facultative suspension does not apply to public takeover bids, provided that the acquired
voting rights are not exercised pending the Authority's decision.

The phase II investigations must lead to the adoption of a decision within 45
calendar days. Such term may be extended once for a further 30 days if the
parties under investigation do not submit information or data available to
them requested by the Authority.

At the end of its investigation, the Authority may prohibit the merger,
approve it conditionally or inform the companies concerned that it has no
objections to its implementation.

All decisions adopted by the Authority may be appealed within 60 days from
their service on the party(ies). The competent authority is the Administrative
Court of Lazio Region (TAR Lazio) in first instance, and the Administrative
Supreme Court (Consiglio di Stato) in second instance. The TAR Lazio has
exclusive jurisdiction on appeals from decisions of the Authority, regardless
of the location or nationality of the parties.

Sanctions

11.116   To enforce the merger control provisions, the Authority has wide-
spread powers to impose punitive sanctions. The amount of the fine will
depend upon the gravity of the offence.

In particular:

(a)   if the parties fail to notify a transaction after its implementation, the
       Authority may impose a fine on the undertaking(s) concerned of up to
       1% of their annual turnover in the preceding year;

(b)   the Authority may also impose on the undertakings concerned a fine
       ranging from 1% to 10% of the turnover of the business forming the
       object of the concentration if:

       (i)   a concentration prohibited by the Authority is implemented; or

       (ii)   the conditions ordered by the Authority to restore effective com-
              petition, are not complied with.

Special rules

11.117 If undertakings which, by virtue of provision of law, operate services of general economic interest or a monopoly intend to trade in different markets, they must both:

(a) operate through separate companies; and

(b) notify the Authority in advance of the incorporation of undertakings and the acquisition of controlling interests in undertakings trading in different markets.

Special thresholds for merger notifications apply to film distribution and to the operation of cinemas. Mergers must be notified in advance to the Authority if, as a result of the merger, an undertaking would hold both:

(a) directly or indirectly, a market share of more than 25% of the turnover from film distribution, and

(b) a market share of more than 25% of the operation of cinemas in at least one of the main 12 Italian cities.

In the banking, insurance and communications industries special competition rules apply, also in consideration of the competence of regulatory agencies in these fields.

The Authority co-operates with the following agencies:

(i) in the banking sector, the Bank of Italy (Banca d'Italia, see Law 1067/1936);

(ii) in the insurance sector, the Insurance Control Body (ISVAP, created by Law 576/1982);

(iii) in the communications sector (telecommunications, audiovisuals and publishing), the Communications Regulatory and Guarantee Authority (Autorità per le Garanzie nelle Telecomunicazioni, see Law 249/1997).

The Authority has also cooperation relationships with other public agencies, in particular with the Authority for Electricity and Gas (Autorità per l'Energia Elettrica e il Gas), which can submit observations to the Authority concerning competition in its sectors of competence.

With respect to mergers in the banking sector, article 20 of the Antitrust Law, as amended by article 19 of the Law n. 262/2005, provides for coordination between the Bank of Italy and the Authority. In particular, article 19(12) establishes that, in cases of concentrations within the scope of article 6 of the Antitrust Law or of acquisitions of at least a 5% capital share in an Italian bank, clearance decisions by both the Bank of Italy (with respect to the issues of financial stability and sound management of banking institutions) and by the Authority (with respect to competition issues) must be issued in a single resolution, to be adopted within 60 days of the filing. In the near future a legislative decree implementing the provisions of Law n. 262/2005 should be enacted. The draft version of such statute contains amendments to the regime described in the foregoing. In particular the draft legislative decree provides that the Authority shall assess only transactions which are 'concentrations' within the scope of the Antitrust Law and that the two authorities must adopt separate resolutions. Moreover, the draft legislative decree provides for an exception to the general merger control rules contained in the Antitrust Law. In fact, upon formal request of the Bank of Italy, the Authority may clear a concentration which may lead to the creation or strengthening of a dominant position, if such clearance is considered to be crucial to the financial stability of one or more of the banks concerned.

In the insurance sector the Authority has full jurisdiction for enforcing the Antitrust Law. In the context of concentration proceedings, the Authority, pursuant to article 20(4) of the Antitrust Law, must require ISVAP for a non-binding opinion. ISVAP has 30 days to issue its opinion. The Antitrust Law provides that if the aforesaid deadline elapses before the Authority receives opinion, it may render its decision without waiting. In practice, the 30-day time limit for the decision by the Authority is suspended until it receives the opinion or until the aforesaid deadline expires. This practice should also be consolidated in the forthcoming legislative decree implementing Law n. 262/2005.

Also in the communications sector (telecommunications, audiovisuals and publishing), the Authority must request the Communications Authority for a non-binding opinion concerning concentrations in its sector of competence, pursuant to article 1, para. 6, lett. c), n. 11, of Law n. 249/1997.

Spain

Introduction

11.118   The Spanish merger control regime is set out in articles 14 to 18 of the Law 16/1989, of 17 July, on the Defence of Competition (the 'Spanish Competition Act'), as amended, and in Royal Decree 1443/2001, of 21 December. Non-binding Guidelines have also been published.

In certain sectors, apart from the approval of the Spanish competition authorities, mergers may also require the authorisation or the non-binding opinion of other relevant authorities (eg the Telecommunications Market Commission). The decision of the Bank of Spain is mandatory concerning a merger transaction that may involve insurance companies.

Furthermore, limitations are imposed with respect to the direct or indirect acquisition of more than 3% of the shares of two or more of the five main operators in certain energy and telecommunications markets. Similarly, Spanish legislation imposes restrictions as regards the possibility of certain operators to increase their current market share, in particular in the hydrocarbons and electric energy sectors.

It must be remarked that since 2005 the Ministry of Economy has published a white paper on the modernisation of the Spanish competition rules and published a bill on Spanish competition rules. This bill is, at the time of writing, under the corresponding legislative procedure and it is expected that it will be passed and will be in force by May 2007[1].

1. For further details about its main novelties, please see a few details in **11.126** below.

Competent authorities

11.119 Merger control rules in Spain are enforced by the following authorities:

(a) Servicio de Defensa de la Competencia ('SDC'): general directorate within the Ministry of Economy which conducts investigations and, concerning merger control, conducts the First Phase proceedings (as defined below in **11.123**). Merger notifications must be addressed to the SDC.

(b) Minister of Economy: has the following powers concerning merger control proceedings: (i) refer a merger notifications to Second Phase proceedings (as defined below in **11.124**) upon proposal by the SDC; (ii) authorise a merger if the remedies proposed by the parties during the First Phase proceedings are deemed sufficient; and (iii) lift the suspension obligation imposed on the implementation of concentrations before final clearance is obtained from the Council of Ministers.

(c) Tribunal de Defensa de la Competencia ('TDC'): autonomous body which exercises its functions in a fully independent way. The TDC renders non-binding reports at the request of the Minister of Economy when Second Phase proceedings are open.

(d) Council of Ministers (cabinet): has the power to finally approve or block a transaction at the end of Second Phase proceedings.

Regional competition authorities do not have powers on merger control rules.

Concept of merger

11.120 The Spanish Competition Act defines a concentration as any transaction that implies a stable change in the control structure of the undertakings concerned, by means of:

(a) a merger of two or more previously independent undertakings;

(b) a takeover of all or part of an undertaking or undertakings by any legal means or business; and

(c) the creation of a joint venture and, in general, the acquisition of joint control over an undertaking when the latter permanently carries out the functions of an independent economic entity and does not have the fundamental objective or effect of co-ordinating the competitive behaviour of undertakings that continue to be independent.

For the purpose of application of the Spanish Competition Act, 'control' means the possibility of exercising decisive influence on a company's activities. In particular 'control' exists when a decisive influence is exercised over the composition, discussions or decisions adopted by the company's bodies.

Unless the merger falls within the scope of EU Regulation 139/2004, 20 January, on concentration of undertakings, a merger must always be notified to the SDC whenever the following thresholds are met:

(i)   a market share equal to or higher than 25% in any relevant Spanish product or service market is attained or exceeded as a result of the concentration; or

(ii)   the combined turnover in Spain of all the companies taking part in the concentration exceeds the amount of €240.4M in the last accounting year, as long as at least two of the participant undertakings have an individual turnover in Spain of more than €60.1M.

With regard to the market share threshold, the 'relevant market' is usually defined according to the practice of the Spanish Competition Authorities and European Commission in previous cases.

For the purpose of calculating the turnover in Spain of the undertakings involved in the concentration, the aggregate turnover of all the undertakings belonging to the same group of companies should be taken into account[1]. In the event of joint control of a company, the volume of the company's turnover is allocated in equal parts to the controlling parties.

The Spanish Competition Act provides for special rules regarding the turnover of credit and other financial institutions, as well as insurance companies.

It is important to note that concentrations between undertakings outside Spain may also be caught by the Spanish Competition Act provided that either of the above thresholds is met. Therefore, no local presence is required.

The Spanish Competition Act expressly provides the possibility of referring any Spanish merger notification to the European Commission in accordance with EU Regulation 139/2004. Likewise, the Spanish Competition Authorities may request the referral of cases of a community dimension for its analysis in accordance with the Spanish Competition Act.

1. Parameters established by the European Commission in the Notice, published 2 March 1998, on calculation of sales volumes will be followed.

Merger notification requirements

11.121 Notification to the Spanish Competition Authorities prior to the execution of a concentration is compulsory where either of the thresholds is met (please see **11.120** above). Likewise, clearance of the concentration must be provided prior to its execution except when the Minister of Economy grants derogation from the suspension obligation – upon request of the filing party – at the end of the First Phase investigation.

Only with regards to concentrations through takeover bids for securities listed on a stock exchange in Spain, there is a time period requirement: concentrations must be notified within five days following approval by the Spanish Securities and Exchange Market Commission ('Comisión Nacional del Mercado de Valores'), as set out in Royal Decree 1197/1991[1].

The filing of a merger notification must comply with the following requirements:

(a)   The notification must be filed by the party or parties that acquire either exclusive or joint control. In case of companies, a public deed granting powers of attorney in favour of the signing person must be filed.

(b)   The notification must be filed using the official form attached to Royal Decree 1443/2001. It requests the provision of information and documentation concerning the parties, details of the transaction, turnover figures, control structure, and definition and characteristics of the relevant markets.

(c)   A copy of the agreement or letter of intent. In this latter case, it is possible that if the competition authorities consider that no serious merger agreement is to be reached they delay the merger analysis until filing the merger agreement signed.

(d)   Receipt of payment of a filing tax which ranges from €3,005 to €60,000, depending on the total Spanish sales of the parties involved in the transaction.

(e)   The merger notification needs to be made in Spanish; likewise, any document provided in a non-official language in Spain must be translated into Spanish.

Failing to comply with the notification requirement may imply the following consequences:

(i)   A fine of up to €30,000 may be imposed on the parties.

(ii)   The SDC may (i) request them to notify the concentration, in which case the notification should be filed within 20 days or (ii) initiate the procedure 'ex officio'.

(iii) Periodic penalty payments of up to €12,020 for each day of delay in filing the merger after the 20 day-period granted by the SDC.

In addition, the implementation of a concentration before approval is obtained, thus infringing the suspension obligation, may imply (i) the imposition of fines up to 10% of the turnover in Spain of the undertaking concerned and (ii) in case the transaction is not finally cleared or is cleared with remedies, divesture of the measures adopted.

1. Please note that the legislation on transactions through takeover bids for securities listed on a stock exchange in Spain is currently under review and a new bill is expected to be passed by summer 2007.

Notification procedure

11.122 A concentration notification analysis may comprise two different investigation phases and, in this latter case, take a maximum period of four months. However, if the information contained in the merger notification is deemed incomplete, the SDC may send the notifying party(ies) either an informal request for information –the referred period of time will not be suspended – or a formal request. This latter request must be answered within ten days and suspends the legal period until the information is duly provided.

11.123

(a) The First Phase investigation starts with the merger notification to the SDC. Within one month the SDC must study the case and make a proposal to the Minister of Economy and the latter must decide on the referral of the case to the TDC (Second Phase).

(b) If by the end of said one-month period the case has not been referred to the TDC, the merger shall be deemed tacitly authorised. Indeed, in most of the cases there is a written decision stating that the merger is tacitly approved.

(c) It could be possible that, should the SDC consider that the merger does not hinder competition if fulfilling certain conditions, the merger is finally cleared through a negotiated procedure during the First Phase. In this regard, it is possible that the notifying party(ies), previous request of the SDC, proposed amendments (remedies) to the Minister of Economy in order to delete any potential competition concern and, therefore, clear the transaction. This negotiated procedure can last 20 days.

Second Phase

11.124

(a) The Second Phase starts with the decision of the Minister of Economy on the referral of the case to the TDC. Within two months the TDC must render and provide the Minister of Economy with a non-binding report.

(b) The TDC must consult with any third party that may be affected by the transaction. In this regard, the TDC drafts a brief note – that submits to the consideration of the notifying party(ies) – on the main features of the merger and communicates it to any affected parties. The Spanish Competition Act expressly provides for the right of third parties who have a legitimate interest to (i) have access to the file (excluding confidential information), (ii) make observations and (iii) be heard during the Second Phase.

(c) Based on said TDC's non-binding report the Minister of Economy submits a proposal to the Council of Ministers. Within one month the
Council of Ministers must finally decide on (i) the approval of the
transaction, (ii) its approval subject to certain remedies – eg, divestiture
or any other structural or behavioural conditions – or (iii) prohibiting it.
However, should the Council of Ministers not adopt a decision within
the one-month period, the concentration will be deemed tacitly
approved.

The Spanish Competition Authorities, when assessing a merger transaction,
can use all its investigative powers that allow them to (i) request further information, (ii) investigate and search the premises of the companies concerned,
(iii) copy and seize all kinds of documents and computer records for a 10-day
period (with the exception of attorney-client privileged correspondence), (iv)
the employees of the investigated companies any questions they consider relevant, etc. Failure to provide the SDC with the requested information in due
time may be sanctioned with fines between €60.10 and €3,005 per day of
delay.

The Spanish Competition Authorities, when analysing a merger notification,
take into account whether it may hinder the maintenance of effective competition in the Spanish market, in terms similar to the 'substantial impediment
to effective competition' test adopted by the new EU Merger Regulation.

In general terms, the following elements will always be assessed and
analysed in greater detail: (i) the party's position in the relevant market(s) and
their evolution over the last three years, (ii) competitors' market power, (iii)
market characteristics and barriers to entry for new operators, (iv) the countervailing power of the demand (or offer) and the control of public authorities, (v) the creation of a potential (collective) dominant position and (vi) as
a second level matter, the contribution of the merger to the improvement of
production and marketing systems and economic progress.

The filing of a notification before the SDC is published immediately by
announcing the parties to the same and the type of merger transaction and the
relevant market. First Phase is confidential until the Minister of Economy
adopts the decision to refer the case to the TDC. A no confidential version of
the decision of the Minister of Economy (full competition assessment of the
notified merger) is published after justifying and negotiating with the notifying party(ies) the confidential elements of the same; published data and not
strictly commercial or trade secrets are never deleted from the version of the
decision to be published.

Likewise, a no confidential version of the TDC non-binding report is published before the Council of Ministers has decided on the whole transaction.

Both decisions of the Minister of Economy and the TDC are published
through their respective websites. The decision of the Council of Ministers is
also published in the Spanish Official Bulletin.

Prior to notifying a merger, the potential parties to it may file the SDC a formal request. Through this proceeding the parties can request the opinion of the SDC concerning any issue related to the analysis of the same: does this merger 'X' need to be notified? How would the SDC assess compliance of the threshold requirements in this other case?, etc. However, in practice this type of proceeding requires a substantial amount of information (similar to that when filing a merger notification).

Final decision

11.125 A clearance decision covers restrictions which are directly related to the operation (eg non-compete or non-solicitation clauses). In their assessment, Spanish competition authorities will follow the practice of the European Commission[1].

The decision of the Minister of Economy not to refer the case to the TDC may be subject to judicial review by the National Court (Audicencia Nacional). Judgments of the National Court may be, in turn, appealed before the Supreme Court (Tribunal Supremo).

The decision of the Council of Ministers, either authorising or prohibiting a transaction, may be directly appealed to the Supreme Court.

The time limit to take action against merger falling under the Spanish Competition Act is four years from its execution.

1. For further details, please see European Commission Notice, dated 5 May 2005, on restrictions directly related and necessary to concentrations.

New Spanish Competition Bill

11.126 The new Spanish Competition Bill ('Bill') expected to be approved in mid 2007, adopts the following most relevant changes to the current legislation as regards merger control:

(a) The market share thresholds would be increased and, therefore, only mergers that may imply a final market share equal to or higher than 30% in any relevant Spanish product or service market will be caught by the obligation to notify.

(b) The SDC and TDC would be replaced by one single administrative Competition Authority: the Comisión Nacional de la Competencia.

The notification merger proceedings would be more flexible:

(i) there would be a simplified procedure for mergers that may not affect the market substantially;

(ii) the concept of 'merger' will include any full function joint ventures;

(iii) the derogation from the suspension obligation may be obtained at any time during the merger analysis;

(iv) the basis for the government not to follow the decision of the Comisión Nacional de la Competencia would be limited to those cases listed in the Bill.

The notification proceedings may last up until four and a half months. Any merger notification may be subject to 4 phases: (1) First Phase before the Comisión Nacional de la Competencia (up to 1 month); (2) Second Phase before the Comisión Nacional de la Competencia (up to 2 months); (3) Third Phase before the Minister of Economy (up to 15 days); and (4) Fourth Phase before the Council of Ministers (up to 1 month).

There would be one single judicial review concerning the decisions falling under the Bill.

Poland

Relevant legislation

11.127 Rules on merger control in Poland are contained in the Act on the Protection of Competition and Consumers of 15 December 2000 (Consolidated text: Journal of Laws of 2005, No 244, item 2080, as amended) (the 'Act').

The method of calculating the turnover of undertakings that are the subject of a planned concentration is set out in the Regulation of the Council of Ministers of 23 May 2001. Detailed requirements concerning the pre-merger notification are set out in the Regulation of the Council of Ministers of 3 April 2002 on the notification of intention to concentrate undertakings (the 'Regulation').

The President of the Office for the Protection of Competition and Consumers (the 'President of the Office') is responsible for enforcing the Act.

Definition of concentration

11.128 The Act applies to 'concentrations' which encompass the following:

(a) the acquisition by one or more undertakings – whether by purchase or subscription of shares or other securities of all or part of the assets or through any other means – of direct or indirect control of the whole or parts of one or more other undertakings,

(b) the creation by undertakings of a joint undertaking;

(c) the merger of two or more undertakings.

The following events constitute notifiable concentrations:

(i) the acquisition of shares of another undertaking which confer 25 per cent or more of the eligible votes at the general shareholders' meeting of the undertaking;

(ii) the exercising of a managing or controlling function by the same person in competing undertakings;

(iii) the exercising of rights conferred by shares acquired temporarily by financial institutions whose normal activity includes trading in securities (there is an exemption from the notification obligation if the shares are intended for resale within one year and if the financial institution exercises voting rights during that time only for the purpose of resale of the entire enterprise or part thereof, its property or the shares);

(iv) the exercising of rights conferred by shares acquired temporarily for the purpose of securing a debt (the notification is not required if exercising of rights refers to the resale of the shares);

(v) and those arising in the course of insolvency proceedings, where the undertaking intending to take over control is a competitor, or belongs to the capital group to which belong competitors of the target.

Jurisdictional thresholds

11.129 The pre-merger notification requirement of the Act applies to concentrations in which the aggregate turnover of all participating undertakings in the year prior to notification exceeded EUR 50 million. The turnover of the entire capital groups of the participating undertakings must be taken into account. Such turnover is deemed to be the amount derived in the preceding year from the sale of goods (excluding intra-group sales, rebates and discounts, VAT and other turnover-related taxes). When a concentration consists of the acquisition of a part of the assets of an undertaking or of part of its enterprise, only the turnover achieved by this part is included in the calculation.

A concentration arising from the acquisition of control as well as the acquisition of a minority interest is exempted from the notification obligation if the turnover in Poland of the undertaking subject to control (that is, the target company) did not exceed the equivalent of EUR 10 million in each of the two years preceding the planned transaction. Note that the turnover derived from sales in Poland of the entire capital group of the target must be taken into account. In the case of a concentration which consists of the acquisition of a part of the assets of the target or a part of its enterprise, only the turnover achieved by this part is included in the de minimis calculation.

The de minimis based turnover exemption, however, only applies to a concentration in which a dominant market position is not created or strengthened.

Concentrations concluded within a single capital group are exempted from the notification obligation (intra-group transactions). A capital group is defined by the Act as all undertakings controlled directly or indirectly by a single undertaking (the ultimate parent), including the ultimate parent entity.

Foreign-to-foreign transactions

11.130 Foreign-to-foreign transactions are subject to merger control in Poland in so far as they have or may have an effect within Poland. According to the official interpretation of the President of the Office (first published on the Office's website in September 2005), the effects of extra-territorial concentrations in Poland may exist if at least two of the participating undertakings to the concentration belong to capital groups that each have a subsidiary in Poland.

Notification, procedure and timetable

11.131 The Act makes filing mandatory if the turnover thresholds described above are met and the transaction cannot be exempted from the notification requirement on the basis, for example, of the de minimis 'turnover threshold in Poland' test.

A merger or the creation of a joint venture must be notified jointly by the parties to the merger or joint venture. In the case of an acquisition of control, the notification should be filed by the undertaking acquiring control. For an acquisition of more than 25 per cent, the notification obligation rests with the acquiring party. When a managing or controlling function in competing undertakings is to occur, the notifying entity will be the one in whose executive body the managing function is intended to be exercised. When a concentration occurs through at least two subsidiaries, notification should be made by their common parent company.

The filing fee is currently PLN 1,000 (approx. EUR 260 based upon November 2006 rates).

An undertaking obliged to notify can do so at any time from the moment the concentration intention is first documented (for example, on signing a letter of intent, etc) until shortly before the transaction is to be completed.

The Office's review of a notification may take up to two months or longer. The two-month statutory waiting period begins only when a completed notification has been submitted to the President of the Office. The two-month period may be further extended should the Office request additional information (which it often does). The Act does not provide for any simplified procedure.

Parties to a notified transaction must suspend the implementation of the notified concentration until a decision by the President of the Office is rendered or until the statutory review period lapses (two months plus additional periods during which the Office waits for the submission of requested information or documents). The suspension requirement does not apply to the implementation of a public bid that has been notified to the President of the Office provided that the acquirer does not exercise any voting rights attached to the securities in question, or does so only to maintain the full value of its

investment or to prevent serious damage occurring to undertakings participating in a concentration.

The notification is made in the Polish language by completing and filing an
official form, which details the information required. The notification form
(questionnaire) is the attachment to the Regulation that is as detailed as the
Form CO under the EC Merger Regulation. A considerable amount of market
information must be provided, including information concerning the parties
and the transaction. The documentation for a notification typically consists of
30 to 40 pages and four to ten attachments.

Decisions in merger cases and substantive test of clearance

11.132 During the pre-merger examination proceedings, the President of
the Office analyses whether a concentration may lead to a restriction of competition in the market. The President of the Office may issue a decision prohibiting the transaction only if a concentration significantly restricts
competition in the market, specifically, as a result of the creation, or strengthening of a dominant market position. In the case of a concentration which
raises significant competition concerns, the President of the Office may also
propose conditions which the parties must fulfil in order to obtain clearance.

Judicial review

11.133 Any notifying party may appeal to the Court for Protection of
Competition and Consumers against any decision by the President of the
Office. In turn, a party may appeal against the verdict of this court to a second
instance court. A judgment of the second instance court may be further overturned by the Supreme Court after an application for cassation is filed and
accepted.

Sanctions

11.134 The Act allows the President of the Office to fine an undertaking
which, even unintentionally, concluded a transaction that was subject to the
obligation to notify. The fine is a maximum of 10 per cent of annual revenue
in the financial year prior to the imposition of the fine. A separate fine (of up
to 50 times average monthly salary within the industry sector) may be
imposed on a person holding a managerial post or who is a member of a managing authority of the undertaking. When deciding upon the amount of a fine,
the President of the Office is obliged to take into account the period of delay,
scope and circumstances of the infringement of the Act. Moreover, in the
event of failure to notify a concentration which restricts competition, and if
competition cannot be restored in any other way, the President of the Office
may order a division of the merged undertaking, the sale of all or part of its
assets, the sale of controlling interests, or termination of a joint venture. Such
a decision by the President of the Office cannot be rendered if a period of five
years has elapsed from the date of completion of the concentration.

Changes in legislation

11.135 A new competition law ('New Act') is expected to be enacted at the beginning of 2007.

The New Act refers to the duty to notify a 'concentration', which is defined as:

(a)   a merger of two or more independent undertakings;

(b)   the acquisition by one or more undertakings, whether by purchase or subscription for shares or other securities, or through any other means of direct or indirect control of one or more undertaking;

(c)   the creation of a joint venture by undertakings; and

(d)   the acquisition by an undertaking of part of assets of another undertaking (the whole or part of an enterprise) where the turnover generated by the acquired assets in Poland – in each of the last two financial years preceding the notification – exceeds the equivalent of EUR 10 million.

The New Act proposes raising jurisdictional worldwide turnover thresholds from the current EUR 50 million to EUR 1 billion. Furthermore, under the current wording of the New Act, transactions would fall within this threshold if the total turnover of parties to a transaction (including their capital groups) in Poland exceeds EUR 50 million; this is an alternative threshold (domestic turnover threshold). According to the justification of the New Act published on the Competition Authority's website, a transaction will be subject to the notification obligation if at least one of the above-mentioned turnover thresholds is reached. In other words, a transaction will not be subject to pre-merger control if the total global turnover of participants to a concentration (including their capital groups) does not exceed EUR 1 billion, and if the turnover of concentration participants in Poland (including their capital groups) did not exceed EUR 50 million during the year preceding the year of the transaction.

The New Act additionally specifies that the assumption of control over another undertaking shall be exempt from the notification obligation, even if it fulfils any of the above-mentioned financial thresholds if the turnover of the targeted undertaking in each of the two years preceding the concentration did not exceed the equivalent of EUR 10 million (according to the New Act, this turnover will refer only to that of the target company plus all of its direct and indirect subsidiaries). The New Act introduces a rule that the turnover to be considered will only relate to the target company and to its subsidiaries (and not, as is currently the case, to the entire capital group of the seller).

Under the New Act, there will no longer be an obligation to notify certain transactions that currently constitute 'notifiable' concentrations. The acquisition of minority interests, the exercise of management or controlling function by the same person in competing undertakings, and the exercise of share or stock rights assumed or acquired without prior notification by financial institutions will no longer be notifiable under the New Act.

Ireland

Introduction

11.136 The regime governing Irish merger control is established in Part 3 of the Competition Act 2002 as amended ('The Competition Act'). The relevant authority responsible for the enforcement of competition law in Ireland is the Competition Authority, an independent statutory body, the functions of which are governed by the Competition Act. The Chairperson of the Competition Authority is currently Mr. William Prasifka, who took up the post on 3 April 2006. There are also four other members of the Competition Authority, each of whom head a Division within the Competition Authority. Dr Paul Gorecki is the Director of the Mergers Division. The role of the Competition Authority is to ensure that the competition rules in Ireland are respected and it administers the merger control regime. There is a special regime in place for media mergers.

Relevant mergers

11.137 The Competition Act applies to a 'merger or acquisition' which satisfies certain thresholds or constitutes a 'media business'. The circumstances under which a merger or acquisition is deemed to occur are set out in section 16 of the Competition Act. This test mirrors the test set out in the EC merger Regulation ('ECMR') (Council Regulation (EC) No 139/2004 of 20 January 2004). A merger or acquisition occurs if:

(a) two or more undertakings, previously independent of one another, merge, or

(b) one or more individuals or other undertakings who or which control one or more undertakings acquire direct or indirect control of one or more other undertakings, or

(c) the result of an acquisition by one undertaking (the 'first undertaking') of the assets, including goodwill, (or a substantial part of the assets) of another undertaking (the 'second undertaking') is to place the first undertaking in a position to replace (or substantially to replace) the second undertaking in the business or, as appropriate, the part concerned of the business in which that undertaking was engaged immediately before the acquisition.

A merger also occurs if a joint venture is created to perform, on an indefinite basis, all the functions of an autonomous economic entity.

Section 16(2) of the Competition Act sets out that control shall be regarded as existing if decisive influence is capable of being exercised with regard to the activities of the undertaking. The Competition Authority has indicated that notifying parties and their advisers can look to the European Commission Notices and Guidelines for guidance on matters not specifically covered by the Competition Authority such as the concept of control. The European Commission Notices and Guidelines include (i) the Notice on the concept of concentration (OJ C 66, 02.03.1998, p. 5), (ii) the Notice on the concept of full-function joint ventures (OJ C 66, 02.03.1998, p.1), (iii) the Notice on the concept of undertakings concerned (OJ C 66, 02.03.1998, p.14) and (iv) the Notice on calculation of turnover (OJ C 66, 02.03.1998, p.25).

Thresholds

11.138 Pursuant to the Competition Act, it is mandatory to notify mergers and acquisitions that reach the financial thresholds set out in section 18, which are as follows:

(a)   the worldwide turnover of each of two or more of the undertakings involved in the merger or acquisition is not less than €40,000,000;

(b)   each of two or more of the undertakings involved in the merger or acquisition carries on business in any part of the island of Ireland; and

(c)   the turnover in the State of any one of the undertakings involved in the merger or acquisition is not less than €40,000,000.

On 12 December 2006, the Competition Authority clarified its understanding of the term 'carries on business' in Ireland, following a public consultation. The Competition Authority now understands that term as including undertakings that either:

(a)   have a physical presence on the island of Ireland (including a registered office, subsidiary, branch, representative office or agency) and make sales and/or supply services to customers on the island of Ireland; or

(b)   have made sales into the island of Ireland of at least €2 million in the most recent financial year.

In the amended Notice, the Competition Authority clarified its understanding of 'turnover in the State' to comprise sales made or services supplied to customers within the State, ie the Republic of Ireland.

In clarifying its understanding of the term 'carrying on business', the Competition Authority has ensured that mergers which should be caught by the merger regime are in fact being caught by it and also that mergers which do not have sufficient nexus to Ireland are not being caught by the merger regime and tying up valuable Competition Authority resources.

Media mergers are notifiable to the Competition Authority irrespective of meeting the financial thresholds set out above. A media merger occurs where at least one of the parties to the merger carries on a media business, ie is engaged in the publication of newspapers or periodicals consisting substantially of news and comments on current affairs; broadcasting services; or providing a broadcasting services platform in Ireland.

Notifying mergers to the Competition Authority

11.139 Mandatory merger notifications should be made to the Competition Authority within one month of the conclusion of an agreement or the making of a public bid. All parties are obliged to make a notification, although often in practice the parties file a joint notification. A notification will not be accepted prior to the conclusion of a binding agreement or the making of a public bid, therefore, a notification will not be accepted on the basis of a memorandum of understanding, letter of intent or heads of agreement.

A fee of €8,000 is prescribed for the purposes of a notification under section 18(8) of the Competition Act, further to Statutory Instrument No. 623 of 2002.

All merger notifications must be notified to the Competition Authority on the revised standard form for notifications (available on www.tca.ie).

Voluntary notifications

11.140 The Competition Authority also has a system for voluntary merger notifications which seeks to take account of the possible application of sections 4 and 5 of the Competition Act to a merger which does not meet the financial thresholds set out above nor constitutes a media merger, and is thus referred to as a non-notifiable merger. A decision as to whether or not a merger should be notified, if it does not reach the thresholds set in section 18, should be made based on a consideration of the markets that will be affected by the prospective merger and the approach that the Competition Authority has previously adopted in decisions relating to this market. The Competition Authority's Guidelines for Merger Analysis (N/02/004), which explain the Competition Authority's position on substantive issues in merger control, suggest that parties should consider the following situations which highlight a particular concern: (a) where a dominant firm acquires a smaller rival or new entrant whose turnover was below €40m; (b) the acquisition of a maverick firm or new entrant by another player in an otherwise oligopolistic market; or (c) the acquisition of a dominant Irish player by a strong player in a neighbouring market that had otherwise intended to enter the Irish market. Since the operation of the Competition Act in 2003, the Competition Authority has made public two preliminary assessments of below notification threshold mergers, one of which was notified to it.

Regardless of whether a merger qualifies for a mandatory or voluntary notification, the parties may request pre-notification discussions with the Mergers division of the Competition Authority. Pre-notification discussions are welcomed by the Competition Authority as they assist the parties in the preparation of a notification and help the Mergers Division of the Competition Authority to understand the nature of competition in the relevant market(s).

Competition Authority's assessment process

11.141 There is a two-phase examination process by which the Competition Authority examines mergers. The test the Competition Authority uses when assessing a merger is that of a 'substantial lessening of competition', ie if the merger does not substantially lessen competition in the market for goods or services, it will be cleared.

On 1 March 2006, two documents published by the Competition Authority in February 2006 came into effect. The documents set out revised procedural rules in relation to merger notifications and are entitled 'Revised Procedures for the Review of Mergers and Acquisitions' ('Revised Merger Procedures') and 'Procedures for Access to the file in Merger Cases' ('Access Procedures'). The Revised Merger Procedures deal in particular with how the Competition Authority deals with Phase II investigations.

Phase I

11.142 Once a merger is notified to the Competition Authority it enters into Phase I proceedings. Phase I is an initial period of one month during which the Competition Authority must assess the proposed merger and decide to either authorise it on the grounds that it would not substantially lessen competition, or alternatively carry out a more detailed investigation. This one-month period may be extended to forty five days if competition concerns are raised and the parties and the Competition Authority negotiate undertakings or commitments to address the potential competition issues identified in the Phase I investigation.

Section 20(1)(a) of the Competition Act gives third parties who wish to comment on a merger the opportunity to do so. It provides that within seven days following the receipt of the merger, the Competition Authority is obliged to publish a notice of receipt inviting third parties to comment. The Revised Merger Procedures stipulate that a third party wishing to make a submission about a merger must do so within ten days of the publication of the notice on the Competition Authority's website. The Competition Authority has a discretion to change this time limit in respect of individual cases should it wish to do so depending on the specific circumstances.

During the Phase I investigation, the Competition Authority may exercise its right under the Competition Act to 'stop the clock' and make a formal request for further information. The one-month investigation will recommence as soon as the requested information has been gathered ie the clock restarts all over again. If, at this stage the Competition Authority still has concerns that the proposed merger will substantially lessen competition in the market, it may clear the merger at the end of a Phase I investigation but subject to certain commitments satisfying competition concerns, or alternatively it may refer the merger to a Phase II investigation. While commitments may only be volunteered in Phase I, the Competition Authority may impose conditions on its determination after a Phase II investigation.

Phase II

11.143 Once a Phase II investigation has commenced it can run for up to four months from notification or from receipt of the response to an information request if applicable (ie normally an additional three months onto Phase I). During this time the Competition Authority has to investigate the merger and decide whether it should be cleared, blocked, or cleared subject to conditions. Once the Phase II investigation has commenced notifying parties are given an initial period of 21 days to make additional submissions to the Competition Authority. A Phase II investigation involves a more detailed investigation of the relevant market(s) and may also involve an oral hearing at the request of the parties. During a Phase II investigation the Competition Authority may negotiate undertakings or commitments with the parties to address any concerns it may have about the effects of the proposed merger on competition in the market.

In line with the Revised Merger Procedures, the Competition Authority may issue a clearance decision or a clearance subject to conditions after eight weeks from the opening of the Phase II investigation. Within the eight-week period, or shortly thereafter, the Competition Authority will furnish a written assessment to the notifying parties and in this the competition concerns that have arisen in the course of investigations will be addressed. Notifying parties in a Phase II investigation are provided access to the Competition Authority's file during the three-week period between receipt of the written assessment and their response. Notifying parties are granted access to all documents on file with the exception of internal working documents of the Competition Authority and confidential documents. The Access Procedures available on the Competition Authority's website, set out the Competition Authority's practice on access to non-confidential documents and its procedures for ensuring protection of confidentiality.

Pursuant to section 22(3) of the Competition Act, on completion of a full investigation the Competition Authority shall make whichever of the following determinations it considers appropriate, namely that the merger or acquisition: (a) may be put into effect, (b) may not be put into effect, or (c) may be put into effect subject to conditions specified by it being complied with – on the ground that the result of the merger or acquisition will or will not, as the case may be, substantially lessen competition in markets for goods or services in the State or, as appropriate, will not be to substantially lessen such competition if the specified conditions are complied with.

Since January 2003, eleven cases have been the subject of Phase II investigations: *Scottish Radio Holdings/FM 104* (Competition Authority Merger Notification No. M/03/33) (cleared subject to conditions after the full four-month period); *Dawn Meats/Galtee Meats* (Competition Authority Merger Notification No. M/03/029) (cleared after the first six weeks of Phase II); *Stena/P&O* (Competition Authority Merger Notification No. M/04/016) (withdrawn); *Uniphar/Whelehan* (Competition Authority Merger Notification No. M/04/020) (cleared ten weeks after initiating a Phase II investigation); *IBM/Schlumberger* (Competition Authority Merger Notification No. M/04/032) (blocked); *Grafton/Heiton* (Competition Authority Merger Notification No. M/04/051) (cleared ten weeks after initiating a Phase II investigation); *UGC (Chorus)/NTL* (Competition Authority Merger Notification No. M/05/024) (cleared subject to conditions ten weeks after initiating a Phase II investigation; *Tetra Laval/Carlisle* (Competition Authority Merger Notification No. M/06/027) (cleared 13 weeks after initiating the Phase II investigation), *Coillte/Weyerhaeuser* (Competition Authority

Merger Notification No. M/06/57) (cleared 7 weeks after initiating the Phase II investigation) and *Applied Materials, Inc./Brooks Software* (Competition Authority No. M/06/087) (cleared 7 weeks after initiating the Phase II investigation). To date just two mergers have been blocked, namely *IBM/Schlumberger* and *Kingspan/Xtratherm*. On the 26 October 2006, the Competition Authority announced after a full four-month Phase II investigation, that it had made its decision to block the proposed *Kingspan/Xtratherm* merger (Competition Authority Merger Notification No. M/06/039) because it considered that the transaction would substantially lessen competition in the manufacture and provision of insulation materials, in particular Polyurethane (PU) and polyisocyanurate (PIR), in the State. The Competition Authority considered the nature of the market for PU and PIR in the State and considered that it was characterized by a homogenous product, high concentration, high market shares by the merging entities, limited import competition and sufficient excess capacity to prevent entry. The Competition Authority believed that the merger would have led to a significant lessening of competition as a vigorous competitor would be removed from the market; and because post-merger Quinn Therm, a substantial competitor active in the State, would be likely to accommodate likely price increases of the merged entity. It is only the second time that the Competition Authority has blocked a proposed merger since the provisions of the Competition Act regarding merger control came into effect in January 2003.

It is interesting to note that of the eleven cases that have gone to a Phase II investigation, two of these have been media mergers (*UGC (Chorus)/NTL* and *Scottish Radio Holdings/FM 104*), both of which were cleared subject to conditions. Two mergers in the construction sector also resulted in a Phase II investigation (*Grafton Group plc/Heiton Group plc* and *Kingspan/ Xtratherm*), one of which was cleared subject to conditions and the latter of the two which was blocked, as discussed above.

Once the Competition Authority has determined that the merger or acquisition may be put into effect after either Phase I or Phase II, the notifying parties must complete the merger or acquisition in question within 12 months of the date of the determination.

Media mergers

11.144   Media mergers, regardless of the financial thresholds involved, must be notified to the Competition Authority. Once the initial notification is made to the Competition Authority, a copy is sent to the Minister for Enterprise, Trade and Employment ('the Minister') by the Competition Authority. Once the Competition Authority has made its assessment, it is obliged to refer the merger to the Minister. If, after the Phase I investigation the Competition Authority is satisfied the merger will not result in a substantial lessening of competition, it must refer the merger to the Minister, who then has a period of ten days in which he/she may decide, on the basis of specified 'public interest' criteria, to direct the Competition Authority to open a Phase II investigation. If, at the end of a Phase II investigation, the Competition Authority decides to clear a merger or alternatively, clear the merger subject to conditions, the Minister may then, within 30 days, prohibit the merger or impose new or stricter conditions on the parties. The Minister does not have the power to implement a media merger if the Competition Authority has prohibited it on competition grounds.

The public interest criteria used by the Minister when assessing a media merger are: (a) the strength and competitiveness of indigenous media business; (b) the spread of ownership or control of media businesses in the State; (c) the spread of ownership and control of particular types of media business in the State; (d) the extent to which the diversity of views prevalent in Irish society are reflected through the activities of the various media businesses in the State; and (e) the market share of the parties. Since the operation of the Competition Act, the Minister has not blocked any merger.

In 2005, the Competition Authority initiated a Phase II investigation of a media merger concerning the acquisition of NTL by UPC Ireland (Competition Authority Merger Notification No. M/05/024). On 4 November 2005, the Competition Authority announced that the merger could be put into effect subject to a series of conditions. These conditions addressed issues relating to cross ownership interests which were highlighted by the Competition Authority in its Phase II investigation. The transaction was then referred to the Minister for review. The Minister did not make an order prohibiting the merger from being put into effect. Therefore, the media merger was cleared, subject to conditions, on 2 December 2005.

Appeals process

11.145 The Competition Act provides for an appeal to the High Court against a determination of the Authority to block a merger. The Competition Act provides no right of appeal against a decision to clear a merger, however the remedy of judicial review could be availed of in such circumstances. An appeal must be made within one month after the date on which the undertaking is informed by the Competition Authority of the determination concerned. Any issue of fact or law concerning the determination may form the subject of an appeal. The procedure for appeals is somewhat accelerated, in that the High Court should, by virtue of section 24(6) of the Competition Act 2002, in so far as it is practicable, hear and determine an appeal within two months after the date on which the appeal is made to it. An appeal to the Supreme Court against a decision of the High Court under any of the foregoing provisions of this section shall only lie on a point of law.

Sanctions

11.146 If an undertaking or group of undertakings fail to notify a notifiable merger to the Competition Authority, the person in control of an undertaking is subject to a criminal offence punishable by fines if it can be demonstrated that the failure to notify was knowing and wilful. The merger will be deemed void by the Competition Authority until such time as the Competition

Authority issues a clearance. Undertakings may also be guilty of an offence if they have failed to notify the merger within the specified period or if they have failed to supply information required by the Authority within a specified period. This sanction is applied to parties to a merger since the obligation is on all the undertakings involved to make the notification. Undertakings could be liable on summary conviction, to a fine not exceeding €3,000 or on conviction on indictment, to a fine not exceeding €250,000 and per diem fines of €300 (summary) and €25,000 (on indictment) for each day of continuing infringement. Section 11 of the Competition Act specifies a person in control of an undertaking as: (i) any officer of the body corporate who knowingly or wilfully authorises or permits the contravention, or (ii) in the case of a partnership, each partner who knowingly and wilfully authorises or permits the contravention, or (iii) in the case of any other form of undertaking who knowingly and wilfully authorises or permits the contravention.

In 2004, the Competition Authority was faced with a media merger that had contravened the rules specified above. In *Radio 2000 Limited/Newstalk 106* (Competition Authority Merger Notification No. M/04/003) the parties failed to notify the transaction to the Competition Authority within the time period set out in the Competition Act. The Competition Authority took the view that, in a further breach of the law, the acquisition by Radio 2000 of NewsTalk 106 had been put into effect before clearance had been received from the Authority. However, the Competition Authority, after having fully considered the matter, found insufficient evidence to seek a criminal penalty, as it was not apparent that any officer of NewsTalk 106, Radio 2000 or Communicorp knowingly and wilfully authorised or permitted the breach of the law. In its determination the Competition Authority said that any merger or acquisition that has been implemented prior to Competition Authority clearance remains void until such time as the Authority issues a clearance determination.

In addition to the Competition Authority's power to bring summary proceedings, it may also bring applications to the courts for an interim injunction/injunctive relief. The Competition Authority may apply for an injunction if it believes that a merger has or will be put into effect without the appropriate Competition Authority approval. The Competition Authority may bring civil or criminal proceedings for the enforcement of compliance with the terms of a commitment, a determination or an order. The Courts have the power to grant an injunction on the motion of the Competition Authority or of any other person to enforce compliance with the terms of a commitment, a determination or an order.

The Competition Authority published a press release on 'gun-jumping' on 13 May 2003. If parties are found to have breached the pre-merger waiting period, ie gun jumping, then the transaction will be deemed void. In this press release the Competition Authority sought to clarify its views on this issue and ensure that industry and its legal counsel are aware of the rules. The Competition Authority indicated that it will give priority to investigating any allegations that merging parties have put a merger into effect in advance of Competition Authority clearance.

In July 2006, a case officer in the Mergers Division of the Competition Authority published a practice note in the Irish Law Society Gazette outlining the circumstances, specified in the Competition Act, in which companies are required to notify the Competition Authority of proposed mergers and describing in detail the consequences for failure to notify. The practice note considered the outcome of implementing a transaction prior to Competition Authority clearance. The practice note stated that, 'the merger that has been implemented is void, therefore no merger has taken place at all. The parties, therefore, are notifying a proposed merger, which the Competition Authority can review in the usual way. If the Competition Authority clears it, it may be lawfully implemented. This may involve the parties re-doing legal acts such as contracts and appointments of staff among other things. If the Competition Authority should block such a merger, it would mean that the purported new entity would have to undo the merger'.

Special rules

11.147 Section 19 of the Competition Act sets out the limitations on a merger or acquisition being put into effect. Section 19(1) provides that a merger may be put into effect if the period within which the Competition Authority should have made its determination lapses without the Competition Authority having informed the undertaking involved of its determination in relation to the proposed merger or acquisition. The proposed acquisition by Topaz Energy Group Limited of Statoil Ireland Limited was notified to the Competition Authority on 12 July 2006. The Competition Authority conducted a very extensive Phase I investigation and as a result of this investigation, it is understood that the Competition Authority identified three areas in which preliminary views were expressed that the proposed acquisition would lead to competition concerns. Pursuant to the Competition Act, the Competition Authority was due to make its determination by 9 October 2006. Having identified the competition concerns prior to this date, the Competition Authority had been in discussions with Topaz, wherein Topaz had offered certain commitments. Owing to an administrative error the Competition Authority did not make its Phase I determination by 9 October 2006. Therefore, on 10 October 2006, the Competition Authority issued a statement saying that the date on which the Phase I determination in this matter could have been made passed on 9 October without any determination having been made and that as a result, the parties were free to put the merger into effect. Despite being allowed to put the merger into effect without conditions addressing the competition concerns, Topaz subsequently entered into further discussions with the Competition Authority and offered commitments to the Competition Authority. The provisions of Section 19 of the Competition Act therefore caused controversy due to the Topaz/Statoil merger being put into effect after an extended Phase I investigation when the merger had evoked competition concerns. As a result of this administrative error, the Competition Authority clarified its understanding of the phrase 'within one month after' as used in section 18(1) and section 21(2) of the Competition Act, by inserting a new Article 5 into the amended Notice, referred to in section **11.138** above. Article 5 provides in essence that where that phrase is used in either section, the month will be calculated by including the date after which the month is expressed to run. Thus, where notification must be made 'within one month after' the date on which an agreement has been concluded, the date of the conclusion of the agreement will be counted as the first day of the calendar month. The month will then expire on the day before the corresponding date in the following month.

Sweden

Introduction

11.148 The main rules on mergers and acquisitions are contained in the Competition Act 1993 (Konkurrenslagen 1993:20), which applies to all concentrations and full-function joint ventures. The merger rules were modelled on Regulation (EEC) No. 4064/89 on the control of concentrations between undertakings (since replaced by Regulation (EC) No. 139/2004 on the control of concentrations between undertakings (Merger Regulation)).

The Swedish Competition Authority (Konkurrensverket) is responsible for merger control. The Authority applies the Competition Act and the EC guidelines for merger control.

Relevant jurisdictional triggering events/thresholds

Triggering events

11.149 The first criterion to examine is whether there is a concentration as defined in the Competition Act. A concentration is deemed to arise if any of the following occur (*section 34, Competition Act*):

(a) Two or more previously independent undertakings merge.

(b) One undertaking, directly or indirectly, obtains control over another undertaking, by way of an acquisition, agreement or any other means.

(c) A joint venture performing all the functions of an autonomous economic entity is created on a lasting basis (full function joint venture).

Thresholds

11.150 The second criterion to examine is whether the notification thresholds are triggered. If a concentration exists but the turnover thresholds are not met, notification is not mandatory unless ordered by the Authority. A concentration must be notified if both:

(a) The aggregate worldwide annual turnover of the undertakings concerned exceeded SEK4 billion in the preceding financial year.

(b) Each of at least two of the undertakings concerned had a turnover in Sweden exceeding SEK100 million in the preceding financial year.

The undertakings concerned are:

(i) In a merger, the merging entities; purchaser and target entity.

(ii) In a full-function joint venture; the parents of the joint venture and the joint venture entity itself.

It should be noted that the Authority has suggested new rules for turnover thresholds for concentration notifications to the government (see Section 9 'Reform' below).

The whole company group of each undertaking is included in the calculation of turnover.

Substantive test

11.151 There is no specific substantive test for the Authority when deciding whether or not to proceed with a special investigation. A concentration can be prohibited if it creates or strengthens a dominant position, which significantly impedes (or is liable to impede) the existence or development of effective competition on the Swedish market or a substantial part of it, unless a prohibition would interfere with important national interests of security or resources of supply.

It should be noted that there are no special rules for specific industries.

Notification requirements

11.152 The Authority cannot examine a merger if it does not constitute a concentration. Notification of a concentration is mandatory if the turnover thresholds are met. If a concentration exists and the first but not the second turnover threshold is met (that is, the aggregate worldwide annual turnover of the undertakings concerned exceeded SEK 4 billion million in the preceding financial year, notification is not mandatory unless ordered by the Authority. Special reasons must exist for this (for example, if there are several minor acquisitions or when an undertaking with a large market share acquires a new entrant in a highly concentrated market to reduce competition). If necessary, the order can be under penalty of a fine. If parties believe that special reasons exist, they can notify the transaction voluntarily. The Authority rarely orders notifications but as an example requested a shipping company to notify a merger subject to fines (Decision of 22 June 2005, case no. 597/2005).

No time limit exists for submitting the notification. In principle it is possible to implement a concentration before it is approved by the Authority. However, in practice, parties are subjected to a standstill obligation once they notify. The Authority prefers the parties to have signed the concentration documents before notification, but it can start proceedings on a draft document which is almost finalised and submitted jointly by the parties. In the case of a public offer, the offer document should be made public before notification.

The Authority can hold confidential, informal pre-notification talks to clarify the information required for notification. These talks can also identify and discuss sensitive areas of the case, although the Authority is reluctant to predict its outcome.

In the case of a merger, the parties to the concentration are responsible for the notification. In all other cases, the party acquiring control must notify.

Notifications should be submitted to the Authority on a standard form (Regulation KKVFS 2006:3). Notifications must be submitted in Swedish. However, the Authority has so far accepted supporting documents in English. There is no filing fee for any procedures before the Authority, Stockholm District Court or Market Court.

The parties must not take any action to complete the concentration during the initial 25-day period that the Authority has to issue a decision or initiate a special investigation (standstill obligation). If parties breach the standstill obligation the Authority can order them to stop completion, and if necessary, impose a fine. If requested by the Authority, the Stockholm District Court can prohibit the parties and other participants from taking any measure to put the concentration into effect until a final decision has been made. If special reasons exist, the Authority can grant an exemption from the standstill provision.

Publicity and confidentiality in merger inquiries

11.153 Informal pre-notification meetings are kept confidential, including all documentation supplied during the meetings.

When a formal notification is filed, a notice is published on the Authority's website. The normal rules on secrecy apply to merger notifications. This means that all information held in the Authority's files, with the exception of business secrets and some personal information, is open to the public. This also applies to submissions made by third parties to the Authority in relation to the merger.

If a file is requested for inspection, the Authority must decide, on the basis of the Secrecy Act 1980 (Sekretesslagen 1980:100), which information must be kept secret. It usually consults the undertaking concerned for this and it is customary for an undertaking to indicate in notifications and correspondence with the Authority that certain information is considered to be a business secret. In practice, the Authority sends requested documents with business secrets blanked-out.

Procedure and timetable

11.154 Parties to a transaction must establish whether there is a concentration and whether the turnover thresholds are met. If so, the transaction must be notified to the Authority. When the Authority is satisfied that it has received a complete notification, it has 25 business days to issue a decision either approving the concentration or initiating a special investigation. During this period, the parties are subject to a standstill obligation.

The Authority has three months to initiate a special investigation. The Stockholm District Court can, at the request of the Authority, extend this period by not more than one month at a time either if the parties agree or if 'exceptional grounds' exist. It is not specified what circumstances are considered to be exceptional grounds.

At the end of the three-month period, the Authority must decide whether the concentration should be:

(a) **Approved.** If it wishes to attach any agreed conditions to its approval, the Authority can file a request to the Stockholm District Court to have them sanctioned with a penalty.

(b) **Prohibited.** Although the Authority can approve a concentration, it cannot prohibit it. A prohibition must be decided by the Stockholm District Court, following an application by the Authority (which can only be submitted after a special investigation has taken place).

If the Authority applies to prohibit the concentration, the Stockholm District Court must issue its decision within six months (or longer if special reasons exist). It can order that the concentration is:

(i) Approved with an order that the parties take certain pro-competitive actions (see **11.156**). This cannot be done more than two years after the date of the contract.

(ii) Prohibited (in which case it becomes void).

A concentration cannot be prohibited:

(A) more than two years after the date of the contract; or

(B) when an acquisition is made on public stock markets (instead, the acquirer can be ordered to sell the acquired shares).

Right to appeal

11.155 A decision of the Stockholm District Court can be appealed to the Market Court. A decision of the Stockholm District Court can be appealed by the parties to the decision to the Market Court within three weeks. The Market Court must issue a decision within three months after the expiry of the period allowed for appeals (or longer if the parties consent or if there are exceptional grounds).

A third party cannot appeal against a decision to approve a concentration.

Conditions of clearance

11.156 Provided they are sufficient to eliminate competition concerns, the Authority (normally at the end of its special investigation) and the Stockholm

District Court (after reviewing an Authority application for prohibition) can accept commitments offered by the parties as conditions of clearance to prevent an application for prohibition being made, such as:

(a)   Divestments.

(b)   Other measures that have a positive effect on competition.

(c)   The Parties may offer such commitments also within the 25 first days in order to avoid a special investigation procedure. However, the time frame is dependent upon the Authority's finding of the competition concern.

If conditions of clearance are not put into effect, undertakings can be fined. Fines can be imposed by the Stockholm District Court at the request of the Authority.

Reforms

11.157 The Authority has suggested new rules as regards turnover thresholds for concentration notifications to the government. The proposed rules are the following:

(a)   The aggregate annual turnover in Sweden of the undertakings concerned exceeded SEK1 billion in the previous financial year.

(b)   Each of at least two of the undertakings concerned had a turnover in Sweden exceeding SEK200 million in the previous financial year.

According to the Authority the new rules would result in fewer concentration notifications and would allow the review procedure to be better focused. At present, about 97% of the notifications do not result in any legal measures being taken.

Contact details

11.158 The Competition Authority (*Konkurrensverket*) (Authority)

Head. Claes Norgren (Director General)

Address for correspondence: SE-103 85
Stockholm
Sweden
Address for visits: Sveavägen 167
Stockholm
Sweden
T + 46 8 700 1600
F + 46 8 24 5543

E ikonkurrensverket@kkv.se

W http://www.kkv.se/eng/eng_index.shtm

Czech Republic

Applicable legislation

11.159 Merger control in the Czech Republic is governed by Act No. 143/2001 Coll, on the Protection of Economic Competition and Modification of Other Laws (the Act on the Protection of Economic Competition), as amended (the 'Czech Competition Act'). The Czech Competition Act became effective on 1 July 2001 and replaced the previous Act on the Protection of Economic Competition, which became effective on 1 March 1991.

On 1 May 2004, the Czech Republic became a member of the European Union; therefore, a merger with a 'Community Dimension' must be assessed under the Merger Regulation (provided, however, that the concentration is not referred from the European Commission to the Czech Competition Office (as defined below) in accordance with such regulation).

Competition Authority

11.160 The Office for the Protection of Economic Competition, with its registered office at třída Kpt. Jaroše 7, 604 55 Brno, Czech Republic (the 'Czech Competition Office'), is the competent authority to assess concentrations under the Czech Competition Act. Further details are available at the web site of the Czech Competition Office, *www.compet.cz*.

In addition, the Czech Telecommunication Office exercises state administration in the area of electronic communications and postal services, including market regulation and the determination of business conditions (i) to substitute for the missing effects of economic competition, and (ii) to establish conditions for the proper functioning of economic competition and for the protection of users and other market actors until a fully competitive environment is achieved. However, merger notifications must be submitted to and decided by the Czech Competition Office.

Concentration

11.161 Under Section 12 of the Czech Competition Act, a concentration between undertakings arises:

(a)   upon the merger of two (2) or more previously independent undertakings;

(b)   in case of the acquisition of an enterprise of another undertaking or a part thereof (purchase of assets); or

(c)   when one (1) or more undertakings acquire the possibility to exercise direct or indirect control over a previously independent undertaking, especially (a) through the acquisition of shares, or (b) through an agreement, or by any other means that confer the possibility of determining, or exercising influence on the competitive conduct of the controlled undertaking. A concentration may also arise when sole control over a company changes to joint control and vice versa;

(d)   upon the establishment of joint control over an undertaking that performs, on a lasting basis, all the functions of an autonomous economic entity ('full function joint venture').

Under Czech law, only a permanent change in the nature of the control over an undertaking on a lasting basis is deemed to result in the formation of a concentration. From the notification obligations, the Czech Competition Act expressly excludes a temporary acquisition of control by (i) a bank during a rescue operation or financial reconstruction and/or (ii) an investment services provider, who acquires shares, in case the shares in question are acquired for the purpose of their sale, and the voting rights relating thereto are not exercised.

Thresholds

11.162   In case a concentration between undertakings occurs, the duty to have the transaction approved by the Czech Competition Office arises if the following turnover thresholds are met (provided, however, that the given concentration does not have a Community Dimension in which case the Merger Regulation, subject to the referral of the concentration from the European Commission to the Czech Competition Office, applies and the concentration in question is examined by the European Commission):

(a)   Either: The combined net (aggregate) turnover achieved in the last accounting period in the Czech market exceeds CZK 1.5 billion (aprox. EUR 50 million) for all undertakings concerned **AND** at least two (2) of the undertakings concerned each achieved a net (aggregate) turnover of over CZK 250 million (aprox. EUR 8 million) in the last accounting period in the Czech market;

(b)   Or: The net (aggregate) turnover achieved in the last accounting period in the Czech market:

   (i)   (if the concentration assumes the form of a merger by absorption or amalgamation), by at least one (1) of the parties to the merger;

   (ii)   (if the concentration takes the form of the purchase of an enterprise or a part thereof (the purchase of assets)), by the acquired enterprise or its respective acquired part;

   (iii) (if the concentration takes the form of an acquisition of control), by the undertaking over which control is acquired; or

   (iv)   (if the concentration takes the form of a joint-control acquisition over a 'full function joint venture'), by at least one (1) undertaking creating the joint venture;

   exceeds the amount of CZK 1.5 billion **AND** the worldwide net (aggregate) turnover achieved in the last accounting period by at least one (1) other undertaking concerned exceeds CZK 1.5 billion.

Mandatory notification and procedure

11.163 A prior notification to the Czech Competition Office is mandatory if the above-mentioned thresholds are met. There is no time limit within which the filing must be made. The undertakings concerned usually give notification of concentrations following the conclusion of the agreement, the announcement of the public bid or the acquisition of a controlling interest. Notwithstanding, under Czech law, notification is also possible where undertakings concerned satisfy the Czech Competition Office of their intention to enter into an agreement concerning a proposed concentration and demonstrate to the Czech Competition Office that their plan for that proposed concentration is sufficiently concrete. However, a concentration which is subject to notification may be implemented only after clearance is granted, or is deemed to be granted, by the Czech Competition Office.

The notification must be made in the Czech language and must contain the information stipulated in the Czech Competition Office's regulation No. 368/2001 Coll., on Details Concerning the Terms of Notification, as amended, as well as documents evidencing the decisive facts for the concentration, including the agreement, based on which the concentration is to occur, and annual reports and financial statements of the undertakings concerned for the last accounting period.

Within 30 days of receiving a completed notification (the first phase), the Czech Competition Office must (i) decide whether the concentration is subject to its clearance and if not, issue a decision to that effect, or (ii) issue a decision approving the concentration if such concentration does not significantly impede competition. Within the same time limit, the Czech Competition Office may commence an in-depth investigation (the second phase). In the second phase, the Czech Competition Office is obliged to issue its clearance or prohibition of the implementation of the concentration within five months of receiving the completed notification. If neither of the above decisions are issued during the first phase (or as the case may be, during the second phase) clearance is deemed to be issued by the Czech Competition Office on the final date of the first phase (or as the case may be, on the final date of the second phase).

The Czech Competition Office will not issue its clearance if the concentration could result in a substantive distortion of competition on the relevant market, namely if the concentration would give rise to the creation, or reinforcement of a dominant position of the undertakings concerned, or any one of them. If the aggregate market share of the undertakings concerned does not exceed 25% on the relevant market, it is presumed that the concentration does not cause substantive distortion of competition, unless proved otherwise during the concentration assessment.

Filing fees

11.163a A notification fee amounting to CZK 100,000 is payable to the Czech Competition Office before the notification is filed (if paid later, the deadline for decision (see below) will start to elapse no earlier than the date when evidence proving payment of the fee is delivered to the Czech Competition Office).

Ancillary restraints

11.164 Granting clearance applies also to competition restrictions declared by undertakings in their notification to the Czech Competition Office, which are directly related to the concentration, and are indispensable for its implementation.

Sanctions

11.165 The Czech Competition Office may impose financial penalties for breach of the merger control regulation. The penalties amount to CZK 10,000,000 or 10% from the net income for the last accounting period for an intentional or negligent breach of the prohibition to implement the concentration before the Czech Competition Office gives its clearance. The Czech Competition Office may impose a penalty of up to CZK 300,000 (or up to 1% of the net turnover of the relevant competitor for the last accounting period) for an intentional non-submission or partial submission of documents or information to the Czech Competition Office. Acting in breach of an enforceable decision of the Czech Competition Office may result in a penalty of up to CZK 1,000,000.

The Czech Competition Office also has been endowed with powers to challenge the transaction after the clearance. It may revoke the decision on clearance if the decision was issued based on documents and information provided by the undertaking concerned which were completely or partially untrue or incomplete, or if clearance was issued as a result of the Czech Competition Office being misled by the undertakings concerned or if the undertakings concerned do not comply with the conditions, limits or liabilities imposed by the Czech Competition Office. The Czech Competition Office may initiate proceedings to revoke its decision within one year after it discovered the above facts, but not later than within five years after such events occurred.

Hungary

Merger control issues

11.166 Hungary's EU accession and the previous law approximation have resulted in significant changes in Hungarian competition law. As regards merger control issues, the most important impact of the accession is that concentrations subject to notification under Council Regulation No. 139/2004/EC ('Merger Control Regulation') and simultaneously reaching the thresholds stipulated in the Hungarian Act LVII of 1996 on the prohibition of unfair and restrictive market practices ('Competition Act') do not need to be notified to the Hungarian Competition Authority (in Hungarian: Gazdasági Versenyhivatal; 'HCA'). Therefore, the Competition Act shall only be applied to concentrations, which fall out of the scope of the Merger Control Regulation.

Concentrations

Concentrations subject to authorisation

11.167 According to section 23(1) of the Competition Act, a concentration between undertakings arises if:

(a)   two or more previously independent undertakings merge or an undertaking is integrated with another or a part of an undertaking becomes part of another undertaking which is independent of the first one;

(b)   an undertaking or more undertakings jointly acquire direct or indirect control over the whole or parts of one or more previously independent undertaking(s)[1];

(c)   more than one undertaking, which are independent of each other, jointly create an undertaking controlled by them, which is permanently able to perform all the functions of an independent undertaking (full function joint venture).

1. Part of an undertaking means assets or rights, including the clientele of an undertaking, the acquisition of which, solely or together with the assets and rights which are at the disposal of the acquiring undertaking, is sufficient for enabling market activities to be pursued.

Concentrations not subject to authorisation

11.168 Temporary acquisition of control or ownership for a period of one year at the maximum by insurance companies, credit institutions, financial holding companies, holding companies with mixed activities, investment companies or property managing organisations for the purpose of preparing resale shall not qualify as concentrations, provided that they do not exercise their control rights or exercise them only to an extent which is indispensable to the attainment of these objectives. The HCA may extend such one-year period upon request if the undertaking concerned proves that it was not possible to carry out the disposal within one year.

Establishment of control

11.169 As section 23(2) of the Competition Act provides, direct control may be established if an undertaking or more undertakings jointly:

(a)   hold more than 50% of the voting rights in another undertaking based on a shareholding interest, or hold more than 50% of the voting rights on a contractual basis, or

(b)   are entitled to elect, designate or revoke the majority of another undertaking's executives, or

(c) based on an agreement, are entitled to influence significantly another undertaking's decision-making, or

(d) as a matter of fact, are able to influence significantly another undertaking's decision-making (de facto control).

Indirect control refers to the situation where an undertaking ('A') controls another undertaking ('B') through a third undertaking ('C') that is controlled, either directly or indirectly, by the first undertaking, 'A'.

Thresholds

11.170 The Hungarian merger control system is based on obligatory preliminary authorisation; therefore, a concentration must be notified to the HCA provided that the following conditions are met:

(a) the aggregate net turnover of:

  (i) all the groups of undertakings concerned; and

  (ii) the undertakings jointly controlled by members of the groups of undertakings concerned and other undertakings

  exceeded HUF 15 billion (approximately EUR 58 million, based on a 260 EUR/HUF exchange rate) in the business year prior to the date of the concentration; and

(b) the net turnover of each of at least two of the groups of undertakings concerned, together with the net turnover of the undertakings jointly controlled by undertakings members of the respective group of undertakings and other undertakings, exceeded HUF 500 million (approximately EUR 1,9 million, based on a 260 EUR/HUF exchange rate) in the business year prior to the date of the concentration.

It should be noted that in assessing whether the above HUF 500 million threshold is met, concentrations – not subject to authorisation – that took place within a two-year period preceding the concentration concerned between (a) the group of undertakings acquiring control and (b) undertakings of the group of undertakings, the controlling powers of which cease as a conclusion of the concentration, shall also be taken into account.

In the course of the calculation of the turnover thresholds, the intra-group company turnover must be ignored. Moreover, in the case of a foreign undertaking, only the turnover generated in Hungary must be taken into account. (For undertakings resident in Hungary, their worldwide turnover shall be taken into account.) The net turnover of undertakings jointly controlled by two or more undertakings shall be apportioned equally to each undertaking having control over them. For the purpose of such apportioning, controlling undertakings which belong to the same group of undertakings shall be deemed to be one single undertaking. For parts of undertakings, the net turnover realised in the preceding year by the use of the assets and rights by the undertaking which sold them shall be taken into account.

In case of insurance companies, investment service providers and funds, credit institutions and financial enterprises, the Competition Act stipulates special rules for the replacement of the net turnover, eg for insurance companies, the gross insurance premiums shall be taken into account instead of the net turnover.

The rules of the Competition Act on groups of undertakings concerned

11.171 According to section 26(5) of the Competition Act, a group of undertakings concerned consists of the direct participants and the indirect participants.

Direct participants are the acquirer undertaking and the target undertaking.

As section 26(3) of the Competition Act provides, indirect participants are the other members of the group of undertakings, to which the direct participants belong. An undertaking belongs to the same group of undertakings which:

(a)   are under the direct or indirect control of it, or

(b)   have direct or indirect control over it, or

(c)   are under the direct or indirect control of the undertakings referred to in point (b) above, or

(d)   are under the joint control of two or more of the undertakings referred to in points (a)-(c) above.

For the meaning of direct and indirect control, please see **11.170** above.

It is also worth mentioning that merger control focuses on the status that comes into existence as a result of the concentration. Therefore, in establishing the indirect participants, the undertakings whose right to control will cease as a result of the concentration, must be left out.

Notification

11.172 If the above thresholds are met, the authorisation of the HCA is required. The notification is statutory and shall be made prior to the merger. The Competition Act has extra-territorial effect, the jurisdiction of the HCA is based on the Hungarian sales of the undertakings, ie Hungarian merger control procedure may even take place, if all the participants are foreign undertakings but their Hungarian sales exceed the thresholds mentioned above.

Responsibility for notification

11.173 In the event of merger or integration, the merger control notification shall be filed by the direct participants, while in any other cases, it shall be filed by the party acquiring the part of undertaking or the direct control.

Timing of notification

11.174 The merger control notification must be filed within 30 days of the date of the publication of the takeover bid, the conclusion of the contract for the acquisition or the acquisition of the controlling rights, whichever is the earliest. In contractual relationships, this is typically handled in the manner that the contract is signed but the HCA approval is treated as a condition precedent to the closing of the transaction. The notification shall be submitted by filing the standard fill-in-form published by the HCA together with all necessary attachments [sections 28(2), 68(2) of the Competition Act]. The form is available at the website of the HCA, *www.gvh.hu*. In the form, detailed information is required, inter alia, on the participants, on other interested undertakings (eg suppliers) and on the relevant product(s) and the geographical market.

Procedural issues

Pre-merger consultation

11.175 The HCA may be consulted on how to answer the questions of the form (the form requires rather extensive and detailed information). Such pre-notification consultation may help to resolve interpretation problems and to identify the relevant information, but this informal consultation is not part of the official proceedings.

Simplified and full procedure

11.176 According to section 63(3)(a) of the Competition Act, the concentration must be approved within 45 days if:

(a)   the transaction does not constitute a concentration; or

(b)   based on the net turnover figures of the participants, the thresholds mentioned above are not met; or

(c)   granting authorisation for the concentration may clearly not be refused (simplified procedure). The deadline may be extended by another 20 days.

Otherwise, the decision must be granted within 120 days (full procedure), whereas the deadline may be extended by another 60 days. If the HCA requires additional information or documents, the time period whilst these are produced must be added to the normal time period of the procedure.

As a general rule, the competition council (in Hungarian: versenytanács) shall pass its decision without holding a hearing. However, each party may request passing the decision with holding a hearing [section 74(1) of the Competition Act].

Filing fees

11.177 The fee of a merger control procedure is HUF 2 million (approximately EUR 7,700, based on a 260 EUR/HUF exchange rate) in case of a simplified procedure and HUF 10 million (approximately EUR 38,500, based on a 260 EUR/HUF exchange rate) if the approval is granted after a full procedure [Section 62 of the Competition Act]. The fee of the simplified procedure shall be paid at the time of filing the notification, and, if the case is decided in a full procedure, the additional fee shall be paid following the receipt of the decision of the HCA.

Sanctions

11.178 According to section 79 of the Competition Act, if the responsible participant fails to notify the concentration to the HCA, the HCA may impose a fine of HUF 50.000 (app. EUR 190) per day.

Judicial review

11.179 The decision of the HCA may be reviewed by the court. The statement of claim shall be submitted within 30 days of the conveyance of the HCA's decision.

Substantive issues

Dominant position

11.180 According to the Competition Act, the HCA shall not deny granting the approval if the concentration does not create or strengthen such dominant position on the relevant market, which impedes the creation, maintenance or development of effective competition on the relevant market or on a substantial part thereof. In the course of the procedure, the HCA will have to evaluate the advantages and disadvantages connected to the concentration. The HCA will examine, among others:

(a)   the structure of the relevant market; existing or potential competition on the relevant market; procurement and marketing possibilities; the conditions and the costs of entry into the market and the exit from the market and the technical, economic and legal conditions thereof; the impact of the concentration on the competition on the market;

(b)   the market position and strategy, economic and financial capacity, business conduct, internal and external competitiveness of the participants; and

(c)   the impact of the concentration on the suppliers and intermediate and final consumers.

Based on the practice and the guidelines of the HCA, as a rule of thumb it may be stated that in the case of a 40% market share, dominant position is presumed. If the market share is in the range of 30-40%, the HCA will carefully scrutinize the markets in more depth than in the case of a market share between 20% and 30%, when the review will not be so detailed [eg 116/1999 Competition Board Decision]. Finally, under 20%, the HCA's practice tends to give an automatic green light to the concentration [eg 151/2002 Competition Board Decision].

However, even if the aggregate market share is relatively high (eg around 50%), this fact in itself will not bar the concentration from being approved. There are cases in the practice of the HCA where concentrations with an aggregate market share above 50% per cent have been approved [eg 131/1997 Competition Board Decision]. However, according to the practice of the HCA, the market shares are only of secondary importance in the case of bidders' markets. It is also important to stress that in the last years' practice of the HCA, the approval to concentrations was only rejected in very few cases.

Simplified procedure

11.181 As mentioned in **11.176** above, if certain conditions are met, the concentration may be approved in a simplified procedure, within 45 days from the filing of the application. The considerations in differentiating between concentrations subject to authorisation in simplified or full procedure are laid down in Notice No. 1/2003 of the president of the HCA and the chairman of the competition council of the HCA. The notice is not binding, its function is to state how the HCA will apply the legal provisions and to explain the factors and considerations used by the HCA when deciding whether to assess an application under simplified or full procedure in respect of concentrations subject to authorization (ie **11.176**(c) above).

According to the above notice, those concentrations may be authorised in a simplified procedure, which clearly do not create or strengthen a dominant position, therefore, the HCA applies the simplified procedure to the following types of concentrations:

(a)   The concentration has no horizontal, vertical or portfolio effects, ie:

   (i)   there is no relevant market on which at least two participating groups of undertakings are active; and

   (ii)   there is no relevant market on which any two participating groups of undertakings are/may be in a supplier – buyer relationship; and

   (iii)   the participating groups of undertakings are in no way (production, distribution, etc.) involved in any activity on the markets of complementary products.

Even if the above conditions are satisfied, the concentration may be assessed in a full procedure, if, as a result of conglomerate effects, the group of undertakings with previously weaker financial status: (a) would substantially reinforce its financial status, (b) would increase its market share to over 30 % on any of the relevant markets, and (c) taking into account the features of the market, there is a reasonable danger that restrictive strategies (eg predatory pricing) might be applied relying on the improved positions.

(b) The concentration has horizontal and/or vertical and/or portfolio effects; but:

(i) there is no relevant market on which the combined market share of the participating groups of undertakings exceeds 20%;

(ii) there is no relevant market connecting any two participating groups of undertakings on which the market share of either the supplier-group or the buyer-group exceeds 25%; and

(iii) there is no relevant market affected by portfolio effects on which the market share of any participating groups of undertakings exceeds 25%.

(c) If the combined market share of the participating groups of undertakings exceeds the 20% threshold mentioned in point (b)(i) above on the relevant market, but the increase of the concentration resulting from the transaction on this relevant market is insignificant, ie:

(i) without having regard to the group of undertakings concerned, the market share of which is higher than that of any other group of undertakings concerned on this relevant market, the combined market share of the other groups of undertakings concerned does not exceed 5% on this relevant market; and

(ii) on this relevant market, there is a competitor with a market share which is similar to that of the largest participating group of undertakings; and

(iii) the concentration may not substantially reduce potential competition as it can be reasonably expected that the shares of undertakings currently having low market shares would not increase to an appreciable extent in the future.

As the market share of the participating groups of undertaking is a significant issue for the assessment of the above criteria, the definition of the market share, based on unambiguous, objective and verifiable information, is a precondition for the simplified procedure.

Special rules

11.182 Besides the merger control rules described above, there are several other legal rules which may affect the execution of a merger. Without aiming at completeness, the following issues may have importance in connection with a merger:

(a) The Capital Market Act and the Business Associations Act stipulate certain notification and disclosure obligations in connection with takeovers.

(b)   There are prior approval and notification requirements relating to the acquisition of interest in investment enterprises, financial institutions and insurance companies, as well as in authorised operators in the energy sector.

(c)   If the merger qualifies as employer's legal succession, the rules of the Hungarian Labour Code pertaining to consultation obligation, liability, etc. of the employer shall also be applied.

(d)   The Radio and Television Broadcasting Act, in order to secure impartial information, contains several restrictions, eg it (i) restricts foreigners' acquisition of ownership in national broadcasters, (ii) excludes the sole ownership in case of national televisions, (iii) restricts the cross ownership of the electronic and printed press.

(e)   Under the Privatisation Act, the state holds a golden share in more than 30 privatised companies, which provides veto right to the state in several strategic decisions.

United States

11.183   Given the importance of the US market and the fact that many multinational mergers require a consideration of both EU and US merger control legislation, this section sets out the main US regulatory obligations. The principal statutory instrument in the United States for regulating acquisitions or mergers is section 7 of the Clayton Act (15 U.S.C. section 18). Section 7 forbids the consummation of an acquisition or a merger the effect of which 'may be substantially to lessen competition, or to tend to create a monopoly'. However, in an enforcement action, the United States Department of Justice may also proceed under section 1 of the Sherman Act, which forbids concerted action, namely a 'contract, combination or conspiracy' that is 'in restraint of trade' (15 U.S.C. section 1). This summary will focus primarily on the regulation under section 7 of the Clayton Act as it applies to horizontal mergers, the type of merger most likely to have anti-competitive effects.

Pre-merger reporting requirements

Hart-Scott-Rodino filings

11.184   The Clayton Act was amended in 1976 to add section 7A, the Hart-Scott-Rodino Antitrust Improvements Act of 1976, as amended ('HSR Act') (15 U.S.C. section 18a). The HSR Act requires parties contemplating an acquisition of voting securities, non-corporate interests or assets that meets certain thresholds to file a pre-merger notification report form with the Federal Trade Commission ('FTC') and the Antitrust Division of the United States Department of Justice ('DOJ'), pay a minimum of $45,000 as a filing fee and observe a 30-day waiting period before consummating the transaction (15 U.S.C. section 18a(a) and (b)). The waiting period can also be extended if the DOJ or FTC makes a secondary request for information.

The first major revisions to the HSR Act became effective on 1 February 2001 and were finalised on 18 March 2002. These changes are reflected below. Additional amendments to the regulations are now finalised and are noted at the relevant sections of the text. The most significant change is the treatment of the acquisition of 'non-corporate interests.' The term 'non-corporate interest' means 'an interest in any unincorporated entity that gives the holder the right to any profits of the entity or in the event of dissolution of that entity the right to any of its assets after payment of its debts. These unincorporated entities include, but are not limited to, general partnerships, limited partnerships, limited liability partnerships, limited liability companies, cooperatives and business trusts' (16 Code of Federal Regulations ('CFR') Part 801.1(f)(1)(ii)). The purpose of this change in the regulations was to make the treatment of non-corporate interests the same as the treatment of corporations.

Note below that each threshold value is now adjusted annually based on the change in gross national product (15 U.S.C. section 18a(a)(2)). Current thresholds can be found on the FTC's website. (http://www.ftc.gov/os/2006/01/Section_7AThresholdsfrn.pdf).

The reporting requirements of the HSR Act apply to a transaction only if three threshold jurisdictional tests are met:

(a) Commerce Test: Either the acquiring person or the acquired person must be engaged in United States commerce or in some activity affecting United States commerce (15 U.S.C. section 18a(a)(1)). An 'acquiring person' is any person that, as a result of an acquisition, will hold voting securities or assets, either directly or indirectly (16 CFR Part 801.2(a)). An 'acquired person' is the issuer of voting securities being acquired or a person meeting certain criteria regarding affiliation with the entity whose assets, non-corporate interests or voting securities are being acquired (16 CFR Part 801.2(b)).

(b) Size of the Parties Test: One person to the transaction must have at least $100 million (as adjusted) in total assets or annual net sales and the other person must have total assets or net sales of $10 million (as adjusted) or more to meet this threshold (15 U.S.C. section 18a(a)(2)). In the case of a joint venture, one party to the joint venture must have at least $100 million (as adjusted) in annual net sales or total assets, the joint venture itself must have at least $10 million (as adjusted) in total assets and one other contributor to the joint venture must have $10 million (as adjusted) in annual net sales or total assets; or, the joint venture must have at least $100 million (as adjusted) in total assets and two contributors must have at least $10 million (as adjusted) in annual net sales or total assets (16 CFR Part 801.40(b)). Under the HSR regulations, the 'person' referred to in the HSR regulations can be a natural person, a corporation, an unincorporated entity (such as a limited liability company or LLC) or a trust. A 'person' is defined as the 'ultimate parent entity' (UPE), that is, an entity that is not controlled by any other entity and which includes all other entities that are controlled, directly or indirectly, by the UPE (16 CFR Part 801.1(a)(1)). The control test for corporations is whether the entity holds 50% interest or more of the outstanding voting securities of an issuer (16 CFR Part 801.1(b)(1)(i)). For non-corporate entities such as LLCs or partnerships, the control test is economic, that is, control is the right to 50% of the profits of the entity or 50% of the assets upon dissolution (16 CFR Part 801.1(b)(ii)). Having the contractual power to designate 50 percent or more of the directors of a for-profit or not-for-profit corporation or in the case of certain trusts would also confer control. Thus, when the HSR regulations refer to a 'person', person is the UPE and all of the entities which it controls directly and indirectly and it is the total assets or annual net sales of the UPE that determines the 'size of the party' and certain exemptions below (16 CFR Part 801.1(b)(2)). Please note that if the value of the transaction is in excess of $200 million (as adjusted), the 'size of the parties' test does apply.

(c)   Size of the Transaction Test: This test is met if, as a result of the acquisition, the acquiring person will hold assets or voting securities valued in excess of $50 million (as adjusted). Transactions valued in excess of $200 million (as adjusted) are reportable regardless of the 'size of the parties'. Transactions valued in excess of $50 million (as adjusted) but less than $200 million (as adjusted) are still subject to the 'size of the parties' test. There are special rules that apply in valuing a transaction. The value of an asset transaction is the acquisition price or the fair market value, whichever is greater (16 CFR Part 801.10). Additionally, the value of an asset transaction would include any premium paid to assume executory contracts (such as a lease), the assumption of any accrued liabilities by the acquiring person, or the issuance of a guarantee or a covenant not to complete. If the acquisition is a purchase of voting securities, the value of an acquisition of voting securities under the HSR Act is the value of all of the voting securities that will be held as a result of the acquisition (16 CFR Part 801.10). For example, if the acquiring person purchased the stock in stages, the value of all of the stock held, not just that acquired at a particular stage, would be the value of the transaction. If the stock is publicly traded, the value of the shares to be acquired is either 'Market Price' or the acquisition price, whichever is greater. Market Price for publicly traded shares is the lowest closing quotation within 45 or fewer calendar days that are prior to the consummation of the acquisition but not earlier than the day prior to the execution of the contract, agreement in principle or letter of intent (16 CFR Part 801.10(c)(1)(ii)). If the stock is not publicly traded, and the exact purchase price is contingent or unknown, the HSR Act requires that a fair market value determination of the entire transaction be made (16 CFR Part 801.10(a)(iii)). For acquisitions of non-corporate interests that confers control of an existing or newly-formed entity, the value would be the acquisition price plus the fair market value of any such interests held prior to the acquisition (16 CFR Part 801.10(d)). Fair market value must be determined, in good faith, by the board of directors of the acquiring person or its delegee within 60 days of filing or, if no filing, within 60 days of closing (16 CFR Part 801.10(c)(iii)(3)). The delegation can be implied and no special valuation technique is required.

If these three jurisdictional tests are met, then each of the parties must file a HSR pre-merger notification report form, pay the fee and observe the waiting period unless an exemption applies. The statute designates eleven types of acquisitions and persons that are exempt from HSR Act's coverage (15 USC, section 18a(c)). It also authorises the FTC to promulgate further exemptions of persons and transactions that are not likely to violate the antitrust laws. Thus, even if a transaction satisfies the statutory jurisdictional thresholds, it may still be exempt from the HSR Act's notification and waiting period requirements.

The most important exemptions to non-US companies are the two 'foreign acquisition' exemptions contained in the regulations at 16 CFR Parts 802.50 and 802.51. Under Part 802.50, an acquisition of non-US assets is exempt if:

(a)   the acquiring person is a US person; and

    (i)   the assets are located outside of the US; and

    (ii)   the non-US assets that the acquiring person will hold as a result of the acquisition generated sales in or into the U.S. aggregating $50 million (as adjusted) or less during the acquired person's most recent fiscal year; or

(b)   even if sales exceeded $50 million (as adjusted) in or into the US, the acquisition shall be exempt if:

    (i)   both acquiring and acquired persons are non-US; and

    (ii)   aggregate sales of the acquiring and acquired person in or into the US are less than $110 million (as adjusted) in their respective most recent fiscal years; and

    (iii)   the aggregate total assets located in the US (other than investment assets, securities of another person, or credit extensions or guarantees) are less than $110 million (as adjusted); and

    (iv)   the acquisition is valued at $200 million (as adjusted) or less.

Under 16 CFR Part 802.51, acquisitions of voting securities of a non-US issuer are exempt:

(a)   by a US person unless:

    (i)   the issuer (including all entities controlled by the issuer) holds assets located in the US (other than investment assets, securities of another person or credit extensions or guarantees) having an aggregate total value of greater than $50 million (as adjusted); or

    (ii)   the issuer made aggregate sales in or into the US of over $50 million (as adjusted) in its most recent fiscal year;

(b)   by a non-US person unless:

    (i)   the acquisition will confer control of the issuer; and

    (ii)   the issuer (including all entities controlled by the issuer) either holds assets located in the United States (other than investment assets, securities of another person, or credit extensions or guarantees) having an aggregate total value in excess of $50 million (as adjusted); or

(iii) the issuer (including all entities controlled by the issuer) made aggregate sales in or into the US of over $50 million (as adjusted) in its most recent fiscal year;

(c) by a non-US person even if the thresholds in section (b) are exceeded if:

(i) both the acquiring and acquired persons are non-US persons; and

(ii) the aggregate sales of the acquiring and acquired persons in or into the US are less than $110 million (as adjusted) in their respective most recent fiscal years; and

(iii) the aggregate total assets located in the US (other than investment assets, securities of another person and credit extensions or guarantees) of the acquiring and acquired persons are less than $110 million (as adjusted); and

(iv) the acquisition is valued at $200 million (as adjusted) or less.

Note that for the purpose of these exemptions, if interests of multiple foreign issuers are acquired from the same UPE, the assets located in the US or the sales in or into the US must be aggregated to determine whether the $50 million (as adjusted) threshold is exceeded (16 CFR Part 802.51(a)(2) and (b)(2)).

Non-corporate entities

11.185 Limited Liability Companies ('LLCs') and partnerships are now treated the same as corporations under the HSR Act. These rules were revised extensively and discussed above. In particular, the formation of a non-corporate entity is reportable if there is an acquisition of a controlling interest by one or more of the forming parties and the transaction meets the thresholds discussed above (16 CFR Part 801.50). However, if the new unincorporated entity is being formed in connection with a financing transaction it is exempt as well as the acquisition of a controlling interesting in an existing unincorporated entity if (1) the acquiring person is contributing only cash to the unincorporated entity; (2) for the purpose of providing financing; and (3) the terms are such that the acquiring person will no longer control the entity after it realizes its preferred return (16 CFR Part 802.65).

Fees

11.186 For transactions valued at less than $100 million (as adjusted), the filing fee is $45,000. For transactions valued in excess of $100 million up to $500 million (as adjusted), the fee is $125,000. For transactions valued in excess of $500 million (as adjusted), the filing fee is $280,000.

Enforcement actions

11.187 Enforcement of the HSR Act is rigorous and can be severe. The penalties for not filing an HSR premerger notification report form are $11,000 a day from the day a party should have filed until the actual filing is made. Deficient filings are treated as if a filing was never made. For example, one company made a material omission in an HSR filing and was fined $2.785 million and the officer who signed the HSR filing was fined personally $50,000. In a recent case, The Hearst Trust, paid a civil penalty of $4 million to resolve charges that the company failed to produce key documents required to have been supplied along with its premerger notification of the acquisition of Medi-Span. The DOJ filed the lawsuit at the request of the FTC, and the civil penalty is the largest a company has ever paid for violating antitrust premerger requirements. It is recommended that, if a transaction implicates the HSR Act, the parties seek the advice of HSR counsel.

Additionally, the DOJ has brought a number of 'gun jumping' cases where companies begin to integrate during the HSR waiting period. The acquiring and acquired persons must remain separate and apart during the HSR waiting period, which means no common management, no disclosure of trade secrets or other confidential information except in a limited manner during due diligence or other similar integration of businesses. Recent enforcement actions by the DOJ resulted in multi-million dollar fines. (See, eg, *United States v Computer Associates*, Civ. No. 01–02062(GK) 2002 W.L. 31961456 (D.D.C. 2002); *United States v Gemstar-TV Guide International*, Civ. No. 030198, (D.D.C. 2003)).

HSR Premerger Notification and Report Form

11.188 The HSR Form, the instructions and updated thresholds are available at www.ftc.gov. The HSR Form asks for information regarding the UPEs of the parties and the transaction. Filing persons are required to report revenue data using the North American Industry Classification System ('NAICS'). Information regarding the NAICS can be found in North American Industry Classification – United States, 2002, published by the Executive Office of the President, office of Management and Budget and should be used to locate NAICS industry codes. Information is also available at www.census.gov.

Exon-Florio filings

11.189 Another premerger filing that may be necessary is an Exon-Florio notification under 50 U.S.C. section 2151 et seq. The Exon-Florio Amendment to the Omnibus Trade and Competitiveness Act 1988 established a federal government review process for certain foreign investments in the US. The statute authorises the President to investigate acquisitions, mergers or takeovers by or with foreign persons that could result in foreign control of US companies. The President is further authorised to suspend or prohibit transactions to prevent foreign control of a US company that may threaten to impair US national security. This authority has been delegated to the Committee on Foreign Investment in the United States ('CFIUS'). The joint filings, deemed 'voluntary' under the regulations, are made to the Office of International Investment as part of the United States Department of the Treasury and have a 30-day waiting period. The regulations governing the scope of the statute and the content of the filings can be found at 31 CFR Parts 800.001 to 800.505. Mostly recently, post 9/11, the scrutiny paid to these filings has become more intense and could cause delay in the transaction.

Section 7 of the Clayton Act

11.190 The fact that no reporting is required under the HSR Act does not provide a 'safe harbour' from substantive antitrust enforcement. The HSR program was created to enable the DOJ and the FTC to challenge anti-competitive acquisitions before they are consummated. However, an acquisition may be unlawful even if the HSR Act is not triggered. Thus, to avoid an enforcement action, any anti-competitive effects should be analysed under section 7 of the Clayton Act.

Section 7 of the Clayton Act is enforced by (i) the DOJ, (ii) the FTC and (iii) private parties. Whether, in any given instance, the DOJ or the FTC initiates an investigation of an acquisition is entirely a matter of non-public arrangements between the two agencies. Normally, the agency with expertise or interest in a given industry at any particular period of time will assume 'jurisdiction' over a particular merger investigation. The normal relief sought by either federal agency is divestiture or a similar 'unwinding' and an injunction against similar action for a specified period. A private party can sue for money damages for losses directly caused by a violation of section 7; however, such cases are infrequent.

Traditionally, substantive analysis of section 7 has been divided into three categories equivalent to the types of mergers historically reviewed under that law: (a) vertical, (b) horizontal and (c) conglomerate:

(a) Vertical mergers: Vertical mergers are agreements or mergers of firms within the same chain of distribution of a product, typically the equivalent of acquiring a supplier. The general test for legality of vertical integration was whether a potential competing supplier or customer was foreclosed from access to the market by the acquisition. Most enforcement efforts are directed at horizontal not vertical acquisitions.

(b) Conglomerates: This analysis focuses on the 'potential competition doctrine' which was developed in the 1960s as a method for finding violations of section 7 when a proposed merger removed a potential competitor from the market. The 'potential competition' theory found very little acceptance through the 1980s. Recently, almost all federal courts have declined to find violations under section 7 in cases involving only alleged 'potential competition'.

(c) Horizontal acquisitions: The third way to analyse a merger is as a 'horizontal' merger, an acquisition that eliminates an actual competitor from the marketplace. The present enforcement policy of the DOJ and the FTC are embodied in the 1992 Horizontal Merger Guidelines ('the Guidelines'). The Guidelines describe the analytical process that the FTC and the DOJ ('the Agencies') employ in determining whether to challenge a horizontal merger. They basically apply five factors in this analysis.

The first factor applied by the Agencies is 'whether the merger would significantly increase concentration and result in a concentrated market, properly defined and measured'. They review the product market (eg, coal), the geographic market (eg North America) and the concentration in that defined market. The Agencies use the Herfindahl-Hirschman Index ('HHI') to determine market concentration. The HHI is calculated by squaring each market share then adding them up both before and after the merger. The difference between the HHI pre-and post-merger measures the increase in concentration in the market as a result of the merger. The Agencies consider both the post-merger market concentration and the increase in concentration in determining the competitive effect of a merger. If the post-merger HHI is below 1,000, the market is not concentrated, if it is between 1,000 and 1,800 it is moderately concentrated, and if it is over 1,800, the market is highly concentrated. Once market concentration is determined, the agencies analyse the increase in the HHI. If the market is unconcentrated, any merger in that market is unlikely to have any adverse effects on competition. If the market is moderately concentrated, any increase in HHI over 100 points will 'raise significant competitive concerns' depending on the remaining four factors under the Guidelines. If the market is highly concentrated, any increase in HHI over 50 points will 'raise significant competitive concerns'.

The second factor reviewed is the potential adverse effects of the merger. The Agencies consider whether a merger diminishes competition by enabling the selling firm in the market to engage in 'co-ordinated interaction' that could harm consumers, such as unilaterally raising prices and/or suppressing output.

The third factor the Agencies consider is the likelihood of competitors entering the market in response to an increase in prices after a merger. The merger or acquisition raises no antitrust concern if market entry could be timely, likely, and sufficient in its magnitude, character and scope to deter or counteract any anti-competitive effects.

The fourth factor concerns some mergers that might otherwise be challenged but are reasonably necessary to achieve significant net efficiencies.

The final factor considered is whether the firm would have failed but for the merger, and if so, then competition is no worse off than had the merger not taken place.

Conclusion

11.191 The above discussion provides an overview of the major considerations under federal law whether relevant to an acquisition in the United States or of a United States corporation. The analysis is varied and complex. In addition, state anti-competition laws affecting acquisitions in the United States must also be considered.

Finland

Applicable rules

11.192 The provisions on merger control ('Finnish Merger Control') are included in Chapter 3a of the Act on Competition Restrictions (480/1992) ('Competition Act').

These provisions are supplemented by the Decision of the Ministry of Trade and Industry on the Obligation to Notify a Concentration (499/1998) and the Decree of the Ministry of Trade and Industry on the Calculation of Turnover of a Party to the Concentration (377/2004).

The Finnish Competition Authority has in the end of 1998 published Merger Guidelines. Partial amendments to the Guidelines were published in May 2004, when the Finnish Competition Authority introduced a short form notification mainly for such joint ventures that only have a minimal effect on the Finnish market.

Generally speaking it can be noted that in its main points the Finnish Merger Control follows the rules and principles set out in the EC Merger Regulation and related Commission's notices.

Competition authority

11.193 The competent authority to assess concentrations in Finland is the Finnish Competition Authority ('FCA').

Definition of concentration

11.194 According to the Competition Act a concentration is defined as:

(a)   an acquisition of control;

(b)   an acquisition of an entire business operation or a part thereof;

(c)   a merger; and

(d)   a creation of a joint venture, which shall perform on a lasting basis all the functions of an autonomous economic unit (full-function joint venture).

The provisions on the control of concentrations do not normally apply to intra-group arrangements.

Firstly, the acquisition of control includes an acquisition of the majority of voting rights or the right to appoint the majority of members of the executive body or the body with this right. Secondly, an acquisition of 'corresponding actual control' is also taken into consideration. In practice the acquisition of 'corresponding actual control' covers situation in which a minority shareholder is able to exercise decisive influence over the relevant strategic business decisions of another company. Such strategic decisions cover, for example, the appointment of directors and the adoption of the business plan or budget. The ability to block such decisions also constitutes an actual control

The acquisition of control includes the acquisition of sole control, joint control, indirect control and change in shareholding in the case of joint control. Joint control may be obtained, for example, through unanimity requirements, requirements concerning a qualified majority or veto rights in the Shareholders' Agreement. Normally there is joint control if the parent companies must reach agreement on major decisions concerning the controlled undertaking (possibility of a deadlock situation). Even in the absence of specific veto rights, two or more undertakings acquiring minority shareholdings in another undertaking may obtain joint control on a de facto basis.

The definition of a concentration also covers the acquisition of an entire business operation or a part thereof. In practice the FCA's interpretations concerning the acquisition of a business operation have been very wide and acquisitions of property in which business can be carried out or to which turnover can be allocated has also been considered a concentration that must be notified.

In addition, the concept of 'concentration' covers mergers and full-function joint ventures. The definition of a full-function joint venture under Finnish Merger Control is very much in line with the EC Merger Regulation.

Turnover thresholds

11.195 The provisions of the Finnish Merger Control shall apply to concentrations where the two following cumulative conditions are met:

(a) the combined worldwide turnover of the parties to the concentration exceeds €350 million; and

(b) the turnover of a minimum of two parties each derived from Finland exceeds €20 million.

In accordance with the Competition Act, a party to a concentration refers to the acquirer of control; the acquirer of business operations or a part thereof; the object of control; the acquired business operation; an entity or foundation party to a merger and the founder of a joint venture.

The calculation of turnover is very much in line with that of the EC Merger Regulation. The turnover taken into account for the first threshold is the annual worldwide turnover of each party to the concentration based on the most recent profit and loss account drawn up. When calculating the turnover of the acquirer(s), the turnover of the whole group of companies to which it belongs needs to be taken into consideration. Turnover generated within the group is not included.

When calculating the turnover for the second threshold, the turnover accrued from Finland includes the gross sales which have accrued from the sales of products or offering of services in Finland. Turnover is allocated to the location where the customer is located at the time of the transaction and, thus, imports to Finland are also taken into consideration.

According the above, the parties to the concentration do not have to have any presence in Finland in order for the Finnish Merger Control to apply. Thus, the Finnish Merger Control also applies in foreign to foreign transactions that exceed the turnover thresholds set out in the Competition Act.

More specific instructions on the calculation of turnover are given in the Decree by the Ministry of Trade and Industry on the Calculation of Turnover of a Party to a Concentration (377/2004) and in the FCA's Merger Guidelines.

Notification

11.196 In accordance with the Competition Act, a concentration must be notified to the FCA within a [1] week from:

(a) acquisition of control;

(b) acquisition of business operations or a part thereof;

(c) announcement of a public bid referred to in the Securities Market Act;

(d) decision to merge in the merging operations; or

(e) decision to set up a joint venture in a founding meeting, whichever event happens first.

The notification must be made in accordance with the Decision on the Obligation to Notify a Concentration by the Ministry of Trade and Industry (499/1998) unless the FCA has granted derogation with respect to the certain content of the notification. The Decision includes a notification form where the required information is defined in detail. A simplified notification form has been introduced for certain joint venture situations.

The information required in the notification form includes, for example, the basic data about the parties, the type of the concentration, detailed turnover figures, market definitions and market figures, competitor, supplier and customer information, effects of concentration, possible ancillary restrictions, etc.

The notification must be made in Finnish or Swedish (the official languages of Finland). One original and four copies of the notification and its annexes must be delivered to the FCA.

In accordance with the Competition Act, all undertakings are obliged to provide the FCA with all the information it requests for the investigation of a concentration, whether this information is commercially sensitive or not. An undertaking providing the FCA with documents containing confidential information and business secrets should clearly mark all such confidential information. The decisions of the FCA are published in a non-confidential form.

The FCA provides additional information and guidance. The party obliged to notify has the possibility to have pre-notification discussions with the FCA. These preliminary negotiations facilitate the drafting of the notification and help the FCA to process the matter quickly. Thus, it is highly recommended to have pre-notification contacts with the FCA on the basis of a pre-notification memorandum or a draft notification prior to the submission of the final notification.

Ancillary restraints

11.197 In the same process and as part of a concentration, the FCA may also approve competition restrictions which are directly related to the concentration and which are necessary for its implementation.

The FCA's Merger Guidelines set out the main principles according to which ancillary restrictions are assessed. Typical ancillary restrictions accepted are non-competition and non-solicitation obligations, obligations to licence industrial property rights and purchase and supply obligations. The assessment of ancillary restrictions by the FCA is very much in line with the Commission Notice regarding restrictions ancillary to the concentrations.

Clearance of the ancillary restrictions is not automatic, it needs to be specifically requested and motivated in the notification.

Procedure and timetable

11.198 The concentration may not be implemented prior to the FCA's approval.

During the waiting period, all actions affecting the commercial conduct or market behaviour of the target are prohibited. However, it is possible to apply for an exemption to the prohibition on completing the concentration before clearance.

The prohibition to implement a concentration does not prevent the implementation of a public bid. Thus, it is possible to purchase the shares in question. However, a decision of the Market Court prohibiting the concentration would lead to an obligation to sell the shares.

The official process has two stages:

(i)   The so-called first stage takes one month. If the notification is significantly incomplete, the time will not begin running. When the acceptability of a concentration is evaluated, the main competitors of the parties, the customers, and the suppliers are always heard. If the acquisition clearly does not have restrictive effects on competition or if the restrictive effects can be prevented by setting conditions to the FCA's approval, the acquisition will be cleared during stage I.

(ii)   In potentially problematic cases, the FCA will make a decision to initiate further proceedings (stage II) during which the transaction and its competitive effects are thoroughly investigated. The FCA normally only decides to conduct an in-depth investigation in cases where a concentration is deemed to raise serious competition problems in the Finnish market. The acquisition may still be cleared as such or approved as conditional. Stage II takes normally three months at most. However, the Market Court may extend this time by two months.

According to the Competition Act, the Market Court may, upon the proposal of the FCA, prohibit or order a concentration to be dissolved or attach conditions on the implementation of a concentration, if, as a result of the concentration, a dominant position would arise or be strengthened which would significantly impede competition in the Finnish market or a substantial part thereof. The Market Court must issue its decision within three months from the FCA's proposal.

The decision of the Market Court may be appealed to the Supreme Administrative Court.

The primary way to eliminate harmful competition restraints is to impose conditions on the concentration. It is the task of the notifying party, to propose conditions/remedies. The conditions/remedies accepted by the FCA can be both behavioural and structural in nature. However, structural remedies such as divestment of a company or a business are normally preferred.

The Competition Act sets out a time periods within which the FCA and the Market Court are obliged to reach their decisions in concentration cases. If a decision is not made within such time period, a concentration is considered approved.

Sanctions

11.199 An undertaking, which fails to notify or implements a concentration in breach of the provisions of the Finnish Merger Control can be fined a penalty payment. The amount of that fine can be up to 10% of the previous year's turnover of each undertaking involved (the turnover of the whole group to which the party to the concentration belongs can be taken into consideration). In accordance with the Competition Act, a penalty payment shall be imposed, unless the conduct is deemed to be minor or the imposing of a fine otherwise unjustified with respect to safeguarding competition.

In addition, the Market Court may, based on a proposal by the FCA, prohibit or order a concentration to be dissolved if the deal has been implemented in breach of the provisions of the Finnish Merger Control or if the parties have supplied false or misleading information which has had a substantial effect on the decision, provided that the parties to the concentration are informed of the proposal of the FCA no later than one year from the implementation of the concentration.

There are no criminal sanctions for not notifying. However, there are criminal sanctions for submitting false or misleading information to the FCA.

Acknowledgements

11.200   The author of this chapter gratefully acknowledges the assistance of Paolo Sbuttoni and Kate Stanyer, Nabarro Nathanson in updating the section on EU and United Kingdom Merger Control; Guus Kemperink, Partner, VanDoorne, Amsterdam in relation to his section on The Netherlands Law of Merger Control; Mr Frank Lipworth, Partner and Ms Iris Bellanger of Cabinet Lipworth, Paris in contributing the section on French merger control; Dr Michael Stobbe, Partner and Christian Kirschke of GSK Gassner Stockmann & Kollegen, Berlin for their section on German merger control law; Enrico Adriano Raffaelli, Partner, and Antonio Debiasi of Rucellai and Raffaelli, Milan for their section on Italian merger control legislation; Carles Prat, Partner, Baker &McKenzie, Barcelona for contributing the section on Spanish merger control; Ms Allison A Davis, Partner of Davis Wright Tremaine LLP, Attorneys at Law, San Francisco, in contributing the section on US merger control; Helen Kelly, Partner and Niamh Connery, Senior Associate of Matheson Ormsby Prentice, Dublin for the section on Irish merger control law; Eva-Maj Mühlenbock, Partner, Lindahl, Stockholm for the section on Swedish merger control law; Hannu Pokela, Partner and Ms Sari Hiltunen, Partner of Castrén & Snellman, Helsinki for the section on Finnish merger control law; Ms. Daniela Musilová of Prochazka Randl Kubr, Prague for the section on merger control in the Czech Republic; Gábor Damjanovic, Partner and Zsófia Füzi of Forgó, Varga & Partners, Budapest for the section on Hungarian merger control law; Andrzej Madala, Wardyński & Partners, Warsaw for the section on Polish merger control law.

Chapter 12

Strategy and Tactics

At a glance

- Acquisition strategy should be set within the context of the overall business and financial strategy of the company and should be complementary to the strategy for organic growth.

- A statement of acquisition strategy should set out the objectives, target criteria and approach to resourcing acquisitions, as well as clearly stating the risks involved.

- The company should make a realistic assessment of the competence and capacity of its management to manage an acquisition or acquisitions of the scale and type intended.

- Acquisition strategy influences organisational structure and culture in a number of ways, especially if the company intends to make a series of significant acquisitions.

- For each acquisition project a team should be formed with clarity of role, responsibility, resources and authority.

- The company should take appropriate external advice in developing its acquisition strategy and in executing individual transactions.

- If the company intends to make a series of acquisitions then it needs to be mindful of its reputation as an acquirer.

Developing an acquisition strategy

12.1   This chapter assumes that the company has a good process for developing, implementing and reviewing strategy as a whole. If it doesn't, then it shouldn't be considering making acquisitions. After all, if a prospective bidder has not already applied such professional analysis to its own activities it is unlikely to do so with a target. Moreover, it is clearly harder to communicate the strategic rationale of an acquisition to shareholders, potential financiers, staff and other key audiences if there isn't one.

The legal and financial aspects of making acquisitions covered in this volume are important and they consume considerable amounts of management time and expense during the acquisition process. However, it is the quality of the strategic judgements made which will determine whether that expenditure of time and money will deliver real growth in value.

There are many approaches to developing corporate strategy and much has been written on the subject. A good summary of the various methods, models and issues involved is contained in Richard Koch's book *The Financial Times Guide to Strategy.*

The strategic analysis, which generally leads to the need for a coherent acquisition strategy, is typically that relating to the structure of the industry and its competitive environment. Michael Porter's seminal work *Competitive Strategy* contained the chart, below, which has probably been at the heart of many acquisition strategy papers.

Porter's five competitive forces

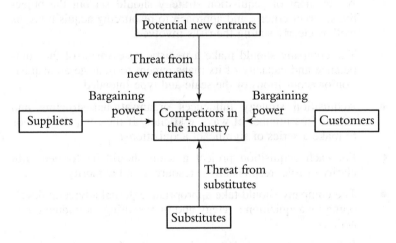

Out of such analysis the typical drivers which lead to the need for acquisitions to support growth are likely to be related to:

- increasing market share or reach;

- extending product and brand portfolios;

- gaining technological advantage; or

- vertical integration to gain a higher share of industry profit.

One argument frequently used in favour of using acquisitions instead of relying on alternatives, such as organic growth, is that the pace of change in business is increasing. The time available to enter new markets or to introduce new products against competition is decreasing, so that acquisition may be the only route quick enough to enable the company to achieve the defined objectives. This can be true, but if this is the primary reason for acquisition it is worth remembering the words of Ghandi:

'People remember how well you do things not how quickly you do them.'

and avoiding the danger of compromising quality for speed.

Acquisitions which support the management of risk or improvement in operational performance are those which meet some or all of the following objectives:

- reducing competitive pressure;

- increasing control of distribution channels;

- gaining economies of scale;

- applying the buyer's greater management capability to the target's assets and market opportunity; and

- acquiring management talent or improved processes.

Few companies today would consider their growth opportunities and competitive challenges to be solely domestic. Industry consolidation and globalisation are two powerful forces behind the strategic logic of many acquisitions. Whether it is simply a small extension of the product portfolio or a geographical expansion that is driving the company's acquisition strategy or a grander plan to transform the business or the industry itself, the company needs to be clear why it wants to make acquisitions in general and how a specific acquisition fits within the acquisition strategy.

It also has to be recognised that there are occasions where the real driver of acquisition strategy relates to the personal rather than the corporate ambitions of the chief executive. In Nancy Hubbard's excellent book *Acquisition Strategy and Implementation* she lists some of the following as classic personal motivations:

- sending the right signals to the City;

- impressing the competition;

- deflecting attention from issues within the business; and

- retrieving face.

In the US where scale and status are possibly more closely linked than in Europe you could probably add the motivation of running the biggest company in the patch, whether that be the local patch or the industry patch. Whatever the personal motivation if it diverges from what is in the best interests of the company then value is in danger. The most effective independent non-executive directors and chairmen have always been alive to this issue, vigilant in recognising its presence and rigorous in dealing with the consequences.

The other driver for the unsuspecting chief executive officer (CEO) is hubris and there is an excellent example of this in Jack Welch's autobiography *Straight from the Gut*. Welch was the legendary CEO of General Electric.

'Jack what are you going to do next? Buy McDonalds?'

The remark came from a foursome of guys across the seventh fairway at Augusta as I was teeing off from the third hole in April 1986. Four months after announcing the deal to buy RCA, I had just acquired Kidder, Peabody, one of Wall Street's oldest investment banking firms.

While the guys were only kidding, there were others who really didn't think much of our latest decision. At least three GE board members weren't too keen on it, including two of the most experienced directors in the financial services business Citibank Chairman Walt Wriston and J.P. Morgan President Lew Preston. Along with Andy Sigler, then Chairman of Champion International, they warned that the business was a lot different from our others.

'The talent goes up and down the elevators every day and can go in a heartbeat,' said Wriston. 'All you're buying is the furniture.'

At an April 1986 board meeting in Kansas City, I had argued for it and unanimously swung the board my way.

It was a classic case of hubris. Flush with the success of our acquisitions of RCA in 1985 and Employers Reinsurance in 1984, I was on a roll. Frankly, I was just too full of myself. While internally I was still searching for the right feel for the company, on the acquisition front I thought I could make anything work.

Soon I'd realise that I had taken it one step too far.

In addition to the underpinning commercial logic of an acquisition strategy, three other areas are critical to apply thought to and these relate to brand strategy, corporate culture and the degree of integration.

Defining brands is a big industry in itself, for the purposes of this chapter we will use a simple definition.

'A brand is what is inside people's heads about your company.'

A complex mix of variables will determine what a customer, supplier, employee or any one else who matters to the company thinks about the business. Most companies will have a deliberate strategy for developing their corporate brand and, where relevant, the brands of different parts of their business. They will be clear about who the key audience groups are and carry out regular research to check the status of the brand competitively and alert them to issues they need to address. Underpinning any brand strategy will be a clear positioning for the company in its markets, a set of agreed values and an identity/image which matches. Difficulties arise if there is divergence between the company's attempted positioning and its execution.

Well-experienced and successful acquirers have developed clear policies for dealing with each of the important areas of brand management. They plan ahead so that communication of what is required in the acquired company is effective and dilution of brand equity is avoided. They deliberately use the opportunity of the acquisition to enhance, rather than dilute, their brand equity. Despite the example given above General Electric was very successful in doing this in a number of sectors through the 1990s and has sustained this performance during this decade as well.

The range of cultures and styles of leadership vary widely from business to business, even in the same sector. Watching the behaviour and listening to the words of the world's most successful business leaders it is apparent that they are very clear about the culture they are building. The folksy tough no nonsense penny wise styles of Berkshire Hathaway's Warren Buffet is markedly different from the highly entertaining bold style of others. A strong brand and culture which is highly respected can make acquisition strategy easier. However, it can also make it more difficult, if it is so distinctive it is hard for others to join in. What matters is that the potential acquirer possesses a high level of awareness, has a strategy for dealing with the issues involved and recognises the challenges to its own culture of a significant acquisition of a business with a very different culture. If corporate culture is the personality of a business, who wants a confused personality?

In this context any acquisition strategy should be clear about the conditions the company would be prepared to consider making contested or hostile bids. The cultural integration issues are clearly very different under these circumstances. Businesses with very strong brands, cultures and processes will probably consider the contested bid for a smaller entity considerably less risky than those who lack these strengths.

The degree of integration of companies acquired will depend upon a number of factors in addition to brand strategy. There is a spectrum of integration possibilities from 'complete' ie from corporate identity to every item of policy, control and management practice, to 'autonomy' where the acquired company remains as a separate entity in almost every regard other than financial control. This is covered in more detail in **Chapter 10 Post Acquisition Management**.

Once an overall acquisition strategy has been agreed detailing the broad financial and market objectives for acquisitions, the next step is to plan in detail how to bring this strategy into action. The more research undertaken and work done to prepare the acquisition strategy the easier this will be. Essentially this next phase is about establishing the right team of people, internal and external, to do the job, agreeing the resources which will be at their disposal and setting clear objectives and processes.

Establishing the team

12.2 Having gained board approval for the acquisition strategy, the next step is to form a core team with the purpose of converting the strategy into action. Successful acquisitions involve a high degree of organisation and management of a wide range of people inside and outside the company. A tight knit highly motivated core team who have the knowledge, skills and style needed to do the job will greatly improve the chances of success, and will reduce the time and costs involved.

In determining the best team for the job, the chief executive needs also to be conscious that as the process moves forward the core team will need to enlist the support of many others and, therefore, the leader of the acquisition team needs to possess relevant leadership and communication skills. The chief executive and other board members must ensure that appropriate confidentiality is maintained at each stage of the process and that everyone involved understands what is required of them in this regard. This is especially true for the leader of the acquisition team.

A project leader should be nominated for each planned acquisition. They should be a senior person who is given the authority from the outset to administer and guide each individual acquisition project through each stage, and who has the credibility to speak, deal and negotiate with all internal and external persons and parties, at all levels, through all those stages. They need to be someone who has a good broad base of knowledge, a strong organisational network, high credibility and excellent communication skills. One person may be able to perform this role for more than one acquisition at a time, depending on the size, complexity, location or other features of the targets concerned.

It may be the case that the project leader is not going to be the one ultimately responsible for managing the acquired business. For example, a highly acquisitive business which is acquiring a bolt on for a division, may have an acquisition specialist who heads up the acquisition process. If this is the case, the person who ends up having the responsibility for the success of the acquisition should be a key and actively involved member of the team and bought into the key decisions.

If one of the reasons for making an acquisition is to acquire management talent and the leader of the acquired business is to replace an incumbent in the acquirer then this needs managing carefully. The risk of making the bid is greater in these circumstances because if the deal falls apart for some reason then the acquirer may suffer the additional loss of a competent manager.

Understanding the motivations of all the many people involved in the acquisition process is critical. Acquisitions can be make or break moments for people's careers and are a source of considerable fee income to advisers. Managing conflicts of interest is a core skill for any business leader, as is exercising good judgement.

The core team should be small in number but large in experience and normally be led by a divisional or group CEO with input from the marketing, finance and operations teams. Their compatibility is important and given the high volume of work involved in any acquisition it is essential that members of this group are action oriented as well as good thinkers and talkers.

When considering the best team for the job, the board should ensure that there is a good fit between the company's advisers and the nature of the transaction or transactions proposed. It should be prepared to change advisers or employ different advisers for a particular deal if appropriate. A good example of where this might be needed is where the company is acquiring a business in a country where it is unfamiliar or where there will be a greater level of scrutiny from competition authorities. Picking appropriate advisers and managing them takes time and skill. The basic criteria for selecting advisers should apply namely:

- track record and reputation of the firm and the individuals in the specific fields required;

- quality of their processes and service ethic;

- ability to deliver within the requisite timeframe;

- relevant international or sectoral capability;

- fit with the business and chemistry with the key people;

- cost and process for agreeing variances from budget; and

- conflicts of interest are identified.

The core team should be a small group of people, but the range of people and teams likely to become involved in the acquisition process, as can be seen from the selection below, can be quite broad. Whether these individuals are employees or advisers will depend upon the scale of the business, whether it is a public company, whether the company is planning regular acquisitions and the nature of the specific acquisition.

(a) *Auditors.* The company's auditors will be involved at various stages of the process providing advice on technical accounting issues and producing and verifying information. They will also be liaising with the buyers, other financial advisers and those of the target company.

(b) *Environmental.* It is important for a purchaser to establish whether there are any environmental issues it needs to deal with as a result of making an acquisition. Increasingly, environmental consultants are appointed to conduct an environmental audit of the target.

(c) *Finance.* The finance functions of the company and key financial advisers will be deeply involved in most transactions at a corporate, treasury, accounting, tax and operational level. They will also be actively involved in the due diligence process and in planning integration to ensure that risks are minimised, operational integrity is assured and financial information systems are effective. External financial advisers are dealt with below.

(d) *Human resources.* Planning and managing the people issues at each stage of the acquisition and supporting the board in terms of professional input to assessing key people in the target company, determining who should hold the key positions, organisational structure, dealing with remuneration disparities, employment contracts, employee share schemes, etc.

(e)   *Information Systems.* Given the scale of investment in IT infrastructure and its critical role in operational effectiveness there should be awareness of the IT implications of an acquisition. In some situations, IT incompatibility could undermine the commercial logic of a deal.

(f)   *Internal Communications.* There may or may not be a formal internal communications function, but someone has to ensure that the communication of acquisition within the existing business and the target is well managed and that staff understand the rationale for the transaction, how it will affect them and what is expected of them. Maintaining momentum is critical.

(g)   *Investment Banks.* The roles of investment and merchant banks in acquisition processes vary considerably. As with any other adviser their role needs to be clear and managed. Corporate finance, and tactical support are the two key roles.

(h)   *Investor relations.* If the company has shareholders other than management, it will need to ensure that it has the necessary formal and informal support required to effect a transaction, especially if the transaction requires external funding.

(i)   *Legal and Company Secretarial.* The company's in-house lawyers, company secretariat and external legal advisers will need to be prepared to deal with the wide range of legal issues covered in **Chapter 8 Legal Aspects of Acquisitions**. They will also be responsible for ensuring appropriate compliance and governance throughout the transaction.

(j)   *Marketing.* Branding, communication, product positioning, pricing, distribution channel and other marketing issues will need to be planned and managed.

(k)   *Market intelligence.* A company's market intelligence function and advisers are likely to have been involved from the outset in competitive and market opportunity analysis. They may also be heavily involved in the due diligence process and in determining the likely market reaction and issues arising from the acquisition itself.

(l)   *Operations.* Whether there are significant synergistic benefits planned or not an acquirer needs to understand the operations of the company to be acquired and to be clear which aspects need changing and have a plan ready to implement upon taking control.

(m)   *Patent Agents.* Where evaluation of intellectual property assets and risks is required, and for advice on the transfer or disposal of rights.

(n)   *Pensions.* To analyse and advise on pension schemes. Pension issues are covered in more detail in **Chapter 9 Pension Aspects of Acquisitions**. The company may have in-house pensions expertise but may still require the services of a firm of actuaries.

(o)   *Property and facilities management.* Acquisitions generally involve a number of property issues in addition to due diligence, for example the merging of head office or other facilities. If moving people is a significant element of the plan, property issues need to be identified, decided upon and managed from an early stage. With an increasing element of outsourcing in this area, expertise is required to manage the selection and integration of various suppliers.

(p) *Public relations and advertising consultants* for public and press relations, including informing or influencing customers, suppliers, shareholders and employees.

(q) *Search firms.* It has become a feature of many larger acquisitions for management audits to be undertaken prior to acquisition and formal selection processes to be established with a view to selecting the best person from either company for key roles.

(r) *Stockbrokers.* In public company transactions and/or where there is a coincident external capital raising, stockbrokers will be required for Stock Exchange liaison, pricing and placing of stock, etc.

(s) *Tax.* The company's finance director, in-house tax specialist and tax advisers will need to ensure that there are tax efficient structures in place and that there is appropriate due diligence on tax matters together with relevant taxation warranties and indemnities. Tax issues are covered in more detail in **Chapter 13 Tax Planning**.

Identifying targets

12.3   With a clear acquisition strategy it ought to be a fairly straightforward step to develop some detailed criteria which potential acquisition targets should meet, especially if the strategy is based on logical extension of product or geography. The criteria will need to be sufficiently focussed and broad enough to create opportunities, yet narrow enough to spot them.

The most common criteria relate to the following:

(a) *Products.* This may be very specific and describe ranges, individual products or components of products.

(b) *Customers.* There may be particular segments of the market the company is looking to target. These may be identical to the company's current customer profile or an extension into a different segment.

(c) *Geography.* The company may only wish to acquire in certain countries.

(d) *Technology.* Or technological capabilities.

(e) *Distribution channels.* Extending distribution channels may be a driver of acquisition strategy; alternatively the company may have a particular expertise in certain types of channels. There may be types of distribution channel that the company has expertise in and is only prepared to structure and system (which may add to, parallel or conflict with the bidder's);

(f) *Financial profile.* For example, only companies generating cash flow or those which have low levels of debt.

(g)   *Method of purchase.* For example, the company may only want to acquire for shares and not for cash or the reverse. It may only be prepared to acquire with an element of deferred consideration

(h)   *Scale.* In terms of scale of organisation to be acquired or acquisition price.

(i)   *Competitive position.* There may be constraints in terms of what would be acceptable to competition authorities. Issues relating to the regulatory aspects of acquisitions in the European Union are covered in **Chapter 11 Regulatory Aspects of Acquisitions in the EU.**

When criteria have been intelligently decided, they should be responsibly maintained. Acquisition criteria decided by the prospective bidder may be positive or negative. For example: 'We will only acquire companies who have...' or: 'We are not prepared to acquire companies who...' Making successful acquisitions demands discipline, from the Chief executive down, so that resources are not dissipated on ad hoc chases or purchases, which do not meet the company's decided criteria.

One piece of direct and strong advice, which seems to be needed more often than it should be, is: *'Don't buy hamster wheel businesses'.* A very common trap is for companies to compromise on the size criteria. An acquisition of a much smaller company, with a very small market share, which the acquiring company hopes to build up, quite often fails because it subsequently proves too difficult to build from such a small base. Further, the gap between the management styles and the main management preoccupations in companies which differ greatly in their absolute sizes or relative market shares can prove too wide to be bridged successfully. The managers end up like the proverbial hamster running round but going nowhere.

As a generalised guideline, an acquisition which 'will make very little impact' on a company's business is probably not worth the trouble making, or the trouble managing thereafter. Naturally there are exceptions, for example when it is decided to acquire sole rights to a specialised technology, or even to a single product, which can be absorbed smoothly into an existing part of the acquirer. However, given the time, the costs and the traumas of change, then it is better to grow the company with significant, noticeable moves, not with such small moves that they seem almost accidental.

A company's chosen criteria can be influenced by fashion, this often results in failure. At various points in corporate history it has been fashionable for UK companies to acquire in the United States. Post the collapse of communism and the fall of the Berlin Wall, it was fashionable to acquire in Eastern Europe. The last big fashion to cause considerable destruction of wealth and reputations was at the end of the 1990s and the beginning of this decade when the fashion for technology, especially telecom and Internet related companies, reached fever pitch. The inevitable collapse of many of these deals came close to damaging the development of genuine hi-tech companies.

Assuming the company has a good set of highly commercially driven criteria and has avoided some of the dangers described above, there is one final test worth performing. This is to challenge whether with these criteria the company does really have the capacity and competence to make an acquisition of the type envisaged. A good way to do this is to consider the chart below.

Chart: Organisational Effectiveness and pressure

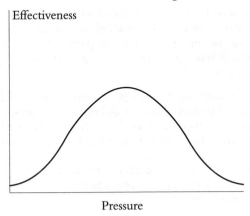

The principle of the chart is straightforward, if there is no pressure there is no output, the right amount of pressure and the organisation delivers its best performance, but too much pressure and the organisation becomes dysfunctional. If the company is realistic about where it is on the curve pre-acquisition and has a good idea of the increased pressure the acquisition will involve it can decide whether the risk is appropriate or whether it needs to bolster management resources before proceeding.

Armed with detailed criteria, the next job is to identify targets which meet the desired characteristics. Whether the company has in-house researchers or engages outside specialists to conduct the search, the sources of information are likely to be the same. Most of these are available in electronic form and via the Internet, even if subscriptions are necessary.

If the company has retained an investment bank or a corporate finance house they should also be able to provide a good first list of targets which meet the criteria and an assessment of the feasibility for each company on the initial target list. If they can't then you should question whether you have made the right appointment.

The main advantage in using an in-house team is that they should know their company and its markets well. They ought to have a good understanding of the strategy and their board as well as their preferences, prejudices and eccentricities. Using external specialists, on the other hand, provides professional independent judgements, free of internal politics and prejudices, at strictly time-limited fees. They may also have a broader range of information sources at their disposal.

Either way, the following is a natural sequence in preparing a target list.

(a)   *Using the company's knowledge.* If the target criteria are concerned with logical product or geographical extensions or vertical integration, then it is most likely that many of the main prospective targets are known in greater or lesser detail by those who meet them as competitors, suppliers or customers.

(b)   *Using advisers' knowledge.* Suggestions from bankers, brokers, auditors, suppliers, customers and other close contacts of the company can be added to the initial list. If a company is known to be a regular acquirer it will find that it receives a regular stream of suggestions from corporate finance houses.

(c)   *Rigorous research.* Trade sources including trade directories, supplier directories and buyers' guides, exhibition catalogues, trade literature, trade journals, industry surveys, the Internet and comments from companies and individuals working in the targeted trade sector.

Experienced searchers will have their preferred sources and individual sequences. They will know that no one source is ever comprehensive, and that all or most must be at least perused.

They will use some or all of the following published sources most of which are now web based, with some only being available through subscription:

(i)   General industrial directories which list relevant manufacturers and distributors, together with their ultimate holding company information.

(ii)   Specific Trade Directories.

(iii)   Trade Journals.

(iv)   Trade Associations.

(v)   Exhibition catalogues and industry surveys.

(vi)   The Internet. There is a huge amount of data available on the Internet but there are two thoughts worth remembering when using it. One is that the information you find is available to anyone who looks, and the other is that its quality is variable. Having identified basic information, the researcher will want to undertake preliminary financial analysis. This can be performed by using web-based company financial databases such as Thomson Financial Extel or ICC, reference checking databases such as Dun and Bradstreet or Infocheck, and Companies House.

Issuing target criteria to intermediaries and on the Internet or as part of public relations exercises on other issues can also generate useful suggestions. The objective overall is to ensure that not only are you aware of the businesses which meet your target criteria, but that you are on their list if they ever think of selling. A simple thing to do is to ensure that all the advisers of the companies on your target list are aware of your target criteria.

Approaching targets

12.4   Before making contact, careful consideration needs to be given as to the timing and method of approach and, most importantly, as to whom the approach should be made. An inappropriately directed first approach can kill off the chances of a successful deal. In an ideal world the target company will not be in a formal sales process and an approach would be made chairman to chairman or chief executive to chief executive. The potential buyer will want to avoid getting into a competitive situation and in order to do so must have a compelling proposition as to why a sale to them makes the most sense.

If the company is being professionally marketed the sales memorandum will make it clear what the formal process is. However, the objective of any keen buyer is to avoid as much competition as possible for the target and to bust any process which might lead to a full blown auction without alienating the company's advisers. The smart buyer prefers to win on non-price factors and not succeed simply through paying the highest price. Consequently, the formal approach is seldom sufficient to win the target at the desired price.

Whether there is a formal sales process or not, in order to determine how to play this very critical stage of the acquisition process the prospective buyer will need to address the following questions first.

(a)   Is the company really for sale and if so why?

(b)   How familiar is the company with yours and how are you perceived?

(c)   Who are the real decision takers and how do decisions of this nature get made?

(d)   What would a sale of the company mean for each of the key shareholders and directors?

(e)   Will they sell the company to your organisation?

(f)   Whose support within the target are you likely to obtain and whose opposition do you expect?

(g)   What will be the reaction of the non-executive directors?

(h)   What will be the reaction of the potential target company's advisers?

(i)   Is there a compelling rationale for the proposed acquisition?

(j)   Do you have the appropriate level of support from your board to make an approach?

Highly professional chairmen understand that it is their duty to consider all serious and credible approaches and, if approached in an appropriately respectful manner, will handle the situation properly. However boards are stocked with human beings of a wide variety of ability and motive and it is essential for the prospective buyer to do their homework and have a good idea how the chairman of a target is likely to respond. Assuming the company isn't being marketed professionally, a typical start is for the chairman of the buyer to suggest an informal first meeting. This might be best as a lunch, to 'compare notes on the industry', 'see if there are any areas where we can collaborate' or something equivalently subtle.

Before this first meeting or lunch takes place, the chairman of the potential acquirer will want to be as well prepared as possible and understand the key issues if acquisition discussions were to proceed. The objective of this meeting is to establish or develop the relationship and gauge feasibility.

Most chairmen of potential targets will understand the ritual and respond accordingly. Wise chairmen of acquisitive groups will tend to have had these sorts of meetings with most of the key players in the sector anyway. So it may simply be a case of developing an already established relationship.

When it comes to how many companies to be approaching at the same time there is a balance to strike between keeping it low to achieve focus and keeping it broad to avoid losing opportunities. It is important to search in parallel rather than series, if only to strengthen one's negotiating position.

When the target is an independent company, the prospective bidder should approach the chairman of the target's board, rather than the managing director, because acquisition is a shareholder rather than management matter. When the target is a small subsidiary of a larger group, the normal etiquette is to make simultaneous approaches to the chairman of the subsidiary's board and to the managing director of the group of companies in which the subsidiary resides. In practice, in the majority of British groups, these two people are the same. When the subsidiary is a larger part of that group, and its sale is likely to require a group holding board decision, then the simultaneous approach should be made to the chairman of the group holding board. Naturally, there will be cases where the bidder decides to approach the holding company, only, to discuss the possible acquisition of a subsidiary – perhaps to preserve commercial secrecy, to avoid flushing good individual managers in the subsidiary or to avoid panicking the rest. Frequent bidders may indeed adopt this course as a routine.

It is sometimes suggested that initial approaches can be made by intermediaries. However, when approaching a public company, any independent intermediary used to make this initial approach must disclose the name of his principal, so there is no question of preserving secrecy. Whatever kind of company is approached, public or private, small or large, there are likely to be a range of reactions from the target's directors from the 'threatened' at one end of the spectrum to the 'pound notes in the eyes' at the other.

Whatever the circumstance the approach should be direct, but the content of the initial conversation establishing the first meeting can be indirect. When public companies are involved, as bidders or targets, there are rules covering every step. These rules are detailed in the City Code on Takeovers and Mergers and the company secretary and key advisers should be well aware of them.

If rebuffed firmly by a private company or a small public company in which the majority of the shares are almost certainly held in person or proxy by the directors, the bidder should move on to the next on the short-list of priorities. There is seldom value in consuming time in considering whether to try to stimulate minority shareholders in such reluctant targets to press their board to invite the bidder to a more formal, collective discussion of a proposed acquisition. The bidder has to make a judgement as to whether a rebuff is really a bluff, in which case another line of approach can be tried before considering eliminating the prospect. The legislation today, while in theory enabling the minority to act against 'unfair prejudice', in practice, following case precedents leaves minority shareholders in a weak position.

The options are naturally very different when the offeror is rebuffed by a large or listed public company where there is no single dominant shareholder or no small controlling group of shareholders. If an initial 'friendly' approach is rebuffed in this case the potential acquirer might decide to launch a 'hostile' bid. If it is to do this then it must take into account the following:

(a)   it may well have to pay a higher price to win the deal;

(b)   expert advice will need to be enlisted in terms of corporate finance, legal and public relations;

(c)   management within the target may resist and obstruct the process despite their formal duties not to do so. Due diligence is therefore often more limited;

(d)   the target is then 'in play' and may attract other potential suitors;

(e)   a longer acquisition process may result, costs may be greater and the target may suffer a greater loss of momentum than in a 'friendly' situation;

(f)   management of the target company is seen as more available and open to offers from the headhunters; and

(g)   if the bid is unsuccessful the bidder may be putting themselves in play.

If an initial approach is welcomed to the extent of the target company being prepared to move to the next step and enter a serious exploratory discussion then a longer more detailed meeting is arranged to agree a process and agree who will be involved. It is normal at this stage for a Confidentiality Agreement to be issued by the target and to be signed by both parties. This is an essential, but quite straightforward, document and contains the following clauses:

(i)   Range of information required by each party from the other.

(ii)   Reasons for that requirement, if not self-evident.

(iii)   Record of named individuals (not just their organisations) to receive the information on a 'need to know' basis.

(iv)   Prohibition of further disclosure beyond those names in (iii) above.

(v)   Recipients of information provided are prohibited from using it in their own businesses.

(vi)   (Normal exclusions for information which is already in public domain, or already known to recipients.)

(vii)   Time limits where relevant – may be unlimited.

(viii) Arbitration – governing law.

If the target agrees:

(A)   Exclusivity of information exchange and exclusivity of negotiation for a defined period. (This helps avoid an uncontrolled auction, avoids confusing key staff, or arousing customers or business associates.)

If the target does not agree to the inclusion of *clause (1)* above, the bidder may choose to withdraw, at least until any other parties have moved out of the way. Occasionally the target will agree to the inclusion of the exclusivity clause on the condition that the bidder signs a Letter of Intent (sometimes called a Memorandum of Understanding or Memorandum of Agreement). The contents of a typical Letter of Intent include:

(1)   names and addresses of bidder and target;

(2)   description of the businesses or company to be sold;

(3)   price range for the anticipated offer which would follow detailed investigation of target;

(4)   possible structure of the payment, shares/cash/loan/mixed, method and timing of the payment;

(5)   the scope of the detailed investigation which the bidder wishes to make, and by whom it is to be made;

(6)   the position of directors and contracted senior managers of the target post-acquisition;

(7)   position of other employees post-acquisition. (A factor which is often neglected.);

(8)   restrictive covenants;

(9)   warranties and indemnities;

(10)   any special conditions (eg future profitability targets);

(11)   timetable for investigation, agreement, announcements, exchange of contracts and completion;

(12)   if an 'exclusivity' clause has not been included in the Confidentiality Agreement, then it should be included here – the target can hardly require a Letter of Intent without the bidder having exclusivity; and

(13)   a statement that 'this letter is in good faith but not legally enforceable'.

It is possible to record within the Letter of Intent that specified clauses are legally enforceable and that the others are not. Better practice is to record and agree that none of it is legally enforceable, as in *clause (13)* above. A seller will naturally insist on 'Heads' whereas the buyer will often want to delay until the seller is emotionally hooked.

Valuing the target

12.5   Before considering appropriate methodologies for the valuation of a target business, it is important to remember that the buyer will be seeking to understand the value of the company to the vendor, the value of the company to itself and the value in the eyes of likely competitors. Beauty is very much in the eye of the beholder.

A range of valuation methods or metrics can be used, and the most common are described below. As to which ones are the most useful, well that ultimately depends on whether you are buying or selling. A buyer will want to use metrics which provide the rational to argue for a lower price. A seller will naturally choose those which will show the highest values. If there have been a number of transactions in the sector of similar businesses there may also be a sense of a 'going' or 'market' rate. Ultimately the balance of power between buyer and seller will determine the price; valuation methodologies are really used to support the logic for a price and for buyers and sellers to really understand the value of the acquisition to them. No buyer should rely upon one method alone and every buyer should be armed with a basic asset, market, earnings and cash flow based valuation before they start to negotiate.

(a)   *Net Assets or Book Value.* Put simply, total assets minus total liabilities. This method is not as widely used today as it once was because it ignores the future return that the assets can produce. It tends to be employed in situations where the company has substantial assets but low earnings. If it is used then normally the *'book value'* of assets and liabilities, as stated in the last balance sheets, are reviewed to reflect any changes since the balance sheet date and to incorporate latest market value. The resultant figure produced is then the latest estimate of Net Assets. A buyer relying on this method must ensure that they fully understand the accounting policies used to derive the valuation and always check in detail assets under the category of *'intangibles'* and liabilities under the heading *'contingent'*. In addition, off balance sheet assets or liabilities should also be reviewed to assess their real impact on value.

(b)   *Price Earnings:* This approach is based on the principle that value today is related to the future benefits which will flow from ownership. A multiple is applied to the earnings of the company, usually the EBITDA earnings, before interest, taxation, depreciation and amortisation. It is commonly used in private company acquisitions. In these circumstances the multiple is usually derived from the price earnings multiple of quoted companies in the sector less a discount of 20-40%. Volatility of earnings should be taken into account in arriving at this discount.

Although there is often much haggling over what is the exact multiple to use and whether the comparable companies are really comparable, the real fun in this method is in calculating the earnings figure. The seller will want to add back to the earnings items which are exceptional or non-recurring to produce a 'real' earnings figure. The buyer or seller may also want to make adjustments to the earnings figure for directors' emoluments where these are at *'non-market'* levels. If earnings have been volatile there may also be debate about what is an appropriate average to use and care is required to avoid double treatment of such factors in the earnings figure and the multiple. EBITDA has tended to be a popular basis for calculating earnings because it removes many of the significant distortions which can arise out of capital structures and accounting policies.

(c) *Discounted cash flow ('DCF')*. Underlying DCF methodology is based on the principle that cash is the real measure of value, and it is free from the influences of accounting policies. A value of the acquisition target may be calculated applying this method to the cash flows of the target on a stand-alone basis and a value of the acquisition project can be calculated by then including all other relevant items such as increased capital expenditure, reorganisation costs, transaction fees, etc. Clarity over what is actually being valued is essential as what the buyer is prepared to pay the vendor may be the most significant cost in an acquisition, but it is not the only one. Moreover, the buyer will want to avoid paying the vendor for value which is going to be created by the buyer him or herself.

The first step is to calculate the future free cash flows of the acquisition target for a period into the future. All items of expenditure should be included which support the income. Then this cash flow is discounted by the firm's weighted average cost of capital (WACC)and a risk factor, commonly known as a beta. WACC is the average cost of all the capital used in the business, including debt and equity. The risk factor or beta is an adjustment that uses historic data to measure the sensitivity of the company's cash flow, for example, through business cycles. This means that companies in highly cyclical businesses will have a high beta to reflect the volatile nature of their cash flow.

The DCF method is a strong valuation tool, as it concentrates on cash generation potential of a business. However, the risk factor, measured by the beta, is impossible to measure precisely. A DCF analysis should always be performed because it forces the buyer to consider in detail all of the cost and income items to produce and can often surprise the buyer in terms of the real implications of proceeding with the acquisition. It will also allow the potential buyer to compare this acquisition project with other growth projects, such as significant capital expenditure to support organic growth.

(d) *Premium to market:* If the target is a quoted company, the bidder will normally have a valuation to start from, namely the current market capitalisation of the business. This is simply calculated by multiplying the share price by the number of shares in issue and produces the value that the market at a point in time is putting on the company. It is, therefore, influenced by the condition of the stock market and the concerns and opportunities that are seen for the company in the sector or market in which it operates. Another influence is the investor's view of the ability of management to deliver a return on the capital he or she is using. There may or may not be an element of bid premium in the price already, depending upon whether the company is seen as an acquisition target.

Bidders in a *'normal'* market will pay a premium of approximately one third. *'Normal'* means that there is good liquidity in both the company's stock and the market as a whole. The premium percentage varies significantly with illiquid smaller quoted companies.

(e) *Revenue multiple.* Here a multiple is applied to the sales revenue of the current year. This approach, which is used more in smaller companies and in valuing professional service firms, has little or no scientific methodology behind it. It has, however, determined the 'going' or 'market rate' in many service or retail sectors historically. In situations where profit margins are declining or there are large contracts it can produce dangerous valuations.

(f) *Technology or Intellectual Property.* It is not unusual in technology sectors for companies to be loss making and to have few tangible physical assets to be sold for significant sums if they possess a technology or intellectual property. In these cases the buyer is making an assessment of the extra value they can extract by having ownership of the technology or intellectual property and the cost and time involved in developing it for themselves.

(g) *Industry Metrics.* Apart from the going or market rate described above there may be measures which pertain to a particular industry at a particular point in time. An example of this would be in businesses such as the mobile telephone or cable television industries in their early phases of growth where numbers of subscribers, average spend per customer and 'churn' rate, the rate at which customers withdraw, were key metrics in determining value.

There are some other more general points to consider on valuation no matter what valuation method is being used. These are that:

(i) a buyer should not rely solely on one method of valuation;

(ii) the buyer should pay as little as possible for value which he or she is going to create post acquisition;

(iii) so often it is the assumptions rather than the methodology which lead to flawed valuations;

(iv) accounting policies need to be clearly understood, especially with regard to profit recognition and valuation policies;

(v) buyers should always have a figure beyond which they will not go and stick to it. Gradual price creep during negotiations can lead to a flawed price at the end; and

(vi) it is better to slightly over pay for an excellent business than to slightly underpay for a 'dog'.

Detailed investigation

12.6   This phase of the acquisition process is primarily to achieve three things:

(a)   Validating the facts that have been presented and the assumptions made until this point. Are you buying what you think you are buying?

(b)   Validating the investment case and, if this includes significant synergistic benefits, ensuring that these are realistically assessed.

(c)   Providing as much detailed insight into the target to enable the plan for post-acquisition management to be as strong as possible.

Of these things, validating the investment case is the most important. Due diligence is generally seen in a defensive light and in the context of reducing risk, which is absolutely right, however the primary purpose of this phase of detailed investigation has to be ensuring that the reasons for making the acquisition are valid and that the potential projection of value to be created is realistic.

Given the long list of items that the prospective buyer will want to investigate, it is essential that the project leader has a clear view of the priorities. It is essential to focus on those things which underpin the investment case and ascertain whether the target company really does in fact meet the target criteria.

The investigation will focus on key areas such as market, finance and operations but should also include investigation of human resources, technology, legal, environmental, property, insurance, pensions and many other detailed aspects. Each firm of professional advisers will have its own due diligence checklist for its specific area. The list described in **12.7** is a fairly standard one and if the vendor is advised by a quality professional adviser one would normally expect that these would be readily available.

An area which frequently is under investigated is management. In friendly situations it is possible to perform extensive assessment of the management of the acquired company and in many transactions these days full blown management audits take place. Even if the buyer cannot undertake such diligent and sophisticated processes they can undertake extensive referencing. Most major search firms have experience of conducting this nature of work and if the buyer hasn't got an established relationship they are likely to receive approaches from firms offering their services the moment an acquisition is announced.

Cultural fit is discussed in detail in **Chapter 10 Post Acquisition Management**, but again this is something it is vital to understand as early as possible. Many deals fail to complete at later stages of the process because it suddenly dawns on one of the parties that it just isn't going to work. In acquisitions that fail to deliver value frequently it is because of the dysfunction caused through poor cultural fit. If the cultural fit is poor not only will the acquired business suffer, but so will the acquirer's.

The buyer should ask for as much detail as he can possibly get but be conscious of the fact that the vendor will want to give as little commercially sensitive information away as possible just in case the transaction collapses. A balance needs to be struck between obtaining as high a level of insight as possible and putting off the vendor. There is much greater flexibility with private company acquisitions than with public companies or 'controlled auction' processes. The contents list below is from a typical sales memorandum from an investment bank, in this case it is for the sale of a mid-sized technology business.

A typical contents list for a sales memorandum from an investment bank is shown below. The numbers of pages devoted to each section is always interesting, as is what is emphasised in the executive summary. Sales Memorandum should be viewed as being sophisticated versions of estate agents' particulars and treated with the same degree of caution.

Section	Page
I. Executive Summary	1
II. Technology	6
A. The Market Opportunity	6
B. ABC Ltd's Product Performance Benefits	10
C. Commercialisation of ABC Ltd's Product	14
D. ABC Ltd's Manufacturing Process Advantages	16
III. Business Description	19
A. ABC Ltd's Patents and Intellectual Property	19
B. Revenue Model and Patent Exploitation Strategy	26
C. Research and Development	34
D. ABC Ltd's Other Products	41
IV. Industry Overview	46
A. Introduction	46
B. Overview of Principal Technologies	47
C. Industry Forecasts	50
D. Competition	53
V. Corporate Information	55
A. History	55
B. Structure and Management	56
C. Employees	62
D. Premises	64
E. Legal Issues	66
F. Central Functions	67
VI. Financial Information	69
A. Financial Information	69
B. Product Licensing	70
C. Product Licensing Management Discussion and Analysis	72
D. Forecast Financial Information	78
E. Share Capital	82
Appendices.	83

Although contested bids between major public companies receive considerable media coverage, by far the largest number of acquisitions made involve the purchase of private companies in which there is one dominant shareholder with whom negotiations are conducted, or just one shareholder, as in the case of the purchase of a wholly-owned subsidiary which is being divested by its holding group. There is sometimes a cultural clash between corporate and entrepreneurial styles and if it is anticipated that most of the targets are of this nature it needs to be factored in the decision on whom is the project leader.

Prospective buyers should maintain a healthy degree of scepticism throughout the process and should understand why the vendor really wants to sell. For example, if succession is the reason given for sale then the buyer needs to check whether the founder-chairman really is wanting to retire from his happy and successful business. It could be that he has a bunch of frustrated, depressed executives whom he can no longer handle; he sees his business as ex growth and succession is simply a convenient rationale rather than genuine reason. Most corporate executives would prefer to describe a subsidiary for sale as 'non-core' rather than to be honest and call it 'a loss making dog of a business'. For these reasons trend analysis of key performance measures within the business is especially important. The potential buyer should be suspicious of abrupt changes in performance, sudden increases in profitability alongside equally abrupt increases in the level of creditors, etc. Every seller will attempt to 'gild the lily' but the degree to which some vendors and their advisers are prepared to go can surprise the uninitiated.

Finally, Directors have, at all times and in all circumstances, a legal responsibility to exercise skill, care and due diligence, and might later be judged 'unfit' if they do not do so. They must also balance what is responsible against what is unreasonably excessive, and design the detailed investigation so as to avoid 'paralysis by analysis' or from spending major amounts of time or money on the valuation of minor items. They should view every list of work from an adviser as a menu to choose from and control fees carefully throughout the process.

An information checklist

12.7

Market

- Description of product portfolio and key markets, including relevant literature and marketing collateral.
- Market share and competitive analysis.
- Customer analysis, showing revenue and margin by customer.
- Analysis of pricing strategy.
- Product life cycle analysis by product.
- Description of distribution channels and key intermediary contracts.
- Details of salesforce structure and rewards.
- All relevant market analysis conducted by external advisers.

- Company press releases.
- Articles relating to the company or its industry.

Operations

- Details of the company's main operational facilities and processes.
- Organisation chart for operations.
- Description of the process flow for main activities of the company.
- Supplier information.
- An appraisal, including age of all equipment and fixed assets.
- Expansion plans.
- Patents, trademarks and other intangible assets.

Research and development

- Review of research in progress with critical path analysis to revenue generation for each key item.
- Commercial analysis of R&D over the last five years.
- Description of R&D policies and processes.

Finance

- Audited financial statements for the last 10 years, including income statements, balance sheets, statements of cash flow and changes in equity position.
- Management accounts for the last three years.
- Budgets and financial projections.
- Business plans.
- Description of accounting policies and practices and key financial controls and systems.
- Organisation chart for finance function.
- Details of company's financial advisers.
- Copies of the management letters from the company's auditors for the last three years.
- Accounts receivable analysis.
- Accounts payable analysis.
- Analysis of any extraordinary income or expenses.
- Analysis of any material write-downs or write-offs.
- Summary of any bad debt experience.
- details of any outstanding contingent liabilities.

- any reports from external consultants or accountants on the company's financial condition.
- Summary of the company's financing arrangements including terms, conditions, covenants.

Human Resources

- Profiles of all board members and senior executives of the company, together with any management audit reports undertaken in the last three years.
- If the company is private and the directors are shareholders the buyer needs to understand the implications of a sale and the motivations of each of the directors.
- The buyer will want to understand the nature of the relationships between the directors.
- Organisational chart, including numbers currently employed and projections in each function or activity.
- Details of remuneration and incentive schemes, including pension, option, profit sharing, deferred compensation and pension arrangements.
- Confidentiality agreements with employees.
- Consulting agreements.
- Details of staff turnover.
- Copies of employee policies and procedures.
- If appropriate, details of key union arrangements and agreements including descriptions of any past disputes of a material nature.
- Details of the company's internal communication processes and examples, eg company newsletters, etc.

Investor relations (if company is public or has other professional or institutional shareholders)

- Shareholder analysis.
- Investment agreements with shareholders (e.g. private equity firms) where relevant.
- Analyst reports for the last three years, together with analyst contact details.
- Results presentations and scripts for the last three years.
- Copies of any market research undertaken with shareholders and analyst communities.
- Contact details for the top 20 shareholders.
- Organisation chart and curriculum vitaes for the investor relations team.

- Description of the company's culture and core values.

Legal and company secretarial

- Articles of incorporation.
- Minutes of board of directors, committee and shareholder meetings.
- Documents furnished to shareholders and directors over the last three years.
- Certificates from all states and jurisdictions where the company and subsidiaries are authorised to do business.
- Sample copies of stock certificates, warrants and options.
- Shareholder data, including dates of issuance, number of outstanding shares and details of registrars.
- Detail of any outstanding preferred stock, options, warrants or convertible securities.
- Description of share option, share purchase and other employee share ownership schemes.
- Joint venture and partnership agreements.
- Licence agreements.
- Purchase agreements.
- Liens, equipment leases, mortgages or any other outstanding loans.
- Insurance contracts and agreements.
- Any additional agreements or contracts relevant to the business of the company, including contracts with suppliers, vendors and customers.
- Description of any current litigation, including potential damages.
- Description of any potential litigation, including potential damages.
- Settlement documentation for any previous litigation.
- List of all real property owned by the firm.
- Recent appraisals and property surveys.
- Titles, mortgages, deeds of trust and any other agreements relating to company-owned real property.
- Detail of any easements or other encumbrances.
- Leases and sub-leases.

Tax

- Full details of company's tax returns and current tax position.
- Details of company's tax advisers.
- Description of any fines or penalties the company has had to pay in the last five years relating to tax.

Governmental regulations

- Copies of any permits and licences and, if the company is operating in a fully regulated industry, all other relevant details.

- Copies of reports made to government agencies

- Detail of any enquiries made by any local or national government agencies.

Financing the acquisition

12.8 Just as an acquisition strategy needs to fit into the context of the company's overall strategy, so the financing strategy for an individual acquisition should fit into the financing strategy for acquisitions in general and the company's overall financial strategy. The principle that if there is high business risk there should be low financial risk is so often forgotten when it comes to acquisitions that this should be the first principle when considering the financing strategy.

Numerous textbooks are devoted to corporate finance from the very readable and concise summary *Corporate Financial Strategy* by Ruth Bender and Keith Ward, to the heavyweight classics such as Brearley and Myers *Principles of Corporate Finance*. The key issues, other than the very important one at the start of this section and that anticipated returns need to be sufficient to compensate for the risks of the project, are:

- The method of payment may influence price.

- Cash is worth more to a vendor than paper, ie the acquirer's shares.

- Cash today is worth more than cash tomorrow.

- Purchase using equity is less risky to the buyer than using cash.

- Issuing shares involves dilution.

- Using debt can increase returns to shareholders in the long term.

- The repayment profile of the debt needs to be understood and planned for. Interest rate risk can be dealt with by negotiating interest rate caps, floors and collars but at a cost.

- Any significant debt issue is likely to involve covenants and the borrower must understand the commercial implications of operating within them and the consequences of failing to do so.

- Potential external financiers of the acquisition will want to understand the risk, yield and potential capital upside involved for them. The acquiring company seeking the finance needs to help them do this and awareness aids negotiation.

- If the transaction is of an international business the buyer must understand any increased currency risks it will be taking on and have a strategy for dealing with them.

- Tax efficiency is important to buyer and seller but sometimes results in over complexity and constraining structures.

- Deferred consideration offers some protection but the buyer must ensure they can finance the total amount deferred at the outset.

- If the buyer thinks the projected returns, given a valuation, adequately compensate for the risks, they must have clearly identified the risks, the consequences of the risks becoming a reality and are clear what their strategy for dealing such circumstances will be.

- The best time to raise cash is when you don't need to.

- If the company can't raise the capital externally for the acquisition the potential buyer should question whether they should be doing the deal at all.

A fine example of the lower risk involved in using a company's shares as purchase consideration compared with using cash can be seen by contrasting the fortunes of Vodafone PLC and Marconi PLC during the late 1990s and early part of this decade. Both companies enjoyed and then suffered the dramatic growth then collapse of confidence in the telecoms sector. Vodafone, led then by Sir Christopher Gent, made a series of large transformational acquisitions including Airtouch in the USA and Mannesman in Germany. It chose the equity issue route to finance these deals. When the market went into a severe downturn the company saw its stock market capitalisation dive but had no cash crunch and was able to carry on developing its business. It was even able to take advantage of other distressed companies' misfortunes in the sector to make further acquisitions. Marconi on the other hand started with a considerable cash pile of over £1bn and not only spent it but increased debt to pay for acquisitions. When the crunch came for the market it came for them also and the company's chairman and chief executive resigned.

Cash forms a higher part of the price in years when the Stock Market is low, and equity forms a higher part when the markets are high, assuming interest rates are the same in each case. If the company is public, highly regarded, has good investor relations and the acquisition has a straightforward rationale then it is likely to find it easy to issue equity to finance it. Some companies however even in a raging bull market will find it tough because some or all of the aforementioned characteristics apply.

A useful illustration of the continuum of financial products is provided in Ruth Bender and Keith Ward's *Corporate Financial Strategy*.

Financial products

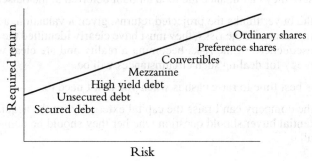

A buyer may also see deferred consideration or the use of earn-outs as a way of financing the deal.

Deferred consideration

12.9 This can be a useful mechanism for the buyer to receive a little extra protection against things which have not emerged in due diligence or warranties. It can also sometimes prove tax efficient for the vendor. Put simply, it is an agreement to pay a part of the price, usually no more than a third, at a later date. Unlike an 'earn-out', which is described in **12.10** below, it is not usually contingent upon performance or other milestones, but it could be. Any vendor who is sensible and well advised will want to ensure, as far as is possible, that the buyer can guarantee future payment. As has been mentioned above, the buyer must ensure that they have the funds in place to meet commitments entered into through this mechanism.

Earn-outs

12.10 A typical earn-out splits the purchase consideration between what is paid upfront upon completion of the deal and what is paid later dependent upon performance. The difference between this and deferred consideration is that the amount is variable. Typical measures which drive the amount of future payments are forecast profits, revenue, product developments or other strategic milestones.

Earn-outs tend to be used:

- in order to bridge the price gap which emerges when there is a wide difference in the perception of value between buyer and seller;

- to reduce risk for the buyer – they only pay if performance is delivered;

- to provide an incentive for the vendor to be open about issues pre-acquisition; and

- to encourage management to stay on and be motivated post-acquisition.

However, before using an earn-out the potential buyer needs to consider the following issues:

- the level of complexity, many earn-out mechanisms fail to deliver the desired benefits because they are simply too complicated and hard to make work in practice;

- finding the most appropriate measures used may focus on the wrong things, may not be those best for developing value and ultimately constrain long-term performance post the earn-out period;

- it doesn't work well if one expects high degree of integration or anticipates making similar acquisitions which might produce synergies with the target if integrated.

- from the buyer's point of view, may end up paying more overall and have less control over the business;

- risk;

- if the earn-out applies to several people and not all stay, how is the earn-out to be adjusted?;

- must ensure they have funds later on to pay;

- suggesting an earn-out may weaken the competitive position if there are other cash bidders; and

- tax implications for buyer and seller, these are covered in **Chapter 13 Tax Planning**.

If a buyer elects to use the earn-out mechanism they will need to take good professional advice and be very careful in structuring it. A seller accepting an earn-out will generally want as much control as possible over the use of assets and people and will want to take on as a little 'Group cost' as possible. Sellers will also want to incorporate clauses protecting them from changes in circumstances in the buyer. For example 'If the buyer is later taken over itself, the earn out pays out in full at the maximum anticipated level of £Xm.'

Often the main benefit of discussing the possibility of an earn-out with a vendor is to flush out issues you might not establish in other ways.

Pension funds

12.11 Pension funds are not company assets of the acquired company, and the question of who owns them has long been under professional and government review in the UK. The subject is covered more fully in **Chapter 9 Pensions Aspects of Acquisitions**, but valuation of the target's pension scheme is essential in *steps seven* and *eight* described in this present chapter. If underfunded, the acquiring company will need to assess the additional cash cost of topping-up. On the other hand, if over-funded, the acquiring company may be able to benefit from further 'contribution holidays', or 'clawbacks'. This is not a secondary matter to be squeezed into the investigation agenda at the last moment; it is complex, politically sensitive, time-consuming, and certainly requires actuarial assistance. It can also involve sums, or even surplus sums, which are greater than the acquisition price itself.

Chapter 13

Tax Planning

At a glance

- If the substantial shareholding exemption applies to a share sale, a corporate seller may be reluctant to sell assets rather than shares.

- If the stamp duty cost is not significantly greater, an asset sale may be preferable to a share sale for the purchaser.

- The purchaser should ensure that the seller's proposed structure is consistent with its own tax planning.

- Where the consideration for a share sale is to be paid in a form other than cash, it should be possible for the seller to defer realising any capital gain.

- A seller should be asked to give contractual protection to the purchaser in respect of the target company's historic tax liabilities.

- The parties should ensure that any relevant tax clearances or consents are obtained.

- The purchaser and the seller should discuss the target's particular tax attributes, and whether these will affect the target after its sale to the purchaser.

- On a public takeover, where there is a large number of selling shareholders, care needs to be taken to ensure that the tax implications of the proposed transaction are acceptable to different categories of shareholder.

Introduction

13.1   The tax implications of any company sale or purchase need to be considered at a very early stage. The seller will clearly want to maximise the net proceeds that it receives for the company. By contrast, the purchaser will want to ensure that the target company is in as beneficial a tax position as possible following the sale. Both the seller and the purchaser will want to ensure that any tax losses or other tax benefits are used efficiently and not wasted. The parties will also need to discuss to what extent the purchase price should be increased to reflect any future tax benefits that are available to the target company.

This chapter aims to summarise the relevant tax planning issues that need to be considered. The main part of the chapter looks at the UK tax issues that might arise on the sale of 100% of the shares in an unlisted UK-resident company. It concentrates on the issues arising for a UK tax-resident purchaser and seller.

It is worth restating the need to consider the tax treatment of a company sale at a very early stage. Certain tax planning opportunities may only be available if they are implemented before negotiations with a purchaser have proceeded beyond preliminary discussions. In addition, a seller will normally be in a stronger negotiating position if it presents its preferred structure to the potential purchaser at the beginning, rather than if it tries to restructure the transaction at a later stage. Of course, if the seller's preferred structure is not attractive to the purchaser, the seller may well be persuaded to accept a revised structure; tax is simply a cost of the transaction and so long as the purchase price paid by the purchaser provides the seller with an acceptable amount of proceeds after tax, the seller may well accept a structure that is less tax efficient. Conversely, a purchaser may simply reduce the price it is prepared to pay if the structure is disadvantageous to it for tax purposes.

The first decision for both seller and purchaser is what is to be sold. Although there are a number of non-tax issues that are relevant to this decision, tax considerations are likely to be important.

The options might include:

(a)   a sale of the company;

(b)   a sale of the company's holding company;

(c)   a sale of the company's business as a going concern;

(d)   a sale of particular assets owned by the company, separate from the relevant business; and

(e)   a hive down of some or all of the company's assets to a new company followed by a sale of the shares in that company.

Share sales and asset sales

13.2   Traditionally, it has generally been the case that, whilst a seller would prefer to sell shares, a purchaser would prefer to acquire assets. This trend has been emphasised by the introduction of the substantial shareholding exemption ('SSE') from capital gains tax ('CGT'), which is only available if the seller is a corporate and sells shares, and the new regime for intangible assets, which allows a corporate purchaser who purchases intangible assets to depreciate those assets for corporation tax purposes.

The stamp duty cost of an asset sale was, however, often significantly higher than a share sale. Following the substantial changes to stamp duty which took effect from 1 December 2003, this is only likely to be the case where the assets to be sold include a significant amount of UK land.

Share sale

13.3 The main tax advantages of selling shares rather than assets are as follows.

First, a share sale will often be exempt from CGT due to the availability of SSE. Even if SSE is not available (eg where the seller is an individual), a share sale may involve a lower tax charge than a disposal by the target company of its assets, although this will depend on a comparison of the seller's CGT base cost and taper relief position in respect of the target's shares as compared with the target company's base cost in its assets. In many cases, however, the target company will have little or no base cost in assets such as goodwill.

Secondly, a share sale may avoid an additional tax charge should the proceeds from a sale need to be returned to the target company's shareholders. On a share sale, the proceeds are received by the selling shareholders rather than by the target company. This avoids the further tax charge that might otherwise arise if the sales proceeds were extracted from the target, either by way of dividend (which would depend on the availability of distributable reserves and would be subject to income tax in the hands of individual shareholders) or by liquidation (which would constitute a further CGT disposal by the shareholders).

Thirdly, although stamp duty is payable on a share sale at the rate of 0.5% of the consideration, this may compare favourably with the stamp duty land tax payable on the asset sale where the assets include significant amounts of UK land.

If the target company has carried forward tax losses that are to be preserved for the benefit of the purchaser, the purchaser must either acquire the shares in the company which incurred the losses or the shares in a company to which the trade of the loss-making company has been hived down before the sale (see **13.47** below).

Asset sale

13.4 Although the purchaser will need to compare the stamp duty costs, there can be advantages for the purchaser in buying some or all of the assets constituting the company's business rather than its share capital. For a more detailed evaluation of this area, see **Chapter 8 Legal Aspects of Acquisitions**.

The main (non-tax) attraction of an asset purchase is that it gives the purchaser the right to choose which assets he does and does not want, and to purchase those assets clear of any undisclosed liabilities. An asset acquisition therefore avoids the need for the seller to give complicated tax warranties and indemnities because any crystallised or contingent tax liabilities will generally be left with the seller.

From a corporation tax perspective, a corporate purchaser of intangible assets, such as goodwill, will be entitled to claim tax depreciation in respect of the consideration allocated to those assets broadly in accordance with the accounting treatment of those assets. This will often be a significant benefit when compared to a share acquisition.

Additionally, a purchaser who acquires assets that fall outside of the intangibles regime should obtain a CGT base cost equal to the price he pays for those assets. This will most likely result in a lower chargeable gain on any subsequent disposal of those assets. Where he buys a company's share capital, however, the company will retain its historic base cost for those assets, which may be much lower than their current market value.

Finally, although the selling company will suffer a clawback of capital allowances, the purchaser will be able to claim capital allowances on buying assets such as plant and machinery or industrial buildings. By contrast, on a share sale there is no clawback of capital allowances and the target company continues with its capital allowance position unchanged.

Business asset roll-over

13.5   If an asset sale is the preferred route but the seller would realise a significant taxable gain on selling the assets, it may be possible for the seller to shelter the gain by claiming business asset roll-over relief under *section 152* of the *Taxation of Chargeable Gains Act 1992 (TCGA 1992)*.

Section 152 applies where certain types of asset are disposed of and the proceeds are reinvested in replacement assets to be used either in the same business or in another trade carried on by the seller or another member of the seller's CGT group. Where the relief is claimed, no chargeable gain arises on the disposal of the old asset, but the CGT base cost of the replacement asset is reduced by the amount of the rolled-over gain. This will mean that, if and when the replacement asset is sold, an increased capital gain may arise, although this gain may usually be the subject of a further roll-over claim.

The main types of asset to which the relief applies are buildings and land occupied and used for the purposes of the trade, fixed plant and machinery. The replacement asset must be acquired within the three years following the disposal of the old asset or within the year preceding the disposal.

From 1 April 2002, the *Finance Act 2002* has also introduced a roll-over relief for intangible assets. The relief works in a similar way as business asset roll-over, although it also provides for roll-over into shares acquired in a company which holds intangible assets. The effect of the roll-over is to allow the tax charge arising on the disposal of intangible assets to be rolled over into newly acquired intangible assets, reducing the tax depreciation that would otherwise be obtained in respect of the new assets.

VAT

13.6   A sale of shares is an exempt supply for VAT purposes. By contrast, a sale of assets will (subject to the special rules for a transfer of a business as a going concern described below) generally be a taxable supply for VAT purposes. It is important for the parties to agree the VAT treatment of an asset sale before completion. In particular, if the sale agreement is silent on the subject, the consideration is treated as VAT inclusive and the seller must pay the VAT on the purchase price out of the amount received from the purchaser [*Value Added Tax Act 1994, s 19*].

The extent to which any VAT payable by a purchaser of assets represents a real cost to him will depend on the purchaser's ability to recover that VAT against the VAT that he charges on his own supplies. If the purchaser uses the assets acquired to make only exempt supplies for VAT purposes, any amount in respect of VAT paid by the purchaser would not be recoverable. Conversely, to the extent that the purchaser uses the assets to make taxable supplies, the VAT paid should be recoverable.

Where a business is transferred 'as a going concern', the transfer can effectively be disregarded for VAT purposes [*Value Added Tax (Special Provisions) Order 1995, SI 1995/1268, Art 5*]. In order to fall within this provision, the transfer must satisfy certain conditions. These include:

(a)   the assets must represent a business, or part of a business that is capable of separate operation (and not simply a collection of assets that falls short of a business);

(b)   the assets must have been used in the transferor's business (which needs to be borne in mind when any pre-sale reorganisation is considered – see, for example, *Re Kwik Save Group plc* [1994] VATTR 457);

(c)   the transferee must use the assets to carry on the same kind of business, whether or not as part of an existing business; and

(d)   if the transferor is a taxable person for VAT purposes, the transferee must be, or must immediately become as a result of the transfer, a taxable person.

In addition, to the extent that the assets transferred consist of land or buildings, and the transferor has elected to waive the exemption from VAT in respect of such assets, the transferee must also elect to waive the exemption in respect of these assets. The transferee must make the election and notify HMRC of it before any supply is made of those assets to the transferee. It should be noted that the time of supply for VAT purposes is subject to some complicated rules, and will often fall before completion (see, for example, *Higher Education Statistics Agency Ltd v C&E Comrs* [2000] STC 332.

13.7 *Tax Planning*

The HMRC leaflet 'Transfer of a business as a going concern' (Notice 700/9 March 2002) gives some helpful guidance as to the distinction between a transfer of a business as a going concern and a mere transfer of assets. There is, however, no formal clearance procedure and HMRC have said that it will not as a matter of course give confirmation as to whether the provisions will apply. Indeed, as the application of the provisions depends on the purchaser's use of the assets after completion, it cannot technically be cleared in advance.

An asset sale agreement typically provides that no VAT will be charged on completion but that, if HMRC later determine that VAT is chargeable, the purchaser will pay an additional amount in respect of VAT on receipt of a VAT invoice. [In addition, the agreement should make it clear whether the transferor is to apply to HMRC for permission to keep any VAT records relating to the business or whether the records will be transferred to the transferee in accordance with *section 49* of the *Value Added Tax Act 1994*.]

The VAT capital goods scheme covers computers and items of computer equipment of a VAT-exclusive value of [£50,000] or more, and land and buildings of a VAT-exclusive value of [£250,000] or more. Where these items are acquired as capital items for use in a business, the extent to which a buyer can recover the VAT element in the purchase price will not depend solely on the initial use to which he puts them. Instead, although the initial VAT recovery is made by reference to the initial usage of the assets, the use to which the computers, land or buildings are put is monitored over a period of time (five years for computers and, generally, ten years for land and buildings). Adjustments are then made to reflect any change of use.

When a business is transferred as a going concern, the purchaser of the business must therefore continue to monitor the use of the assets and operate the adjustment process by reference to the use to which he puts the computers, land or buildings after he has bought the business. This means that any purchaser of a business must check whether what he is buying includes any such capital goods which are still within their adjustment period. If the purchaser's intended use of the assets is different to that initially assumed by the seller, VAT adjustments may become payable for the remainder of the adjustment period.

Stamp duty

13.7   Over the years, stamp duty has been a significant cost of asset sales Since 2000, the stamp duty payable on an asset sale where the total consideration exceeds £500,000 has been 4% of the consideration paid.

Since 2003, stamp duty on the transfer of most assets (including, eg receivables and book debts) has been abolished, with stamp duty land tax ('SDLT') replacing stamp duty for transfers of UK land, payable at broadly equivalent rates.

These changes mean that the stamp duty cost of an asset sale will now depend on the value of any UK land being sold. Despite the reduction in the scope of stamp duty, it will often still represent a significant cost of many asset sales. In addition, and in contrast to stamp duty, SDLT is a tax on transactions rather than on the execution of documents and, therefore, planning techniques involving, eg holding documents offshore are no longer effective.

It will be apparent that, from a stamp duty perspective, the purchaser should consider carefully how the consideration is apportioned between stampable and non-stampable assets. So long as any apportionment is made on a *bona fide* basis, it should be respected for stamp duty purposes. Of course, such an apportionment would also apply for the purposes of capital gains tax and capital allowances, where, for example, apportioning substantial amounts of consideration to trading stock may not be so attractive.

Share sales – seller's tax planning

13.8 Once the parties have agreed that the transaction is to be structured as a share sale, the seller should determine the tax costs of such a sale and consider ways of reducing such costs.

The following discussion (and the discussion of the purchaser's tax planning that follows) assumes that the target is not a close company and is not listed. It also assumes that the target does not have valuable tax losses or other reliefs that the purchaser is seeking to preserve, and that neither the target nor the purchaser is subject to the *Corporation Tax (Treatment of Unrelieved Surplus Advance Corporation Tax) Regulations 1999 (SI 1999/358)* (the '*Shadow ACT Regulations*'). The specific tax issues raised by the above are dealt with separately later on in this chapter.

A seller's tax planning check list might be as follows.

(a) Is the seller subject to CGT?

(b) Is the substantial shareholding exemption ('SSE') available?

(c) If not, what is the base cost in the shares? Is there another company (eg the target company's immediate parent company) in which there is a higher base cost?

(d) What is the effect of indexation allowance and/or taper relief?

(e) Are any capital losses available? If so, where are they?

(f) Will reinvestment relief under *Schedule 5B* to *TCGA 1992* be available?

(g) Will roll-over relief under *section 135* of *TCGA 1992* be available?

(h) Does the target company owe any amounts to the seller or other group companies?

(i) Does the target company have distributable reserves which would enable it to pay a pre-sale dividend?

(j)   Does the target company own any assets which are not to be sold to the purchaser?

(k)   Will an exit charge arise under *section 179* of *TCGA 1992* on the sale of the target company?

(l)   Does the target company surrender or claim group relief from other group companies?

Scope of CGT

13.9   CGT (or corporation tax on chargeable gains) is payable by UK residents and by non-UK residents to the extent that they dispose of assets held for the purposes of a branch or agency through which the non-UK resident is trading in the UK. There are special rules that apply where a company ceases to be resident in the UK, where an individual ceases to be UK-resident for less than five complete tax years, and where an asset ceases to be used by a non-UK resident for the purposes of a UK branch or agency.

Substantial Shareholding Exemption

13.10   A chargeable gain which arises when a company (but not an individual) disposes of a 'substantial shareholding' in another company will usually be exempt from CGT (and no capital loss can arise) due to *Schedule 7AC* of *TCGA 1992*. This provision means that a seller will usually prefer to sell shares, rather than assets, if the seller is holding the business at a capital gain.

A holding of shares is likely to be substantial if it consists of 10% or more of the target company's ordinary share capital. To qualify, the disposing company must generally have retained the substantial shareholding throughout a 12-month period in the two years prior to the sale. In addition, the disposing company and the target must each have been either a trading company or a member of a trading group from the beginning of the 12-month period referred to above until immediately after the disposal.

A group (which consists of the parent company and its 51% subsidiaries) is a trading group when at least one of its members carries on trading activities and, when taken together, the activities of the group's members do not include to a substantial extent activities other than trading activities. A trade includes any trade, profession or vocation which is conducted on a commercial basis with a view to profit. There are special rules to deal with investments in trading joint ventures.

It is worth noting that, where the seller would have otherwise made a capital loss on the disposal of the shares, such a loss will not be realised if the transaction falls within the scope of SSE. The SSE rules include a number of provisions designed to ensure that a seller cannot structure such a loss-making transaction so as to fall outside of SSE.

Base cost

13.11   The detailed rules governing the CGT base cost of shares are beyond the scope of this chapter. The following points are, however, worth noting.

If the shares in the target company were acquired before 31 March 1982, their base cost may simply be their value at that date. Otherwise, their base cost will often be their acquisition cost. There are special rules which apply where, for example, there has been any reorganisation of the share capital of the target company or the shares have been the subject of a share-for-share exchange.

Indexation allowance/taper relief

13.12   The amount of capital gain chargeable to CGT can be reduced by the operation of the indexation allowance or by taper relief. From April 1998, indexation allowance continues to accrue only for taxpayers who pay corporation tax, while the taper relief rules now apply to individuals, trustees and personal representatives.

Indexation allowance was introduced in 1982 with a view to relieving the element of a capital gain attributable to the effects of inflation. This is achieved by effectively increasing the acquisition cost of the asset disposed of (i.e. the consideration and any incidental costs of acquisition) in line with any increase in the retail prices index between the date of acquisition and the date of disposal. It should be noted that indexation cannot be used to produce a capital loss.

As stated above, taper relief applies only to non-corporate taxpayers. Taper relief reduces the amount of a taxable chargeable gain after current year and brought forward allowable losses have been deducted.

A gain will be eligible for taper relief if either (i) it is a gain on the disposal of a business asset which has been held for at least one year or (ii) it is a gain on the disposal of a non-business asset which has been held for at least three years. For non-business assets acquired before 17 March 1998, an additional year is added to the holding period used in calculating the taper relief available on any gain.

Shares in a trading company, or the holding company of a trading group, are a business asset if:

(a)   the company is unquoted; or

(b)   the company is quoted and either the taxpayer is an employee of the company (or a connected company) or the taxpayer can exercise 5% of the voting rights in the company.

Assets other than shares are business assets if they are used in a trade or employment carried on by the individual taxpayer, or are owned by the individual but used by a company whose shares qualify as business assets in relation to that individual.

The amount by which the gain is reduced by taper relief is calculated according to how long the asset has been held and whether the asset is a business or non-business asset. Broadly, after the relevant minimum holding period, gains on non-business assets are reduced by 5% per year up to a maximum of 40%. For a business asset, 50% of the gain is taxable after one year and 25% of the gain after two or more years.

Although taper relief replaces the indexation allowance, the two operate together where an individual disposes of an asset acquired before April 1998. In this case, indexation accrues until April 1998. Capital losses are then deducted from the indexed gain and the remaining gain is relieved by taper relief.

Capital losses

13.13   Capital losses may be set off against capital gains to reduce the tax charge arising on a gain. Capital losses may not be carried back, and so the capital loss must either accrue in the accounting period in which the capital gain arises or in an earlier accounting period.

Capital losses may not be surrendered by way of group relief. Two companies within a CGT group may, however, jointly elect that an asset which has been disposed of outside of the group by one of them may be treated for tax purposes as if it had been transferred between them immediately before that disposal. This enables losses and gains on assets within the CGT group to be matched in a single company. The relevant election must be made within two years of the end of the accounting period in which the actual disposal was made.

A capital loss arising on a disposal to a connected person is only deductible from capital gains arising on other disposals to that same person. *Schedule 7A* to *TCGA 1992* contains provisions that prevent the losses that accrue prior to a company joining a CGT group being set off against later capital gains. These provisions go beyond their stated intention, namely to prevent the market in companies with surplus capital losses. There are further provisions designed to prevent the setting off of losses against gains that accrue before a company joins a group.

[There are a number of provisions that prevent or restrict the offset of capital losses where, for example, the loss arises on the disposal of an asset to a connected person, the loss or gain accrues to a company prior to that company joining a CGT group, or the creation of the loss was contrived.]

CGT deferral – Enterprise Investment Schemes

13.14   An individual who realises a chargeable gain on the disposal of any asset may defer the whole or part of that gain by making a 'qualifying investment'. A 'qualifying investment' is, broadly speaking, a cash subscription for new ordinary shares in an unquoted trading company, or the parent company of a trading group, although certain trades are not permissible. The deferred gain becomes taxable if the shareholder disposes of these shares, if the shareholder ceases to be UK-resident within a specified period or if the shares cease to be a qualifying investment. This relief replaces the business expansion scheme relief that applied until 1993, and the reinvestment relief that applied from 1994 until 1998. There are a series of anti-avoidance provisions that could apply to prevent the deferral being available, or to cause the deferred gain to be crystallised.

Roll-over relief

13.15   The provisions of *sections 135* and *136* of *TCGA 1992* prevent certain 'paper-for-paper' transactions being treated as disposals for CGT purposes. These provisions are discussed in more detail at **13.33** *et seq.* below.

Target indebtedness

13.16   The seller is unlikely to want any loans or other debts which the target company owes to the seller to remain outstanding after completion. There are, however, certain pitfalls in this area.

If the sale agreement provides that the consideration for the shares includes an obligation on the purchaser to repay target indebtedness, the amount of the repayment might be argued to form part of the consideration received by the seller for the target shares for both CGT and stamp duty purposes. It would be more usual for the purchaser to undertake that it will procure that the target will repay any such debts at or immediately after completion. This should prevent the repayment of the debt being added to the consideration.

Alternatively, the purchaser could agree to acquire the debt from the seller. If the purchaser acquires the debt at a discount, it will need to consider whether a later repayment of the debt could cause it to realise a taxable profit. Where the underlying debt gives rise to a 'loan relationship' and the purchaser is a company within the scope of the rules set out in the *Finance Act 1996*, it is unlikely that a purchaser would be prepared to acquire the debt at a discount to its par value. This is because, as the purchaser and the target company would be connected for the purposes of the loan relationship rules, the purchaser would be taxable on this discount, either immediately or, perhaps more likely, over the remainder of the term of the loan.

If the purchaser is not prepared to acquire the debt, the seller could subscribe for additional shares in the target to enable the target to repay its debt. The seller should not assume that it will necessarily increase its base cost in the target company's shares as a result of such a subscription. Any increase in base cost would depend on the extent to which the value of the target company's shares increases as a result of the subscription.

Finally, the seller could consider simply releasing the target from its obligation to repay the debt. To the extent that the debt represents a loan relationship, this release should not cause any tax charge to arise in the target company, as the seller is connected with the target company. Where, however, the debt is not a loan relationship, the forgiveness of the debt could create a deemed trading receipt for the target company (see *section 94* of the *Taxes Act 1988 (TA 1988)* and *IRC v Falkirk Ice Rink* [1975] STC 434).

Pre-sale dividends

13.17   Where the target company has distributable reserves, the seller should consider whether it would be attractive for the target company to pay a dividend to the seller prior to the sale. From the perspective of the purchaser, this is likely to be attractive, as it will reduce the purchase price payable by the purchaser and, therefore, the amount of stamp duty arising on the sale.

From the seller's perspective, if SSE does not apply it may also be attractive for such a pre-sale dividend to be paid. The effect of the dividend will be to reduce the sale price for the target company shares. This should reduce the capital gain arising on the sale of the shares. In addition, where the seller is a company, the dividend will be tax free in its hands.

The position is slightly more complicated for individual sellers. First, all individuals have the benefit of an annual exemption from capital gains tax. In the tax year 2006/2007 this means that an individual may realise capital gains of up to £8,500 before any tax liability arises. By contrast, although an individual who does not pay tax at the higher rate of income tax does not have any additional tax to pay when he receives a dividend from a UK company, higher rate taxpayers do have additional income tax to pay on dividends. This income tax liability will, however, often be significantly less than the additional CGT payable in the absence of the pre-sale dividend.

The tax treatment of dividends received by UK-resident individuals has become increasingly complicated. The position is now as follows.

Where a UK-resident individual receives a cash dividend of £80.00, this dividend carries a tax credit of £8.89 (which is one-ninth of the cash dividend received). This means that the individual receives gross income of £88.89, but the rate of income tax on dividends applicable to individuals other than higher rate tax paying individuals is such that no additional income tax is payable in respect of the dividend. The tax credit attaching to dividends is not reclaimable.

Where the individual pays income tax at the higher rate, additional tax is payable at the rate of 32.5% of the gross income. This means that additional tax of £20.00 is payable in respect of a cash dividend of £80.00, leaving a net cash receipt of £60.00, and imposing an additional tax liability equal to 25% of the cash dividend received.

To illustrate the advantages of paying a pre-sale dividend, the following example (which ignores indexation and taper relief) may be helpful.

Suppose that the seller has a base cost of £50,000 in its shares in the target company, but the target company is currently worth £75,000. Suppose that the target company has distributable reserves of £25,000. If the seller is a company but SSE does not apply to the share sale, it is likely to make sense for the target company to pay a pre-sale dividend of £25,000. This would mean that the seller would not make any capital gain on the sale of the target company, and the seller would not be liable to tax on the dividend that it receives.

Where the seller is an individual subject to the higher rate of income tax, a dividend of £25,000 would create an income tax liability of £6,250 compared with a CGT liability of £10,000 (40% of £25,000). Here the pre-sale dividend represents a net tax saving of £3,750. Instead of receiving a pre-sale dividend, the seller may prefer to retain the flexibility of, for example, reinvestment relief, which would not be available in respect of any amount paid as a pre-sale dividend. Even if a pre-sale dividend is attractive, it may make sense for the level of the dividend to be set so as to leave an amount of value in the target company which will give rise to a capital gain equal to the seller's annual exemption from CGT when the target company is sold.

It should be noted that the depreciatory transaction provisions in *sections 176* and *177* of *TCGA 1992* may prevent the creation of a capital loss by the payment of a pre-sale dividend. HMRC has, however, confirmed that the depreciatory transaction provisions will not be applied in respect of dividends paid out of post-acquisition profits.

The value shifting provisions in *sections 29* to *34* of *TCGA 1992* may also be relevant where the payment of a pre-sale dividend materially reduces the value of the target company shares and the recipient of the dividend is a company that is not subject to tax on the dividend and therefore receives a tax-free benefit. The provisions would not be relevant where the dividend was paid to an individual shareholder who pays income tax on the dividend. If the provisions apply, their effect is to increase the capital gain arising on the sale of the target company by an amount which is 'just and reasonable'. There is an exemption in *section 31* of *TCGA 1992* for dividends paid by the target company to another member of its CGT group, so long as the dividend is not paid from distributable profits arising from a no gain/no loss transfer of assets, a 'share-for-share' roll-over or a revaluation of an asset in the target company's accounts.

Pre-sale asset strip

13.18   If the target company owns any assets which are not to be sold to the purchaser, these assets will need to be transferred out of the target company before its sale. To make such a transfer on a tax efficient basis, the transfer should be made as early as possible, in order to ensure that the relevant grouping tests are still passed at the time of the transfer.

Pursuant to *section 171* of *TCGA 1992*, assets held by the target company but which are not to be sold to the purchaser may be transferred by the target company to another UK company in the same CGT group as the target company without triggering any capital gain. The detailed CGT group definition is complicated and beyond the scope of this chapter, but the following observations may be useful.

The CGT grouping test is based around a principal company, its 75% subsidiaries, those subsidiaries' 75% subsidiaries and so on. It is not necessary for members of a CGT group (including the principal company) to be UK-resident. A company may only be a member of one CGT group. A company is a 75% subsidiary of another company if 75% of its ordinary share capital is owned by that other company. Ordinary share capital excludes fixed rate preference shares.

In addition, a CGT group requires the principal company to have more than 50% economic ownership (judged on direct or indirect entitlement to both income distributions and capital on a winding-up) in all of the members of the group. There are no 'arrangements' or 'option arrangements' provisions (see **13.20** below) applicable to the CGT group definition. This is probably due to the effect of *section 179* of *TCGA 1992* (which is discussed at **13.19** below).

Even if the assets to be transferred include UK land, it should be possible for the land to be transferred by the target company to another member of the seller's group without giving rise to a liability to SDLT. *Schedule 7* to the *Finance Act 2003* exempts from SDLT transfers between group companies. The test for determining whether two companies are members of the same group is set out in *paragraph 1* to *Schedule 7*. It is a wide 'economic ownership' test, taking account of ownership of ordinary share capital, beneficial entitlement to profits and to assets on a winding-up. The requisite threshold in each case is 75% ownership or entitlement.

Schedule 7 also contains certain anti-avoidance provisions that deny this intra-group transfer relief in certain circumstances. *Paragraph 2* provides that relief will not be given if the transfer is made in pursuance of, or in connection with, an arrangement (which need not be legally binding) under which:

(a)   all or part of the consideration for the transfer was to be provided or received, directly or indirectly, by a person outside the group; or

(b)   the interest being transferred was previously transferred directly or indirectly by a person outside the group; or

(c)   the transferor and transferee were no longer to be part of the same group because the transferor or a third company was to cease to be the transferee's parent.

In addition, intra-group transfer relief will be withdrawn under *paragraph 3* of *Schedule 7* if, while still owning the land, the transferee ceases to be a member of the same group as the transferor within three years of the transfer, otherwise than due to the transferor leaving the group.

Intra-group transfer relief should therefore be available where, prior to a sale of the target company, the target company transfers an asset to another member of the seller's group; although the target company will cease to be associated with the seller following the sale, this is due to the transferor's, and not the transferee's, leaving the group, so *paragraphs 2* and *3* do not apply.

It will sometimes be necessary to consider whether loan finance for the purchase by the transferee could cause *paragraph 2* to apply. The Stamp Office has stated, however, in the context of the equivalent provision under the old stamp duty regime, that relief will normally be available as long as the intra-group transfer is not followed by a further sale of the asset transferred, and it is thought that the same reasoning should apply in the context of *Schedule 7*.

Section 179 exit charge

13.19   Transfers of assets between members of a CGT group are made on a no gain/no loss basis for CGT purposes. In order to prevent this being used as a method to avoid CGT on a sale to a third party, *section 179* of *TCGA 1992* applies when a company leaves a CGT group and still owns such assets. The general effect of *section 179* is that the company leaving the group is treated as disposing of all the assets that it acquired intra-group in the previous six years for the market value of the assets at the date on which it acquired those assets. There is an exemption for assets acquired from another company that is leaving the CGT group at the same time.

If a *section 179* charge would arise on a sale of the target company, the seller might consider selling the relevant asset of the target company to the purchaser instead. This would avoid the tax charge arising in the target company (for which the purchaser would require indemnification) and might enable the seller to use capital losses or other reliefs to shelter a tax charge on the disposal of the asset.

Group relief

13.20   Where two companies are members of the same 75% group (i.e. one is a 75% subsidiary of the other or both are 75% subsidiaries of another company), then one company may surrender its current year surplus UK (and in certain limited transactions non-UK) tax losses to the other ('the claimant company'). The claimant company may then set off those tax losses against its UK taxable profits. The tax losses that may be surrendered in this way are current year trading losses, capital allowances, excess charges on income, excess Schedule A deductions and excess management expenses of investment companies. Surrenders and claims may be made by members of the group that are UK-resident or are carrying on a trade in the UK through a UK branch or agency. There are similar provisions that allow the surrender of losses by or to a consortium company and its members, although these provisions only allow the member to access its appropriate proportion of the consortium company's profits and losses.

The economic ownership tests for group relief purposes are wider than those for CGT grouping (see **13.18** above). In particular, the existence of legally binding option arrangements over the target company's shares will prevent the existence of a group relief group.

In addition, *section 410* of *TA 1988* provides that, where there are arrangements (which need not be legally binding) for a company to leave a group relief group, its accounting period is deemed to end for the purposes of group relief surrenders and group relief ceases to be available for the accounting period deemed to begin thereafter. The profits of the actual accounting period are apportioned between the two deemed accounting periods on a time basis or such other basis as is just and reasonable.

Arrangements for the purposes of *section 410* of *TA 1988* may arise due to the existence of non-legally binding heads of agreement. HMRC Statement of Practice SP3/93, however, states that, when a sale of a subsidiary requires shareholders' approval, no arrangements will come into existence until that approval has been given, 'or until the directors become aware that it will be given' and that 'straightforward negotiations' for the sale of shares will not give rise to the existence of arrangements before the point at which an offer is accepted subject to contract or on a similar conditional basis.

Notwithstanding these helpful statements, SP3/93 continues:

> 'If following negotiations with potential purchasers a holder of shares or securities concentrates on a particular purchaser this will not of itself be regarded as bringing "arrangements" into existence. But "arrangements" might exist if there were an understanding between the parties in the character of an option. For example, an offer, whether formally made or not, might be allowed to remain open for an appreciable period so that the potential purchaser was allowed to choose the moment to create a bargain.'

This clearly raises a degree of uncertainty, although if the seller can show that it was continuing discussions with other potential purchasers, or at least that it considered itself free to do so, this should be sufficient to fall within the scope of the Statement of Practice.

A seller might choose to end the target's actual accounting period at the time of the sale. This might make the apportionment of profits for group relief purposes easier, although it would still be open to HMRC to claim that arrangements were in place at some earlier date. It is, however, not necessary to end an accounting period, and it may have the disadvantage of accelerating the target company's tax payment date(s).

Practical issues on grouping tests

13.21   Most pre-sale restructuring relies on one or more of the grouping reliefs. Whilst there are a number of specific anti-avoidance provisions, it is also necessary to bear in mind the need to fall within the terms of the basic group definition. All of this points to the desirability of effecting any pre-sale reorganisation at as early a stage as possible.

The basic grouping tests generally require the seller beneficially to own a certain percentage of the target company's share capital. The decision in *Wood Preservation v Prior* [1969] 1 All ER 364 shows it is possible for beneficial ownership to be lost before legal or beneficial ownership is passed to the purchaser. In *J Sainsbury PLC v O'Connor* [1991] STC 318, however, the Court of Appeal thought that beneficial ownership was lost when the rights retained were such as to represent only 'a mere legal shell'. The seller must therefore demonstrate that it retains the 'fruits' or economic benefits of ownership of the shares at the time that any restructuring takes place. For example, an agreement that the target company would not pay any further dividends to the seller would be unhelpful in demonstrating that the seller had retained beneficial ownership in the target company's shares.

Share sales – purchaser's tax planning

13.22 The purchaser also needs to consider certain tax planning issues before the acquisition. A purchaser's tax planning checklist might be as follows.

(a) Who is to be the purchaser?

(b) What form will the consideration take?

(c) How will any cash consideration be financed?

(d) Will the shares in the target be a business asset for CGT taper relief purposes?

(e) Is there any way to mitigate the stamp duty cost of the acquisition?

(f) Is the purchaser content with any proposed pre-sale restructuring?

(g) Is the purchaser intending to dispose of any of the target's assets?

(h) Is the purchaser intending to terminate the employment of any of the target's employees or directors?

Identity of purchaser

13.23 Where the target is a UK tax-resident company, and the purchaser already has other operations in the UK, the purchaser will want to ensure that the target and the purchaser's existing operations will form a group for UK tax purposes. A group for these purposes may now be traced through both UK and non-UK resident companies, so this is no longer likely to cause any particular difficulties.

Purchase consideration

13.24 In many cases, the purchaser will agree to purchase the target for cash. The cash purchase price is often payable at completion, but may be deferred. Alternatively, the parties may agree that the seller will receive shares or other paper consideration, with differing tax implications (see **13.31** *et seq.* below).

Financing any cash consideration

13.25   If the purchaser is to pay cash for the target, it needs to consider how such cash is to be financed. If the cash is to be financed by debt, the purchaser will want to ensure that it is entitled to a tax deduction for any interest paid, and that it has sufficient taxable profits to absorb that tax deduction, either within its existing group or within the target group. The purchaser also needs to consider its obligations to withhold tax from any interest payments.

If the purchaser group has sufficient funds to finance the purchase within the group, but those funds are not within the purchaser itself, the group needs to decide how the funds are to be passed to the purchaser. Although it may be attractive from a UK tax perspective for the purchaser to borrow the necessary funds from other members of the group, where the lender is not UK-resident the UK transfer pricing rules need to be considered. The effect of these rules is often that the purchaser needs to be funded at least in part by way of equity.

In the context of debt financing, the transfer pricing rules will apply where a loan is made between two affiliates and the terms on which the loan was made (including whether the loan would have been made at all) differ from those that would have been imposed between independent enterprises. The loan must also confer a UK tax advantage, but this will almost always be the case where the borrower is a UK-resident company and seeks to claim a tax deduction for the interest expense. The rules apply whether or not the lender is UK resident, although a UK-resident lender may apply for the interest that it is deemed to receive to be reduced to equal the amount of interest for which the borrower is entitled to claim a deduction, making the effect of the rules in this situation broadly UK tax neutral.

There is another provision that may adversely affect the purchaser's deduction for interest paid to a non-UK-resident affiliate. The UK corporate debt rules generally allow a UK-resident company to claim a deduction for interest on an accruals basis. Where, however, the interest is due to an affiliate that is not within the charge to UK corporation tax and the interest has not actually been paid within the period of 12 months following the end of the accounting period of the borrower in which such interest accrued, that interest will only be deductible when it is actually paid.

Where the purchaser is to be funded directly by loans from third party lenders, the transfer pricing rules are still relevant to the extent that an affiliate guarantees the debt or otherwise supports the borrower's obligations to the lender. Unless the borrower can demonstrate that the effect of the guarantee is only to reduce the rate of interest payable on the loan, and that the lender would still have lent the same principal amount to the lender in the absence of the guarantee, the purchaser will be denied a deduction for some or all of the interest payable under the loan. A UK resident guarantor may apply for the interest deduction that is denied to the borrower to be transferred to it, so making the effect of the rules in this situation broadly UK tax neutral.

It is also necessary to consider the borrower's obligation to deduct tax from any interest payment that it makes. Unless one of the exemptions applies, the borrower must withhold tax at the rate of 20% from any interest payment that it makes. The principal exemptions are as follows.

(a)   Tax need not be withheld from interest other than yearly interest. The distinction between 'yearly' and 'short' is not always entirely clear-cut, but as a general rule interest will be yearly interest if it is paid on a loan that is capable of being outstanding, or if it is the intention of the parties that it should be outstanding, for at least 365 days.

(b)   From 1 April 2001, interest may be paid without deduction between two companies, so long as the recipient is subject to UK corporation tax on the interest.

(c)   Interest may be paid on 'quoted Eurobonds' without withholding tax. A 'quoted Eurobond' is basically a bond that is listed on a recognised stock exchange.

(d)   If the lender has the benefit of a suitable double tax treaty with the UK, it may be entitled to claim an exemption from withholding tax or the right to have tax withheld at a lower rate, in accordance with the provisions of that treaty. This exemption generally requires the interest payable on the loan not to exceed the amount that would have been payable in the absence of any 'special relationship' between the lender and the borrower. For these purposes, a 'special relationship' includes a parent company guarantee of a subsidiary's obligations under a loan from a third party.

(e)   If the lender is within the EU, and either the lender directly owns at least 25% of the share capital of the borrower (or vice versa) or a third company directly owns at least 25% of the share capital of the borrower and the lender, the lender may be entitled to claim exemption under the provisions of sections 757 onwards of the *IT (Trading and other Income) Act 2005*, which enacts the EU Directive on interest and royalty payments made between associated companies (the 'Directive').

Where the lender in an intra-group loan seeks to take advantage of a double tax treaty with the UK or the Directive in order to avoid UK withholding tax, it is quite common for the parties to agree with HMRC in advance the amount and terms of the debt that the borrower would have been able to raise from a third party lender in the absence of any 'special relationship'. HMRC will look at the borrower's ratio of debt to equity and its interest cover ratio (the ratio of profits before interest and tax to the interest payable). It is open to the borrower and the lender to demonstrate that in the particular industry in which the borrower operates the ratios required by a third party lender are different from those normally encountered.

If the purchaser itself has insufficient UK taxable profits to absorb the tax deduction for the interest accrued in any accounting period, it may surrender any surplus to other members of the UK tax group by way of group relief. For this reason it will be important to ensure that the target is the member of the same group relief group as the purchaser, so that the target's UK corporation tax liability may be reduced by this interest deduction. Where the interest deduction available exceeds the available taxable profits in that accounting period, the surplus may be carried forward, but may not then be surrendered by way of group relief in subsequent periods.

It will not always make sense for the purchaser to be funded by debt. Where, for example, the target's UK operations are not generating substantial taxable profits, and the target's non-UK operations are generally in highly taxed jurisdictions, there may be insufficient UK taxable profits to absorb any interest deduction. In these circumstances, it may make sense for the interest deduction to be taken outside the UK. It may also be attractive to maximise the tax deductions available in the jurisdictions that impose tax at the highest rates.

Care needs to be taken if the debt funding proposed is intended to rely on an arbitrage between the tax rules in the borrower's and the lender's jurisdictions (for example, if the interest is not taxed as interest in the hands of the lender), because of the specific tax avoidance provisions that may apply to deny a deduction to a UK borrower in these circumstances.

Business assets

13.26   If the purchaser is an individual, he or she will need to consider whether it is possible for the shares in the target to qualify as business assets for the purposes of taper relief. As discussed at **13.12** above, business assets qualify for greater amounts of taper relief than non-business assets. All shares in unquoted trading companies will constitute business assets. In addition, shares in quoted trading companies will qualify as business assets for these purposes if either the individual is an employee of the company (or a connected company) or the individual controls at least 5% of the votes in the company.

Stamp duty

13.27   Stamp duty is payable on the sale of shares at the rate of 0.5% of the consideration. Given that stamp duty is only now payable on asset sales to the extent that the assets consist of UK land (although the rate applied to UK land is up to 4%) the stamp duty cost of a share sale may now exceed that of an asset sale. Any steps which can be taken to mitigate or eliminate that cost should therefore be considered carefully by both the seller and purchaser.

It is not generally possible to avoid stamp duty on the transfer of shares in UK incorporated companies by executing the stock transfer form offshore. First, the purchaser may only become the registered owner of the shares to the extent that he can produce a duly stamped stock transfer form. Secondly, even if stamp duty is avoided, the purchaser will be liable to stamp duty reserve tax ('SDRT') on an agreement to transfer the shares in a UK incorporated company.

If the purchaser is in a position to acquire shares in a company incorporated outside the UK, it should be possible to avoid UK stamp duty on the transfer, as there is unlikely to be a requirement outside the UK to present a stamped transfer document in order to be registered as shareholder and, once registered as a shareholder, the purchaser need no longer rely on the transfer documentation. It should be noted that a company need not be incorporated in the UK to be UK tax-resident.

Stamp duty planning techniques have been used in the past to seek to avoid stamp duty on the transfer of shares in UK incorporated companies. Such techniques have generally either been subject to a successful challenge before the Courts or to a change of law, and there are few planning opportunities remaining.

Pre-sale restructuring

13.28   The purchaser will want to understand any pre-sale restructuring implemented by the seller. It is obviously preferable if the purchaser can approve any steps before they are taken by the seller, although in practice this may not be feasible for two reasons. First, the seller will be keen to ensure that the target is still grouped within the seller's group for tax purposes when the restructuring takes place. This will encourage the seller to implement any restructuring before negotiations with the purchaser are too advanced. Secondly, the seller may conclude that its negotiating position is stronger if the restructuring has already been implemented before the purchaser has had a chance to review the steps. The purchaser will undoubtedly want to seek protection in the sale documentation by appropriate warranties and indemnities for any tax liability which could fall on the target company as a result of any pre-sale restructuring.

Disposal of target's assets

13.29   The purchaser may intend to retain the target in its entirety. In some situations, however, the purchaser may know that it will want to dispose of some of the target's assets soon after completion. This may be because there is some duplication between the target's assets and those of the purchaser's existing business. For example, the target may have office space that is surplus to the purchaser's group's requirements. Alternatively, the seller may have only been prepared to sell the whole of the target to the purchaser, although the purchaser might only have wanted to acquire part of the target's business.

If the purchaser intends to dispose of some of the target's assets, it will want to know the tax cost of effecting such a disposal before it agrees a valuation of the target with the seller. The purchaser might therefore ask the seller to warrant, for example, the CGT base cost in the target's assets that are to be disposed of.

Similar issues may arise if the purchaser wishes to integrate the target's business with its existing operations, although in these circumstances it is likely that the various reliefs for transfers between members of the same group may reduce the tax cost of such transfers.

Termination of employment contracts

13.30   To the extent that any payment made on the termination of an employment contract is made pursuant to an express clause under that contract, the payment will be subject to income tax under Schedule E and national insurance, and should be deductible for tax purposes by the target company. Where, however, the target pays other termination payments to the departing employee, the tax position may be different.

Sections 401 and *403* of *ITEPA 2003* provides that, where payments which would not otherwise be taxable under Schedule E are paid to an employee on termination of his or her employment, such payments are only taxable to the extent that the amount paid exceeds £30,000. A payment of up to £30,000 will generally be tax free provided it is paid as damages for breach of contract and not as a payment in lieu of notice. In *EMI Group Electronics v Coldicott* [1999] STC 803, however, the Court of Appeal confirmed that, where a contract of employment contains a clause allowing the employer to make a payment in lieu of notice, such a payment is a contractual payment, and therefore cannot fall within the £30,000 exemption. Where there is an express payment in lieu clause in the contract but the parties seek to argue the payment to be made is damages rather than an emolument of employment there will be a presumption that the payment is taxable in full unless there are strong indications to the contrary (*Richardson (HM Inspector of Taxes) v Delaney* [2001] IRLR 663). Where there is no express payment in lieu clause, HMRC will be alert to the payment of notice being an automatic response to dismissal by the employer, so that custom and practice may mean a payment is taxable in full.

Statutory redundancy payments are exempt from income tax under Schedule E, and therefore are only taxable under *sections 401* and *403* to the extent that the £30,000 exemption is exceeded. In addition, Inland Revenue Statement of Practice SP1/94 confirms that payments under non-statutory redundancy schemes are taxed on the same basis so long as they are genuinely made solely on account of redundancy.

To the extent that a payment falling within *sections 401* and *403* exceeds £30,000, the employer must account for PAYE on any excess. If the employer delays the payment until after it has issued the P45 form to the employee, the employer is only required to deduct income tax at the basic rate from such excess. Otherwise, PAYE needs to be deducted on the usual basis, using the employee's appropriate tax coding.

Section 408 ITEPA provides that a special contribution to a registered pension scheme for the benefit of a departing employee would not be taxable in the hands of the employee. This may be an attractive alternative where the departing employee is close to retirement age. This provision replaces what was Statement of Practice SP 2/81.

The target will need to consider whether any such lump sum payment made to the employee is deductible for corporation tax purposes. In particular, where the payment is non-contractual, it may be necessary to demonstrate that the payment is made wholly and exclusively for the purposes of the target's trade. Where the payment is made in connection with the sale of the target, HMRC are likely to require the target to demonstrate that the payment was made for the purposes of its trade, and not in connection with the sale of the target. In a situation where the relevant employee is also the seller, it is HMRC's view that it is unlikely that the payment is made solely for the purposes of the target's trade. HMRC rely on the Court of Appeal decision in *James Snook & Co Ltd v Blasdale* (1932) 33 TC 244, where a payment made to a company's directors under an agreement for the sale of the shares in that company was held not to be an allowable deduction for the company because the company's motive was not limited to a trading purpose.

Additionally, where the employee or director is a seller, and therefore a shareholder in the target, there is a significant risk that a discretionary payment made on termination of the employee's employment would constitute a distribution by the target company. If this is the case, the payment would not be deductible by the target. HMRC has, however, confirmed that it will give 'sympathetic consideration' to this point in a situation where the payment is both reasonable in amount, having regard to past services and length of service, and admissible as a deduction for corporation tax purposes.

Consideration

13.31 The consideration payable for the shares in the target may comprise cash, shares, debentures or a combination of these. It may be payable at completion or deferred to a later date. Where payment is deferred, the parties may agree that the amount payable at the later date may vary, perhaps by reference to the performance of the company between completion and the payment date.

Cash consideration

13.32 If the consideration for the sale is made up entirely of cash payable at completion, the tax position is relatively straightforward. It should, however, be noted that, for CGT purposes, the date of disposal by the seller and acquisition by the purchaser is the date on which the contract becomes unconditional, which will often be earlier than the completion date.

If the payment of all or part of the cash consideration is deferred until some date after completion, the total consideration payable must be brought into account at the time of the disposal for CGT purposes. No account is taken of any delay before such amounts are received [*TCGA 1992, s 48*].

Section 280 of *TCGA 1992*, however, allows a seller to apply to pay his CGT liability in instalments where he himself is paid the consideration in instalments over a minimum of 18 months from the date of sale. The terms of the instalment arrangements are at the discretion of HMRC, but the tax may not be payable over a period in excess of eight years. It is likely that HMRC would look at the resources raised by the seller from the transaction itself in order to determine the terms of such instalment arrangements.

Where the parties have agreed to calculate the consideration on this basis, the interest element of the consideration may have to be paid to the seller subject to withholding tax. It is clear from the decision in *Chevron Petroleum (UK) Limited v BP Petroleum Development Limited* [1981] STC 689 that this type of payment is a payment over time for the use of money, and so is interest. The seller would therefore be taxable on this amount as interest, and not as part of the consideration received for the target shares for CGT purposes. Similarly, if the consideration is increased by an interest-like amount to reflect its deferral, that amount is likely to be taxed in the same way as interest in the hands of a corporate seller, under *section 100* of the *Finance Act 1996*.

Shares

13.33   There are a number of reasons why a purchaser might consider an issue of shares to the seller as consideration for the target shares. First, this could reflect the fact that the 'acquisition' is in reality a merger of the two companies and that the seller is simply to become a shareholder in the combined group. Alternatively, it may provide the purchaser with a simple mechanism by which to raise the funds required for the purchase. Indeed, by combining an issue of shares by the purchaser with a placing of those shares on behalf of the seller, it may be possible to combine the funding requirements of the purchaser with a cash purchase price for the seller.

Where the seller is to receive and retain shares in the purchaser, the seller will generally want to ensure that the provisions of *section 135* of *TCGA 1992* apply. Where these apply, the seller will avoid a disposal of the target shares for CGT purposes and instead be able to treat the new shares acquired as the same asset as the target shares for UK tax purposes. This means that any capital gain on the target shares will be rolled over into the new shares and will not be realised for CGT purposes until the seller disposes of the new shares. There are, however, situations where a seller might not want *section 135* to apply. For example, if the seller would realise a capital loss on a disposal of the target shares for cash, the seller might prefer to make a taxable disposal of the target shares, rather than roll over that loss into the new shares.

In order for *section 135* of *TCGA 1992* to apply, the following conditions will need to be satisfied.

(a) The transaction must be a share sale, and not an asset sale (although the target does not have to be a UK-resident company).

(b) The purchaser must be a company (although, again, the purchaser need not be UK tax-resident).

(c) The purchaser must issue the shares to the seller in exchange for the seller's shares in the target. It should be noted that this means that the same company in the purchaser's group must acquire the target and issue the shares. If, for example, the purchaser is not to be the parent company of the group, but the seller wishes to receive shares in the parent company, this might be solved by the parent's acquiring the target initially and then transferring the target around the group subsequently. If the purchaser issuing the new shares is not the top company within the UK tax group, it is important to consider whether the issue of the new shares could de-group the purchaser. This should not be an issue if the new shares are fixed rate preference shares, as defined in *paragraph 1(3)* of *Schedule 18* to *TA 1988*.

(d) The purchaser must hold, or must as a consequence of the transaction be expected to hold, either more than 25% of the ordinary share capital in the target or more than 50% of the voting power in the target, or the exchange must be made as a result of a general offer to the target shareholders which is initially conditional on control of the target being obtained.

(e) If the seller (together with connected persons) holds more than 5% of any class of shares in or debentures of the target company, the roll-over will only be available if the exchange is effected for bona fide commercial reasons and does not form part of a scheme or arrangement of which one of the main purposes is avoiding CGT or corporation tax [*TCGA 1992, s 137*]. There is a clearance procedure set out in *section 138* of *TCGA 1992* under which HMRC can be asked to confirm in advance that *section 137* will not apply to deny the roll-over (see **13.43** below).

Loan notes

13.34 It is possible for the seller to benefit from a tax deferral over pursuant to TCGA 1992 where the seller receives debentures in the purchaser, rather than shares of the purchaser. Again, the seller effectively defers realising the capital gain attributable to the target shares until the loan notes are redeemed or otherwise disposed of.

Loan notes may be attractive to the seller even when commercially the seller might prefer to receive cash consideration. For example, the deferral of the gain might allow an individual seller to access more than one year's annual exemption from CGT, or might enable the seller to defer the gain until a later period when capital losses are available to shelter the gain. (As mentioned above, capital losses may not be carried back to set off against gains realised in earlier periods.) The parties should consider these issues when agreeing the terms of the loan notes so that, for example, they include a number of redemption dates in order that the seller can arrange its tax affairs in the most beneficial way.

The tax treatment of an exchange of target shares for loan notes depends on whether the loan note is a qualifying corporate bond or 'QCB'. Confusingly, there are different definitions of a QCB, depending on whether the holder is subject to corporation tax.

For non-corporation taxpayers, a QCB is basically any plain vanilla debenture [*TCGA 1992, s 117*]. The definition of a QCB excludes, however, a bond which is repayable other than in sterling, and a bond which does not constitute a 'normal commercial loan', broadly as defined for the purposes of *Schedule 18* to *TA 1988*.

The definition of a QCB for companies which are subject to UK corporation tax was amended by the *Finance Act 1996*. Under *section 117(A1)* of *TCGA 1992*, any asset representing a loan relationship is now a QCB. This means that the definition of a QCB for corporation taxpayers is wider than for other taxpayers. It does not, however, include 'asset-linked' or convertible debt if, in the case of convertible debt, there is a more than a negligible likelihood that the conversion right will be exercised.

Where the debenture issued by the purchasing company is a QCB, the rollover provisions in *section 135* of *TCGA 1992* do not technically apply to the exchange. Instead, the tax implications of the exchange are set out in *section 116* of *TCGA 1992*. Although both sets of provisions allow a deferral of a capital gain arising on the disposal of the target shares, there are material differences between the provisions. The summary of these differences is as follows.

(a)   No indexation relief or taper relief accrues from the date on which the shares are exchanged for the QCBs. This may be a significant disadvantage where the seller has a significant base cost in the target shares that would otherwise continue to benefit from indexation allowance or taper relief.

(b)   If, following the exchange, the QCB becomes a bad debt, the gain which has been deferred from the target shares is still crystallised, even though the seller might not actually receive any cash consideration for the target shares.

(c)   It is not possible to effect a subsequent roll-over of the gain at a later date. Even if the loan notes are exchanged for further shares or loan notes, the gain held over from the target shares will be realised when the original loan notes are disposed of or redeemed.

It can therefore be seen that, in many cases, it will be attractive to the seller to try to ensure that the loan notes issued as consideration for the target shares are not QCBs. It should be noted that this will often not be the case for an individual who holds the target shares as a business asset for taper relief purposes.

For non-corporation taxpayers, a non-QCB loan note might include a provision allowing for redemption of the loan note in a currency other than sterling. Alternatively, for non-corporation taxpayers, the loan notes could include a right for the holder of the loan note to subscribe at par for additional securities. In order to avoid a risk of the interest payable on the loan note being treated as a distribution, it is usual for the issuer of the additional securities to be a company other than the issuer of the loan stock. Furthermore, as the additional securities solution would cause the loan note not to be a normal commercial loan for the purposes of *Schedule 18* to *TA 1988*, it will be important to ensure that the issue of such a loan note does not de-group the purchaser for UK tax purposes. This will not be an issue if the purchaser is the top company within the UK tax group.

As noted above, neither of these suggestions will cause a loan note not to be a QCB in the hands of corporation taxpayers. Under the new loan relationship rules, however, a corporation taxpaying holder of a QCB loan note will often be able to claim bad debt relief if the loan note issued by the purchaser becomes a bad debt. Bad debt relief will not, however, be available if the purchaser and the seller fall within the connection rules set out in *section 87* of the *Finance Act 1996*. The seller and purchaser should not normally be connected where the seller holds no interest in the purchaser other than the loan notes.

Where the seller receives loan notes rather than shares, it would still be usual to obtain a clearance under *section 138* of *TCGA 1992* for any seller that holds more than 5% of any class of shares in or debentures of the target company. HMRC are reluctant to give such a clearance if the earliest redemption date for the loan stock is too soon after the date of issue. HMRC's argument is that where the loan note has only a short life, the 'bona fide' condition of section 137 of TCGA 1992 is not satisfied, as the loan note is in effect simply a postdated cheque for cash consideration. Although HMRC's position does vary from case to case, it is usual for clearance to be denied if the first redemption date is within six months of the issue date of the loan note.

Earn-outs

13.35   It is quite common for shares in a company to be sold for a certain amount of upfront consideration plus further consideration which is of an uncertain amount at completion, but which is calculated on the basis of the target company's future performance.

In *Marren v Ingles* (1980) 54 TC 76 it was decided that, for the purposes of tax on chargeable gains, the gain on the disposal of the shares is calculated as if the earn-out element was a separate chargeable asset. Accordingly, it is necessary to value this separate asset, and add that value to the upfront consideration, to calculate the chargeable gain accruing on the disposal of the target shares.

If and when any amount is payable by the purchaser to the seller under the earn-out, this is treated as a disposal of the separate earn-out asset, and so causes a further chargeable gain to arise if the amount actually received under the earn-out exceeds the value put on the earn-out asset for the purposes of calculating the chargeable gain on the shares (plus any indexation or taper relief). If the amount actually received is less than the upfront valuation, an allowable loss will arise.

It should be noted that this rule will not apply unless the consideration is unascertainable at completion. If the amount is simply unascertained (although it could be ascertained) the rules relating to deferred consideration will apply (see **13.31** above). Where, for example, the consideration is to be calculated by reference to completion accounts, this will usually be unascertained but ascertainable consideration at completion.

The rather harsh rule in *Marren v Ingles* may be avoided if the conditions of *section 138A* of *TCGA 1992* are fulfilled. This provision will apply if the earn-out will, once the amount due has been ascertained, be satisfied by the issue of new shares or debentures. *Section 138A* then causes the separate earn-out asset to be treated as a security for the purposes of *section 135* of *TCGA 1992*, and *section 135* is then applied again to the exchange of the earn-out right for the new shares or debentures. It will therefore generally be beneficial for the seller to agree to accept such securities in satisfaction of the earn-out right, as this should defer the tax charge on the earn-out until cash is actually received by the seller. With effect for earn-outs granted after 9 April 2003, *section 138A* will apply automatically unless the seller elects that it should not apply.

[Amendments were made to the *Income Tax (Earnings and Pensions) Act 2003* by *Schedule 22* to the *Finance Act 2003* which affect the tax treatment of 'employee securities'. There was initially some concern that these provisions could cause income tax and national insurance contribution charges to arise on the grant of an earn-out right to an individual seller to be satisfied by the issue of securities.

Although there remains a technical concern in this area, in most cases HMRC's Question and Answer 5(l) (which was published on 22 July 2003) will apply so that no such income tax or national insurance charges will arise where it can be shown that the earn-out is granted as further consideration for the disposal of the shares in the target, rather than as value obtained by reason of employment. Advice should, however, be taken in this area, particularly if the seller continues to be employed in the business and:

(a)   is not to be fully remunerated for his continuing employment;

(b)   the earn-out is conditional on future employment (beyond a reasonable requirement to stay to protect the value of the business being sold); or

(c)   the earn-out includes personal performance targets for the seller.

Target debt

13.36   As set out above, if the sale agreement provides that part of the consideration for the target shares is that the purchaser will repay amounts owed by the target to members of the seller's group, this could form part of the consideration for the sale of the target for stamp duty and CGT purposes. It is therefore preferable to ensure that any such target indebtedness is not dealt with in this way, perhaps by using one of the solutions set out above to ensure that the target effectively ceases to owe amounts to the seller's group after completion.

Warranties and indemnities

13.37 Tax warranties and indemnities are generally only necessary on a share sale, since on a sale of assets virtually all tax liabilities are left behind with the selling company. The limited exceptions to this rule are that certain assets may be charged, or subjected to other restrictions, under provisions in the inheritance tax and VAT legislation. Additionally, as discussed at **13.6** above, the VAT rules for certain categories of computers, land and buildings can impose a continuing obligation to monitor the use to which those assets are put following the sale of a business that constitutes the transfer of a business as a going concern.

Chapter 8 Legal Aspects of Acquisitions discusses the overlapping purposes of a warranty and an indemnity. In summary, an indemnity obliges the covenantor to make good the indemnified liability on a pound-for-pound basis. The indemnified party does not need to prove damage to the target or the purchaser if the liability in question crystallises. A warranty, on the other hand, is simply a contractual statement about the affairs of the target. If that statement proves untrue, the purchaser may have the right to rescind the contract or to claim breach of contract. As warranties are made subject to what is revealed in the seller's 'disclosure letter', they effectively offer the purchaser a means of eliciting more information about the target.

It is usual on a share sale for the purchaser to require both a tax indemnity or covenant and tax warranties. Given the greater protection afforded by an indemnity, this will usually be regarded as the purchaser's primary protection in relation to tax.

Warranties

13.38 As a rule, a seller should resist giving warranties unless the information that is disclosed as a result is genuinely required – for the valuation of the target, for instance. A seller should not be required to go to considerable lengths to provide detailed information about the target's tax liabilities merely to assist the purchaser's future tax planning.

As regards past tax liabilities, a purchaser should generally only be interested in knowing that these have been properly calculated and, where they have not been paid, that proper provision has been made in the company's accounts. This is what distinguishes tax warranties from other types of warranty: past liabilities are unlikely to affect the present value of the company (unlike, for example, a bad record in environmental compliance or past litigation concerning a defective product that the company may still sell). Typical tax warranties concerning past liabilities would provide that:

(a)   full provision has been made in the target's accounts;

(b)   all returns have been duly made; and

(c)   there are no outstanding disputes with the tax authorities.

As regards present and future tax liabilities, there are certain situations in which tax disclosure will help a purchaser value the target company. Usually in the case of present and future tax liabilities, however, the seller can quite legitimately argue that the purchaser is adequately protected by the tax indemnity and does not need warranties.

For this reason, it is best to avoid automatically including numerous 'standard form' warranties in the share purchase agreement. From both the seller's and purchaser's perspective, it is better if the tax warranties are aimed specifically at eliciting information about the tax affairs of the target which is likely to have an impact on the value of the target or on the purchaser. Two examples are:

(i)   where the purchaser is buying the target in contemplation of stripping out some of its assets and selling them off, he will want information and protection from warranties concerning the target's tax position in relation to those assets, particularly their CGT base cost and the possibility of any balancing charges for capital allowance purposes; and

(ii)   where the purchaser is attracted by tax losses in the target, he should seek specific warranties as to the availability of those losses, particularly where those losses are specifically valued for the purposes of valuing the target.

Tax indemnity versus tax covenant

13.39   It used to be that the seller would give a tax indemnity in favour of the target company. The position has since changed, so that it is now standard practice for the seller to give a covenant to pay the purchaser, not the target, if certain liabilities of the target crystallise. (Strictly speaking, an indemnity is a promise to compensate a person for a loss or liability that is incurred by that person and not by a third party; where the seller promises to pay the purchaser, rather than the target, for a loss or liability of the target, it is more correct to talk of a covenant than an indemnity.)

The reason behind the change from tax indemnity to tax covenant is the case of *Zim Properties Limited v Proctor* [1985] STC 90. In this case, it was held that a client's right of action against a firm of solicitors who were negligent in a conveyancing transaction was an asset for the purposes of capital gains tax. Therefore, if any sum was received by way of settlement of the dispute between the client and solicitors, the client would be deemed to have disposed of this asset and a charge to capital gains tax would then arise on the proceeds received.

By extension of the principle set out in the *Zim* case, where a seller makes payment to the target under the terms of an indemnity, the payment could be regarded as the proceeds of the disposal of an asset of the target (its right of action against the seller). Since the target company has not given any consideration for the indemnity, its base cost in the asset will be nil and the proceeds will amount to a pure taxable gain.

A prudent purchaser would in this situation ask for a provision in the contract to require the seller to gross-up the amount payable to the target under the indemnity to take into account the capital gains tax payable by the target on receipt of the indemnity payment.

Although the purchaser will usually require a gross-up provision, the seller and purchaser will, in practice, tend to rely on HMRC's Extra-Statutory Concession D33, entitled 'Capital Gains Tax on Compensation and Damages', which mitigates the effect of the Zim principle. In the concession, HMRC states that the Zim principle is not regarded as applicable to payments under a warranty or indemnity included as one of the terms of a sale and purchase agreement. This concession applies only to payments made by the seller to the purchaser as an adjustment to the purchase price for the target, and not to payments to the target company.

Under the terms of the concession, if a payment is made by the seller to the purchaser under an indemnity or warranty, the purchaser's base cost in the target and the seller's disposal proceeds from selling the target are reduced under *section 49* of *TCGA 1992*.

Tax covenant

13.40   It is accepted practice on a private share sale for there to be a blanket tax covenant. It is often embodied in a deed which is separate from the main sale agreement. The use of a blanket covenant gives the purchaser comprehensive protection against the tax liabilities of the target. It also means that there is no need to have a long list of tax warranties. Indeed, as any disclosure against the warranties does not generally limit claims under the tax covenant, a seller will be reluctant to give excessive warranties, as it then would have to waste time and effort in making valueless disclosures against such warranties.

Where the price is based on earnings or the target's future profit-making potential, a seller may argue that he should merely warrant the tax position, obliging the purchaser to prove the damage he has suffered if a tax liability materialises. This is because, although an undisclosed tax liability will affect the company net assets, it may have little impact on the company's earnings position. This argument rarely succeeds in practice, however, since earnings potential generally relies on an adequate capital base.

In addition to the general tax covenant, the purchaser may also require specific provisions dealing with:

(a)   any secondary liability falling on the target for tax unpaid by a member of the seller's group under *section 132* of the *Finance Act 1988* or *sections 190* of *TCGA 1992* or for a tax charge on the target that arises under *section 214* of *TA 1988*;

(b)   the 'de-grouping' charge which can be triggered under *section 179* of *TCGA 1992* on chargeable assets transferred on a no gain/no loss basis for CGT purposes to the target from companies remaining in the seller group; and

(c)   the tax treatment of any pre-disposal restructuring that the seller may have effected.

Liability of seller(s)

13.41   Where there is only one seller of a company, then the purchaser will look primarily to that seller to make good any loss covered by a tax warranty or tax covenant. Where there is more than one selling shareholder, each may seek to limit his liability to his pro rata share in the proceeds of sale. Generally, a purchaser should resist this, and argue that the liability of the sellers must be joint and several, leaving them to sort out the position as between themselves 'behind the scenes'.

In relation to tax warranties, since these serve the dual function of providing the purchaser with information as well as protection, it is not uncommon to seek warranties from the directors of the target (at least if they are executive directors) and, less usually, from senior management. This is justified on the basis that information is best provided by those who have or should have that information, whether or not they are selling shares in the target company. Conversely, in a management buy-out the seller can resist giving warranties on the basis that the management should already know what state the affairs of the company are in.

Protecting the seller

13.42   There are certain tax-related problems which the purchaser or the target can cause the seller following the sale. The seller should therefore consider asking the purchaser for certain warranties or covenants on the tax front. The following points are relevant in this context:

(a)   The seller will want to ensure that the target does not disturb any group relief or capital allowance claims for periods prior to completion.

(b)   The seller will also want to ensure that the purchaser will co-operate with the seller in relation to the preparation and submission of tax returns and claims for periods before completion.

(c)   The seller will want reciprocal protection against secondary liabilities that it has offered to the purchaser (see **13.40** above). This will protect the seller's group from liabilities to tax that may arise as a result of the actions of the target after completion.

(d) There are certain anti-avoidance provisions under which the seller could become liable to tax because of an act or omission of the target or the purchaser. These include *sections 703* to *709* of *TA 1988* (transactions in securities); *section 776* of *TA 1988* (artificial transactions in land); *section 765* of *TA 1988* (migration of companies); and *section 767A* of *TA 1988* (change in ownership of a company and failure to meet tax liabilities).

Clearances and consents

13.43   The UK tax system does not currently oblige HMRC generally to grant advance clearance of the tax implications of a transaction. Under HMRC's Code of Practice 10, HMRC will currently give its interpretation of new legislation, where it has a settled view. The Varney Report, published in November 2006, recommended that these rulings should not be limited to new legislation, and that in addition businesses should be able to apply to HMRC for binding rulings on the tax treatment of commercial transactions.

In the context of the sale and purchase of a company, there are three specific tax provisions that entitle (in the case of clearances) or require (in the case of consents) the taxpayer to apply for a clearance or consent. These provisions are:

(a)   an (optional) HMRC clearance under *section 138* of *TCGA 1992*;

(b)   an (optional) HMRC clearance under *section 707* of *TA 1988*; and

(c)   a Treasury consent under *section 765* of *TA 1988*, which is not optional; indeed it is a criminal offence to carry out a transaction which falls within *section 765* without first obtaining such a consent.

An HMRC clearance or Treasury consent may only be relied on if the application has fully and accurately disclosed all material facts. Any application letter must therefore be reviewed with care to ensure that all relevant facts are disclosed. In addition, if there is a change in the proposed transaction, HMRC or the Treasury must be notified of such change, and a confirmation obtained that the clearance or consent remains valid.

Section 138 of TCGA 1992

13.44   As discussed at **13.33** *et seq.* above, it is possible for shareholders effectively to roll over or hold over any gain on the disposal of their shares in the target into shares or loan stock issued by the purchaser to the seller. The new shares or loan stock are treated as the same asset as the target shares for CGT purposes, so that any capital gain on the target shares is deferred until a disposal of the new shares or loan stock.

If the seller (together with connected persons) holds more than 5% of any class of shares in or debentures of the target company, the roll-over will only be available if the exchange is effected for bona fide commercial reasons and does not form part of a scheme or arrangement of which one of the main purposes is to avoid CGT or corporation tax. In this situation, it is usual to apply for an advance clearance under *section 138* of *TCGA 1992*, asking HMRC to confirm that this 'bona fide' condition will not apply to deny the roll-over. HMRC is not obliged under *section 138* to give any assurance that the other technical conditions for the roll-over are satisfied by the proposal. Although this is strictly speaking a question for the relevant taxpayer's Inspector of Taxes, in practice HMRC may indicate that in its view the other technical conditions are not so satisfied.

It is worth noting that no such clearance need be obtained if no seller who is intending to rely on the roll-over provisions holds (with connected parties) more than 5% of any class of shares in or debentures of the target company. Given the complexity of the connected party definition for these purposes, it will be difficult to determine whether or not there are any such shareholders from the share register alone, particularly in the context of a public acquisition. It is, however, relatively routine to apply for a clearance under *section 138* even where the parties are not aware of there being any such shareholder.

Section 138 of *TCGA 1992* requires that the clearance application is made by or on behalf of the target or the purchasing company. In practice, it is sensible for the form of the clearance to be approved by all of the parties prior to its submission.

An application for a clearance under *section 138* should be sent to:

[Non-market Sensitive]	[Market Sensitive]
Mohini Sawhney Clearance and Counteraction Team Anti-Avoidance Group Intelligence HMRC First Floor 22 Kingsway London WC2B 6NR E-mail: reconstructions@hmrc.gsi.gov.uk Fax: 020 7438 4409	Eric Gardner (Team Leader) Clearance and Counteraction Team Anti-Avoidance Group Intelligence HMRC First Floor 22 Kingsway London WC2B 6NR

As a matter of courtesy, a copy of the application (and any application under *section 707* of *TA 1988*) is often sent to the relevant Inspectors of Taxes.

A clearance application should usually include the following information:

(a) details of the seller, the target and the purchaser, including their tax districts and reference numbers and a copy of their latest accounts;

(b) the background to the transaction where relevant, including details of any related transactions;

(c) details of the sale and the form of consideration;

(d) the commercial objectives of the transaction;

(c)   a request for confirmation that HMRC is satisfied that the transaction will be effected for bona fide commercial reasons such that *section 137* of *TCGA 1992* will not apply.

It may also be helpful to give an indication of the timetable and to provide a contact name and telephone number and ask that any request for further information is initially made by telephone. Where any press release or share-holder's circular has been issued, it would be usual to enclose a copy of this with the application.

HMRC will confirm receipt of the application, giving a reference number for the application. HMRC then has 30 days in which to grant or refuse the clearance, or to ask for further information. In the latter case, a new 30-day period begins to run following receipt by HMRC of the further information requested. Where the transaction is on a tight timetable, it therefore clearly makes sense to provide as much information as possible initially, so as to avoid a request for further information.

Section 707 of TA 1988

13.45   *Sections 703* to *709* of *TA 1988* enable HMRC to counteract tax advantages obtained in relation to certain transactions in securities where one of five circumstances (which are set out in *section 704* of *TA 1988*) applies. Under *section 707* of *TA 1988* a taxpayer may ask HMRC in advance for confirmation that it will not exercise its powers under these provisions.

These provisions were introduced at a time when the rate of tax applied to capital gains was significantly lower than the rate that applied to income, and the provisions were originally intended to apply where taxpayers sought to convert income into capital for tax purposes. The provisions are, however, drafted very widely. In the context of the sale of a company, the provisions might apply, for example, to the payment of a pre-sale dividend.

A *section 707* clearance application will need to contain substantially the same information as that provided for the purposes of a clearance under *section 138* of *TCGA 1992* and is sent to the same address as set out above. Where appropriate, a single letter may apply for consent under both provisions.

As for the *section 138* clearance application procedure, HMRC has 30 days from receipt of the application in which to grant or refuse the clearance, or to ask for further information.

Section 765 of TA 1988

13.46   *Section 765* of *TA 1988* requires Treasury consent to be obtained for certain transactions involving the issue or transfer of shares and/or debentures in a company resident outside the UK. As stated above, the failure to obtain consent under *section 765* for a transaction to which the section applies is a criminal offence.

Section 765 of *TA 1988* only applies if the relevant company that is resident outside the UK is controlled by a company resident in the UK. *Section 765* might therefore apply, in the context of company acquisitions, where the target is resident outside the UK, but the seller is a UK-resident company. In addition, *section 765* might apply where the purchaser is a non-UK-resident company, but is controlled by a UK-resident company and is to issue shares or debentures to the seller in consideration of the purchase of the target.

In many cases it will be unnecessary to apply for a specific consent under *section 765*. This may be for one of two reasons.

First, *section 765A* of *TA 1988* will apply where the transaction represents the movement of capital between two persons that are resident in different members states of the EU. This would cover, for example, the sale of shares in a non-UK-resident company by a person resident in the UK to a person resident in another member state of the EU. Similarly, *section 765A* would apply to an issue of shares by a company resident in a member state of the EU to a person resident in a different member state of the EU.

Where *section 765A* applies, there is no requirement to obtain a prior consent to the transaction, although the relevant company that is resident in the UK and controls the non-UK-resident company must notify HMRC of the details of the transaction within six months of its being carried out. There is, however, no requirement to notify a transaction under *section 765A* if the transaction would also have fallen within the general consents (see below).

The second situation in which it is not necessary to apply for a specific consent under *section 765* of *TA 1988* is where the transaction falls within the general consents issued by the Treasury. For example, where a UK company is selling a non-UK company to an unconnected purchaser, so long as the sale is for full consideration paid by the purchaser, and there are no arrangements for anyone connected with the seller to obtain or to acquire any interest in the shares transferred, the general consent will usually apply. In addition, where a non-UK-resident purchaser is issuing shares to a seller in consideration for the transfer of the target, and the seller and the purchaser are not connected, the general consent will usually apply if similar conditions are met.

If a specific consent under *section 765* is required, an application should be made to:

Mary Sharp, Peter Steeds or Des Hanna
CT and VAT (International CT)
100 Parliament Street
London
SW1A 2BQ

The application should contain details of each of the parties (including their residence, tax references and latest accounts and details of their businesses) and full details of the proposed transaction. Although there is no statutory time limit for the grant or refusal of a Treasury consent, these applications are generally dealt with quickly, particularly where the matter is urgent.

Tax losses

13.47 Where the target company has previously made trading losses for tax purposes, these losses can be set against future profits in the same trade. It would therefore appear that a target with carried forward trading losses is more valuable than one without, as a purchaser will benefit from the offset of these losses against the target's profits in the future. In practice, however, although the losses may have this effect, a purchaser is usually reluctant to pay additional consideration for a target with carried forward losses. This is because, due to the provisions described below, the purchaser cannot be certain that those losses will be available to the target following its acquisition by the purchaser.

First, it should be noted that the carried forward losses may only be set off against profits arising from the same trade. Accordingly, if the purchaser is intending to cause the target to change its trade, the benefit of the losses may be lost.

In addition, in certain circumstances:

(a) *section 768* of *TA 1988* prevents the carry forward of trading losses incurred before a company is sold;

(b) *section 768B* of *TA 1988* prevents the carry forward of excess management expenses and interest deductions incurred before the company is sold; and

(c) *section 768A* of *TA 1988* prevents the carry back of losses arising after the sale to a period before the sale.

Broadly, all these provisions apply where, within a three-year period, there is both a change in ownership of the company and a major change in the nature or conduct of the trade or business carried on by the company. When the purchaser acquires the target, there is clearly a change in ownership of the target. It is then necessary to look to see if there is any major change in the target's trade or business both before and after the sale, as the provisions simply require the change of ownership and the major change in the trade to have occurred within a three-year period.

It is often difficult to determine whether or not a major change in the nature or conduct of a trade or business has occurred. This is particularly the case because, if the purchaser is buying a loss making company, it may well believe that it has to make changes to the way that the business is carried on in order to ensure that the target becomes profitable.

A major change in the nature or conduct of a trade includes a major change in the type of property dealt in, or services or facilities provided, or a major change in the customers, outlets or markets of the trade. In Statement of Practice SP10/91 (which was revised in 1996) HMRC attempts to set out its interpretation of a major change in the nature or conduct of a trade or business. The Statement identifies certain factors which HMRC will have regard to such as the location of the company's business premises, the identity of the company's suppliers, management, or staff, the company's methods of manufacture, or the company's pricing or purchasing policies. The Statement of Practice also indicates that HMRC will not regard a major change in the nature or conduct of the trade as having occurred when all that happens is that a company makes changes to increase its efficiency or to keep pace with developing technology, or where a company rationalises its product range by withdrawing unprofitable items.

If the purchaser is reflecting the value of any losses in the purchase price, it is reasonable for the purchaser to seek warranty and/or indemnity protection should the losses prove to be unavailable due to a major change in the trade or business of the target that occurred in the three-year period ending on the date of the sale. The seller will need to ensure that this warranty and/or indemnity does not cover any such change that occurs after the sale. In practice, this distinction is not easy to draw, as a change of this nature rarely occurs instantaneously, and may involve changes that commenced prior to the sale but are not fully implemented until after the purchaser acquires the target.

Where the target has carried forward trading losses or capital allowances, but the purchaser does not want to buy the target (with its other assets and inherent liabilities), the losses may be preserved for the benefit of the purchaser if the target transfers the relevant business to a new subsidiary and the purchaser then acquires that subsidiary. Under *section 343* of *TA 1988*, the new subsidiary should step into the shoes of the target as regards trading losses and capital allowances. The provisions outlined above will continue to apply on the change of ownership of the new subsidiary when it is acquired by the purchaser. The hive down should preferably occur a little while before the sale to the purchaser, in order to ensure that *section 343* applies. In addition, if any liabilities attributable to the relevant business are not transferred to the new subsidiary, *section 343(4)* of *TA 1988* is likely to restrict the amount of the losses that pass to the new subsidiary.

Although the initial transfer of the assets by the target to the new subsidiary will benefit from the no gain/no loss treatment set out in *section 171* of *TCGA 1992*, when the purchaser acquires the new subsidiary any gain will be crystallised under *section 179* of *TCGA 1992*, as the new subsidiary will leave the seller's CGT group. As this degrouping charge is a liability of the new subsidiary, the purchaser will require an indemnity for it. It should be noted that it may be inconvenient for the capital gain to be realised in this way, rather than on the actual disposal of the assets of the business. For example, the seller will be unlikely to be able to set any available capital losses against the gain, and business asset roll-over relief will not be available. The seller might therefore consider taking steps to avoid *section 171* applying to the initial transfer.

Unless the hive down is implemented at a time when there were no arrange-ments in place for the sale of the new subsidiary to the purchaser, stamp duty relief under *section 42* of the *Finance Act 1930* is unlikely to be available on the hive down due to *section 27(3)* of the *Finance Act 1967*.

Close companies

13.48   The UK tax system has traditionally had specific rules that apply to certain private companies that are under the ultimate control of only a few shareholders. The reason for these rules was to prevent individuals avoiding income tax and instead benefiting from the more generous corporation tax regime by leaving profits within a company. These anti-avoidance rules are now far less significant, but a purchaser will still want to ascertain whether the target is or has ever been a close company, perhaps by asking for an appropriate warranty from the seller.

The definition of a close company is complicated and far-reaching. Indeed, there are companies that are listed on the London Stock Exchange that are close. The general rule, however, is that a company is close if it is under the control of five or fewer persons, or is under the control of its directors. The definition of control is a wide one, and it is necessary to aggregate the inter-ests of connected persons when applying this test. Where a company is con-trolled by companies that are not close, or where a company is quoted and shares carrying more than 35% of the voting power in it are held by the pub-lic, then, notwithstanding this definition, the company is treated as not being close.

Where the target is a close company, the purchaser should be aware of the fol-lowing points, and seek adequate protection in the documentation:

(a)   Where expenses are incurred by a close company for the benefit of a shareholder or his associate, this will be treated as a distribution by the company. Following the abolition of ACT, this provision should have no implications for the company itself, but the purchaser might want to ensure that any liability to ACT that arose in respect of any such distri-bution made before April 1999 has been met by the target.

(b)   Where shareholders in a close company borrow funds from the com-pany, the company is liable, in the accounting period in which the loan is made, for an additional amount of corporation tax equal to 25% of the amount borrowed. This tax is refunded to the company as and when the borrowing is repaid.

(c)   A transfer of value involving a close company may cause the company to be liable to inheritance tax.

Where a purchaser is an individual and is acquiring ordinary shares in a close trading company, the purchaser may be able to obtain income tax relief in respect of the interest on any loan to fund the acquisition. This will only be the case, however, if the purchaser holds a material interest in the close com-pany. Although the company must be a close company at the time when the shares are acquired, it need not continue to be close beyond the initial acquisition (see HMRC Statement of Practice SP3/78). The interest held by the purchaser must, however, continue to be a material one.

An interest is a material interest if it represents 5% or more of the ordinary share capital of the company, or entitlement to assets on a winding up of the company, or if the purchaser works for the greater part of his time in managing the business of the company or an associate company. In order to manage the business, the purchaser must either be a director or must have significant managerial or technical responsibilities relating to the overall running and policy making of the company as a whole.

Public mergers and acquisitions

13.49 A public merger or acquisition will involve a quoted target and (often) a quoted bidder. Many of the issues discussed above in relation to tax planning apply equally to public takeovers. There are, however, some distinguishing features between public and private transactions, and these have an effect on tax planning.

Distinguishing features

13.50 Typically, in a public takeover there are a large number of target shareholders. There may also be option holders under employee share option schemes. While each shareholder and option holder may have a slightly different tax position, it will be necessary to consider the typical tax position of various categories of target shareholders (eg individual shareholders, corporate shareholders and tax exempt shareholders) under any proposed structure. Although it will not always be possible to achieve the optimum tax structure for all shareholders, some attempt is usually made to ensure that the structure is not unduly tax inefficient for any class of shareholder.

Due to the larger number of shareholders, it may be more difficult to implement certain restructuring schemes in advance of a public takeover. On the other hand, there may be other possibilities such as the use of court-approved Schemes of Arrangement.

Where a transaction is governed by the City Code on Take-overs and Mergers ('the Take-over Code'), it may not be possible for a transaction to be delayed while a pre-sale restructuring is carried out. This is because the restructuring may require details of the transaction to be publicly disclosed, which would lead to the imposition of a timetable on the parties under the Take-over Code (although it may be possible to announce an offer subject to a pre-condition). In addition, it is unlikely that the potential purchaser will be able to do significant amounts of due diligence work in respect of the target, but instead will have to rely on publicly available information.

Lastly, in relation to a public transaction, there will usually be no seller who will provide contractual protection in relation to the target's historic tax position. The purchaser will therefore not normally have the benefit of any tax warranties or indemnities.

The one exception to this rule might be where a company is listed for the first time. In this situation, the underwriters might require the original shareholders to indemnify the company for certain historic tax liabilities, although these will generally be limited to tax liabilities that only arise because of the company's prior status. For example, if the company was a close company prior to its listing, the company might be indemnified for any tax liabilities that arose due to its close status; if the company was previously a member of a larger group, the company might be indemnified for any liability under *section 179* of *TCGA 1992* due to the company leaving the CGT group on listing.

Shareholders' tax planning

13.51   Where a listed target company is to be acquired by another listed company, each shareholder will have a slightly different tax position. The following may, however, be a useful summary of the issues that usually arise.

For tax purposes, there is a basic distinction between an income distribution and a capital receipt. Where a shareholder sells his shares, he will generally be treated as receiving a capital receipt and this will be taxed within the CGT rules. By contrast, if the shareholder receives a dividend from the company, this will be treated as an income distribution. Where a company repurchases its own shares, the amount paid to shareholders will generally be treated as in part a capital receipt and in part an income distribution.

It is likely that a significant proportion of the target's shareholders will be pension funds and other tax exempt investors. Such shareholders will not be subject to tax on any gain that arises on the sale of the shares in the target, but are no longer able to claim any tax credit payment in respect of income distributions. They are therefore simply concerned with maximising their proceeds from the sale and are generally indifferent as to whether they receive these proceeds on a sale of the shares or via a dividend or other income distribution.

Individual shareholders who pay tax at the higher rate of income tax will typically prefer to receive their proceeds in consideration for the disposal of their shares, rather than as an income distribution. Such shareholders have an additional income tax liability in respect of any income distribution (see **13.17** above). By contrast, any proceeds from the disposal of the shares will form part of their capital gains tax computation, with the benefit of their base cost in the shares, indexation and taper relief. In addition, it may be possible for an individual's annual exemption from CGT or for capital losses to be used to reduce or eliminate the tax charge, or for the proceeds to be reinvested in a qualifying investment for EIS purposes.

Individual shareholders who do not pay tax at the higher rate of income tax have no additional tax liability in respect of income distributions, and so may prefer to receive some of their proceeds in this form. Individuals who hold their shares via a PEP or an ISA are still entitled to a tax credit payment in respect of income distributions, which makes such distributions particularly attractive to them for tax purposes.

UK corporate shareholders are not subject to corporation tax on dividends received from other UK companies. Where however, the distribution arises on a repurchase of shares, the fact that part of the repurchase price is treated as an income distribution does not prevent it also being included in the consideration that the shareholder is deemed to receive for CGT purposes on the disposal of the relevant shares. It may therefore be more efficient for corporate shareholders to receive a dividend from the company, rather than for the company's shares to be repurchased.

Special dividends

13.52   If the target company has sufficient distributable profits for company law purposes, it may be attractive for the target to pay a special dividend to shareholders just prior to the sale. This would enable the purchaser to reduce the purchase price for the target, and therefore the stamp duty payable on the acquisition. Unfortunately, as set out above, a special dividend may not be attractive to certain categories of shareholder.

Mix and match offers

13.53   It may be attractive to offer shareholders a variety of consideration packages, with each shareholder able to select the package that suits his commercial and tax objectives. This might involve, for example, a shareholder electing to take its consideration in the form of cash, loan notes and shares in the purchaser. Following the Special Commissioners decision in *Snell v Revenue and Customs Commissioners* [2006] STC (SCD) 296, there is some evidence that HMRC will examine such arrangements more carefully before granting a clearance under *section 138 TCGA 1992*.

Even where the target is to be acquired in whole or part for cash, the purchaser will often offer a loan note alternative to target shareholders. As discussed at **13.34** *et seq.* above, this loan note will be structured so as not to constitute a qualifying corporate bond. In this situation, as shareholders are free to take their consideration entirely in the form of cash and would only take the loan notes for tax planning purposes, it would be usual for the interest rate payable on the loan notes to be slightly less than the market rate of interest. For this reason, the loan notes can also represent attractive funding for the purchaser.

Partial mergers and spin offs

13.54   It may be that the bidder would like to acquire only some of the target group's businesses ('the target businesses'). The purchaser could acquire the target, and then sell those parts of the business that it did not want to retain ('the surplus businesses'). This would, however, involve the purchaser bearing the cost, including the tax cost, of the disposal of the surplus businesses.

In addition, the target's shareholders might actually prefer to retain the surplus businesses. The simplest way to achieve this would clearly be for the purchaser to purchase the target businesses from the target company. To the extent that the proceeds are surplus to the seller's future business requirements, the seller could distribute these proceeds to shareholders. This would, however, involve the seller being subject to CGT on the disposal of the target businesses and the shareholders then receiving a dividend, rather than realising a capital gain. This may not be particularly tax efficient.

There are other possibilities: first, it might be possible, before the bidder acquires the target, for the surplus businesses to be spun out to and retained by the target shareholders in a tax efficient manner; secondly, it might be possible for the target businesses to be spun out to shareholders and for the purchaser then to acquire the target businesses directly from the shareholders. The tax issues raised by these transactions are complicated and are beyond the scope of this chapter. In summary, however, it will not be possible in this situation to rely on the tax exempt demerger provisions in *sections 213* to *217* of *TA 1988*, due to the change of control of the target businesses on their acquisition by the purchaser. Instead, it is necessary to rely on *section 136* of *TCGA 1992* (for shareholders) and *section 139* of *TCGA 1992* or, where available, SSE (for the seller) in order for the transaction to be effected tax efficiently.

Employee share schemes

13.55   Where the target is a listed company, it is quite likely that it will operate one or more share option schemes for the benefit of its employees (see **Chapter 5 Employee Share Schemes**). The detailed rules that govern these schemes are beyond the scope of this chapter, but the following issues need to be considered in the context of an offer for the target.

Where the Take-over Code applies, the purchaser is obliged to make an 'appropriate' offer to ensure that the interests of the target's option holders are protected. Even where the Take-over Code does not apply, it will generally be in the interests of all parties to ensure that the sale of shares in the target does not deprive its employees of their accumulated rights under any share scheme nor leave the purchaser with a small minority of employees holding shares in the target.

Under the rules of the target's share option schemes, where there is a change in control of the target, option holders will often have a fixed period in which to exercise their options, after which the options will lapse. It will be necessary to see whether the proposed transaction causes any such provision of the scheme to apply. If it does, then the purchaser might decide to extend its offer for the target's shares to option holders. Option holders could become shareholders in the target by exercising their options under the rules of the scheme, and then accept the purchaser's offer. The option holders may then benefit from any mix and match elections that are being offered to other target shareholders.

Another solution might be for the purchaser to offer to pay the option holder a cash sum for the release of his option equal to the difference between the exercise price payable under the option and the value of the consideration offered by the purchaser for the shares in the target. This reduces the number of shares in the target that are to be acquired by the purchaser, and so the stamp duty payable by the purchaser on the acquisition of the target's shares. Option holders will, however, generally suffer an income tax charge on the receipt of the cash payment and National Insurance contributions will be payable. By contrast, if an option granted more than three years earlier under an 'approved' scheme had been exercised this income tax and National Insurance liability would have been avoided.

It may also be possible for the option holders to exchange their existing target share options under the option scheme for options over shares in the purchaser without triggering any charge to tax. In the case of approved SAYE or CSOP schemes, this can only be done, preserving the favourable tax treatment, if the terms of the share option schemes provide that, where one company obtains control of another company, an option holder may agree to release his old rights in consideration of the grant to him of new rights which are equivalent to those released. If the purchaser agrees to make such an offer, the terms of the new option would have to be equivalent in economic terms to the original option, and must satisfy the other conditions for approval. The terms of the exchange would, in the case of approved schemes, need to be approved by HMRC.

It will be necessary to consider the effect of any proposals on the availability of Corporation Tax relief under *Schedule 23 FA 2003*. For example, where the target is acquired by an unlisted company that is not itself the subsidiary of a listed company, that Corporation Tax relief will cease to be available when shares in the target cease to be listed. It may be desirable therefore for the exercise of options to take place prior to listing ceasing. Payment of a cash sum for the release of options may be less attractive than allowing option exercise because that payment will not attract Corporation Tax relief for the purchaser.

Cancellation schemes

13.56   *Section 425* of the *Companies Act 1985* (or *sections 895* and *896 Companies Act 2006*) allows a company to enter into a broad range of arrangements with its shareholders (and creditors). It is possible for a merger of two companies to be implemented in this way. For example, under such a scheme the existing shares in company A may be cancelled and new shares in company A issued to company B in consideration for the issue of shares by company B to company A's former shareholders pro rata to their previous holdings.

A section 425 scheme has the advantage of only requiring the support of 75% (by value) of the shareholders present at the relevant shareholders' meeting. In addition, on a cancellation scheme, where there is no transfer of the shares in the first company, stamp duty is avoided on the merger.

Shareholders may, however, still be entitled to a roll-over in respect of such a merger transaction. Although there is no exchange of shares (so that *section 135* of *TCGA 1992* cannot apply), *section 136* of *TCGA 1992* should apply to the extent that the transaction is a scheme of reconstruction or amalgamation and the shareholders in company A receive shares in company B in proportion to their shares in company A.

Depositary receipts

13.57   Non-UK shareholders in a UK company will often only hold shares in a form that may be traded on local exchanges. This typically means a clearance system or, in the case of US shareholders, in the form of depositary receipts.

Once shares are held in a depositary or clearance system, the shares may effectively be traded free of UK stamp duty and SDRT. In order to avoid a loss of UK stamp duty revenue, the UK imposes a charge to stamp duty or SDRT of 1.5% when the shares first enter the system.

Where a non-UK company is to be taken over by a UK company and shares are to be issued in the UK company, there are likely to be a significant number of non-UK shareholders that will want to hold their shares in the UK company in a depositary or clearance system. The SDRT entry charge would in this situation typically be borne by the acquiring company and will be a significant cost of the transaction.

Where shares are issued into a depositary or clearance system on a merger in exchange for shares in a UK company that are already held in such a clearance system, no further entry charge should be payable. Where, however, the existing shares are not UK shares, the entry charge will be payable on such an exchange.

Identity of the bidder

13.58   Where the target is a listed company, it is common for the bidder to acquire a stake in the target by purchasing shares in the market before or after announcing its bid. If the bidder then decides not to launch the bid, or the bid fails, the bidder may then dispose of these shares. For this reason, it may make sense for the initial stake to be acquired by a company resident outside the UK, so that any profit made in this situation escapes UK CGT. At a later stage, the shares could be sold by the initial purchaser to a UK-resident bidding vehicle.

As discussed above at **13.25**, where the bidder is making a purchase for cash and is intending to fund the purchase price with borrowings, the bidder may intend to surrender the tax deduction for the interest cost to the target itself by way of group relief. In a public takeover, however, there may be some delay between the bidder incurring this debt and acquiring sufficient share capital in the target for the target to become a member of the same group relief group as the bidder. As the interest is deductible on an accruals basis, this may mean that the interest relief for this period is unusable unless the bidder's group has other UK taxable profits against which this relief may be set.

Chapter 14

Corporate Acquisitions involving Real Estate

At a glance

- Most businesses have properties and how they are to be dealt with must be considered as part of any company acquisition.

- The strategy to be adopted for dealing with property assets will tie into the chosen corporate structure for the sale and purchase. However, the properties may have an impact upon this if they are a major part of the assets of the company in question and therefore the parties ought to liaise early in the process to agree how they should be dealt with.

- Properties will follow the share transfer in a share purchase and no separate property transaction is required, but the parties will need to consider whether the target company holds any properties as part of its assets that need to be extracted prior to sale.

- In asset deals, there will need to be a separate property transaction requiring specialist property legal input.

- The level of due diligence to be undertaken in respect of the properties in a corporate portfolio will need to be decided. Often the cost of a full due diligence exercise for properties is prohibitive, so strategies need to be put in place to agree what level of due diligence can be undertaken realistically and at what cost and risk.

- There are a number of different approaches to carrying out the legal due diligence for properties, including full investigations of title and certificates of title. The correct approach has to be worked out for each deal.

- There are pitfalls in dealing with leasehold properties in an asset transaction around obtaining landlord's consent to assignment or underletting. These need to be factored into the transaction and a strategy for addressing the problems realised.

Introduction

14.1   Almost every business has some property interests. For a large number of businesses, the property interest will merely be a head office from which the business must be run containing the usual management functions. Many other types of business will have a far bigger interest in properties. For instance, conventional 'bricks and mortar' retail businesses will operate from shop premises and distribution facilities; industrial businesses will require factories and warehouses, and leisure businesses (eg cinemas, restaurants) will require a location from which the leisure activity can be carried out. Even if one of the rationales for the acquisition of one business by another is to cut costs by, amongst other things, closing down duplicated property interests (such as head offices), it is still important to understand what the property interests are and what are the potential risks and liabilities in taking them on in a new combination.

A distinction must also be drawn between properties of strategic importance and properties that are less important. A retail or pubs business involving a large chain of shops or pubs may have no individual shop that is more important than any others unless one or some are making a greater profit or are for some reason in a higher profile location. A business such as, say, Harrods with a single trading store, will inevitably regard that asset as being vital to its success. Almost all businesses will have head office functions that will need to be inspected closely. In reviewing the property work to be undertaken in a corporate acquisition, therefore, the lawyers will need some guidance on the relative importance to the business of the assets they hold and individual properties within a portfolio. This guideline should be given at the outset of a transaction to avoid the need for unnecessary work being undertaken.

Shares or assets?

14.2   The corporate structure of the transaction will guide whether a purchase is to be by way of a share purchase or an asset purchase. In the case of corporate transactions involving either lots of valuable, or otherwise significant property interests, there may be good reason for considering the structure of the properties and the best way of dealing with them in the context of the proposed transaction. We will deal with this in more detail below. However, in most cases it is likely that the way in which the property interests are dealt with will be driven more by the needs of the corporate and tax structuring than the other way around and property advice will need to fit into that context rather than try to drive it.

All property in England and Wales is registrable (upon a transaction taking place) at the Land Registry. This is now dealt with in the *Land Registration Act 2002* (*2002 Act*), which is a major update on the procedures and processes set out in the *Land Registration Act 1925*. This does not mean that all properties are yet registered and there is a substantial national estate of properties that has not yet been registered. However, the vast majority of commonly traded properties are now registered pursuant to the *2002 Act*.

Currently, any lease with a term of more than seven years upon grant or remaining upon assignment must be registered also and it is the Land Registry's intention that leases with a term of more than three years will soon be registerable. Also, easements granted pursuant to leases of seven years or less are required to be registered.

The registration burden has, in respect of asset transactions therefore, increased substantially and this will need to be considered in the formality of arrangements dealing with corporate transactions.

Considerations for share sales and purchases

14.3   A share purchase is the acquisition of shares only, and as there is no actual transfer of any property, the property considerations are somewhat different from those which might be applied to an ordinary property asset purchase. There is no transfer of the legal estate in the land, as the shares in the target company are transferred instead. Therefore, there should be no need to deal with any land registry formalities relating to any transfer of the land. In the case of leasehold property there will be no requirement for landlord's consent to assignments as the tenant will, so far as the landlord is concerned, remain the same both before and after the share transfer. There is one small caveat to that statement. In a very small minority of cases, leases contain a control provision requiring landlord's consent upon a change in the ultimate ownership of the tenant company. However, this is very rare in England and Wales.

As there will be a change in the ultimate ownership via the sale and purchase of shares, due diligence does still need to be carried out and we will deal with that in paragraphs **14.7–14.10** below. In addition, there are some specific requirements that will need to be considered in relation to the share purchase agreement.

One potential disadvantage of dealing with a transaction by means of shares as opposed to assets is a potential lack of knowledge of the history of the company. Companies will have contingent liabilities within them for all sorts of reasons. **Chapter 7 Environmental Responsibilities** will deal with the potential liabilities for contaminated land. As for pure property interests these cannot necessarily be discovered by means of a conventional property due diligence and the buyer must receive protection by some other method. We will consider this in more depth at paragraph **14.8**.

Considerations for asset sales and purchases

14.4   There may be many good reasons why a corporate transaction is done by way of a transfer of the underlying assets of a business rather than a sale of the shares. This will in particular be the case when a company is selling off a division which it has not formalised within a separate group company. Again, as mentioned previously, it is unlikely that the property itself will be the driving force behind this decision, although it may influence it.

From a purely property perspective, an asset transaction is much more like a conventional property deal than a share purchase, in that the actual property asset must be transferred in the normal way. It is not in the scope of this chapter to comment in detail upon the transfer of property assets, but we will draw out one or two important issues to consider in the context of a corporate transaction. We will also review the documentation required for such a transaction.

The Law Society has within its rules Practice Rule 6A which governs sellers dealing with more than one prospective buyer in relation to the conveyancing of freehold and leasehold property. This rule is designed to protect residential purchasers from gazumping at the stage when sales are in the hands of solicitors. However, it is not limited to residential transactions and technically affects commercial properties also. Briefly, it states that for any transaction that involves sending out a second contract for the conveyance of land, the solicitor acting for the seller must notify the first prospective buyer when the second contract is sent out. It does not impose a contract race as such, but merely an obligation to inform the first party. It does not apply in respect of auctions, but does technically apply for general corporate transactions involving the sale of an asset. It could, therefore, affect a corporate transaction which consists in part of such a conveyancing transaction, even if that is only a small part of the transaction.

Tie in to corporate document

14.5   In the case of a share sale, the property aspects will almost certainly be dealt with within the share purchase agreement, which will require a description of the properties and property warranties. Depending upon the circumstances of the individual transaction, other contractual provisions relating to the properties may need to be incorporated in the share purchase agreement.

In the case of an asset sale, as this is in itself a substantive property transaction, more contractual provisions will be required. These can either be part of the main corporate asset agreement or a separate agreement dealing with the property transactions, but in all likelihood tied into the terms of the main corporate transaction. In any event, it will be important to liaise with the lawyers running the main corporate transaction in order to ensure that the documents interlink and cover the transaction as a whole.

Assessing the importance of property in target

14.6   As mentioned at the outset, different transactions will have differing types of property within them. The extent to which the property within a target company needs to be considered will depend very much upon its importance as part of the transaction as a whole. It is important for the bid team to consider carefully what work they should be undertaking given factors such as the importance of the property portfolio or individual properties within it, timing and the cost of undertaking work.

One discussion that needs to take place is as to whether it is possible to reduce the due diligence exercise to be undertaken in some way, either by passing it to a third party or by reducing the extent of the due diligence. In this latter case, certain transactions lend themselves to some sort of a sampling exercise, whereby a full due diligence is only undertaken for a minority of a portfolio, with the remaining part of the portfolio either unreviewed or reviewed only to a limited extent. This works well for large portfolios, such as a chain of high street retail shops or pubs.

In the case of a chain of shops, a bidder for the portfolio may take the view that the shops are similar and are all likely to have similar problems and advantages. To the extent that any individual shops have problems, say, an inability to trade, this would be set off against the remaining portfolio being acquired and a portfolio risk can be taken. A sample of the shops to review may, therefore, be chosen upon one or (more likely) a combination of factors which may include the following:

(a) Valuable properties.

(b) Competing sites (ie where it is likely disposals will be needed).

(c) Properties with high rents.

(d) Properties where the lease term is coming to an end shortly.

(e) Properties in certain locations (eg shopping centres, small towns, large cities).

(f) Highly profitable properties.

(g) Loss making or unacceptably low profit making properties.

For a sampling exercise, it is likely that a full due diligence (as set out in paragraph **14.9** below) would be carried out for the sample chosen with a limited exercise carried out for the remaining properties, which may involve a review of specific aspects or areas of specific interest. It is common, for instance, for a review to be undertaken in all circumstances of any clauses that may (following *Homebase Ltd v Allied Dunbar Assurance plc* [2002]) require under-lettings to be carried out at the higher of the best and passing rent when it is likely that disposals will need to take place for all or part of a portfolio. Sometimes, the bidder will choose to do no due diligence at all on certain aspects of a portfolio.

Property due diligence

14.7   It is beyond the scope of this chapter to go into a great deal of detail about the extent of the property due diligence that may need to be carried out on an acquisition, suffice it to say that some level of due diligence will be needed. Bidders for a company will need to decide upon their approach to property due diligence from amongst the options set out below.

Warranties

14.8 In most corporate transactions, of either assets or shares, the sellers will be required to give warranties. **Chapter 8 Legal Aspects of Acquisitions** deals with warranties generally; this section will pick them up only insofar as they relate to the property elements of a transaction.

It is possible, although highly unusual, for warranties to cover the entirety of the due diligence needed to be done in respect of the property contained in the corporate transaction. If it is intended only to rely upon warranties, then these will need to cover all aspects that would otherwise be undertaken by means of an investigation of title. In particular, the disclosures against the warranties will be very limited and specific only to matters that affect the individual warranties that have been given.

A conventional disclosure against a warranty that, for example, the owner of a property has good and marketable title, would be that the buyer takes subject to all matters referred to in the deeds to the property and any information in respect of the property capable of being discovered by means of a search of public authorities. In other words, the only benefit for that warranty would be in respect of matters in the knowledge of the company and not disclosed.

For this reason, it is unusual to rely entirely upon warranties in a property transaction and normally only certain warranties are used (although this shortlist may be expanded depending upon the actual circumstances of the transaction). The most commonly used warranties are the following:

(a) **List of properties**

It is usual in any sort of corporate transaction to have a list of properties owned by the company. In an asset transaction, this is self explanatory and it will be necessary to transfer each of these properties on an individual basis. In a share transaction, where the properties do not need to be individually transferred, it is important for the buyer to have an understanding of what properties are within the target. It makes a Seller think about the properties needed so as to avoid a false disclosure.

Properties in this context includes freehold and leasehold properties and in all likelihood any properties held only by means of a contractual interest, such as those held pursuant to a licence to occupy. The list of properties will lead then to the nature and extent of the due diligence to be undertaken.

(b) **Contingent liabilities**

As a matter of contract law, a company remains liable as original contracting party to any document that it entered into as such. From a property perspective this will in particular include original tenant liability where a company may have signed up as tenant of a property and then assigned the lease to a third party. Should that third party or its successor disappear due perhaps to an event of insolvency, the landlord may pursue the party with whom it had its original contract and this liability will continue notwithstanding any sale or other transaction involving that company. It is important, therefore, in the context of property warranties to insist upon having a warranty dealing with contingent liabilities so as to have protection against this risk.

By means of the *Landlord and Tenant (Covenants) Act 1995 (Covenants Act)*, tenant liability as the original contracting party (normally called original tenant liability) was altered and has reduced. The *Covenants Act* stated that a tenant will only be liable under the covenants contained in a lease as original contracting party for the length of time that it is actually a tenant, subject to a possible obligation upon lawful assignment to enter into an authorised guarantee agreement as defined by *section 16* of the *Covenants Act*. This guarantees the liability of an assigning tenant's immediate successor, but no one beyond that. Accordingly, you would expect a seller of shares in a company with contingent liabilities to make disclosure of original lease liabilities that may be continuing (remembering, of course, that these liabilities may be from some years ago) and against authorised guarantee agreements that the company has signed up to since the *Covenants Act*.

There are still numerous leases that pre-date the *Covenants Act* changes (being those granted before and in very limited circumstances after 1 January 1996), but they are becoming less common as they expire over time. Therefore, with the exception of authorised guarantee agreement liabilities, the contingent liability issue is becoming less of a concern as time passes.

Obviously, any failure to disclose such contingent liabilities will be limited in time and extent to the limitations placed upon the warranties generally as part of the main transaction. This should always be borne in mind when taking any form of warranty.

From the perspective of the warrantor, it is important to try to examine company records to ascertain whether there are any potential contingent liabilities, usually being leases that have been assigned or authorised guarantee agreements that have been entered into as set out above. Unfortunately, it is not common for there to be any good record of such liabilities, as, although a contingent liability remains, the corporate view taken is normally that it is remote and there is no registry of such liabilities.

(c) **Replies to enquiries**

As part of a full investigation of title (for which see paragraph **14.9** for greater detail), replies to enquiries from the seller will be part of the package. For share purchase, it is necessary to pick up a contractual reliance upon these replies to enquiries and this is commonly dealt with by having a warranty that the replies are true and accurate in all respects. If it later turns out that a reply has been inaccurately given in breach of this warranty, there is an opportunity to pursue the warrantor for the breach subject to the terms of the warranties as discussed above.

For an asset purchase, contractual reliance may be dealt with by way of a misrepresentation argument in the property contract if there is a separate property contract. This is the way that liability would normally adhere in a conventional property transaction. We cover more detail on this in paragraph **14.9** below.

(d)   **Certificate of title**

If a certificate of title or certificates of title are to be given (see paragraph **14.10** for more details), it is necessary to tie these also in the contract with a warranty that the certificates are true and accurate in all respects and the company has given the certifying solicitor all the information necessary for the certificate to be issued. The principle is the same as for a warranty in respect of replies to enquiries.

Part of any warranty exercise will be the need to disclose against the warranties in a disclosure letter, which will be an activity undertaken by the corporate lead. The property feed into this will need to consider both the general disclosures made and any specific disclosures against the individual warranties. General disclosures would include a disclosure of all documentation provided (which is likely in the case of property to include title deeds and supporting documents) together with anything that the buyer might find out from any search undertaken of the usual public registries. In cases where an investigation of title is being carried out, this should be acceptable. It will not be acceptable in the case of a warranty as to the contents of the certificate of title for the underlying documents supporting the certificate to be disclosed. We will deal with why this is in a little more detail in paragraph **14.10**.

Investigation of title

14.9   It is beyond the scope of this chapter to cover in detail the way in which an investigation of title may take place (upon which specific advice will be needed depending upon the particular property portfolio), save to the extent that it can be outlined for a corporate acquisition.

The basic principle behind an investigation of title is that the buyer is subject to caveat emptor (in that it will be deemed to have all knowledge available in respect of the asset save to the extent that the contract otherwise deals with this). Investigations of title are the same for a share or an asset transaction, as you are investigating the title held by the seller to the underlying asset and not dealing with the manner in which it is transacted.

There are three main parts to a title investigation which we can deal with separately:

(a)   **Title documents**

As mentioned previously (in paragraph **14.2**), land in England and Wales is subject to registration in most circumstances upon a transaction being undertaken. The vast majority of land that is now transacted is already registered at the Land Registry and, therefore, an investigation of the title held by the seller to property will in most cases include a review of Land Registry documentation. The Land Registry, however, does not give the whole story of the land and there are various other documents that may be necessary to add up the paper title. These will include in particular leases and supporting leasehold documents (for instance licences to assign, licences to alter etc) which are not capable of registration and unregistered interests which override the registered title (set out in *Schedule 3* of the *Land Registration Act 2002*). In addition, planning documents are not normally registered on the Land Registry entries, so a separate review of planning permissions will need to be undertaken. If a property has undergone a substantial development in recent years, then it is likely to be subject to an agreement under *section 106* of the *Town and Country Planning Act 1990* relating to planning gain. Although this agreement will bind all parties with an interest in the land from the date of the agreement, it is not in itself capable of registration at the Land Registry. There may well be other agreements of a similar nature relating to utilities, such as water supply and sewage.

In the case of unregistered land, the title is based upon conveyancing documents showing transactions dating back at least 15 years with good information to identify the property and referring to all documents affecting the title. Unregistered conveyancing is now becoming a very specialist area, as few young lawyers have done much of it and it can be quite tricky and time consuming.

(b) **Replies to enquiries**

Any property transaction would normally require, in addition to the information obtained from the title deeds and public searches, any information available in the hands of the seller itself by means of replies to enquiries before contract. There are now a standard set of pre-contract enquiries in the Commercial Property Standard Enquires (CPSE) forms covering general enquiries, specific enquiries to deal with assignments of leases, specific enquiries for the grants of new leases and specific enquiries for the transfer of property subject to leases. These enquiries are very detailed and will in most cases be adequate for the purposes of the transaction, although it may be necessary to deal with supplemental enquiries or specific ones for unusual properties.

The enquiries should deal with matters in the knowledge of the seller and there is often a debate as to which individual within the selling organisation has adequate knowledge to be able to give the replies. From a seller's perspective, it is usual to ensure that the contract limits the identity of the person who gives the replies to one or two individuals, so that knowledge in other areas of the company is not imputed to the company as a whole and may thereby lead to a warranty claim.

In a conventional property-only transaction, contractual force is given to the replies to enquiries by means of making them a representation in the contract, such that it is affirmed that the buyer has entered into the contract as a result of the replies given to enquiries and any representation in the enquiries that turns out to be a misrepresentation is a breach of contract. This is governed by the *Misrepresentation Act 1967* and may result in setting aside a conveyance for fraudulent or even innocent misrepresentation or damages being payable.

This approach will work well in the case of a separate asset contract for sale of properties as part of a corporate transaction. However, it is not normally acceptable in a share sale context, where the matter will be dealt with by means of a warranty as to the replies to enquiries as set out at paragraph **14.8**(c) above. In the event that no such warranty is given, there can be no means of contractually pursuing any representations given in replies to enquiries that turn out to be incorrect.

(c)   **Enquiries of public authorities**

A buyer of a property will be expected to carry out searches of relevant public authorities to find out information that will be available from them. The most important such search is a local authority search, which will reveal matters relating to the property in the knowledge of the local authority and local land charges which are registered in the local land registers by the *Local Land Charges Act 1975*. Such local land charges will include planning entries, including information on listed buildings and conservation areas, *section 106* agreements, grants, statutory notices served by the local authority (including, for instance, food hygiene notices) and local public developments, for instance road works or transport infrastructure works. A local search is, therefore, very important and should in all events be obtained, unless an adequate warranty is available from the seller (without disclosure of the public records) as to the contents of such a search. In theory, a seller should have all knowledge that is within the local search on the basis that it should have been served with all the notices and be aware of any agreements affecting the property and matters in the vicinity. However, this is not necessarily always the case in practice.

Although the time for receipt of local searches has improved in recent years, it is still fairly slow and likely to take about two weeks. In the context of a very urgent corporate transaction, there may be pressure to undertake a personal local search which can be done by search agents. These, however, are of limited use and will not necessarily obtain all the information that is available to the local authority. A client relying upon personal searches should be warned of the risks. By *section 10* of the *Local Land Charges Act 1975*, a person who is adversely affected by an incorrect formal search result or a misregistration is entitled to compensation from the local authority. This protection only applies to incorrect entries so will not be available against search agents performing a poor service.

The Land Registry now allows a search against the names of registered proprietors (in form PN1). This should always be carried out in share purchases. It indicates every registered title held in a particular proprietor's name and allows a buyer to double check whether there are any properties registered in the names of the target about which they otherwise have no information.

There are numerous other searches that may need to be carried out. One important search which is in part dealt with in the local search is a highways search, as it is vital to ascertain that a piece of land either adjoins a public highway or has adequate private access rights to a public highway. A local authority search will give indication of roads that are publicly maintained, but will not necessarily give enough detail to indicate any random strips that might adjoin the land and, therefore, it is good practice to obtain a specific search from the highways authority which will give more detail.

Other searches may be needed on a regional basis (eg coal authority searches) or due to the specific requirements of the land (utilities searches in respect of development land).

Certificates of title

14.10 Transactions are often undertaken now with a supporting certificate of title given by a reputable law firm. This is designed to support a property valuation.

A certificate of title is a formalised report on title undertaken upon a full investigation of the title that a land owner has to a property. It is carried out on the principle of a series of statements against which disclosures are made in the certificate. There are two common forms of certificate of title used which have been developed by the City of London Law Society Land Law Sub-Committee, being the long form and the short form certificates. The most commonly used is the long form certificate (now in its fifth edition). Other forms are used by firms of solicitors on a case-by-case basis.

Certificates are particularly useful when more than one party will need to rely upon a property investigation, for instance in transactions where there is bank funding or private equity buy out where a management team and other investors and a bank may need to rely upon title investigations. They are best undertaken by the land owner's solicitors who will have the greatest knowledge personally and via the land owner and the greatest ability to pursue further information. To the extent that the solicitors give an opinion in the certificates, if they are negligent there is a right of action by the addressees against the solicitors. To the extent that the solicitors have been given information by the owner of the property then this will be dealt with by means of the warranty referred to in paragraph **14.8**(d) above giving a cause of action against the company for its confirmation that the certificate is accurate.

Certificates rely upon the underlying documentation that supports their being prepared not being disclosed as part of the transaction. Therefore, no title information should be part of a disclosure package if any certificate is being given. Also, it is important that documents (other than plans) are not attached to the certificates as these will be deemed to be disclosed to the reader of the certificate.

From the perspective of the property buyer, the certificate should be capable of being read and understood, although parts of it may require 'translation' and a solicitor acting for a party receiving a certificate of title will often prepare an overall summary of the certificate picking out any points of particular importance or interest.

Certificates of title have certain limitations, some of which are as follows:

(a)   If they are being prepared by a seller, the seller's solicitors will not be instructed upon the particular purposes that a buyer may have in mind for a property. The certificate may not, therefore, deal well with matters of particular importance to the buyer for any later action that the buyer may wish to carry out in respect of that property.

(b)   Certificates only work well for properties that are largely static, so are not undergoing intense management or being developed. In particular, the disclosure in the certificate of construction on the property is inadequate for a development. Documentation relating to a development will need to be dealt with separately.

(c)   Certificates do not deal well with planning. If a property is subject to complicated planning restrictions or is in the process of going through planning, the certificate will not be capable of dealing with this well given its limits.

Property developments

14.11   The basic rules set out in this chapter work well for conventional property estates. They do not, however, work well for corporate transactions involving any element of development. A property which is in the course of being developed has a great many more considerations to bear in mind than a property which is either occupied for the purposes of a business or let to a third party. In particular, there is a need to understand and review construction arrangements undertaken for a property that is being developed and think about how these are best transferred to new owners. However, as it is fairly rare to transact a corporate involving a property subject to a development, we will not deal with this in any greater detail.

Property documents

14.12   There are numerous additional documents that may be required for the property aspects of an asset deal. A brief outline of these follows.

(a)   **Contract for sale of property**

This may either be a schedule to the corporate agreement or a stand-alone agreement which will govern the specific manner in which the properties are to be transferred. It will also act as a framework agreement to the remainder of the documents listed in this section.

(b) **Land Registry transfer**

Registered land or unregistered land which is to be registered will be transferred by means of a prescribed Land Registry form of transfer (normally a TR1).

(c) **Assignment of lease**

A lease which is not registered and not registrable will be transferred by means of an assignment.

(d) **Authorised guarantee agreement**

This will normally be required to be entered into by an outgoing tenant when assigning its lease.

(e) **Rental support document**

This may be required to support the covenant strength of an incoming tenant under an assignment or a new lease. It can take many forms, most common being parent or director guarantee, rent deposit and bank guarantee.

(f) **Licence to underlet/assign**

A licence required from the landlord of a lease being assigned or underlet giving consent to the transaction.

(g) **New lease**

This may be needed if a new lease is being granted as part of the transaction.

Note that as a result of the action of *section 141* of the *Law of Property Act 1925* the landlord's interest in a lease (the reversion) passes automatically upon any sale of that interest (eg a sale of a freehold subject to a lease). So, no document is needed to govern such a transaction.

Dealing with landlords

14.13   In share transactions, it is unlikely that a buyer will need to have any direct involvement with a landlord of any leasehold properties that are being acquired as part of the share purchase. This is because there will be no individual transfers of land. In asset deals, however, there will be a substantial need to deal with landlords on the acquisition of any leasehold property. In the majority of cases involving leasehold land, landlord's consent will be required for the transaction to be undertaken. The rare exceptions to this are likely to be in respect of leasehold property that has a value (and where a landlord is paid only a ground rent at best). It is important, therefore, in the context of a corporate transaction to think about how this may be approached, given that corporate transactions are often dealt with rapidly with no involvement of third parties and often highly confidentially.

s to assignment

14.14   In most rack rented occupational leases (ie those which will be used by the vast majority of businesses to occupy their premises if they do not hold the freehold), the landlord will retain control over alienation (being an assignment or underletting of the lease or any other change in control by the tenant or sharing of occupation). Conventionally, and in particular prior to the *Covenants Act*, there would be a statement in a lease that a landlord may not unreasonably withhold or delay consent to an assignment. The provisions regarding underletting would normally be more complex and distinct for individual properties, but generally most leases would allow subletting of whole or certain parts subject to subleases being in accordance with the terms of the headlease.

Since the *Covenants Act*, given the loss of original tenant liability, landlords have become more alive to the need to have certainty on the covenant strength of tenants. As a result, lease alienation clauses have become more convoluted to try to protect the landlord better. Broadly, landlords need to be satisfied that tenants are capable of taking on the leasehold liabilities. They will normally require outgoing tenants to enter into authorised guarantee agreements. There are often restrictions upon alienation to group companies so as to avoid tenants transferring properties into insubstantial group companies.

Landlord's control on alteration is restricted by the *Landlord and Tenant Act 1988*. This states that a Landlord must respond in a reasonable time to requests for consents. The case law (eg *Go West v Spigarolo* [2003], *Auborgine v Lakewood* [2002]) has left the tenant in a strong position to force through an assignment (even against the landlord's wishes) if the landlord acts unreasonably slowly. The cases here indicate that even a letter of consent may be adequate to give consent and a formal licence to assign may not be needed. The cases also make some comment on timing of landlord's responses indicating that three weeks may be a reasonable period for a landlord to consider the assignment on a simple matter, but the actual period is dependent upon the detailed circumstances. If following that time, no consent has been forthcoming, then a tenant may be capable of either applying to the court pursuant to the *Landlord and Tenant Act 1988* for a declaration that the landlord is unreasonably withholding consent or proceeding directly to an assignment in any event. These are, of course, quite aggressive steps and a tenant will need to be secure of its ground before pursuing them and ensure that the assignee will agree a course of action.

Fundamentally, the law as now stated is that landlords will be unreasonable in withholding consent if an incoming tenant can demonstrate that it is capable of complying with the tenant's liabilities under the lease. Most landlords will expect an assignee to have at least three years worth of after tax profits of no less than three times the annual rent under a lease. In the event that a tenant cannot demonstrate this level of quality financial strength, a landlord will probably be reasonable in asking for further security, such as a rent deposit, bank guarantee or guarantee from a parent company or directors.

Getting round the landlord's requirements is something that will need to be investigated on a case-by-case basis.

Post-completion alienation consideration

14.15 In many cases, corporate transactions are by their nature confidential and the parties will not wish to inform landlords that they are taking place until completion has occurred. In this case, in an asset transaction, it is vital that the contractual drafting deals with the post-completion position.

The normal position is that following completion of the transaction, the seller will agree to sell any leasehold properties, but hold them on trust for the buyer pending application being made to the landlord for consent to assignment. The contract will need to deal in detail with the process for making such an application and dealing with the consequences of it, including the need for any supporting security that may be required. Normally, the documentation would enable an application to be made for a subletting if an assignment is unavailable (as a landlord will be less reasonable in refusing an application for subletting than it will for an assignment). The contract will also need to deal with the default position. If consent cannot be obtained for any form of alienation, then the property will need to remain with the seller and appropriate compensation provisions may need to be built into the contract to deal with this position.

Leases that are incapable of alienation in any circumstances whatsoever are surprisingly common. Obviously, a landlord will be entirely within its rights in the case of such a lease to refuse consent to assignment or subletting and it may be that such a property will have to drop out of the transaction if consent cannot be obtained from the landlord outside the terms of its lease. Similar factors apply for a lease where landlords are not required to be reasonable in respect of the specific application that is being made as part of the transaction.

Virtual assignments

14.16 Virtual assignments are a mechanism that has arisen as a result of the property outsourcing market which has developed in recent years. In effect, they are trust arrangements whereby a property owner holds a property on trust for the beneficiary and undertakes to act as trustee, but the economic interest is held by the buyer who will direct the seller as trustee to act in accordance with its instructions. They are useful for property outsourcing transactions as they enable the outsourcing company to have control over the property interests without taking on the lease liabilities directly, but leaving them within the company who is outsourcing its functions. They also enable the outsourcing to be undone merely by undoing the virtual assignment rather than having to assign a lease back to the original owner.

Virtual assignments are less likely to be used in a conventional corporate transaction where a seller will wish to dispose of its interest absolutely rather than having it potentially revert in due course. After *Abbey National plc v HM Revenue & Customs* [2006], the courts have also held that VAT treatment is not the same in virtual as opposed to actual assignments, so there will probably be irrecoverable VAT in such an arrangement, which decreases its attractiveness.

New leases and licences to occupy

14.17   It is quite common in many corporate transactions for there to be a need for new leases to be granted or licences to occupy to be entered into for short periods to enable transitional arrangements to take effect. These will need to be negotiated and granted on a case-by-case basis.

Under the *Landlord and Tenant Act 1954*, a tenant has prima facie security of tenure for any occupation of land pursuant to a lease (which can include an oral lease) for a period of greater than six months. It has always been possible to avoid this taking effect by contracting out of the security of tenure provisions of the Act. However, until recently, this required the obtaining of a court order by consent which, although rarely controversial, was always time consuming. Since the *Regulatory Reform (Business Tenancies) (England and Wales) Order 2003*, a court order is no longer needed and the contracting out of the Act can be dealt with by way of a notice being given by the landlord and the tenant responding with a declaration accepting that it will not have security of tenure. An ordinary declaration is required to be given 14 days before the lease is actually granted, but this can be avoided by the tenant obtaining a statutory declaration to this effect. Therefore, the landlord's risks of a tenant remaining in place on a temporary basis as a result of a short-term arrangement have been restrained and eased under this procedure.

Post completion

14.18   There is nothing out of the ordinary in corporate transactions for the post-completion obligations that need to be undertaken. The Land Registry requirements for any property transaction will need to be dealt with and stamp duty land tax will need to be paid. As stamp duty land tax changes on a regular basis, the particular provisions will need to be considered in the light of the law as it stands at the time a transaction is carried out, but a buyer should normally expect to pay stamp duty of 4% upon any property transaction unless the property is of low value.

Overseas properties

14.19   Many businesses have properties overseas which will need to be dealt with as part of the corporate transaction. Whilst we cannot comment upon individual countries' laws or practices, it is, obviously, necessary to consider the impact that overseas properties may have from as early as possible in the process so as to ensure that there is nothing within them that can upset the main corporate transaction being processed. The lawyers dealing with overseas properties should, therefore, be carefully project managed to ensure that they give an indication of the required timescales in their juris-diction, what can be undertaken and what cannot be undertaken and proceed in accordance with the timescale needed to ensure the transaction can be completed in time.

Chapter 15

Private Equity Finance and Buyouts

At a glance

- This Chapter considers the role of private equity and buyouts in the M&A market, and the impact that the involvement of a private equity fund is likely to have on the acquisition process and terms.

- Private equity funds are an important buyer and seller of companies, both private and public.

- The way in which their funds are structured, their investment objectives and contractual obligations to their investors are all important to understand the way in which buyouts are structured. Funds seek to generate profits for their investors, usually by seeking to make operational improvements to a business that increase its market value during the fund's period of ownership.

- The main focus of this chapter is on the typical terms that the private equity house will negotiate with a management team and the other providers of finance. It also briefly reviews how the presence of a private equity buyer is likely to affect the terms of the acquisition itself.

Introduction

15.1   In 2006, private equity accounted for over 25% of the European M&A market (according to mergermarket), and plays a critical role – either as a seller or prospective buyer (or both) – in many corporate disposals. The industry is now very large: in 2005 alone, European private equity funds raised over €71.8, and invested €47 billion in 7,207 different businesses[1]. In most auction sales, there will now be more private equity bidders than trade, and many household name UK companies are, or have in the recent past, been owned by buyout houses (see below).

15.2   *Private Equity Finance and Buyouts*

Examples of private equity financed businesses²

> The AA
> Center Parcs
> Debenhams
> Halfords
> Homebase
> Kwik-Fit
> Little Chef
> NCP
> Somerfield

But, despite the huge influence of the industry, there are still a number of mis-conceptions about private equity. Often portrayed by politicians and the media as 'asset strippers' and financial engineers with short-term goals, the objectives of private equity funds are frequently misunderstood. The aim of this chapter is to explain what a fund's objectives will be when it looks at a potential acquisition, and what those working with private equity – especially a management team – can expect when they partner with these financial investors.

1. European Venture Capital Association, 'Annual Survey of Pan-European Private Equity & Venture Capital Activity – EVCA Yearbook 2006' (2006).
2. Companies that are currently owned by private equity investors, or have been in the past.

What is private equity?

15.2   First, it is important to explain some terminology. Private equity is sometimes used as a generic term to cover both buyouts, when investors buy (often in combination with a team of managers) an established business, and venture or growth/development capital, which is when they invest relatively small sums into new or early stage businesses. While there are some private equity funds who invest in early stage businesses, growth capital and buyout situations (like 3i), most now focus on one or the other.

In this chapter we are looking only at buyouts (because they involve the *acquisition* of a business), and not at venture capital, where – despite some similarities – different investment structures are used and different invest-ment strategies are deployed.

There are a number of different types of buyout (see **15.20** below), but the hallmark of this type of transaction is the fact that one or more financial investors (as opposed to a trade buyer) acquires a controlling stake in an established business with the objective of selling that business at a profit within a defined and relatively short period of time.

Where does the money come from?

15.3   Private equity funds have been very successful at raising money in the past few years. Their funds come from a range of investors, who are usually sophisticated, and most are institutional (rather than retail). **Figure 1** shows that, of the €71.8 billion raised in Europe in 2005, 24.8% came from pension funds, 17.6% from banks, 13.1% from funds of in 2005, 24.8% came from pension funds, 17.6% from banks, 13.1% from funds of funds and 11.1% from insurance companies. Only 6% came from private individuals.

Figure 1 – Source of Private Equity Funds Raised – 2005 (EVCA)

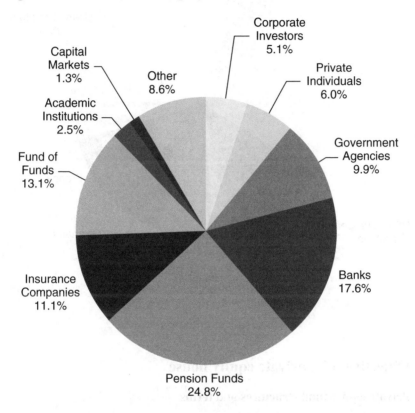

The geographical origins of the money invested in private equity funds are also diversified. **Figure 2** shows that 65% of the funds raised by European funds came from European investors (with 28% from the UK), 24% came from the United States and 6% from Asia.[1]

1. European Venture Capital Association, 'Annual Survey of Pan-European Private Equity & Venture Capital Activity – EVCA Yearbook 2006' (2006).

Figure 2 – Geographical Source of Funds Raised – 2005 (EVCA)

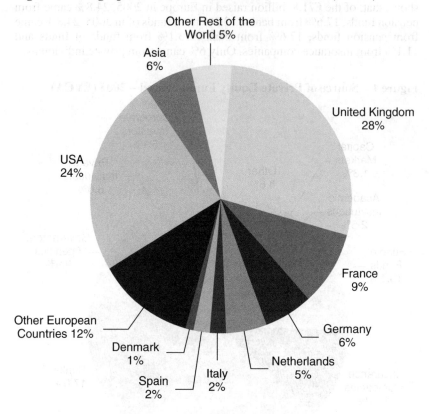

Objectives of a private equity house

Private equity fund structures and terms

15.4   It is helpful to say a few words about the structure and terms of private equity funds, as this will help to explain some of the investment objectives, structures and priorities of a private equity investor.

Fund structures

15.5   Most private equity funds are organised as limited partnerships or similar vehicles. These types of vehicle usually meet the fund's main structuring objectives, which are:

(a)   Limited liability for the fund's investors.

(b)   No double taxation for investors, which means that the vehicle has to be tax exempt or tax transparent so that there is no tax at the fund level.

(c) An appropriate level of regulation, to take account of the fact that the funds are not generally available to unsophisticated or retail investors, and relatively easy to administer. In the UK, the fund's manager will usually need to be regulated by the Financial Services Authority.

(d) Capable of being marketed to a range of sophisticated and institutional investors across Europe, the United States, Asia and elsewhere.

(e) The ability to incorporate a tax efficient fee and profit share for the fund's managers (see below).

(f) No charge to VAT on the fund's management fees.

Self liquidating v evergreen funds

15.6 Private equity funds are usually, although not always, 'self-liquidating'. That means that the funds are (with only limited exceptions) only invested once, and on realisation of an investment the proceeds are returned to investors. The investors themselves (not the limited partnership) are responsible for paying tax on any profits according to their own tax position (and many – like UK pension funds – are actually tax exempt, so they pay no tax at all on capital profits).

For funds that are not self-liquidating (so called 'evergreen' funds), where the proceeds are not returned to investors but reinvested in further transactions, a tax exempt structure (like the UK's Investment Trust) is needed. That is because tax transparent structures would require investors to pay tax as profits are made even though they are not being distributed, which is not attractive for investors. Investors in evergreen funds also need some way to realise their investment, which is why many evergreen funds are quoted on a stock market, allowing realisation through sales of shares in the fund.

But evergreen funds are not the norm, and the fact that most funds are self-liquidating has some important consequences for a fund's investment strategy and priorities. Fund managers are required to raise successor funds every few years, or they will rapidly run out of cash to invest. In order to do that successfully they will usually need to show realised returns from previous funds, and that imposes additional pressures on fund managers to exit from their investments and return the proceeds to investors reasonably fast.

Fees and incentives

15.7 Another important aspect of the terms of private equity funds is the way in which fees and incentives are structured. Most buyout funds charge management fees of between 1.5% and 2% on the amount of funds committed to the fund, usually reducing to the amount actually invested after an initial 'investment period' has ended. Funds also charge a 'carried interest', which is a share of investment profits made by the fund. That usually amounts to 20% of profits, payable only once an initial 'hurdle rate' of return has been made for investors and only on realisation of the actual profit (not on a notional valuation, as is usually the case with hedge funds). This structure means that there is an incentive for funds to realise investments, and to make capital profits from them, rather than to hold them for long periods and enjoy an income stream.

Investment decision-making process

15.8   Before a fund (or, commonly, its manager) makes the decision to invest in an underlying company, it will generally follow an internal approval process. This process typically follows three steps:

(a)   An individual executive will usually draft an investment paper assessing the economic and strategic reasons to invest in the target and describing the proposed acquisition structure and key terms.

(b)   The investment paper is considered by an investment committee, often made up of the senior members of the fund's management team; if the investment is approved by the investment committee, the acquisition process continues.

(c)   As the investment committee's approval is generally given before any offer is officially made by the fund for the target, it is common for a final investment committee approval to be given once the final terms of the deal are agreed.

This process can obviously impact on the timetable for the investment process, although usually it can be accommodated within the timetable with minimal impact. The key point is that there will need to be parallel processes running: the approval process, the negotiation of the equity documentation with the management team and the acquisition itself. The logistics of these processes can be challenging, but they are crucial and need to be managed carefully.

Drawdown of funds

15.9   One other term of the fund which is worth mentioning in this context is the fact that (in most cases) the funds are not drawn down from investors in self-liquidating funds at the outset, but on an 'as needed' basis. The 'hurdle rate' and the returns from the fund are usually calculated on the basis that money is not invested until it is drawn down, so the later the funds can be drawn down, and the earlier they can be repaid, the better for fund managers. This structural issue has implications for the way in which deals are executed, and – for example – means that the fund has to allow time to draw down funds, and helps to explain why private equity houses are very reluctant to give any warranties when they sell an investment. If they did so, they might have to reserve against that potential liability before distributing proceeds to their investors, which would reduce the 'rate of return' ultimately received by investors.

Investment objectives

Alignment of interests

15.10   It is often said that private equity is, to a large extent, about align-ment of interests. The way in which the fund manager is compensated is closely related to the profits that it makes for investors in the fund (through the carried interest referred to above), and that objective also drives the struc-ture of investments in underlying companies. Some argue that the reason buyout funds have out-performed public equities in recent years is that this alignment of interests reduces the 'agency costs'[1] that can arise when a man-agement team has incentives which are out of step with the objectives of the shareholder group.

The private equity house aims to achieve an 'exit' – when it realises its investment, usually through a sale or flotation – within a defined time period, and to make a capital gain at that time. In practice the way in which private equity investors tend to align interests with management (and, often, a num-ber of the other key employees) is to ensure that they have a significant equity stake in the business. They will tend to insist that management hold their shares until the private equity investor has achieved an exit, and if a member of the team leaves the business early they will want to ensure that they have to sell their shares, usually for less than their full value (it being only possible to realise full market value on a full exit). It will often be the case that the management team will stand to make significant personal gains if they achieve the exit that the private equity house wants, but will not stand to make so much money if they choose to leave the company before that has been achieved.

1. 'Agency costs' is a term used to describe the additional costs (financial and non-financial) that can arise (and are usually ultimately borne by the shareholders) when a company's man-agers have incentives that differ from those of its owners.

Involvement in the board and management

15.11   Typically, private equity houses are active investors. They seek to add value to their investments in a number of ways.

At the outset, the private equity house will usually be involved in determin-ing the business plan for the acquired company, or at least agreeing it with management. They will assist in strategic planning, and – through their sec-toral and financial expertise, and their extensive networks – will assist in the implementation of that plan.

Usually, one or more representatives of the investor(s) (or sometimes an independent person with relevant expertise that they nominate and with whom they have an ongoing relationship) will sit on the board of the portfo-lio company as chairman and/or as non-executive director(s) (or member of the supervisory board), and will help management to set the strategic direc-tion for the company and will participate in important decisions. In the initial period after the investment has been made, and during any particularly difficult periods (such as following the departure of a key manager, or when there are financial difficulties in the business), the involvement of the investor's nominated director(s) can be quite intensive.

On an ongoing basis the investor will expect to be kept informed of the progress of the business, through the provision of management accounts and other information.

Holding periods

15.12   From the moment that a private equity buyer begins evaluating a business, it will be considering the way in which it will be able to 'exit' from that business, usually by a trade sale or public flotation (for a detailed discussion of different exit routes, see **15.67 et seq**).

However holding periods vary – occasionally, the exit can be within a year or less of acquisition, and other investments can remain in the portfolio for well over five years – but most funds will typically seek to exit fully within a three- to seven-year period from the date of any investment.

Value creation strategies

15.13   There are a variety of ways in which private equity investors seek to make returns on their investments, and in many cases there will be more than one factor which will contribute to the success (or failure) of a deal.

Buying a company for less than its full market value is clearly one way that a buyer can make money, and in less efficient markets or special situations that may be possible. However, in most of Europe today – where sellers are sophisticated and professionally advised, and most businesses are sold by auction – that is usually very hard to do.

'Financial engineering' – ensuring that a company has the optimum capital structure and is accessing capital at the lowest available cost – is often said to be a key driver of value. But many of the benefits of these techniques will be reflected in the price paid (sometimes even through a financing package devised by the seller as part of the auction process – so called 'stapled finance'), since most buyers will be able to utilise them. There is, therefore, likely to be only limited scope for a buyout house to capture the upside itself in a sophisticated market.

Another way in which returns can be made is through 'multiples arbitrage' – buying a business when the accepted price/earnings multiple for that sector is x, and selling it some years later when the accepted multiple has grown to more than x. In this way, it may be possible to make a good return on an investment without increasing its intrinsic value by exploiting rising prices, either generally or in a particular sector. That would be a dangerous strategy to employ alone, and is easy to imitate (and therefore in the medium term not sustainable). It is not usually relied upon as a principal source of returns at the outset. However, it has been an important source of private equity returns in the recent past.

Most private equity houses focus on improving the intrinsic value of their investments as their major source of returns, either through earnings growth, improved operational efficiency, or strategic changes. In many cases, these strategies are executed through a strong and focused management team – which is why, when asked to identify the most important driver of value creation in portfolio companies, most buyout practitioners will say that it is the quality of the management team[1].

One way in which intrinsic value is enhanced is through 'buy and build' strategies, or 'platform deals', where two or more separate businesses are acquired and merged together to create a larger and more successful single company (see *Example: Yellow Brick Road*). In other cases, a refocus on a core business, or an entirely new strategy can deliver the out-performance.

1. SJ Berwin, The Human Capital Equation, 2002, www.sjberwin.com.

Example: Yellow Brick Road (Source: 3i)

> 3i successfully achieved an internal rate of return of 111% on their investment in Yellow Brick Road, a European directories business.
>
> The origins of Yellow Brick Road date back to 1997, when 3i backed Gary List to buy out Thomson Directories, the UK's second largest operator, in a €133m buyout that turned 3i's original €38m into nearly €200m – more than five times the original investment. 3i identified the yellow pages sector as a promising sector, at a time when the telecoms bubble had just burst and operators were offloading their directories businesses.
>
> In 2002 3i bought Fonecta for €112m. 3i's Finnish venture capital team's relationship with telecoms group Sonera provided the inside track, whilst their Thomson Directories experience gave it the credibility. In 2003, 3i and Veronis Suhler Stevenson ('VSS') then led further buyouts, alongside new management teams, of De Telefoongids (€500m) from KPN in the Netherlands and Mediatel (€270m) in Austria and central Europe from Verizon Inc. Gary List joined the Board of De Telefoongids.
>
> Benefiting from the Thomson experience, 3i supported management in driving through cost savings (especially in printing), developing electronic media, improving sales efficiency and taking advantage of the fast growing eastern European markets. 3i were actively involved in implementing over 15 smaller bolt-on acquisitions, especially in Finland. Earnings grew from a pro-forma €126m in 2002 to €160m in 2005. Cash flow was particularly strong with over €400m generated over the course of three years.

In 2004, working with advisers and management from 17 different nationalities, 3i merged Fonecta, De Telefoongids and Mediatel to form Yellow Brick Road ('YBR'), a leading, fast growing, diversified European Directory player with an enhanced strategic value beyond the limits of the individual country operations. 3i brought back Gary List to act as chairman and help drive through a number of organisational changes. A refinancing of the combined group raised €1bn of new debt and delivered cash returns for 3i of €224m (a cash-to-cash multiple of 1.5×).

In May 2005, 3i and VSS agreed to sell YBR for €1,825 million to a consortium led by Macquarie Capital Alliance Group and including Macquarie Bank Limited, Caisse de dépôt et placement du Québec and Nikko Principal Investments Limited.

Under the ownership of 3i and VSS, YBR's management team had successfully grown the business, both organically and through acquisitions, and had begun to realise the benefits arising from the combination of the company's regional businesses and the sharing of best practices.

Valuation

15.14   When a private equity house is seeking to acquire a business, it will clearly try to do so at the lowest possible cost. It may, therefore, place a value on the business which is greater than the amount it bids, although the valuation would usually provide a cap on the amount that the investor is willing to pay.

Company valuation is highly complicated and is outside the scope of this chapter, but the following is a very basic introduction to the approach likely to be adopted by a private equity investor.

There are a variety of valuation techniques, but most private equity investors will focus on expected future cash flows integrated into a target financial structure for the company, with an EBITDA (Earnings Before Interest, Tax, Depreciation and Amortisation) multiple being applied to determine an expected 'terminal value' for the business at exit.

The value that this methodology will typically provide is a 'debt free, cash free' value. In other words, this value provides the enterprise value for the whole business, assuming that it has no debt and no excess cash (other than cash required to deliver the earnings used as the basis for the valuation, such as normal working capital). Therefore, if there is any debt in the business which will not be repaid before acquisition, then this will need to be deducted from the value, and if there is any excess cash that is not being left with the seller then this will have to be 'valued' and that amount added to the valuation. Note that a buyer may not be willing to pay £ for £ for cash, because it may be hard to extract or there may be costs associated with extracting it (for example, it could be trapped in a company that has insufficient reserves to make dividend payments).

Debt (senior and junior)

15.15   A private equity buyer will usually try to maximise the use of debt finance in order to enhance its own return if the investment is successful.

Of course, the more debt that there is in a business the greater the risk to the residual equity holders, since it is more likely that the company will be unable to meet its contracted repayments and be forced into liquidation[1]. However, as a general rule a private equity house will seek to maximise the debt that it can obtain without significant risk of default.

There are a variety of different layers of debt that are available – see **Figure 3** below. The first layer will be senior debt, secured on the assets of the target company. The primary source of senior debt will be the leading commercial

Figure 3 – European Divestments (EVCA)

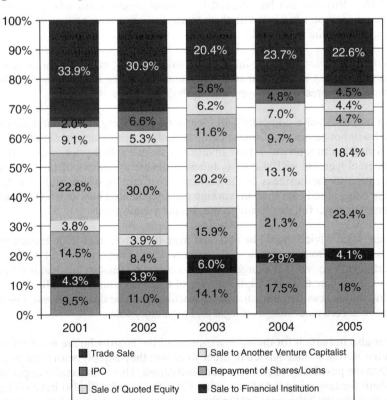

banks, which will usually syndicate some or all of it to other banks, or hedge funds or other funds specialising in debt instruments. The senior debt may be split into various tranches, carrying different coupons (interest rates) and maturing over different periods.

There may also be one or more layers of junior debt, which could take a number of different forms – 2nd lien, mezzanine, PIK notes and so on. Junior debt may include some equity style upside, and/or a higher coupon (interest rate) to reflect its higher risk. Debt structures can be multi-tiered and very complex in a buyout, in order to provide as much debt capacity as possible for the target company, and to do so at the lowest possible cost of capital.

1. For a discussion of the risks related to debt in private equity transactions, see *Financial Services Authority Private equity: a discussion of risk and regulatory engagement* published in November 2006 (pp. 61-63).

The buyout process

Initiation of a buyout

15.16   Buyouts can be initiated by a management team who look for a financial investor to work with them to acquire a business, by a private equity house, or by the seller itself.

Where the buyout is being initiated by an incumbent management team it is very important for those managers to understand the obligations that they owe to their present employers and to abide by them.

An employee of a company will clearly owe obligations of confidentiality and will not be able to disclose commercially sensitive or other confidential information to a private equity investor without explicit prior consent from his employer. He will also owe duties to devote the whole of his time and attention to the business of the company that employs him, and so before expending significant time in working on any potential buyout it will be necessary to make full disclosure to the company concerned.

Clear legal advice should be obtained from the outset in order to reduce any risks arising from these potential conflicts. That is important in all deals, but particularly so where the target is a listed company (that is, the deal is a 'take private') where there is a higher degree of regulation, and there is likely to be some 'price sensitive information' that will have to be dealt with responsibly and in accordance with strict legal and regulatory rules.

It is also important for the other members of the board who are not involved in the buyout to take advice in order to ensure they comply with their duties when the possibility of a buyout has been raised. This is especially important where the target is a listed company, since the board will also have obligations under the Takeover Code in these circumstances. A private equity house might originate a buyout, by identifying a potential target (whether publicly listed or private) and seeking to acquire it (either with or without the help of an existing or new management team).

However, it is increasingly common for buyouts – especially larger ones – to be initiated by the seller through an auction process. In this case, the procedure for that auction is usually set by the seller's investment bank.

Business plan

15.17 Once initiated, the buyout process usually starts with the preparation of a business plan for the target. This step is generally implemented by the management of the target or, in the case of an auction, by the seller. The business plan basically describes the current situation of the target and what it could become after completion of the buyout. It is often on the basis of the business plan (in addition to the investment paper drafted by the fund manager – see section 2.1(d)) – that the fund's investment committee takes its provisional decision to continue – or not to continue – with the acquisition.

Due diligence

15.18 Financial, legal and other due diligence is generally undertaken by the private equity fund or its advisers, as on most M&A deals.

Negotiation, signing and closing

15.19 The remainder of the buyout process proceeds like any typical M&A deal (with the variations described in this Chapter), but with the added complexity of the arrangements that have to be reached with the management team, and other finance providers. Those arrangements are the principal subject of the remainder of this Chapter.

The structure of a buyout

The parties involved

The main parties

15.20 As previously mentioned, the fundamental characteristic of a buyout is that one or more financial investors acquire a controlling stake in a business – there is a change of ownership. In many cases, the financial investor(s) will have combined forces with a team of managers before making the acquisition, although this is not always the case.

Glossary

MBO (Management Buyout)	a buyout where the existing management team combine with one or more private equity investors to acquire a target company or business
MBI (Management Buy In)	a buyout where one or more private equity investors combine with a new management team to acquire a target company or business
BIMBO (Buy In Management Buy Out)	a buyout where one or more private equity investors combine with some new and some incumbent managers to acquire a target company or business
IBO (Institutional Buyout) or Bought Deal	a buyout where one or more private equity investors buy a target company or business without a management team, usually with the intention of sourcing a management team after the deal is completed
Club deal	a buyout where more than one private equity investor is involved and are working together to undertake a buyout
PTP (Public to Private) or Take Private	a buyout that involves de-listing a quoted target company, usually involving the added complexity of a public offer to buy the shares in the company from the public
Secondary (or Tertiary or even Quaternary) Buyout	a buyout where the seller is another private equity house exiting from an earlier buyout
PIPEs (Private Investment in Public Equity)	the acquisition of a strategic (but usually minority) stake in a publicly quoted company
IRR or Internal Rate of Return	an industry standard measure of return generated by a private equity backed company or a portfolio of companies making up a fund, measuring the annual returns to investors

In most buyouts, therefore, the main parties are the private equity investor(s), the management team, and the debt holders (including a senior debt provider, and any junior debt providers). In addition, there will be the usual parties to an M&A transaction, most importantly, the seller(s) of the target business. There will also be a range of advisers, including lawyers and accountants, acting for the buyer, the seller and the management team.

For legal and tax reasons (see below), the private equity house and the management team, if there is one, will usually establish a new company to act as the acquirer of the target (commonly referred to as 'Newco'). There may also be additional new companies in the structure – see **Figure 4** for an example of a simplified UK buyout structure. Some or all of those companies will often be parties to the equity documents. The timing of the establishment of Newco, and the subscription of shares by the management team, can be important for tax reasons.

Figure 4 – The Layers of Debt and Equity (Michael Dance)

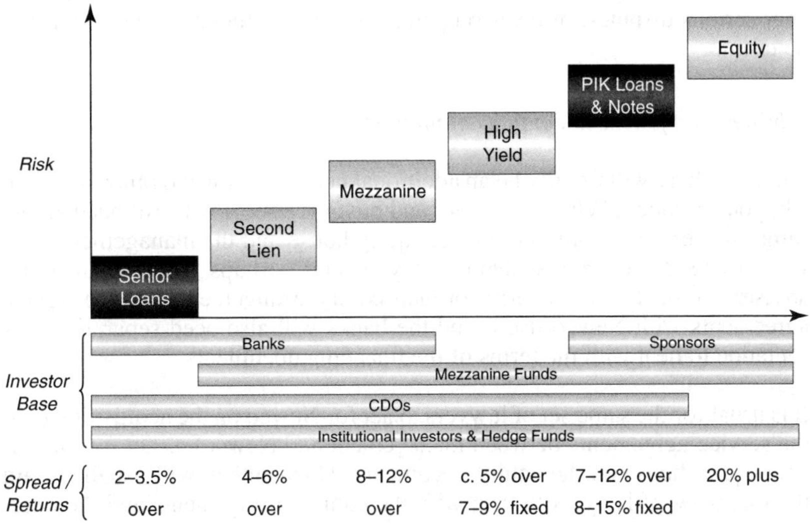

| Spread / | 2–3.5% | 4–6% | 8–12% | c. 5% over | 7–12% over | 20% plus |
| Returns | over | over | over | 7–9% fixed | 8–15% fixed | |

Note: Spreads are approx. and may vary from estimates especially in case of PIK loans and notes

Club deals and syndication

15.21   In many deals, there will be a group of private equity investors coming together to fund the buyout, or the investor who invests at the outset will want to syndicate it to other investors afterwards. The equity documentation (ie the documentation which reflects the financing arrangements of the deal – see **15.32 et seq**) needs to cater for this.

First, there needs to be an ability for the investor to sell down part of the equity and other instruments to any subsequent investors. In addition, it is important to consider the way in which this is going to be done from a tax and legal point of view, to ensure that there are no unnecessary tax costs. Stamp duty is a particular concern, and this could arise if there is a simple transfer from the original investor to the new one. The other main method is for Newco to issue convertible loan notes at the outset, and then to issue new loan notes and/or new shares to the new investor when required. The original notes can then be redeemed from the proceeds.

The other key issue is the way in which the investors relate to each other. There will often be a lead investor who takes a dominant role and exercises all the various investor rights. Behind that, there will usually be a mechanism to facilitate decisions by the investor group, especially where no single investor is clearly dominant. The mechanism can range from consultation obligations on the lead investor, through to a voting mechanism, so that each investor has to be consulted on major investor decisions and has a vote on any decisions taken in proportion to its share of the total investment.

These mechanisms are very important, especially where there are a large number of roughly equal investors; otherwise there is the potential for some very serious disputes, or decision paralysis, when difficult decisions have to be taken.

Advisers and potential conflicts of interest

15.22 There will usually be an additional need for legal and other advice in a buyout situation. Whilst the seller and buyer (Newco) will still need all the same advisers as before, the private equity house and the management team will also need to be represented by lawyers (and, perhaps, financial and other advisers) to deal with the terms of their equity arrangements and the service agreements with Newco itself, and the banks will also need separate representation to deal with the terms of the financing documents.

It is usual for the same set of lawyers to act for Newco on the acquisition (and the service agreements between management and Newco) as act for the private equity house on the equity documents. Management will usually retain their own set of lawyers to deal with the equity arrangements and their service agreements.

With the addition of an extra party – management – there is clearly greater scope for conflicts of interest for the advisers, especially when one set of lawyers will usually be acting for Newco, and therefore in effect both management and the private equity house as joint owners of Newco, and for the private equity house only in relation to the terms of the deal with the investor. Clearly, advisers have to remain vigilant to the risk of conflicts of interest arising and have to deal with them professionally if they do. As long as management have separate advisers looking after their interests, this is not usually a problem.

Structuring considerations

15.23 Structuring a buyout can be a very complicated business, because there are a wide range of tax, regulatory and legal issues which can affect the deal. Some of these are the same as on any M&A deal, but many are peculiar to private equity.

The solutions to these structuring issues will differ according to the jurisdiction concerned and the particular characteristics of the fund and its investors.

Structuring a buyout: the main aims

15.24

- Achieve a tax deduction for debt finance
- Favourable tax treatment: capital gains on exit, and ideally only payable at ultimate investor level

- Minimising employment income taxes
- Minimising withholding taxes
- Structural subordination of junior debt
- Compliance with applicable laws and regulation.

Tax deductibility

15.25 As a general principle, debt is a tax deductible expense for a company and reduces its taxable income, and dividends are not. That principle applies to third party debt (including senior and junior) debt, and to loans provided by shareholders. It is common for some of the private equity finance provided by the private equity house to be structured as loan, as well as equity, and clearly it is helpful for that loan to benefit from a tax deduction.

For third party debt, it is clearly important that the company which borrows the finance to acquire the target has some taxable income against which to offset the interest costs. As Newco will usually not be the main operating company, it is important that the target company is ultimately in the same tax group as Newco, in order to make sure that the interest costs at the top level can be offset against operating income at the lower level.

When looking at the value and free cash within an investment, the liability to tax is clearly an issue that relates to both – cash not sent to the tax authority is extra value for the investors. It also impacts on the serviceability of debt – and therefore the debt capacity of the target. In the UK, there are some restrictions on the deductibility of debt finance, particularly when this is provided by the shareholders rather than a third party – such as the bank – and the structure needs to work within those restrictions to make sure the tax deduction is as large as possible.

The UK restrictions are known as the 'transfer pricing' rules, and apply to transactions between parties that are 'related' under the test laid down by the legislation. In general, parties are 'related' if one of them controls the other, or if they are under common control, and in some cases the interests of certain persons can be combined (in particular, when they are 'acting together in relation to financing of a company'). That means that the rules will apply in many buyout situations, where one or more private equity investors will generally control the acquisition vehicle.

When a 'related party' finances a company with shareholder loan (or other debt) and that company seeks to obtain a tax deduction for the interest on that loan, the tax authorities will only allow the deduction to the extent that the loan is on an 'arm's-length' basis. That means that a deduction will only be available if a third party would have lent that amount to the target company, and at that rate. Certain compensating adjustments are available for UK groups of companies, but these rules are complex, and have to be worked through in every case.

Capital gains on exits

15.26   All shareholders – managers and private equity investors – will usually want to receive a capital gain on exit, rather than proceeds which are subject to income tax. That is, in general, because effective capital gains tax rates tend to be lower than effective income tax rates. This is especially true for management shareholders, who will benefit from a variety of tax reliefs that will make a big difference to their after-tax returns. But it is also true for investors and carried interest holders.

For the shares held by the management team, there are some complex rules introduced in 2003 that need to be navigated. The legislation tries to make sure that any shares given to management shareholders are within the meaning of the term 'employment related'. It is hard to argue that management shares are ever outside this definition, although there are some ways to do so (such as by using LLPs instead of companies).

Just for historical interest: the rules are often referred to as 'Schedule 22', because they were first introduced by *Schedule 22* to the 2003 *Finance Act*. Actually they are now somewhere else entirely – *Part 7* of the *Income Tax (Earnings and Pensions) Act 2003 (ITEPA)* – but the now misleading name has stuck.

The rules, although they apply to all managers' shares, mainly have an impact if the shares are 'restricted' in some way. In practice, of course, that is usually the case. As we shall see, management 'leavers' usually have to give up their shares if they leave, and unless they are good leavers, they usually receive less than market value for them. That constitutes a 'restriction' on the shares that reduces their market value, and so brings them within this regime.

That will mean that when the restrictions fall away – so if the shares vest fully in the manager, or they are sold – employment income tax and national insurance charges will arise. Under these rules, any amounts attributable to the difference between what the shares would have been worth originally if they had no restrictions and what was actually paid for them will be chargeable to tax at 40%, and 1% employee and 12.8% employer national insurance is also triggered.

Not only does that give rise to a problem for the company – which is not at that time getting any value at all, even though it has to collect PAYE tax and pay national insurance – but it also results in more tax being due than would be the case if capital gains tax were payable. In general, if the manager has held the shares for two years or more, the capital gains tax rate (with the benefit of business asset taper relief) will be 10%, and on top of that there may be other capital gains tax reliefs available to reduce the rate even further. No national insurance obligations arise either.

There is a procedure which allows an election to be made when the shares are initially issued to the manager. If the employer and the employee jointly elect to do so, income tax on the difference between the unrestricted value of the shares – the amount they would be worth if they had no restrictions – and what the manager actually pays for them will be payable at the outset, and that then disapplies the rules which would tax subsequent proceeds as employment income. Instead, such proceeds will, if applicable, be eligible for capital gains tax treatment. In practice, private equity houses will want to make that election.

But the election does also raise a difficult question. In the section above we said that, at the time of the election, a manager will pay income tax by reference to the unrestricted value of the shares. The question of course is what that value is.

When these rules came into force, the BVCA worked with HMRC on two 'memoranda of understanding' – agreements about how the rules would be applied[1]. One of these related to carried interest, and the other to management equity. Basically, these MoUs give us a way to value the shares at the outset, allowing an election to be made.

In essence, if the deal meets certain conditions laid down in the MoU, the tax authority will accept that the price that management paid was the amount the 'unrestricted shares' were actually worth. In other words, if the deal is 'MoU compliant', there is no difference between what was paid and what the shares were worth, and so there is no income tax to pay at that time. The election theoretically needs not be made because no amounts can be attributed to the difference between what was paid and the unrestricted market value, provided that HMRC has accepted there is no difference. However, 'protective' elections are common since the MoU is not technically enforceable. Either way, capital gains tax treatment is secure for the future (for example, when restrictions are lifted or when the shares are sold).

There are two 'safe harbours' in the management equity MoU – one applying where there is a ratchet and one applying where there is not. For a deal without a ratchet, these are the most important qualifying features:

- Managers receive ordinary shares with the same basic rights and entitlements as the private equity investor.

- Managers acquire their shares at the same time as the private equity investor.

- Managers pay the same amount for their shares as the private equity investor.

- Managers are properly remunerated.

- Subordinated debt or preference share amounts invested by the private equity house is provided on terms which are not less expensive to the investee company than the most expensive tranche of third party debt.

The last point is important. The interest rate on shareholder debt – or dividends on preference shares if they are being used instead of shareholder loan – must be at least as high as the most expensive third party debt. So if a mezzanine provider is charging 12%, the private equity house's debt must cost the investee company at least that much. The idea is that the manager's returns are not skewed upwards because the private equity house is leaving too much money on the table for the ordinary shareholders. It is taking a commercial return on its investment, and the upside for the managers is therefore more limited.

For deals that have ratchets the rules are basically the same, with a requirement that the ratchet has to operate downwards not upwards. In other words, the entitlement of management must ratchet down if a certain exit value is not achieved, rather than to ratchet up if it is.

1. See the HMRC website *www.hmrc.gov.uk/manuals/ersmmanual/ERSM30520.htm* for a copy of the MoU.

Employment income taxes

15.27 For management shareholders, there is an even bigger problem with income rather than capital gain. There may well be national insurance contributions to pay on the value of the income received, which is also a problem for the investee company, which might then also have to pay employer's national insurance on any such income. That can be a significant additional cost.

Withholding taxes

15.28 These are amounts of tax which have to be paid directly by an investee company to a tax authority so that the recipient of interest or dividends only receives the net amount. There may be ways for the recipient to reclaim the tax or to get a credit for it, but in general it is better to avoid any obligations to withhold tax if at all possible. That can affect the choice of jurisdiction of any holding company, especially on a pan-European deal.

Structural subordination and tax reasons for multiple Newcos

15.29 One reason that there may be multiple companies in the structure (see **Figure 4** above) is that the debt holders may want additional comfort that any claims by more junior debt holders, and the equity holders, are clearly subordinated to any claims that they may have. One way to make this more secure than by just using a contractual subordination arrangement is to insert separate companies, with different layers of debt at different levels. That way, any claims that a senior debt holder may have very clearly rank ahead of more junior creditors, including those providing the shareholder loan.

There may also be tax reasons to separate the shareholder debt and the equity into different companies, especially if they are 'stapled' together[1], which can sometimes lead to an extra company in the structure.

1. In this context, 'stapled' means that the instruments can only ever be dealt with together, in many ways as if they were a single instrument.

Compliance with law and regulation

15.30   As well as tax and legal issues, there may be regulatory issues to deal with. For example, in many funds, a number of the investors will be subject to 'ERISA', which is US legislation applying to certain pension fund investors. In such a case, it will usually be necessary (in order to come within an exemption from the full rigours of the rules) to ensure that the fund which includes the affected investors has 'management rights' over the underlying portfolio company. Those management rights are generally encapsulated in a right to appoint a director to the board, but a special clause is usually used which ensures that the relevant rights are given to the correct investors to satisfy the requirements of the US legislation[1].

There may also be anti-trust issues to contend with which impact the deal structure chosen, or accounting rules that need to be avoided.

1. The ERISA rules were reformed recently, making it easier for private equity funds to rely on a different exemption. Where the fund is relying on that other exemption, as is becoming more common, they will no longer need the 'management rights' referred to here.

Choice of vehicle and jurisdiction

15.31   A key question is where the acquisition vehicle(s) should be based. In a straightforward UK deal, this will almost always be a UK company. But where the investee company – or its management team – is based outside the UK, or where it is pan-European, it may be advantageous to consider a location other than the one that otherwise seems natural. There may be a good reason to put it somewhere with a favourable tax regime, such as Luxembourg.

The next critical analysis that has to be done is to consider what type of income is likely to be generated. In most cases, the main cash is likely to be generated by way of a capital gain on exit, but some investments – especially those that have a longer time horizon like infrastructure assets – may also produce significant amounts of income on an ongoing basis. The nature of the likely cash outflows will be an important question in deciding which vehicle to use.

The other key question is what type of investors there are in the fund. Are they tax exempt, like pension funds? Are they based in countries with a good network of tax treaties? The reality is that there is likely to be a mix, and advisers will have to devise a structure that works well for all or most of them.

In considering the various potential vehicles, the advantages and disadvantages of each need to be considered. In summary, the answer is usually – for a UK deal – that you will use one or more UK based Newcos, structured as private companies. There may also be an offshore company (often Luxembourg) in the structure to ensure that there is no withholding tax on any interest payments. However, for non-domestic deals, or those that produce lots of income on an ongoing basis, other corporate structures may be appropriate.

Type of vehicle	Advantages	Disadvantages
UK private company	Subject to Companies Acts rules but not subject to the strict regulatory framework governing public companies. Liability of shareholders is limited. Shares are unlisted – a number of tax advantages e.g. any share in an unlisted trading company is a business asset for taper relief purposes. Shares in unlisted companies qualify for 100% relief from inheritance tax (subject to two-year ownership requirement). Eligible to form a tax group with other companies.	Potential double taxation: at level of company and in hands of shareholders on distributions.
UK public company (plc)	Liability of shareholders is limited. Eligible to form a tax group with other companies.	Subject to stricter regulatory framework, including prohibition on 'financial assistance'. Tax – shares in listed company only qualify for business asset taper relief if held by officer or employee or if 5% stake owned. Shares in listed company only qualify for business property relief from inheritance tax if the holding owned is sufficient to give control of the company. Potential double taxation – at level of company and in hands of shareholders on distributions.
UK Limited Liability Partnership (LLP)	Tax transparent for UK purposes (income and gains attributed to individual members and not taxed at partnership level). Treated as bodies corporate but have internal flexibility of a partnership. LLP member taxed as self-employed, so no employer NIC liability.	Members taxed on LLP profits whether or not profits distributed. LLP cannot offer incentives e.g. EMI, share option schemes. Cannot establish occupational pension scheme for members. LLP cannot form a group with another company (except for VAT purposes).
Luxembourg SICAR	Flexible and tax-favoured vehicle for investment in risk bearing capital. Regulated in a flexible way and largely exempt from tax, but with access to benefits of Luxembourg tax treaty network and EU parent/ subsidiary directive.	Can only be used for investment in assets that represent an element of risk. Currently subject to investigation by the European Commission on the basis that it constitutes an illegal state aid.

Type of vehicle	Advantages	Disadvantages
Luxembourg SICAV	Corporate structure with limited liability with variable capital depending upon its net assets.	Subject to various investment and gearing restrictions.
Dutch BV	Private limited company. Liability of shareholders is limited. Access to benefits of the Netherlands' tax treaty network and EU parent/ subsidiary directive	Shares in a BV are not freely transferable. Tax obstacles: taxation arises in various ways when payments are made by the Dutch holding company to the fund, and exemption from taxes may lead to difficult interpretation and uncertainty.

Key legal documents

15.32   When documenting a buyout, there are, of course, all the usual documents associated with an M&A transaction: including an acquisition agreement, with associated warranties and disclosures. In many ways, those documents are unaffected by the fact that the acquisition vehicle is a new company which is financed by private equity investors, although there are some differences which are discussed below (see **15.61 et seq**).

However, in addition to those documents, there will be a number of other documents that will be needed to reflect the financing arrangements of the deal. These are commonly referred to as the 'equity documents'. In addition to those, there will be the financing documents dealing with the various layers of debt finance that are being provided to Newco.

If an M&A deal can be compared to a divorce, in that the parties are making arrangements for the separation of the target company from its present owner, then the equity and financing documents on a buyout can, perhaps, be compared to a marriage. While in many cases (although not all, especially if transitional services are required or there is some form of vendor finance in place) the seller of the target business and the new owner will have very little or no ongoing relationship, the management team, the private equity investors and the banks and other providers of debt finance have to establish the terms for their future lives together. Therefore, as well as dealing with the terms of the investment and lending arrangements, the documents also have to set out the framework for future decision-making about the business and the role of each party in the way the business is run. It is important that they operate fairly between the parties in order to ensure that the relationship does not break down as soon as an issue arises.

The two most important equity documents will be the Investment Agreement and the Articles of Association of Newco, or equivalent constitutional document in other countries.

The Investment Agreement – Form

15.33   Although these documents can vary in style and content, a typical Investment Agreement is likely to follow the following format:

Parties	Generally the parties will be the Newco(s), the private equity investors and the management team members.
Definitions	This section will include a list of all defined terms used in the document.
Subscription	This will include details of the number and type of instruments to be subscribed by the private equity house and management team, including any shares and loan notes. The actual terms of the shares and loan notes will be dealt with elsewhere.
Conditions Precedent	Any conditions that have to be satisfied before completion of the private equity investors' investment, often listed in a Schedule, and including satisfaction of any conditions relating to financing, the entry into by management of service agreements and applications to subscribe for their shares.
Completion	Setting out the arrangements for completion of the investment, which will include board meetings and general meetings of the Newco(s) to approve and enter into the service agreements, to issue the shares and loan notes to the private equity house and managers, and to appoint the board of directors.
Warranties	The warranties to be given by the management team to the private equity investors, which will usually be included in a schedule, and the limitations on the liability of the management team members.
Board of Directors	Provisions relating to the membership and operation of the board of directors of Newco, including details of the committees to be formed by the board (commonly an audit and remuneration committee is required), and arrangements relating to the frequency of board meetings and the required notice period and quorum. There will usually also be a provision allowing the investors(s) to appoint one or more persons to the board (often including a non-executive Chairman) and/or to appoint one or more observers.
Financial information	This section will deal with the investors' rights to receive management accounts and other regular financial reports on the company and its progress, and to receive copies of audited accounts and any proposed business plans. There may also be rights for the investor(s) to appoint independent accountants to examine the state of the company's finances.
Consent matters	There will usually be a list of matters (often set out in a schedule) that the company is not permitted to do without the consent of the investor(s). These will generally be major strategic matters, rather than day-to-day management.
Restrictive covenants	The management team will usually agree to certain restrictive covenants, which (for legal reasons referred to below) generally appear in the investment agreement as well as in their service agreements. These will prevent them from soliciting employees,

	customers etc and from competing with the business for a certain period after they leave it.
Undertakings	The managers will also typically give some undertakings to the investor(s) on a variety of matters, including an undertaking to vote any shares that they own, and to act as directors of the company, in such a way as to give effect to the provisions of the investment agreement, to take out and maintain appropriate insurances and to take action to enforce certain documents in the manner requested by the investor(s).
ERISA	If there is a requirement for 'management rights' to ensure that the investment comes within the relevant exemption from ERISA (see above), a clause will usually be included in the agreement to that effect.
Transfers of shares	There will usually be severe restrictions on the disposal of shares by members of the management team.
Assignment	Generally the managers will not be permitted to assign their rights under the investment agreement, but the investor(s) will usually be allowed to do so when they have transferred their shares.
Exit	There will often be a non-binding statement of intent that the parties intend to work towards a trade sale or flotation of the company within a specified period, and a non-binding agreement to work together to achieve that aim.
Deed of adherence	There will usually be provisions stating that any new shareholder in the company must agree to adhere to the investment agreement.
Miscellaneous	There will be a variety of 'boilerplate' provisions, which will include sections dealing with confidentiality, announcements, termination, costs and expenses, entire agreement, amendments, further assurance, counterparts, notices, further assurance, governing law and jurisdiction.
Schedules	These will usually give further details of the Newco(s) and the other parties, list the conditions to completion and completion matters, the consent matters and the detailed warranties and indemnities, and the form of the deed of adherence.

Articles – Form

15.34   The Articles (or other constitutional document of Newco outside the UK) will usually follow the following format:

Definitions	The defined terms will usually be listed at the beginning of the document.
Table A	The articles will specify which articles from Table A (the default articles which would otherwise apply to the company) will be disapplied. Often, all that is used is a statement that the Table A in force when the company was formed will apply except to the extent excluded or modified by the articles.

Share capital	The amount of the company's authorised share capital, and the number, nominal value and designation of the various classes of shares.
Dividend rights	The rights attaching to the various classes of shares to receive dividends, including any rights for preference shareholders to a dividend in priority to any ordinary shareholders, which will usually accrue (with interest) if it is not paid annually.
Capital	The rights to participate in the company's capital for each of the various classes of shares, and the order of priority for any such payments.
Redemption	If any shares are to be redeemable (as is commonly the case for preference shares, when used instead of shareholder loan), the dates and mechanism for redemption are set out.
Voting	Usually the ordinary shareholders will have one vote for every share, and the preference shares will not carry any rights to vote. If the company is in default of its obligations under the investment agreement or the financing documents, or preference dividends or coupons on shareholder loan cannot be paid, there may be rights for the investors to take voting control of the company (whether through their preference shares or their holding of ordinary shares).
Class rights	This establishes whether the rights attaching to the different classes of shares issued to managers and to the investor(s) can be changed only by separate votes of those classes, or by a general vote of all shareholders.
Issue of shares	There will usually be rights of pre-emption for existing shareholders before any new shares can be issued by the company, although there may be exceptions; for example, if a 'rescue issue' is needed to capitalise the company when it is in default of its obligations or at risk of becoming so. The investor will have to consent to any such issue.
Transfers of shares	There will usually be severe restrictions on the transfer of shares by members of the management team. The definition of 'transfer' is likely to be broad to ensure that any transfer of beneficial interest, as well as transfers of legal title, are prohibited. There are also likely to be pre-emption rights applying on transfers of shares by the management team. The investors will probably be permitted to transfer shares more freely, especially to other investment funds or to their own investors.
Compulsory transfers of shares	Provisions will require management shareholders to transfer their shares if they leave the company, the price at which they are required to sell them depending on the circumstances in which they leave.
Drag along and Tag along rights	The investor will have the right to force management shareholders to sell if a buyer for the whole of the company has been identified ('drag along rights'), and there may also be an obligation for an investor who is selling to also procure that other shareholders are able to sell their own shares at the same time and on the same terms ('tag along rights').

General meetings and resolutions	The quorum for general meetings will generally include at least one investor representative, and the shareholders will usually be permitted to use written resolutions.
Directors and board meetings	There will be provisions stipulating the quorum board meetings (usually including one director nominated by the investor(s)), the notice requirements and provisions allowing telephone board meetings to take place and written resolutions to be passed. The right for the investor(s) to nominate one or more directors may be included in the articles as well as (or instead of) in the investment agreement (it being generally easier to enforce in the articles). These provisions will also typically deal with removal of directors, alternate directors (who can act in place of the directors) and indemnification of directors).
Miscellaneous	There will be other provisions dealing with a number of other matters of company law or company administration (for example, the Article in Table A dealing with notices to shareholders will often be modified).

Financing documents

15.35   The other important category of documents are the financing documents that will be put in place with the banks and other providers of debt finance. Perhaps the most important of these is the Facilities Agreement, which will include the terms of the senior debt, including the conditions to the drawdown of the loan, and the financial covenants that the company will be required to comply with (see **15.36** below). There will also be an Intercreditor Deed, which will govern the priorities of the various lenders to enforce their rights, and security documents (including a debenture) taking fixed and floating charges over the assets of the target company.

Financial covenants in loan documentation

15.36   The Facilities Agreement will include a number of financial covenants with which the company will be required to comply on an ongoing basis. Breach of these covenants can result in the loan becoming immediately repayable, so it is very important that the company considers carefully whether it will be able to meet the various ratios on an ongoing basis.

The usual starting point for the financial covenants will be those recommended by the Loan Market Association ('LMA'), who have recently released a set of covenants to be used in conjunction with their model leveraged facility agreement.

As the LMA suggests in their Users Guide to the financial covenant provisions, the recommended ratios (which the company covenants to maintain) represent those most often seen in European leveraged finance acquisition facilities and include the following:

- Cashflow Cover, which measures Cashflow to Debt Service and indicates the ability of the borrowing group to produce adequate cash to cover its debt servicing costs (including any scheduled amortisation).

- Interest Cover, which measures EBITDA to Finance Charges and is indicative of the ability of the borrowing group to produce enough operating profits before tax to service aggregate interest, fees, and other finance charges/payments. There is a further ratio, which looks at Senior Interest Cover and relates to transactions where there is mezzanine or other junior debt and only Senior Finance Charges are relevant.

- Leverage, which measures Total Debt to EBITDA and indicates borrowing group debt to pre-tax operating profit before deducting interest, fees and other finance charges/payments. Again, there is a further option to use a Senior Leverage ratio where there is a mezzanine or other junior debt component and only Senior Total Debt is relevant.

- Capital Expenditure, where limits are set for each Financial Year.

In each case, there may be additional complexity included in the formula (for example, to reflect whether it is calculated on a 'net' or 'adjusted' basis).

Before the security documents can be entered into, it will usually be necessary to go through a 'financial assistance whitewash' in the UK. Financial assistance issues are particularly important on a buyout because the debt incurred by Newco in order to fund the acquisition will almost always be secured on the assets of the target company and its subsidiaries. To give that security would generally constitute financial assistance, which is (at present[1]) prohibited by *section 151* of the *Companies Act 1985*. Therefore, a 'whitewash' will be required, using the procedure set out in *sections 155–158* of the 1985 Act, which will permit the target company to enter into a guarantee of Newco's obligations, and provide security for that guarantee.

1. The *Companies Act 2006* has abolished the prohibition on financial assistance for private companies, but that change is not in force yet (January 2007).

Service agreements

15.37   There will also be a number of other ancillary documents that will be required to give effect to the equity and financing arrangements of the buyout. Perhaps the most significant of these, at least so far as management is concerned, will be their service agreements, which will record the terms of their employment relationship with Newco.

The service agreement will not differ materially from any usual employment agreement, and will include details of salary and benefits, restrictive covenants applying on termination, notice periods and so on. In a buyout, however, given the dual nature of the relationship of a member of the management team with Newco (that is, shareholder and employee) it is particularly important, from Newco's perspective, to ensure that any compensation following from a potential wrongful termination of the employment relationship does not include any losses incurred as a result of the leaver provisions in the Investment Agreement/Articles. Typically, the Investment Agreement or the Articles will provide that an executive must give up his shares on the termination of his employment with Newco (see **15.33** and **15.34** above).

In order to avoid liability for any loss suffered in respect of the early release of shares, Newco should first ensure that the fact of the shareholding is, as far as is possible, kept separate from the employment relationship. The service agreements and the investment documents should therefore be stand-alone: specifically, the provision of the shares should not be set out as an entitlement in the service agreement.

Second, the service agreement would usually include what is known as a discretionary pay in lieu of notice clause (a 'discretionary PILON'). This clause permits Newco to dismiss the executive immediately by making a payment rather than permitting him or her to work out the notice period. The inclusion of a discretionary PILON means that Newco has the option of an immediate dismissal, without being in breach of the terms of the service agreement. Where there is no breach of the service agreement, there is no wrongful dismissal, and thus any argument about wrongful dismissal compensation will not arise. (Of course, the executive may well have a statutory claim for unfair dismissal, and the right to bring such a claim cannot be excluded or limited other than by way of a compromise agreement: however unfair dismissal claims are of less concern as compensation is currently capped at £60,600, based on financial losses). The actual wording of the PILON clause should be considered carefully: specifically, it is possible to limit the value of the PILON itself by calculating this by reference to salary only, or potentially also including the value of specific benefits during what would have been the notice period. In a management buyout situation, any losses arising as a result of the early sale or release of shares on the termination of the employment should be excluded from the calculation of the PILON.

Finally, both the service agreement and the investment documentation should also include a catch-all provision that makes it clear that damages for any breach of contract by the company (for example, on a wrongful termination) will not include any damages for loss resulting from any obligation to transfer shares for less than market value under any 'leaver' provisions in the Articles or the Investment Agreement (a 'Micklefieldclause'). There is some debate as to whether such an exclusion clause is enforceable or subject to the *Unfair Contract Terms Act 1977*. Currently, in England and Wales, a clause such as this in the Investment Agreement or the Articles will be upheld, provided that the Investment Agreement or the Articles is a 'primary' agreement and not collateral to the service agreement – this was established by the Micklefield case itself[1]. However, the position is different in Scotland, where UCTA does apply to securities contracts, and such a clause has been held to be unenforceable[2].

The simplest way to limit liability for wrongful dismissal compensation is to include a properly drafted and appropriate discretionary pay in lieu of notice clause in the service agreement itself: this means that there is no wrongful dismissal, and so no compensation for wrongful dismissal, which renders any argument about the quantum of such compensation academic.

1. *Micklefield v SAC Technology Ltd* [1990] IRLR 218.
2. *Chapman v Aberdeen Construction Group plc* [1991] IRLR 505.

The main terms of a buyout

15.38   It is possible to separate the main terms of the equity documents into three distinct categories: (a) the investment itself, and its terms; (b) the historical position of the target company; and (c) the ongoing relationship between the management team and the private equity house. We shall deal with each in turn.

The investment

15.39   One important set of terms will relate to the way in which the private equity investors and the management team make their investment in Newco.

The management stake

15.40   Most obviously, a key term to be negotiated at the outset will be the proportion of the shares in Newco that are subscribed by the management group and the price that management will pay for those shares. Usually a private equity house will require a management team to invest some money into Newco, but they will not usually be required to invest in the full 'strip' of equity and loan notes (or preference shares), so their overall 'return' will be greater than that received by the investor(s), albeit with a higher level of risk. For tax reasons (see **15.26** above), management will usually pay the same price for their ordinary shares as the investors do. Their ordinary shares are sometimes referred to as 'sweet equity' because it is not combined with an obligation to subscribe other instruments which have a capped return.

The result of the negotiations on the size of management's stake will depend very much on the circumstances, but an MBO team that have initiated the deal would expect (all other things being equal) a greater stake than a buy-in team in a deal initiated by the private equity investor.

The fund investment

15.41   At the very least, the private equity house will want to make sure that, on its base case assumptions for the business and its exit valuation, they achieve their targeted return on the investment. As a very general rule of thumb, that would be between two and three times their investment and an annualised return of around 20% or higher. Again, as a very general guide, management could expect to target ten times their investment, but less (perhaps five times) if they were rolling over part of their proceeds from a previous buyout (see below). Of course, the returns actually achieved may be more or less than these 'targets'.

As discussed above (see **15.25**), the investor(s) will usually try to invest some of their 'strip' by way of shareholder loan so that a deduction for the interest on the loan can be obtained by Newco. However, in some cases they will use preference shares instead of (or as well as) loan notes. The decision here is usually tax driven, and has little effect on management. In either case, the use of instruments which have priority over those taken by management gives the investors some additional downside protection – they will get the bulk of their money back before the ordinary shareholders are entitled to any proceeds.

It is also typical to differentiate the ordinary shares by designating them separately as 'A' and 'B' ordinary shares (or as 'ordinary' and 'preferred ordinary' shares) and by issuing one class to management and the other to the investor(s). This allows the shares to include slightly different rights – for example, the transfer provisions which apply to management's shares are likely to differ from those that apply to the investor.

Ratchets

15.42 The deal may also include a 'ratchet', which is a mechanism to allow management's proportionate entitlement to proceeds to increase if the base case return expectations are exceeded. For tax reasons (see **15.26** above), the ratchet will often operate so that the proportion of ordinary shares that management holds starts at the highest possible entitlement under the terms of the ratchet, and then reduces according to the returns actually received. This is typically achieved by a conversion of some of management's ordinary shares into worthless deferred shares.

The historical position

Warranties

15.43 As in any normal M&A transaction, the buyer (in this case, Newco) will usually expect a full set of warranties from the seller of the business (although see below in relation to secondary buyouts). These warranties are primarily aimed at price protection – meaning that a claim will arise if the buyer paid too much for the business because there was something wrong with it of which it was unaware.

However, in a buyout, the private equity investor will usually also expect to get warranties from the management team. The main purpose of these warranties is not price protection – it is, in any case, unlikely that the management team will have sufficient personal wealth to meet a substantial claim (and, if the investment is performing poorly, there will be little value in setting off warranty claims against their shares or loan notes). Here the private equity investor is more concerned to ensure that the management team has made full disclosure to it of all material information, and has taken all reasonable care in preparing any business plans or projections on which the investor is relying.

The warranties in the investment agreement are therefore likely to be much shorter than those in the acquisition agreement, and will focus on information provided by management to the investor and used by them in determining the terms of their investment. Clearly management will not provide any guarantees of future performance, but will usually be willing to say that they have prepared their business plans diligently and have made appropriate disclosure to the investors. In situations where management have greater knowledge of the target company than the investor (for example, on an MBO), managers may also be asked to warrant some of the due diligence material and report. Where the seller is resisting full warranty protection because the management team had greater knowledge of the business than it did, then increased reliance may be placed upon the management team warranties which would therefore be more extensive. In some cases, there may be a general warranty that management are not aware of any matter that would constitute a breach of warranty under the acquisition agreement.

As well as the management team, Newco is sometimes also asked to provide warranties. This may give the investor some additional rights to make recovery in the event that the investment is a complete failure but there are some proceeds available after the secured lenders have been repaid out of which a warranty claim could be met.

Limitations of liability

15.44   A key focus for the negotiations between the management team and the private equity house, apart from the extent of the warranties, will be the limitations on liability that go with them. As a general rule, the investor will be satisfied with a limit that is reasonable in the context of a manager's personal wealth. The level of personal wealth is important, because the investor wants to make sure that the amount is sufficient to act as a real incentive to the manager to make full disclosure and to be as diligent as possible in preparing forward looking information. Therefore, the amount may be related to the salary level under the service contract (around three times salary would be typical), but should also take account of other assets that the manager has (if any), including any proceeds that are being extracted from the deal itself – which is especially important in a secondary buyout where some cash is being taken out by a continuing management team.

The warranties will also be subject to similar limitations as those which apply to the acquisition warranties, and a time limit which is usually related to one or two full audits of the company to allow the investors to make a reasonable assessment of whether they have a claim. There will also be provisions (again, similar to those in the acquisition agreement) providing for the way in which claims have to be made and prosecuted.

Joint and several liability

15.45   One area for debate is the extent to which the management team are a 'team', and are all jointly and severally liable for warranty claims, or whether they should only be liable for their own proportion of any loss sustained. Generally, the investor will want joint and several liability, meaning that a claim for the full amount of any loss can be recovered from any of the warrantors, but with a right for that manager to seek a contribution from the others. In many cases, the warrantors will enter into a separate contribution agreement between themselves to govern their respective share of any claims, but this will not affect the right of the investor to pursue a claim for the full amount against any one or more of them.

The ongoing relationship

15.46   A large part of the equity documentation will be concerned with regulating the ongoing relationship between the private equity house, the management team, and Newco.

The board of Newco

15.47   An important set of clauses will concern the composition and duties of the board, and other key corporate governance mechanisms. Although the private equity investor(s) will commonly have a majority shareholding position in the company, they will not want to be involved in the day-to-day operation of the company – at least not on an ongoing basis. For an initial period after the deal (while formulating and executing a '100-day plan'), the investor(s) may be quite heavily involved with the company, and at certain difficult periods during the company's life (for example, if a key member of the management team is removed or leaves the company) it might also be necessary for the investor to take a 'hands on' role. But for most of the time, the investor(s) will typically appoint one or more non-executive directors to the board, and may appoint an independent non-executive chairman, and will then only get involved in board level decisions and key strategic matters.

Establishment of the board, and putting in place some of the key structures through which it will operate – usually including an audit and remuneration committee – will therefore be important.

The Chairman

15.48   Private equity houses are often said to be better at effecting necessary changes to their investee companies, including to the management team, than shareholders of listed companies. One of the reasons for this is that they are more actively involved in the business and are more likely to identify underperformance earlier than shareholders in a listed company are able to do. However, in order for them to be able to identify and carry through the necessary changes they will often rely on a good independent Chairman, part of whose role will be to monitor the performance of the management team, and to provide stability and continuity at times of traumatic change. The ability to appoint a strong Chairman is therefore usually important to a private equity investor.

THE 3I BUYOUT BOARD MODEL (SOURCE: 3I)

15.49   As a guide, at 3i the expected roles of the investor, the Chairman and the executive team in a buyout are as follows:

Investor	Chairman	Executive team
Sets/agrees investment strategy	Implements investment strategy/exit	Develop business plan
Establishes legal ground rules	Judges the executive team on operational/financial performance	Deliver business plan
Focuses on: Value Chairman performance Operational performance	Responsible for management change	Maintain financial and operational integrity
Puts in place: Incentives for delivery Monitoring/review mechanisms		
Initiates change of chairman & use of legals		

Directors' duties and 'consent matters'

15.50   It will be very important for the director(s) nominated by the investor(s) to understand their legal obligations to Newco. Where (as in the UK) they have been appointed to sit on a unitary board (as opposed to the supervisory board in a two-tiered structure) then, even though they have been nominated to the board by a majority shareholder, they still owe the same fiduciary obligations to the company as any other director. That means that they could find themselves liable to the company – or to its creditors following an insolvent liquidation – if they have not complied with their legal duties. The most important of those duties is probably to act in good faith in the best interests of the company, and that can sometimes create conflicts of interest; for example, if the interests of the investor are not the same as the interests of the company. It is critical that the directors recognise when such conflicts arise, and deal with them responsibly.

In most cases, the investor has – as a shareholder – a right to prevent the company from taking any major strategic steps without prior consent. This list of 'consent matters' is usually included as a schedule to the investment agreement, and includes most decisions that are not day-to-day management – see the following example.

Example: some typical consent matters

> The following are the types of action that the board is typically not allowed to undertake without specific consent from the investor(s).

(Note that this list is not exhaustive and is illustrative only.) Typically it applies to Newco, and to all of its subsidiaries.

- Alter the share capital, issue or redeem shares or grant share options outside of agreed share option schemes.

- Pay dividends or otherwise distribute income or capital to shareholders.

- Change the company's constitution.

- Enter into major transactions (usually those greater than a specified value or which, in aggregate, exceed a specified value over a 12-month period), subscribe for or buy shares in other companies or sell the company's business and assets or a significant part of it.

- List the company on a stock market.

- Liquidate the company or enter into any formal or informal insolvency procedure.

- Make material changes to the business, its countries of operation, or undertake any act which is outside its ordinary course of business.

- Change the auditors, bankers, accounting reference date or accounting policies (except as recommended by the auditors).

- Enter into any mortgages or charges, factor debts, give guarantees or indemnities or make loans.

- Incur capital expenditure beyond certain financial limits.

- Appoint or terminate the appointment of senior employees (usually identified by reference to annual salary), or change their terms of employment.

- Appoint additional directors.

- Engage in significant litigation (other than ordinary course of business debt collection).

- Enter into long-term or onerous contracts.

- Establish or materially alter a pension scheme.

As a shareholder, the investor is free to use that right freely and owes no fiduciary duties in relation to the way it is exercised. It is usually important, where there is a conflict of interest for the nominated director, that this separate shareholder approval mechanism is used to prevent the company from proceeding in the way proposed, rather than through the board processes.

Following the decision in *Russell v Northern Bank* ([1992] 3 All ER 161), which said that a company may not fetter its statutory powers to undertake certain actions, it is common for the consent rights to be a matter of agreement between the investor and the management team only in the Investment Agreement (without the company being a party to that clause), so that management agree to procure that the company will not do any of the restricted matters without consent. To the extent that the company undertakes not to do these things, it is better for it to do so in a separate, severable clause. It may also be advisable to remove from the list of matters to which the company agrees those matters which constitute 'statutory powers', such as the right to increase share capital and issue shares (which was the right at issue in the *Russell* case).

Example: conflicts of interest for the nominated director

The most common way in which a conflict of interest arises for a nominated director is where the course of action that is most advantageous for the company is not in the best interests of the investor(s) that he or she represents. For example, an issue of new shares, where the company needs additional finance to expand but the investor neither wants to provide it nor wants its own shareholding to be diluted.

Observers

15.51 In some cases, especially where the company is in financial difficulties and there are liability concerns, the investor(s) may decide not to appoint a director to the board. Invariably they will also have the right to appoint 'observers' as well as or instead of directors, and if they take this right up the appointed observer has a right to notice of board meetings, to the board papers and to attend, but not vote at, board meetings. In such a case, especially if the motivation for doing this is to avoid legal liabilities, then it is very important that the director does not become a 'shadow director', by frequently influencing the board's decisions. A 'shadow director' is defined in *section 741(2)* of the *Companies Act 1985* as 'a person in accordance with whose directions or instructions the directors of the company are accustomed to act'.

Information rights

15.52 The private equity investor will also expect to receive regular information on Newco and its subsidiaries. These information rights will be included in the investment agreement, and will include rights to receive detailed management accounts on a regular (usually monthly) basis, comparisons to budget, audited accounts and business plans. The investors will usually also want regular reports on compliance with the covenants in the banking documents.

Investors usually have the right to send their own nominated accountants to inspect the books of the company, and to prepare the information to which they are entitled if it is not provided.

Sales and transfers of shares

15.53 As noted above, an important aspect of a private equity investor's approach to investing is the desire to ensure that, so far as possible, the interests of the management team and the investors are aligned. That is one of the reasons why buyouts are usually characterised by a relatively high level of share ownership by managers, who tend to see most of their return only on exit and who will usually only take a relatively modest salary from the company.

That also explains why transfers of shares by management are so closely regulated by the articles of association. There are two distinct aspects to that regulation. First, managers are not generally allowed to sell or transfer their shares (other than to family trusts or other tax planning devices) before an exit is achieved. Secondly, there will be provisions requiring managers to sell their shares if they cease to be employed by the portfolio company. These provisions are designed to ensure that the managers remain fully incentivised until the investors achieve their exit, and to avoid external shareholders becoming involved with the company.

So far as the prohibition on share transfers is concerned, it will usually be acceptable to the investors for the managers to transfer their shares to a trust established for the benefit of their family, or to other immediate family members, in order to take advantage of any tax planning opportunities that may exist. However, it will be important that the list of 'permitted transferees' is kept as limited as possible, to avoid undue complexity and outside interference, and it is also important for the documents to include a mechanism to ensure that the shares can be recovered from their 'owner' if the manager concerned leaves the company.

The restrictions on transfer of shares by the investor group will usually be less severe, and will often allow (again, by way of 'permitted transfers') for transfers that facilitate administration of the fund, or the sale of the investment to a new investor in a secondary portfolio sale. It is also important that any changes in investors in the fund itself do not fall within any share transfer restrictions or trigger the pre-emption procedures. This can be a problem, for example, where the fund is a limited partnership and there is a change in the identity of the partners in that fund. Unless the articles have been carefully drafted, such a technical change in the composition of the fund could fall foul of a prohibition on transfer, or result in a requirement to go through pre-emption.

Leavers

15.54 For managers that leave the company (including by reason of death or permanent incapacity), or whose contract of employment is terminated by the company, there will be a mechanism requiring them to sell their shares. There may be circumstances (especially on a secondary buyout) when the managers are able to argue that some of their shares have 'vested' prior to the buyout, and that they should be able to keep those even if they leave the company. Generally, however, the debate will focus not on whether manager shares have to be sold, but at what price.

The price paid for a departing manager's shares will usually depend on the circumstances in which he leaves, and when. A 'good leaver' will typically be paid a higher price for his shares than a 'bad leaver'; typically a good leaver will get 'market value', determined by an independent valuation (if the value cannot be agreed), while a 'bad leaver' will get the lower of: i) the price paid for the shares and ii) their current market value. Clearly, there may be a very substantial difference between these prices.

Typically, a 'good leaver' will be someone who dies or is permanently incapacitated, or perhaps who leaves on some other pre-agreed basis, and anyone else who departs before exit will be treated as a 'bad' leaver. Sometimes the length of service of the leaver may be a factor in determining whether he or she is treated as a good or bad leaver. In that case, there may be a vesting schedule stipulating that some shares have to be sold at market value and others at the lower of cost and market value; over time, the proportion of the shares that are sold at market value increases to reflect the longer length of service (and, presumably, the greater contribution made by the leaver to any increase in value of the shares).

Generally, a leaver's shares will be offered to other members of the management through the normal pre-emption procedure (see below), but usually the investors will have the right to stipulate that they should be reserved for a new (often replacement) manager or to direct that they be repurchased by the company or transferred to an employee trust.

In order to secure the operation of the forced sale rights, the investor usually requires that Newco is appointed as the managers' attorney.

Drag along rights

15.55   In order to be able to achieve the exit that is so important to the private equity investor, it will generally require a 'drag along right' in the articles, which will enable it to force the management shareholders to sell their shares in the event that the investor finds a buyer for the entire share capital.

The way that this clause generally operates is to require the investor to issue a notice to the management shareholders requiring them to sell their shares to the prospective buyer at the same time and on similar terms to those agreed by the investor. It is important to think carefully about what terms the management team are obliged to accept, and whether they have to be identical to the terms being offered to the investor.

The enforceability of drag along clauses is not beyond doubt, and it is very important to ensure that the terms of the drag along are very clearly laid out, and that they operate fairly on the management team, in order to improve the chances that a court will enforce them.

Tag along rights

15.56 The articles will also usually include provisions to ensure that, if the investor transfers some or all of their shares to a third party (that is, achieves an exit or partial exit), then it is also required to procure that the same buyer offers to buy all or the same proportion of management's shares on the same terms. Here again, there is a desire to ensure that interests are aligned; in this case, the investor is committing not to exit the company without achieving a similar result for the management group.

Pre-emption provisions

15.57 Unless transfers of shares are 'permitted transfers' by management or the investors, and when they are not prohibited by the other sale restrictions, a sale will usually be subject to an obligation to first offer the sale shares to the other shareholders, usually with those in the same class having the first right of refusal. These provisions are usually triggered when a manager is forced to sell shares because he or she has left the company (see above), but they apply more generally to other sales as well.

Positive covenants by management

15.58 The investment agreement will typically include some positive covenants or undertakings on the part of the managers. The list of matters to which the managers will agree may include taking out suitable insurance for the company, protecting its intellectual property, maintaining key man insurances and using their powers of voting to ensure that all obligations of the management group and the company in the equity and financing documents are met.

Restrictive covenants

15.59 The investment agreement is likely to include covenants by the management team that restrict them from competing with the company while employed by it, and from taking actions that could damage it for a period (often between one and two years) afterwards. These post-termination covenants will typically restrict them from:

- competing with the company;
- damaging the goodwill of the company;
- soliciting, or dealing with, customers, suppliers, agents and distributors of the business;
- soliciting key employees.

Restrictive covenants of this type have to be drafted carefully, because as a matter of public policy they will be held to be void as a restraint of trade unless they go no further than necessary to protect legitimate business interests, and are reasonable in scope, balancing the interests of the company against those of the individual concerned. In particular, the courts will only uphold such post-employment restrictions if they prevent competition which is unfair: such clauses cannot be used to prevent competition per se. Therefore the time limit of the restrictions, their geographical scope and their ambit (particularly in terms of the restricted activities) should be considered on a case-by-case basis. For example, a blanket obligation not to poach staff is unlikely to be enforceable as it is unlikely that where an executive solicits a more junior employee to take up new employment, for example, this could amount to unfair competition. A restriction which is, however, limited to key employees of the business whose presence is necessary for the business to continue to operate effectively, and with whom the former executive has had personal dealings, is more likely to be enforceable, as it is clearly limited, and potentially reasonable.

Covenants of this type are also likely to appear in the directors' service agreements, but there is case law[1] which makes it clear that they are more likely to be enforceable in the context of investment arrangements with the management team, as there is more likely to be equality of bargaining power between the parties, dealing as they are as commercial parties. Another reason for including them here is that they are likely to be enforceable even if the employer has committed a breach of the service agreement (for example, by terminating without notice), even though the covenants in the service agreement itself may not remain enforceable in those circumstances[2].

1. *Systems Reliability Holdings plc v Smith* [1990] IRLR 377 (17-month restriction upheld following a business sale by a majority shareholder); also, for example: *Dawnay, Day v De Braconier D'Alphen* [1997] IRLR 285 which is authority for the proposition that covenants should be considered in the light of the commercial context in which they were entered into; and more recently *LTE Scientific Ltd v Thomas* [2005] EWHC 7(QB) which confirms the fact that the court's approach is less strict in cases where there is greater equality of bargaining power between the parties.
2. See, for example, *General Billposting Co Ltd v Atkinson* [1909] AC 118 HL. There may be ways to address this issue in the service agreement itself; for example, by including a term permitting the employer to dismiss without notice but give pay in lieu of notice.

Exit planning

15.60 As discussed above, achieving an exit within a reasonably short timeframe is an important goal of a private equity investor, and even from the moment of the investment this will be at the forefront of the investor's mind. It is for this reason that the drag along right (see above) is an important protection, to ensure that management can be forced to sell their shares if the investor wants to exit, and why management's incentives will be heavily weighted to their capital gain on exit.

The investment agreement itself will also normally include a non-binding statement that the parties will all work towards a trade sale or listing within a particular period (usually up to five years). Although this cannot be enforced in itself, it is regarded as a useful statement of intentions, and will also usually make it clear at the outset that on any sale management will be expected to give warranties to the buyer, but the investors will not (other than in relation to their title to the shares).

Impact on the M&A deal

15.61 Although the M&A deal will largely follow its normal course on a buyout, and much of the deal will be the same as if the buyer was a trade buyer, there will be some important differences where the buyer is a financial investor. These are highlighted in this section.

Warranties

15.62 One important consequence of an MBO, where the incumbent management team is working with a private equity house to buy a company, will be that the seller may claim that it has only limited knowledge of the target business, and that the management team (which has the knowledge) should give the warranties instead. This argument will usually be strongly resisted, on the basis that the warranties in the acquisition agreement are mainly a price protection mechanism, and the knowledge of the seller is not relevant. However, it can in practice make the warranty negotiation more difficult and may lead to greater reliance being placed on the warranties being given by management in the investment agreement.

In any case, one clause that will be important in the acquisition agreement is a waiver of any claims that the seller may have against management following a claim against the seller for breach of a warranty in the acquisition agreement. If this clause is not included, there is a possibility that the seller may argue that it was the negligence or non-disclosure of a member of the management team that led to a successful warranty claim being brought, and will then seek to make recovery against the manager(s) concerned. This could obviously be detrimental to the target business.

Newco and guarantees

15.63 As the purchaser is likely to be a newly incorporated company, with no assets other than the equity and debt that is being provided to finance the acquisition, additional guarantees for any obligations that are undertaken by Newco may be required, especially if these obligations arise before any the acquisition funding has been provided – for example, a break fee that is agreed to be paid by the potential acquirer if a proposed acquisition does not proceed. These are common on public to private deals in particular, but also on most large private M&A deals (especially where regulatory or competition reasons require a gap between signing and completion).

Price adjustment: completion accounts and 'locked box'

15.64 Because the price will often have been calculated on the basis of a cash free/debt free valuation of the target company, and because the amount of 'cash' and 'debt' is likely to fluctuate from time to time, it will be important to have some mechanism to adjust or fix the price.

Completion accounts are a common price adjustment mechanism. They provide a statement of the target company's financial position on the day of completion and facilitate any adjustments to the price that may be required. However, in many private equity deals recently, especially secondary buyouts, the parties have used a 'locked box' mechanism.

The locked box approach uses a balance sheet as at a date prior to actual closing. The idea is that the economic interest in the business effectively transfers at that date. In order to achieve that, interest is likely to be paid on the consideration by the buyer from that date and no cash or other benefit can be extracted by the seller after that date. Many financial buyers and sellers prefer the certainty that this mechanism delivers: the seller wants to distribute the exit proceeds to its investors as soon as possible without the risk of a downward adjustment to the purchase price, and the buyer may wish to avoid the cashflow risk of an upward adjustment.

Pensions

15.65 Pensions issues are clearly important on any M&A deal, and are dealt with in detail in Chapter [ ], but where the buyer is using debt to acquire the target company and is then using the target company's assets to secure that acquisition finance there may be particular concerns for the trustees of the pension fund of any defined benefit scheme, and for the pensions regulator. As explained in Chapter [ ], a buyer will often want to apply to the Pensions Regulator for clearance, especially where any additional debt obligations are being taken on. Although the regulator has said that he does not, in general, have a problem with leveraged acquisitions, anything which makes the target company's obligations to the pension fund less secure will clearly need to be taken into account as part of any clearance that is applied for.

Secondary buyouts

15.66 Secondary buyouts – where one private equity house buys from another – have become common in recent years (see **15.69** below).

In many ways, a secondary buyout is no different from a normal trade acquisition, except that the seller is another private equity house and management team. However, there are a number of features of the deal that will differ when buying from a private equity seller.

First, there is a further potential for conflicts of interest to arise. The management team may be part of the seller group and the buyer group at the same time. For example, if the existing management team are going to stay on after the buyout then they will, as shareholders in the target, have an interest in getting as high a price as possible for the target company (which puts them in conflict with the buyer), but will also be keen that the seller sells to a buyer that will give them the best equity deal going forward (which may not be the seller that is offering the most money, and could therefore bring them into conflict with the seller).

Secondly, the selling private equity house is unlikely to give any warranties, except brief warranties as to title to its shares and its capacity to sell them. This can create problems for the buyer, who will look for this customary protection from the seller. As discussed above, increased reliance may be placed on management and, in the context of a secondary buyout – where management are usually realising significant value on the sale (even if a large proportion of it is being rolled over) – they are more likely to accept a larger cap on their liability and to accept that (as sellers) they should give wide-ranging warranties. However, the cap on their liability is still likely to be significantly less than the total consideration. Sometimes this gap will be met by warranty and indemnity insurance, or occasionally the selling private equity house may agree to an escrow or retention.

Thirdly, there may discussions with management shareholders about whether the investment that they roll over into Newco is 'vested' and therefore not subject to the leaver provisions (discussed in **15.54** above) obliging them to sell their shares if they leave the company. Management may argue that their rolled over investment – or at least part of it – is a genuine investment and should belong to them outright. The private equity house will still be keen to ensure that the managers' incentives are aligned with their own, and that the company does not have outside shareholders. In some cases, this issue is resolved by accepting that some proportion of management's investment is made on similar terms to the private equity house, so that they also invest in loan notes or preference shares alongside the ordinary shares, but that the leaver provisions do not apply to that part of the investment.

Finally, since the management group is likely to roll over some of its gain on the sale of target into new shares in the buyer group, there will be additional tax issues to consider.

Exit routes

15.67   Figure 5 shows the most common exit routes for each of the years from 2001 to 2005.

IPO

15.68   Historically, IPOs (and sales of quoted equity after them) have been a very common form of exit. However, as **Figure 5** shows, in 2005 they only amounted to just under 10% of all exits. The relative weakness in the capital markets has been one reason for this, and longer 'lock-up periods' (often from 6 to 12 months) have also contributed. These 'lock up' periods are imposed on private equity houses (and other shareholders) to prevent them from selling their shares for a period after an IPO and they put them at risk of adverse price movements.

Figure 5 – A Simplified UK Buyout Structure

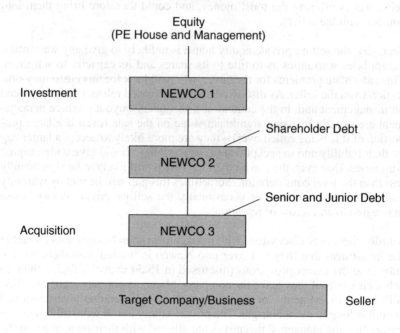

Secondary buyouts

15.69   Secondary buyouts have increased over the last few years with the UK now seeing some tertiary (and even a quaternary) buyouts: in 2001 and 2002, sales to other private equity houses only accounted for around 4% of all exits, but that figure jumped to around 20% in 2003. The proportion fell back to 13.1% in 2004, but rose again to 18.4% in 2005.

There are a number of reasons for the increasing numbers of secondary buy-outs, including the success of private equity fund-raising in recent years and the consequent amount of investment available to fund managers, and the need for private equity houses to focus on exits even in markets where trade buyers are scarcer and IPOs more difficult.

For the consequences of secondary buyouts on the transaction process, see **15.66**.

Trade sale

15.70   Trade sales were the second most common exit routes in 2005 accounting for around 23% of all 'exit events'.

Recapitalisations

15.71   Recapitalisations (repayment of share capital and shareholder loan, often out of new third party debt) amounted to nearly a quarter of all exit events in 2005. In fact, a recapitalisation is not an exit, because the investor will still own the company afterwards. However, it is one way of realising returns from an investment, and has been a common way to accelerate realisations from portfolio companies in recent years (and thereby improve IRRs for underlying investors). The debt markets have been very strong over this period, and it has become easier to obtain low cost third party debt to replace some of the capital initially invested by the investor. **Figure 5** illustrates that trend.

List of Figures

15.72

- Figure 1 – Source of Private Equity Funds Raised – 2005 (EVCA).
- Figure 2 – Geographical Source of Funds Raised – 2005 (EVCA).
- Figure 3 – The Layers of Debt and Equity (Michael Dance).
- Figure 4 – A Simplified UK Buyout Structure.
- Figure 5 – European Divestments (EVCA).

Glossary of Terms

ACAS The Advisory, Conciliation and Arbitration Service was established by *section 1* of the *Employment Protection Act 1975* to promote the improvement of industrial relations. Contact regional offices for further information.

Accrued benefits Benefits due to an employee for service up to a given point in time, calculated in relation to projected or current earnings.

Acquisition An acquisition is a transfer of ownership of at least one of the combining companies.

Acquisition accounting The method of accounting prescribed by FRS 6 for all business combinations that do not meet the strict definition of '*merger*' laid down in that standard.

Administration A status which an insolvent company may enter by one of several different routes, the common effect of which is the imposition of a moratorium upon creditor action, with the view to achieving one of a hierarchy of purposes, the primary among which is expressed to be the saving of the company. A *licensed insolvency practitioner* is appointed as administrator to oversee the process.

Administrative receivership The process by which a secured creditor appoints a *licensed insolvency practitioner* under a security, typically a mortgage debenture, to realise the value of the charged assets for the benefit of the appointor. An administrative receiver is a person so appointed.

All employee share ownership plan A new arrangement introduced by the government in the Finance Act 2000 to enable shares to be awarded to employees. It operates in a similar way to a *profit sharing scheme* but with more flexible terms. Provided that various conditions are satisfied – in particular that the shares are kept in the trust for a certain period – they can be distributed to employees without giving rise to any tax charge.

Asset(s) sale An asset(s) sale is the sale of a range of individual business assets, where the sale price is paid to the company rather than to the shareholders as in a *share sale*. The purchaser is only obliged to take over those liabilities which he specifies in the agreement rather than all the liabilities of the business (although some liabilities cannot be separated from the assets).

BIMBO (buy in management buyout) A buyout where one or more private equity investors buy a target company or business without a management team, usually with the intention of sourcing a management team after the deal is completed.

Bonus issue An issue of shares to existing shareholders using retained profits. Does not involve any payment of cash.

Buy out The purchase by Trustees of an occupational pension scheme, of an insurance policy in the name of a member or other beneficiary, in lieu of entitlement to benefit from the scheme, terminating the scheme's liability to provide that benefit.

Business combination The bringing together of separate entities into one economic entity as a result of one entity uniting with, or obtaining control over the net assets and operations of, another.

Call option A right given to one person to acquire an asset (e.g. shares) from another person on stated terms.

Capital loss A capital loss arises where a *chargeable asset* is disposed of for a price which is less than the base cost of the asset to the seller. Subject to certain anti-avoidance rules, a capital loss may be set against a chargeable gain in order to reduce or eliminate it. An unused capital loss may be carried forward, but it may not be sold or surrendered to another company in the same group.

CAPM The capital Asset Pricing model which uses the risk-free rate, a measure of risk compared to the market and the market premium of a company to calculate the cost of a company's equity.

Cash placing A cash placing is the issue of shares to investors for cash.

Central management and control Broadly, the concept of central management and control is directed at the highest level of control of the company's business, rather than the place where its operations are found. For many companies, residence will in practice be determined by the place where its Board of Directors regularly meets.

Chargeable asset A chargeable asset is one which can give rise to a chargeable gain or allowable loss for the purposes of CGT or corporation tax on chargeable gains.

Clawback offer In a clawback offer, the shareholders of the purchaser are given the right to call for the new shares (issued under a *cash placing* or a *vendor placing*), in which case they are not delivered to the placees who originally agreed to take them, but are sold to the shareholders instead.

Close company A company is a close company if it satisfies any of the following tests:

(a)   it is controlled by five or fewer 'participators';

(b)   it is controlled by its directors; or

(c)   five or fewer participators, or participators who are directors, together possess or are entitled to acquire such rights as would, in the event of a winding-up, entitle them to receive the greater part of the assets available for distribution among participators.

Exceptions: a non-resident company, a company controlled by the Crown or by one or more open companies. A quoted company is not close if its shares carrying 35% or more of the voting power of the company are held by members of the public.

Club deal A buyout where more than one private equity investor is involved and are working together to undertake a buyout.

Combined Code The Combined Code on Corporate Governance was issued in June 2005 and gives principles and provisions that a company should abide by where it is listed or seeking a listing.

Company share option scheme (revenue approved) A category of *share option scheme* introduced in 1984 under which selected employees in a company may be granted options which are afforded beneficial tax treatment. There are a number of detailed rules which must be satisfied in order for approval to be given.

Company voluntary arrangement ('CVA') An arrangement proposed by a company to its creditors to accept less than their respective dues. If approved by the requisite majority of creditors, it is binding on all.

Confidentiality Undertaking An agreement by the potential purchaser that any information disclosed during the sale negotiations will be considered confidential and therefore must not be disclosed to other parties or used by the potential purchaser to the detriment of the seller.

Contracted-out pension scheme Refers to a pension scheme whose members are contracted out of the earnings related pension arrangements provided by the State (ie the State Earnings Related Pension Scheme before 6 April 2002; and the State Second Pension after 5 April 2002. Both employer and employee are liable to pay lower National Insurance contributions. The scheme is required either to provide a minimum level of benefits relating to final salaries of the members or to provide protected rights if contracted-out on a money purchase basis.

Cost of capital A weighted average of a company's cost of finance from debt, equity or any other instrument.

Covenant A promise to pay a particular amount.

Debt on employer A debt on employer or *section 75* debt is a debt due to be paid to an occupational pension scheme by a participating employer. This debt is generally triggered if the scheme is wound-up or if an employer ceased participation in a multi-employer scheme. The amount of debt for a defined benefit scheme is generally the employer's share of the scheme deficit measured on an assumed buy-out basis.

Deemed trading receipt A transaction which is treated by the Revenue for tax purposes as a trading receipt, even though not expressly characterised as such.

Deferred pensioner One who is no longer an active member of a pension scheme but who will be entitled to receive benefits from the scheme at a later date.

Delisting When a public company listed on a stock exchange goes through a process of delisting its shares to become a private company.

Disclosure letter A disclosure letter is produced by the seller and lists certain matters of importance to the company which, if left undisclosed, would be likely to subject the seller to actions in breach of *warranty* after the sale.

Discretionary increase An increase in a pension (either being paid or to be paid in future) which is made without reference to an established system of escalation or indexation.

Distribution When made by a UK company, the recipient of a distribution is assessable for income tax under Schedule F. A distribution is not deductible in computing the profits of the company. As well as dividends, the tax legislation sets out other transactions which are taxed as distributions.

Due diligence The process undertaken by a prospective buyer of a business to firstly ensure they are buying what they think they are and secondly to validate their investment thesis and feel satisfied that the acquisition is likely to produce the returns envisaged.

Employee benefit trust A trust established by the company under which the trustees use the funds (gifted or loaned by the company) to acquire shares in the company. The trustees then distribute such shares to employees or directors in accordance with the terms of a share option arrangement or long-term incentive arrangement.

Enterprise management incentive scheme ('EMI') An option arrangement introduced in the *Finance Act 2000* under which a qualifying company can grant options up to a certain limit to selected employees. Provided that various conditions are satisfied, the options are afforded beneficial tax treatment.

Envy ratio In a private equity situation this is the ratio of the capitalisation of the company from the private equity firm's point of view (i.e their risk capital dived by their equity percentage) compared with that of the management teams.

Fair value The amount at which an asset or liability could be exchanged in an arm's-length transaction between informed and willing parties, other than in a forced or liquidation sale.

Final salary scheme A scheme where the pension benefit is calculated according to the member's pensionable earnings for a period ending at or near to his normal pension date.

Floating charge A charge over certain assets of a company which in their nature are intended to circulate (e.g. stock) which attaches to and becomes a fixed charge on individual items of that class of asset then in the possession of the company only upon the occurrence of specified events (e.g. a cessation of trade, the appointment of an administrator, administrative receiver etc) – events known as 'crystallisation'.

Funding level The relationship between the actuarial liability and the actuarial value of assets at a specified date.

Gearing The ratio of a company's debt to its equity. Also known as leverage.

IBO (institutional buyout) or bought deal A buyout where one or more private equity investors buy a target company or business without a management team, usually with the intention of sourcing a management team after the deal is completed.

ICE Regulations The *Consultation of Employees Regulations 2004 (SI 2004/3426)* (the '*ICE Regulations*') which give employees in larger firms (those with 50 or more employees), rights to be informed and consulted about the business they work for.

Impairment of fixed assets and goodwill A reduction in the recoverable amount of a fixed asset or goodwill below its carrying amount.

Indemnity A contractual obligation by which one party agrees to keep another protected from a specific loss.

Individual buyout policy An insurance company policy, giving deferred pension on retirement, which is purchased with a transfer value.

IPO A flotation of a company on a stock market. IPO stands for Initial Public Offering.

IRR or internal rate of return An industry standard measure of return generated by a private equity backed company or a portfolio of companies making up a fund, measuring the annual returns to investors.

Licensed insolvency practitioner A person licensed by one of a number of recognised professional bodies (e.g. the Institute of Chartered Accountants in England and Wales) to hold office as a liquidator, administrator, administrative receiver or supervisor.

Liquidation The process by which a company's assets are liquidated into cash and distributed amongst its creditors in accordance with their individual and class rights. Liquidation can be compulsory (by order of the court) or voluntary (by resolution of the members), A liquidator is in either case the *licensed insolvency practitioner* charged with the task of liquidation and distribution, appointed either by the court or by the creditors.

Listing Rules The United Kingdom Listing Authority listing rules were published on 1 July 2005 by the FSA as part of the final version of the new listing regime which governs any entity seeking to have its securities listed on the UK stock exchange. The Listing Rules focus on eligibility requirements, listing application procedures and ongoing obligations of listed issuers.

Long-term incentive scheme An arrangement under which a director or employee of a company is allowed to acquire shares in that company, either free or at a discount to their market value, subject to the satisfaction of performance conditions and/or continued employment for a designated period.

MBI (management buy in) A buyout where one or more private equity investors combine with a new management team to acquire a target company or business.

MBO (management buyout) A buyout where the existing management team combine with one or more private equity investors to acquire a target company or business.

Merger A pooling of existing interests such that the voting rights and equity interests in the combined group are allocated to the former shareholders of the combining companies in such a way as to reflect the agreed values of their respective companies.

Merger accounting The method of accounting prescribed by FRS 6 for business combinations that meet the strict definition of '*merger*' laid down in FRS 6.

Merger relief An accounting practice which relieves a company issuing shares from the requirement of crediting to a share premium account any premium at which such shares are issued above their nominal value. It will apply to most ordinary share-for-share acquisitions.

Minimum Funding Requirement ('MFR') The minimum amount of fund which a final salary pension scheme must have as required by the *Pensions Act 1995*. Schemes will be required to meet 90% of the MFR in 2003 and 100% in 2007.

Minimum statutory early leaver benefits The minimum amount of pension benefit payable to a person who ceases to be an active member of the scheme (other than by death) who will not be granted an immediate retirement pension.

Money purchase scheme A scheme to which contributions by either or both employer and members are at agreed rates, the ultimate benefits being dependent on the size of the fund built up, annuity rates at retirement date etc. Also known as a 'defined contribution' scheme.

Mortgage debenture (or debenture) A security granted by a company typically consisting of a series of fixed charges over certain assets and a floating charge over the balance.

NAV The Net Asset Value of a company. A common measure used in company valuations especially if the company is not producing earnings and has high fixed assets.

Nominee An insolvency practitioner proposed as the supervisor of a *CVA*.

Occupational pension scheme A scheme organised by an employer (or on behalf of a group of employers) to provide pension or other benefits to employees on retirement or death.

Option The right to do something. The most common usages in an acquisition context are the right to buy shares in the company under particular circumstances on or a specific date.

Pac-man defence An unusual bid defence tactic under which the target launches a retaliatory bid for the offeror.

Participating employer An employer, some or all of whose employees have the right to become members of an occupational pension scheme.

P/E ratio The ratio of company's share price per share divided by its earnings per share. A common metric in valuing a company. The higher the P/E ratio the higher the implied potential of the company.

Personal pension/personal pension plan An individual contract which enables an employee or a self-employed person to make contributions to his or her own pension plan.

Phantom share option scheme A cash bonus arrangement under which the amount payable to a director or employee is dependent on the increase in the company's share price.

PIPEs (private investment in public equity) The acquisition of a strategic (but usually minority) stake in a publicly quoted company.

Poison pills Might involve a clause requiring exceptional voting requirements for the implementation of mergers or the removal of directors included in the Articles of Association; or where special shares carrying extraordinary voting or dividend rights are issued to existing shareholders which are triggered when a hostile bid is made.

Profit sharing scheme (revenue approved) An arrangement under which a company pays over amounts to trustees who use those amounts to acquire shares in the company, which are then appropriated to employees in the company. Provided that various conditions are complied with, in particular that the shares are kept in the trust for a certain period, they can be distributed to employees without giving rise to any tax charge.

Protected rights Benefits which are provided in a specified form and derive from minimum contributions or minimum payments made as a condition of contracting-out on a money purchase basis.

PTP (private to public) or take private A buyout that involves de-listing a quoted target company, usually involving the added complexity of a public offer to buy the shares in the company from the public.

Public company A company which is a public company must be designated as such, usually by the letters 'plc' – public limited company – and must have a minimum issued capital (which is currently £50,000) and the shares must have been paid up to the extent of 25%.

Purchased goodwill The difference between the cost of an acquired entity and the aggregate of the fair values of that entity's identifiable assets and liabilities. Positive goodwill arises when the acquisition cost exceeds the aggregate fair values of the identifiable assets and liabilities. Negative goodwill arises when the aggregate fair values of the identifiable assets and liabilities of the entity exceed the acquisition cost.

Qualifying service Service to be taken into account which will entitle a member to short service benefit (at present the condition is at least two years' qualifying service).

Ratchet Usually used in the context of an 'earnout' where it is the mechanism for increasing or decreasing the amount paid depending upon future earnings. However also used to describe a performance incentive for management teams in buyouts where the better the performance or the higher the valuation that company is eventually sold for the higher the equity percentage that management ultimately obtain.

Recovery plan   If an actuarial valuation shows that the statutory funding objective is not met, the pension scheme trustees will have to prepare a 'recovery plan' setting out the steps to be taken (and over what period) to make up the shortfall.

Restricted or convertible share schemes An arrangement under which a director or employee of a company acquires shares (usually free) which are subject to restrictions thus reducing their value. The restrictions fall away on the attainment of performance targets.

Return on equity The profits available for ordinary shareholders divided by the company's equity.

Return on investment The profits before any financing charges divided by the total amount invested in the specific investment under consideration. This is done on a pre- or post-tax basis.

Savings-related share option scheme A Revenue approved scheme under which participants save between £5 and £250 per month from their salary. The savings will be used to fund the exercise cost when the participants exercise options to acquire shares in the company at a future date.

Scorched earth defence A bid defence strategy whereby the offeree's assets are depleted through sale to a friendly party.

Secondary (or tertiary or even quaternary) buyout A buyout where the seller is another private equity house exiting from an earlier buyout.

Section 67 *Section 67* of the *Pensions Act 1995* requires that trustees obtain members' consents, or a certificate from an actuary before making any modification to an occupational pension scheme approved under Chapter 1, which would or might affect members' entitlements or accrued rights in respect of service before the modification.

Section 75 *Section 75* of the *Pensions Act 1995* contains requirements relating to a debt on employer.

SERPS The State Earnings Related Pension Scheme which provides an earnings-related pension in addition to the basic state pension. SERPS was superseded by the State Second Pension in April 2002.

Share option scheme An arrangement under which a director or employee is granted an option to acquire at a future date shares in the company he works for (or its holding company) usually at a price equal to the market value of the shares when the option is granted. There are three sorts of share option scheme which are capable of approval by the Revenue. These are *savings-related share option schemes*, *company share option schemes* and *enterprise management incentive schemes*. Approval of the scheme enables participants to obtain certain tax advantages in respect of their options.

Share sale The purchase of shares from shareholders in the target company; the purchase price is therefore paid to the shareholders rather than to the company as it is in an *asset(s) sale*. The purchaser acquires the company with all its rights and obligations, both disclosed and undisclosed, whether he wishes to or not.

Stamp duty reserve tax ('SDRT') A separate tax from stamp duty, the main charge of stamp duty reserve tax is 0.5% on agreements to transfer 'chargeable securities' for a consideration. Where stamp duty and SDRT are both payable the payment of stamp duty franks the need to pay SDRT.

State second pension ('S2P') The State Earnings Related Pension Scheme which provides an earnings-related pension in addition to the basic state pension. This replaced SERPS from April 2002.

Supervisor A *licensed insolvency practitioner* responsible for the implementation and supervision of a *CVA* advanced by a company to, and approved by, its creditors.

Takeover Code The City Code on Takeovers and Mergers is a Code of Practice administered by The Panel on Takeovers and Mergers – comprised of representatives of the principal bodies engaged in financial activities in the UK, including, *inter alia*, the Association of British Insurers, the Confederation of British Industry, the London Stock Exchange and the Institute of Chartered Accountants in England and Wales – which regulates offers for public companies in the UK, Channel Islands and Isle of Man.

Tax advantage A relief or increased relief from, or repayment or increased repayment of, tax, or the avoidance or reduction of a charge to tax or an assessment to tax or the avoidance of a possible assessment to tax, whether the avoidance or reduction is effected by receipts accruing in such a way that the recipient does not pay or bear tax on them, or by a deduction in computing profits or gains. [*TA 1988, s 709*].

Transfer value A payment made from one pension scheme to another, or to an insurance company to purchase a buyout policy, which is in lieu of the amount of members' accrued benefits, to enable the scheme receiving the payment to provide alternative benefits.

TUPE The *Transfer of Undertakings (Protection of Employment) Regulations 2006 (SI 2006/246)* which apply to the transfer of an undertaking or business.

Underwriting An arrangement where a party, usually an investment bank, agrees to acquire something if others end up not doing so. Its most common use is in an IPO.

UK-resident company A company incorporated in the UK, or a company incorporated outside the UK whose *central management and control* is exercised in the UK, will be generally treated as resident in the UK for UK tax purposes. Such a company is, however, treated as resident outside the UK if it is regarded for the purposes of any double tax treaty as resident outside the UK and not resident in the UK. The significance of UK residence is that a UK-resident company is liable to UK tax on its worldwide income, whereas a non-resident company is liable to tax only to the extent that it trades in the UK through a branch or agency, or receives UK source income.

Unapproved share option scheme Any type of *share option scheme* other than a *savings-related share option scheme*, a *company share option scheme* or an *enterprise management incentive scheme*.

Vendor placing A vendor placing occurs where the purchaser issues new shares to the seller but arranges with a merchant bank or broker for the immediate resale of such shares in the market and guarantees in the sale and purchase agreement that the sale of the shares will yield the seller the right amount of consideration. A vendor placing requires the co-operation of the seller.

Vendor rights scheme Similar to *vendor placing* but, in a vendor rights scheme, the merchant bank, acting as broker, will first offer the shares to the bidder's existing shareholders in proportion to their existing shareholdings to avoid dilution of interest. (This scheme is also referred to as a 'vendor placing with clawback').

Warranty A warranty is an assurance by the seller that a particular state of affairs exists. Breach of warranty entitles the purchaser to claim damages which equal any amount reasonably foreseeable at the time of the contract as likely to flow from the breach.

White knight A third party which makes a higher offer for an offeree in response to a hostile bid from another party.

White squire An investor, probably corporate, who purchases a substantial share stake in an offeree to assist in the defence of a hostile bid.

Winding-up The process of termination of an occupational pension scheme (or less commonly a personal pension scheme), usually by applying the assets to the purchase of immediate annuities and deferred annuities for the beneficiaries, or by transferring the assets and liabilities to another pension scheme, in accordance with the scheme documentation or statute (*section 74 of the PA 1995*).

Workout A contractual arrangement reached between (a) a company and its creditors, and (b) the creditors among themselves, to achieve an agreed end without the entry into of a formal insolvency procedure such as liquidation, administration, administrative receivership or a CVA.

Specimen: Confidentiality Undertaking

[letterhead of seller]

To   [name and address of the potential purchaser] [date]

STRICTLY PRIVATE AND CONFIDENTIAL

Attention: [ ]

Dear Sirs,

You have expressed an interest in the Proposal (as defined below) and in consideration of the Company (as defined below) [and the other members of the Group (as defined below)] and our agents and advisers making available to you and your advisers the Confidential Information (as defined below) you hereby agree with and acknowledge and undertake to us on the terms set out below.

1. Interpretation

1.1 In this letter:

'Agents' means directors, officers, employees, agents, professional advisers or contractors

'Company' means [name/code name of target];

'Confidential Information' means:

(A)   all Information relating directly or indirectly to the Proposal including the existence of the Proposal and this letter and of the discussions and negotiations between you and us and our willingness to enter into such discussions and negotiations with you or any other party; and

(B)   all Information relating to the Company [and/or any member of the Group] including, without limitation, information relating to the property, assets, business, trading practices, plans, proposals and/or trading prospects of the Company [and/or any member of the group],

disclosed by or acquired in any way (and whether directly or indirectly) from us or the Company [and/or any member of the Group] or from any of our or their Agents and includes Information prepared by you or your advisers which contains or otherwise reflects or is generated from such Information

BUT EXCLUDING:

(A)   all Information that is in, or has, after disclosure to or acquisition by you or your Agents, entered the public domain otherwise than as a consequence of any breach of any undertaking contained in or given pursuant to this letter;

(B)   all Information that you can show by your written records is properly and lawfully in your possession prior to the time that it is disclosed by or acquired from (and was not acquired in any way directly or indirectly from) us or the Company [and/or any member of the Group] or from any of our or their advisers and provided that such information is not known by you to be subject to any other duty of confidentiality owed to us or the Company [or any member of the Group];

'Information' means all information in whatever form including, without limitation, all data, proposals and plans whether in writing, conveyed orally or by machine-readable medium;

['**Group**' means the Company and its subsidiary undertakings and associated undertakings;]

'Order' means the *Financial Services and Markets Act 2000 (Financial Promotion) Order 2005*;

'Proposal' means the acquisition of the Company [and the other members of the Group];

'subsidiary undertaking' and **'associated undertaking'** shall have the meanings ascribed to them in the Companies Act 1985 (but for this purpose ignoring paragraph 20(1)(b) of Schedule 4A to the Companies Act 1985).

1.2   The obligations are given in our favour on behalf of ourselves [and our subsidiary undertakings and associated undertakings (including the Group)] and on behalf of our directors, officers, employees, agents, contractors and professional advisers.

2.   Confidential Information

2.1   You will treat and keep all Confidential Information as secret and confidential and will not, without our prior written consent (which may be given on such terms as we consider appropriate), directly or indirectly communicate or disclose (whether in writing or orally or in any other manner) Confidential Information to any other person.

2.2   You will not use any Confidential Information for any purpose (including, but not limited to, any competitive or commercial purpose) other than directly in connection with your appraisal of the Company [Group] for the purpose of negotiations in connection with the Proposal.

3.   Exceptions

The restrictions in sub-paragraph 2.1 of this letter do not apply to the disclosure of Confidential Information:

(A)   which is disclosed to those of your directors, officers, employees and professional advisers who have been identified to us prior to such disclosures being made and strictly need to receive and consider Confidential Information for the purposes of the Proposal; and

(B)   which is required by law or the rules of any applicable regulatory organisation (but subject to paragraph 5 below).

4.   Records and return of Information

You will keep a record of the Confidential Information provided to you or your advisers and, so far as is reasonably possible, of the location of that Confidential Information and of any persons holding that Confidential Information. You and your advisers will, upon demand by us or if you cease to be interested in the Proposal, (a) return to us all documents and all other materials which are in a form capable of delivery (including, without limitation, computer tapes and disks) containing or reflecting any Confidential Information and of all copies thereof which have been made by or on behalf of you or your advisers and (b) erase all Confidential Information from any computer, word-processor or other device containing such information, in each case within [seven] days of such demand or cessation of interest. In addition, you and your advisers will, in these circumstances, provide to us within such [seven] day period a certificate addressed to us and signed by one of your directors confirming your compliance with this paragraph.

5.   Announcements and Disclosure

You will not make, or permit or procure to be made or solicit or assist any other person to make, any announcement or disclosure of your prospective interest in the Proposal without our prior written consent (which may be given on such terms as we consider appropriate). If you should agree to purchase the Company [Group], no announcement of the transaction will be made except by agreement between you and us. If, however, you become compelled by law or the rules of any applicable regulatory organisation to disclose any Confidential Information, you will immediately notify us (at the address set out above) so that we may seek an appropriate means to prevent that disclosure or waive compliance with the provisions of this letter and you will take such steps as we may reasonably require for that purpose.

6.   Approaches to the Company [or other member of the Group]

6.1   For a period of [one year] after the date of this letter, neither you nor any of your advisers will, without our written consent, directly or indirectly initiate or engage in or have any contact of any kind whatsoever with any of the directors or employees of the Company [or any member of the Group] unless you have completed the acquisition of the Company [Group].

6.2   You will not

(A)   while negotiations for the proposed acquisition of the Company [Group] are taking place; or

(B)   if the proposed acquisition does not take place for any reason, during the period of [one year] after the date of this letter,

directly or indirectly solicit, endeavour to entice away or offer to employ any person who is at any time during those negotiations employed in a senior capacity by the Company [or any member of the Group], whether or not that person would commit any breach of his or her contract or service in leaving the employment of the Company [or the member of the Group concerned].

6.3   You will not, while negotiations for the proposed acquisition of the Company [Group] are taking place, directly or indirectly make contact with any customer or suppliers of the Company [any member of the Group] in connection with the discussions and negotiations regarding the Proposal.

7.   Duration

The obligations undertaken by you and your advisers under this letter shall be continuing and, in particular, they shall survive the termination of any discussions or negotiations between you and us regarding the Proposal, provided that if the acquisition of the Company [and the Group] is successfully completed then the obligations contained in this letter shall not apply to the extent that the Confidential Information relates solely to the Company [or any other member of the Group].

8.   Principal

You confirm that you are acting as principal and not as nominee, agent or broker for any other person and that you will be responsible for any costs incurred by yourselves or your advisers in considering or pursuing the Proposal and in complying with the terms of this letter.

9.   Procedure

You understand that the procedure for the sale of the Company [Group] may be changed or terminated at any time and without notice and you agree that we will be under no obligation to accept any offer or proposal which may be made by you or on your behalf in the course of any negotiations.

10.   Advisers

You will ensure that your Agents comply with the terms of this letter and any action by them will be treated as yours for the purposes of this letter and if required by us, you will ensure that your Agents execute written undertakings as to confidentiality on terms and in the form approved by us.

11.   Offer

You agree that documents, whether containing Confidential Information or otherwise, made available to you or your Agents prior to, in the course of, or for the purpose of, negotiations in relation to the Proposal, will not constitute an offer or invitation by, or on behalf of, ourselves, nor will those documents nor the information contained in them form the basis of, or any representation in relation to, any contract.

12.   Representations

You will be responsible for making your own decision on the Confidential Information and on the information and data contained in any document of the kind referred to in paragraph 11 of this letter (the **'Material'**) and you acknowledge that you will have no right of action (except in the case of fraud) against us or any of our Agents or any other person in relation to the accuracy, reasonableness or completeness of any of the Confidential Information, including the Material except to the extent that any representation or warranty relating to such information made in any binding sale and purchase agreement is enforceable by you. Accordingly, neither we nor any of our Agents nor any other person shall be liable for any direct, indirect or consequential loss or damage suffered by any person as a result of relying on any statement contained in or omitted from the Confidential Information.

13.   [Restrictions on share dealings [if Seller is a listed company]]

[You agree that you shall not and shall procure that none of your Agents to whom Confidential Information has been disclosed shall acquire or seek to acquire directly or indirectly, without our prior written consent, an interest (as defined in Part VI of the Companies Act 1985) in our share capital until there is a public announcement of the Proposal or, if you decide not to proceed with the Proposal, until the later of (i) the date on which the Confidential Information ceases, in our reasonable opinion, to be inside information (as defined in the Criminal Justice Act 1993) in relation to our share capital and (ii) the date two years from the date of this letter, or such later date as we may reasonably determine, when in our reasonable opinion the Confidential Information ceases to be commercially relevant to us.]

14.   [Standstill [if Seller is a listed Company]]

[You will not (and will procure that none of your subsidiary undertakings or associated undertakings will), for a period of twelve months from the date of this letter directly or indirectly, by purchase or otherwise, conditionally or otherwise, acquire, offer to acquire or agree to acquire ownership of or options to acquire such ownership or derivatives relating to or any rights whatsoever in respect of, any share capital of the Company (or otherwise act in concert with any person which so acquires, offers to acquire or agrees to acquire).]

15.   Expertise

You confirm that you are a person who:

(A)   is an investment professional within the meaning of *Article 19(5)* of the *Order*; or

(B)   falls within *Article 49(2)(a)* to *(d)* ('high net worth companies, unincorporated associations etc') of the *Order*; or

(C)   is situated outside of the United Kingdom

and that in each case you are able to receive the Confidential Information without contravention of any unfulfilled registration requirements or other legal restrictions in the jurisdictions in which you reside or conduct business.

16.   Insider dealing and market abuse

You acknowledge that:

(A)   the Confidential Information is given in confidence and that you will not base any behaviour in relation to qualifying investments (within the meaning of *Part 6* of the *Financial Services and Markets Act 2000* (*'FSMA'*) and the Code of Market Conduct made pursuant to *FSMA*) which would amount to market abuse for the purposes of *FSMA* on the Confidential Information until it has been generally made available; and

(B)   the Proposal and some or all of the Confidential Information may be inside information for the purposes of the *Criminal Justice Act 1993* (*'CJA'*) and accordingly by receiving such Confidential Information you may become an 'insider'. You consent to being made an insider by virtue of the disclosure or acquisition of price-sensitive information and acknowledge that, subject to and in accordance with applicable law, you should not deal in securities that are price-affected securities (as defined in the *CJA*) in relation to the inside information, encourage another person to deal in price-affected securities or disclose the information except as permitted by the *CJA* before the inside information is made public.

17.   Adequacy of damages

Without affecting any other rights or remedies that any party may have, you acknowledge and agree that damages alone would not be an adequate remedy for any breach by you or any of your advisers of any of the provisions of this letter.

18.   Indemnity

You will be responsible for any breach of any of the terms of this letter by you or by any of your advisers. You will indemnify us and our Agents from and against all costs, expenses, losses or damages (including but not limited to legal expenses) which may arise directly or indirectly from the unauthorised disclosure or use of Confidential Information by you or your Agents or from any other breach of the terms of this letter.

19.   Remedies

No failure or delay in exercising any right, power or privilege under this letter will operate as a waiver of it, nor will any single or partial exercise of it preclude any further exercise or the exercise of any right, power or privilege under this letter or otherwise.

20.   Contracts (Rights of Third Parties) Act 1999

19.1   The provisions of this letter confer benefits on the persons specifically referred to in sub-paragraph 1.2 of this letter (each, a 'Third Party') and, subject to the remaining terms of this paragraph 19, are intended to be enforceable by each Third Party by virtue of the Contracts (Rights of Third Parties) Act 1999.

19.2   Notwithstanding sub-paragraph 19.1 of this letter, this letter may be rescinded or varied in any way and at any time without the consent of any Third Party.

19.3   Notwithstanding sub-paragraph 19.1 of this letter, no Third Party may enforce, or take any step to enforce, any of the provisions of this letter without our prior written consent, which may, if given, be given on and subject to such terms and conditions as we may determine.

21.   General

20.1   This letter shall enure to the benefit of, and be enforceable by, our successors and assigns and you agree to procure that its terms are observed by any successors and assigns of your business or interests or any part thereof as if they had been party to this letter.

20.2   The provisions of this letter shall be severable in the event that any of the provisions hereof are held by a court of competent jurisdiction to be invalid, void or otherwise unenforceable, and the remaining provisions shall remain enforceable to the fullest extent permitted by law.

22.   Governing law

This letter will be governed by, and construed in accordance with, English law and you hereby irrevocably submit to the exclusive jurisdiction of the English courts in connection with this letter. [If you are not incorporated or registered in England and Wales you hereby irrevocably appoint the person identified below as your agent for service of process in England and Wales.]

We should be grateful if you would confirm your acceptance of the terms of this letter by signing and returning to us the enclosed copy of this letter.

Yours faithfully,

....

for and on behalf of

[Seller]

On the copy:

To: [Seller]

We agree to the matters set out in your letter dated [ ] (of which this is a copy).

Dated ....

....

for and on behalf of

[ ]

duly authorised officer

Index

[*all references are to paragraph number*]

A

Abstraction of water
  environmental responsibilities, and,
    7.26
Accountants' report
  pre-contractual considerations, and,
    8.14
Accounting
  acquisition accounting
    balance sheets, 2.18
    basic principle, 2.14
    cost of acquisition, 2.17
    date of acquisition, 2.15
    fair value, 2.16
    goodwill, 2.20–2.21
    impairment, 2.21
    intangible assets, 2.19
    introduction, 2.11
    summary, 2.18
  acquisition costs, 2.22
  asset purchases, and, 2.41
  associates
    generally, 2.39
    introduction, 2.38
  cash flows, 2.26
  Companies Act 1985, and, 2.2
  conclusion, 2.43
  consolidated financial statements
    excluded subsidiaries, 2.9
    generally, 2.6
    intermediate parent company, 2.7
    small and medium-sized groups, 2.8
  disclosures
    acquisitions, 2.25
    cash flows, 2.26
    introduction, 2.23
    mergers, 2.24
    substantial acquisitions, 2.27
  framework, 2.2
  FRS, 2.2
  FRSSE, 2.10
  future developments, 2.42
  GAAP
    consolidated financial statements,
      2.6–2.9

Accounting – *contd*
  GAAP – *contd*
    introduction, 2.3
    merger relief, 2.5
    parent company's individual
      accounts, 2.4
    share-for-share transactions, 2.5
  IFRS
    allocation of costs, 2.33
    business combinations (IFRS 3),
      2.30
    cost of acquisition, 2.32
    entities under common control, 2.35
    generally, 2.2
    goodwill, 2.34
    introduction, 2.28
    overview, 2.29
    parent company balance sheet and
      distributable reserves, 2.36
    reverse acquisition, 2.31
    transitional rules, 2.37
  introduction, 2.1
  joint ventures
    generally, 2.20
    introduction, 2.38
  merger accounting
    balance sheets, 2.18
    conditions, 2.12
    introduction, 2.11
    method, 2.13
    summary, 2.18
  merger relief, 2.5
  parent company's individual accounts,
    2.4
  pension schemes, and, 9.34
  share-for-share transactions, 2.5
  small companies, 2.10
  SSAP, 2.2
  substantial acquisitions, 2.27
  UK GAAP, 2.3–2.6
Accounting Standards Board (ASB)
  generally, 2.2
Accounts
  pre-contractual considerations, and,
    8.14

Acquisition accounting
  balance sheets, 2.18
  basic principle, 2.14
  cost of acquisition, 2.17
  date of acquisition, 2.15
  fair value, 2.16
  goodwill, 2.20–2.21
  impairment, 2.21
  intangible assets, 2.19
  introduction, 2.11
  summary, 2.18
Acquisition costs
  accounting treatment, and, 2.22
'Acquisition of control'
  merger control, and, 11.9
Acquisition strategy
  approaching target company, 12.4
  detailed investigation of target
      company, 12.6–12.7
  development, 12.1
  establishing a team, 12.2
  financing acquisition
    deferred consideration, 12.9–12.11
    earn-outs, 12.10
    introduction, 12.8
    pension funds, 12.11
  identifying target company, 12.3
  information checklist, 12.7
  introduction 12.1
  valuing target company, 12.5
Administration
  appointment of administrators, 3.7
  Chapter 11 US Code, and, 3.8
  corporate trading name, 3.10
  employees, and, 3.12–3.17
  generally, 3.4–3.6
  initial procedure, 3.7
  introduction, 3.1–3.3
  pre-packs, 3.9
  purpose, 3.4
  substantial property transactions, 3.11
  trading name, 3.10
Air pollution control
  environmental responsibilities, and,
      7.23
Allocation of costs
  IFRS, and, 2.33
Allocation of risks and liabilities
  see also Environmental
      responsibilities
  bespoke provisions, 7.46
  contractual provisions, 7.42–7.46
  indemnities, 7.44–7.45
  relevant factors, 7.41
  warranties, 7.43

Appeals
  German merger control, and, 11.107
  Irish merger control, and, 11.145
  Swedish merger control, and, 11.155
  UK merger control, and
    generally, 11.70
    role of CAT, 11.50
Approved withdrawal arrangements
  effect, 9.22
  generally, 9.20
  Regulator's approval process, 9.21
Articles of association
  pre-contractual considerations, and,
      8.15
  private equity transactions, and, 15.34
Asbestos
  environmental responsibilities, and,
      7.35
Asset sales and purchases
  accounting treatment, and, 2.41
  employment issues, and, 6.32
  environmental responsibilities, and,
      7.4
  private company acquisitions, and,
      8.3
  property transactions, and, 14.4
Assignments
  property transactions, and, 14.12
  tax planning, and, 13.4
Assets and liabilities
  fair value, and, 2.16
Associates
  generally, 2.39
  introduction, 2.38
Authorisations
  see also Environmental
      responsibilities
  abstraction of water, 7.26
  air pollution control, 7.23
  COMAH, 7.29
  discharge consents, 7.24
  discharges to sewers, 7.25
  discharges to water, 7.24
  emissions trading scheme, 7.32
  greenhouse gas emissions, 7.32
  hazardous substances, 7.28
  integrated pollution prevention and
      control, 7.23
  major accident hazards, 7.29
  packaging waste, 7.31
  radioactive substances, 7.27
  trade effluent consents, 7.25
  waste management licence, 7.30
Authorised guarantee agreements
  property transactions, and, 14.12

'Autonomous economic entity'
merger control, and, 11.12

B
Balance sheets
acquisition accounting, and, 2.18
merger accounting, and, 2.18
Board minutes
private company acquisitions, and,
8.10
Business asset roll-over
tax planning, and, 13.5
Business combinations (IFRS 3)
allocation of costs, 2.33
cost of acquisition, 2.32
entities under common control, 2.35
generally, 2.29
goodwill, 2.34
introduction, 2.28
overview, 2.29
parent company balance sheet and
distributable reserves, 2.36
reverse acquisition, 2.31
transitional rules, 2.37
Business, purchase of
employment, and
application of TUPE, 6.35
effect of TUPE, 6.36
'employee liability information',
6.42
employment dismissed before time
of transfer, 6.39
employment 'immediately before'
transfer, 6.38
exceptions from effect of TUPE,
6.40
generally, 6.34
liabilities acquired, 6.37
position of employee, 6.43
reorganisations, 6.44 6.51
summary, 6.33
transfer before completion, 6.41
Business-specific information
pre-contractual considerations, and,
8.16

C
Capital restructuring
defensive measures, and, 4.7
Cash consideration
private company acquisitions, and,
8.21
Cash flows
disclosures, and, 2.26

Certificates of title
property transactions, and, 14.10
Change of place of work
internal reorganisations, and, 6.26
Change of terms and conditions
reorganisations, and, 6.48
share purchases, and, 6.27–6.29
Chapter 11, US Code
generally, 3.8
Clearances
pensions, and
and see Pension schemes
applications, 9.30
directors' role, 9.29
general principles, 9.27
trustees' role, 9.27
Swedish merger control, and, 11.156
tax planning, and
introduction, 13.43
s 138 TCGA 1992, and, 13.44
s 707 TA 1988, and, 13.45
UK merger control, and
Competition Commission's duties,
11.54
OFT's duties, 11.53
public interest mergers, 11.55–11.58
Close companies
tax planning, and, 13.48
Club deals
private equity transactions, and, 15.21
COMAH
environmental responsibilities, and,
7.29
Commitments
merger control, and, 11.30
Community dimension
and see EC Merger Regulation
introduction, 11.14
turnover, 11.16
'undertaking concerned', 11.15
Companies Acts
accounting treatment, and, 2.2
private company acquisitions, and,
8.63
Company name
private company acquisitions, and,
8.52
Company share option schemes
see also Employee share option
schemes
generally, 5.4
**Company voluntary arrangements
(CVA)**
see also Insolvency
generally, 3.2

Competition Appeals Tribunal
 and see UK merger control
 generally, 11.50
Competition Commission
 and see UK merger control
 duties, 11.54
 generally, 11.48
Completion
 private company acquisitions, and,
 8.11
Completion accounts
 private equity transactions, and,
 15.64
'Concentrations'
 and see EC Merger Regulation
 'acquisition of control', 11.9
 Czech Republic merger control, and,
 11.161
 German merger control, and,
 11.185–11.190
 Hungarian merger control, and,
 11.167–11.169
 introduction, 11.7
 Italian merger control, and, 11.110
 Polish merger control, and, 11.184
 'previously independent
 undertakings', 11.8
Conduct of litigation
 private company acquisitions, and,
 8.48
Conduct of negotiations
 private company acquisitions, and,
 8.17
Confidential guidance
 UK merger control, and, 11.62
Confidentiality undertaking
 private company acquisitions, and,
 8.52
Conflicts of interest
 private equity transactions, and,
 15.22
'Consent matters'
 private equity transactions, and,
 15.50
Consents
 private company acquisitions, and,
 8.31
 property transactions, and, 14.14
 tax planning, and
 introduction, 13.43
 s 765 TA 1988, and, 13.46
Consideration
 cash
 generally, 8.21
 tax planning, 13.32

Consideration – *contd*
 delayed payment, 8.23
 earn-outs
 generally, 12.10
 tax planning, 13.35
 financial assistance issue, and, 8.22
 financing acquisition, and
 deferred consideration,
 12.9–12.11
 earn-outs, 12.10
 introduction, 12.8
 pension funds, 12.11
 introduction, 8.18
 loan notes
 generally, 8.20
 tax planning, 13.34
 pension schemes, and, 9.15
 shares
 generally, 8.19
 tax planning, 13.33
 tax planning, and
 cash, 13.32
 earn-outs, 13.35
 introduction, 13.32
 loan notes, 13.34
 share sales (purchaser's planning),
 13.24–13.25
 shares, 13.33
 target debt, 13.36
Consolidated financial statements
 excluded subsidiaries, 2.9
 generally, 2.6
 intermediate parent company, 2.7
 small and medium-sized groups, 2.8
Constitution of company
 pre-contractual considerations, and,
 8.15
Constructive dismissal
 generally, 6.28
 reasonableness, 6.29
Consultation
 see also Employment
 additional legislation, 6.61
 commencement, 6.58
 liability for failure, 6.59
 redundancies, 6.54
 remedy for failure to consult, 6.60
 transfers, 6.55–6.57
Contaminated land
 see also Environmental
 responsibilities
 generally, 7.16
 water pollution, 7.17
Contingent liabilities
 fair value, and, 2.16

Continuation of services
private company acquisitions, and,
8.27
Contracts for sale of property
property transactions, and, 14.12
Contracts of employment
generally, 6.2
Contribution Notices
pension schemes, and, 9.24
Convertible share schemes
see also Employee share option
schemes
generally, 5.12
Corporate rescue
administration
and see Administration
generally, 3.4–3.11
hive-downs, 3.19
introduction, 3.1–3.3
pensions, 3.18
super-priority, and
background, 3.31
classes of DIP funding, 3.32
conclusions, 3.37
general principles, 3.33–3.36
introduction, 3.30
transfer of undertakings, 3.12–3.17
work-outs
accountants' investigation, 3.22
common features, 3.25
company/participants agreement,
3.28
documentation, 3.27–3.29
general structure, 3.21
'intensive care', 3.23
introduction, 3.20
participants agreement, 3.29
public companies, and, 3.24
risks, 3.26
Corporate social responsibility
environmental responsibilities, and,
7.22
Cost of acquisition
acquisition accounting, and, 2.17
IFRS, and, 2.32
Costs
private company acquisitions, and,
8.52
Covenants
see also Warranties
comparison wit h warranties and
indemnities, 8.33
generally, 8.34
introduction, 8.32
tax planning, and, 13.39–13.40

Czech Republic (merger control)
ancillary restraints, 11.164
competition authority, 11.160
concentrations, 11.161
introduction, 11.159
notification requirements, 11.163
sanctions, 11.165
thresholds, 11.162

D
Date of acquisition
acquisition accounting, and, 2.15
Debtor in possession finance
see also Corporate rescue
background, 3.31
classes of funding, 3.32
conclusions, 3.37
general principles, 3.33–3.36
introduction, 3.30
Debts on employers
and see Pension schemes
defined contribution employers, on,
9.19
generally, 9.17
industry-wide schemes, 9.18
'De-consolidation pack'
private company acquisitions, and,
8.52
Defensive measures
after announcement of bid
generally, 4.7
summary, 4.6
'capital restructuring', 4.7
conclusion, 4.8
'defence bible'
contents, 4.5
introduction, 4.4
'golden parachutes', 4.7
introduction, 4.1
'Pac-man' defence, 4.7
'poison pills', 4.7
prior to bid
'defence bible', 4.5
generally, 4.4
summary, 4.3
public companies, and, 4.1
regulatory environment, 4.2
'scorched earth' defence, 4.7
'shark repellents', 4.7
Takeover Code, and, 4.1–4.2
Deferred consideration
earn-outs, 12.10
introduction, 12.9
pension funds, 12.11

Defined benefit pension schemes
and see Pension schemes
funding, 9.32
generally, 9.3
section 75 debts, 9.17–9.18
Defined contribution pension schemes
and see Pension schemes
generally, 9.3
section 75 debts, 9.19
Delayed payment of consideration
private company acquisitions, and,
8.23
Depositary receipts
tax planning, and, 13.57
Directors
'garden leave' clauses, 6.9
general considerations, 6.5
'golden parachutes', 6.8
negotiations with departing directors,
6.11
notice of termination, 6.6
post-termination restrictions, 6.10
removal, 6.7–6.10
remuneration, 6.12
restrictive covenants, 6.10
share purchases, and, 6.7–6.8
summary, 6.4
Directors' liability
environmental responsibilities, and,
7.19
Discharge consents
environmental responsibilities, and,
7.24
Discharges to sewers
environmental responsibilities, and,
7.25
Disclosure letter
format, 8.30
generally, 8.39
introduction, 8.10
Dividend payment
private company acquisitions, and, 8.52
Discharges to water
environmental responsibilities, and,
7.24
Disclosures
acquisitions, 2.25
cash flows, 2.26
introduction, 2.23
mergers, 2.24
private company acquisitions, and
format, 8.30
generally, 8.39
introduction, 8.10
substantial acquisitions, 2.27

Drag along rights
private equity transactions, and,
15.55
Drawdown of funds
private equity transactions, and,
15.9
Due diligence
see also Environmental
responsibilities
authorisations
abstraction of water, 7.26
air pollution control, 7.23
COMAH, 7.29
discharge consents, 7.24
discharges to sewers, 7.25
discharges to water, 7.24
emissions trading scheme, 7.32
greenhouse gas emissions, 7.32
hazardous substances, 7.28
integrated pollution prevention and
control, 7.23
major accident hazards, 7.29
packaging waste, 7.31
radioactive substances, 7.27
trade effluent consents, 7.25
waste management licence, 7.30
contaminated land, 7.16–7.17
contract, 7.20
corporate social responsibility, 7.22
directors' liability, 7.19
environmental permits, 7.14–7.15
instructing local lawyers, 7.12
introduction, 7.10
legal issues, 7.13–7.22
contaminated land, 7.16–7.17
contract, 7.20
corporate social responsibility,
7.22
directors' liability, 7.19
environmental permits, 7.14–7.15
introduction, 7.13
pressure groups, 7.22
regulatory enforcement, 7.18
splitting permits, 7.15
tort, 7.21
water pollution, 7.17
pressure groups, 7.22
private company acquisitions, and,
8.7
property transactions, and, 14.7
regulatory enforcement, 7.18
splitting permits, 7.15
tort, 7.21
use of consultants, 7.11
water pollution, 7.17

E

Early leavers
employee share option schemes, and,
5.15
Earn-outs
deferred consideration, and, 12.10
tax planning, and, 13.35
EC Merger Regulation
'acquisition of control', 11.9
ancillary restrictions
generally, 11.35
intellectual property licences, 11.36
joint venture restrictions,
11.39–11.42
non-compete clauses, 11.36
purchase and supply obligations,
11.38
application, 11.6
'autonomous economic entity', 11.12
commitments, 11.30
Community dimension
introduction, 11.14
turnover, 11.16
'undertaking concerned', 11.15
'concentrations'
'acquisition of control', 11.9
introduction, 11.7
'previously independent
undertakings', 11.8
consents, and, 8.31
fines, 11.33–11.34
Form CO
contents, 11.21–11.25
control, 11.23
introduction, 11.17
market conditions, 11.25
market information, 11.24
ownership, 11.23
parties, 11.22
transaction, 11.22
Form RS, 11.17
general issues, 11.4
historical background, 11.5
intellectual property licences
joint ventures, 11.41
mergers and acquisitions, 11.37
introduction, 11.1–11.2
investigation
commitments, 11.30
introduction, 11.27
Phase I, 11.28
Phase II, 11.29
joint venture restrictions
generally, 11.39
intellectual property licences, 11.41

EC Merger Regulation – *contd*
joint venture restrictions – *contd*
non-compete clauses, 11.40
purchase and supply obligations,
11.42
joint ventures
'autonomous economic entity', 11.12
introduction, 11.10
joint control, 11.11
other considerations, 11.13
restrictions, 11.39–11.42
market conditions, 11.25
market information, 11.24
non-compete clauses
joint ventures, 11.40
mergers and acquisitions, 11.36
notification
method, 11.20
relevant persons, 11.17
required information, 11.21–11.25
ownership, 11.23
penalties, 11.33–11.34
pre-notification, 11.18
'previously independent
undertakings', 11.8
principal aims, 11.3
private company acquisitions, and,
8.31
procedure
introduction, 11.17
investigation, 11.26–11.30
notification, 11.17–11.20
pre-notification, 11.18
simplified notice, 11.32
substantive assessment, 11.31
suspension of concentrations, 11.26
time limits, 11.27–11.30
purchase and supply obligations
joint ventures, 11.42
mergers and acquisitions, 11.38
scope, 11.6
Short Form, 11.17
simplified procedure notice, 11.32
substantive assessment, 11.31
suspension of concentrations, 11.26
turnover, 11.16
'undertaking concerned', 11.15
EEA Agreement
merger control, and, 11.43
EFRBs
and see Pension schemes
generally, 9.3
EGM documentation
private company acquisitions, and,
8.10

Electrical and electronic equipment
environmental responsibilities, and,
7.39
Emissions trading scheme
environmental responsibilities, and,
7.32
Employee share schemes
approved schemes
company share option scheme, 5.4
enterprise management initiative
scheme, 5.7
introduction, 5.2
SAYE scheme, 5.5
share incentive plan, 5.6
types, 5.3
company share option scheme, 5.4
convertible share schemes, 5.12
'early leavers', and, 5.15
effect of acquisition, 5.14
enterprise management initiative
(EMI) scheme, 5.7
institutional investors' guidelines,
5.13
introduction, 5.1
long-term incentive scheme, 5.11
phantom share option scheme, 5.10
post-acquisition schemes, 5.18
public companies, and, 5.16
restricted share schemes, 5.12
savings-related share option (SAYE)
scheme, 5.5
share incentive plan (SIP), 5.6
Takeover Code, and, 5.16
tax planning, and, 13.55
types, 5.3
unapproved schemes
convertible share schemes, 5.12
introduction, 5.2
long-term incentive scheme, 5.11
phantom share option scheme, 5.10
restricted share schemes, 5.12
share option scheme, 5.9
types, 5.8
unapproved share option scheme, 5.9
Employment
asset purchases, and, 6.32
business purchases, and
application of TUPE, 6.35
effect of TUPE, 6.36
'employee liability information',
6.42
employment dismissed before time
of transfer, 6.39
employment 'immediately before'
transfer, 6.38

Employment – *contd*
business purchases, and – *contd*
exceptions from effect of TUPE,
6.40
generally, 6.34
liabilities acquired, 6.37
position of employee, 6.43
reorganisations, 6.44–6.51
summary, 6.33
transfer before completion, 6.41
change of place of work, 6.26
change of terms and conditions,
6.27–6.29
collective issues
consultation, 6.54–6.61
post-acquisition changes, 6.53
pre-acquisition investigation, 6.52
purchases from insolvent company,
6.62
trade unions, 6.52
constructive dismissal
generally, 6.28
reasonableness, 6.29
consultation
additional legislation, 6.61
commencement, 6.58
liability for failure, 6.59
redundancies, 6.54
remedy for failure to consult, 6.60
transfers, 6.55–6.57
contracts of employment, 6.2
corporate rescue, and
see also Transfer of undertakings
background, 3.13
contractual variations, 3.17
effect of regulations, 3.14
extent of relief, 3.15
introduction, 3.12
pensions, and, 3.16
directors
'garden leave' clauses, 6.9
general considerations, 6.5
'golden parachutes', 6.8
negotiations with departing
directors, 6.11
notice of termination, 6.6
post-termination restrictions, 6.10
removal, 6.7–6.10
remuneration, 6.12
restrictive covenants, 6.10
share purchases, and, 6.7–6.8
summary, 6.4
employees
asset purchases, 6.32
business purchases, 6.33–6.51

Employment – *contd*
employees – *contd*
introduction, 6.13–6.14
share purchases, 6.15–6.31
employment status, 6.2
executive directors
'garden leave' clauses, 6.9
general considerations, 6.5
'golden parachutes', 6.8
negotiations with departing
directors, 6.11
notice of termination, 6.6
post-termination restrictions, 6.10
removal, 6.7–6.10
remuneration, 6.12
restrictive covenants, 6.10
share purchases, and, 6.7–6.8
summary, 6.4
information
additional legislation, 6.61
commencement, 6.58
remedy for failure to inform, 6.60
transfers, on, 6.55–6.56
internal reorganisation (share
purchases)
change of place of work, 6.26
change of terms and conditions,
6.27–6.29
constructive dismissal, 6.28–6.29
introduction, 6.24
reasonableness, 6.29
redundancy, 6.30–6.31
transfer from one company to
another, 6.25
introduction, 6.1
managers, 6.13
place of work, and, 6.26
pre-contractual considerations, 6.3
redundancy, 6.30–6.31
reorganisations
change of terms and conditions,
6.48
examples, 6.45
introduction, 6.44
key issues, 6.50–6.51
purchaser requires dismissal by
transferor, 6.46
purchaser wishes to integrate
workforces, 6.47
re-employment of dismissed
employees, 6.49
share purchases, and
directors, and, 6.7–6.8
generally, 6.16
internal reorganisation, 6.24–6.31

Employment – *contd*
share purchases, and – *contd*
summary, 6.15
unfair dismissal, 6.17–6.20
wrongful dismissal, 6.21–6.23
terms and conditions, and, 6.27–6.29
transfer from one company to another,
6.25
TUPE, and
business purchases, 6.34–6.43
internal reorganisations, 6.36
share purchases, 6.15
unfair dismissal
fair reasons, 6.19
generally, 6.18
introduction, 6.17
remedies, 6.20
wrongful dismissal
damages, 6.22–6.23
generally, 6.21
introduction, 6.17
**Enterprise management initiative
(EMI) scheme**
see also Employee share option
schemes
generally, 5.7
Environmental information
environmental responsibilities, and,
7.48
Environmental Liability Directive
environmental responsibilities, and,
7.38
Environmental permits
environmental responsibilities, and,
7.14–7.15
Environmental responsibilities
abstraction of water, 7.26
air pollution control, 7.23
allocation of risks and liabilities
bespoke provisions, 7.46
contractual provisions, 7.42–7.46
indemnities, 7.44–7.45
relevant factors, 7.41
warranties, 7.43
asbestos, 7.35
asset purchases, and, 7.4
authorisations
abstraction of water, 7.26
air pollution control, 7.23
COMAH, 7.29
discharge consents, 7.24
discharges to sewers, 7.25
discharges to water, 7.24
emissions trading scheme, 7.32
greenhouse gas emissions, 7.32

Environmental responsibilities – *contd*
authorisations – *contd*
hazardous substances, 7.28
integrated pollution prevention and control, 7.23
major accident hazards, 7.29
packaging waste, 7.31
radioactive substances, 7.27
trade effluent consents, 7.25
waste management licence, 7.30
COMAH, 7.29
contaminated land
generally, 7.16
water pollution, 7.17
contractual provisions
bespoke provisions, 7.46
generally, 7.42
indemnities, 7.44–7.45
warranties, 7.43
corporate social responsibility, 7.22
directors' liability, 7.19
discharge consents, 7.24
discharges to sewers, 7.25
discharges to water, 7.24
due diligence
authorisations, 7.23–7.32
contaminated land, 7.16–7.17
contract, 7.20
corporate social responsibility, 7.22
directors' liability, 7.19
environmental permits, 7.14–7.15
instructing local lawyers, 7.12
introduction, 7.10
legal issues, 7.13–7.22
pressure groups, 7.22
regulatory enforcement, 7.18
splitting permits, 7.15
tort, 7.21
use of consultants, 7.11
water pollution, 7.17
electrical and electronic equipment, 7.39
emissions trading scheme, 7.32
'environmental', 7.6
environmental information, 7.48
Environmental Liability Directive, 7.38
environmental permits, 7.14–7.15
general legislation
asbestos, 7.35
electrical and electronic equipment, 7.39
Environmental Liability Directive, 7.38
hazardous substances, 7.40

Environmental responsibilities – *contd*
general legislation – *contd*
introduction, 7.33
oil storage, 7.36
ROHS Directive, 7.40
statutory nuisance, 7.37
waste, 7.34
waste electrical and electronic equipment, 7.39
greenhouse gas emissions, 7.32
hazardous substances
generally, 7.28
ROHS Directive, 7.40
identification of relevant issues
allocation of risks, 7.41–7.46
due diligence, 7.10–7.40
introduction, 7.7
purchasers, for, 7.8
sellers, for, 7.9
indemnities, 7.44–7.45
instructing local lawyers, 7.12
integrated pollution prevention and control, 7.23
introduction, 7.1
legal issues
contaminated land, 7.16–7.17
contract, 7.20
corporate social responsibility, 7.22
directors' liability, 7.19
environmental permits, 7.14–7.15
introduction, 7.13
pressure groups, 7.22
regulatory enforcement, 7.18
splitting permits, 7.15
tort, 7.21
water pollution, 7.17
liabilities, 7.2
major accident hazards, 7.29
money laundering, 7.47
oil storage, 7.36
other jurisdictions, and, 7.5
packaging waste, 7.31
permits and transfer process, 7.49
pressure groups, 7.22
purchasers, and, 7.8
radioactive substances, 7.27
regulatory enforcement, 7.18
ROHS Directive, 7.40
sellers, and, 7.9
share purchases, and, 7.3
splitting permits, 7.15
statutory nuisance, 7.37
tort, 7.21
trade effluent consents, 7.25
use of consultants, 7.11

Environmental responsibilities *contd*
warranties, 7.43
waste, 7.34
waste electrical and electronic
equipment (WEEE), 7.39
waste management licence, 7.30
water pollution, 7.17
'Evergreen' funds
private equity transactions, and, 15.6
Exchange-completion hiatus
private company acquisitions, and,
8.28
Execution of documents
private company acquisitions, and,
8.10
Exit charges
private equity transactions, and, 15.26
Exit routes
and see Private equity transactions
introduction, 15.67
IPOs, 15.68
recapitalisations, 15.71
secondary buyouts, 15.69
trade sales, 15.70

F
Fair value
acquisition accounting, and, 2.16
False information
UK merger control, and, 11.66
Fees
private equity transactions, and, 15.7
UK merger control, and, 11.68
Final salary pension schemes
and see Pension schemes
generally, 9.3
Financial assistance
consideration, and, 8.22
Financial limitations
private company acquisitions, and,
8.41
Financial Reporting Standards (FRS)
generally, 2.2
Financial Support Directions
pension schemes, and, 9.25
Financing acquisitions
deferred consideration, 12.9–12.11
earn-outs, 12.10
introduction, 12.8
pension funds, 12.11
Fines
merger control, and, 11.33–11.34
Form CO
and see EC Merger Regulation
contents, 11.21–11.25

Form CO – *contd*
control, 11.23
introduction, 11.17
market conditions, 11.25
market information, 11.24
ownership, 11.23
parties, 11.22
transaction, 11.22
Form RS
merger control, and, 11.17
France (merger control)
employee consultation, 11.79
generally, 11.77
mixed economy companies, 11.81
non-resident investment issues,
11.78
privatisations, 11.81
quoted companies, 11.80
regulated professions, 11.83
sector regulators, 11.82
FRS
accounting treatment, and, 2.2
FRSSE
accounting treatment, and, 2.10
Future events
private company acquisitions, and,
8.45

G
GAAP
consolidated financial statements
excluded subsidiaries, 2.9
generally, 2.6
intermediate parent company, 2.7
small and medium-sized groups,
2.8
introduction, 2.3
merger relief, 2.5
parent company's individual accounts,
2.4
share-for-share transactions, 2.5
'Garden leave' clauses
directors, and, 6.9
Germany (merger control)
acquisition of control, 11.88
administrative offences, 11.106
appeals, 11.107
asset purchases, 11.87
bank transactions, 11.92
causal connection, 11.98
clearance, 11.103
competence, 11.101
conditions and thresholds, 11.86
consideration clause, 11.100
control thresholds, 11.96

Germany (merger control) – *contd*
  controlled concentrations,
      11.85–11.90
  creating dominant position, 11.97
  de minimis rule, 11.94
  'domestic effect', 11.85
  dominant position, 11.96
  gradual increase of concentration,
      11.91
  instituting merger control proceedings,
      11.95
  insurance transactions, 11.92
  introduction, 11.84
  minor market clause, 11.94
  post-merger notification, 11.105
  prediction, 11.99
  pre-merger notification, 11.102
  procedure, 11.100
  prohibitions, 11.103–11.104
  share purchases, 11.89
  significant influence on another
      undertaking, 11.90
  strengthening dominant position,
      11.97
  turnover threshold values, 11.93
Golden parachutes
  defensive measures, and, 4.7
  directors, and, 6.8
Goodwill
  acquisition accounting, and
      generally, 2.20
      impairment, 2.21
  IFRS, and, 2.34
Greenhouse gas emissions
  environmental responsibilities, and,
      7.32
Guarantees
  private equity transactions, and,
      15.63

H
Hazardous substances
  see also Environmental
      responsibilities
  generally, 7.28
  ROHS Directive, 7.40
Hive-downs
  see also Corporate rescue
  generally, 3.19
HMRC consents
  private company acquisitions, and,
      8.31
Holding periods
  private equity transactions, and,
      15.12

Hostile bids
  and see Defensive measures
  generally, 4.1–4.8
Hungary (merger control)
  concentrations, 11.167–11.169
  dominant position, 11.180
  establishment of control, 11.169
  filing fees, 11.177
  groups of undertakings, and, 11.171
  introduction, 11.166
  judicial review, 11.179
  notification requirements,
      11.172–11.174
  pre-merger consultation, 11.175
  procedural issues, 11.175–11.179
  sanctions, 11.178
  simplified procedure, 11.176, 11.181
  special rules, 11.182
  substantive issues, 11.180–11.182
  thresholds, 11.170

I
Identity of seller
  private company acquisitions, and,
      8.24
IFRS
  allocation of costs, 2.33
  business combinations (IFRS 3), 2.30
  cost of acquisition, 2.32
  entities under common control, 2.35
  generally, 2.2
  goodwill, 2.34
  introduction, 2.28
  overview, 2.29
  parent company balance sheet and
      distributable reserves, 2.36
  reverse acquisition, 2.31
  transitional rules, 2.37
Immovable property
  private company acquisitions, and,
      8.25
Incentives
  private equity transactions, and, 15.7
Indemnities
  see also Warranties
  assignment, 8.51
  comparison with warranties and
      covenants, 8.33
  environmental responsibilities, and,
      7.44–7.45
  generally, 8.34
  introduction, 8.32
  tax planning, and, 13.39
Informal advice
  UK merger control, and, 11.61

Information
see also Employment
additional legislation, 6.61
commencement, 6.58
remedy for failure to inform, 6.60
transfers, on, 6.55–6.56
Information-gathering
private company acquisitions, and, 8.13
Insolvency
administration
and see Administration
generally, 3.4–3.11
hive-downs, 3.19
introduction, 3.1–3.3
pensions, 3.18
transfer of undertakings, 3.12–3.17
Institutional investors' guidelines
employee share option schemes, and, 5.13
Insurance cover
private company acquisitions, and, 8.46
Intangible assets
acquisition accounting, and
generally, 2.19
impairment, 2.21
Integrated pollution prevention and control
environmental responsibilities, and, 7.23
Integration
post-acquisition management, and 10.4
Intellectual property licences
and see EC Merger Regulation
joint ventures, 11.41
mergers and acquisitions, 11.37
Interest on purchase money
private company acquisitions, and, 8.52
Intermediate parent company
consolidated financial statements, and, 2.7
Internal reorganisation (share purchases)
see also Reorganisation
change of place of work, 6.26
change of terms and conditions, 6.27–6.29
constructive dismissal, 6.28–6.29
introduction, 6.24
reasonableness, 6.29
redundancy, 6.30–6.31
transfer from one company to another, 6.25

International Financial Reporting Standards (IFRS)
generally, 2.2
Intra-group debts
private company acquisitions, and, 8.52
Intra-group relations
private company acquisitions, and, 8.27
Investigation
and see EC Merger Regulation
commitments, 11.30
introduction, 11.27
Phase I, 11.28
Phase II, 11.29
Investigation of title
property transactions, and, 14.9
Investment agreement
private equity transactions, and, 15.33
IPOs
private equity transactions, and, 15.68
Ireland (merger control)
appeals, 11.145
assessment process, 11.141
introduction, 11.136
media mergers, 11.144
notification requirements, 11.139
Phase I proceedings, 11.142
Phase II proceedings, 11.143
relevant mergers, 11.137
sanctions, 11.146
special rules, 11.147
thresholds, 11.138
voluntary notifications, 11.140
Italy (merger control)
calls for market comments, 11.113
competition authority, 11.109
'concentration', 11.110
filing fees. 11.114
introduction, 11.108
jurisdiction, 11.111
market comments, 11.113
notification, 11.112
pre-notification contacts, 11.113
procedure, 11.115
sanctions, 11.116
special rules, 11.117
thresholds, 11.111
timetable, 11.115

J
Joint and several liability
private equity transactions, and, 15.458

Joint ventures
accounting, and
generally, 2.20
introduction, 2.38
'autonomous economic entity', 11.12
introduction, 11.10
joint control, 11.11
other considerations, 11.13
restrictions
generally, 11.39
intellectual property licences, 11.41
non-compete clauses, 11.40
purchase and supply obligations,
11.42
Junior debt
private equity transactions, and, 15.15

L
Land Registry transfers
property transactions, and, 14.12
Leases
property transactions, and, 14.12
Legal issues
accountants' report, 8.14
accounts, 8.14
articles of association, 8.15
asset purchase, 8.3
basic structure
completion, 8.11
due diligence, 8.7
execution of documents, 8.10
introduction, 8.5
negotiation, 8.9
objectives, 8.6
preparation of documentation, 8.8
Board minutes, 8.10
business-specific information, 8.16
cash consideration, 8.21
checklists
completion, 8.61
introduction, 8.57
post-completion, 8.62
prior to completion, 8.60
prior to signature, 8.59
taking instructions, 8.58
Companies Acts, and, 8.63
company name change, 8.52
completion, 8.11
conduct of litigation, 8.48
conduct of negotiations, 8.17
confidentiality undertaking, 8.52
consents, 8.31
consideration
cash, 8.21
delayed payment, 8.23

Legal issues – *contd*
consideration – *contd*
financial assistance issue, and, 8.22
introduction, 8.18
loan notes, 8.20
shares, 8.19
constitution of company, 8.15
continuation of services, 8.27
costs, 8.52
covenants
comparison with warranties and
indemnities, 8.33
generally, 8.34
introduction, 8.32
'de-consolidation pack', 8.52
delayed payment of consideration,
8.23
disclosure letter
format, 8.30
generally, 8.39
introduction, 8.10
dividend payment, 8.52
due diligence, 8.7
EC Merger Regulation consent, 8.31
EGM documentation, 8.10
environmental responsibilities, and
contaminated land, 7.16–7.17
contract, 7.20
corporate social responsibility, 7.22
directors' liability, 7.19
environmental permits, 7.14–7.15
introduction, 7.13
pressure groups, 7.22
regulatory enforcement, 7.18
splitting permits, 7.15
tort, 7.21
water pollution, 7.17
exchange-completion hiatus, 8.28
execution of documents, 8.10
financial assistance, and, 8.22
financial limitations, 8.41
future events, 8.45
HMRC consents, 8.31
identity of seller, 8.24
immovable property, 8.25
indemnities
assignment, 8.51
comparison with warranties and
covenants, 8.33
generally, 8.34
introduction, 8.32
information-gathering, 8.13
insurance cover, 8.46
interest on purchase money, 8.52
intra-group debts, 8.52

Legal issues – *contd*
intra-group relations, 8.27
introduction, 8.1
Listings Rules, and, 8.55
loan notes, 8.20
matters within seller's knowledge,
8.43
memorandum of association, 8.15
mitigation, 8.46
name change, 8.52
negotiations
conduct, 8.17
introduction, 8.9
objectives, 8.6
pensions documentation, 8.10
powers of attorney, 8.10
practical steps
completion, 8.61
introduction, 8.57
post-completion, 8.62
prior to completion, 8.60
prior to signature, 8.59
taking instructions, 8.58
pre-contractual considerations
accountants' report, 8.14
accounts, 8.14
business-specific information, 8.16
constitution of company, 8.15
information-gathering, 8.13
introduction, 8.12
preparation of documentation, 8.8
'private company', 8.1
private company acquisition, on
basic structure, 8.5–8.11
introduction, 8.2–8.4
Prospectus Rules, and, 8.56
protection for seller
conduct of litigation, 8.48
disclosure letter, 8.39
financial limitations, 8.41
future events, 8.45
insurance cover, 8.46
matters within seller's knowledge,
8.43
mitigation, 8.46
provisions, 8.47
rescission, and, 8.44
reserves, 8.47
security for warranties, 8.49
time limits, 8.42
warranty limitations, 8.40
provisions, 8.47
purchase consideration
cash, 8.21
delayed payment, 8.23

Legal issues – *contd*
purchase consideration – *contd*
financial assistance issue, and, 8.22
introduction, 8.18
loan notes, 8.20
shares, 8.19
regulatory consent, 8.31
rescission, and, 8.44
reserves, 8.47
resignation letters, 8.10
restrictive covenants, 8.26
sale and purchase agreement, 8.29
security for warranties, 8.49
seller's identity, 8.24
service agreements, 8.10
share purchase, 8.3
shareholder consent, 8.31
shares, 8.19
stock transfer forms, 8.10
Substantial Acquisitions of Shares
Rules, and, 8.54
Takeover Code, and, 8.53
tax covenant, 8.10
tax returns, 8.52
use of experts, 8.4
warranties
assignment, 8.50
comparison with indemnities and
covenants, 8.33
conduct of litigation, 8.48
coverage, 8.38
disclosure letter, 8.39
future events, 8.45
generally, 8.35
insurance cover, 8.46
introduction, 8.32
limitations, 8.40–8.49
matters within seller's knowledge,
8.43
nature, 8.37
provisions, 8.47
rescission, and, 8.44
reserves, 8.47
secondary purpose, 8.36
security, 8.49
time limits, 8.42
Licences to occupy
property transactions, and, 14.17
Licences to underlet/assign
property transactions, and, 14.12
Limitations of liability
private equity transactions, and, 15.44
Listings Rules
private company acquisitions, and,
8.55

Loan notes
  private company acquisitions, and,
    8.20
  tax planning, and, 13.34
Loans
  private equity transactions, and, 15.36
'Locked box'
  private equity transactions, and, 15.64
Long-term incentive scheme
  see also Employee share option
    schemes
  generally, 5.11
Losses
  tax planning, and, 13.47

M
Major accident hazards
  environmental responsibilities, and,
    7.29
Management post-acquisition
  communication, 10.6
  degree of integration, 10.4
  failure of acquisitions, and 10.2
  introduction, 10.1
  legal issues checklist, 8.62
  people issues, 10.5
  success of acquisitions, and, 10.3
Managers
  employment, and, 6.13
Market conditions
  merger control, and, 11.25
Market information
  merger control, and, 11.24
Matters within seller's knowledge
  private company acquisitions, and,
    8.43
Media mergers
  Irish merger control, and, 11.144
  UK merger control, and, 11.58
Memorandum of association
  private company acquisitions, and,
    8.15
Merger accounting
  balance sheets, 2.18
  conditions, 2.12
  introduction, 2.11
  method, 2.13
  summary, 2.18
Merger control
  'acquisition of control', 11.9
  ancillary restrictions
    generally, 11.35
    intellectual property licences, 11.36
    joint venture restrictions,
      11.39–11.42

Merger control – *contd*
  ancillary restrictions – *contd*
    non-compete clauses, 11.36
    purchase and supply obligations,
      11.38
  application, 11.6
  'autonomous economic entity',
    11.12
  commitments, 11.30
  Community dimension
    introduction, 11.14
    turnover, 11.16
    'undertaking concerned', 11.15
  'concentrations'
    'acquisition of control', 11.9
    introduction, 11.7
    'previously independent
      undertakings', 11.8
  consents, and, 8.31
  Czech Republic, in
    ancillary restraints, 11.164
    competition authority, 11.160
    concentrations, 11.161
    introduction, 11.159
    notification requirements, 11.163
    sanctions, 11.165
    thresholds, 11.162
  EC Merger Regulation, and
    'acquisition of control', 11.9
    ancillary restrictions, 11.35–11.42
    application, 11.6
    'autonomous economic entity',
      11.12
    Community dimension,
      11.14–11.16
    'concentrations', 11.7–11.9
    fines, 11.33–11.34
    Form CO information, 11.21–11.25
    general issues, 11.4
    historical background, 11.5
    intellectual property licences,
      11.37
    introduction, 11.1–11.2
    joint ventures, 11.10–11.13
    non-compete clauses, 11.36
    notification procedure, 11.17–11.20
    penalties, 11.33–11.34
    pre-notification, 11.18
    'previously independent
      undertakings', 11.8
    principal aims, 11.3
    purchase and supply obligations,
      11.38
    scope, 11.6
    simplified procedure notice, 11.32

Merger control – *contd*
EC Merger Regulation, and – *contd*
substantive assessment, 11.31
suspension of concentrations,
11.26–11.30
turnover, 11.16
'undertaking concerned', 11.15
EEA Agreement, and, 11.43
fines, 11.33–11.34
Form CO
contents, 11.21–11.25
control, 11.23
introduction, 11.17
market conditions, 11.25
market information, 11.24
ownership, 11.23
parties, 11.22
transaction, 11.22
Form RS, 11.17
France, in
employee consultation, 11.79
generally, 11.77
mixed economy companies, 11.81
non-resident investment issues,
11.78
privatisations, 11.81
quoted companies, 11.80
regulated professions, 11.83
sector regulators, 11.82
general issues, 11.4
Germany, in
acquisition of control, 11.88
administrative offences, 11.106
appeals, 11.107
asset purchases, 11.87
bank transactions, 11.92
causal connection, 11.98
clearance, 11.103
competence, 11.101
conditions and thresholds, 11.86
consideration clause, 11.100
control thresholds, 11.96
controlled concentrations,
11.85–11.90
creating dominant position, 11.97
de minimis rule, 11.94
'domestic effect', 11.85
dominant position, 11.96
gradual increase of concentration,
11.91
instituting merger control
proceedings, 11.95
insurance transactions, 11.92
introduction, 11.84
minor market clause, 11.94

Merger control – *contd*
Germany, in – *contd*
post-merger notification, 11.105
prediction, 11.99
pre-merger notification, 11.102
procedure, 11.100
prohibitions, 11.103–11.104
share purchases, 11.89
significant influence on another
undertaking, 11.90
strengthening dominant position,
11.97
turnover threshold values, 11.93
historical background, 11.5
Hungary, in
concentrations, 11.167–11.169
dominant position, 11.180
establishment of control, 11.169
filing fees, 11.177
groups of undertakings, and,
11.171
introduction, 11.166
judicial review, 11.179
notification requirements,
11.172–11.174
pre-merger consultation, 11.175
procedural issues, 11.175–11.179
sanctions, 11.178
simplified procedure, 11.176,
11.181
special rules, 11.182
substantive issues, 11.180–11.182
thresholds, 11.170
intellectual property licences
joint ventures, 11.41
mergers and acquisitions, 11.37
introduction, 11.1–11.2
investigation
commitments, 11.30
introduction, 11.27
Phase I, 11.28
Phase II, 11.29
Ireland, in
appeals, 11.145
assessment process, 11.141
introduction, 11.136
media mergers, 11.144
notification requirements, 11.139
Phase I proceedings, 11.142
Phase II proceedings, 11.143
relevant mergers, 11.137
sanctions, 11.146
special rules, 11.147
thresholds, 11.138
voluntary notifications, 11.140

Merger control – *contd*
  Italy, in
    calls for market comments, 11.113
    competition authority, 11.109
    'concentration', 11.110
    filing fees. 11.114
    introduction, 11.108
    jurisdiction, 11.111
    market comments, 11.113
    notification, 11.112
    pre-notification contacts, 11.113
    procedure, 11.115
    sanctions, 11.116
    special rules, 11.117
    thresholds, 11.111
    timetable, 11.115
  joint venture restrictions
    generally, 11.39
    intellectual property licences, 11.41
    non-compete clauses, 11.40
    purchase and supply obligations, 11.42
  joint ventures
    'autonomous economic entity', 11.12
    introduction, 11.10
    joint control, 11.11
    other considerations, 11.13
    restrictions, 11.39–11.42
  market conditions, 11.25
  market information, 11.24
  Netherlands, in
    collective labour agreements, 11.76
    Competition Act, under, 11.71
    Merger Code, 11.74
    procedure, 11.72–11.73
    works councils, 11.75
  non-compete clauses
    joint ventures, 11.40
    mergers and acquisitions, 11.36
  notification
    method, 11.20
    relevant persons, 11.17
    required information, 11.21–11.25
  ownership, 11.23
  penalties, 11.33–11.34
  Poland, in
    concentrations, 11.184
    foreign-to-foreign transactions, 11.186
    introduction, 11.183
    judicial review, 11.189
    legislative changes, 11.191
    notification requirements, 11.187
    sanctions, 11.190

Merger control – *contd*
  Poland, in – *contd*
    substantive test of clearance, 11.188
    thresholds, 11.185
    timetable, 11.187
  pre-notification, 11.18
  'previously independent undertakings', 11.8
  principal aims, 11.3
  private company acquisitions, and, 8.31
  procedure
    introduction, 11.17
    investigation, 11.26–11.30
    notification, 11.17–11.20
    pre-notification, 11.18
    simplified notice, 11.32
    substantive assessment, 11.31
    suspension of concentrations, 11.26
    time limits, 11.27–11.30
  purchase and supply obligations
    joint ventures, 11.42
    mergers and acquisitions, 11.38
  scope, 11.6
  Short Form, 11.17
  simplified procedure notice, 11.32
  Spain, in
    competent authorities, 11.119
    Competition Bill, 11.126
    final decision, 11.125
    introduction, 11.118
    merger concept, 11.120
    notification requirements, 11.121–11.124
  substantive assessment, 11.31
  suspension of concentrations, 11.26
  Sweden, in
    appeals, 11.155
    clearance, 11.156
    confidentiality, 11.153
    contact details, 11.158
    introduction, 11.148
    notification requirements, 11.152
    publicity, 11.153
    reforms, 11.157
    substantive test, 11.151
    thresholds, 11.150
    timetable, 11.154
    triggering events, 11.149
  turnover, 11.16
  UK, in
    and see UK merger control
    appeals, 11.70

Merger control – *contd*
UK, in – *contd*
  assessment process, 11.65
  clearance process, 11.53–11.58
  decision making process, 11.67
  Enterprise Act 2002, under, 11.45
  false information, 11.66
  fees, 11.68
  institutions, 11.46–11.50
  introduction, 11.44
  misleading information, 11.67
  notification requirements,
    11.60–11.64
  relevant mergers, 11.51–11.52
  undertakings in lieu of reference,
    11.69
  water and sewerage mergers,
    11.59
'undertaking concerned', 11.15
United States, in
  Clayton Act (s 7), 11.134
  conclusion, 11.135
  enforcement actions, 11.131
  Exon-Florio filings, 11.133
  fees, 11.130
  Hart-Scott-Rodino filings, 11.128
  HSR Form, 11.132
  introduction, 11.127
  non-corporate entities, 11.129
  pre-notification requirements,
    11.128–11.134
Merger relief
accounting treatment, and, 2.5
Mergers
disclosures, and, 2.24
Misleading information
UK merger control, and, 11.67
Mitigation
private company acquisitions, and,
  8.46
Mix-and-match offers
tax planning, and, 13.53
Money laundering
environmental responsibilities, and,
  7.47
Money purchase pension schemes
and see Pension schemes
generally, 9.3
Moral hazard provisions
and see Pension schemes
clearance, and, 9.27–9.30
Contribution Notices, 9.24
Financial Support Directions, 9.25
introduction, 9.23
Restoration Orders, 9.26

Moratorium
see also Insolvency
generally, 3.2

N
Name change
private company acquisitions, and,
  8.52
National security mergers
UK merger control, and, 11.56
Negotiations
conduct, 8.17
introduction, 8.9
Netherlands (merger control)
collective labour agreements, 11.76
Competition Act, under, 11.71
Merger Code, 11.74
procedure, 11.72–11.73
works councils, 11.75
Non-compete clauses
and see EC Merger Regulation
joint ventures, 11.40
mergers and acquisitions, 11.36
Notice of termination
directors, and, 6.6
Notification procedure
and see EC Merger Regulation
Czech Republic merger control, and,
  11.163
Hungarian merger control, and,
  11.172–11.174
Irish merger control, and, 11.139
method, 11.20
Polish merger control, and, 11.187
relevant persons, 11.17
required information, 11.21–11.25
Spanish merger control, and,
  11.121–11.124
Swedish merger control, and, 11.152
UK merger control, and
  confidential guidance, 11.62
  informal advice, 11.61
  introduction, 11.60
  regular procedure, 11.64
  voluntary pre-notification process,
    11.63

O
Occupational pension schemes
and see Pension schemes
generally, 9.3
Office of Fair Trading
duties, 11.53
generally, 11.47

Oil storage
environmental responsibilities, and,
7.36
Ownership
merger control, and, 11.23

P
Packaging waste
environmental responsibilities, and,
7.31
'Pac-man' defence
defensive measures, and, 4.7
Parent company's individual accounts
UK GAAP, and, 2.4
Participation period
pension schemes, and, 9.13
Penalties
merger control, and, 11.33–11.34
Pension documentation
private company acquisitions, and,
8.10
Pension Protection Fund
and see Pension schemes
generally, 9.33
Pension schemes
accounting standards, 9.34
adjustment to purchase consideration,
9.15
approved withdrawal arrangements
effect, 9.22
generally, 9.20
Regulator's approval process, 9.21
benefits, 9.10
clearance
applications, 9.30
directors' role, 9.29
general principles, 9.27
trustees' role, 9.27
conclusion, 9.35
contract-based schemes, 9.3
Contribution Notices, 9.24
corporate rescue, and, 3.18
debts on employers, and
defined contribution employers, on,
9.19
generally, 9.17
industry-wide schemes, 9.18
defined benefit schemes
funding, 9.32
generally, 9.3
section 75 debts, 9.17–9.18
defined contribution schemes
generally, 9.3
section 75 debts, 9.19
EFRBs, and, 9.3

Pension schemes – *contd*
establishing new scheme, 9.9
final salary schemes, 9.3
Financial Support Directions, 9.25
interested parties
buyer, 9.8
seller, 9.7
trustees of buyer's pension scheme,
9.6
trustees of seller's pension scheme,
9.5
introduction, 9.1–9.2
money purchase schemes, 9.3
moral hazard provisions
clearance, and, 9.27–9.30
Contribution Notices, 9.24
Financial Support Directions, 9.25
introduction, 9.23
Restoration Orders, 9.26
occupational schemes, 9.3
participation period, 9.13
Pension Protection Fund, 9.33
Pensions Regulator
approved withdrawal arrangements,
9.20–9.22
clearance, 9.27–9.30
funding defined benefit schemes,
9.32
generally, 9.16
moral hazard provisions, 9.23–9.26
section 75 debts, 9.17–9.19
practical issues, 9.9
private equity transactions, and, 15.65
regulatory framework
Pension Protection Fund, 9.33
Pensions Regulator, 9.16–9.32
relevant issues, 9.4
Restoration Orders, 9.26
retirement benefits, 9.3
S2P, and, 9.3
sale agreement clauses, 9.14
section 75 debts
defined contribution employers, on,
9.19
generally, 9.17
industry-wide schemes, 9.18
SERPS, and, 9.3
transfer of undertakings, and, 3.16
transfer provisions
calculation of transfer payment,
9.12
generally, 9.11
TUPE, and, 9.31
types, 9.3
unapproved arrangements, 9.3

Pensions Regulator
and see Pension schemes
approved withdrawal arrangements
  effect, 9.22
  generally, 9.20
  Regulator's approval process, 9.21
clearance
  applications, 9.30
  directors' role, 9.29
  general principles, 9.27
  trustees' role, 9.27
funding defined benefit schemes, 9.32
generally, 9.16
moral hazard provisions
  clearance, and, 9.27–9.30
  Contribution Notices, 9.24
  Financial Support Directions, 9.25
  introduction, 9.23
  Restoration Orders, 9.26
section 75 debts
  defined contribution employers, on,
    9.19
  generally, 9.17
  industry-wide schemes, 9.18
Phantom share option scheme
see also Employee share option
  schemes
generally, 5.10
Place of work
internal reorganisations, and, 6.26
'Poison pills'
defensive measures, and, 4.7
Poland (merger control)
concentrations, 11.184
foreign-to-foreign transactions,
  11.186
introduction, 11.183
judicial review, 11.189
legislative changes, 11.191
notification requirements, 11.187
sanctions, 11.190
substantive test of clearance, 11.188
thresholds, 11.185
timetable, 11.187
Positive covenants
private equity transactions, and,
  15.58
Post-acquisition management
communication, 10.6
degree of integration, 10.4
failure of acquisitions, and 10.2
introduction, 10.1
legal issues checklist, 8.62
people issues, 10.5
success of acquisitions, and, 10.3

Post-termination restrictions
directors, and, 6.10
Powers of attorney
private company acquisitions, and,
  8.10
Pre-contractual considerations
accountants' report, 8.14
accounts, 8.14
business-specific information, 8.16
constitution of company, 8.15
information-gathering, 8.13
introduction, 8.12
Pre-emption rights
private equity transactions, and, 15.57
Pre-merger notification
EC merger control, and, 11.18
German merger control, and, 11.102
Hungarian merger control, and,
  11.175
UK merger control, and, 11.63
Pre-packs
administration, and, 3.9
Preparation of documentation
private company acquisitions, and, 8.8
Pressure groups
environmental responsibilities, and,
  7.22
'Previously independent undertakings'
merger control, and, 11.8
Price adjustment
private equity transactions, and, 15.64
'Private company'
private company acquisitions, and, 8.1
Private company acquisition
and see under individual headings
assignments, 8.50–8.51
basic structure, 8.5–8.11
checklists, 8.57–8.62
conduct of negotiations, 8.17
consents, 8.31
consideration, 8.18–8.23
continuation of services, 8.27
documentation, 8.29–8.30
identity of seller, 8.24
immovable property, 8.25
introduction, 8.2–8.4
other considerations, 8.52
pre-contractual considerations,
  8.12–8.16
regulations, 8.53–8.56
restrictive covenants, 8.26
seller protection and limitations,
  8.39–8.49
warranties, indemnities and covenants,
  8.32–8.38

Private equity transactions
advisers, 15.22
aims of buyout, 15.24
alignment of interests, 15.10
articles of association, 15.34
board involvement, 15.11
buyout process
business plan, 15.17
due diligence, 15.18
initiation, 15.16
negotiation, signing and closing,
15.19
buyout structure
considerations, 15.23–15.30
jurisdiction, 15.31
parties, 15.20–15.22
vehicle, 15.31
Chairman's role, 15.48–15.49
club deals, 15.21
completion accounts, 15.64
conflicts of interest, 15.22
'consent matters', 15.50
debt, 15.15
directors' duties, 15.50
documentation
articles of association, 15.34
financing covenants, 15.35–15.36
introduction, 15.32
investment agreement, 15.33
loans, 15.36
service agreements, 15.37
drag along rights, 15.55
drawdown of funds, 15.9
employment income taxes, 15.27
'evergreen' funds, 15.6
exit charges, 15.26
exit planning, 15.60
exit routes
introduction, 15.67
IPOs, 15.68
recapitalisations, 15.71
secondary buyouts, 15.69
trade sales, 15.70
fees, 15.7
financing, 15.3
financing covenants, 15.35–15.36
fund structures, 15.5–15.6
guarantees, 15.63
holding periods, 15.12
incentives, 15.7
information rights, 15.52
introduction, 15.1
investment agreement, 15.33
investment decision-making,
15.8

Private equity transactions – *contd*
investment objectives
alignment of interests, 15.10
board involvement, 15.11
debt, 15.15
holding periods, 15.12
junior debt, 15.15
management involvement, 15.11
senior debt, 15.15
valuation, 15.14
value creation, 15.13
IPOs, 15.68
joint and several liability, 15.45
junior debt, 15.15
jurisdiction, 15.31
leavers, 15.54
legal compliance, 15.29
limitations of liability, 15.44
loans, 15.36
'locked box', 15.64
management involvement, 15.11
management stake, 15.40
meaning, 15.2
objectives, 15.4
observers, 15.51
on-going relationship with
management, 15.46–15.48
parties to buyouts
advisers, 15.22
club deals, 15.21
generally, 15.20
syndication, 15.21
pensions, 15.65
positive covenants, 15.58
pre-emption rights, 15.57
price adjustment, 15.64
ratchets, 15.42
recapitalisations, 15.71
regulatory compliance, 15.30
restrictive covenants, 15.59
secondary buyouts, 15.66, 15.69
'self liquidating' funds, 15.6
senior debt, 15.15
service agreements, 15.37
subordination, 15.29
syndication, 15.21
tag along rights, 15.56
tax deductibility, 15.25
terms of buyouts
fund investment, 15.41
introduction, 15.38
investment, 15.39–15.42
joint and several liability, 15.45
limitations of liability, 15.44
management stake, 15.40

Private equity transactions – *contd*
terms of buyouts – *contd*
on-going relationship with
management, 15.46–15.48
ratchets, 15.42
warranties, 15.43
trade sales, 15.70
transfer of shares, 15.53
valuation, 15.14
value creation, 15.13
vehicle for buyout, 15.31
warranties, 15.43, 15.62
withholding taxes, 15.28
Property transactions
assessment of importance, 14.6
asset sales and purchases, 14.4
assignments, 14.12
authorised guarantee agreements,
14.12
certificates of title, 14.10
consents to assignments, 14.14
contracts for sale of property, 14.12
dealings with landlords
consents to assignments, 14.14
introduction, 14.13
licences to occupy, 14.17
post-completion alienation, 14.15
virtual assignments, 14.16
development of property, and, 14.11
due diligence, 14.7
introduction, 14.1
investigation of title, 14.9
Land Registry transfers, 14.12
leases, 14.12
licences to occupy, 14.17
licences to underlet/assign, 14.12
overseas properties, 14.19
post-completion obligations, 14.18
rental support documents, 14.12
share sales and purchases, 14.3
structure of transaction, and, 14.2
virtual assignments, 14.16
warranties, 14.8
Prospectus Rules
private company acquisitions, and,
8.56
Protection for seller
conduct of litigation, 8.48
disclosure letter, 8.39
financial limitations, 8.41
future events, 8.45
insurance cover, 8.46
matters within seller's knowledge,
8.43
mitigation, 8.46

Protection for seller – *contd*
provisions, 8.47
rescission, and, 8.44
reserves, 8.47
security for warranties, 8.49
time limits, 8.42
warranty limitations, 8.40
Provisions
private company acquisitions, and,
8.47
Public companies
defensive measures, and, 4.1
employee share option schemes, and,
5.16
Public interest mergers
UK merger control, and
generally, 11.55
media, 11.58
national security, 11.56
special situations, 11.57
water and sewerage, 11.59
Purchase and supply obligations
and see EC Merger Regulation
joint ventures, 11.42
mergers and acquisitions, 11.38
Purchase consideration
cash, 8.21
delayed payment, 8.23
financial assistance issue, and, 8.22
introduction, 8.18
loan notes, 8.20
pension schemes, and, 9.15
shares, 8.19

R
Radioactive substances
environmental responsibilities, and,
7.27
Ratchets
private equity transactions, and, 15.42
Recapitalisations
private equity transactions, and, 15.71
Redundancy
see also Employment
generally, 6.30–6.31
Regulatory consent
private company acquisitions, and,
8.31
Regulatory enforcement
environmental responsibilities, and,
7.18
Remuneration
directors, and, 6.12
Rental support
property transactions, and, 14.12

Reorganisations (purchase of business)
see also Internal reorganisation
change of terms and conditions, 6.48
examples, 6.45
introduction, 6.44
key issues, 6.50–6.51
purchaser requires dismissal by
transferor, 6.46
purchaser wishes to integrate
workforces, 6.47
re-employment of dismissed
employees, 6.49
Rescission
private company acquisitions, and,
8.44
Reserves
private company acquisitions, and,
8.47
Resignation letters
private company acquisitions, and,
8.10
Restoration Orders
pension schemes, and, 9.26
Restricted share schemes
see also Employee share option
schemes
generally, 5.12
Restrictive covenants
directors, and, 6.10
private company acquisitions, and,
8.26
private equity transactions, and, 15.59
Retirement benefits
pension schemes, and, 9.3
Reverse acquisition
IFRS, and, 2.31
ROHS Directive
environmental responsibilities, and,
7.40

S
S2P
and see Pension schemes
generally, 9.3
Sale and purchase agreement
pension schemes, and, 9.14
private company acquisitions, and,
8.29
**Savings-related share option (SAYE)
scheme**
see also Employee share option
schemes
generally, 5.5
'Scorched earth' policy
defensive measures, and, 4.7

Secondary buyouts
private equity transactions, and,
15.66, 15.69
Secretary of State
UK merger control, and, 11.49
Section 75 debts
and see Pension schemes
defined contribution employers, on,
9.19
generally, 9.17
industry-wide schemes, 9.18
Security for warranties
private company acquisitions, and,
8.49
'Self liquidating' funds
private equity transactions, and, 15.6
Seller's identity
private company acquisitions, and,
8.24
Senior debt
private equity transactions, and, 15.15
SERPS
and see Pension schemes
generally, 9.3
Service agreements
private company acquisitions, and,
8.10
private equity transactions, and, 15.37
Sewerage mergers
UK merger control, and, 11.59
Share-for-share transactions
UK GAAP, and, 2.5
Share incentive plan (SIP)
see also Employee share option
schemes
generally, 5.6
Share sales and purchases
employment, and
directors, and, 6.7–6.8
generally, 6.16
internal reorganisation, 6.24–6.31
summary, 6.15
unfair dismissal, 6.17–6.20
wrongful dismissal, 6.21–6.23
environmental responsibilities, and,
7.3
private company acquisitions, and,
8.3
property transactions, and, 14.3
tax planning (purchaser's planning)
business assets, 13.26
consideration, 13.24
disposal of target's assets, 13.29
financing cash consideration, 13.25
introduction, 13.22

Share sales and purchases – *contd*
tax planning (purchaser's planning) –
  contd
  pre-sale restructuring, 13.28
  purchaser's identity, 13.23
  stamp duty, 13.27
  termination of employment
    contracts, 13.30
tax planning (seller's planning)
  base cost, 13.11
  capital losses, 13.13
  deferral of CGT, 13.14
  Enterprise Investment Schemes,
    13.14
  exit charge, 13.19
  group relief, 13.20–13.21
  indexation allowance, 13.12
  introduction, 13.8
  overview, 13.2–13.3
  pre-sale asset strip, 13.18
  pre-sale dividends, 13.17
  roll-over relief, 13.15
  scope of CGT, 13.9
  substantial shareholding exemption,
    13.10
  taper relief, 13.12
  target company indebtedness,
    13.16
Share schemes for employees
approved schemes
  company share option scheme, 5.4
  enterprise management initiative
    scheme, 5.7
  introduction, 5.2
  SAYE scheme, 5.5
  share incentive plan, 5.6
  types, 5.3
company share option scheme, 5.4
convertible share schemes, 5.12
'early leavers', and, 5.15
effect of acquisition, 5.14
enterprise management initiative
  (EMI) scheme, 5.7
institutional investors' guidelines,
  5.13
introduction, 5.1
long-term incentive scheme, 5.11
phantom share option scheme, 5.10
post-acquisition schemes, 5.18
public companies, and, 5.16
restricted share schemes, 5.12
savings-related share option (SAYE)
  scheme, 5.5
share incentive plan (SIP), 5.6
Takeover Code, and, 5.16

Share schemes for employees – *contd*
types, 5.3
unapproved schemes
  convertible share schemes, 5.12
  introduction, 5.2
  long-term incentive scheme, 5.11
  phantom share option scheme,
    5.10
  restricted share schemes, 5.12
  share option scheme, 5.9
  types, 5.8
  unapproved share option scheme, 5.9
'Shark repellents'
defensive measures, and, 4.7
Shareholder consent
private company acquisitions, and,
  8.31
Shares
private company acquisitions, and,
  8.19
Short Form
merger control, and, 11.17
Simplified procedure notice
merger control, and, 11.32
Small companies
accounting treatment, and, 2.10
Small and medium-sized groups
consolidated financial statements, and,
  2.8
Spain (merger control)
competent authorities, 11.119
Competition Bill, 11.126
final decision, 11.125
introduction, 11.118
merger concept, 11.120
notification requirements,
  11.121–11.124
Special dividends
tax planning, and, 13.52
Spin-offs
tax planning, and, 13.54
Splitting permits
environmental responsibilities, and,
  7.15
SSAP
generally, 2.2
Stamp duty
generally, 13.7
share sales, 13.27
**Statements of Standard Accounting
  Practice (SSAP)**
generally, 2.2
Statutory nuisance
environmental responsibilities, and,
  7.37

Stock transfer forms
private company acquisitions, and,
8.10
Strategy
approaching target company, 12.4
detailed investigation of target
company, 12.6–12.7
development, 12.1
establishing a team, 12.2
financing acquisition
deferred consideration, 12.9–12.11
earn-outs, 12.10
introduction, 12.8
pension funds, 12.11
identifying target company, 12.3
information checklist, 12.7
introduction 12.1
valuing target company, 12.5
Subordination
private equity transactions, and,
15.29
Substantial acquisitions
disclosures, and, 2.27
**Substantial Acquisitions of Shares
Rules**
private company acquisitions, and,
8.54
Substantial property transactions
administration, and, 3.11
Substantive assessment
merger control, and, 11.31
Super-priority
see also Corporate rescue
background, 3.31
classes of DIP funding, 3.32
conclusions, 3.37
general principles, 3.33–3.36
introduction, 3.30
Suspension of concentrations
merger control, and, 11.26
Sweden (merger control)
appeals, 11.155
clearance, 11.156
confidentiality, 11.153
contact details, 11.158
introduction, 11.148
notification requirements, 11.152
publicity, 11.153
reforms, 11.157
substantive test, 11.151
thresholds, 11.150
timetable, 11.154
triggering events, 11.149
Syndication
private equity transactions, and, 15.21

T
Tag along rights
private equity transactions, and, 15.56
Takeover Code
defensive measures, and, 4.1–4.2
employee share option schemes and,
5.16
private company acquisitions, and,
8.53
Tax covenant
private company acquisitions, and,
8.10
Tax planning
asset sales, 13.4
business asset roll-over, 13.5
clearances
introduction, 13.43
s 138 TCGA 1992, and, 13.44
s 707 TA 1988, and, 13.45
close companies, 13.48
consents
introduction, 13.43
s 765 TA 1988, and, 13.46
consideration
cash, 13.32
earn-outs, 13.35
introduction, 13.32
loan notes, 13.34
share sales (purchaser's planning),
13.24–13.25
shares, 13.33
target debt, 13.36
covenants, 13.39–13.40
earn-outs, 13.35
indemnities, 13.39
introduction, 13.1
loan notes, 13.34
losses, 13.47
public mergers
bidder's identity, 13.58
cancellation schemes, 13.56
depositary receipts, 13.57
employee share schemes, 13.55
features, 13.50
introduction, 13.49
mix-and-match offers, 13.53
partial; mergers, 13.54
shareholding planning, 13.51
special dividends, 13.52
spin-offs, 13.54
seller protection, 13.42
share sales (purchaser's planning)
business assets, 13.26
consideration, 13.24
disposal of target's assets, 13.29

Tax planning – *contd*
  share sales (purchaser's planning) –
    contd
    financing cash consideration, 13.25
    introduction, 13.22
    pre-sale restructuring, 13.28
    purchaser's identity, 13.23
    stamp duty, 13.27
    termination of employment
      contracts, 13.30
  share sales (seller's planning)
    base cost, 13.11
    capital losses, 13.13
    deferral of CGT, 13.14
    Enterprise Investment Schemes,
      13.14
    exit charge, 13.19
    group relief, 13.20–13.21
    indexation allowance, 13.12
    introduction, 13.8
    overview, 13.2–13.3
    pre-sale asset strip, 13.18
    pre-sale dividends, 13.17
    roll-over relief, 13.15
    scope of CGT, 13.9
    substantial shareholding exemption,
      13.10
    taper relief, 13.12
    target company indebtedness, 13.16
  stamp duty
    generally, 13.7
    share sales (purchaser's planning),
      13.27
  VAT, 13.6
  warranties, 13.37–13.38
Tax returns
  private company acquisitions, and,
    8.52
Terms and conditions
  reorganisations, and, 6.48
  share purchases, and, 6.27–6.29
Tort
  environmental responsibilities, and,
    7.21
Trade effluent consents
  environmental responsibilities, and,
    7.25
Trade sales
  private equity transactions, and, 15.70
Transfer of undertakings (TUPE)
  business purchases, and, 6.34–6.43
  corporate rescue, and
    see also Corporate rescue
    background, 3.13
    contractual variations, 3.17

Transfer of undertakings (TUPE) –
  contd
  corporate rescue, and – *contd*
    effect of regulations, 3.14
    extent of relief, 3.15
    introduction, 3.12
    pensions, 3.16
  internal reorganisations, and, 6.36
  pensions, and
    GENERALLY, 9.31
    introduction, 3.16
  share purchases, and, 6.15
Turnover
  merger control, and, 11.16

U
UK GAAP
  consolidated financial statements
    excluded subsidiaries, 2.9
    generally, 2.6
    intermediate parent company, 2.7
    small and medium-sized groups,
      2.8
  introduction, 2.3
  merger relief, 2.5
  parent company's individual accounts,
    2.4
  share-for-share transactions, 2.5
UK merger control
  see also Merger control
  appeals
    generally, 11.70
    role of CAT, 11.50
  assessment process, 11.65
  clearance process
    Competition Commission's duties,
      11.54
    OFT's duties, 11.53
    public interest mergers, 11.55–11-
      58
  Competition Appeals Tribunal, 11.50
  Competition Commission
    duties, 11.54
    generally, 11.48
  confidential guidance, 11.62
  decision making process, 11.67
  Enterprise Act 2002, under
    appeals, 11.70
    assessment process, 11.65
    clearance process, 11.53–11.58
    decision making process, 11.67
    Enterprise Act 2002, under, 11.45
    false information, 11.66
    fees, 11.68
    introduction, 11.45

UK merger control – *contd*
  Enterprise Act 2002, under – *contd*
    misleading information, 11.67
    notification requirements,
        11.60–11.64
    relevant mergers, 11.51–11.52
    undertakings in lieu of reference,
        11.69
    water and sewerage mergers, 11.59
  false information, 11.66
  fees, 11.68
  informal advice, 11.61
  institutions
    Competition Appeals Tribunal,
        11.50
    Competition Commission, 11.48
    introduction, 11.46
    Office of Fair Trading, 11.47
    Secretary of State, 11.49
  introduction, 11.44
  media mergers, 11.58
  misleading information, 11.67
  national security mergers, 11.56
  notification requirements
    confidential guidance, 11.62
    informal advice, 11.61
    introduction, 11.60
    regular procedure, 11.64
    voluntary pre-notification process,
        11.63
  Office of Fair Trading
    duties, 11.53
    generally, 11.47
  public interest mergers
    generally, 11.55
    media, 11.58
    national security, 11.56
    special situations, 11.57
    water and sewerage, 11.59
  relevant mergers
    'ceasing to be distinct', 11.52
    generally, 11.51
  Secretary of State, 11.49
  special situations, 11.57
  undertakings in lieu of reference,
      11.69
  voluntary pre-notification process,
      11.63
  water and sewerage mergers, 11.59
Unapproved share option scheme
  see also Employee share option
      schemes
  generally, 5.9
'Undertaking concerned'
  merger control, and, 11.15

Undertakings in lieu of reference
  UK merger control, and, 11.69
Unfair dismissal
  fair reasons, 6.19
  generally, 6.18
  introduction, 6.17
  remedies, 6.20
United States (merger control)
  Clayton Act (s 7), 11.134
  conclusion, 11.135
  enforcement actions, 11.131
  Exon-Florio filings, 11.133
  fees, 11.130
  Hart-Scott-Rodino filings, 11.128
  HSR Form, 11.132
  introduction, 11.127
  non-corporate entities, 11.129
  pre-notification requirements,
      11.128–11.134
Urgent Issues Task Force (UITF)
  generally, 2.2

V
Valuation
  private equity transactions, and,
      15.14
  target companies, and, 12.5
VAT
  tax planning, and, 13.6
Voluntary pre-notification process
  UK merger control, and, 11.63

W
Warranties
  assignment, 8.50
  comparison with indemnities and
      covenants, 8.33
  conduct of litigation, 8.48
  coverage, 8.38
  disclosure letter, 8.39
  environmental responsibilities, and,
      7.43
  future events, 8.45
  generally, 8.35
  insurance cover, 8.46
  introduction, 8.32
  limitations
    conduct of litigation, 8.48
    future events, 8.45
    generally, 8.40–8.41
    insurance cover, 8.46
    matters within seller's knowledge,
        8.43

Warranties – *contd*
limitations – *contd*
provisions, 8.47
rescission, and, 8.44
reserves, 8.47
security, 8.49
time limits, 8.42
matters within seller's knowledge,
8.43
nature, 8.37
private equity transactions, and,
15.43, 15.62
property transactions, and, 14.8
provisions, 8.47
rescission, and, 8.44
reserves, 8.47
secondary purpose, 8.36
security, 8.49
tax planning, and, 13.37–13.38
time limits, 8.42
Waste
environmental responsibilities, and,
7.34
**Waste electrical and electronic
equipment (WEEE)**
environmental responsibilities, and,
7.39

Waste management licence
environmental responsibilities, and,
7.30
Water and sewerage mergers
UK merger control, and, 11.59
Water pollution
environmental responsibilities, and,
7.17
Withholding taxes
private equity transactions, and, 15.2
Work-outs
accountants' investigation, 3.22
common features, 3.25
documentation
company/participants agreement,
3.28
introduction, 3.27
participants agreement, 3.29
general structure, 3.21
'intensive care', 3.23
introduction, 3.20
public companies, and, 3.24
risks, 3.26
Wrongful dismissal
damages, 6.22–6.23
generally, 6.21
introduction, 6.17